CURRICULUM & INSTRUCTION

ALTERNATIVES IN EDUCATION

Edited by

HENRY A. GIROUX
Senior Editor
Boston University

ANTHONY N. PENNA
Carnegie Mellon University

WILLIAM F. PINAR
University of Rochester

McCutchan Publishing Corporation
2526 Grove Street
Berkeley, California 94704

ISBN 0-8211-0615-5
Library of Congress Catalog Card Number 80-84142

© 1981 by McCutchan Publishing Corporation. All rights reserved
Printed in the United States of America

Cover design by Terry Down, Griffin Graphics
Typesetting composition by Marin Typesetters

This book is dedicated to Jeanne F. Brady, whose intellect, sense of caring, and social consciousness make her one of the finest human beings and teachers I have ever met. The book is also dedicated to those teachers and students who are working to create a more just and democratic world.

H.A.G.

Contributors

Jean Anyon, Rutgers University
Michael W. Apple, University of Wisconsin, Madison
Stanley Aronowitz, Columbia University
George Beauchamp, Northwestern University
James H. Block, University of California, Santa Barbara
Dale Carlson, California Department of Education
Robert Donmoyer, The Ohio State University
Robert Gagné, Florida State University
Henry A. Giroux, Boston University
Madeleine Grumet, Hobart and Williams Smith Colleges
Dwayne Huebner, Teachers College, Columbia University
Philip W. Jackson, University of Chicago
Mauritz Johnson, Jr., State University of New York, Albany
M. Frances Klein, Pepperdine University
Ulf Lundgren, Stockholm Institute of Education, Sweden
John D. McNeil, University of California, Los Angeles
Anthony N. Penna, Carnegie-Mellon University
William F. Pinar, University of Rochester
W. James Popham, University of California, Los Angeles
Thomas S. Popkewitz, University of Wisconsin, Madison
Joseph J. Schwab, Center for Democratic Institutions
Daniel Tanner, Rutgers University
Laurel N. Tanner, Temple University
Ralph W. Tyler, Center for Democratic Institutions
Decker F. Walker, Stanford University
Robert S. Zais, Kent State University

Contents

Introduction and Overview to the Curriculum Field   1

SECTION I: CURRICULUM

Three Perspectives on Curriculum   13

Traditionalists

1   Specific Approaches to Curriculum Development
      Ralph W. Tyler   17

2   Conceptions of Curriculum and the Curriculum Field   *Robert S. Zais*   31

Conceptual-Empiricists

3   The Concept of the Structure of a Discipline
      Joseph J. Schwab   51

4   Basic Components of a Curriculum Theory
      George Beauchamp   63

5   Definitions and Models in Curriculum Theory
      Mauritz Johnson, Jr.   69

Reconceptualists

6   The Reconceptualization of Curriculum Studies
      William F. Pinar   87

7   Toward a New Sociology of Curriculum
      Henry A. Giroux   98

8	On Analyzing Hegemony	Michael W. Apple	109
9	Toward a Political Economy of Curriculum and Human Development	Dwayne Huebner	124
10	Autobiography and Reconceptualization	Madeleine R. Grumet	139

SECTION II: INSTRUCTION

Three Perspectives on Instruction · · · · · · · · · · · · 147

Traditionalists

| 11 | Instructional Decisions in Curriculum M. Frances Klein | 149 |

Conceptual-Empiricists

| 12 | Promoting Excellence Through Mastery Learning James H. Block | 161 |
| 13 | The Learning Basis of Teaching Methods Robert Gagné | 177 |

Reconceptualists

| 14 | Frame Factors in Teaching | Ulf Lundgren | 197 |
| 15 | Social Education in the Classroom: The Dynamics of the Hidden Curriculum Henry A. Giroux and Anthony N. Penna | 209 |

SECTION III: EVALUATION

Three Perspectives on Evaluation · · · · · · · · · · · · 233

Traditionalists

| 16 | How Can the Effectiveness of Learning Experiences be Evaluated? | Ralph W. Tyler | 237 |
| 17 | Evaluating the Curriculum John D. McNeil | 252 |

Conceptual-Empiricists

| 18 | Deep Dark Deficits of the Adversary Evaluation Model W. James Popham and Dale Carlson | 271 |

19	What Curriculum Research? *Decker F. Walker*	281

Reconceptualists

20	Educational Research: Values and Visions of Social Order *Thomas S. Popkewitz*	297
21	Social Class and the Hidden Curriculum of Work *Jean Anyon*	317
22	The Evaluator as Artist *Robert Donmoyer*	342

SECTION IV: DIALOGUE AND DEBATE

23	Curriculum and Its Discontents *Philip W. Jackson*	367
24	Emancipation From Research: The Reconceptualist Prescription *Daniel Tanner and Laurel N. Tanner*	382
25	A Reply to My Critics *William F. Pinar*	392
26	Hegemony, Resistance, and the Paradox of Educational Reform *Henry A. Giroux*	400
27	The Abstract and the Concrete in Curriculum Theorizing *William F. Pinar*	431
28	Politics and Higher Education in the 1980s *Stanley Aronowitz*	455

Introduction and Overview to the Curriculum Field

Curriculum as a field of study is relatively young. Most place its birth during the second or third decade of this century, often with the publication of Franklin Bobbitt's *The Curriculum* in 1918, sometimes with Denver superintendent Jesse Newlon's use of teachers in curriculum development during the early 1920s.[1] Because the field is young and because it was born, in part, of administrative convenience rather than intellectual necessity, the study of curriculum has yet to establish itself clearly as a discipline. During the next twenty years or so we expect this to occur.

In this text you will be introduced to the issues germane to the present state of the field and its future. In the next few pages, we will sketch the history of the field, concluding with the origin of the three modes of curriculum writing that roughly make up the field today. The bulk of the text comprises examples from each of these three modes. Concluding the volume is a section that makes explicit the thematic and methodologic grounds on which the struggle to establish curriculum as a discipline is waged.

Central to an understanding of the curriculum field is an appreciation of its origins. Superintendent Newlon saw the importance of systematically attending to the curriculum in the various subject areas, across subject areas at the same grade level (that is, horizontal integration), and across grade levels (vertical integration). Perhaps teachers who had indicated interest in these matters were selected. Regardless, teachers who had been trained in a variety of disciplines were selected. It is still true today that curriculum specialists represent the spectrum of disciplines: social studies, mathematics, science, business, humanities, and the arts. By the end of the 1920s courses of study that focused on curriculum were available in universities, generally housed in departments of educational administration or secondary education.[2] In 1938 the first department of curriculum and teaching was established at Teachers College, Columbia University. Today, most schools or colleges of education have a department of curriculum.

It is important to note that the study of curriculum did not begin as an addition to an extant field, say as a subfield of psychology or philosophy. Rather, it began in administrative convenience: professional responsibility for curricular matters. Thus, curricularists came from every academic background imaginable. What they shared was an interest in and responsibility for the curriculum. This particular history has meant that several different kinds of thinking—from the scientific to the artistic—have emerged in the curriculum field. Consequently, attempts to achieve consensus regarding the limits of our concerns and the methods by which we investigate them—indeed, even consensus concerning the definition of curriculum itself—has been impossible to achieve. At the present time, however, this effort to achieve consensus has become urgent for economic and political reasons we shall mention, but before elaborating this issue, let us briefly review the salient characteristics of the traditional curriculum field.

The field's beginning in administrative convenience meant that it was initially and powerfully dominated by administrative notions. Thus, for instance, rather than being viewed as a complex presence in the schools requiring understanding, curriculum was viewed as the organization of time and activities to be managed according to sound business principles. Kliebard terms this style of curriculum "bureaucratic," and he cites Ellwood Cubberly as a representative spokesman for it.

Every manufacturing establishment that turns out a standard product or a series of products of any kind maintains a force of efficiency experts to study methods of procedure and to measure and test the output of its works. Such men ultimately bring the manufacturing establishment large returns by introducing improvements in process and procedures and in training the workmen to produce larger and better output. Our schools are, in a sense, factories in which the raw products (children) are to be shaped and fashioned into products to meet the various demands of life. The specifications for manufacturing come from the demands of twentieth-century civilization, and it is the business of the school to build its pupils according to the specifications laid down. This demands good tools, specialized machinery, continuous measurement of production to see if it works according to specifications, the elimination of waste in manufacture, and a large variety in the output.[3]

To achieve these ends, an idea of "scientific management" was articulated, perhaps most prominently by Frederick W. Taylor. In Taylor's model the principles of efficiency, control, and prediction were central.[4] Franklin Bobbitt extended this model into the curriculum domain, arguing that to achieve maximum efficiency the curriculum must be efficiently managed and outcomes precisely predicted. This model meant that the classical ideals of education, that is, the cultivation of intelligence and sensitivity, were no longer useful; the goals of the curriculum must be specified. In this effort Bobbitt was joined by David Snedden and W. W. Charters.[5]

Introduction and Overview

Charters conducted a curriculum study for Stephens College of Columbia, Missouri. His task was to develop a program to train young women for the "specific job of being a woman."[6] How this training might be accomplished was by analysis of the activities of women. Women throughout the country were asked to describe what they did during a typical week, and 95,000 women answered. With these replies Charters classified the activities into 7,300 categories, such as food preparation and cleaning. With these categories as his "knowledge base," Charters developed the curriculum for the college. As Kliebard notes, these tendencies remain present today, as emphases upon behavioral objectives and observable and measurable competencies indicate.[7]

There are other tendencies or issues that emerge from an examination of the traditional curriculum field. Among these are an ahistorical posture and an ameliorative orientation; both follow from the administrative origin of the field. Kliebard notes, for example, that in many Ph.D. programs in curriculum, there is no requirement to study the history of the field and the work of such early curricularists as Bobbitt, Charters, and Snedden. Perhaps because succeeding generations have known little of these early tendencies, they tend to repeat them, such as the contemporary interest in specifying objectives in behaviors. Kliebard observes:

Generally speaking, the foremost scholars in other fields continually engage in a kind of dialogue with their ancestral counterparts—rejecting, revising, or refining the early formulations and concepts. No such cumulative approach to the content of the curriculum field has yet emerged, and this has had the telling effect on the relative permanence of curriculum thinking. Issues tend to arise *de novo*, usually in the form of a bandwagon and then quickly disappear in a cloud of dust. Sometimes these issues have their counterparts in an earlier period, but this is rarely recognized. The field in general is characterized by an uncritical propensity for novelty and change rather than funded knowledge or dialogue across generations.[8]

We are suggesting that this ahistorical posture results from the fundamentally managerial interest and function of the field. Ironically, it may be that the narrowly managerial and service-oriented nature of the field has worked to diminish its capacity to either manage or serve effectively.

This ahistorical posture, with its emphasis on efficiency and service, became crystallized in a small book published by the University of Chicago Press in 1949. There were four questions asked by Ralph Tyler in his *Basic Principles of Curriculum and Instruction*: (1) What educational purposes should the school seek to attain? (2) How can learning experiences be selected that are likely to be useful in attaining these objectives? (3) How can learning experiences be organized for effective instruction? (4) How can the effectiveness of learning experiences be evaluated? These questions came to epitomize the traditional scope of the field. The commonsensical tone of the book underscores its origins in an administrative or bureaucratic mode of rationality, a kind of thinking that depoliticizes issues and removes them from a historical context. There is no disciplinary coherence or rationale in either asking or answering Tyler's four "basic" questions. Yet they articulate the businesslike instrumentality of school administrators as they insist on knowing in advance how to handle "practical" problems of curriculum development, implementation, and evaluation. This specific notion of the relation between theory and practice, namely that theory exists exclusively to guide practice, has dominated intellectual thinking in the West since the rise of science in the seventeenth century.[9] (It is this notion of the relation between theory and practice that is coming under increasing attack, as some of the reconceptualist readings in this volume demonstrate.)

For example, Tyler's book became widely used in college courses on curriculum and also played an influential role in the theoretical development of the field itself. Building on Tyler's four curriculum questions, Hilda Taba identified seven steps to guide curriculum developers in her text titled *Curriculum Development*.[10] In many volumes of this genre, such as Tanner's and Tanner's *Curriculum Development*,[11] a compendium of items is presented. The underlying idea in these books seems to be to anticipate problems a curriculum developer might encounter during the course of his or her professional studies. In this sense traditional curriculum theory guides practice as it anticipates and attempts to control it.

Increasing criticism about the quality of the elementary- and secondary-school curriculum surfaced during the 1950s. For example, curriculum models that had "life adjustment" as a primary goal were attacked by Admiral Hyman Rickover and others as an indicator of the "softness" of the American school system. Responding to this criticism, various academic, discipline-based groups began the task of reforming the school's curricula. In 1952 the University of Illinois Committee on School Mathematics began its work of revising the school's mathematics curriculum. Likewise, Jerrold Zacharias of MIT had been instrumental in establishing the Physical Sciences Study Committee (PSSC), which designed a new secondary school physics course in 1956. These scientists and mathematicians were conceptual-empiricists and not associated with the traditionalist school in curriculum. They attempted to inspire by teaching about a discipline's structure and its proof process, that is, its method of investigation.

The activities of these scientists accelerated with the launching of the Soviet satellite, *Sputnik*, in 1957. This event and the national curriculum reform movement that followed it further isolated the traditionalists from the mainstream of curriculum activity during the 1950s and 1960s. The Soviet success became the burden of American schools, as it demonstrated how "far behind" we were and by implication indicated the traditionalists' influence in the curriculum field. As the national curriculum reform effort became organized, it became increasingly clear that the structure of content was the primary goal of the movement. As a result curriculum specialists were bypassed during the selection of leadership for the movement.

Natural and behavioral scientists, mathematicians, humanists, and representatives from many other disciplines were in the vanguard of the reform movement, and most were influenced by the discussions conducted at Woods Hole, Massachusetts, in 1959 and summarized in 1960 in the most influential little volume published during the early years of the movement, *The Process of Education*, by the noted cognitive psychologist Jerome Bruner. It was of no small consequence that discipline-based specialists looked to a behavioral scientist and not to a curricularist for guidance on what to teach and how to teach content in the new curricula.[12] The effect upon the curriculum field would be slow but powerful. Conceptual-empiricists from the many academic disciplines had replaced traditionalists in the curriculum field as policymakers and innovators. Private philanthropic foundations as well as federal agencies did not regard curricularists as worthy of leading a reform movement that bore their specialization's name.

During this period a development occurred within educational departments that further eroded the position of the traditionalists and enhanced the stature of the empirical-conceptualists. Philosophers, psychologists, sociologists, and historians of education were allying themselves more closely with their colleagues in departments of philosophy, psychology, sociology, and history. Educational administration became more closely tied to management theory and industrial psychology. This movement closer to the "parent" discipline was propelled in part by criticism from spokesmen of these intellectual parents that, for instance, educational philosophers were not "doing" philosophy. Such criticism was literal and accurate to some extent, but it was symbolic as well and as such represented part of the period's reaction against educationalists and the education establishment.

By 1980 we find the practice of hiring Ph.D.'s in one of the disciplines, such as sociology, who have an "interest" in curriculum. This practice is still limited to the most prestigious schools of education, but it represents a continuation of this trend. Under these conditions it is easy to see how vulnerable the curriculum field could become. It never had a close disciplinary affiliation; the circumstances of its origin did not allow one, and its traditional function did not ask for one. While the specific theoretical character of traditional curriculum writing made it easily accessible to school personnel—and thereby made curriculum as a specialization one of the most popular in graduate schools of education—it now made the field vulnerable to criticisms of academic weakness and conceptual muddiness and flabbiness. Initially, curricularists could and did ignore these attacks, temporarily safe in the protection of healthy enrollments and the country's needs for new teachers and administrators responsible for the curriculum. But the decline in student population and the deterioration of the American economy during the 1970s would underscore how temporary and fragile that safety was.

The effects of these developments upon the field were quite serious. There were more prospective teachers than jobs for them to take. A majority of working teachers, especially in the Northeast, were now permanently certified, further reducing graduate enrollments. During the 1960s many schools of education grew rapidly; many education colleges and departments had more faculty than their current enrollment of students could justify. Part of this economic stress was relieved by federal funding for educational research, but this was of marginal relief to traditional curriculum specialists since most funds went to empiricists. Traditionalists had no discipline in the conventional sense, and they conducted no research. Their constituency was shrinking rapidly. Criticisms of intellectual weakness from colleagues could no longer be ignored. The economic foundation of the traditional field was collapsing.

There had been several attempts of varying sorts and of varying duration to establish an intellectually serious field—a discipline—of curriculum. For instance, the Association for Supervision and Curriculum development, still the largest professional association devoted to curriculum problems, convened a Commission on Curriculum Theory during the 1960s. However, this commission failed to come to a consensus regarding the shape and scope of the field. Independently of the commission, a number of individuals tried to specify the nature of the field. George Beauchamp outlines the major elements of a scientific curriculum field.[13] Also in this vein are articles by Mauritz Johnson[14] and the Ohio State group.[15] While Professor Beauchamp currently completes work on a fourth edition, and Johnson's students, such as George Posner at Cornell University and A. Leon Pines at the University of Maine, carry on aspects of his work, it must be concluded that the effort to establish a scientific field of curriculum has not yet succeeded. By 1970 it was possible for philosopher Joseph Schwab, in a well-known and influential essay, to characterize the curriculum field as "moribund."[16] It was a judgment pronounced throughout the decade,[17] and it seemed possible that the field might slowly disappear.

But a "third force" appeared during the 1970s that claimed to reconceptualize the field. Drawing upon a tradition of critique that extends from the early 1947 curriculum conference at the University of Chicago to the more recent conferences at Ohio State University in 1967 and Stanford University in 1969, a diverse group of educators appeared in the early 1970s to mount a new challenge and criticism of the assumptions underlying existing modes of curriculum theorizing.[18]

In the early stages of this development, theorists such as James Macdonald, Dwayne Huebner, Maxine Greene, William Pinar, and Michael Apple played a significant role in "reconceptualizing" the major issues, concerns, and

Introduction and Overview

modes of educational inquiry that provided a focus for curriculum theory and practice.[19] Drawing selectively on such European intellectual traditions as existentialism, phenomenology, psychoanalysis, and neo-Marxism, these theorists attempted to offset the relatively apolitical, ahistorical, and technological orientation that has characterized the curriculum field for the last fifty years.[20] For example, Pinar has attempted to illuminate the importance of using a psychoanalytical framework in analyzing experiential and gender issues in the schooling process;[21] Huebner has provided an extended critique of the technocratic rationality that permeates the underlying structural principles of existing curriculum thinking;[22] Kliebard has written historical accounts of the "scientism" that has not only influenced curriculum development but also lies at the center of the relationship that ties schools to the logic of capitalism;[23] Greene has written extensively about the value of the arts for developing meaning in the classroom encounter;[24] finally, Macdonald[25] and Apple have voiced similar concerns about subjecting the curriculum field to political and social critiques.[26]

By the latter part of the 1970s a number of curriculum conferences and a growing list of articles, journals, and debates attested that the influence of these early critics, such as Macdonald and others, had spread significantly. For example, Apple and Pinar's work, though quite different, was now attracting considerable attention and criticism from educators outside of the boundaries of the reconceptualizing tradition[27] and in fact had reopened a heated debate in a field recently declared moribund. In addition, some of the earlier modes of reconceptualizing were now being further developed to include perspectives drawn from the Frankfurt School version of critical theory and ethnographic school studies grounded in a neo-Marxist perspective. The latter is particularly exemplified in the more current work of Henry A. Giroux and Jean Anyon.

While it is too early to speak of the work of the reconceptualists a distinct and integrated school of thought, it is probably appropriate to refer to it as a mode of theorizing whose supporters reject the positivistic and conservative nature of existing curriculum theory and practice. At the core of this form of theorizing is an attempt, which takes many forms, to make the human subject a primary focus of concern and to develop modes of criticism and social practices whose ultimate aim is captured by Giroux when he writes that educational theory and practice can be

> generally construed as a paradigm that combines theory and practice in the interest of freeing individuals and social groups from the subjective and objective conditions that bind them to the forces of exploitation and oppression. This suggests a critical theory that promotes self-reflection aimed at dismantling forms of false consciousness and ideologically frozen social relations, all of which usually parade under the guise of universalistic laws. . . . This suggests a learning process in which thought and action would be mediated by specific cognitive, affective, and moral dimensions.[28]

Suffice to say that now with the appearance of the reconceptualists the field could be loosely categorized into three modes: the traditional, the conceptual-empirical (as these terms are used in the social scientific tradition), and the reconceptualist. In the next section we will define these categories further.

The text you are about to read, therefore, has a dual purpose. One is to introduce you to the field of curriculum by offering exemplars from each of the three major modes of work that comprise it. Second, we offer a sketch of a field in progress. In most introductory texts, a field of study is presented as a fait accompli, as something final. While some fields do achieve consensus for a period of time, all fields are in process and have a history and a future that is created through debate and through response to "external" factors such as recessions, declining birth rates, Russian satellites, and "internal" disputes, as you will see in the last section. Because curriculum has always involved political and economic as well as epistemological considerations, we consider it appropriate to lay bare these aspects of a field in evolution. We hope that from your study you will gain insight into the processes that underlie a field's formation and regeneration as well as into those of this particular field in formation. Further, we hope you will be moved to participate in it, and we welcome you.

Notes

1. L. Cremin, "Curriculum Making in the United States," in *Curriculum Theorizing: The Reconceptualists,* ed. W. Pinar (Berkeley: McCutchan Publishing, 1975).
2. Ibid.
3. Quoted in H. Kliebard, "Bureaucracy and Curriculum Theory," in Pinar, *Curriculum Theorizing*, p. 52.
4. Ibid., p. 53.
5. Ibid., p. 60.
6. Ibid.
7. Ibid., pp. 63–67.
8. H. Kliebard, "Persistent Curriculum Issues," in Pinar, *Curriculum Theorizing*, p. 41.
9. L. Nicholas, *Theory and Practice* (Notre Dame: University of Notre Dame Press, 1967).
10. H. Taba, *Curriculum Development* (New York: Harcourt, Brace, and World, 1962).
11. D. Tanner and L. Tanner, *Curriculum Development,* 2d ed. (New York: Macmillan, 1980).
12. Cremin, "Curriculum Making," p. 28.
13. G. Beauchamp, *Curriculum Theory*, 3d ed. (Wilmette, Illinois: Kagg Press, 1975).
14. M. Johnson, Jr., "Definitions and Models in Curriculum Theory," *Educational Theory* 17:2 (April 1967):127–140.

15. J. K. Duncan and J. R. Frymier, "Explorations in the Systematic Study of Curriculum," *Theory into Practice* 6:4 (October 1967):180–200.

16. J. Schwab, "The Practical: A Language for Curriculum," *School Review* 77 (November 1969):1–23.

17. D. Huebner, "The Moribund Curriculum Field: Its Wake and Our Work," Division B Address, 1976 Meeting of AERA. Also, W. Pinar, "Notes on the Curriculum Field 1978," *Educational Researcher* 7:8 (September 1978):5–12.

18. J. Miller, "Curriculum Theory: A Recent History," *Journal of Curriculum Theorizing* 1:1 (1978):28–43.

19. All of these authors are represented in Pinar, *Curriculum Theorizing*, 1975.

20. For a critical overview of reconceptualist thinking see K. Mazza, "Reconceptual Inquiry as an Alternative Mode of Curriculum Theory and Practice: A Critical Study (Doctoral dissertation, Boston University, 1980).

21. W. Pinar and M. Grumet, *Toward a Poor Curriculum* (Dubuque, Iowa: Kendall/Hunt, 1976).

22. See the various articles by Huebner in Pinar, *Curriculum Theorizing*, 1975.

23. H. Kliebard, "The Drive for Curriculum Change in the United States, 1890-1958, I—The Ideological Roots of Curriculum as a Field of Specialization," *Journal of Curriculum Studies* 2:3 (1979):191–202.

24. M. Greene, *Teacher as Stranger* (Belmont, Calif.: Wadsworth, 1973); and *Landscapes of Learning* (New York: Teachers College Press, 1978).

25. J. Macdonald, "The Quality of Everyday Life in Schools," in *Schools in Search of Meaning*, ed. J. McDonald and E. Zaret (Washington, D.C.: Association for Supervision and Curriculum Development, 1975); "Curriculum, Consciousness, and Social Change," in *The Hidden Curriculum and Moral Education*, ed. H. Giroux and D. Purpel (Berkeley: McCutchan, in press); also see Macdonald's work in Pinar, *Curriculum Theorizing*, 1975.

26. M. Apple, *Ideology and Curriculum* (Boston and London: Routledge & Kegan Paul, 1979).

27. See D. Tanner and L. Tanner, "Emancipation from Research: The Reconceptualist Prescription," *Educational Researcher* 8:6 (June 1979):8–12.

28. H. A. Giroux, "Toward a New Sociology of Curriculum," *Educational Leadership* 37:3 (December 1979): 248. This theme is more fully developed in H. A. Giroux, *Ideology, Culture, and the Process of Schooling* (Sussex, England: The Falmer Press, 1981).

Section I
CURRICULUM

Three Perspectives on Curriculum

After reading the following section, you will realize that the term *curriculum* is used in diverse though categorizable ways by writers in the field. The commonsensical definition is a "course of study." Rarely, however, has this definition been widely employed by curriculum specialists. For example, Franklin Bobbitt in *The Curriculum* defines it as a "series of experiences which children and youth must have by way of attaining . . . objectives."[1] An even broader definition still focused on "experience" is Vernon Anderson's; in his view, curriculum is "the whole of interacting forces of the total environment."[2] For many, curriculum as a field includes curriculum theory, development, implementation (that is, instruction), and evaluation.[3] Johnson, on the other hand, restricts the definition to "intended learning outcomes."[4] Beauchamp suggests that "a legitimate use of the term *curriculum* is to refer to a *curriculum system*. . . . A curriculum in schools is the system within which decisions are made about what the curriculum will be and how it will be implemented."[5] More recent definitions include curriculum as "social text,"[6] as the "running of the course,"[7] and as the "relationship between the knower and the known."[8]

We can categorize these definitions as either traditional, conceptual-empirical, or reconceptualist. Bobbitt's and Anderson's are traditional. Johnson's and Beauchamp's are conceptual-empirical; the final three are reconceptualist. Giroux describes these categories as theoretical frameworks that govern specific approaches to curriculum issues. Each of these frameworks can be characterized by the dominant and subordinate assumptions that govern the knowledge and values which underlie their respective modes of inquiry.

While each of these frameworks contain rather broad boundaries, their distinctiveness rests with their identifying problematic. The problematic of a theoretical framework is not only the questions that it asks but also the questions it does not ask. As such, the problematic refers to the relationship between questions asked and questions ignored by each of these frameworks. For instance, the traditionalist may ask what goals the school should seek to attain but not what goals specific socioeconomic classes should seek to attain and in what ways the schools as presently organized block the attainment of class goals. The traditionalist framework raises questions about the best or most efficient way to learn a specific kind of knowledge (the "cultural heritage"), to create moral consensus, and to provide a curriculum that keeps the existing society functioning. Outside of its framework are questions concerning the school as an agent of reproduction in a class-divided society and questions that deal with power, ideology, and class conflict. Questions concerning the intersubjective basis of establishing meaning, knowledge, and legitimating social relationships are ignored. The question of how people generate meaning tends to be obscured in favor of how people can master someone else's meaning, thus depoliticizing both culture and classroom pedagogy.

Traditional curriculum notions have lent themselves to transmission forms of instruction. Since they place high priority on knowledge that is functional, thus given and taken for granted, this approach appears to leave little room for analyzing the notion of the hidden curriculum in classroom encounters or linking patterns of instruction to corresponding patterns in the larger social order.

The allegiance of the conceptual-empirical position is to a model of logic and investigation based on the physical sciences. Its interests include certainty, control, and prediction. It supports a unitary scientific method and tends to deny the importance of other modes of knowing such as the literary or the artistic. Facts are considered as clearly separable from values.

A number of thematic strands can be associated with the reconceptualist framework or problematic. There is a strong hermeneutical tradition with its emphasis upon subjectivity, existential experience, the art of interpretation, and the centrality of intentionality to understanding human action. There is as well a strong political strand with emphasis upon class conflict, the reproduction of power relations, a concern for resistance, and the inherently political character of culture, meaning, and knowledge. Giroux develops these categories in more detail in his chapter on the "new sociology of curriculum"; Pinar discusses them in his "The Reconceptualization of Curriculum Studies."

As you see, there are and have been diverse and even conflicting definitions of the term *curriculum*. As you read this section, you might ponder how each definition suggests its own theoretical agenda for the field. You might also begin to develop your own assessment of the various definitions and start to sketch in your own agenda within the field of curriculum.

Notes

1. F. Bobbitt, *The Curriculum* (Boston: Houghton Mifflin Co., 1918),p. 42.
2. V. Anderson, *Principles and Procedures of Curriculum Improvement* (New York: Ronald Press, 1956), p. 9.
3. R. Tyler, *Basic Principles of Curriculum and Instruction* (Chicago:University of Chicago Press, 1950).
4. M. Johnson, Jr., "Definitions and Models in Curriculum Theory,"*Educational Theory* (April 1967): 127–40.
5. G. Beauchamp, *Curriculum Theory* (Wilmette, Illinois: Kagg Press, 1975), p. 6.
6. See the work of H. Giroux or M. Apple in this text.
7. See "Autobiography and Reconceptualization" by M. R. Grumet in this text.
8. W. Pinar, "The Voyage Out," *Journal of Curriculum Theorizing* 2:1, (Winter 1980).

Traditionalists

1 Specific Approaches to Curriculum Development

Ralph W. Tyler

Introduction

In this essay Ralph Tyler draws upon his rich history of involvement with schools to define and demonstrate the nature of curriculum theory and development. Tyler's main point appears to be that curriculum development is by and large a systematic attempt at problem solving focused on a particular school problem, namely, the understanding and guidance of learning in the schools. Tyler's work has been the subject of a heated debate for the last decade.
- What relationship does Tyler present between schools and the wider society?
- What conceptual guidelines does he point to in developing a model of curriculum theory?
- In more specific terms, what are some of the underlying assumptions that support his call for viewing curriculum development as a response to a perceived "problem" situation?
- What, if anything, do you think Tyler leaves out of his model of curriculum development?

The term *curriculum* is used in several different ways in current educational literature. In its most limited sense, it is an outline of a course of study. At the other extreme, the curriculum is considered to be everything that transpires in the course of planning, teaching, and learning in an educational institution. In this chapter the term will be used to include the plans for an educational program. The phrase *curriculum development*, then, will refer to developing the

Reprinted from *Strategies for Curriculum Development*, eds. Jon Schaffarzick and David H. Hampson (Berkeley, Calif.: McCutchan, 1975), pp. 17–33.

plans for an educational program, including the identification and selection of educational objectives, the selection of learning experiences, the organization of the learning experiences, and the evaluation of the educational program.

Approaches to curriculum development are likely to vary with different kinds of educational institutions: those used in professional schools are not usually like those used in liberal arts colleges, and those appropriate for colleges may not be feasible in elementary schools. The focus of this chapter is on approaches to curriculum development in American public elementary and secondary schools.

The term *approach* also has a variety of meanings in contemporary educational discourse. Here it will be used to include the various aspects of the developmental process, including the assumptions, the purposes, the criteria, the procedures, and the participants in curriculum development projects.

The content of this chapter is derived from my experience in curriculum development beginning in Nebraska in 1925. Although many of the projects I have been involved in have been in colleges or professional schools, a considerable part of my activities has been with elementary and secondary schools, for example, the Eight Year Study with high schools and the Neighborhood Education Center involving four elementary schools in an inner-city "disadvantaged" area.

The Nature of Curriculum Development

Curriculum development is a practical enterprise—not a theoretical study. It endeavors to design a system to achieve an educational end and is not primarily attempting to explain an existential phenomenon. The system must be designed to operate effectively in a society where a number of constraints are present and with human beings who all have purposes, preferences, and dynamic mechanisms in operation. Hence, an essential early step in curriculum development is to examine and analyze significant conditions that influence the construction and operation of the curriculum.

Preliminary Analysis

One important factor for early analysis is the need or problem that has led to the decision to construct or reconstruct a curriculum. For example, the many recent attempts to develop new curricula for disadvantaged children have largely been stimulated both by the recognition that children from low-income families—especially minorities—are making little progress in their academic work and by the pressure on the schools exerted by active minority groups. The several national curriculum-development projects in science and mathematics were mainly promoted by scientists and mathematicians who pointed to the out-of-date content that they found in high school textbooks and who were concerned by the small percent of high school students taking advanced courses in science and mathematics.

The current interest in building new curricula for "career education" appears to derive from several needs or problems that are now becoming recognized. One problem is the widespread lack of understanding on the part of children and youth of the modern world of work. Another is the increasing alienation of youth from the adult society, which includes a lack of plans or planning for their future occupations. A third is the current high level of unemployment of youth between the ages of sixteen and twenty-one, and a fourth is the lack of vocational courses in the high school for job areas that are experiencing increasing demand.

Most curriculum approaches do not involve a systematic analysis of the needs or problems that stimulated the initial interest in the curriculum. As a result, it is likely that some of the curriculum-development efforts will not adequately provide for these needs or solve the problems, or else the local schools will not adopt the new curricula because they do not appear to be responsive to the problems that are recognized locally. For example, the most expensive curriculum-development project undertaken to that time was the high school physics course produced by the Physical Science Study Committee.[1] In spite of the large expenditures, both in development and in teacher institutes to help physics teachers understand and utilize the materials, schools using them today as the committee intended them to be used are in a distinct minority. Part of this ineffectiveness can be attributed to other factors, but one obvious error made by PSSC was its failure to work with local schools to know what problems and difficulties they were experiencing in physics courses and to see that the new physics curriculum would indeed provide a way to solve some of these problems or overcome some of the difficulties.

Far too often the following questions are asked: "How can we get the schools to change?" or "Why aren't the schools innovative?" The school ought not change for the sake of change nor innovate for the sake of innovation. The school has a mission that it performs more-or-less well. Where the school seems to be succeeding in its mission, there is no reason to change. Where the school encounters problems or discovers it is failing in its mission, school personnel are usually interested in doing something likely to solve the problem. The schoolpeople accepted the diagnosis of the physicists that the content of high school physics textbooks was out of date, and they welcomed the efforts of PSSC to produce authentic up-to-date material. They did not, however, recognize the necessity for a new kind of learning experience and a new kind of teaching strategy. Hence, as Goodlad and his colleagues found in their observations of a sample of PSSC classrooms,[2] the PSSC materials were being utilized in the same way that previous textbooks had been used. It is doubtful, furthermore, whether many high schools considered the relatively small enrollment in advanced physics classes as a serious problem. Had they done so, they might have helped the Physical Science Study Committee analyze possible causes for this enrollment situation and develop more effective plans than were represented by the PSSC course. It is interesting that neither the PSSC nor Project Physics has stopped the downward trend in enrollment in high school physics classes.

Another important facet of analyzing a curriculum problem is to identify the particular category of students who are having difficulties with the present curriculum or for whom no satisfactory learning system is available. In the field of primary reading, for example, 75 to 80 percent of American children achieve the skills required to comprehend typical newspaper items and children's stories by age thirteen. However, 20 to 25 percent do not learn to read adequately. These children are usually found in the inner cities and in very rural areas. They commonly come from low-income families where the parents have had little education. Designing a more effective reading curriculum for these categories of children is a different task than the effort needed to develop a curriculum to be used for all primary children.

Similarly, an analysis of the problem of the individualization of learning reveals certain categories of children who devise their own individual sequence of learning and proceed at their own rate while others require a curriculum specifically designed to enable them to learn and to progress sequentially. It is an inefficient use of resources to design an individualized curriculum for those who develop one for themselves.

It is still early enough in the development of major curriculum projects in career education to analyze the problems more fully before actually designing curricula to deal with them. The proponents of some of these programs are nevertheless telling the community, and especially low-income parents, that the new curriculum—when in operation—will largely guarantee the employment of graduates who do not go on to postsecondary schools. An analysis of the problem would have shown that it is not primarily the lack of occupational skills that prevents the large-scale employment of seventeen-year-olds. Most employing institutions will not hire youth under age twenty-one no matter how skilled they are. If this is true, the implication for the design of curricula for occupational-skill training would connect it directly with employment, possibly through cooperative education or through postsecondary technical training. The main point I wish to make is that curriculum development projects must begin with an analysis of the needs or problems that have stimulated the decision to develop a new or revised curriculum.

Related to the analysis of the relevant problems, the approach should examine the contemporary educational environments, including the home, the peer group, the larger community, and the school in order to identify dynamic factors that influence the problem and the constraints that must be considered in designing an effective curriculum. For example, an analysis of the large environment of young children in a slum neighborhood might reveal a per-

Specific Approaches to Curriculum Development 21

vasive negative attitude toward the school and schooling that strongly influences the children's work in school; thus many of the children consider their time in school not only irrelevant but also boring, unhappy, and often painful. In this situation curriculum that assumes that the students want to learn what the school has to teach will be ineffective. Some way of influencing the out-of-school environment is necessary, or else a curriculum must be designed with highly potent internal rewards.

Particular attention should be given to teachers when one is considering the positive and negative dynamic factors that must be taken into account in the curriculum development project. A curriculum designed as a complete, almost teacher-proof learning system will not usually be acceptable to teachers in any field in which they feel confident they can teach and do not dislike the teaching role. The curriculum preferred and more likely to be used by teachers is one with components from which the teacher can make selections and/or adaptations in terms of what he perceives to be necessary for the conditions he works under and what he believes best utilizes his skills, ingenuity, and personal style. A rigid learning system that permits or requires very little artistry on the part of the teacher is likely to be accepted only when the teacher dislikes the teaching task—as in routine drill in spelling, handwriting, or computation—or feels that he does not have the competence to teach the task well. The curriculum development plan will, in most cases, need to include means for working with teachers to assure that the curriculum meets their needs and that they can handle their roles effectively.

One of the limiting factors requiring attention in many curriculum projects is the conscious or unconscious assumption on the part of the school that it is fully as much a sorting institution as it is an educational one. In the past these two functions largely went together. Many children from families with educated parents went to school with some notion of what they were expected to learn and how to go about learning it. This made it possible for them to be guided by the existing curriculum, including textbooks and other learning materials, and to use them successfully. A number of other students did not, however, understand the purposes or the learning tasks they were assigned and saw no connection between the curriculum and those things that were important to them. The class activities and the learning materials neither caught their attention nor stimulated their efforts. Normal school practice was to assign high marks to those who found meaning and satisfaction in the curriculum and low marks to those who did not carry on the learning tasks successfully. Thus "good students" were encouraged to continue their education, while "poor students" were discouraged and dropped out or were pushed out.

It has been common in the past to place responsibility for failure on the quality of students rather than on the adequacy of the curriculum, and—since the society did not appear to suffer when "poor students" did not learn—the school was not attacked for sorting them out. Now, however, an uneducated person is a costly liability to American society, and the schools are expected to educate all children. It is also widely recognized that every child who has no serious physical handicap is capable of learning the kinds of behavior emphasized by the schools.

This change in expectation necessitates not only a new orientation on the part of many teachers but also new understanding and skills. In curriculum development it requires the formulation of learning objectives that are understood by both teachers and students and believed by both to be desirable and attainable. An approach that seeks to develop a curriculum that will be meaningful and helpful to students who have not learned much heretofore involves working with such children and their teachers to clarify meaningful educational goals and to find learning experiences that stimulate the children's attention and interest and that they can carry through successfully.

Some constraints arise from the traditional role of the public schools in America. In the past children and youth learned most of what was required to be a constructive adult outside of school. They gradually were inducted into adult life because the barriers separating them from adults were neither many nor rigid. By the time they were fifteen or sixteen, they had participated with adults in most of life's arenas: home, work, church, playing field, and social and civic activities. But the school was expected to expand the horizon of children by opening up the resources of scholarship, which went far beyond firsthand experience in the community. The school was not to be a substitute for direct experience but a means of enlarging it. Reading, writing, history, geography, literature, mathematics, science—these were subjects that could open up a vast world of experiences, ideas, and knowledge that could free young people from the limitation of their parochial environment. Hence, teachers were sought who had had scholarly preparation.

Now, a bachelor's degree is a minimum requirement for teacher certification in all states. Scholarly interests and background are assets for much teaching, but they may be a constraint when teachers are expected to provide vocational guidance relating to occupations that are foreign to academic college programs. Ginzberg's study of career guidance[3] shows its inadequacy in the typical American high school. A scholarly teacher is unlikely to know much about blue-collar jobs or to be a role model for them; he is also likely to have low esteem for such jobs and to communicate this to his students. Such a constraint needs to be considered in planning career education curricula in order to determine what is possible in a school and what will have to be learned elsewhere.

Although I have used career education as an extreme example of a constraint that must be recognized in the typical teaching staff, most curriculum development projects will find that teachers or other school personnel have not yet acquired the attitudes, understanding, or skills necessary to guide some of the desirable learning experiences. Where such constraints are identified, they need to be dealt with by providing for necessary teacher education, by allocating the learning activities to other institutions or individuals, or by eliminating them from the curriculum.

When the education or preparation of teachers, administrators, parents, or others is an essential part of the curriculum plan, the feasibility in terms of the efficient allocation of resources for this task is frequently overlooked. In Israel, for example, the Science Teaching Center developed a new science curriculum that required extensive further education of teachers in order for them to properly guide the learning of their students. After the materials were developed, the expenditures for the teacher education program were estimated. Much to the consternation of the project staff, it was found that the cost of educating Israel's high school science teachers to use the new course would require all of the in-service education funds of the Ministry of Education for ten years. And there was, in the meantime, great demand for curriculum development in the field of social studies. The total requirements, including personnel, equipment and supplies, consultations, and the further education of teachers, should be carefully estimated when a major curriculum project is undertaken. In the past many—if not most—such projects have failed to come to fruition because the practical requirements could not be met.

Rationale for Curriculum Building

After identifying the needs or problems to which the curriculum development project should be responsive and the constraints under which the curriculum must operate, the curriculum builders have a clearer picture of the requirements the curriculum will have to satisfy; then it is possible to work on the several components of the total project. To guide these activities, a rationale is helpful if not essential. Various rationales are described in the current educational literature, and several of them have been used successfully. However, I prefer the one outlined in my syllabus, *Basic Principles of Curriculum and Instruction*,[4] because it is comprehensive and has been employed effectively in a number of curriculum projects.

In this rationale, four major tasks serve as the focuses of curriculum construction: the selection and definition of the learning objectives, the selection and creation of appropriate learning experiences, the organization of the learning experiences to achieve a maximum cumulative effect, and the evaluation of the curriculum to furnish a continuing basis for necessary revisions and desirable improvements. In the case of projects that seek to reconstruct the total school curriculum, the selection and definition of the learning objectives will commonly be attacked first. But a project that deals with only one subject or curriculum area may begin with the evaluation of an earlier curriculum and then move to objectives, learning experiences, and organization. In some cases, as in building a curriculum in the field of literature, the first step may be the selection of literary works that appear to offer a variety of new experiences for students and then to consider what can be learned from the reading of these materials that is important for the students. Whichever of the four major tasks is undertaken first, the complete development project will involve them all, often moving to and fro several times as ideas emerge that are checked and rechecked among the several components of the curriculum.

Selecting and Defining Objectives

Curriculum building is not a process based on precise rules, but rather it involves artistic design as well as critical analysis, human judgments, and empirical testing. In selecting objectives, for example, curriculum makers need current data and future estimates about opportunities and problems in various sectors of society—occupational, sociocivic, home and family, recreational. These data should be accurate and reliable, but the interpretations as to what students can learn so they can respond to opportunities or help solve problems are judgments that are not precise, and these judgments become more dependable only as they are tested in actual curriculum practice. Similarly, information about the interests of particular students, their abilities, and their problems should be accurate and reliable, but the interpretations drawn from them as to what these students can learn that will broaden their interests as well as satisfy them, that will furnish a more comprehensive set of abilities as well as build on those already acquired, and that will enable them to deal successfully with their problems—these are judgments that become more dependable as they are tested in the operation of the curriculum. Even more a matter of human judgment are the decisions concerning what students can learn of significance from a given subject-matter field—its concepts, generalizations, questions for inquiry, methods of inquiry, skills, attitudes, and facts. When it comes to the enhanced emotional responses that can be learned from the study of literature and other arts, human judgments and the results of actual curriculum practices are the major bases for selecting objectives.

Recognizing the importance in selecting objectives that human judgments based on experience as well as relevant data systematically collected and analyzed play, I recommend the procedure of group deliberation described by Joseph J. Schwab[5] and illustrated in some detail by Seymour Fox at the AERA Convention in 1971. Suggestions and judgments of teachers, subject-matter specialists, curriculum specialists, psychologists, sociologists, and specialists in human development can be considered and their probable consequences can be deliberated in some ways that lead to constructive decisions that in turn form the basis of initial objectives to be tested for their attainability and their effects in real curriculum projects.

This procedure of deliberation is also helpful in defining the level of generalization on which to focus an objective. Since 1910 American curriculum practice has alternated between two extremes: learning objectives stated so generally that they failed to clarify the kind of behavior the student was to be

Specific Approaches to Curriculum Development

helped to learn and objectives that are so specific that they fail to provide for the level of behavior generalization of which human beings are capable. To state that an objective of arithmetic is to teach students to "think" is obviously too general to guide the selection of learning experiences, the activities of the student or of the teacher, but to formulate more than three thousand objectives of arithmetic as E. L. Thorndike[6] did more than fifty years ago is to caricature human learning. Children can, for example, acquire the "idea" of addition and learn to add with a score of illustrative examples without practicing on each of the one hundred combinations of one-digit numbers taken two at a time. When I wrote in 1931 of the need for stating objectives in terms of behavior, I made definite reference to the fact that an objective could be clearly defined in terms of generalized behavior if the students involved were able to generalize at that level. An objective can be clear without being specific.

During World War II, when large numbers of workers had to be quickly trained to carry on specific tasks like soldering electronic circuitry, the training directors emphasized specific objectives. After the war this approach was carried over into education without scrutinizing the difference between objectives appropriate for very short training programs for specific jobs and the long-term educational programs in schools. In making judgments about the level of generality to be the focus of a given educational objective, one should use the process of deliberation carried on by the types of groups suggested above.

The syllabus mentioned earlier comments on the use of the schools's educational philosophy as a screen or set of criteria for selecting objectives, particularly for distinguishing the more important from the less important ones. The syllabus also points out the way in which knowledge of the psychology of learning can be used to estimate the probability of attaining a given objective under the conditions found in a particular school. It is obvious that the effort to develop learning experiences for an objective that has small likelihood of being attained would be wasted.

The selection and definition of objectives for a curriculum are a complex but necessary—and continuing—task. It continues both as the rest of the curriculum tasks are carried on and after the curriculum is operating because new external conditions and experiences with the curriculum in the school will provide new information and the bases for new judgments about objectives. A curriculum must be ever relevant in the best sense of that word.

Selecting and Creating Learning Experiences

Creating learning experiences is an even more artistic enterprise than the selection of objectives. It is true that certain conditions must be met for an experience to aid the student in reaching the objective. The student must, for example, carry on the behavior that is the learning objective in order to learn it. The learner must, furthermore, obtain satisfaction (reinforcement) from the desired behavior in order for it to become part of his repertoire of behavior. Opportunities for practicing the behavior and for feedback to inform the learner when his performance is not satisfactory so that he can try again are also conditions to be met by a set of learning experiences. But these are criteria largely used in appraising possible learning experiences, not means of creating them. Not all teachers or curriculum builders are able to create new and effective learning experiences. One procedure I have found useful is to ask each of those involved in the curriculum development project to suggest a few learning experiences that seem appropriate and then use the deliberative process to review, criticize, and identify those offering enough promise for further development. The persons who, in this preliminary exercise, created some experiences that held up under deliberative review are then encouraged to produce more.

In creating learning experiences, it is important to use the perspective of the different kinds of students for whom they are designed. The initial activities should attract the attention of each student and seem worth doing because they can help him learn something he wants to learn, because they are interesting to do, or because persons he respects are doing them. These activities should also be well within his present ability to carry on successfully so that he can gain confidence in going on to further activities. Although practice is essential in learning, repetitive drill soon becomes boring, and the student does not give adequate attention to it. This effort to use the student's perspective is often overlooked in creating learning experiences. It is necessary to keep firmly in mind that human learners rarely, if ever, want to be "shaped" by others. Each one has purposes and interests of his own and utilizes much energy and effort to further his purposes and satisfy his interests. If a school activity is perceived as interesting and/or useful for his purposes, he enters into it energetically, whereas if it seems irrelevant or boring or painful, he avoids it, or limits his involvement as much as he can. I have found that observing and interviewing students when they are actively engaged in learning things they think are important helps me to develop initial outlines for experiences that will then help these students learn things the school seeks to teach.

Another important principle to keep in mind is to make use of peer-group influences as far as they can be appropriately employed in the development of the desired objectives. Solitary activities are hard for children to carry on for long periods of time. Group projects and games, group discussions, group attacks on problems, and group planning of emotionally charged experiences are illustrations of activities that provide powerful learning experiences. A two-student group is a special case in which learning can be enhanced. The two may be of different ages in a tutoring relationship, of the same age in a cooperative endeavor, or of the same age in a competitive contest. When participants in a curriculum development project are encouraged to explore the many types of social learning, they are usually able to create a wider range of effective learning experiences than they produced before.

Learning experiences that facilitate transfer usually require explicit attention. Every educational program seeks to help students develop new ways of thinking, feeling, and acting that can be used by them in various appropriate situations they encounter in their lives. Education has been unsuccessful if the student does not transfer what he learns in school to his life outside. Because many things to be learned in school are new ways of viewing situations, new ways of attacking problems, new ways of understanding and explaining phenomena, new ways of responding emotionally to aesthetic experiences, new kinds of interests, and new social, intellectual, and communication skills, they are often in sharp contrast to the habits, ideas, and practices of many students. Without learning experiences that furnish help to apply these new things to life situations the student is encountering, he may not transfer school learning to his life outside the classroom. Hence, for every objective, the participants in curriculum development will find it helpful to consider the ways in which and the conditions under which the behavior being learned can be appropriately employed by the student outside the classroom. Thus, an important criterion for a set of learning experiences is the inclusion of several that stimulate the student to use what he is learning in school outside of school. Too frequently the curriculum omits this important component.

Organizing Learning Experiences

The syllabus referred to earlier discusses the relatively minor changes in student behavior that result from single, isolated learning experiences. However, when they are organized so that each subsequent experience builds on what has been learned in earlier ones and so that the student can perceive the connection between what he is learning in one field and what he is learning in another, the cumulative effect in changes in the learner's behavior is greatly enhanced. The purpose guiding the task of organizing learning experiences in the curriculum is that of trying to maximize their combined impact. In obtaining a larger cumulative effect, attention should be given both to the sequence of experiences within each field of learning, such as mathematics, social studies, and occupational planning, and the extent of integration among the fields. By integration is meant the learner's perception of meaningful connectives from one field to another so that what he learns day by day in the several fields will be part of his repertoire of behavior, and he can draw upon this combined learning as he encounters appropriate situations or problems.

To plan for sequence and integration, organizing elements—such as concepts, skills, and values—are helpful. This means, for example, that the curriculum makers identify major concepts that are useful in explaining and controlling phenomena and that are sufficiently complex and pervasive to enable the student to gain increasing depth of understanding and increasing breadth of application of them as he progresses from week to week and year to year in the curriculum. Some concepts may also be related to phenomena in other fields or problems that cut across several fields so that they are useful elements for aiding integration of learning.

Curriculum makers can also identify significant skills that are sufficiently complex and pervasive to serve as organizing elements to achieve sequence and integration. And, for objectives involving attitudes, appreciations, interests, and personal commitments, curriculum makers can identify important values that can serve as organizing elements.

The syllabus comments on the variety of organizing principles that are found in current curriculums. I doubt if there is a single organizing principle that is to be preferred because it clearly contributes to a greater cumulative effect of the learning experiences. The principles can generally be selected on the grounds that they furnish a sequence or an integration that is meaningful and effective with the students and teachers who are expected to use them.

In addition to criteria, elements, and principles of organization, the curriculum makers must deal with the problem of the organizing structures, such as courses, units, topics, lessons, and their relative rigidity or flexibility. The recent debate on individualization of instruction furnishes an initial list of issues and criteria with regard to the size and definition of useful structures, while the debates on the open classroom fairly well outline the issues and criteria to guide in developing an appropriate balance between flexibility and rigidity.

Curriculum Evaluation

The term *evaluation* is used in several different ways in current educational publications, ranging from the inclusion of all information needed by decision makers in education to the other extreme in which it is restricted to the use of an objective testing program. I shall employ the term to include the process of comparing the ideas and assumptions involved in curriculum development with the realities to which they refer. Most of the planning, monitoring, and reporting of curriculum activities is guided by conceptions the participants have about the persons, processes, and objects involved. Unless there is continuous checking to ascertain the probable validity of these notions, the curriculum-development project will have little relation to the actual situations that are being encountered. Evaluation is this checking process.

The checking process should be applied at four different stages in curriculum development. When one or more ideas are proposed for developing a program, a set of materials, or an instructional device, evaluation should be undertaken to find out whether there is any evidence from earlier experiments or experience that indicates the probable effectiveness of the idea. In reviewing recent curriculum-development projects, I am disappointed to see how frequently ideas are accepted that have been tried or tested in the past and found fallacious. It is unfortunate that so many of the project directors are newcomers to curriculum development and are unfamiliar with its detailed history, because much wasted effort could be avoided by critical evaluation at the idea stage.

Evaluation is also essential in the implementation stage. When a plan is presumably in operation, an actual check of the school situations usually reveals a number of places reporting that the plan is in operation when, in fact, it is not. In some cases this is due to a lack of understanding of the essential features of the plan so that the implementation lacks salient conditions essential to the idea. In other cases those implementing the plan feel that it will not work, and so they establish a program that they think is better. There are even cases where an old procedure is continued while it is professed that the new idea is in operation. I found in the study of activity schools in New York City in 1942 that less than half the classrooms in these schools were actually carrying on activity programs.

Various techniques have been developed for sampling the actual implementation of educational programs. John Goodlad and his colleagues have devised a rather comprehensive schedule for his current *Study of Schooling in the United States*.[7] Seymour Fox and his colleagues in the Hebrew University of Jerusalem have developed an analysis procedure that relates the actual operations to the purposes and guiding principles of the plan. In our study of activity schools, we used a check list of sixty-one items based on an analysis of the plan for these schools.

A third stage in which evaluation contributes to the effectiveness of the curriculum is during its actual operation, both in guiding its development during early trials and also in monitoring its continuing use. Placement tests, mastery tests, and diagnostic tests can keep students and teachers in touch with the actual learning process and can furnish information to guide them. An assessment program conducted once or twice a year can provide data that serve to alert the principal or the central administration regarding problems needing special attention. The yearbook of the National Society for the Study of Education entitled *Evaluation: New Roles, New Means*[8] describes some of these procedures.

Finally, evaluation needs to be conducted to find out the extent to which students are actually developing the patterns of behavior that the curriculum was designed to help them learn. Before curriculum makers had developed sophisticated achievement tests, this kind of evaluation was conducted with norm-referenced achievement tests that were not based on a sample of behavior that the students were expected to learn but only on those exercises which differentiated among pupils. This often meant that the exercises did not reflect what the curriculum was designed to help students learn but involved behavior not in the curriculum; this sharply differentiated students who came from backgrounds where they had experienced these things from students who had not. Because schools attempt to help all children learn, the exercises that sample what the children are really learning in school often do not differentiate sharply among them.

Curriculum makers have recently become more interested in using criterion-referenced tests rather than norm-referenced ones. They have also become aware of various other devices that indicate what students have learned. It seems likely that evaluation of the outcomes of new curricula will be increasingly valid.

Conclusion

The approach outlined in this chapter is pragmatic. It assumes limited resources for curriculum development and effective implementation. It seeks, therefore, to utilize available knowledge and experience at each step. A grand, comprehensive, total-school curriculum is assumed to be impracticable to develop and implement with the resources usually available. Hence the first step is to identify serious difficulties or problems within the present curriculum that should be given primary attention. The second step is to explicitly outline the constraints under which a new curriculum must operate. To maximize the constructive participation in curriculum development, a group procedure—including group deliberation—is suggested. The construction process itself is outlined in terms of four major tasks: selecting objectives, developing learning experiences, organizing learning experiences, and evaluation. This approach has been successful in my own experience, and I believe it has value for others.

Notes

1. The Physical Science Study Committee, chaired by Jerold Zacharias of the Massachusetts Institute of Technology, obtained in 1959 the first grant from the National Science Foundation to produce a new high school physics course.

2. J. Goodlad et al., *Looking Behind the Classroom Door* (Worthington, Ohio: Charles A. Jones, 1974).

3. E. Ginzberg, *Career Guidance: Who Needs It, Who Provides It, Who Can Improve It* (New York: McGraw-Hill, 1971).

4. R. Tyler, *Basic Principles of Curriculum and Instruction* (Chicago: University of Chicago Press, 1949).

5. J. J. Schwab, "The Practical: A Language for Curriculum," *School Review* 78:1 (August 1971): 493–542.

6. E. L. Thorndike, *Psychology of Arithmetic* (New York: Macmillan, 1922).

7. Goodlad et al, *Looking Behind the Classroom Door*.

8. R. Tyler, ed., *Evaluation: New Roles, New Means* (Chicago: University of Chicago Press, 1969).

2 Conceptions of Curriculum and the Curriculum Field

Robert S. Zais

Introduction

This selection from Robert Zais's book *Curriculum: Principles and Foundations* exemplifies, perhaps, the best of the traditional curriculum literature. Its tone is cautious; it treats several viewpoints on the issue of definition impartially. (It excludes several as well, however.) The work is traditional as it attempts to present a compendia of items representative of several major strands of thought. In this sense it attempts an overview, as if the author were standing outside the field. Its major organizing concepts are basically—though not strictly—Tylerian (design, development, implementation). Beauchamp's notion of "curriculum engineering" is also employed.

Zais breaks with reconceptualist work most clearly in the last section on curricular versus noncurricular issues. Here he insists that economic and political issues are not simultaneously curricular issues. Many reconceptualists would not only disagree but would in fact argue that the concepts of design are in the service of larger political and economic tendencies in the culture.

As you read, you might begin with the following questions:

- What evidence can you find in the text to support the argument that while impartial in tone, the chapter is not impartial in fact?
- With what parent discipline would you associate this writing—history, English, journalism? Why?
- After reading these opening two selections, what is your sense of the traditional conception of curriculum?

Reprinted from Robert S. Zais, *Curriculum: Principles and Foundations* (Thomas Y. Crowell Company), pp. 3–21. Copyright © 1976 by Harper & Row, Publishers, Inc. Reprinted by permission of the publisher.

It is most important that those who are constructing our school curriculum shall maintain an overview of the total situation.

Harold Rugg

The term *curriculum*, like most words in our language, is used in many different ways. Indeed, even among professional educators, it is used in so many different ways that communication is often hampered. Although curriculum specialists have, in the interests of clarity, attempted to limit the meaning of *curriculum*, disagreement still exists with respect to what constitutes legitimate definitions of the word.

In the broadest sense the term *curriculum* is ordinarily used by specialists in the field in two ways: (1) to indicate, roughly, a plan for the education of learners and (2) to identify a field of study.[1] Curriculum as a plan for the education of learners is usually referred to as *a* curriculum or *the* curriculum. At present, there is significant disagreement among curriculum specialists with regard to the ingredients of the plan. Curriculum as a plan for the education of learners is part of the subject matter of the curriculum field.

Curriculum as a field of study, like most specialized fields, is defined by (1) the range of subject matters with which it is concerned (the substantive structure) and (2) the procedures of inquiry and practice that it follows (the syntactical structure).[2] Thus, the curriculum field, for our purposes, may be described in terms of the subject matters that are treated in schools and the many processes (for example, curriculum development and curriculum change) with which specialists are characteristically concerned.

Origin and Development of Curriculum as a Field of Study

Curriculum has been a consideration of writers on education for centuries. Plato (Greek philosopher, fourth century B.C.), Comenius (seventeenth-century Moravian bishop and educationist), and Froebel (nineteenth-century German educationist), for example, have all given their attention to the curriculum and its problems. But the specialized and systematic study of curriculum and curricular phemomena and the identification of certain individuals as curriculum specialists did not occur until the twentieth century.[3]

The curriculum field had its roots in the Herbartian movement of the late nineteenth century.[4] Johann Friedrich Herbart (1776–1841) was a German philosopher whose educational ideas had wide acceptance in the United States in the latter half of the nineteenth century. Herbart's theories about teaching and learning required that systematic attention be given to the selection and organization of subject matter. This subject-matter emphasis on the part of Herbartians led to a reawakening of interest in curriculum content in American education around the turn of the century, and as Kliebard[5] states, "curriculum became a popular issue."

During the 1890s and early 1900s, a number of significant educational events occurred that intensified interest in curricular concerns. First, the Committee of Ten, under the chairmanship of Harvard president Charles W. Eliot, issued its famous report in 1893. This report dealt with such matters as required courses, electives, college preparatory subjects, and "practical" subjects—all issues concerning curriculum. In 1895 the Herbart Society—now the National Society for the Study of Education—was formed. In the two decades that followed, members of this organization were influential in keeping the question of curriculum content and organization alive. At this same time, John Dewey was engaged in curriculum experimentation and innovation in his famous Laboratory School at the University of Chicago.

Notwithstanding this concentrated attention to curriculum issues, however, no concerned individual at that time was thought of as a "curriculum specialist," and there existed no "readily identifiable field of curriculum specialization."[6] It was not until 1918 that the first book specifically devoted to the curriculum was published. Written by Franklin Bobbitt and titled simply *The Curriculum*, this volume is generally recognized as the milestone that marks the emergence of curriculum as a specialized field of study.

The 1920s are usually regarded as the formative years of the curriculum field. It was during these years, following the publication of Bobbitt's book, that volumes on curriculum began to appear that were written by educational theorists and practitioners who are thought of as curriculum specialists. W. W. Charters of Ohio State University, for example, published *Curriculum Construction* in 1923. In the following year, *How to Make a Curriculum* appeared as Bobbitt's second major work on this subject. And in 1926 the National Society for the Study of Education (NSSE) published an exhaustive 685-page review of the curriculum movement called *The Foundations and Technique of Curriculum Construction*. This two-part yearbook of the society was prepared by a distinguished committee of "curriculum scholars" that included Franklin Bobbitt, W. W. Charters, and Charles Judd, with Harold Rugg as chairman.

During this period the emergence of curriculum as a field of study manifested itself in several other ways. A number of increasingly "curriculum-conscious" school systems inaugurated programs of curriculum revision. In 1922, for example, Denver launched a systemwide curriculum improvement project, and in 1925 St. Louis attracted national attention with its comprehensive curriculum revision program involving hundreds of teachers and a large group of curriculum consultants.[7] Projects such as these were entirely novel to the educational community at that time.

Another manifestion of the growing interest in curriculum was the establishment of university curriculum laboratories. Following the lead of Teachers College, Columbia University, in 1926, a large number of colleges and departments of education founded curriculum laboratories as innovative but indispensable units in their professional programs.

The 1930s brought further developments that established curriculum as a field of study. State departments of education became interested in curriculum revision and improvement and started programs of implementation. Colleges and schools of education, recognizing the significance of curriculum study for education, founded departments of curriculum. The establishment of the Department of Curriculum and Teaching at Teachers College, Columbia University, in 1937 is generally considered a landmark in this regard. Finally, the development of the Association for Supervision and Curriculum Development as the nationally recognized organization for curriculum workers secured for curriculum specialization the status of an acknowledged (if ill-defined) field of study.

The fact that the field of curriculum has persisted and established its legitimacy in the educational community is probably evidence that it addresses itself to a specific core of educational problems that are not treated in a systematic way by any other segment of the profession. Curriculum workers do not entirely agree as to what these problems are, except that there seems to be a reasonably large number of them. One writer in the field has concluded that during its first four decades (roughly 1895–1938), the curriculum movement was characterized by interest in four "especially persistent and significant" problems: (1) the nature of knowledge; (2) the nature of knowing; (3) the domain and limits of the new speciality, curriculum; and (4) the translation of curriculum principles and theories into educational practice.[8] It is Seguel's further contention that since 1938 "there has been remarkably little basic change in the field."[9] In the absence of any comprehensive historical investigation of the curriculum field since 1938, this contention must be viewed as an educated conjecture. If the nature of the curriculum field's central concerns are to be the index, however, there is some evidence that shifts in direction have taken place. For example, Caswell[10] identifies three "matters of central concern" to "most or all of the curriculum movement": (1) the establishment of a consistent relationship between general goals, on the one hand, and specific objectives to guide teaching on the other; (2) the assurance of sound sequence or continuity in curriculum; and (3) the provision for balance in the curriculum.

A survey of eminent curriculum specialists would probably yield a quite disparate list of educational concerns identified as being distinctively curricular in nature, although some issues would undoubtedly emerge more prominently than others. This difficulty in defining the major interests of curriculum study testifies to the relative infancy of the field. Another indication of the developmental state of curriculum is the lack of precision in the meaning of its basic terminology. Among the most persistent difficulties in this regard is the definition of the word *curriculum* when it is used to refer to a plan for edu-

Conceptions of Curriculum

cation. The following section discusses and assesses some of the variant meanings attached to the term as it is used in the curriculum literature.

Concepts of the Curriculum

The word *curriculum* comes from a Latin root meaning "racecourse," and, traditionally, the school's curriculum has represented something like that—figuratively speaking of course—to most people. Indeed until quite recently even the most knowledgeable professional educators regarded curriculum as the relatively standardized ground covered by students in their race toward the finish line (a diploma). It should not be a surprise, then, to find that many current concepts of the curriculum are firmly grounded in this notion that curriculum is a racecourse of subject matters to be mastered.

Curriculum as the Program of Studies

When asked to describe the curriculum of a particular high school, the informed layman often recites a list of the subjects offered (or required) by the school. He is likely to answer, "The curriculum includes English, algebra, history, economics, and so on." A more specific response would involve a listing of the titles of the courses offered by the school: American History, Elementary Algebra, French I, and the like. Except in a very few instances, subject matter designations convey variable and imprecise information on the content and processes of the subject. Furthermore, reflection on our own experience will serve to remind us that course titles ordinarily reveal very little about the learning outcomes and the experiences that students can expect to have while taking the course. For these reasons, therefore, specialists in the field prefer to use the term "program of studies" rather than curriculum to refer to a school's subjects and/or course offerings.

Curriculum as Course Content

The content of particular courses in the program is often regarded as the curriculum. For example, when asked to describe the American history curriculum, a teacher might recite the topical outline of the course: discovery and exploration before 1607, settlement of the southern colonies, colonization of New England, and so forth. This concept of curriculum, like the one described above, was prevalent among most professional educators before the advent of the curriculum movement. It is extremely simple and, indeed, tends toward the naive. It conceives of curriculum solely as the data or information recorded in guides or textbooks and overlooks many additional elements that need to be provided for in a learning plan. Such a conception of curriculum limits planning to the selection and organization of information that learners are to acquire. Clearly, other elements in the educational arena (for example, the conditions under which learners are to interact with content) need to be included in the definition of curriculum.

Curriculum as Planned Learning Experiences

A curriculum conceived of as planned learning experiences[11] is one of the most prevalent concepts among specialists in the field today. For example, Krug[12] refers to curriculum as "all the means employed by the school to provide students with opportunities for desirable learning experiences," and Doll[13] writes: "The commonly-accepted definition of the curriculum has changed from *content of courses of study and lists of subjects and courses to all the experiences which are offered to learners under the auspices or direction of the school.*" This broader definition seems to reflect the educational state of affairs more accurately than the previous definitions. The school, after all, is established in order to educate—that is, to develop along certain lines—the learners placed in its charge. This development is achieved through the experiences that the learners have, and so it seems reasonable to conclude that the curriculum, as a blueprint for education, ultimately consists of the experiences planned for learners to have. While this definition has been criticized by a number of specialists as being far too broad to be functional (see Taba,[14] Johnson,[15] Inlow,[16]), others view this rather expansive definition of curriculum as being too narrow! The latter would argue that the curriculum consists ultimately of all the experiences that learners *in fact do have* under the auspices of the school, whether planned for or not.

Curriculum as Experiences "Had" Under the Auspices of the School

Writers who favor the broader definition of curriculum sometimes refer to the "invisible curriculum" or the "hidden curriculum," that is, those aspects of the curriculum that are unplanned or unintended and therefore overlooked. They point out that certain planned curriculum experiences are designed, for example, to teach students to read, but as a result of certain other experiences "had" by the students, they may *also* learn to dislike reading. Thus, both the experiences that teach students to read and those that teach dislike of reading must be counted as part of the curriculum, even though the latter experiences were not planned for and are unintended. Along these same lines, some critics of the schools have noted that while students experience and learn the various subject areas of the high school curriculum, they also experience the authoritarian structure of the institution and thus learn conformity to authority along with their algebra, history, and English.

The case for this wide-ranging definition of curriculum is difficult to refute if we are at all interested in the *totality* of students' experiences in school. Obviously, however, the definition is not functional at the *planning* stage of curriculum since the experiences that students will actually have as they interact with the curriculum cannot be known. At the *evaluation* stage of the curriculum construction process, however, it is difficult to refute the validity of this broader definition. Certainly, the experiences that students actually have under the auspices of the school comprise valuable data for assessing the quality and effectiveness of the *planned* curriculum.

Curriculum as a Structured Series of Intended Learning Outcomes

Among the writers who view "planned learning experiences" as too broad a definition of the curriculum is Mauritz Johnson. In a widely debated essay, this curriculum theorist points out that "there is . . . no experience until an interaction between the individual and his environment actually occurs. Clearly, such interaction characterizes *instruction*, not curriculum." He argues that because a curriculum constitutes a guide for instruction, it must be viewed as "anticipatory, not reportorial." Curriculum "prescribes (or at least anticipates) the *results* of instruction," and "does not prescribe the *means*, that is, the activities, materials, or even the instructional content to be used in achieving the results." Thus, he maintains, the curriculum can consist only of "a structured series of intended learning outcomes."[17] All else is instruction.

The Curriculum-Instruction Controversy. The problem of the distinction between curriculum and instruction[18] that Johnson is dealing with above is one that has plagued curriculum specialists since the earliest days of the movement. It arose when the inadequacies of the "course of study" and "content" definitions were recognized, and attempts were made to deal with the complexities of curriculum through the "experience" definitions.

The distinction between curriculum and instruction that Johnson draws is significant because of the far-reaching effect it has on many traditionally accepted concepts. By restricting the meaning of curriculum to a structured series of intended outcomes, all other planning (for example, of content, learning activities, and evaluation procedures) is viewed as *instructional*, not curriculum planning. A live classroom situation is regarded as the implementation of the *instructional* plan, not of the curriculum. And an implemented curriculum would logically consist only of achieved learning outcomes.

Johnson's points are attractive and carry impressive logical force, but they nevertheless raise both theoretical and practical difficulties. With regard to the former, we should point out that it is simply not possible, as Johnson proposes, to divorce outcomes from the means used to achieve them.[19] Indeed, the "unintended consequences" generated by the "hidden" curricula discussed above demonstrate this point in the most graphic terms: The methods and content of reading instruction are clearly inextricably tied to a variety of curriculum outcomes. Moreover, many specialists believe that Johnson's definition of curriculum is not helpful in dealing with real-school situations on a practical level. If curriculum specialists limit themselves only to the formulation of structured lists of intended learning outcomes, they abdicate responsibility and concern

for some of the most important processes that have traditionally been included in curriculum work (for example, content selection and the specification of learning activities). The semantic question of whether these processes are labeled "curriculum" or "instruction" seems less important than the persistent fact that they must be dealt with at the planning level. This being the case, it would seem that Johnson's definition is either too narrow or is acceptable only to the extent that curriculum planners change their titles to "curriculum and instruction" planners. For the present, at any rate, some broader conception of curriculum than Johnson's seems to be called for to describe the curriculum construction and development activities that are characteristics of specialists in the field.

Curriculum as a (Written) Plan for Action

The problem of the distinction between curriculum and instruction that Johnson deals with is also treated by Macdonald, another prominent curriculum theorist.[20] In the process of arriving at a solution, this specialist achieves tentative definitions not only for curriculum and instruction but for teaching and learning as well.

Macdonald[21] proposes that schooling be conceptualized as the interaction of four systems. The first of these, teaching, is defined as the "professionally oriented behavior of individual personality systems, called teachers. . . ." The second system, learning, consists of the "actions that students perform which teachers perceive to be task related. . . ." Combining these two systems, Macdonald defines the third, instruction, as "the action context within which formal teaching and learning behaviors take place"—in other words, the teaching-learning system. He points out that while teaching and learning taken separately are personality systems, their combination—instruction—is a social system. The fourth system of schooling is the curriculum system, which—like instruction—is a social system. The curriculum system consists of those individuals whose behaviors eventuate in *a* curriculum. Macdonald then defines *a* curriculum as a plan for action, that is, a plan that guides instruction.

As a plan for the education of students, Macdonald's concept of curriculum is broader than Johnson's since it could contain, in addition to intended learning outcomes, other ingredients, such as content and learning activities. Like Johnson, however, Macdonald uses the principles of *action* or *implementation* of the plan as a basis for the distinction between curriculum and instruction: once the plan is acted upon, these writers say, we are in the realm of instruction.

Curriculum Plan Versus Funtioning Curriculum. Like the two writers discussed above, a number of prominent curriculum theorists draw a distinction between curriculum and instruction, using the criterion of implementation. For example: "A curriculum is a written document which may contain many ingredients, but basically it is a plan for the education of pupils during their

Conceptions of Curriculum

enrollment in a given school."[22] But if we observe a particular classroom in operation, are we not able to "see" the curriculum functioning? Are we not able to "see" the class move toward certain goals, employ certain content, or engage in certain activities? Furthermore, when asked to evaluate a curriculum, are we content only to examine a document? Certainly the quality of the document will be a factor in our final assessment, but who will deny that the acid test of curriculum quality really depends on how well it functions in live situations?

Of course, the evaluation of a functioning curriculum is far more complex and difficult than the evaluation of a curriculum document. For one thing, a curriculum functioning in a classroom situation is "filtered," so to speak, through instruction—that is, through people in teaching-learning situations—and this condition operates to obscure curriculum-instruction distinctions. Furthermore, when it is operative in live teaching-learning situations, the curriculum is far less tangible than is the document that represents, paradoxically, only its potential. But in the last analysis, it is only when curriculum becomes a functioning component of the educational process in live classroom settings that its potential (as a document) is realized.

In light of the points made above, this writer believes that a curriculum can refer either to a written plan for instruction or to the functioning curriculum that operates to guide and govern the environment and activities of live classroom situations. Consequently, when the distinction needs to be made, we will refer to the written plan as the *curriculum document* or *inert curriculum* and to the curriculum in operation in the classroom as the *functioning, live,* or *operative curriculum*. Clearly, this distinction creates as many problems and raises as many theoretical questions as other analyses of the nature of curriculum, but it does have the advantage of including under the aegis of curriculum those crucial aspects of education with which curriculum planners and workers must deal if their efforts are to affect students in any significant way.

A Compromise Concept of the Curriculum

Taba finds the extreme breadth of the "experience" definitions of the curriculum nonfunctional. On the other hand, she feels that "excluding from the definition of curriculum everything except the statement of objectives and content outlines and relegating anything that has to do with . . . learning experiences to 'method' might be too confining to be adequate for a modern curriculum."[23]

Her response to this dilemma of curriculum definition lies somewhere in between these two extremes and is worth quoting at length:

A sharp distinction between method and curriculum seems unfruitful, but some distinctions need to be drawn between aspects of learning processes and activities that are of concern in curriculum development and those that can be allocated to the realm of specific methods of teaching. Only certain objectives can be implemented by the nature of curriculum content, its selection and organization. Others can be implemented only by the nature and organization of learning experiences. Thinking, for example, is one of the latter objectives. It would appear, then, that the criteria for the decisions about learning experiences necessary to implement major objectives belong in the realm of curriculum design.[24]

Clearly, Taba has succeeded in drawing only a very hazy distinction between the aspects of learning processes and activities that are of conern in curriculum and those that are distinctively within the realm of teaching and instruction. The suggestion and the central thrust of Taba's conception of curriculum, however, is that the broader (that is, more general) aspects of purposes, content, and method belong in the realm of curriculum, while the more proximate and specific aspects are properly allocated to teaching and instruction.[25] Taba's conception of curriculum, unlike Johnson's and Macdonald's, does not employ an "implementation" criterion; rather, it depends on a relatively flexible and subjective judgment as to where a dividing line is to be drawn on a continuum that is clearly ultimate-general at the "curriculum" pole and immediate-specific at the "instruction" end (see Figure 2-1).

Figure 2-1

Continuum along which subjective judgments are made to determine the *curricular* or *instructional* nature of educational phenomena

This relatively loose criterion is useful because it can be employed whether we think of curriculum as a document or as a cluster of phenomena in a live classroom situation. For example, in a curriculum document, prescribed content should be specific enough to provide focal thrust for the teacher but general enough to allow for specific content and materials to be selected according to the teacher's personality and teaching style and the students' needs and interests. A curriculum unit on prejudice in this instance might allow for a wide variety of alternative content but certainly would reject attempts to include items from geology or analytic geometry. The same sort of distinction might be drawn in live classroom situations, although the complexities involved would make it much more difficult. Questions to be asked might include: Is the specific content being treated in the classroom consonant with general curriculum content? Are the specific activities that students are engaged in congruent with the intent and thrust of the general activities suggested in the curriculum? Are the unanticipated outcomes observed more a function of curriculum content and activities or of instructional factors?

Put in a more general way, we might say that the curriculum provides direction for classroom instruction, but it does not consist of a series of lesson plans.

It is the teacher's prerogative and responsibility to interpret and translate the curriculum document in terms of her own and her students' experience.

The Necessity of Multiple Concepts

The concepts of curriculum discussed in the previous sections account for only a fraction of the number that have been proposed over the past five or six decades by scholars. Instead of being disturbed by this state of affairs, however, some specialists believe that the definitions of curriculum *should* be variable. Mann, for example, holds that defining curriculum "is a matter of how, for the convenience of enacting a commitment," the student of curriculum "decides to imagine the in fact unsliced and unsliceable pie to be sliced."[26] This definition is not as loose as it immediately appears, since it is tied to "the convenience of enacting a commitment"—in other words, to intended purposes in carrying out curricular decisions. Such a position is supported by Schwab,[27] who asserts that the curriculum field is moribund because of its preoccupation with fine theoretical points (like the precise definition of the term *curriculum*). He insists that the curriculum field will rejuvenate itself only when it becomes concerned primarily with "the practical," a concept he views as action based on defensible decisions. Defensible decisions, of course, must involve the examination of philosophical assumptions and "theoretical" bases, and Schwab's position does not exclude theory in this sense. His contention constitutes, rather, a reaction against abstruse and often esoteric controversy in the curriculum field over such issues as the precise definition of a curriculum.

Schwab's criticism is well taken. The present state of curriculum in the public schools makes it abundantly clear that a search for *the* correct definition of the term is not a very productive enterprise and that scholars might better spend their time dealing with the realities of curriculum making in practical school situations. Beyond this, however, recent developments in the scientific community indicate that the practice of permitting only a single acceptable definition for each referent may not even be *theoretically* sound.

Since the earliest decades of the twentieth century, science has generally ceased to regard definitions (and theories) as descriptions of metaphysical reality. Rather, definitions have come to be viewed more as "policies" or "guides to action."[28] For example, if a layman were to ask a physicist for a definition of light, he would likely be told that light may be a wave phenomenon (wave theory) or it may be composed of particles (corpuscular theory). If the layman insisted that he wanted to know what light "really" is—that is, if he insisted on *the* correct definition of light—the physicist would probably tell him, "That isn't a useful question; physicists have stopped asking it."[29] The reason that physicists no longer are interested in the "correct" definition of light is that it is irrelevant. One definition, within a limited situation, enables scientists to account for certain phenomena; the other definition, in another set of circumstances, is more useful. This concept of the function of definition is similar to that of Mann.

It seems reasonable that specialists in the curriculum field might profit from adopting this same scientific stance in their own investigations. As we have previously pointed out, for curriculum *evaluation* activities, the definition that is most useful is one that includes experiences "had" by learners, planned for or not. On the other hand, the planning stage of curriculum cannot possibly utilize a definition that includes experiences "had" but only one that includes *proposed* content and activities that will produce the planned (or rather "hoped-for") experiences. Also, at the planning stage, it seems reasonable to conceptualize the curriculum as a tangible written document that can be referred to as a plan for action. But again, at the evaluation stage, curriculum unavoidably must be conceived of as a cluster of phenomena embedded in the live classroom situation.

The inference to be drawn from the foregoing observations seems to be that any definition of curriculum will necessarily vary according to the purposes which are to be accomplished. Like the physicist's concept of light, the definition of curriculum that is most useful in achieving the purposes of the situation at hand is the one that is most "correct" for that situation.

Other Aspects of the Curriculum Field

The curriculum field includes a number of concepts and processes that are related to the curriculum as it was discussed above but which at the same time represent quite distinct areas. These areas are represented in the literature by phrases such as "curriculum foundations," "curriculum design," "curriculum construction," "curriculum development," and "curriculum improvement." Unfortunately, there is little agreement among specialists in the field with respect to the precise meaning of such terms, and often they are used loosely and interchangeably. The following sections attempt to clarify the distinctions among the terms and in so doing provide the reader with some idea of the scope of curriculum study.

Curriculum Foundations

Curriculum foundations are those basic forces that influence and shape the content and organization of the curriculum. Curriculum foundations are often referred to in the literature as the sources or the determinants of the curriculum. Although the precise areas included in the term *foundations* are still disputed by specialists, most would agree that some, if not all, of the following areas should be included.

Philosophy and the Nature of Knowledge. Philosophy and philosophical assumptions, of course, undergird all of the foundational areas. However, basic assumptions about philosophy and the nature of knowledge are particularly relevant and influential in curriculum work since education's major focus *is* knowledge and learning. Curriculum objectives and content will vary considerably depending, for example, upon whether one believes that "true" knowledge exists out there in the real world or whether "true" knowledge is located internally, within the subjective recesses of the individual mind. In the former instance the curriculum will emphasize activities that center on objective or "scientific" studies and the learning of fixed and objective ideas and concepts. In the latter instance the curriculum will emphasize symbolic and metaphorical studies, such as literature and art. Inquiring into the nature of knowledge is often referred to in the literature as epistemology.

Society and Culture. Inasmuch as schools were invented by social groups to secure the survival of the cultural heritage, it is not surprising that society and its culture exert an enormous influence on the curriculum. Traditional (and often unconscious) assumptions, values, and ideas about what is important or unimportant, good or bad, are translated into curriculum objectives, content, and learning activities. Some notion of the influence of culture on curriculum may be gained by examining and comparing British and American textbooks that deal with the American Revolution. Not only will the objectives and content of the texts differ, but the prominence and importance accorded the event itself will tend to be much greater in American texts.

The Individual. The nature of the individual human organism influences the curriculum on at least two levels. First, the biopsychological nature of man places certain limits on the content and organization of the curriculum. Humans are capable of learning only what their genes will allow them to learn. Thus, a curriculum intended to teach students to fly unaided by mechanical devices or to learn Chinese in a week would be doomed to failure. Second and no less important, man's philosophical conceptions of his own nature will exert a significant influence on the curriculum. For example, notions about the innate goodness or badness of human beings will greatly affect the curriculum. If humans are perceived as innately good, the curriculum is likely to allow learners substantial latitude in pursuing their studies. But if humans are perceived as innately evil (as in the Calvinist doctrine), the curriculum will be highly prescriptive and even coercive.

Learning Theory. Notions about *how* human beings learn will affect the shape of the curriculum. For example, the nineteenth-century theory (called "faculty psychology") that the mind was analogous to a muscle and would develop its powers through mental exercise led to curricula that emphasized drill in difficult academic subjects such as Latin and mathematics. Another popular theory of learning has held that individuals "learn by doing." This point of view eventuated in curricula that provided students with problems and "raw materials" and required them to "discover" knowledge and skills.

Curriculum Design

Curriculum design most commonly refers to the arrangement of the components or elements of a curriculum. Often the "curriculum organization" is used to indicate curriculum design. Ordinarily, the components or elements included in *a* curriculum are (1) aims, goals, and objectives; (2) subject matter or content; (3) learning activities; and (4) evaluation. Thus, the nature of these elements and the pattern of organization in which they are brought together as a unified curriculum constitute the curriculum design. It should be emphasized here that "curriculum design" identifies a substantive entity; it does not refer to a process.

More often than not, the most prominent feature of curriculum designs is their pattern of content organization. Thus, the nomenclature employed to identify various curriculum designs ordinarily refers to content organization. Some of the more familiar designs that have drawn their organizing principles from content include the subject design, the disciplines design, and the broad-fields design. A design that has not centered on content is the activities curriculum, which draws its organizing principles from the felt needs and interests of learners. The areas-of-living design centers on the social functions that learners will be required to perform as adults, and the social-problems design, as its name implies, is organized around current social problems.

Curriculum Construction

Curriculum construction is a phrase that has traditionally been employed to refer vaguely to all the processes involved in the building or making of curricula. It appears in the literature as a synonym for curriculum development and curriculum engineering. In this paper we shall use the term in a more restricted sense. We define curriculum construction as the decision-making process that involves only the determination of the nature and organization of curriculum components. These decisions would involve answering such questions as the following: What is the nature of a good society? What is the nature of man? What is the good life? What is the nature of knowledge? What should the aims of education be? What curriculum design will most effectively actualize our foundational commitments? What content (knowledge) should all students learn? What activities should learners engage in as they interact with content? How should we assess the merit of educational aims, of content, and of learning activities?

Clearly, though we have sought to limit the meaning of curriculum construction, its parameters remain immense. Curriculum construction is a critical process because, more than any other aspect of the curriculum field, it determines the nature and organization of the curriculum to which learners will be exposed.

Curriculum Development

Like curriculum construction, curriculum development refers to a process. It is intimately related to curriculum construction but is distinguished from it by virtue of the nature of its decisions. Curriculum development is a process that determines how curriculum construction will proceed. It is concerned with the following questions: Who will be involved in curriculum construction —teachers, administrators, parents, students? What procedures will be used in curriculum construction—administrative direction, faculty committees, university consultation? If committees are to be employed, how will they be organized?[30]

In real situations curriculum development does not discretely precede curriculum construction. The processes usually overlap, with development and construction decisions being made at the same time. For example, a curriculum development decision to employ English teachers to structure the high school literature curriculum implies certain prior curriculum construction decisions regarding the nature of English (literature) and the organization of the curriculum along subject lines.

Obviously, the integration of the processes of curriculum construction and curriculum development is unavoidable. The distinction is useful, however, in identifying and focusing on the nature of the decision to be made: curriculum construction is concerned with the curriculum, while curriculum development is concerned with the processes of construction.

Curriculum Implementation

Curriculum implementation is one of the few phases that is used consistently in this field. It means simply putting the curriculum that was produced by the construction and development processes into effect. It should be pointed out here that since the curriculum by definition includes an evaluation component, implementation activities will include provision for an appraisal of the effectiveness of the curriculum. Thus, curriculum implementation by definition provides evaluative feedback to the construction/development processes, in which the data are utilized for curriculum revision and improvement.

A situation in which it were possible to "implement" a "new curriculum" in toto in a "virgin" school setting might appear at first to be the ideal. Not only does such a situation rarely occur, but it may in theory be undesirable. As suggested in the previous paragraphs, the curriculum construction/development/implementation processes are not sequential. They occur both in parallel lines as well as in tandem. Construction and development are usually begun in certain curriculur areas and implemented on a trial basis as an alternative to present practices. Evaluative data are then utilized in the construction/development phases to give direction to further construction/development activities and/or to modify the implemented portion of the curriculum. The entire process is highly complex and requires extremely skillful orchestration of participants and components for effective results.

Curriculum Engineering

Curriculum engineering is a phrase of more recent vintage than the three discussed above. Beauchamp defines curriculum engineering as "all of the processes necessary to make a curriculum system functional in schools." A curriculum system "has three primary functions: (1) to produce a curriculum, (2) to implement the curriculum, and (3) to appraise the effectiveness of the curriculum and the curriculum system."[31] Although Beauchamp has employed somewhat different language and a slightly variant division of functions, his curriculum system roughly corresponds to what we have described as the processes of curriculum construction, development, and implementation. Consequently, we would agree with Beauchamp's concept of curriculum engineering, except that we would prefer to define it as the collective processes of curriculum construction, development, and implementation.

Curriculum Improvement versus Curriculum Change

Curriculum improvement and curriculum change, as well as curriculum revision, are generally synonyms in the literature. However, Taba[32] has drawn a distinction that is not only interesting but significant: "curriculum improvement means changing certain aspects of the curriculum without changing the fundamental conceptions of it or its organization." By contrast, she sees curriculum change involving transformation of the entire curriculum scheme, including design, goals, content, learning activities, scope, and so on. Perhaps most important, curriculum change involves change in the value assumptions on which all the aforementioned areas of the curriculum are based.

Curriculum improvement is usually regarded favorably (and enthusiastically) by most individuals and groups concerned with schooling. Because it essentially involves only a refinement of the status quo with minimal alteration of value orientation, it is a relatively safe enterprise. But curriculum *change* is not so readily accepted. "To change a curriculum means, in a way, to change an institution."[33] This involves change in values, people, society, and culture and basic assumptions about what constitutes education and the good life. It is not surprising, therefore, to find that curriculum change, when it does occur, usually occurs only very gradually and in response to the pressures of historical circumstance. It is very rare that widespread, significant, and lasting curriculum change has been brought about as a result of the efforts of professional educators. Attempts to change the curriculum are almost always vehemently resisted, and individuals who engage in curriculum change should expect to assume the risks that accompany any attempt to reorder the society and its value structure.

Two final points should be made about the nature of curriculum change.

First, change is inevitable; it will occur despite attempts to inhibit it. Second, change itself is neither good nor bad; it is the *direction* of change and the value judgment placed on it that determines its goodness or badness. It seems natural to infer from these two points that since change will occur in any case, it is preferable that it be directed by intelligent human intervention than that it be allowed to occur randomly as a result of accidental historical circumstance.

Curricular versus Noncurricular Issues

We have seen in the previous sections that even curriculum specialists are not entirely clear on the parameters of their area of specialization. There is disagreement on the nature of "the curriculum," for example, and the distinction between curriculum and instruction remains a point of debate. Nevertheless, it is possible in a general way to identify certain issues as being primarily *curricular*, while others—though they affect the curriculum—are better classified as administrative, instructional, economic, political, and so forth.

Typically, curricular issues are those that involve curriculum foundations, curriculum design, the components or elements of the curriculum, curriculum engineering, and curriculum improvement and change. These areas represent the subject matter of curriculum study and constitute (loosely) the *substantive structure* of the curriculum field. Such issues as class scheduling, school plant design, and school finance are clearly noncurricular (though they affect the curriculum) and are rarely treated by curriculum specialists.

Most educational issues, however, are highly complex and involve subject matter that is classifiable in more than one category of specialization. For example, "nongrading" or "continuous progress schooling" could be treated either as an administrative or curriculum problem. The difference in treatment would depend upon the methods of inquiry and the contextual framework employed in dealing with it. The characteristic methodologies and approaches used in particular areas of specialization are called the *syntactical structure* of the field.

In the case cited above, nongrading may be viewed as one of several possible administrative responses to the wider issue of grouping students for instruction. The administrator, typically, would be concerned with procedures for scheduling and grouping the student on a nongraded basis. She might, in addition, be concerned with advantages and disadvantages of nongrading in terms of staff utilization, economy, and efficiency in learning. While some of her attention might be directed at considerations that are curricular in nature, on the whole her activities would be identified as administrative.

By contrast, a curriculum specialist approaching the issue of nongrading would immediately define the problem in terms of the broader issue of grouping students for effective learning. He would inevitably review foundational areas and ultimately make an assessment of the nongrading proposal in terms of the total curriculum—its aims, content, and other components. While strategies for implementing the nongrading proposal would eventually concern him, such matters as scheduling, convenience, and economy would not be central to his deliberations.

Because education involves so many interacting variables, it is impossible to indicate definitively where one domain of special inquiry ends and another begins. Nevertheless, the study of curriculum, broad as it is, clearly excludes extensive segments of the educational enterprise. In general, the areas identified in this chapter constitute what is generally understood as the curriculum field.

Notes

1. G. Beauchamp, *Curriculum Theory* (Wilmette, Illinois: Kagg Press, 1968) proposes a third meaning: "A . . . legitimate use of the term *curriculum* is to refer to *a curriculum system*. . . . A curriculum system in schools is the system within which decisions are made about what the curriculum will be and how it will be implemented." In this text we prefer to employ such compound terms as *curriculum development* and *curriculum implementation* to indicate the processes that Beauchamp includes in the term *curriculum system*.

2. Although some writers question whether the field of curriculum is characterized by a distinctive syntactical structure, there is evidence to suggest that certain methodologies—however loosely structured—tend to recur in curriculum inquiry and practice.

3. H. Kliebard, "The Curriculum Field in Retrospect," in *Technology and the Curriculum*, ed. P. Witt (New York: Teachers College Press, 1968), p. 70.

4. M. Seguel, *The Curriculum Field* (New York: Teachers College Press, 1966), p. 788.

5. Kliebard, "Curriculum Field in Retrospect," p. 70.

6. Ibid., p. 70.

7. H. Caswell, "Emergence of the Curriculum as a Field of Professional Work and Study," in *Precedents and Promises in the Curriculum Field*, ed. H. Robison (New York: Teachers College Press, 1966), p. 2.

8. Seguel, *Curriculum Field*, pp. 180–84.

9. Ibid., p. 183.

10. Caswell, "Emergence of the Curriculum," pp. 5–10.

11. The difficulties generated by imprecise use of the term *experiences* are dealt with in the section "Learning Activities and Learning Experiences" in chapter 15 of Zais's book *Curriculum: Principles and Foundations*.

12. E. Krug, *Administering Curriculum Planning* (New York: Harper & Row, 1956), p. 4.

13. R. Doll, *Curriculum Improvement: Decision-making and Process* (Boston: Allyn and Bacon, 1964), p. 15.

14. H. Taba, *Curriculum Development* (New York: Harcourt Brace Jovanovich, 1962).

15. M. Johnson, Jr., "Definitions and Models in Curriculum Theory," *Educational Theory* (April 1967): 127–40.

16. G. Inlow, *The Emergent in Curriculum* (New York: John Wiley, 1973).

17. Johnson, Jr., "Definitions and Models," p. 130.

18. See the section "Curriculum Learning Activities versus Instructional Learning Activities" in chapter 15 of Zais's book for a supplementary discussion of the curriculum-instruction issue.

19. See "The Problem of Ends and Means" in chapter 13 of Zais's book for an extended discussion of ends and means.

20. See "The Scope and Function of Curriculum in Education: Macdonald's Model" in chapter 4 of Zais's book for additional commentary and a graphic illustration of Macdonald's system.

21. J. Macdonald, "Educational Models for Instruction—Introduction," in *Theories of Instruction*, ed. J. Macdonald and R. Leeper (Washington, D.C.: Association for Supervision and Curriculum Development, 1965), p. 3.

22. G. Beauchamp, *Curriculum Theory* (Wilmette, Illinois: Kagg Press, 1968), p. 6.

23. Taba, *Curriculum Development*, p. 9.

24. Ibid., p. 9.

25. Arno Bellack, another curriculum specialist, tends to agree with Taba: "In some quarters an attempt is made to deduce teaching methods (and learning activities) from certain generally accepted psychological principles of a high order of abstraction like the following: Learning is basically goal-seeking behavior; an individual 'learns' when he is motivated to achieve goals and purposes that are meaningful and significant to him. . . . In accordance with this view, curriculum content . . . is of value to the student to the extent that it facilitates goal-setting and goal-seeking. The problem for schools is how best to make available to oncoming generations the accumulated experiences of mankind for them to use and remake in gaining their satisfactions and meeting their needs.

"But these high level generalizations (curriculum directives) do not dictate specific teaching procedures, nor do they designate the precise way in which content is to be selected and organized. Of necessity, teachers must seek more explicit formulations (instructional directives) of the teaching-learning process to guide classroom practice." A. Bellack, "Selection and Organization of Curriculum Content: An Analysis," in *What Shall the High Schools Teach?* (Washington, D.C.: Association for Supervision and Curriculum Development, 1956).

26. J. Mann, "The Curriculum Worker," quoted in "In Search of Ambiguity" by Patricia Mills, *Educational Leadership* (April 1971), p. 731.

27. J. Schwab, "The Practical: A Language for Curriculum," *School Review* (November 1969), pp. 1, 2.

28. J. Conant, *Modern Science and Modern Man* (Garden City, N.Y.: Doubleday Anchor Books, 1952), p. 55ff.

29. Ibid., p. 80.

30. *Curriculum development* is a term that most educationists use to refer broadly to all the processes of constructing and implementing curricula. While the more restrictive definition that we propose breaks with this traditional usage and thus creates some degree of confusion, we believe that the increased precision achieved can ultimately improve communication among curriculum specialists.

31. Beauchamp, *Curriculum Theory*, p. 108.

32. Taba, *Curriculum Development*, p. 454.

33. Ibid.

Conceptual-Empiricists

3 The Concept of the Structure of a Discipline

Joseph J. Schwab

Introduction

It is customary to associate discussions about "structure" in the academic disciplines and the adaptation of these disciplines for curriculum design with the writings of Joseph Schwab. As a scientist, Schwab's work influenced the form if not the content of many nationally funded curriculum-reform project of the 1960s (for example, BSCS biology, CHEM study, ESCP earth science, to name but a few). In fact, his influence extended beyond the physical and life sciences to include the humanities and social sciences (for example, Project Social Studies and Project English). The "structure of the disciplines" became the intellectual underpinning for the curriculum-reform movement of the sixties. And this essay as well as the conference report titled *The Process of Education* by Jerome Bruner provided teachers, curriculum developers, and researchers with intellectual justification for organizing content according to the "structure of the disciplines."

In the pages that follow, Schwab defines structure and elaborates on its importance for education. As you read, think about the following questions:

- What is the meaning of conceptual structure and syntactical structure?
- Of the six related but different significances of structure to education, which are most important to you as an educator?

Reprinted from *The Educational Record* 43 (July 1962), pp. 197–205. Reprinted by permission.

In 1941 my colleagues and I offered for the first time a course in the structure of the disciplines. We had devoted an entire year to developing its plan and content. But we had spent no time at all on the problem of how to teach it. The first few weeks, in consequence, were a severe trial of our students' patience. Finally, one of them cornered me.

"Tell me," she said, "what this course is about."

I did so—in twelve minutes. I was impressed by my clarity as much as by my brevity. So, apparently, was my student. For she eyed me a moment and then said, "Thank you. Now I understand. And if the truth is that complicated, I am not interested."

The young lady was right on two of three counts. First, the concept of a structure of a discipline is concerned in a highly important sense with truth, not with truth in some vaguely poetic sense, but with answerable, material questions of the extent to which and the sense in which the content of a discipline is warranted and meaningful. Second, study of the structures of the disciplines is complicated—at least by contrast to the simple assumptions about truth and meaning that we have used in the past in determining the content and the organization of the school curriculum.

On the third count, however, the young lady was wrong. We cannot afford to be uninterested in the structures of the disciplines. We cannot so afford because they pose problems with which we in education must deal. The structures of the modern disciplines are complex and diverse. Only occasionally do we now find among them a highly esteemed body of knowledge that consists simply of collections of literal statements standing in one-for-one relation to corresponding facts. Instead of collections, we find organizations in which each member statement depends on the others for its meaning. And the verifying relations of such organizations to their facts are convoluted and diverse. This complexity of modern structures means that problems of comprehension and understanding of modern knowledge now exist which we in education have barely recognized. The diversity of modern structures means that we must look not for a simple theory of learning leading to a one best learning-teaching structure for our schools, but for a complex theory leading to a number of different structures, each appropriate or "best" for a given discipline or group of disciplines.

In brief, the structures of the disciplines are twice important to education. First, they are necessary to teachers and educators: they must be taken into account as we plan curriculum and prepare our teaching materials; otherwise, our plans are likely to miscarry and our materials, to misteach. Second, they are necessary in some part and degree *within* the curriculum, as elements of what we teach. Otherwise, there will be failure of learning or gross mislearning by our students.

Let us turn now to examination of a structure, using the sciences as an example. Forty years ago it was possible for many scientists and most educators

Concept of the Structure of a Discipline   53

to nurse the illusion that science was a matter of patiently seeking the facts of nature and accurately reporting them. The conclusions of science were supposed to be nothing more than summaries of these facts.

This *was* an illusion, and it was revealed as such by events in the science of physics that began in the late 1890s. The discovery of radioactivity suddenly revealed a world within the world then thought to be the only world. The study of that world and of its relations to the already known world led to a revolution in the goals and the structures of physics. By the mid-twenties, this revolution in physics had gone so far that we were faced with the fact that some of the oldest and least questioned of our ideas could no longer be treated as literally true— or literally false. Classical space had been a homogeneous, neutral stage on which the dramas of motion and existence were acted out. The flow of classical time was always and everywhere the same. The mass and length of bodies were each elementary properties independent of other properties. Bodies occupied a definite location and a definite amount of space.

The new physics changed these notions. In its knowledge structure, space was something that could be distorted, and its distortions affected bodies in it. The magnitude and position of subatomic particles could not be described as we describe the magnitude and position of a 1-inch cube here and now.

But these new assertions did *not* come about because direct observations of space, place, time, and magnitude disclosed that our past views about them were merely mistaken. Rather, our old assertions about these matters were changed because physicists had found it fruitful to treat them in a new way— neither as self-evident truths nor as matters for immediate empirical verification. They were to be treated, instead, as principles of inquiry—conceptual structures that could be revised when necessary, in directions dictated by large complexes of theory, diverse bodies of data, and numerous criteria of progress in science.

Today, almost all parts of the subject-matter sciences proceed in this way. A fresh line of scientific research has its origin not in objective facts alone but in a conception, a deliberate construction of the mind. On this conception, all else depends. It tells us what facts to look for in the research. It tells us what meaning to assign these facts.

A moment's thought is enough to show us how this process operates. That we propose to investigate a chosen subject is to say, of course, that we are, in large part, ignorant of it. We may have some knowledge, based on common experience or on data garnered in preliminary study. But this preliminary knowledge is only a nibbling at the edges. We barely know the superficial exterior of our subject, much less its inner character. Hence, we do not *know* with certainty what further facts to look for, what facts will tell us the significant story of the subject in hand. We can only *guess*.

In physiology, for example, we did not know but only supposed that the functioning of the human organism is carried out by distinct parts, that each part has a character and a fixed function in the economy of the whole. Hence, we did not *know* that the facts we ought to seek in physiological research should be facts about the structure of each organ and what happens when each organ is removed. On the contrary, the conceptions of organ and of function were developed prior to sure knowledge of these matters and were developed precisely to make such knowledge possible through research. The conceptions are guiding principles of inquiry, not its immediate fruits.

In physics, similarly, we did not *know* from the beginning that the properties of particles of matter are fundamental and determine the behavior of these particles, their relations to one another. It was not verified knowledge but a heuristic principle needed to structure inquiry that led us to investigate mass and charge and, later, spin.

It may, indeed, be the case that the particles of matter are social particles, that their most significant properties are not properties of their very own but properties which accrue to them from association with other particles, properties that change as the associations change. Therefore, it may be that the more significant facts to seek in physical inquiry are not facts about the properties of particles but facts about kinds of associations and the consequences of associations. Similar alternatives exist for physiology. There are conceptions of the organism that yield, when pursued in inquiry, a more profound knowledge than that afforded by the notions of organ and function.

In short, what facts to seek in the long course of an inquiry and what meaning to assign them are decisions that are made before the fact. The scientific knowledge of any given time rests not on *the* facts but on *selected* facts—and the selection rests on the conceptual principles of the inquiry.

Moreover, scientific knowledge—the knowledge won through inquiry—is not knowledge merely of the facts. It is of the facts *interpreted*. This interpretation, too, depends on the conceptual principles of the inquiry. The structure-function physiologist does not report merely the numerous changes displayed by an experimental animal from which an organ has been removed. He interprets these changes as indicative of the lost function once performed by the organ removed. It is this interpretation of the facts that is the conclusion drawn from the experiment and reported as a piece of scientific knowledge, and its meaning and validity depend on the conception of organ and function as much as they depend on the selected facts.

Here, then, is a first approximation of what is meant by the structure of a discipline. The structure of a discipline consists, in part, of the body of imposed conceptions that define the investigated subject matter of that discipline and control its inquiries.

The significance to education of these guiding conceptions becomes clearer if we repeat once more the way in which they act as guides. First, they severely restrict the range of data which the scientist seeks in inquiry. He does *not* study the whole of his subject, but only some aspect of it, an aspect which his then-current principles of inquiry lead him to treat as the significant aspect. The conclusions of that line of inquiry may be true, but most certainly they are not the whole truth about the subject matter. They are not about some aspect of nature taken in its pristine state but about something which the principles of the inquiry have made, altered, or restricted. Furthermore, what the scientist makes of these data, what he takes them to mean, is also determined not by full knowledge of their significance but by the tentative principles of the inquiry.

Now the subject matter may be—in fact, almost always is—far richer and more complex than the limited model of it embodied in the conclusions of the restricted inquiry. Thus, the first significance to education of the structure of a discipline: we cannot, with impunity, teach the conclusions of a discipline as if they were about the whole subject matter and were the whole truth about it. For the intelligent student will discover in time—unless we have thoroughly blinded him by our teaching—that any subject behaves in ways that do not conform to what he has been told about it. His bodily illnesses, for example, are often not reducible to the malfunctioning of specific organs or the presence of a specific bacterium. His automobile does not appear to obey the "laws" of the particular science of mechanics which he was taught. Legislatures and executives do not behave as a dogmatic political science says they do.

It is the case, however, that a structure-function physiology, a Newtonian mechanics, or some particular reading of political behavior throws *some* light on the behavior of our bodies, our automobiles, or our democracy. Or it would if the body of knowledge were understood in light of the restricted circumstances in which it is valid and known in connection with the restricted range of data that it subsumes. In short, the bodies of knowledge *would* have defensible and valuable meaning to those who learn them had they been learned not in a context of dogma, but in a context of the conceptions and data that determine their limited meaning and confer their limited validity. This is one significance of the structure of the disciplines to education.

A second significance becomes visible if we look at a further consequence of the operation of a conceptual structure in inquiry. It renders scientific knowledge fragile and subject to change; research does not proceed indefinitely on the basis of the principles that guided its first inquiries. On the contrary, the same inquiries that accumulate limited knowledge by the aid of assumed principles of inquiry also test these principles. As the selected principles are used, two consequences ensue. Knowledge of the subject unfolds; experimental techniques are refined and invented. The new knowledge lets us envisage new, more adequate, more telling conceptions of the subject matter. The growth of technique permits us to put the new conceptions into practice as guiding principles of a renewed inquiry.

The effect of these perennial renewals of inquiry is perennial revision of scientific knowledge. With each change in the conceptual system, the older knowledge gained through use of the older principles sinks into limbo. The *facts* embodied are salvaged, reordered, and reused, but the *knowledge* that formerly embodied these facts is replaced. There is, then, a continuing and pervasive revision of scientific knowledge as principles of inquiry are used, tested, and supplanted.

Furthermore, our scientific and scholarly establishment is now so large, so many people are now engaged in inquiry, that the rate of this revision is exceedingly rapid. We can expect radical reorganization of a given body of scientific knowledge not once in the coming century, but several times, at intervals of five to fifteen years. This means, of course, that our students—if they continue to receive all their learning in a dogmatic context outside the structure of the disciplines—will confront at least once in their lives what appears to be a flat contradiction of much that they were taught about some subject. The effect of this lie-direct to teaching in the schools can only be exacerbation to an intolerable degree of the confusion, uncertainty, and cynicism that our young people already exhibit with respect to *expertise*, to schooling, and to bodies of organized knowledge.

Our students and our nation could be protected from the consequences of such misunderstanding if, again, our students learned what they learned not as a body of literal and irrevocable truths but as what it is: one embodiment of one attack on something less than the whole of the matter under investigation. This is a second significance of the conceptual structure of the disciplines to education.

Whereas the second significance to education arises from the existence of a process of revision, the third and fourth significances emerge from the outcomes of this process—from the advances it has made possible. In the process of revision, improvement of principle is sought in two different directions. On the one hand, more *valid* principles are sought, principles that will embrace more and more of the richness and complexity of the subject under investigation. On the other hand, principles of wider *scope* are sought, principles that will embrace a wider and wider range of subject matters, which will reduce what were before considered as separate and different phenonema to related aspects of a common kind or source. (Thus, Newtonian mechanics united the movements of the heavenly bodies with the behavior of objects thrown and dropped by man on earth, rendering these formerly diverse phenomena to be but varying expressions of a common law. Similarly, the physics of the century just past found new principles that united the formerly separated phenomena of light, electricity, and magnetism.)

The successful search for more *valid* principles—for more adequate models of investigated phenomena—has led to scientific knowledge of a new "shape" or character, in sharp contrast to older knowledge. Older knowledge tended toward the shape of a catalogue. Old descriptive biology, for example, was necessarily a catalogue—of the organs, tissues, or kinds of cells that made up the body. Another part of descriptive biology was a catalogue of the species, genera, classes, and so on of the living organisms that populated the earth. Even the experimental physiology of years only recently past tended toward a similarly encyclopedic character—for example, lists of parts of bodies with their functions, meticulous itemizing of hereditary units and their consequent traits. Chemistry, in similar fashion, tended to be a classificatory scheme of elements and of the more complex substances that arose from their combination.

Modern scientific inquiry, conversely, tends to look for patterns—patterns of change and patterns of relations—as their explanatory principles. When such patterns are found, they throw a new and more complex light on the items of our old catalogues. The items lose their primary significance and lose their independence. On the side of significance, an item ceases to be something that simply is and becomes, instead, one of possibly many "somethings" that fulfill conditions required by the pattern. On the side of dependence-independence, an item ceases to be something that can be understood by itself; it becomes, instead, something that can be understood only by knowing the relations it bears to the other items that fill out the pattern or blueprint.

Thus, it was once possible to teach something about the significance of glucose to the living body by reciting a formula for it—naming the three elements that compose it, indicating the number of each—and naming it as an energy source. Today, it is necessary to talk about the basic pattern of a carbohydrate molecule, how the elements are connected to one another, what happens when connections are made or broken, and so on. This story of pattern is embedded, in turn, in a still larger pattern—the pattern of processes by which energy is captured, stored, transferred, and utilized in the body. The educational significance of this emphasis on pattern in the sciences is more clearly indicated by the further point that, a few years ago, we could tell the story of energy sources merely by cataloguing glucose and two or three other substances as the common energy sources of the body. Today, the story must be the story of where and when and under what circumstances each of these substances functions as an energy source, and how, in a sense, they function as *interchangeable* parts to fulfill the conditions of the determining pattern.

This shift from catalogues to patterns in the disciplines means, in turn, that teaching and learning take on a new dimension. Instead of focusing on one thing or idea at a time, clarifying each and going on to the next, teaching becomes a process of focusing on points of contact and connection among things and ideas, of clarifying the effect of each thing on the others, of conveying the way in which each connection modifies the participants in the connection—in brief, the task of portraying phenomena and ideas not as things in themselves but as fulfillments of a pattern.

The successful search for principles of greater scope has led to developments of a parallel kind. As the scope of a set of principles enlarges, so does the coherence of the body of knowledge that develops from it, the interdependence of its component statements, a fifth significance. Thus, in a theory that embraces electricity and magnetism as well as light, an assertion about the nature of light borrows part of its meaning and part of its warrant from statements about electricity and magnetism. The significance of the assertion about light cannot be grasped by understanding only its terms and the light phenomena to which it applies, for these terms are defined in part by terms in other statements about other phenomena.

This kind of coherence in scientific knowledge means that our most common way of applying the old query "What knowledge is of most worth?" is no longer entirely defensible. We can no longer safely select from the conclusions of the disciplines the separate and different bits and pieces that we think would be most useful to the clients of the schools. We cannot because the separation of these bits, their removal from the structure of other statements that confer on them their meaning, alters or curtails that meaning. The statements will no longer convey the warranted and valid knowledge they convey in context but something else or something less.

For students of some ages or of very limited learning competence, such bits and pieces may be appropriate as limited guides to limited actions, limited understanding, and a limited role in society. For many children at many ages, however, we need to face the fact that such a disintegrated content is not only a distorted image of scientific knowledge but a distorted image of the physical world it purports to represent; it will betray itself.

This means, in turn, that teaching and learning, as we have suggested above, need an added dimension. As patterns replace lists and catalogues, learning and remembering of parts remain necessary conditions of learning but cease to be sufficient conditions. A new flexibility is required, a capacity to deal with the roles of things as well as with things as such and to understand the relations among roles. The following crude metaphor may suggest the nature of this flexibility. Natural phenomena as now conceived by the sciences must be understood as a dynamic, a drama. The drama unfolds as the outcome of many interacting roles. Therefore, the relation of each role to others must be understood. Second, each role may be played by more than one actor; different "actors," despite their apparent diversities, must be recognized as potential players of the same role. Third, each potential player of a role somewhat modifies the role he plays and, through this effect, also modifies the roles played by other actors. Hence, the unfolding, the climax, and outcome of the drama are flexible, not one rigid pattern but variations on a theme.

A sixth significance of conceptual principle to education is quickly told. Different disciplines have widely different conceptual structures. Despite the passionate concern of some philosophers and some scientists for a unity of the sciences, biologists and physicists, for example, continue to ask widely different questions in their inquiries, seek different kinds of data, and formulate their respective bodies of knowledge in widely different forms. It is not quite obsolete in biology, for instance, to ask what system of classes will best organize our

Concept of the Structure of a Discipline

knowledge of living things and to seek data primarily in terms of similarities and differences. The physicist, however, continues to find it most rewarding to ask what relations among what varying quantities will best organize our knowledge of the behavior of matter; consequently, he seeks data which consist primarily of measurements of such changing quantities.

Such differences among sciences are so persistent and so rewarding that it is hard to avoid the conviction that there are real and genuine differences among different bodies of phenomena, that differences in questions put and data sought are not merely the products of historical habits among the different disciplines but also reflect some stubbornnesses of the subjects. One subject matter answers when one set of questions is put. Another answers to another set. And neither will answer the questions to which the other responds.

Among these differences of conceptual structure, there are some that deserve special attention from educators because of the confusion they create if ignored. These are the specific differences among conceptions which two or more disciplines apparently hold in common. Two large-scale examples occur to me: the concept of *time* and the concept of *class*.

Time is deeply imbedded in the conceptual structure of both physics and biology. In many respects, the concept of time is the same in both sciences. In one respect it is radically different. Time for the biologist is unavoidably vectorial and has direction from past to future, like the time of common sense. It cannot in any sense be considered reversible. Time, as it appears in most physical equations, in contrast, has no notion of past and future attached to it; it permits, in a certain sense, reversibility.

The concept of class is, perhaps, a more telling instance of difference for the purposes of education. The class of biology is a loose and messy affair compared to the class with which traditional logic (and much of mathematics) is concerned. The logical class consists of members that are all alike in some defining respect. The biologist's class, however, consists of members of which it can be said, at best, that most of them have most of many properties which, together, define the class.

The special problem posed by such differences as these is easily seen. The *logical* class, consisting of members alike in some defining respect, permits us to infer with confidence knowledge about members of the class from knowledge of the class. The *biological* class permits no such confident inference. What is true for the class may or may not be true of some members or subclass. Obviously, instruction that permitted this crucially instrumental conceptual difference to go unnoted by teachers and students would lead to all sorts of later confusion and error.

I remarked earlier that a body of concepts—commitments about the nature of a subject matter, functioning as a guide to inquiry—was *one* component of the structure of a discipline. Let us turn briefly to another which I shall call the syntactical structure of the disciplines. By the syntax of a discipline, I mean the pattern of its procedure, its method, how it goes about using its conceptions to attain its goals.

Most of us were taught a schoolbook version of a syntax under the guise of "scientific method." Though oversimple, full of error, and by no means the universal method of the sciences, it will suffice as an example. This schoolbook story (borrowed, incidentally, from an early work of Dewey) tells us that science proceeds through four steps. There is, first, the noting of data relevant to our problem. Second, there is the conceiving of a hypothesis. Third, the hypothesis is tested by determining whether consequences expected if the hypothesis were true are in fact found to occur. Finally, a conclusion is stated, asserting the verification or nonverification of the hypothesis.

So we are given the impression that the goal of all the sciences is a congeries of well-verified hypotheses. We are left with the impression that verification is of only one kind—the discovery that expected consequences occur in fact.

If this were all there were to the syntax of the disciplines, it would be of little importance to teaching, learning, and the curriculum. Unfortunately, this is not all there is, for different disciplines have different starting points and different goals. That is, their subject matters may be conceived in vastly different ways, so also may what they conceive to be sound knowledge or fruits of the inquiry. Consequently, the path, the syntax, the process of discovery and verification is also different.

Such differences in method of verification and discovery hold even for the similar disciplines called the sciences. They hold, *a fortiori*, between the sciences on one count, mathematics on another, and history on a third.

Among the sciences, let us contrast once more biology and physics. Biology, until very recently, has been the science that comes closest to fulfilling the schoolbook version of science. It has consisted in large part of a congeries of tested hypotheses. Its inquiries have turned from the verification of one to the verification of another with little twinge of conscience. Biologists have rarely hesitated to formulate hypotheses for different problems that differed widely from one another, that had little indeed of a common body of conceptions. Thus, verification for biology was largely a matter of chasing down, one by one, many and various expected consequences of many and various hypotheses.

Physics, on the other hand, has for centuries held as its goal not a congeries of almost independent hypotheses but a coherent and closely knit body of knowledge. It has sought to impose on its diverse formulations of diverse phenomena a body of conceptions that would relate them to one another and make of them one body, inferable from the conceptions that bound them together. Hence, for physics, verification has often meant something far otherwise than its meaning in biology. It has meant, in many cases, that expected consequences had been observed. In a few cases, however, the first reason for accepting a certain hypothetical had nothing to do with observed consequences. Rather, the hypothetical in question was accepted in order to save another conception, one that lay deep in the structure of physical knowledge and had ramifications extending over most of its conclusion. Thus, the "verifying" circumstance had to do with the structure of existing knowledge rather than the structure of existing things. (In one such case, the hypothetical in question—the neutrino—was verified some years later by the discovery of expected consequences, to the great relief of many physicists. In still another case—that of the parity principle—the principle itself was discarded and replaced.)

Where physics and biology differ in their goals, science and mathematics differ primarily in their starting points, that is, their subject matters. The consequent differences in their syntax are vast. Let us take algebra as our example and agree for the moment that the subject matter of algebra is number. Now, whatever number may be, one thing is certain: it does not consist of a body of material things, of events accessible to our senses. The idea of testing for the presence of materially existential consequences is meaningless in algebra. The algebraist may conceivably use something called data in a science that studies a material, sense-accessible subject matter. Yet, there can be error as well as truth in algebra, hence, some means of discovery and of test. Clearly then, the means, the syntax of mathematics, must be vastly different from the syntax that has a material subject matter.

A similar great difference holds between most history and the sciences. Few historians would hold that their goal, like the goal of science, is the discovery of general laws. They do not take as their starting points things and events which they think of as repeated instances of a *kind* of thing or event. On the contrary, most historians take as their goal the recovery or the reconstruction of some selected, time-limited or space-limited group of past and unique events. But again, there are such things as better history and worse history—the more and the less well verified. Yet only by the wildest of equivocations can we assert that the historian discovers and verifies in the same way as does the investigator of living things, of falling bodies, or of numbers.

In brief, truth is a complicated matter. The conceptual structure of a discipline determines what we shall seek the truth about and in what terms that truth shall be couched. The syntactical structure of a discipline is concerned with the operations that distinguish the true, the verified, and the warranted in that discipline from the unverified and unwarranted. Both of these—the conceptual and the syntactical—are different in different disciplines. The significance for education of these diverse structures lies precisely in the extent to which we want to teach what is true and have it understood.

4 Basic Components of a Curriculum Theory

George Beauchamp

Introduction

Curriculum theory is an often neglected area of explication and analysis. It is this statement that undergirds the harsh judgment that the curriculum field is moribund. As the field's critics are quick to point out, it lacks underlying and explicit structures, ideas and assumptions about learning and schooling, and greater ideological links to the society at large.

In order to correct these deficiencies, conceptual-empiricists maintained that a number of issues needed to be addressed if the curriculum field was to acquire respectability as a field of inquiry and as a discipline. First, the technical language of curriculum needed to become unambiguous and disciplined. Second, principal curriculum issues had to be investigated through a process of classification, contingencies, and making relationships. To illustrate this weakness in the curriculum field, George Beauchamp points out a fundamental flaw in the uses of language and in the choice of definitions used for the term *curriculum*.

In the text of the essay that follows, Beauchamp defines and interprets the following terms: curriculum, curriculum system, and curriculum as a field of study. He points out that the word *curriculum* is the most important technical word in the investigative process because it is a prerequisite for understanding the phrases curriculum system and curriculum as a field of study. Second, it tells us that what (in terms of content) ought to be taught is of primary importance.

As you read the following essay by Beauchamp, think about these questions:

- What are the basic theory-building processes of a curriculum theory?

- What are the different and sometimes confusing definitions of the word *curriculum* and which one do you subscribe to as a teacher, curriculum designer, and educator?
- How would you systematically outline Beauchamp's theory of curriculum?

In this article, I present a point of view on the basic components of a curriculum theory. I have broken the discussion into three topics: (1) a brief statement of theory-building processes, (2) a discussion of sources of potential curriculum postures, and (3) a statement outlining my own curriculum-theory position. My major purpose in writing this article is to help stimulate more dialogue on the subject of curriculum theory.

Basic Theory-Building Processes

There is general agreement that a theory is a set of related statements explaining some series of events. From theory to theory, there may be variations in definition and in the character of the statements made, and the sets of events are, admittedly, always peculiar to the field within which the theorizing takes place. Nonetheless, any theorist is obligated to generate statements that provide satisfactory explanations for the particular sets of events he or she has under consideration.

The fundamental behaviors of a theorist, particularly in the social sciences, seem to be quite common. They are sufficiently common that we can identify certain rules for behavior in theorizing. A first and necessary task for a theorist is to fence in the field of inquiry. An important mechanism for doing so is to identify the technical language, including unique or specialized terms, subjects, and processes that appear to be essential to the set of events the theorist is to delineate and explain. Once the technical language has been identified, a theorist must carefully define and consistently use it throughout his theoretical work. By performing this set of tasks, the theorist satisfies the first rule in theorizing: namely, to discipline his use of technical terms. The identification and definition of technical terms assist the theorist in defining his field and, to a great extent, in establishing the rough boundaries of the field.

In order to further the definition of the field and begin the process of explaining the characteristics of the sets of events and the relationships among them, two more basic tasks of theorizing must be undertaken. One is to classify the accumulated information within the sets of events presumed to be in the field of inquiry. A second is to describe the circumstances and conditions under which the identified sets of events occur. When these two tasks are complete, a theorist has satisfied a second rule in theorizing: that is, to identify the principal ingredients essential to the field of concern.

Then the theorist can move to the more sophisticated processes of theory building, which result in the establishment of relationships among the identified phenomena in the field. The performance of the complicated tasks involved here satisfies the third role of theorizing, which is to identify relationships among the various parts, or the theoretical statements, and to explain the character of those relationships. Most theories are complex wholes. The various parts may have individual meaning or significance, but meaning and significance are enhanced as the parts are related to the whole. We hear a lot about prediction as a sophisticated process in theory building, but it takes a great deal of study of theoretical events before predictive relationships among them can be established.

The above are relatively simple rules for theory building. Defining, describing, classifying, relating are fundamental to the more general process of explanation, which is the primary purpose of theory building. I believe they are of cardinal importance in the development of any curriculum theory.

Sources of Curriculum Postures

In my judgment, most of the discourse on curriculum theory avoids the principal issues that must be faced if theory development in the field of curriculum is to mature. So far, I have briefly sketched what I consider to be the principal rules of theory building that tend to be ignored. In particular, the rule with respect to the careful definition of technical terms has been violated.

The field of curriculum has grown up with a proliferation of meanings associated with key technical terms, and the associated meanings are often in conflict; that is, distinctly different meanings may be associated with the same term. The most critical term for theory building in the field of curriculum is *curriculum*. The term *curriculum* is most critical because the associated meanings accepted by the theorist identify the dimensions of the total set of events to be explained by the theory. Different meanings would involve different sets of events, and explanations for different sets of events would produce different theories.

Persons who use different meanings of *curriculum* fall into three groups. One group thinks of a curriculum as a plan for subsequent action. In this case, a curriculum is principally organized so as to reveal the decisions of the planners in response to the question of what ought to be taught in the school, or schools, for which the curriculum is intended. Normally, the intended subsequent action is instruction. In most cases, the plan is assumed to be in written form. The intended characteristics of the written form may vary considerably, but these variations provide food for discourse on the nature of curriculum design.

Basic Components of a Curriculum Theory

A significant number of curriculum authorities—the majority, in fact—operate as if *curriculum* and *instruction* were synonymous or a unified concept. There are differences in emphasis within this majority group, however. Critical to these differences is the degree to which curriculum planning and instructional planning are to be explained under the heading "curriculum," as well as distinctions among various arenas for curriculum planning and planning for instruction. For example, one person may advocate a series of steps including curriculum planning by scholars in the disciplines, curriculum planning for an individual school, and the development of specific instructional strategies by individual teachers—all under the caption of curriculum. Another might add to these the action of the classroom. A third person might propose that curriculum planning and instructional planning be accomplished simultaneously. No doubt there are others. There have been attempts within professional organizations to discriminate between curriculum theory and instructional theory but to no avail; and in my judgment, the failure to develop theoretical postures in the two areas is due primarily to the unwillingness of people to discriminate between curriculum and instruction as two different but related dimensions of schooling.

Others—a smaller group of curriculum authorities—take an even broader view of the term *curriculum* than those referred to in the paragraph above do. For them, *curriculum* is a very broad term that includes the psychological processes of the learner as she acquires educational experiences. In a sense, proponents of this interpretation subsume instruction, learning, and often evaluation within the concept of curriculum. What happens to the school pupil is so important to these authorities that they would state that each pupil has her own curriculum. I believe that advocates of this position use the term *curriculum* as synonymous with experience in the sense in which John Dewey used the term.

These different conceptual interpretations of the term *curriculum* should lead to the development of alternative curriculum theories because of variation induced in the sets of events. But all who engage in curriculum theory formulation are obligated to follow the basic rules of theory building.

A Position on Curriculum Theory

Now I will use my own posture in curriculum theory to illustrate some of the consequences of selection from basic conceptual notions about curriculum as well as the application of theory-building rules. Since an initial decision that must be reached by a theorist is his or her interpretation of the word *curriculum*, I shall begin there. I choose to use the word in three ways: (1) to refer to a curriculum, (2) to refer to a curriculum system, or (3) to refer to curriculum as a field of study. A curriculum is a document designed to be used as a point of departure for instructional planning. A curriculum system refers to what has conventionally been called curriculum planning, curriculum implementation, and curriculum appraisal. These events I choose to call curriculum engineering. Curriculum as a field of study, or a field of inquiry, encompasses: (1) curriculum design, (2) curriculum engineering, and (3) the research and theory building necessary to explain curriculum design and curriculum engineering.

As I previously stated, the word *curriculum* is the most important technical term within the field. All of its associations must be clearly defined by the theorist in order to prescribe the boundaries of the events she or he is explaining, to communicate this position to others, and to consistently do the kinds of theoretical work necessary to establish relationships among the phenomena within this field. In this connection, operational definitions are of very great value to theorists. Certainly, any single curriculum theory cannot be based upon all of the diverse ways in which the word *curriculum* is used in the present literature. To try to do so would be a violation of the rule of consistency in the definition and use of technical terms and a failure to fence in the theoretical field. It has helped me to formulate a few positive assertions with respect to each of the three ways I use the word.

The first is that *what* ought to be taught in schools is the primary curriculum question. Responses to this primary curriculum question would define the subject matter of a school, and the subject matter for a school constitutes the bulk of the content of a curriculum. *Why* that material ought to be taught is in partial justification for the "ought to" decision. Frequently, responses to why content should be taught in a school are spelled out in the form of objectives. *How* the subject matter of a school ought to be taught is a question for the domain of instruction, and therefore is not a primary problem for the curriculum theorist. *What happens* as a result of instruction is the primary question to be evaluated with inferences for both curriculum and instruction. From this rationale, I conclude that a curriculum is a written plan for subsequent action. Basically, a curriculum plan should include a statement of goals for the school and the content (subject matter, if you please) that has been selected for the achievement of these goals. There may be other ingredients added to a curriculum, but goals and content seem to me to be essential. The form and arrangement of goals and content in accordance with the administrative organization of the school constitute the basic dimensions of curriculum *design*.

In order for curricula to be created, implemented in schools, and appraised, it is necessary for curriculum workers to establish some means of engineering those decisions within the schools. This I choose to call a curriculum system. The fundamental processes of a curriculum system are the choice of the arena in which curriculum decisions are to be made; the selection of personnel to work within the system; the selection, ordering, and execution of working procedures; the establishment of implementation procedures; and the establishment of procedures for appraising and revising the curriculum. The primary output of a curriculum system is, of course, a curriculum.

The location of a curriculum system has a great deal to do with the choices a theorist makes with respect to the fundamental processes of the system. In countries like France, Italy, Spain, and Sweden, the arenas of decision making are split. Curriculum planning takes place in the national arena, but implementation processes are invoked at local school levels. In the United States, most decisions about what shall be taught in schools are made at the level of the local school district. Politically, the local board of education is responsible for the decisions. Ideas about curriculum content generated through national projects, textbooks, state laws, or the work of scholarly groups may be treated as influences upon or inputs to curriculum systems located in local school districts.

To me, curriculum as a field of inquiry and as an arena for theory building is defined by all of the concepts and processes associated with curriculum design and curriculum engineering. The task of the curriculum theorist is to identify, classify, and otherwise explain these various sets of events associated with design and engineering. In my opinion, some of my colleagues who write in the area of curriculum theory tend to restrict themselves to one or the other of these dimensions of the total field. I believe that this is a fundamental error, except in those cases where the individuals tacitly assume that theoretical work in design or in engineering are recognized subordinate components to the total field of curriculum theory. Certainly, we need both, but it is unrealistic to claim that one of these constitutes the entire field.

Every serious curriculum thinker realizes that research is the fundamental tool to be used by the theorist as she or he attempts to reach acceptable generalizations that explain or predict relationships within the field of curriculum. Most of the research that to date has been done in the field of curriculum has been in the area of curriculum engineering, and, needless to say, there is a lot more that needs to be done. We drastically need research in curriculum design. Curriculum designers today have too few choices available to them. The vast majority of the curricula that have been planned for schools are subject or discipline centered. Any variations are within this basic construct. We have some proposals for variation in the contents of curriculum, but even those variations are subject centered.

Concluding Comments

In the preceding paragraphs, I have identified some basic theory-building processes that ought to be utilized by anyone concerned with the development of curriculum theory. Sources for potentially different curriculum postures were identified. Finally, I outlined the principal ingredients of my own theoretical position.

A curriculum theorist who starts with a conceptual posture different from mine necessarily works with different sets of events, and he will arrive at different conclusions. However, it is my conviction that those who adopt different positions should proceed in a systematic way. For instance, those who take the position that curriculum and instruction are all one ball of wax should explain the complex set of events inherent in the position by carefully defining their technical terms, by describing the character of the events, and by identifying relationships among them. Obviously, the resulting propositions about curriculum design and curriculum engineering would be vastly different from those I have set forth. No doubt different research demands would be indicated. Such theoretical postures are not clearly presented in the literature at the present time, and we need them to stimulate organized dialogue on curriculum theory.

5 Definitions and Models in Curriculum Theory

Mauritz Johnson, Jr.

Introduction

A pragmatic view of curriculum has dominated thought and action in the field. In effect the traditionalists have shaped the structure of the field by being overly concerned with practical considerations and classroom applications at the expense of curriculum theory, research, and understanding. In the selection that follows, Mauritz Johnson argues persuasively that an overzealous effort to use curriculum in order to improve education inhibits opportunities to develop curriculum theory and more effectively influence curriculum practice.

The organization of this selection provides the reader with an opportunity to explore conflicting definitions and explanations of curriculum structure, sources of curriculum, and the selection of curriculum items. Taken together, these differing interpretations of the components of curriculum allow readers to understand the areas of confusion that divide proponents of the curriculum field. Johnson's paper aids us in the process of understanding the confusions existing in the field by clarifying the various meanings associated with the term curriculum and those linked to it.

In the final sections of this paper, Johnson presents the relationships between curriculum and instruction, evaluation and research, and he provides a schema for understanding the many aspects of curriculum better. As you read, think about the following questions:
- Of the many definitions of curriculum that you have read about in this paper, which one or two seems compatible with your understanding of the curriculum field?
- How would you describe the distinctions between curriculum, instruction, evaluation, and research after reading this article?

Educational researchers have traditionally been more concerned with improving education than with understanding it. This observation by Lazarsfeld and Sieber[1] seems valid for educationists in general, whether engaged in research or some other endeavor such as "curriculum development." And, indeed, the noneducationist scholars who have of late interested themselves in curriculum reform projects are also more concerned with *improving* school programs than with gaining increased insight into the nature of curriculum. As scholars, all of them are of course interested in some kind of theory but not in *curriculum* theory. Their views regarding curriculum may be sound, but they are no more firmly grounded in theory than those of education professors.

At the same time, educational practitioners—teachers, administrators, and even those with titles indicating specific responsibility for curriculum development—while interested in curriculum, are not particularly concerned with curriculum *theory*. After all, they feel, their concern is the practical one of improving the curriculum, not studying it. A perusal of the curriculum literature of the past twenty years will reveal, moreover, that the professors of education who have achieved reputations as "curriculum specialists" have chiefly been experts on *how* to organize and direct professional and lay groups effectively for curriculum improvement by applying principles of group dynamics and human relations. These specialists have seemed more concerned with improving the *process* of curriculum development than with any specific improvement in the curriculum itself; and whatever interest they may have had in *organizational* theory and the psychology of groups, they have evidenced little concern for curriculum theory.

Thus the majority of educationists, educational practitioners, and scholars active in curriculum reform are oriented toward improvement rather than understanding, action and results rather than inquiry. Nevertheless, a small but increasing number of students of education are directing their attention to questions of curriculum theory for no other immediate purpose than to increase understanding of curricular phenomena. The theoretical clarification they bring about may ultimately benefit both scholars and practitioners in their efforts to improve curriculum, but this possibility is not the immediate motive for attempting to construct a curriculum theory. The theorist cannot allow himself to be forced into justifying his inquiry solely on the basis of its immediate utility.

Theories and Platforms

Current theoretical work on curriculum is of two types—programmatic (doctrinal) and analytic. Phenix,[2] who subtitled his book *A Philosophy of the Curriculum for General Education*, engaged in both analysis and prescription.

He analyzed various disciplines and built a taxonomy of meanings. He also proposed certain criteria for curriculum selection and organization. But at the same time he advocated a specific program of general education.

Similarly, Broudy, Smith, and Burnett[3] subtitled their work *A Study in Curriculum Theory*; and while they, too, examined criteria and classified the uses of knowledge, they also delineated a program of general education for the secondary schools. Beauchamp likewise explored in some detail the problems of formulating a theory, but his own illustrative model of a curriculum theory was programmatic with respect to process (planning) rather than substance or structure. He acknowledged that his own "curriculum position was imposed upon the field of curriculum theory as organized in the classification scheme...."[4]

All of these current scholars are well aware of the difference between a curriculum position and curriculum theory. In the past, however, even the "giants" of the profession seemed not to note this distinction. One of the most remarkable collaborations of eminent educational thinkers occurred in 1924–26 when Bagley, Bobbitt, Bonser, Charters, Counts, Courtis, Horn, Judd, F.J. Kelly, Kilpatrick, H. Rugg, and Works joined in preparing a composite statement on "The Foundations of Curriculum-Making." Despite the fact that every member felt obliged to append his own reservations about the report, the committee's fifty-eight "principles" represented a consensual *position* rather than a curriculum theory. That the committee considered it to be a theory is evident, however, from an announcement in the introductory section that "each member . . . has not insisted upon the acceptance of his own curriculum theory...."[5] On the other hand, it had been stated previously that the group was explicitly concerned with ". . . writing a platform of *practical forward steps* in curriculum-making...." In this same paragraph the confusion is increased by Rugg's reference to ". . . this platform of curriculum theory...."[6]

Clearly, platforms and theories are two different things. Platforms propose policies, theories provide explanations. Included among the "principles" proposed by the 1926 Committee were many normative statements. Not until the twenty-eighth item was any definition of curriculum provided, and that was clearly "programmatic," as Scheffler uses the term.[7] "The curriculum," stated the committee, "should be conceived . . . in terms of a succession of experiences and enterprises having a maximum of lifelikeness for the learner."[8] By considering "experiences and enterprises" to be the essential elements of curriculum, the committee obscured the distinction between curriculum and instruction; by qualifying these elements with "lifelikeness," it engaged in exhortation instead of explanation.

But the committee was aware of the problem of terminology. "From the beginning of our discussion," Rugg reported, "it was apparent that we did not understand each other. The chief task which we confronted was the erection of a common vocabulary."[9] Vocabulary is still one of the chief problems in curriculum theory. Note, for example, the confusion evidenced as late as 1962 in the ASCD pamphlet, "What are the Sources of the Curriculum?"[10] in which "curriculum" is confused with "curriculum development" and "source" is confused with "determinant."

Curriculum and Instruction as Systems

Some current theorists (Macdonald, Faix[11]) favor a "systems" or process model for curriculum in which the elements are inputs, processes, outputs, and feedbacks. They recognize the necessity of explicating the relation between curriculum and instruction, but in viewing curriculum cybernetically, they, too, confuse curriculum per se with the curriculum development process. Macdonald has included both content and process in his "curriculum system," but since the system ". . . is made up of people as its basic units . . ."[12] and its output is "transmitted . . . to the instructional setting (also a separate social system),"[13] one finds it difficult to identify the curriculum itself, either *as* or *in* the system. Surely curriculum does not consist of people.

In Macdonald's model some of the variables conventionally labeled as "sources" are considered to be "inputs."[14] This only makes sense if the system in question is construed as the "curriculum development system." To consider these variables inputs into the curriculum itself makes no more sense than to consider them sources of the curriculum.

Maccia[15] and Macdonald disagree on the relationship of curriculum to instruction. To Macdonald these are separate concepts (systems?) that overlap to some extent. Maccia, on the other hand, holds that curriculum is a component of instruction by virtue of being a variable in "teacher behavior."[16] Thus, she sees curriculum not as a system but as "instructional content." This content consists of "rules." Rules are conceived as "structures," which in sets constitute "disciplines."[17]

The role of curriculum in instruction is implicit in Maccia's definition of instruction as "influence toward rule-governed behavior." Since curriculum equals rules,[18] its function must be to *govern*, that is, regulate, behavior. But there are two levels of discourse here. Whose behavior does curriculum govern? Is curriculum the set of rules that *learners* are influenced through instruction to govern their behavior by or does curriculum as rules govern the *teacher's* behavior in instruction? By Maccia's formula, $B_t = I_c R M_c$ (the only one in which curriculum, I_c, appears), it seems to be the teacher's behavior that curriculum governs. But the teacher's behavior in instruction influences students' behavior toward governance by rules. Are these the same rules that constitute curriculum? What *is* a curriculum?

The Concept of Curriculum

Accepted usage identifies curriculum with "planned learning experiences." This definition is unsatisfactory, however, if *curriculum* is to be distinguished from *instruction*. Whether experiences are viewed subjectively in terms of the sensibility of the experiencing individual or objectively in terms of his actions in a particular setting, there is in either case no experience until an interaction between the individual and his environment actually occurs. Clearly, such interaction characterizes *instruction*, not curriculum.

A concept of curriculum that limits it to a post hoc account of instruction is of little value. Surely curriculum must play some role in *guiding* instruction. If so, it must be viewed as anticipatory, not reportorial. Curriculum implies intent.

Surely, too, a useful concept of curriculum must leave some room for creativity and individual style in instruction. In other words, decisions regarding the learning experiences to be provided are the result of instructional planning, not of curriculum development. The curriculum, though it may limit the range of possible experiences, cannot specify them. Curriculum must be defined in other terms.

In view of the shortcomings of the currently popular definition, it is here stipulated that curriculum is a *structured series of intended learning outcomes*. Curriculum prescribes (or at least anticipates) the *results* of instruction. It does not prescribe the *means,* that is the activities, materials, or even the instructional content to be used in achieving the results. In specifying outcomes to be sought, curriculum is concerned with *ends* but at the level of attainable learning products, not at the more remote level at which these ends are justified. In other words, curriculum indicates *what* is to be learned, not *why* it should be learned.

This view of curriculum seems to be in substantial accord with that of Gagné who defines curriculum as ". . . a series of content units . . . ," a content unit being ". . . a capability to be acquired under a single set of learning conditions. . . ."[19] Eisner, too, appears to endorse this view when he states that a teacher is engaged in curriculum building when he decides " . . . what to teach and how to order what he teaches"[20] but then appears to depart from it when he stipulates later that ". . . the basic unit of the curriculum is an activity."[21] The central thesis of the present paper is that curriculum has reference to what it is intended that students *learn*, not what it is intended that they *do*.

There seems to be rather general agreement as to what *can* be learned, that is, what the categories of learning outcomes are. Three "domains" are commonly recognized: the cognitive,[22] the affective,[23] and the psychomotor. Other classification schemes may be preferred, but the component types of outcomes are well recognized and accepted. They include factual knowledge, symbolic equivalents, concepts, generalizations, intellectual skills, manipulative skills, attitudes, interests, values, and appreciations.

The nature of a particular intended learning outcome limits the range of possible appropriate learning experiences and thus guides instructional planning. A learning experience has an activity component and a content component, that is, it involves some kind of activity with some kind of content.

A curriculum item that deals with a skill-type outcome restricts the range of appropriate activities but may or may not impose any limitations on the content. On the other hand, an item that concerns facts, concepts, or generalizations specifies content but leaves considerable option with respect to activity. When an affective outcome is specified, neither content nor activity may be greatly restricted, although most affects have fairly definite referents (implying content), and schools are concerned that most affective outcomes be intellectually grounded (implying activity).

No curriculum item fully defines instructional *content*. Instructional content includes not only that which is implied or specified in the curriculum, but also a large body of *instrumental* content selected by the teacher, not to be learned but to facilitate the desired learning. Concepts and generalizations are not learned directly but rather through numerous encounters with specific manifestations, the selection of which is an instructional rather that curricular function.

Every curriculum item defines instructional *activity* to some degree. Although there are many ways of developing a concept of a skill, the accepted approaches to each kind of outcome are finite. When the intended outcome is specified, therefore, certain possible activities are ruled out and others favored.

The *order* of learning experiences also is influenced by curriculum. A curriculum is not a random series of items but a *structured* one, even if only to the extent of indicating that the order in which certain outcomes are achieved is immaterial. Insofar as the sequence of development is not considered to be a matter of indifference, the curriculum must be specific about the proper order. But structure is not merely a matter of temporal sequence. It also refers to hierarchical relations among items.

Curriculum Structure

That curriculum implies such ordering is obviously the assumption underlying the widespread current attention to the structure of knowledge, especially of that knowledge derived from inquiry which constitutes the disciplines. It is implicit in the analysis by Phenix[24] and explicit in that of Schwab[25] that disciplines are structured both conceptually and syntactically (methodologically). Presumably, therefore, curriculum items assume their significance and meaning from their relationship to one another and to the mode of inquiry on the basis of which this relationship was derived or verified.

Thus, if a and b are appropriate curricular items, then aRb is likely to be appropriate also. If a and b are concepts, aRb is a generalization. It may be classificatory (e.g., addition and multiplication are binary operations), correlational (e.g., men tend to be taller than women), a function (e.g., $F = ma$), a definition of another concept (e.g., density is mass per unit of volume), or in some other way relate two concepts within some structure.

Curriculum must indicate such relationships. Concepts and generalizations do not occur singly. They form clusters, and a decision to include one of them is often tantamount to a decision to include a whole cluster. A teacher or curriculum developer is not free to include a concept such as "capillarity" and to exclude, for example, "surface tension." These clusters are not equivalent, however, to "instructional units." The curriculum does not specify what organizational units are to be used in instruction, but it does indicate organizational relationships among the intended outcomes. In this sense, curriculum is a *structured* series of intended learning outcomes.

Source of Curriculum

It is necessary to account for the source of these intended outcomes. In most discussions of this question, the sources of the curriculum are regarded to be (1) the needs and interests of the learners, (2) the values and problems of the society, and (3) the disciplines or organized subject matter. All three of these may indeed impose criteria for the selection of curriculum items, but only the third can be considered a *source* of them. At that, it is only a partial source since it ignores the body of unorganized knowledge and related skills and attitudes that lie outside of the recognized disciplines. The source of curriculum—the only possible source—is the total available culture. This was recognized by Bellack in 1956 when he identified ". . . the expanding content of the culture as the source of curriculum content," which he defined, in turn, as ". . . those elements of the content of the culture that are considered appropriate or relevant to the instructional aims of the school."[26] This is not to say what the curriculum *should* be, but what it *is*. When Rugg and Withers[27] say that the curriculum *should be* "culture-centered," they mean something quite different from the present assertion that the curriculum is *necessarily* "culture-derived."

Not all cultural content is of a sort that could be incorporated into the curriculum. Only that which is teachable and available is eligible for inclusion. Artifacts and social institutions are components of a culture, but they are not teachable. Even some knowledge and skills, though teachable and very much a part of the culture, are not available for curriculum, since they are kept secrets by families, craft groups, corporations, or governments.

Selection of Curriculum Items

It is obvious that everything available and teachable in the culture cannot be included in a given curriculum. Selection is essential. Although who does the selecting is an important educational policy question, it is not a concern of curriculum theory. What is of concern, however, is that whatever criteria are used be made explicit.

There are many possible criteria—some sensible, others silly, depending on one's ideology. Some factions insist that curriculum items bear upon persistent problems of living or current social problems; others emphasize the significance of items to the understanding of an organized field of study; still others favor selection on the basis of the experiences and interests of the potential learners. Some of these preferences are more applicable to instructional organization than to curriculum selection. Those who insist on applying them to selection are of course free to do so, but the notion of curriculum clusters restricts their freedom to select items at will without regard for structural considerations.

Moreover, a distinction can be made between curriculum selection for training and for education. Training implies learning for use in a predictable situation; education implies learning for use in unpredictable situations. The development of a training curriculum begins with a job analysis in which the tasks to be performed and the knowledge, skills, and attitudes needed to perform them are identified. The uses of training are, in the terminology of Broudy, Smith, and Burnett,[28] replicative and applicative. The uses of education are associative and interpretative.[29]

Man's systematic efforts to interpret his experiences are represented by those organized bodies of knowledge, skills, and attitudes known as disciplines. An educational curriculum is developed by selecting among and within these disciplines those elements which analysis identifies as having the greatest potential interpretive value. Once the disciplines considered most relevant in the interpretation of experience have been identified, internal selection criteria become dominant. Which specific curriculum items are selected depends on how fundamental and crucial they are to the discipline, how well they explicate its structure, how powerful they are in furthering its characteristic thought processes and modes of inquiry. Phenix has called attention to the simplifying, coordinating, and generative features of disciplines. Appropriate selection criteria would maximize the probability of retaining these features in the curriculum and, hence, in instruction. Phenix holds that "a discipline is knowledge organized for instruction."[30]

Curriculum and Instruction

Although curriculum is not a system, it may be viewed as the output of a "curriculum-development system" and as an input into an "instructional system." (See Figure 5-1.)

The instructional system has three components: planning, execution (instruction), and evaluation. Instructional planning occurs at various levels, varying in their temporal proximity to the actual instruction. Most remote is that strategic planning which results in the design of "courses" and "instructional units" within courses. Here an appropriate number of curriculum items (intended learning outcomes) are selected and organized for instructional

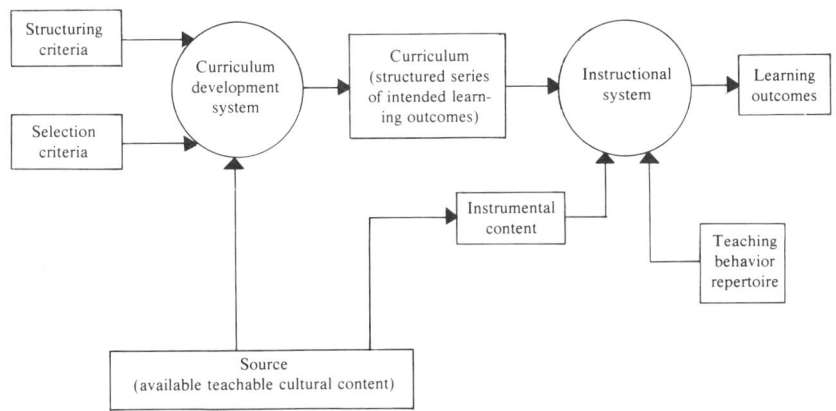

Figure 5-1

A model showing curriculum as an output of one system and an input of another

purposes. Course and unit planners have considerable freedom in their selection and organization so long as they do not violate curriculum stipulations with respect to hierarchy (clusters) and order. In a graded school organization, several versions of each course and unit may have to be planned to take into account differences in students' ability and readiness. Actually, each version is a different course and should be so designated, though this is seldom the case. In a nongraded instructional program, the curriculum can be arranged into a single series of courses through which students pass at varying rates.

Individual teachers continue the process of instructional planning up to and throughout the execution stage. It is they who make the final choice of learning activities and instrumental content in terms of the characteristics of the students, the availability of resources, and the exigencies of the ongoing instructional process. Even at this point, decisions must be governed by the intended outcomes stipulated by the curriculum and incorporated into the course and unit plans.

The evaluation aspect of instruction obviously involves a comparison of actual learning outcomes with the intended learning outcomes. For purposes of such comparison, it is necessary to create a situation in which the student can exhibit behavior indicative that he has learned, that is, has achieved the intended learning outcome. It is in this evaluation context that Mager's injunction[31] applies to specify objectives operationally as terminal behaviors at defined levels of performance under defined conditions. This is not to say, however, that learning consists of a change in behavior or that learning has not occurred if a behavioral change cannot be demonstrated. Nor is it the case that there has been no teaching where learning cannot be shown to have occurred. Teaching occurs whenever appropriate actions intended to produce learning are taken. Because the intentions are not fulfilled or no evidence of their being fulfilled is available does not in any way disqualify the actions as teaching.

Instruction consists of two sets of interaction. One is Dewey's "transaction" between the student and the environment manipulated by the teacher. As indicated earlier, both the content of the environment and the activities of the student are governed by the curriculum. The second interaction is the interpersonal one between the teacher and students. Amidon and Flanders[32] have developed a procedure for analyzing this interaction, and Bellack,[33] Smith,[34] Ryans,[35] and others have examined the linguistic, logical, and information-processing characteristics of the classroom discourse that facilitates the interaction. Maccia[36] has pointed out that the interaction has both motivational and content bases. The content base is clearly either derived from or inspired by curriculum, and unless the motivational base is entirely nonrational (sentimental, hedonistic, or magisterial), it, too, is curriculum-relevant.

It seems evident that many if not most of the so-called "curriculum reform" projects of the past decade have been concerned with instruction far more than with curriculum. Indeed, some of them have never made their curriculum explicit, whereas they have trespassed heavily in the instructional planning domain, going so far as to specify not only the learning activities to be provided but the instructional materials to be used as well. These suggestions may well be excellent ones, so long as it is not assumed that alternative activities and materials could not possibly be devised to carry out the same curriculum as well or better. It seems probable that some of these projects have encroached upon instructional planning in a deliberate, if cynical, effort to make the curriculum "teacher-proof." On the other hand, syllabuses, courses of study, and curriculum guides have for years been freighted with lengthy compilations of suggested activities, materials, evaluation procedures, and other instructional advice, whereas—aside from an extensive list of vague objectives and an expository outline of so-called "content"—they have seldom presented any curriculum at all in the sense the term has been used in this paper.

Curriculum Evaluation and Research

Macdonald[37] has correctly pointed out that curriculum evaluation is all too often conducted at the output point of instruction rather than at the input position. Thus curriculum evaluation is confounded with instructional evaluation. Curriculum serves as the criterion for instructional evaluation; variations in instruction cannot be permitted to enter into the evaluation of curriculum. If curriculum is to be evaluated empirically on the basis of instructional outputs, then differences in instructional effectiveness must be controlled, randomized, or partialed out. Gagné has suggested a scaling method whereby instructional output data may be used ". . . to provide information about

Definitions and Models in Curriculum Theory

the sequence of a curriculum," but notes that it ". . . does not provide an *evaluation* of a curriculum." "It does *not* tell us how good the curriculum is." To determine the effectiveness of an entire curriculum-instruction system, Gagné suggests that "one must actually put the curriculum into use and then measure the results in terms of student achievement or some other specified criterion."[38]

It is probable that feedback from instruction can furnish evidence regarding the *structural* validity of a curriculum. On the basis of instructional experience, curriculum items might be found to be incorrectly ordered, or hierarchical clusters might be found to be incomplete or contain superfluities. But the validity of curriculum *selection*, that is, the omission of significant items and the inclusion of insignificant ones, must rest on some criterion other than instructional results. Cronbach[39] and Stake[40] have explored this problem at some length, and it may be expected that further progress will be made on it at the Center for Instructional Research and Curriculum Evaluation at the University of Illinois. Essential, however, to such progress is a clear delineation of curriculum and instruction.

Similarly, research on curriculum can only be conducted on the basis of some theoretical framework. As Ryans has observed, ". . . the chief function of theory is *not* to describe once and for all how certain kinds of phenomena . . . operate, but rather to provide a framework for observation and analysis."[41] Whether the formulation of curriculum presented here will serve this purpose remains to be seen.

A schema in which curriculum is viewed as something other than "learning experiences" preserves the autonomy of creative instructional planning, free of remote prescription under the guise of curriculum development. It also clarifies the curricular research domain. Immediately susceptible to competent investigation are such questions as: What are the rules relating intended outcomes and more general educational and training objectives? What are the rules for selection of curriculum items within the contexts of education and training? What are the rules for ordering curriculum items and for determining when order is unimportant? What are the rules by which hierarchical clusters of curriculum items are identified? What are the architectonics of nondisciplined cultural content? What standard system of symbols would be most useful in communicating a curriculum?

Summary

Some problems in current efforts at theorizing about curriculum have been discussed. Little interest in curriculum theory has been manifest by educational practitioners, academic scholars, or curriculum specialists. Curriculum theory has been confused with valuative positions regarding curriculum. The conventional definition of curriculum in terms of "planned learning experiences" has prevented a clear distinction between curriculum and instruction. Consequently, many alleged curriculum documents are primarily prescriptions or suggestions for instruction.

Recent considerations of curriculum theory have focused attention on disciplinary structures, but curriculum has been confused with the curriculum-development system of which it is an output, or it has been considered a part of the instructional system of which it is an input. An attempt was made, therefore, to develop a schema in which curriculum was defined as a structured series of intended learning outcomes. For purposes of clarity and convenience, this schema is summarized below.

A Schema for Curriculum

1. A curriculum is a structured series of intended learning outcomes.
   Corollary: Curriculum does not consist of planned learning experiences.
   Corollary: Curriculum is not a system but the output of one system and an input into another.
   1.1 Learning outcomes consist of three classes:
      1.11 Knowledge
         1.111 Facts: items of verifiable information.
         1.112 Concepts: mental constructs epitomizing facts about particular referents.
         1.113 Generalizations: (including laws, principles, rules) statements of relationship among two or more concepts.
      1.12 Techniques (processes, skills, abilities)
         1.121 Cognitive: methods of operating on knowledge intellectually.
         1.122 Psychomotor: methods of manipulating the body and material things effectively with respect to purposes.
      1.13 Values (affects)
         1.131 Norms: societal prescriptions and preferences regarding belief and conduct.
         1.132 Predilections: individual preferential dispositions (attitudes, interests, appreciations, aversions).
   1.2 Whenever a curriculum is used in instruction, the intention (to achieve the outcomes) is implicit regardless of the curriculum's origin or sanction.
2. Selection is an essential aspect of curriculum formulation.
   2.1 The source from which curriculum is selected is the available culture.
      Corollary: Societal problems and the needs and interests of children are not sources of curriculum.
      2.11 Modern communication makes available cultural content that is not indigenous to the society in which the curriculum is formulated.
      2.12 Some indigenous cultural content may be unavailable due to the secrecy of those in possession of it.

Definitions and Models in Curriculum Theory

2.2 Cultural content available for curriculum is of two types: disciplinary and nondisciplinary.

   2.21 The content embodied in organized disciplines is derived from systematic inquiry conducted within a framework of assumptions and procedures accepted by scholars competent to conduct such inquiry.

   2.22 Nondisciplinary content is derived empirically from experience other than deliberate inquiry.

2.3 Various criteria may govern the selection of curriculum from available cultural content.

   2.31 The only necessary, albeit insufficient, criterion for curriculum selection is that the content be teachable.

      2.311 Teachability implies learnability, but the converse does not necessarily hold.

      2.312 Cultural content is teachable if the learning of it by one person can be facilitated by direct or remote interaction with another person.

      2.313 Teaching is the process by which one person interacts with another with the intention of influencing his learning.

         2.3131 There can be teaching where there is no learning.

         2.3132 There can be learning without teaching.

      2.314 Learning is the process by which an individual invests cultural content with meaning, thereby becoming capable of acting differently toward that item, or another item, of cultural content.

      Corollary: Learning does not necessarily change behavior, but it changes the potential for behavior.

         2.3141 Learning can be detected only by contriving a situation in which a change in behavior can be manifested.

         2.3142 Learning is independent of any demonstration of its occurrence.

      2.315 Cultural content is learnable if meaning can be perceived in it.

         2.3151 Cultural content has meaning for an individual to the extent that he recognizes appropriate rules by which his actions toward it may be governed.

         2.3152 Meanings may be symbolic, empiric, esthetic, ethic, synoetic, or synoptic (Phenix 1964).

   2.32 Ideology determines what additional criteria are imposed in curriculum selection.

      2.321 A given society may demand that curriculum be selected in conformity with a specified set of political, social, economic, or moral values.

2.322 Curriculum content may be selected with regard to its utility in the social order or in the present or anticipated life situations of learners.

2.323 Curriculum content may be selected with regard to its significance in the structure of intellectual disciplines.

2.33 The basis of curriculum selection differs for training and for education.

2.331 Training is the process of preparing an individual to perform defined functions in a predictable situation.

2.332 Education is the process of equipping an individual to perform undefined functions in unpredictable situations.

2.333 The selection of curriculum content for training is based on an analysis of the specific functions to be performed and the specific situation in which they are to be performed.

2.334 The selection of curriculum content for education is based on its having the widest possible significance and greatest possible explanatory power.

2.34 The selection of some curriculum items necessitates the selection of related items.

2.341 A set of closely related items is a curriculum cluster.

2.342 A curriculum cluster may consist of one type or mixed types of curriculum items.

3. Structure is an essential characteristic of curriculum.

3.1 Curriculum structure reveals orderings that are mandatory for instruction.

3.11 The ordering of some curriculum items is indifferent.

3.12 The ordering of some curriculum clusters determines the gross ordering of constituent items but not their internal order.

3.13 Some curriculum clusters are ordered internally.

3.14 Curriculum ordering disregards instructional temporal spacing (grade or age placement).

3.2 Curriculum structure reveals taxonomic (hierarchical) relationships, whether or not order of items is significant.

4. Curriculum guides instruction.

4.1 Instruction is the interaction between a teaching agent and one or more individuals intending to learn.

4.2 Instruction engages intended learners in activities with cultural content.

4.21 The teaching agent influences the activities of those intending to learn.

4.22 The range of appropriate instructional activities is limited by the type of curriculum item.

4.23 Instructional content includes both curricular and instrumental content.

4.231 Curricular content is that cultural content explicitly intended to be learned.

4.232 Instrumental content is optional cultural content introduced into the instructional situation, not to be learned but to facilitate the intended learning.

4.24 Instructional planning consists of the selection and ordering of instructional activities and instrumental content on the basis of curriculum.

4.25 A learning experience is the subjective concomitant of activities with instructional content on the part of an individual engaging in them.

4.3 Instruction is episodic.

4.31 An instructional episode consists of a series of teaching cycles relevant to one or more curriculum items.

4.311 A teaching cycle involves perception, diagnosis, and action or reaction by a teaching agent and intended learners (Smith 1961).

4.312 Teaching cycles are initiated by structuring or soliciting moves (Bellack and Davitz 1963).

4.313 Teaching cycles include reflexive response or reaction moves (Bellack and Davitz 1963).

4.314 Actions and reactions in teaching cycles are linguistic, performative, or expressive (Smith 1961).

4.32 Several instructional episodes may relate to the same curriculum item, just as a given instructional episode may relate to a number of curriculum items.

5. Curriculum evaluation involves validation of both selection and structure.

5.1 Empirical evidence based on instruction can identify structural errors and omissions in selection (Gagné 1966).

5.2 Judgmental and consensual methods are required to validate priorities and identify superfluities in selection.

6. Curriculum is the criterion for instructional evaluation.

6.1 The effectiveness of instruction is represented by the extent to which actual outcomes correspond with intended outcomes.

6.2 Comparisons among instructional plans and among instructors using the same instructional plan can be made only in terms of a given curriculum.

Notes

1. P. Lazarsfeld and S. Sieber, *Organizing Educational Research* (Englewood Cliffs, N.J.: Prentice-Hall, 1964), p. 33.

2. P. Phenix, *Realms of Meaning* (New York: McGraw-Hill, 1964).

3. H. S. Broudy, B. O. Smith, and J. R. Burnett, *Democracy and Excellence in American Secondary Education* (Chicago: Rand McNally, 1964).

4. G. A. Beauchamp, *Curriculum Theory* (Wilmette, Ill.: Kagg Press, 1961), p. 116.

5. Harold Rugg et al., *Foundations of Curriculum-Making*. Twenty-sixth Yearbook of the National Society for the Study of Education, pt. II (Chicago: Public School Publishing Co., 1927), p. 11.

6. Ibid., p. 6.

7. I. Scheffler, *The Language of Education* (Springfield, Ill.: Charles C. Thomas, 1970), p. 19.

8. Rugg, *Foundations of Curriculum-Making*, p. 18.

9. Ibid., p. 4.

10. Association for Supervision and Curriculum Development, "What are the Sources of the Curriculum? A Symposium." Mimeographed, 1962.

11. T. L. Faix, "Structural-Functional Analysis as a Conceptual System for Curriculum Theory and Research" (Paper presented at American Educational Research Association meeting, February 1966).

12. J. B. Macdonald, "Curriculum Theory: Problems and a Prospectus" (Paper presented at Professors of Curriculum meeting, Miami Beach, April 3, 1964), p. 6.

13. Ibid., p. 12.

14. His inputs include "cultural heritage," "social pressures," "behavioral knowledge," and "professional knowledge." Macdonald, "Curriculum Theory," p. 5. See similar terminology with respect to sources in Association for Supervision and Curriculum Development, "What are the Sources?"

15. E. S. Maccia, "Curriculum Theory and Policy." Educational Theory Center and Social Studies Curriculum Center, Occasional Paper 65–176, Ohio State University, 1965, mimeographed; "Instruction as Influence Toward Rule-Governed Behavior." Educational Theory Center, Occasional Paper 64–155, Ohio State University, 1964, mimeographed; "The Scientific Perspective: Only One Curricular Model." Center for the Construction of Theory in Education, Occasional Paper 63–143, Ohio State University, 1963, mimeographed.

16. $I = f(B_t R B_s)$ $B_t = I_c R M_c$ where I denotes instruction; B_t, teacher behavior; B_s, student behavior; I_c, instructional content or curriculum; and M_c, motivational content. Maccia, "Curriculum Theory and Policy," p. 8.

17. Maccia, "Curriculum Theory and Policy," p. 8.; "The Scientific Perspective," p. 6.

18. "A rule is a reason or criterion which leads to one behavior rather than another. It is a way of behaving...," "... a way of solving problems...." "In an individual a rule is a cognitive structure." Maccia, "Instruction as Influence," p. 14.

19. R. M. Gagné, "Curriculum Research and the Promotion of Learning" (Invited address to AERA meeting, February 1966, mimeographed), p. 6.

20. E. Eisner, "Levels of Curriculum and Curriculum Research," *Elementary School Journal* 66 (December 1965), p. 156.

21. Ibid., p. 158.

22. B. S. Bloom, ed., *Taxonomy of Educational Objectives. Handbook I: Cognitive Domain* (New York: Longmans, Green, 1956).

23. D. R. Krathwohl, B. S. Bloom, and B. B. Masia, *Taxonomy of Educational Objectives. Handbook II: Affective Domain* (New York: David McKay Co., 1964).

24. Phenix, *Realms of Meaning;* "The Disciplines as Curriculum Content," in *Curriculum Crossroads,* ed. A. H. Passow (New York: Teachers College Press, Columbia University, 1962), pp. 57–65.

25. J. J. Schwab, "Problems, Topics and Issues," in *Education and the Structure of Knowledge,* ed. S. Elam (Chicago: Rand McNally, 1964), pp. 4–42; "Structure of the Disciplines: Meanings and Significances," in *The Structure of Knowledge and The Curriculum,* ed. G. W. Ford and L. Pugno (Chicago: Rand McNally, 1964), pp. 6–30.

26. A. Bellack, "Selection and Organization of Curriculum Content: An Analysis," in *What Shall the High School Teach?* (Association for Supervision and Curriculum Development Yearbook, 1956), p. 99.

27. H. Rugg and W. Withers, *Social Foundations of Education* (Englewood Cliffs, N.J.: Prentice-Hall, 1955), p. 669.

28. Broudy, Smith, and Burnett, *Democracy and Excellence,* pp. 48–54.

29. Ibid., pp. 46–48, 54–55.

30. Phenix, "Disciplines as Curriculum Content," p. 58.

31. R. F. Mager, *Preparing Objectives for Programmed Instruction* (Belmont, Calif.: Fearon Publishers, 1961), p. 12.

32. E. J. Amidon and N. A. Flanders, *The Role of the Teacher in the Classroom* (Amidon and Associates, 1963).

33. A. Bellack and J. R. Davitz, *The Language of the Classroom* (New York: Institute of Psychological Research, Teachers College, Columbia University, 1963).

34. B. O. Smith, "A Concept of Teaching," in *Language and Concepts in Education,* ed. B. O. Smith and R. H. Ennis (Chicago: Rand McNally, 1961).

35. D. G. Ryans, "A Model of Instruction Based on Information System Concepts," in *Theories of Instruction,* ed. J. B. Macdonald and R. L. Leeper. (Association for Supervision and Curriculum Development, 1965), pp. 36–61.

36. Maccia, "Instruction as Influence."

37. J. B. Macdonald, "Researching Curriculum Output: The Use of a General Systems Theory to Identify Appropriate Curriculum Outputs and Research Hypotheses" (Paper presented at AERA meeting, February 1965).

38. R. M. Gagné, "Curriculum Research and the Promotion of Learning," p. 14.

39. L. J. Cronbach, "Evaluation for Course Improvement," in *New Curricula,* ed. R. W. Heath (New York: Harper & Row, 1964), pp. 231–48; "The Psychological Background for Curriculum Experimentation," in *Modern Viewpoints in the Curriculum,* ed. P. C. Rosenbloom (New York: McGraw-Hill, 1964) pp. 19–35.

40. R. E. Stake, "The Countenance of Educational Evaluation," mimeographed (Center for Instructional Research and Curriculum Evaluation, University of Illinois, 1966).

41. Ryans, "A Model of Instruction," p. 38.

Reconceptualists

6 The Reconceptualization of Curriculum Studies

William F. Pinar

Introduction

Within the last five years there has been a great deal of controversy over the issue of whether or not the curriculum field is being revitalized through the development of a new movement in the field of curriculum studies. In this article William Pinar argues strongly that a new movement is indeed visible in the field. In doing so, he examines the parameters of both the existing schools of thought as well as those of the more recent reconceptualization viewpoint, which he defines as a reaction to what the curriculum field has been.

The article begins with a history of the field and an explication of the categories used to organize this book. It would be useful to compare the assumptions and modes of inquiry that characterize each of the positions Pinar discusses. As you read, think about the following questions.

- What are the essential differences of the "schools" that Pinar presents? Are they incompatible?
- Of what use are the categorizations that Pinar develops?
- Also note Pinar's tone; is it favorably disposed toward reconceptualists or does it have the opposite effect?
- Why do you suppose this paper might generate some controversy in the curriculum field?

This is a revised version of a paper presented at the Annual Meeting of the American Educational Research Association in New York in April 1977. Reprinted, with permission, from *Journal of Curriculum Studies* 10, no. 3 (1978), pp. 205-14.

What some observers have designated a "movement" is visible in the field of curriculum studies in the United States. Some have termed it "reconceptualization," others "the new curriculum theory." Both phrases suggest more thematic unity among the curriculum writing characterized as the "reconceptualization" than appears to exist upon close examination. Nonetheless, some thematic similarities are discernible, though insufficient in number to warrant a characterization like "ideology" or composite, agreed-upon point of view. What can be said without dispute is that by the summer of 1978 there will have been six conferences and five books[1] in the past six years that are indications of a sociointellectual phenomenon in this field, and a phenomenon that clearly functions to reconceptualize the field of curriculum studies. Thus, while the writing published to date may be somewhat varied thematically, it is unitary in its significance for the field. If this process of transformation continues at its present rate, the field of curriculum studies will be profoundly different in twenty years time than it has been during the first fifty years of its existence.

What is this reconceptualization? The answer, at this point, is a slippery one, and to gain even an inchoate grip, one looks to the field as it is. This will indicate, in part, what it is not. To a considerable extent, the reconceptualization is a reaction to what the field has been and what it is seen to be at the present time.

Traditionalists

Most curricularists at work in 1977 can be characterized as *traditionalists*. Their work continues to make use of the "conventional wisdom" of the field, epitomized still by the work of Tyler. More important in identifying traditionalists than the allusion to Tyler is citing the *raison d'être* for traditional curriculum work. Above all, the reason for curriculum writing—indeed curriculum work generally—is captured in the phrase "service to practitioners." Curriculum work tends to be field based, and curriculum writing tends to have schoolteachers in mind. In short, traditional curriculum work is focused on the schools. Further, professors of curriculum have tended to be former schoolpeople. In fact, school service of some sort, ordinarily classroom teaching, is still viewed as a prerequisite for a teaching post in the field in a college or university. To an extent not obvious in certain of the other subfields of education (for instance, philosophy and psychology of education, recently in administration and the "helping services"), curricularists are former schoolpeople whose intellectual and subcultural ties tend to be with school practitioners. They tend to be less interested in basic research, in theory development, in related developments in allied fields than in a set of perceived realities of classrooms and school settings generally.

There is, of course, a historical basis for traditional curriculum work. Cremin suggests that it was after superintendent Newlon's work in curriculum revision, in the early 1920s in Denver, that the need for a curriculum specialist became clear.[2] It is plausible to imagine school administrators like Newlon asking teachers who demonstrated an interest in curriculum and its development to leave classroom teaching and enter an administrative office from which they would attend full-time to matters curricular. There were no departments of curriculum in colleges of education in the 1920s; Newlon and other administrators could go nowhere else but to the classroom for curriculum personnel. When the training of curriculum personnel began at the university level in the 1930s, it surfaced in departments of administration and secondary education, further indicating the field's origin in and loyalty to the practical concerns of school personnel. This affiliation, more tenuous and complex at the present time than it was in the 1920s and 1930s, is evident in the programs of the largest professional association of curricularists in the United States, the Association for Supervision and Curriculum Development. The programs of ASCD annual meetings indicate a considerable and growing presence of school personnel. Further, the workshops and papers listed, the authors of which are university teachers, tend to have an explicit thematic focus on whatever school concerns are *au courant.*

There is another sense in which traditionalists carry forward the tradition of the field. The curriculum field's birth in the 1920s was understandably shaped by the intellectual character of that period. Above all it was a time of an emerging scientism when so-called scientific techniques from business and industry were finding their way into educational theory and practice. The early curricularist came to employ what Kliebard has termed the "bureaucratic model."[3] This model is characterized by its ameliorative orientation, ahistorical posture, and an allegiance to behaviorism and to what Macdonald has termed a "technological rationality." The curriculum worker is dedicated to the "improvement" of schools. He honors this dedication by accepting the curriculum structure as it is. "Curriculum change" is measured by comparing resulting behaviors with original objectives. Even humanistic educators tend to accept many of these premises, as they introduce, perhaps, "values clarification" into the school curriculum. Accepting the curriculum structure as it is and working to improve it is what is meant by the "technician's mentality." In a capsule way, it can be likened to adjusting an automobile engine part in order to make it function more effectively. This is also technological rationality, and its manifestations in school practice run the gamut from "competency-based teacher education" to "modular scheduling." The emphasis is on design, change (behaviorally observable), and improvement.

What has tended to be regarded as curriculum theory in the traditional sense, most notably Tyler's rationale,[4] is theoretical only in the questionable sense that it is abstract and usually at variance with what occurs in schools. Its intent is clearly to guide, to be of assistance to those in institutional positions who are concerned with curriculum. Of course, this is a broad concern. Most teachers share it, at least in terms of daily lesson planning. But as well as an element of teaching, curriculum is traditionally thought to include considerations such as evaluation, supervision, and also curriculum development and implementation. The boundaries of the field are fuzzy.

Thematically, there is no unity. From Tyler to Taba and Saylor and Alexander to the current expression of this genre in Daniel and Laurel Tanner's book, Neil's and Zais's writing (all of which attempt an overview of considerations imagined pertinent to a curriculum worker) to the humanistic movement (for instance the work of such individuals as Fantini, Jordan, Simon, Weinstein) is a broad thematic territory.[5] What makes this work one territory is its fundamental interest in working with school people, with revising the curricula of schools. Traditional writing tends to be journalistic, necessarily so, in order that it can be readily accessible to a readership seeking quick answers to pressing, practical problems. The publications of the Association for Supervision and Curriculum Development also exemplify to a considerable extent this writing. ASCD is the traditionalists' professional organization. Relatively speaking, there exists a close relationship between traditional curricularists and school personnel.

Conceptual-Empiricists

A relationship between school personnel and the other two groups of curricularists—*conceptual-empiricists* and *reconceptualists*—also exists. But the nature of this relationship differs from the alliance historically characteristic of the field. This difference becomes clearer as we examine, momentarily, a second group of curricularists, a group which—until reconceptualists appeared—seemed to be the only heir to the field.

I use the word *heir* advisedly, for the traditional curriculum field has been declared terminally ill or deceased by several influential observers, among them Schwab and Huebner.[6] What has caused, in the past fifteen to twenty years, the demise of the field? A comprehensive answer to this important question is inappropriate in the present context. What can be pointed out is twofold. First, the leadership of the so-called curriculum reform movement of the 1960s was outside the field. This bypass was a crippling blow to its professional status. If those whose work was curriculum development and implementation were called on primarily as consultants and only rarely at that, then clearly their claim to specialized knowledge and expertise was questionable. Second, the economic situation of the past six years has meant a drying up of funds for in-service work and for curriculum proposals generally. A field whose professional status was irreparably damaged now lost the material basis necessary for its functioning. How could curricularists work with schoolpeople without money or time for in-service workshops? How could curriculum proposals be implemented without requisite funds?

With the traditional, practical justification of the field attenuated—even teacher-training efforts have slowed dramatically—new justifications appeared. Curriculum and other education subfields have become increasingly vulnerable to criticism regarding scholarly standards by colleagues in so-called cognate fields. The influence of colleagues in the social sciences is particularly evident, parallelling the political ascendency of these disciplines in the university generally. In fact, research in education has in many instances become indistinguishable from social science research. The appearance and proliferation of conceptual-empiricists in the curriculum field is a specific instance of this general phenomenon. There remains, of course, the notion that research has implications for classroom practice, but it is usually claimed that many years of extensive research are necessary before significant implications can be obtained.

This development has gone so far that, examining the work done by a faculty in a typical American college of education, one has little sense of education as a field with its own identity. One discovers researchers whose primary identity is with the cognate field. Such individuals view themselves as primarily psychologists, philosophers, or sociologists with "research interests" in schools and education-related matters. By 1978 it is accurate to note that the education field has lost whatever (and it was never complete, of course) intellectual autonomy it possessed in earlier years and now is nearly tantamount to a colony of superior, imperialistic powers.

The view that education is not a discipline in itself but an area to be studied by the disciplines is evident in the work of those curricularists I have called conceptual-empiricists. The work of this group can be so characterized, employing the terms *conceptual* and *empirical* in the sense social scientists typically employ them. This work is concerned with developing hypotheses to be tested and testing them in methodological ways characteristic of mainstream social science. This work is reported, ordinarily, at meetings of the American Educational Research Association. Just as the Association for Supervision and Curriculum Development is the traditionalists' organization, AERA tends to be the organization of the conceptual-empiricists. (In relatively small numbers, traditionalists and reconceptualists also read papers at AERA annual meetings.)

An illustrative piece of conceptual work from this second group of curricularists was published in the AERA-sponsored *Review of Educational Research*. It is George Posner's (with Kenneth Strike) "A Categorization Scheme for Principles of Sequencing Content." A prefatory paragraph indicates that his view is a social scientist's one, reliant upon hypothesis making, data collection, and interpretation.

We have very little information, based on hard data, regarding the consequences of alternative content sequences and will need a good deal more research effort before we are able to satisfactorily suggest how content *should* be sequenced. Our intention here is to consider the question, What are the alternatives?[7]

The article is a conceptual one, concerned with what the authors view as logically defensible content-sequencing alternatives, and it is empirical in its allegiance to the view of empirical research, one yielding "hard data," typical of social science at the present time.

In a recently published essay, Decker F. Walker, another visible conceptual-empiricist, moves somewhat away from strict social science as exemplified in Posner's work.[8] His essay, or case study as he terms it, is more anthropological in its methodological form, demonstrating a type of curriculum research that Walker's coeditor, Reid, endorses.[9] Anthropology, it should be noted, while regarded as not as "pure" a social science as political science or psychology, is nonetheless generally categorized as a social science.

Taking his cue from Schwab, Walker argues that prescriptive curriculum theories (partly because they do not reflect the actual process of curriculum change) are not useful. Rather than focus on why curriculum developers did not follow the Tyler rationale, Walker concentrates on how, in fact, the developers did proceed. In his study he finds little use for terms like *objectives* and important use for terms such as *platform* and *deliberation.* He concludes that curricularists probably ought to abandon the attempt to make actual curriculum development mirror prescriptive theories, accept "deliberation" as a core aspect of the development process, and apply the intellectual resources of the field toward improving the quality of deliberation and employing it more effectively.

I find this work significant to the field in two ways. First it deals another hard blow to the Tyler rationale and its influence. Second, Walker is moving away from social science. His work remains social science, but it is closer to the work of some reconceptualists than it is to that of Posner and other mainstream conceptual-empiricists. Walker retains the traditional focus upon the practical concerns of schoolpeople and school curriculum, and no doubt he has and will spend a portion of his professional time on actual curriculum projects. Further, his methods seem more nearly those of the ethnomethodologist whose approaches do not easily fit the picture of conventional theories of the middle range as projected by individuals such as the sociologist Robert Merton, who has influenced so many conceptual-empirical studies in the field of sociology. Walker appears to be moving outside mainstream conceptual-empiricism.

Also in the Reid and Walker book is work by another visible conceptual-empiricist, Ian Westbury. With his coauthor Lynn McKinney, Westbury studies the Gary, Indiana, school system during the period 1940–1970.[10] Like Walker's study of the art project, McKinney's and Westbury's study would seem to be outside mainstream conceptual-empiricism, even close to work characteristic of the humanities. The structure of the study, however, indicates its allegiance to social science, thus warranting its categorization as conceptual-empirical. The work is a historical study done in the service of generalization, work that has interest in the particular (the Gary district) as it contributes to understanding of the general. The "general" in this instance is the phenomenon of stability and change, which the authors "now believe are the two primary functions of the administrative structure which surround the schools."[11] Finally what the study demonstrates is "that a concern for goals without a concomitant concern for organizational matters addresses only a small part of the problem of conceiving new designs for schools."[12] This use of the specific to illustrate a general, ahistorical "law" is, of course, a fundamental procedure of mainstream social science.

Reconceptualists

This concern for generalization is not abandoned in the work of the third group of curricularists, the reconceptualists. For example, at the fourth conference at the University of Wisconsin-Milwaukee, Professor Apple reported the results of a study he and a colleague conducted in a kindergarten, substantiating claims he has made before regarding the sociopolitical functions of classroom behavior.[13] His case study is distinguishable from the work of a typical conceptual-empiricist in two significant respects: his acknowledged "value-laden" perspective and a perspective with a politically emancipatory intent. That is, in contrast to the canon of traditional social science, which prescribes data collection, hypothesis substantiation or disconfirmation in the disinterested service of building a body of knowledge, a reconceptualist tends to see research as an inescapably political as well as intellectual act. As such, it works to suppress or to liberate not only those who conduct the research and those upon whom it is conducted but as well those outside the academic subculture. Mainstream social science research, while on the surface seemingly apolitical in nature and consequence, if examined more carefully can be seen as contributing to the maintenance of the contemporary social-political order or contributing to its dissolution. Apple and Marxists and neo-Marxists go further and accept a teleological view of historical movement, allying themselves with the lower classes, whose final emergence from oppression is seen to be inevitable. A number of reconceptualists, while not Marxists, nonetheless accept some variation of this teleological historical view. And many of these, at least from a distance, would seem to be "leftists" of some sort. Nearly all accept that a political dimension is inherent in any intellectual activity.

This political emphasis distinguishes the work of Apple, Burton, Mann, Molnar, and some of the work of Huebner and Macdonald from the work of traditionalists and conceptual-empiricists.¹⁴ It is true that Reid and Walker in their *Case Studies in Curriculum Change* acknowledge that curriculum development is political, but the point is never developed and never connected with a view of history and the contemporary social order. The focus of Walker's case study and of other case studies in the book is limited to literal curriculum change, without historicizing this change, indicating its relationship to contemporary historical movement generally. In the 1975 ASCD yearbook, on the other hand, which is edited by Macdonald and Zaret with essays by Apple, Burton, Huebner, and Mann, this siting of curriculum issues in the broad intellectual-historical currents of twentieth-century life is constant.¹⁵ Macdonald speaks, for instance, of technological rationality, an intellectual mode comparable in its pervasiveness and taken-for-grantedness to the ascendency of technology in human culture at large.¹⁶ Such individuals would argue that comprehension of curriculum issues is possible only when they are situated historically.

The 1975 ASCD yearbook speaks to schoolpeople. It is not that reconceptualists do not speak to this constituency of the curriculum field. But there is a conscious abandonment of the technician's mentality. There are no prescriptions or traditional rationales. What this yearbook offers, instead, is heightened awareness of the complexity and historical significance of curriculum issues. Because the difficulties these reconceptualists identify are related to difficulties in the culture at large, they are not "problems" that can be "solved." That concept, created by technological rationality, is itself problematic. Thus, what is necessary in part is fundamental structural change in the culture. Such an aspiration cannot be realized by "plugging into" the extant order. That is why an elective or two on Marx in high school social studies classes or the teaching of autobiographical reflection in English classes bring indifference and often alarm to most reconceptualists. That "plugging into," "co-opting" it was termed in the 1960s during the student protests, accepts the social order as it is. What is necessary is a fundamental reconceptualization of what curriculum is, how it functions, and how it might function in emancipatory ways. It is this commitment to a comprehensive critique and theory development that distinguishes the reconceptualist phenomenon.

To understand more fully the efforts of the individuals involved in inquiry of this kind requires some understanding of metatheory and philosophy of science. Without such grounding, it is difficult—if not impossible—for curricularists to see clearly their work in the context of the growth of knowledge in general. Max van Manen's paper at the 1976 Wisconsin conference was a significant effort to analyze various structures of theoretic knowledge as they related to dominant modes of inquiry in the field of curriculum.¹⁷ His work builds on basic analyses undertaken by philosophers of science such as Radnitzky and Feyerabend.¹⁸ More work needs to be done along this line.

The reconceptualization, it must be noted, is fundamentally an intellectual phenomenon, not an interpersonal-affiliative one. Reconceptualists have no organized group, such as ASCD or AERA. Individuals at work, while sharing certain themes and motives, do not tend to share any common interpersonal affiliation. (In this one respect their work parallels that of the so-called romantic critics of the 1960s. But here any such comparison stops.) Conferences have been held yearly; the most recent on the campus of Rochester Institute of Technology, Rochester, New York. A journal and a press emphasizing this work are scheduled to appear by 1979.

Conclusion

As an interpreter of metatheories, Richard Bernstein recently analyzed, in detail, individuals at work in four areas—empirical research, philosophical analysis, phenomenology, and critical theory of society.[19] (The first category corresponds to conceptual-empirical, the third and fourth to reconceptualist work.) He ends his study with this conviction:

In the final analysis we are not confronted with exclusive choices: either empirical or interpretative theory or critical theory. Rather there is an internal dialectic in the restructuring of social political theory: when we work through any one of these movements, we discover the others are implicated.[20]

This is so in the field of curriculum studies also. We are not faced with an exclusive choice: either the traditional wisdom of the field or conceptual-empiricism or the reconceptualization. Each is reliant upon the other. For the field to become vital and significant to American education, it must nurture each "moment," its "internal dialectic." And it must strive for synthesis, for a series of perspectives on curriculum that are at once empirical, interpretative, critical, emancipatory.

But such nurturance and synthesis do not characterize, on the whole, the field today. Some of the issues raised by the British sociologist David Silverman are germane here.[21] As a prologue to more adequate social science theorizing, Silverman proposes that we learn how to read Castaneda's account of his apprenticeship to Don Juan in order that we may come to know the kinds of questions that need to be asked. He is convinced that mainstream conceptual-empiricists, regardless of field, do not now know what questions to ask and are indeed intolerant of reconceptualizations that differ from their own. This intolerance is discernible in the American curriculum field. To some extent it can be found in each group of curricularists.

I am convinced that this intolerance among curricularists for work differing from one's own must be suspended to some extent if significant intellectual movement in the field is to occur. Becoming open to another genre of work does not mean loss of one's capacity for critical reflection. Nor does it mean, necessarily, loss of intellectual identity. One may remain a traditionalist while sympathetically studying the work of a reconceptualist. One's own point of view may well be enriched. Further, an intellectual climate may become established in which syntheses of current perspectives could develop, regenerating the field and making it more likely that its contribution to American education be an important one.

Notes

1. Conferences have been held at the University of Rochester (1973), Xavier University of Cincinnati (1974), the University of Virginia (1975), the University of Wisconsin at Milwaukee (1976), Kent State University (1977), and the Rochester Institute of Technology (1978). Books include: W. Pinar, ed., *Heightened Consciousness, Cultural Revolution, and Curriculum Theory* (Berkeley: McCutchan, 1974); W. Pinar, ed., *Curriculum Theorizing: The Reconceptualists* (Berkeley: McCutchan, 1975); W. Pinar and M. R. Grumet, *Toward a Poor Curriculum* (Dubuque, Iowa: Kendall/Hunt, 1976).

At a 1976 conference held at the State University of New York at Geneseo, Professors Apple, Greene, Kliebard, and Huebner read papers. Each of these persons has been associated with the reconceptualists, although the chairmen of this meeting, Professors DeMarte and Rosarie, did not see this seminar as being in the tradition of the others. The papers from this seminar were published in *Curriculum Inquiry* 6:4 (1977).

2. L. Cremin, "Curriculum-making in the United States," in *Curriculum Theorizing*, ed. W. Pinar, pp. 19–35.

3. H. M. Kliebard, "Persistent Curriculum Issues in Historical Perspective" and "Bureaucracy and Curriculum Theory," in *Curriculum Theorizing*, ed. W. Pinar, pp. 39–69.

4. R. W. Tyler, *Basic Principles of Curriculum and Instruction* (Chicago: University of Chicago Press, 1950).

5. H. Taba, *Curriculum Development: Theory and Practice* (New York: Harcourt, Brace and World, 1962); G. Saylor and W. Alexander, *Curriculum Planning for Modern Schools* (New York: Holt, Rinehart and Winston, 1966); D. Tanner and L. N. Tanner, *Curriculum Development: Theory into Practice* (New York: Macmillan, 1975); J. D. Neil, *Curriculum: A Comprehensive Introduction* (Boston: Little, Brown and Co., 1977); R. S. Zais, *Curriculum: Principles and Foundations* (New York: Thomas Y. Crowell, 1976); G. Weinstein and M. D. Fantini, *Toward Humanistic Education: A Curriculum of Affect* (New York: Praeger Publishers, 1971); S. Simons et al., *Values Clarification* (New York: Hart, 1972); D. Jordan, "The ANISA Model" (Paper presented to conference on curriculum at the University of Virginia, 1975, available from Charles W. Beegle, Curry Memorial School of Education, University of Virginia, Charlottesville, VA 22903, USA).

6. J. J. Schwab, *The Practical: A Language for Curriculum* (Washington, D.C.: National Education Association, 1970); D. Huebner, "The Moribund Curriculum Field: Its Wake and Our Work," *Curriculum Inquiry* 6:2 (1976).

7. G. J. Posner and K. A. Strike, "A Categorization Scheme for Principles of Sequencing Content," *Review of Educational Research* 46:4 (1976).

8. D. F. Walker, "Curriculum Development in an Art Project," in *Case Studies in Curriculum Change*, eds. W. A. Reid and D. F. Walker (London: Routledge & Kegan Paul, 1975).

9. W. A. Reid, "The Changing Curriculum: Theory and Practice," in Reid and Walker, *Case Studies in Curriculum Change*.
10. W. L. McKinney and I. Westbury, "Stability and Change: The Public Schools of Gary, Indiana, 1940–70," in Reid and Walker, *Case Studies in Curriculum Change*.
11. Ibid., p. 44.
12. Ibid., p. 50.
13. M. W. Apple and N. King, "What Do Schools Teach?" (Paper presented at the University of Wisconsin and Milwaukee Conference).
14. For discussion of this point see my prefatory remarks in *Curriculum Theorizing* (note 1). See also: P. R. Klohr, "The State of the Field" (Paper presented at the Xavier University Conference on Curriculum); J. L. Miller, "Duality: Perspectives on the Reconceptualization" (Paper presented to University of Virginia Conference); J. B. Macdonald, "Curriculum Theory as Intentional Activity" (Paper presented to University of Virginia Conference (see note 5); J. B. Macdonald, "Curriculum Theory and Human Interests," in Pinar, *Curriculum Theorizing*; B. J. Benham, "Curriculum Theory in the 1970s: The Reconceptualist Movement," (unpublished paper, Texas Technical University, 1976).
15. E. Zaret and J. B. Macdonald, *Schools in Search of Meaning* (Washington, D.C.: Association for Supervison and Curriculum Development, 1975).
16. J. B. Macdonald, "The Quality of Everyday Life in Schools," in Zaret and Macdonald, *Schools in Search of Meaning*.
17. M. Van Manen, "Linking Ways of Knowing with Ways of Being Practical," *Curriculum Inquiry* 6:3 (1977).
18. G. Radnitzky, *Contemporary Schools of Metascience* (Chicago: Henry Regnery Co., 1973); P. K. Feyerabend, "Against Method: Outline of an Anarchist Theory of Knowledge," in *Minnesota Studies in the Philosophy of Science* 4 (Minneapolis: University of Minnesota Press, 1976).
19. R. J. Bernstein, *The Restructuring of Social and Political Theory* (New York: Harcourt Brace Jovanovich, 1976).
20. Ibid., p. 235.
21. D. Silverman, *Reading Castaneda: A Prologue to the Social Sciences* (London: Routledge & Kegan Paul, 1975).

7 Toward a New Sociology of Curriculum

Henry A. Giroux

Introduction

In this article Henry Giroux argues that the curriculum field has been dominated by a mode of reasoning that contains a number of flawed assumptions about the nature of theory, knowledge, and science. As a result, the "traditional" model of curriculum has failed to acknowledge or to raise a number of fundamental questions concerning the ideological underpinnings of curriculum design and evaluation as well as the relationship between schools and the larger social order.

In response to the failure of the traditional approach to curriculum theorizing and practice, a number of educational theorists have emerged to challenge some of the most basic assumptions associated with the dominant approach to the curriculum field. Giroux has loosely grouped these critics under the category of the "new sociology of curriculum" and argues that the new sociology of curriculum movement provides educators with a number of possibilities for developing more flexible and humanizing forms of pedagogy.

As you read this article, consider the following questions:

- What basic assumptions characterize both the traditional as well as the new sociology of curriculum approach to curriculum theorizing?
- Can these two positions be integrated? If so, how?
- Are they mutually exclusive?
- Finally, how might the questions raised by the new sociology of curriculum position be used as a guide to classroom practice?

New Sociology of Curriculum

Anthony Giddens, the English sociologist, once remarked that those who are waiting for a Newton of the social sciences "are not only waiting for a train that won't arrive, they're in the wrong station altogether."[1] Giddens's remark could very well have set the stage for one of the most interesting and urgent debates now taking place in the curriculum field in the United States.

At the heart of this debate is the question of whether the curriculum field can continue to pattern itself after the model of the natural sciences. It is not simply that the curriculum field suffers from serious misconceptions regarding its mode of reasoning and methodology. What is at stake is more than a conceptual problem. The real issue centers on whether the field is moribund, both politically and ethically. Put another way, is the curriculum field in a state of arrest, incapable of developing either emancipatory intentions or new curricular possibilities?[2]

Debate of this sort is not new to the curriculum field. Questions concerning the role that schools and curriculum play in reproducing the values and attitudes necessary for the maintenance of the dominant society have been raised by educators since the turn of the century. What is new is the scope as well as the nature of some of the questions being raised. This should not suggest that a new school or paradigm has appeared in the field. Such an assumption would be both misleading and inaccurate. It would be misleading because those who make up what I will label as the new sociology of curriculum movement represent many critical strands and traditions. It would be inaccurate to call such a movement a paradigm because it would oversimplify its varied members' relatedness and depth of commitment to a new world view, one that speaks to a unifying set of assumptions and guidelines for the development of curriculum theory and practice. Though such a paradigm doesn't exist at the present time, the foundations for such a paradigm can be recognized in some of the broad concerns and related questions voiced by a number of emerging disparate critical traditions.[3]

The singular theme that unites all of these critical traditions is their opposition to what might be called the technocratic rationality that guides traditional curriculum theory and design. This form of rationality has dominated the curriculum field since its inception and can be found in varied forms in the work of Tyler, Taba, Saylor and Alexander, Beauchamp, and others. William F. Pinar claims that between 85 and 95 percent of those who work in the curriculum field share a perspective that is either tied or closely related to the dominant technocratic rationality.[4] Herbert Kliebard has further argued that this form of rationality has evolved in a manner parallel to the

---

Reprinted from *Educational Leadership* 37 (December 1979), pp. 248–253. Reprinted with permission of the Association for Supervision and Curriculum Development. Copyright ©1971 by the Association for Supervision and Curriculum Development. All rights reserved.

scientific management movement of the 1920s and that early founders of the curriculum movement such as Bobbitt and Charters warmly embraced the principles of scientific management.[5] The school-as-factory metaphor has a long and extensive history in the curriculum field. Consequently, modes of reasoning, inquiry, and research characteristic of the field have been modeled on assumptions drawn from a model of science and social relations closely tied to the principles of prediction and control.

The new sociology of curriculum critics see their tasks as more than an attempt to clear up what might be called a conceptual muddle. In the first place, the concepts that underlie the traditional curriculum paradigm serve as guides to action. Secondly, these concepts are inextricably linked to value judgments about standards of morality and questions concerning the nature of freedom and control. More specifically, these assumptions not only represent a set of ideas that educators use to structure their view of curriculum, they also represent a set of material practices embedded in rituals and routines thought of as necessary and natural facts. Thus, they have become forms of sedimented history, commonsense assumptions that have been severed from the historical context from which they developed.[6]

The new sociology of curriculum views the basic assumptions embedded in the traditional curriculum paradigm as the basis for both a critique and a limited situation to be overcome in developing new orientations and ways of talking about curriculum. Hence, it is important that we specify what these assumptions are: (a) theory in the curriculum field should operate in the interest of law-like propositions that are empirically testable; (b) the natural sciences provide the "proper" model of explanation for the concepts and techniques of curriculum theory, design, and evaluation; (c) knowledge should be objective and capable of being investigated and described in a neutral fashion; and (d) statements of value are to be separated from "facts" and "modes of inquiry" that can and ought to be objective.

In the most general sense, the technocratic model of curriculum has been criticized both for its stated claims to the truth and the assumptions implicit in the *kinds* of questions it ignores. Regarding its stated truth claims, critics argue that the traditional model rests on a number of flawed assumptions about the nature and role of theory, knowledge, and science. Moreover, these assumptions have resulted in truncated forms of inquiry that ignore fundamental questions concerning the larger relationship between ideology and school knowledge as well as meaning and social control.[7]

Shortcomings of the Dominant Model

The "new" critics claim that theory in the dominant curriculum model is either ignored altogether or is badly instrumentalized. In other words, theory is important to the degree that it can be rigorously formulated and empirically tested. Its ultimate purpose here is a technocratic one: to reveal lawlike propositions about curriculum design, implementation, and evaluation that can be either factually proven or disproven. Theory is thus reduced to an empirical explanatory framework for social engineering. From this critical perspective, theory appears incapable of stepping outside of its empirical straitjacket in order to raise questions about the nature of truth, the difference between appearance and reality, or the distinction between knowledge and mere opinion. Most importantly, theory in the dominant curriculum paradigm appears unable to provide a rational basis for criticizing the "facts" of the given society. Theory in this case not only ignores its ethical function, it is also stripped of its political function.[8]

Knowledge in the dominant curriculum model is treated primarily as a realm of objective "facts." That is, knowledge appears "objective" in that it is external to the individual and is "imposed" on him or her. As something external, knowledge is divorced from human meaning and intersubjective exchange. It no longer is seen as something to be questioned, analyzed, and negotiated. Instead, it becomes something to be managed and mastered. In this case, knowledge is removed from the self-formative process of generating one's own set of meanings, a process that involves an interpretive relationship between knower and known. Once the subjective dimension of knowing is lost, the purpose of knowledge becomes one of accumulation and categorization. Questions such as "Why this knowledge?" are superseded by technical questions such as "What is the best way to learn this given body of knowledge?" Within the context of this definition of knowledge, curriculum models are developed that stress "mission specificity," "time on task variables," and "feedback obtained to make adjustments."[9] This view of knowledge is usually accompanied by top-to-bottom classroom social relationships conducive to communiques, not communication.[10] Control, not learning, appears to have a high priority in the traditional curriculum model. What is lost here is the notion that knowledge is not simply "about" an external reality, it is more importantly self-knowledge oriented toward critical understanding and emancipation.

A pivotal force in the traditional curriculum model is the claim to objectivity. Objectivity in this case refers to forms of knowledge and methodological inquiry that are untouched by the "untidy" world of beliefs and values. While the severance of knowledge and research from value claims may appear to be admirable to some, it hides more than it uncovers. Of course, this is not meant to suggest that challenging the value-neutrality claims of mainstream curriculum theorists is tantamount to supporting the use of bias, prejudice, and superstition in pedagogical inquiry.

Instead, the notion that objectivity is based on the use of normative criteria established by communities of scholars and intellectual workers in any given field is espoused. Intellectual inquiry and research free from values and norms are impossible to achieve. To separate values from "facts" or social inquiry from ethical considerations is pointless. As Howard Zinn points out, it is like trying to draw a map that illustrates every detail on a chosen piece of terrain.[11] But this is not just a simple matter of intellectual error; it is an ethical failing as well.

The notion that theory, facts, and inquiry can be objectively determined and used falls prey to a set of values that are both conservative and mystifying in their political orientation. As critics such as Paulo Freire have pointed out, schools do not exist in precious isolation from the rest of society. Schools embody collective attitudes that permeate every aspect of their organization.[12] In essence, they are not things but concrete manifestations of specific rules and social relationships. The nature of their organization is value-based. Similarly, curriculum design, implementation, and evaluation always represent patterns of judgments about the nature of knowledge, classroom social relationships, and the distribution of power. To ignore this is to lose sight of the origins and consequences of the belief system that guides one's behavior in the school setting.

Traditional curriculum represents a firm commitment to a view of rationality that is ahistorical, consensus oriented, and politically conservative. It supports a passive view of students and appears incapable of examining the ideological presuppositions that tie it to a narrow operational mode of reasoning. Its view of science ignores the competing elements and frames of reference within the scientific community itself.[13] Moreover, it ends up substituting a limited form of scientific methodology based on prediction and control for critical scientific inquiry.

Instead of promoting critical reflection and human understanding, the dominant curriculum model emphasizes the logic of probability as the ultimate definition of truth and meaning. Not only do the concepts that characterize this model appear less than critical, they appear as blank checks that support the status quo. One example of this can be found in the powerful influence of learning psychologists in the field of education with their endless studies on "performance and the interchange between students and teachers."[14] Some critics view this as a strong measure of the political conservatism that dominates the curriculum field. The learning-psychology perspective fails to examine the way schools legitimize certain forms of knowledge and cultural interests.[15]

The Challenge

The new sociology of curriculum has mounted a serious challenge against many of the deeply held beliefs and assumptions that characterize traditional curriculum. This challenge is far from uniform and has its roots in continental philosophies as diverse as existentialism, psychoanalysis, Marxism, and phenomenology. The new sociology of curriculum speaks a language that might seem strange when compared to the input-output language of the traditional curriculum model. The new language may be difficult, but it is necessary because it enables its users to develop new kinds of relationships in the curriculum field and to raise different kinds of questions. This is not a moot point. It would be spurious indeed to dismiss these critics for drawing upon what might appear to be alien forms of language and thought, and some of their detractors have done just that. However, the real point of concern should be whether the language and concepts used are raising profoundly important questions and issues about the curriculum field itself. While it is not possible to present the various factions and issues that make up the new sociology of curriculum movement, the nucleus of some of the more general ideas that run through this perspective can be analyzed briefly.

The new sociology of curriculum group strongly argues that schools are part of a wider societal process and that they must be judged within a specific socioeconomic framework. In addition, the curriculum itself is viewed as a selection from the larger culture. From this perspective, the new critics argue for a thorough reexamination of the relationship between curriculum, schools, and society. This reexamination focuses on two broad interrelationships. On the one hand, the focus is on the relationship between schools and the dominant society. The focus here is primarily political and ideological; its emphasis is on highlighting how schools function to reproduce, in both the hidden and formal curricula, the cultural beliefs and economic relationships that support the larger social order. On the other hand, the focus is on how the very texture of day-to-day classroom relationships generates different meanings, restraints, cultural values, and social relationships. Underlying both of these concerns is a deep-seated interest in the relationship between meaning and social control.

A number of these critics have been particularly concerned about how meaning is constructed and acted upon in schools. They support the view that the social construction of the principles that govern the operation of curriculum design, research, and evaluation are often ignored by curriculum specialists and classroom teachers. One consequence has been that many educators often operate out of commonsense assumptions that fail to raise fundamental questions about how teachers perceive their classroom experiences and students. Also ignored are questions about how students perceive and generate meaning in the classroom; similarly, questions concerning how particular classroom materials mediate meanings between teachers and students, schools and the larger society, also go unquestioned. Within this limited view of meaning, prejudices and social myths are relegated to the realm of unquestioned habits of mind and experience.

Given this mode of behavior, there is little room for students to generate their own meanings, to act on their own lived histories, or to develop an attentiveness to critical thought. Learning under such circumstances, it is argued, degenerates into a euphemism for a mode of control that imposes rather than cultivates meaning. This is a crucial point. If teachers do not bracket their own basic assumptions about curriculum and pedagogy, they do more than transmit unquestioned attitudes, norms, and beliefs. They unknowingly may end up endorsing forms of cognitive and dispositional development that strengthen rather than challenge existing forms of institutional oppression. Commonly accepted definitions about work, play, achievement, intelligence, mastery, failure, and learning are socially constructed categories that carry with them the weight of specific interests and norms. To ignore this important notion is to relinquish the possibility for students and teachers alike to shape reality in an image other than the one that is socially prescribed and institutionally legitimated. The failure of curriculum workers to appreciate that there are fundamental interests of knowledge other than prediction, control, and efficiency is not just a matter of misunderstanding, it is a serious ethical and political failing.

Critics such as Michael Apple have gone far beyond stressing the need for a model of curriculum that generates interpretive understanding and purposive learning. These critics have raised the debate over curriculum to a new level of criticism by calling for a view of curriculum that defines it as a study in ideology.[16] In this view, questions concerning the production, distribution, and evaluation of knowledge are directly linked to questions of control and domination in the larger society. This can be more fully understood by examining some of the types of questions that would provide the basis for viewing curriculum from this perspective. These questions would include:

1. What counts as curriculum knowledge?
2. How is such knowledge produced?
3. How is such knowledge transmitted in the classroom?
4. What kinds of classroom social relationships serve to parallel and reproduce the values and norms embodied in the "accepted" social relations of the work place?
5. Who has access to "legitimate" forms of knowledge?
6. Whose interests does this knowledge serve?
7. How are social and political contradictions and tensions mediated through acceptable forms of classroom knowledge and social relationships?
8. How do prevailing methods of evaluation serve to legitimize existing forms of knowledge?

At the core of these questions is the recognition that power, knowledge, ideology, and schooling are linked in ever-changing patterns of complexity. The nexus that gives form to these interrelationships is social and political in nature, and it is both a product and process of history. In more concrete terms, curriculum theorists, teachers, and students alike embody certain beliefs and practices, concepts and norms that strongly influence how they perceive and structure their educational experiences. These beliefs and routines are historical and social in nature; moreover, they may be the object of self-reflection, or they may exist unnoticed by the individual they influence. In the latter case, they serve to dominate rather than serve the individual in question.

This approach calls for forms of curriculum that push beyond appreciating that knowledge is a social construction. Also, it stresses the need for examining the constellation of economic, political, and social interests that different forms of knowledge may reflect. To put it another way, curriculum models must develop forms of understanding that relate explanations of social meanings to wider societal parameters in order to be able to judge their claims to the truth.[17]

Significance for the Future

If one purpose of curriculum is to generate possibilities for individual and social emancipation, we will have to develop a new language and new forms of rationality to accomplish such a task. The predicament of the age is no different from the predicament the curriculum field presently faces. And this predicament is as engaging as it is radical: to build the conditions that allow humanity to search for its self-understanding and meaning. The new sociology of curriculum movement provides us with a number of possibilities for developing more flexible and humanizing forms of curriculum.

We must develop a mode of curriculum that cultivates critical theoretical discourse about the quality and purpose of schooling and human life. We need to develop broader perspectives that enrich rather than dominate the field. Critical curriculum theory must be situational. It must analyze the various dimensions of pedagogy as part of the historical and cultural conjunctures in which they occur. And it must do this with the tools that are fashioned from a variety of disciplines. This does not mean that we have to become political scientists or sociologists in order to study curriculum. That is not the case, and it would be inappropriate to do so. Our center of gravity is curriculum, but we need to enrich our focus by drawing upon the concepts and tools that other disciplines offer us.

The foundation for a new mode of curriculum must be as deeply historical as it is critical. In fact, the critical sensibility must be seen as an extension of historical consciousness. The genesis, development, and unfolding of ideas, social relationships, and modes of inquiry and evaluation must be viewed as part of an ongoing development of complex, historically bound social conditions and formations.

The new mode of curriculum must be deeply personal, but only in the sense that it recognizes individual uniqueness and needs as part of a specific social reality. We must not confuse self-indulgence with critical pedagogy. Individual and social needs have to be linked and mediated through a critical perspective tied to notions of emancipation. Curriculum models must address themselves to the concrete personal experiences of specific cultural groups and populations. Curriculum educators must be able to recognize the relevance and importance of accepting and using multiple languages and forms of cultural capital (systems of meaning, tastes, ways of viewing the world, style, and so on). At the same time, educators must acknowledge that the call for cultural pluralism is empty unless it is recognized that the relationship between different cultural groups is mediated through the dominant cultural system. Thus, our task is to unravel these relationships for different cultural groups so as to emancipate them from the imposed kinds of definitions and emotional pain that minorities of class and color have a history of in this country.

A new mode of curriculum must abandon the ideological pretense of being value-free. To acknowledge that the choices we make concerning all facets of curriculum and pedagogy are value-laden is to liberate ourselves from imposing our own values on others. To admit as such means that we can begin with the notion that reality should never be taken as a given but, instead, has to be questioned and analyzed. In other words, knowledge has to be made problematic and has to be situated in classroom social relationships that allow for debate and communication.

Finally, a new mode of curriculum rationality will have to subordinate technical interests to ethical considerations. The question of means must be subordinated to questions that speak to the ethical consequences of our pursuits. Although these suggestions represent a broad theoretical sweep, they do provide a starting point for developing new modes of curriculum inquiry. Also, the somewhat disparate traditions of the new sociology of curriculum have helped to translate some of the larger abstract issues surrounding the purpose and meaning of schooling into concrete curriculum problems and avenues for further study and research.

I began this essay by pointing out that the traditional model of curriculum was moribund, both politically and ethically. I want to go back to that statement and clarify it, lest it be confused with a form of unwarranted optimism. The dominant technocratic curriculum paradigm may be aging, but it is far from a historical relic. The struggle to replace it with principles and assumptions consistent with the vision of the new sociology of curriculum movement will be difficult indeed. But one thing is certain. The struggle for a new mode of curriculum rationality cannot be approached as a technical task only. It must be seen as a social struggle deeply committed to what Herbert Marcuse has aptly termed ". . . the emancipation of sensibility, reason, and imagination in all spheres of subjectivity and objectivity."[18] The new sociology of curriculum has helped to make this struggle just a bit easier. The rest is up to us.

Notes

1. Q. Skinner, "The Flight From Positivism," *New York Review of Books* 25(10):26 (June 15, 1976).

2. Emancipatory intentions in this case can be generally construed as a paradigm that combines theory and practice in the interest of freeing individuals and social groups from the subjective and objective conditions that bind them to the forces of exploitation and oppression. This suggests a critical theory that promotes self-reflection aimed at dismantling forms of false consciousness and ideologically frozen social relations, most of which usually parade under the guise of universalistic laws. Thus, emancipation would render critical thinking and political action complementary. This suggests a learning process in which thought and action would be mediated by specific cognitive, affective, and moral dimensions.

3. Decent collections of writings on the movement can be found in: W. F. Pinar, ed., *Curriculum Theorizing: The Reconceptualists* (Berkeley: McCutchan, 1975); J. Macdonald and E. Zaret, eds., *Schools in Search of Meaning* (Washington, D.C.: ASCD, 1975). One of the better books on the subject published in this country is: M. W. Apple, *Ideology and Curriculum* (Boston and London: Routledge & Kegan Paul, 1979). The continental influence can be found in: J. Karable and A. H. Halsey, eds., *Power and Ideology in Education* (New York: Oxford University Press, 1977). I also deal with this subject in my book, *Ideology, Culture, and the Process of Schooling* (Philadelphia: Temple University Press, 1981).

4. W. F. Pinar, "Notes on the Curriculum Field 1978," *Educational Researcher* 7:8 (September 1978):5–11.

5. H. M. Kliebard, "Bureaucracy and Curriculum Theory," in Pinar, *Curriculum Theorizing*, pp. 51–69.

6. M. F. D. Young, ed., *Knowledge and Control* (London: Collier-Macmillan, 1971).

7. M. W. Apple and N. King, "What Do Schools Teach?" in *Humanistic Education*, ed. R. Weller (Berkeley: McCutchan, 1977), p. 36. See also: H. A. Giroux and A. N. Penna, "Social Education in the Classroom: The Dynamics of the Hidden Curriculum," *Theory and Research in Education* 7:1, (Spring 1979).

8. This should not suggest that the new sociology of curriculum supports the separation of theory from empirical work or rejects empirical investigations altogether. Theory as it is being described in this essay has its center of gravity in its social potential for insight into the nature of truth and the meaning of life. It is linked to specific interests and situates its assumptions and modes of inquiry in *both* understanding and determining ends. What the new sociology of curriculum rejects is empiricism, that is, the use of theory to boost scientific methodology as the ultimate definition of meaning and truth. Empiricism is theory reduced to the instrumentality of finding means for ends that go unquestioned. It stands convicted of ideology in that it is incapable of identifying its own normative foundation or the interests that it serves. See J. Habermas, *Toward a Rational Society* (Boston: Beacon Press, 1970).

9. F. W. English, "Management Practice as a Key to Curriculum Leadership," *Educational Leadership* 36:6 (March 1979): 408–13. An in-depth response to the positivist ideology inherent in English's model can be found in: H. A. Giroux, "Schooling and the Culture of Positivism," *Educational Theory* 29:4 (Fall 1979): 263–84.

10. P. Freire, *Pedagogy of the Oppressed* (New York: Seabury Press, 1973).
11. H. Zinn, *The Politics of History* (Boston: Beacon Press, 1970), pp. 10–11.
12. Freire, *Pedagogy of the Oppressed*.
13. T. Kuhn, *The Structure of Scientific Revolutions,* 2d ed. (Chicago: University of Chicago Press, 1970).
14. T. Popkewitz, "Educational Research: Values and Visions of Social Order," *Theory and Research in Social Education* 6:4 (December 1978): 19–39.
15. Karabel and Halsey, *Power and Ideology in Education,* pp. 1–85.
16. M. W. Apple, *Ideology and Curriculum* (Boston and London: Routledge & Kegan Paul, 1979); H. A. Giroux, "Beyond the Limits of Radical Education Reform: Toward a Critical Theory of Education," *Journal of Curriculum Theorizing* 2:1 (Winter 1980): 20–46; H. A. Giroux, "Paulo Freire's Approach to Radical Education Reform," *Curriculum Inquiry* 9:3 (Fall 1979): 257–272.
17. R. Sharp and A. Green, *Education and Social Control: A Study in Progressive Primary Education* (Boston and London: Routledge & Kegan Paul, 1975).
18. H. Marcuse, *The Aesthetic Dimension* (Boston: Beacon Press, 1978), p. 99.

8 On Analyzing Hegemony

Michael W. Apple

Introduction

In this succinct article Michael Apple outlines many aspects of the theoretical program of politically and economically oriented curriculum scholarship. These include the school as institution, the knowledge forms, and the educator him- or herself. Each of these must be situated within the larger nexus of relations of which it is a constitutive part. That larger nexus is—for Apple—social, economic, and political in nature. Unlike the traditional view, Apple argues that specific curriculum work is saturated by the political and economic practices of those who perform it. One can remain silent regarding one's political views, for instance, but one cannot keep them from infiltrating one's view of course design or evaluation. A politically neutral position is impossible, and thus curricularists are well advised to explore their political views and explicitly acknowledge the influence of these views on their curriculum work.

As you read, you might pay particular attention to your emotional response to this article.
- Do you become uncomfortable? If so, why?
- How can you see the phenomenon of hegemony concretely manifested in the actions and words of your classmates and colleagues?
- How do you suppose a traditionalist would respond to politically oriented curriculum scholars and why?

Reprinted, with permission, from *The Journal of Curriculum Theorizing* 1, no. 1 (Winter 1979), pp. 10–43.

Background

Two or three years ago I was asked to write a personal statement for a volume that was reprinting a number of my papers. In that piece I tried to document the kinds of political and personal commitments that I felt provided an irreducible minimum set of tenets that guided my work as an educator.[1] In summary, I argued strongly that education was not a neutral enterprise, that by the very nature of the institution the educator was involved, whether he or she was conscious of it or not, in a political act. I maintained that in the last analysis educators could not fully separate their educational activity from the unequally responsive institutional arrangements and the forms of consciousness that dominate advanced industrial economies like our own.

Since writing that statement, the issues have become even more compelling to me. At the same time, I have hopefully made some progress in gaining a greater depth of understanding into this relationship between educational and economic structure, into the linkages between knowledge and power. In essence, the problem has become more and more a *structural* issue for me. I have increasingly sought to ground it in a set of critical questions that are generated out of a tradition of neo-Marxist argumentation, a tradition which seems to me to offer the most cogent framework for organizing one's thinking and action about education.

In broad outline, the approach I find most fruitful seeks to:

explicate the manifest and latent or coded reflections of modes of material production, ideological values, class relations, and structures of social power—racial and sexual as well as politico/economic—on the state of consciousness of people in a precise historical or socioeconomic situation.[2]

That's quite a lot for one sentence, I know. But the underlying problematic is rather complicated. It seeks to portray the concrete ways in which prevalent (and, I would add, alienating) structural arrangements—the basic ways institutions, people, and modes of production, distribution, and consumption are organized and controlled—dominate cultural life. This includes such day-to-day practices as schools and the teaching and curricula found within them.[3]

I find this of exceptional import when thinking about the relationship between the overt and covert knowledge taught in schools, the principles of selection and organization of that knowledge, and the criteria and modes of evaluation used to "measure success" in teaching. As Bernstein and Young, among others, have provocatively maintained, the structuring of knowledge and symbol in our educational institutions is intimately related to the principles of social and cultural control in society.[4] This is something on which I shall have more to say in a moment. Let me just state now that one of our basic problems as educators and as political beings, then, is to begin to grapple with ways of understanding how the kinds of cultural resources and symbols schools select and organize are dialectically related to the kinds of normative and conceptual consciousness "required" by a stratified society.

Others, especially Bowles and Gintis,[5] have focused on schools in a way that stresses the economic role of educational institutions. Mobility, selection, the reproduction of the division of labor, and other outcomes, hence, become the prime foci for their analysis. Conscious economic manipulation by those in power is often seen as a determining element. While this is certainly important, to say the least, it gives only one side of the picture. The economistic position provides a less adequate appraisal of the way these outcomes are *created* by the school. It cannot illuminate fully what the mechanisms of domination are and how they work in the day-to-day activity of school life. Furthermore, we must complement an economic analysis with an approach that leans more heavily on a cultural and ideological orientation if we are to completely understand the complex ways social, economic, and political tensions and contradictions are "mediated" in the concrete practices of educators as they go about their business in schools. The focus, then, should also be on the ideological and cultural mediations that exist between the material conditions of an unequal society and the formation of the consciousness of the individuals in that society. Thus, most of my work here and elsewhere has sought to illuminate the relationship between economic and cultural domination, at what we take as given, that seems to "naturally" produce some of the outcomes partly described by those who have focused on the political economy of education.

On Analyzing Hegemony

I think we are beginning to see more clearly a number of things that were much more cloudy before. As we learn to understand the way education acts in the economic sector of a society to reproduce important aspects of inequality,[6] so too are we learning to unpack a second major sphere in which schooling operates. For not only is there economic property, there also seems to be symbolic property—cultural capital—that schools preserve and distribute. Thus, we can now begin to get a more thorough understanding of how institutions of cultural preservation and distribution such as schools create and recreate forms of consciousness that enable social control to be maintained without the necessity of dominant groups having to resort to overt mechanisms of domination.[7]

This is not an easy issue to deal with, of course. What I shall try to do here is to portray, in rather broad strokes, the kinds of questions embodied in this approach. However, given the limited space available in a relatively brief essay, I shall enumerate what I consider to be some essential resources. These should help provide the reader with the conceptual, economic, and political tools to answer the following questions: Where do I as an educator and political actor stand? What position should I embrace? What program should guide my work? In my discussion about some of the necessary preconditions for a politically and educationally potent program of analysis, I shall often draw upon the work of the social and cultural critic Raymond Williams. While he is not too well known among educators (and this is a distinct pity), his continuing work on the relationship between the control of the form and content of culture and the growth of the economic institutions and practices that surround us all can serve as a model, both personally and conceptually, for the kind of progressive arguments and commitments this approach entails.

There are three aspects of the program that need to be articulated here: (1) the school as an institution, (2) the knowledge forms, and (3) the educator him- or herself. Each of these must be *situated* within its larger nexus of relations. The key word here, obviously, is *situated*. Like economic analysts such as Bowles and Gintis, I mean by this that, as far as is possible, we need to place the knowledge that we teach, the social relations that dominate classrooms, the school as a mechanism of cultural and economic preservation and distribution, and finally ourselves as people who work in these institutions back into the context in which they all reside. All of these things are subject to an interpretation of their respective places in a complex, stratified, and unequal society. But we must be careful of misusing this tradition of interpretation. All too often we forget the subtlety required to begin to unpack these relations. We situate the institution, the curriculum, and ourselves in an overly deterministic way. We say there is a one-to-one correspondence between economics and consciousness, economic base "automatically" determining superstructure. This is too easy to say, unfortunately, and is much too mechanistic. For it forgets that there is, in fact, a dialectical relationship between culture and economics. It also presupposes an idea of conscious manipulation of schooling by a very small number of people with power. While this was and is sometimes the case,⁹ the problem is much more complex than that. Thus, in order to go further, we must first clarify what is meant by the notion that structural relations "determine" these three aspects of schools. As I shall argue, the key to understanding this is the concept of *hegemony*.

It is important to note that there are two traditions of using concepts such as "determine." On the one hand, the notion of thought and culture being determined by social and economic structure has been used to imply what was mentioned above, a one-to-one correspondence between social consciousness and, say, mode of production. Our social concepts here are totally prefigured or predicated upon a preexisting set of economic conditions that control cultural activity, including everything in schools. On the other hand, there is a somewhat more flexible position that speaks of determination as a complex nexus of relationships which, in their final moment, are economically rooted, that exert pressures and set limits on cultural practice, including schools.¹⁰ Thus, the cultural sphere is not a "mere reflection" of economic practices.

Analyzing Hegemony

Instead, the influence, the "reflection" or determination, is highly mediated by forms of human action. It is mediated by the specific activities, contradictions, and relationships among real men and women like ourselves—as they go about their day-to-day lives in the institutions that organize their lives. The control of schools, knowledge, and everyday life can be and is more subtle for it takes in even seemingly inconsequential moments. The control is vested in the constitutive principles, codes, and commonsense practices underlying our lives, as well as by overt economic division and manipulation.

Raymond Williams's discussion of hegemony, a concept most fully developed in the work of Antonio Gramsci, provides an excellent summary of these points.

It is Gramsci's great contribution to have emphasized hegemony, and also to have understood it at a depth which is, I think, rare. For hegemony supposes the existence of something which is truly total, which is not merely secondary or superstructural, like the weak sense of ideology, but which is lived at such a depth, which saturates the society to such an extent, and which, as Gramsci put it, even constitutes the limit of common sense for most people under its sway, that it corresponds to the reality of social experience much more clearly than any notions derived from the formula of base and superstructure. For if ideology were merely some abstract imposed notion, if our social and political and cultural ideas and assumptions and habits were merely the result of specific manipulation, of a kind of overt training which might be simply ended or withdrawn, then the society would be very much easier to move and change than in practice it has been or is. This notion of hegemony as deeply saturating the consciousness of a society seems to be fundamental . . . [It] emphasizes the facts of domination.[11]

The crucial idea embedded in this passage is how hegemony acts to "saturate" our very consciousness so that the educational, economic, and social world we see and interact with, and the commonsense interpretations we put on it, becomes the world *tout court*, the only world. Hence, hegemony refers not to congeries of meanings that reside at an abstract level somewhere at the "roof of our brain." Rather, it refers to an organized assemblage of meanings and practices, the central effective and dominant system of meanings, values, and actions which are *lived*. It needs to be understood on a different level than mere opinion or manipulation. Williams makes this clear in his arguments concerning the relationship between hegemony and the control of cultural resources. At the same time, he points out how educational institutions may act in this process of saturation. I would like to quote one of his longer passages, one which I think begins to capture the complexity and one which goes beyond the idea that consciousness is only a mere reflection of economic structure wholly determined by one class consciously imposing it on another. At the same time, the passage catches the crux of how the assemblage of meanings and practices still leads to and comes from unequal economic and cultural control.

[Hegemony] is a whole body of practices and expectations; our assignments of energy, our ordinary understanding of man and his world. It is a set of meanings and values which, as they are experienced as practices, appear as reciprocally confirming. It thus constitutes a sense of reality for most people in the society, a sense of absolute because experienced [as a] reality beyond which it is very difficult for most members of a society to move in most areas of their lives. But this is not, except in the operation of a moment of abstract analysis, a static system. On the contrary, we can only understand an effective and dominant culture if we understand the real social process on which it depends: I mean the process of incorporation. The modes of incorporation are of great significance and, incidently in our kind of society, have considerable economic significance. The educational institutions are usually the main agencies of transmission of an effective dominant culture, and this is now a major economic as well as cultural activity; indeed it is both in the same moment. Moreover, at a philosophical level, at the true level of theory and at the level of the history of various practices, there is a process which I call the *selective tradition*: that which, within the terms of an effective dominant culture, is always passed off as "the tradition," the significant past. But always the selectivity is the point; the way in which from a whole possible area of past and present, certain meanings and practices are chosen for emphasis, certain other meanings and practices are neglected and excluded. Even more crucially, some of these meanings are reinterpreted, diluted, or put into forms which support or at least do not contradict other elements within the effective dominant culture.

The process of education; the processes of a much wider social training within institutions like the family; the practical definitions and organization of work; the selective tradition at an intellectual and theoretical level— all these forces are involved in a continual making and remaking of an effective dominant culture, and on them, as experienced, as built into our living, reality depends. If what we learn were merely an imposed ideology or if it were only the isolable meanings and practices of the ruling class or of a section of the ruling class which gets imposed on others, occupying merely the top of our minds, it would be—and one would be glad—a very much easier thing to overthrow.[12]

Notice what Williams is saying here about educational institutions. It is similar to the point I argued earlier about the possible relationship between the school as an institution and the recreation of inequality. Schools, in the words of the British sociologists of the curriculum, do not only "process people"; they "process knowledge" as well.[13] They act as agents of cultural hegemony, in Williams's words, as agents of selective tradition and of cultural "incorporation." But as institutions they not only are one of the main agencies of distributing an effective dominant culture; among other institutions, they help create people (with appropriate meanings and values) who see no other serious possibility to the economic and cultural assemblage now extant. I want to argue, hence, that this makes the concepts of ideology, hegemony, and selective tradition critical elements in the political and analytic underpinnings of an investigation of the relationship between curriculum and cultural and economic reproduction.

For example, as I have argued elsewhere, the issues surrounding the knowledge that is actually taught in school, surrounding what is considered to be socially *legitimate* knowledge, are of no small moment in becoming aware of the school's problematic so that their latent ideological content can be recovered. Questions such as the following need to be taken quite seriously: Whose knowledge is it? Who selected it? Why is it organized and taught in this way and to this particular group? The mere act of asking these questions is not sufficient, however. One is guided as well by attempting to link these investigations to competing conceptions of social and economic power and ideologies. In this way, one can begin to get a more concrete appraisal of the linkages between economic and political power and the knowledge *made available* (and *not* made available) to students.[14]

The movement, say, in social studies toward "process-oriented" curriculum is a case in point. We teach social inquiry as a set of skills, as a series of methods that will enable students "to learn how to inquire themselves." While this is certainly better than the more rote models of teaching that prevailed in previous decades, at the same time it can actually depoliticize the study of social life. We ask our students to see knowledge as a social construction, in the more disciplinary programs to see how sociologists, historians, anthropologists, and others construct their theories and concepts. Yet in so doing, we do not enable them to inquire as to *why* a particular form of social collectivity exists, *how* it is maintained, and *who* benefits from it. As the British sociologist of education Geoff Whitty so nicely puts it, "The overemphasis on the notion that reality is socially constructed seems to have led to the neglect of the consideration of how and why reality comes to be constructed in particular ways and how and why particular constructions of reality seem to have the power to resist subversion."[15]

There exists in curriculum development and in teaching something of a failure of nerve. We are willing to prepare students to assume only "some responsibility for their own learning." Whether these goals are ever actually reached given what Sarason has called the behavioral regularities of the institution is interesting here but not at issue. Just as important is the fact that what one is "critically reflecting" about is often vacuous, ahistorical, one-sided, and ideologically laden. As has been demonstrated in prior analyses, for instance, the constitutive framework of most school curricula centers around consensus. There are few serious attempts at dealing with conflict (class conflict, scientific conflict, or any other). Instead, one "inquires" into a consensus ideology that bears little resemblance to the complex nexus and contradictions surrounding the control and organization of social life.[16] Thus, the selective tradition dictates that we do not teach, or will selectively reinterpret (and hence will soon forget), serious woman's or labor history. Yet we do teach elite and military history. Whatever economics is taught is dominated by a perspective that grows out of the National Association of Manufacturers or its equivalent. And honest information about countries that have organized themselves about alternative social principles is hard to find. These are only a few examples, of course.

Neutrality and Justice

The very fact that we tend to reduce our understanding of the social and economic forces underlying our unequal society to a set of skills, to how to's, mirrors a much larger issue. It speaks to the technicization of life in advanced industrial economies. In Habermas's terms, purposive-rational, or instrumental, forms of reasoning and action replace symbolic action systems. Political and economic and even educational debate among real people in their day-to-day lives is replaced by considerations of efficiency, of technical skills. "Accountability" through behavioral analysis, systems management, and so on become hegemonic representations. And at the same time, considerations of the *justice* of social life are progressively depoliticized and made into supposedly neutral puzzles that can be solved by the accumulation of neutral empirical facts,[17] which when fed back into neutral institutions like schools can be guided by the neutral instrumentation of educators.

The claim to neutrality is important in this representation, not merely in social life in general but in education in particular. We assume that our activity is neutral, that by not taking a political stance we are being objective. This is significantly falsified, however, in two ways. First, there is an increasing accumulation of evidence that the institution of schooling is not a neutral enterprise in terms of its economic outcomes. As Basil Bernstein, Pierre Bourdieu, and others have sought to show—and as the quotes from Williams have pointed to in this essay—schools may in fact serve the interests of many individuals, and this should not be denied; at the same time though, empirically, they also seem to act as powerful agents in the economic and cultural reproduction of class relations in a stratified society like our own.[18] This is a rather involved issue, yet the literature on the role schools play in economic and cultural stratification is becoming increasingly impressive. This is one of the sections of this essay, hence, where I would like to take the opportunity to suggest a number of pieces that might best be examined to uncover what schools may actually do.

Despite its many weaknesses and its somewhat too heavy reliance on a correspondence theory, *Schooling in Capitalist America,* by S. Bowles and H. Gintis (New York: Basic Books, 1975), is one place to begin the analysis of economic reproduction. The school's role in cultural reproduction, in hegemony, is explored in B. Bernstein's *Class, Codes and Control,* Vol. 3: *Towards a Theory of Educational Transmissions* (2d ed. London: Routledge & Kegan Paul, 1977), in P. Bourdieu's and J. Passeron's *Reproduction in Education,*

Society, and Culture (London: Sage Publications, 1977), in *Knowledge and Control*, edited by M. F. D. Young (London: Collier-Macmillan, 1971), in *Society, State, and Schooling*, edited by M. F. D. Young and G. Whitty (Guilford, England: The Falmer Press, 1977), in R. Dale, et al., eds., *Schooling and Capitalism: A Sociological Reader* (London: Routledge & Kegan Paul, 1976), and in J. Karabel and A. H. Halsey, eds., *Power and Ideology in Education* (New York: Oxford, 1977). These volumes would be a good place to start one's investigation of schooling and economic and cultural control.

Let me note—actually reiterate—the second reason a claim to neutrality carries less weight than it might. The claim ignores the fact that the knowledge that now gets into schools is already a choice from a much larger universe of possible social knowledge and principles. It is a form of cultural capital that comes from somewhere, that often reflects the perspectives and beliefs of powerful segments of our social collectivity. In its very production and dissemination as a public and economic commodity—as books, films, materials, and so forth—it is repeatedly filtered through ideological and economic commitments. Social and economic values, hence, are already embedded in the design of the institutions we work in, in the "formal corpus of school knowledge" we preserve in our curricula, in our modes of teaching, and in our principles, standards, and forms of evaluation. Since these values now work *through* us, often unconsciously, the issue is not how to stand above the choice. Rather, it is in what values we must ultimately choose.

But this brings to the fore another part of the problem as well—those deep-seated values that I mentioned before which already reside not at the top but at the very "bottom" of our heads. The very categories we use to approach our responsibility to others, the commonsense rules we employ to evaluate the social practices that dominate our society, are often at issue. Perhaps the most critical of these categories is our commitment to the abstract individual. For it is the case that our sense of community is withered at its roots. We divorce the individual from larger social movements which might give meaning to "individual" wants, needs, and visions of justice.[19] This is strongly supported by the notion that curriculum research is a "neutral scientific activity" that does not tie us to others in important structural ways.

Our inability to think in other than individualistic terms is nicely expressed once again by Raymond Williams in his argument that the dominance of the bourgeois individual distorts our understanding of our real social relations with and dependence on others.

I remember a miner saying to me of someone we were discussing: "He's the sort who gets up in the morning and presses a switch and expects a light to come on." We are all, to some extent, in this position, in that our modes of thinking habitually suppress large areas of our real relationships, including our real dependence on others. We think of my money, my light, in these naive terms, because parts of our very idea of society are withered at root. We can hardly have any conception, in our present system, of the financing of social purposes from the social product, a method which would continually show us, in real terms, what our society is and does. In a society whose products depend almost entirely on intricate and continuous cooperation and social organization, we expect to consume as if we were isolated individuals, making our own way. We are then forced into the stupid comparison of individual consumption and social taxation—one desirable and to be extended, the other regrettably necessary and to be limited. From this kind of thinking, the physical unbalance follows inevitably. Unless we achieve some realistic sense of community, our true standard of living will continue to be distorted. . . . Questions not only of balance in the distribution of efforts and resources but also of the effects of certain kinds of work both on users and producers might then be adequately negotiated. . . . It is precisely the lack of an adequate sense of society that is crippling us.[20]

Williams's points are many here, yet among them are the following. Our concern for the abstract individual in our social, economic, and educational life is exactly that—it is merely an abstraction. It does not situate the life of the individual (and ourselves as educators) as an economic and social being back into the unequal structural relations that produced the comfort the individual enjoys. It can act as an ideological presupposition that keeps us from establishing any genuine sense of affiliation with those who produce our comforts thus making it even more difficult to overcome the atrophication of collective commitment. Thus, the overemphasis on the individual in our educational, emotional, and social lives is ideally suited to both maintain a rather manipulative ethic of consumption and further the withering of political and economic sensitivity. The latent effects of both absolutizing the individual and defining our roles as neutral technicians in the service of amelioration, therefore, makes it nearly impossible for educators and others to develop a potent analysis of widespread social and economic injustice. It makes their curricular and teaching practices relatively impotent in exploring the nature of the social order of which they are part.

An exceptionally important element in this kind of argument is the idea of *relation*. What I am asking for is what might best be called "relational analyses." These involve seeing social activity—with education as a particular form of that activity—as tied to the larger arrangement of institutions which apportion resources so that particular groups and classes have historically been helped while others have been less adequately treated. In essence, social action, cultural and educational events and artifacts (what Bourdieu would call cultural capital) are not "defined" by their obvious qualities that we can immediately see. Instead of this rather positivistic approach, things are given meaning relationally, by their complex ties and connections to how a society is organized and controlled. The relations themselves are the defining characteristics.[21] Thus, to understand the notions of science and the individual, as we employ them in education especially, we need to see them as primarily ideological economic categories that are essential to both the production of agents to fill existing economic roles and the reproduction of dispositions and meanings in these agents that will "cause" them to accept these alienating roles without too much questioning.[22] They become aspects of hegemony.

Here again a number of volumes are exceptionally helpful in illuminating the nature of relational analysis. B. Ollman's excellent explication of the conceptual apparatus of seeing things relationally in *Alienation* (New York: Cambridge University Press, 1971) is perhaps the best. Other works that are useful here as concrete examples of the actual practice of such inquiries are R. Williams, *The Country and The City* (New York: Oxford University Press, 1973), E. Genovese, *Roll, Jordan, Roll* (New York: Random House, 1974), H. Braverman, *Labor and Monopoly Capital* (New York: Monthly Review Press, 1974), L. Goldmann, *Cultural Creation* (St. Louis: Telos Press, 1976), and P. Willis, *Learning to Labour* (Westmead, England: Saxon House, 1977). The Braverman book is of special interest since it documents the growth of such things as systems management, task analysis, and so forth—items that have become such a large part of the rhetorical arsenal of "efficiency-minded" educators.

So far I have looked rather broadly at what I perceive to be much of the reality behind schools as institutions, the knowledge forms we selectively preserve, reinterpret, and distribute, some of the categories we use to think about these things, and the role of the educator as a "neutral" participant in the large-scale results of schooling. There are still a few final comments to be said about that last aspect of the program, the approach, I am setting forth here though—the educator him- or herself as political being. This is a very personal question, one that is by far the hardest. I am quite aware of the difficulty, in fact often the torture, that one must face in responding to or even adequately asking the question, Where do I stand? This kind of question already presupposes the relationship between cultural captial and economic and social control. It requires an analysis of what social and economic groups and classes seem to be helped by the way the institutions in our society are organized and controlled and which groups are not.

The fact that this question *is* so hard to deal with, the helpless feeling we get when we ask it (What can I as one educator do now?) points to the utter importance of Gramsci's and Williams's arguments about the nature of hegemony. To hold our day-to-day activities as educators up to political and economic scrutiny, to see the school as part of a system of mechanisms for cultural and economic reproduction is not merely to challenge the prevailing practices of education. If it were "merely" this, then we could perhaps change these practices through teacher training, better curriculum, and so on. These practices may need changes, of course, and there is still a place for such ameliorative reform. But the kinds of critical scrutiny I have argued for challenge a whole assemblage of values and actions "outside" of the institution of schooling. And this is exactly the point, for if taken seriously, it must lead to a set of commitments that may be wholly different than those many of us commonsensically accept. It requires the progressive articulation of and commitment to a social order that has at its very foundation not the accumulation of goods, profits, and credentials but the maximization of economic, social, and educational equality.

All of this centers around a theory of social justice. My own inclination is to argue for something to the left of a Rawlsian stance. For a society to be just, it must as a matter of both principle and action contribute most to the advantage of the least advantaged.[23] That is, its structural relations must be such as to equalize not merely access to but actual control of cultural, social, and especially economic institutions.[24] Now this would require more than mere tinkering with the social engine, for it implies a restructuring of institutions and a fundamental reshaping of the social contract that has supposedly bound us together. The theory of social justice that lies behind such a program needs to be generated out of more than personal ideology. It has its basis in a number of empirical claims as well. For example, the gap between rich and poor in advanced industrial nations is increasing. The distribution and control of health, nutritional, and educational goods and services is basically unequal in these same industrialized nations.[25] Economic and cultural power is being increasingly centralized in massive corporate bodies that are less than responsive to social needs other than profit. After some initial gains, the relative progress of women and many minority groups is either stagnant or slowly atrophying. Because of these and other reasons, I am more and more convinced that these conditions are "naturally" generated out of a particular social order. Our educational dilemmas, the unequal achievement, the unequal returns, the selective tradition and incorporation are also "naturally" generated out of this social arrangement. It may be the case that these institutions are organized and controlled in such a way as to require rather large-scale changes in their relationships if progress is to be made in eliminating any of these conditions.

I realize that this is rather controversial, to say the least. Nor do I expect that everyone will accept all that I have written here. However, I did not first come to the position that our educational issues are *at root* ethical, economic, and political and then search for documentation for it. Rather—and this is important—I have been convinced by evidence available to all of us if we are willing to search and question, if we can learn to analyze hegemony. In fact this is part of the approach I would like to explicate here. One thing should be clear, this program requires a good deal of plain old hard intellectual work, as well. It involves more than a modicum of reading, study, and honest debate in areas many of us have only a limited background in. We are unused to looking at educational activity politically and economically, not to say critically, given the very difficult (and time-consuming and emotionally draining) nature of being a decent educator. This task is made even more difficult because of what might be called the politics of knowledge distribution. That is, the kinds of tools and frameworks I have noted here are not readily distributed by the prevailing institutions of cultural preservation and distribution like schools and mass media. These critical traditions are themselves victims of selective tradition. If my arguments here and elsewhere about the nature of whose knowledge gets into schools are correct, this may be unfortunate, but it is to be expected. However, if we do not take it upon ourselves to master these traditions, to relearn them, we ignore the fact that the kinds of institutional and cultural arrangements which control us were built by us. They can be rebuilt as well.

Conclusion

I have argued in this essay that any serious appraisal of the role of education and curriculum in a complex society must have as a major part of its analysis at least three elements. It needs to situate the knowledge, the school, and the educator him- or herself within the real social conditions that "determine" these elements. I have also argued that this act of situating needs to be guided by a vision of social and economic justice if it is to be meaningful. Hence, I have also maintained that the position of educator is neutral neither in the forms of cultural capital distributed and employed by schools nor in the economic and cultural outcomes of the schooling enterprise itself. These issues are best analyzed through the concepts of hegemony, ideology, selective tradition, and relational analysis.

Obviously, a brief article can do more than state these elements. No matter how passionately stated, though, documentation is still often required. Because of this, throughout this essay—both in the body of my analysis and in the footnotes—I have noted a number of resources that should prove helpful in underpinning such a critical program. But we must be cautious here. Documentation does not only come from books. It comes from praxis as well, from reflexively inserting oneself in the political, economic, and cultural struggles to change the unequal and hegemonic conditions out of which this program was originally generated.[26] Thus the question is not merely How do I understand? but "How do I, collectively, act?" Only in such thoughtful commitment is there hope.

Notes

1. M. W. Apple, "Personal Statement," in *Curriculum Theorizing: The Reconceptualists* (Berkeley: McCutchan, 1975), pp. 89–93.

2. D. Lazere, "Mass Culture, Political Consciousness, and English Studies," *College English* 38 (April 1977): 755.

3. Ibid.

4. See, for example, B. Bernstein, *Class, Codes and Control, Vol. 3: Towards a Theory of Educational Transmission* (London: Routledge & Kegan Paul, 1975), p. 158.

5. S. Bowles and H. Gintis, *Schooling in Capitalist America* (New York: Basic Books, 1975).

6. The research on this is described rather clearly in C. H. Persell, *Education and Inequality* (New York: Free Press, 1977).

7. R. Dale et. al., eds., *Schooling and Capitalism: A Sociological Reader* (London: Routledge & Kegan Paul, 1976), p. 3.

8. See the analysis of Althusser's notion of "overdetermination" in M. Glucksmann, *Structuralist Analysis in Contemporary Social Thought* (London: Routledge & Kegan Paul, 1974).

9. This is documented at great length in M. W. Apple and B. Franklin, "Curricular History and Social Control," in *Community Participation in Education*, ed. C. Grant (Boston: Allyn and Bacon, 1978).

10. R. Williams, "Base and Superstructure in Marxist Cultural Theory," in Dale, *Schooling and Capitalism,* p. 202.

11. Ibid., pp. 204–205.

12. Ibid., p. 205.

13. See, for example, M. F. D. Young, ed., *Knowledge and Control* (London: Collier-Macmillan, 1971).

14. M. W. Apple, "Power and School Knowledge," *The Review of Education* 3 (Jan./Feb. 1977): 26–49; and M. W. Apple and N. R. King, "What Do Schools Teach?" *Curriculum Inquiry* 6 (Summer 1977).

15. G. Whitty, "Sociology and the Problem of Radical Educational Change," in *Educability, Schools and Ideology*, eds., M. Flude and J. Ahier (London: Halstead Press, 1974), p. 125.

16. M. W. Apple, "The Hidden Curriculum and the Nature of Conflict," *Interchange* 2:4 (1971): 27–40.

17. T. Schroyer's account of this process is helpful here. See his *The Critique of Domination* (New York: John Braziller, 1973). I have discussed this tendency at greater length in M. W. Apple, "The Adequacy of Systems Management Procedures in Education," in *Regaining Educational Leadership*, ed. R. A. Smith (New York: John Wiley, 1975), pp. 104–121.

18. See, for example, M. W. Apple, "Ideology, Reproduction, and Educational Reform," *Comparative Education Review* 22 (October 1978).

19. Part of what follows here appears in expanded form in M. W. Apple, "Humanism and the Politics of Educational Argumentation," in *Humanistic Education: Visions and Realities,* ed. R. Weller (Berkeley: McCutchan, 1977). See also, M. W. Apple, "Ideology and Form in Curriculum Evaluation," in *Qualitative Evaluation*, ed. G. Willis (Berkeley: McCutchan, 1978).

20. R. Williams, *The Long Revolution* (London: Chatto and Windus, 1961), pp. 298–300.

21. Apple, "Power and Social Knowledge."

22. I. Hextal and M. Sarup, "School Knowledge, Evaluation and Alienation," in *Society, State and Schooling*, eds., M. Young and G. Whitty (Guilford, England: The Falmer Press, 1977), pp. 151–71.

23. J. Rawls, *A Theory of Justice* (Cambridge: Harvard University Press, 1971).

24. For an interesting discussion of the debate in education over the social principle of equality of opportunity, see W. Feinberg, *Reason and Rhetoric: The Intellectual*

Foundations of Twentieth Century Liberal Education Policy (New York: John Wiley, 1975).

25. V. Navarro, *Medicine Under Capitalism* (New York: Neale Watson Academic Publications, 1976).

26. On this point, see the analysis of Gramsci's treatment of the "organic intellectual" in *Gramsci's Marxism*, by C. Boggs (London: Pluto Press, 1976).

9 Toward a Political Economy of Curriculum and Human Development

Dwayne Huebner

Introduction

Dwayne Huebner is one of the intellectual parents of the reconceptualists (along with James B. Macdonald and Paul R. Klohr). His earlier writing criticized the behaviorist language and narrowly instrumental function of traditional curriculum writing, and the titles from these articles illustrate the range of his earlier interests: "Curricular Language and Classroom Meaning," "Curriculum as Concern for Man's Temporality," "The Tasks of the Curricular Theorist," and "Poetry and Power: The Politics of Curricular Development." This last article, read at the 1973 meeting of the Association for Supervision and Curriculum Development, signaled his growing preoccupation with politics. In the article reprinted in this volume (originally read to the 1976 Curriculum Theory Conference held at the University of Wisconsin in Milwaukee) Huebner's interest in politics is indicated by his study of Marx. He writes that he is interested now in understanding how Marxism—"as a structure of social action and thought"—becomes distorted in the individual. To this end he studies Piaget in search of what he terms a "genetic Marxism." Such a Marxism might allow movement toward "a political economy of curriculum."

In a number of places the reader observes Huebner rephrasing conventional questions (see, for instance, the final paragraph). What is your view of his success in this regard; does the different language reconceptualize the issue so that it becomes another, perhaps more soluble issue?

You might also consider the following as you read:
- What stage of development is this "political economy of curriculum?"

Political Economy of Curriculum 125

- How does Huebner use the concept of energy? Is it a materialist usage, consistent with a Marxist perspective?
- Attempt to identify the presence of hermeneutical as well as Marxist influences in his thinking.

The writings of Marx and his followers have too infrequently informed the concerns of the curriculum person and those in related educational fields. The social-political reasons for this underutilization are obvious, inasmuch as the class analysis of the thirties and of this recent critical period were often interpreted as being subversive of United States political and economic institutions. However, the philosophical-historical reasons are less obvious and worthy of significant scholarship, for the historical, dialectical, and material content of his writings describe phenomena that can be interpreted as educational. This paper is intended as a pointer to some of the issues and possibilities that might be considered if a curriculum person were to engage in the critical interpretation of the writings of Marx and his followers. I claim no special competency for this task except interest and a home base in this presumed field of curriculum.

The historical task is a major one if we are to understand why the writings of Marx have been ignored by educators in the United States, except those brave few, some of whom have suffered the consequences. I presume that the reason, in part, revolves around two major figures at the turn of the century, plus or minus twenty years or so—Harris and Dewey. The Hegelianism of Harris had no small impact upon the character of schooling in the United States. Cremin[1] credits Harris with establishing the basic paradigm of the curriculum field that prevails today with minor themes and variations. Perhaps even more important is his impact on the organization of the schools and his concern for textbooks rather than the teacher, as the center of the curriculum. Although one American Hegelian, August Willich,[2] was a colleague of Marx and Engels, the Fuerbachian and Marxian critique and surpassing of Hegel did not make much of an impact on the other American Hegelians. Crucial in this historical picture is Dewey's encounter with Hegel by way of G. S. Morris at Johns Hopkins[3] and his turn to pragmatism. I am unfamiliar with whether Dewey's pragmatism was in part founded by a critical reaction to Marx. However, it is fascinating that both Dewey and Marx cut a philosophical eyetooth or two on Hegel. For reasons perhaps best explained by Novak,[4] Dewey's particular pragmatic surpassing of Hegel dominated educational

Reprinted from *Curriculum Theory*, ed. Alex Molnar and John A. Zahorik (Washington, D.C.: Association for Supervision and Curriculum Development, 1976), pp. 92–107. Reprinted with permission of the Association for Supervision and Curriculum Development and Dwayne Huebner. Copyright ©1976 by the Association for Supervision and Curriculum Development. All rights reserved.

thought to the exclusion of other post-Hegelian philosophies. It seems that the sixty years before the publication of Bobbitt's *Curriculum*[5] might be as important for understanding our intellectual ground as the sixty years following it.

There have been those students of education who have utilized Marx's ideas in *Das Kapital* to analyze the place of schooling in our economic and political structure. In the 1920s and 1930s Langford[6] and Slesinger[7] stand out; and in this critical period the works of Mann[8] and Bowles and Gintis[9] are notable. The analysis has been at the macro level. Concepts of class, labor, alienation, commodity, capital accumulation, and imperialism have been used to describe how schools and other structures of education reproduce the labor force and class distinctions within the capitalistic economy and the political and social institutions that accompany it. These macroanalyses have called our attention to the controlling functions inherent in institutionalized educational structures and point out the masking function of much past and present curricular language that proclaims the school's presumed role in "self-realization" and a more perfect "democratic" society.

With few exceptions in this country, the writings of Marx have not been used to explore the micro aspects of education—the interpersonal or intersubjective—the biography of the individual within specific social locations. One of the reasons for this is given by Joel Kovel,[10] who writes of the dialectical relationship between Freud and Marx. He suggests that Marx, to accomplish his great achievement, necessarily had to be concerned with only those aspects of human life that could be objectified and hence become a commodity. In effect, Marx had to bracket the subjective in order to explain the objective. Kovel suggests that Freud had to bracket the objective in order to deal with the subjective—the interpersonal and fantasy. Because Marx did not attend to the interpersonal and the subjective, the application of his ideas to the evolving biography of the individual within the prevailing objective structures is difficult, although some neo-Marxists have made the effort.[11] Reich[12] has described the dialectical relation between the economic-political structure and the sexual life of individuals. Horkheimer,[13] in his work on the family, has illustrated how the family mediates between the economic structures and the life of the child. He shows how the relations of production carry into the home, thus producing the individual who fits into the capitalistic structures. Today, I suppose that it would be equally easy to show how the commodity structure and consumerism work their way into the home not only via the activity of the parents but also by the mass medium of TV, the commodity which carries the image of all other commodities into the bedroom or kitchen. These mediating structures of home and media are surely important vehicles for describing how the forces and relations of production and the market impinge upon the child.

The historical-dialectical method of Marx, developed in the mid-nineteenth century, must themselves be interpreted historically and dialectically. The genetic epistemology of Piaget,[14] no matter how flawed or partial, is part of the

Political Economy of Curriculum

totality to be considered as the methods and rhetoric of Marx are reinterpreted in the situation of today. The significance which most educators attach to the work of Piaget, namely that he describes the cognitive functioning of the individual during different stages of growth, is, for my purposes, a masking of Piaget's more important contribution. Piaget has described the evolution, in the epistemic subject, of logico-mathematical structures. Piaget's work suggests that the adult decenter. Mathematics is not only what the adult does when computing and operating in science laboratories or in industry; mathematics is also what the child does when he or she groups objects, orders objects according to various attributes, and engages in a host of other transforming activities in the world. Piaget calls our attention to a different definition of knowledge structures. No longer can we see knowledge as finished form built into the behavior of adults and their tools which must then be "taught" to the child. Piaget has asked us to see knowledge structures as evolving—if you wish, as biographical or historical and as dialectical.

Whereas Marx has forced us to see ideologies and social, economic, and political structures within an historical and dialectical focus, Piaget has accomplished the same thing from the perspective of the history of involvement of the individual. Whereas Piaget has attended primarily to the logico-mathematical, and indeed has clearly bracketed out of his consideration metaphysical and ideological knowledge, he makes possible a genetic culture. He brings into our awareness the possibility that all adult forms of knowing and action can be, should be, seen in the perspective of their genesis in the person. No longer should we adults be permitted to see adult forms of knowledge or action as *the* way to interpret knowledge or action. Just as Marx required that we see them as social phenomena and interpret them historically and dialectically, so Piaget asks that we now see them genetically (or historically) and dialectically in the individual person.

The Piagetian task confronting Marxism is to identify and describe the forms or structures of a "genetic" Marxism. How does Marxism, as a structure of social action and thought, evolve and become distorted in an individual? It is normally assumed that Marxism is an adult framework for viewing and acting in adult social life and that the tasks of the Marxist are to develop the class consciousness and political organization of the proletariat to fulfill its historic mission. Given this charge, the Marxist educator must disseminate the political-economic tools for analysis and reconstruction of social life. The use of Marxian tools demystifies the forces of domination, builds political leadership, and develops the class consciousness necessary to mobilize political action of large segments of the people. This is the tack of Bowles and Gintis[15] in education; and indeed it is an important one, whether one shares their political commitments or not.

But if we had a genetic Marxism, the questions of the educator would be different. Assume that Marxian "revolutionary practice" has as its origins biological and social givens and activities of the infant. If the continuities and the discontinuities of this evolving operational structure can be identified, then perhaps we can see how the social and material environment intrudes upon or facilitates the development of so-called mature Marxian thought and action.[16]

This is what I wish to point to in this paper. I do not hope to accomplish the task but merely to point to needed and possible intellectual work. If we can move toward this goal of a "genetic" Marxism, then I think that we can also move toward a political economy of the curriculum and of human development itself. We should then depict more precisely the various mediations between the neophyte and the adult world, not with the intent of improving our educational control over the child, but with the possibility of pointing out the educational significance of the child for the adult and the need to construct more effective means for producing appropriate qualities of life for young and old.

The first task, then, is to map the intellectual tools of Marxism. The function of mapping these tools, these intellectual operations, is to provide a point of origin for genetic analysis. My operation is indeed abstract and conceptual, with the full recognition that the only appropriate method is finally phenomenological and dialectical, which entails bringing to consciousness the child-adult relationship over time—an autobiography of social relations.

The extensiveness, complexity, and detail of Marx's writings make the mapping task almost foolhardy. One is tempted to use already existing maps, such as Ollman's fine work on *Alienation*.[17] But a map is a tool, an instrument of production. Even an intellectual tool or means of production one must own, in order that the production has use value for the person. Thus, in my beginning appropriation of Marx's language tools, I made personal choices with the full recognition that if my production is to have social use value it must become part of the social dialectic and hence critiqued and negated or surpassed by others.

As a point of origin for this particular activity I would identify the following as significant markers: activity, work, labor, labor power; means of production, property; use value, exchange value, commodity; relations of production; alienation, class and class consciousness; surplus value and capital. However, here I shall be concerned only with activity, work, labor, labor power; means of production; and relations of production. My tactic will be to point in the direction that I think a genetic Marxism might take and to suggest the direction of possible implications for curriculum and the way that we adults might talk about child-adult relations over time.

Marx begins his analysis of capitalism in Volume I of *Das Kapital*[18] with the commodity and commodity exchange, but central to his analysis is the labor process. Labor is the process by which nature is appropriated for individual and social use and by means of which use value is produced. The productive process, which is at the same time a process of consumption, requires means of production—the instruments of production and the subject

Political Economy of Curriculum

of production: property. Specialization of labor gradually leads to a separation of the laboring process from the ownership of the means of production, hence the selling of one's labor power and the alienation of one's own being from one's labor and the products of this labor. Capital as surplus labor results, and hence the class distinctions between those who own property and have capital and those who have only their labor power as a commodity to exchange for other commodities. Labor, then, is central to any understanding of Marx's writing and is a key language tool for his economic and political analysis. What are the origins of labor in the person? Or to use Piagetian language, how can genesis of labor be described in the biography of the person and how can its origins be detected in the activity of the young child? Under what circumstances in one's life history does the alienation of labor occur, and when does the person begin to see his or her labor as labor for someone else, as something to be exchanged? Who owns the means of production in the life of the child? How does that ownership contribute to alienation and the loss or increase of power to produce one's own quality of life and to participate willingly in the social production of life?[19]

Marx states that "Labour is, in the first place, a process in which both man and Nature participate, and in which man of his own accord starts, regulates, and controls the material reactions between himself and Nature."[20] In *A Contribution to a Critique of Political Economy* he states that "In the process of production, members of society appropriate (produce, fashion) natural products in accordance with human requirements"[21] and "Production is always appropriation of nature by an individual within and with the help of a definite social organization."[22] For Marx, "The elementary factors of the labor process are (a) the personal activity of man, that is, work itself; (b) the subject of that work; and (c) its instruments."[23] Within the many writings of Marx, Ollman indicates how Marx gradually shifts from the term *activity* to the term *work*. Productive activity is work. Ollman claims that "For Marx, labor is always alienated productive activity."[24]

It is at this point that the specific content of Piaget's writing becomes helpful, not simply his methodology and general commitment to genetic epistemology. There seems to be a striking similarity between Marx and Piaget with respect to significance of activity and the appropriation of nature. You will recall that Piaget grounds logical-mathematical knowledge in the schemata of action.[25] He claims that knowledge and intelligence are transformations of the world, dependent upon the schemata of assimilation and accommodation. For Piaget, as for Marx, the significant aspect of human life is active interchange with the environment from which Piaget draws his genetic conceptions of knowledge and Marx his historical conceptions of labor, alienation, and capital. The foundation of knowledge for Piaget is the body and the biological determinants of the schemata of assimilation and accommodation. The foundation of the social-economic-political structure for Marx is also the material structure of the body in the world (in fact Marx refers to Nature as "man's inorganic body"[26]) from which develops, historically, our ideologies, knowledge structures, and social relations. The basic "instruments" of activity for Piaget are the schemata which are founded in the biological structures. The instruments of activity for Marx are the means of production, property, thus indicating the basic material base upon which they both ground their work.

The obvious hunch at this stage of the interpretation is that Piaget's schemata of action are the subjective correlates of Marx's objective means of production. In fact, Marx, referring to "the factors of the labor process," calls attention to "its objective factors, the means of production, as well as its subjective factors, labor power."[27] The schemata and means of production are not only instruments but become or are vehicles that support activity, give it direction or intentionality, and increase its power. The use of the word *power* is significant, for Marx refers to "labor power" as the commodity that the laborer exchanges for wages. Surplus labor power, the labor power beyond that needed for the maintenance and reproduction of the laborer himself or herself, is the source of surplus value, the source of capital. Surplus labor power, rather than being consumed for social production or for production of the laborer—going beyond his or her own reproduction to produce new personal qualities of life and activity—is used to produce wealth for someone else.

Marx and Piaget both recognize that activity itself produces the person as well as transforms the world or produces use value in the social world. Whereas this is readily seen in the works of Piaget, it stands forth less clearly in the more common interpretations of Marx. Marx states quite specifically that the person "opposes himself to Nature as one of her own forces, setting in motion arms and legs, head and hands, the natural forces of his body, in order to appropriate Nature's productions in a form adapted to his own wants. By this acting on the external world and changing it, he at the same time changes his own nature. He develops his slumbering powers and compels them to act in obedience to his sway."[28]

Thus, both Marx and Piaget ground their work in human activity, which is exhibited at birth. Activity is the manifestation of human life and the starting point of our concern. In the *Economic and Philosophic Manuscripts of 1844*, Marx asked "what is life but activity?"[29] We need not dig beneath the surface to infer motive or biological explanations of activity for purposes of understanding education, although clearly such digging is interesting and valuable. The infant exhibits undifferentiated activity. How is that activity gradually differentiated and focused? How does the stuff of the social-material world shape activity and give it power and direction? Under what circumstances does activity cease being activity for one's self and become activity for another; that is, when does it become alienated labor? In thinking through answers to these questions, both Piaget and Marx are helpful; for Piaget attends to the body (specifically to the cognitive) dimensions of some of the answers, whereas

Marx attends to the social and property dimensions of some of the answers. Thus we have pointed, so far, to the genetic origins of labor and to the possible significance of the means of production in this genetic labor.

We have also called attention, although much too briefly, to the notion of labor power and the significance of power in human life. As educators, we have been more inclined to talk of the person in terms of needs rather than powers, and we have been inclined to speak of needs assessments or deficiencies rather than how a person uses her or his power. But the focus of labor power suggests that we begin to ask how children use their surplus energy beyond that needed for self-maintenance. To what extent do they recognize the power to construct, to produce new qualities of life for themselves, and to produce new qualities of life, new environments for others? To what extent is that surplus energy seen as something negative to be feared, repressed, or sublimated, or used by others; as a source of guilt because it comes up against, and perhaps brings judgments against, the already established that others seek to maintain? In the course of a person's life, when is surplus energy seen as "labor power," a commodity to be exchanged for other commodities? But before these points can be elaborated, we must attend to the social dimension and to the genesis of the relations of production.

Again, Marx is quite clear as to the social dimension in his writings. The significance of social class and class consciousness is the obvious indicator of this social dimension. In the *Grundrisse* he states that: "Each individual's production is dependent on the production of others" and that "private interest is already a socially determined interest."[30] In a sense then, activity for Marx is always social activity, although the social dimension is often hidden by the alienation of labor and commodities. For Piaget, the social dimension is more opaque. In spite of defining cognition as founded on operations that connect the agent and the environment, he fails to ground his cognition of the child in the operations that exist between himself, the experimenter, and the child. It is interesting that as Piaget speaks of the physicist and physics, he states that "the physicist constantly acts, and the first thing he does is to transform objects and phenomena in order to get at the laws validating these transformations."[31] Yet he appears not to acknowledge his own acts. His very knowledge about cognitive development in the young is a consequence of his action; he has transformed the relationships between the child and his environment by manipulating objects, asking questions, or placing puzzles or tasks before the child. His stages of cognitive development are social, a consequence of his very intervention into the life of the child and participation in the activity of the child. Piaget's conceptions of the intellectual development of the child are not only conceptions of the intellectual development of the child but also of the development of the social relationship between the child and the experimenter, in which the social activity of the adult is masked or taken for granted. The correctives against forgetting or masking the activity of the adult are two. First, a phenomenological methodology in which the investigator brackets out his or her own taken-for-granted realities and indeed turns to consciousness of the "thing itself" would help. The thing itself in the Piagetian experiment is not the child and his or her environment but the child, the material environment, and the social environment consisting of the child and the experimenter, which necessarily includes the language activity between them. The other corrective is the empirical literature that seeks to describe the genesis of the social relationship between the neonate and the caregiver. The role or activity of the experimenter must also be reflected upon in this empirical work.

A speculative overview of the problem is found in Macmurray's *Persons in Relations*,[32] wherein the infant is described as a rational person at birth. A person is not an isolated individual but can exist only in relation with others. For Macmurray, the child supplies the motives, the caregiver supplies the intentions; the combination of intention and motive means rationality. The infant can live only through or by means of communication; communication does not develop except through life with another. Language, then, is a consequence of communication, not vice versa. Social relations are foundational for the continuation of individual life.

An empirical approach to the problem is found in *The Effect of the Infant on Its Caregiver*,[33] edited by Lewis and Rosenblum. The studies that they brought together were intended to support the thesis of the editors that: "Not only is the infant or child influenced by its social, political, economic, and biological world but in fact the child itself influences its world in turn."[34] The editors demonstrate with empirical findings that which Marx has demonstrated by way of his dialectical materialism and Piaget by his genetic epistemology— that the activity between the person and the world, even the social world, produces the person and transforms the world. In this volume Bell refers to the fact "that both parent and offspring behave so as to produce or maintain the behavior of the other."[35] The various studies point to the mutual significance of facial, vocal, and gaze behaviors in which the infant is often the instigator and terminator of a series of interactions. In a report on the relationship between blind infants and their mothers, Fraiberg describes how the absence of the infant's gaze changes typical mothering reactions and alters vocalization patterns of mother and infant. Compensation for this lack of visual contact is possible if the mother is helped to respond vocally to the movement cues of the infant and if tactile replaces visual communication and eye play.[36]

Additional information is provided in *Temperament and Behavior Disorders* by Thomas and others, in which the authors identify temperament as a crucial factor in the development of behavior disorders. They hypothesize that the "behavioral style of the individual child . . . the characteristic tempo, rhythmicity, adaptability, energy expenditure, mood, and focus of attention"[37] of a child is a key factor in understanding the social interactions of the child. I interpret this to mean that the physiological characteristics of the individual organism impact on the evolving social relations between the child and her or his caregivers. It seems reasonable to generalize beyond Piaget here. Piaget claims that the logico-mathematical schemata that serve as "specialized organs of regulation in the control of exchanges with the environment"[38] are founded on the biological structures of the child. It would be reasonable to hypothesize that schemata also evolve which serve as organs of regulation in the control of exchanges with other persons and that these are grounded in the biological structures of the infant, hence the significance of temperament in social relationships and their distortions. However, it does not seem reasonable to use the expression assimilation and accommodation with respect to these presumed schemata of regulation in the exchange with others unless we add the qualifier "negotiated" assimilation and "negotiated" accommodation, for the mutuality of impact and the mutuality of self-production must be acknowledged.

I have suggested a parallel between environmental interactions and social interactions, using Piaget formulations of the logico-mathematical as the metaphor. I wish to carry this parallel one step further in order to get a potentially more useful handle on the problem of social relations, the relation of production, and the phenomena of consciousness. Piaget states that "to attribute logic and mathematics to the general coordinates of the subject's action . . . is a recognition of the fact that while the fecundity of the subject's thought process depends on the internal resources of the organism, the efficacy of those processes depends on the fact that the organism is not independent of the environment but can only live, act, or think in interaction with it."[39] Piaget's overall strategy was to begin with the givenness of mathematics and scientific knowledge and to search for their origins in the child. In so doing he has also, of course, reconstructed our knowledge of these disciplines. But he did not start with general notions of schemata of assimilation and accommodation and then find that they led to logico-mathematical formal structures.

The parallel I would suggest is that the forms of language usage are the coordinates of social relations and that the clues to the possible schemata of these social relations are to be found in the functions of speech between and among persons in their many relations. The work of Merleau-Ponty, a phenomenologist, supports this parallel. He describes speech as an extension of the body, in a sense affirming that both logico-mathematical operations and speech are founded in biological givens. He states that "language is a manifestation, a revelation of intimate being and of the psychic link which unites us to the world and to our fellow man."[40] Later he claims that,

There is one particular culture object which is destined to play a crucial role in the perception of other people: language. In dialogue there is constituted between the other person and myself a common ground: my thought and his are woven into a single fabric, my words and those of my interlocutor are called forth by the state of the discussion, and they are inserted into a shared operation of which neither of us is the creator. We have here a dual being, where the other is for me no longer a mere bit of behavior in my transcendental field, nor I in his; we are collaborators for each other in consummate reciprocity.[41]

Paralleling Piaget's reflective abstraction whereby the logico-mathematical structures are constructed, Merleau-Ponty writes that "It is only retrospectively, when I have withdrawn from the dialogue and am recalling it that I am able to integrate it into my life and make it an episode in my private history."[42]

The work of Kohlberg fails to be informed by the methods of phenomenology and the work of Merleau-Ponty. In fact, he misses the fundamental contribution of Piaget in this respect—that knowledge and formal operations are grounded in action. Kohlberg has merely established stages of potential inauthentic or alienated discourse about moral activity. His failure to ground the evolution of moral discourse in the evolving social relations of individuals, in their coordinates of social action, is a major fault of his work.

The studies of the interaction between infant and caregiver indicate that the infant is born into a social relationship and indeed partakes in the structuring of the interactive patterns which make up that social relation. Some of the early studies of language development point to the fact that the communicative relationship between caregivers and infant is foundational for the establishment of dialogue and language. We have inferred from this that the functions of speech in dialogue, the forms that language takes between and among individuals, are reflective of the schemata of social relations. Stated from the other side, social relations are constitutive of language functions. That which needs to be traced empirically and phenomenologically is the gradual transition from these social relations of care and communication to the relations of production. Furthermore, if the above hunches are correct, it should also be possible to detect the shifts in the language exchanges as these gradually express the language of production. Much of the empirical work probably exists. It is obvious, and indeed the work of Horkheimer[43] and Schneider[44] suggests, that the dynamics of family life begin to assume the shape of the relations of production. Horkheimer has shown how the hierarchy of authority in work places carries over to the authority structures in family and hence reproduces in children attitudes and behavior that are required for the work force. The sexual liberation movements of today have also called attention to the penetration of family dynamics by the hierarchical and stereotypical structures in business, industry, and other places of adult occupation. Likewise, it seems rather common knowledge among teachers that the language of the classroom readily and quickly assumes the form of the language of production, with emphasis on production (what one has learned) and external authority. The recent work on communication competence and distorted communication is a possible source of further data and methodologies for exploring the relationships among language functions, social relations, and the relations of production.[45]

The centrality of language in a genetic Marxism is also indicated by the significance of language for consciousness. In *The German Ideology*, Marx states that "Language is as old as consciousness, language is practical consciousness. . . . Consciousness is therefore from the very beginning a social product."[46] Later he claims "that the real intellectual wealth of the individual depends entirely on the wealth of his real connections."[47] I am not certain what he intends by the words "intellectual wealth," but for me it entails consciousness. Again, in education we have been so conditioned to think of the individual and his or her consciousness, his or her language, that we fail to recognize the social and relational aspect of that consciousness and that language. Thus, it is less a matter of changing one's language patterns, of changing his or her consciousness of who he or she is, than of changing his or her relations with others and broadening this range of relationships. It seems to me that psychotherapy illustrates this, for by working through a significant relationship with the therapist, the client speaks differently about her- or himself and others and has a changed consciousness about her- or himself in the world. Hence class consciousness is necessarily a creation of dialectical thinking and awareness. Class consciousness exists when one recognizes those with whom she or he is in relation and those with whom she or he has few or distorted relations, perhaps indeed only relations of production, consumption, or exchange.

Some of the implications of this analysis for curriculum and our "understanding" of human development are easy to generate. If we take seriously the possibility of a genetic Marxism, then further inquiry might produce more useful knowledge about the dialectical relationship between adults, the structures of the adult world and the child. Central to such inquiry would not be cognition or affect but the shape of human activity throughout the lifetime of the person, the developing power of the person for self and social production, the evolving social relations of the person, the relationship of self activity to social activity, the evolving functions of language as manifestations of social relations and consciousness, including class consciousness, the functions of production and ownership, and the use value of the materials of production for children, the relationships of these materials to the schemata of assimilation and accommodation of the child, and the relationship of these materials to the productive forces within the society.

Inquiry into such phenomena is part of our problem, for it is a division of labor that produces elites and develops not consciousness but knowledge, which becomes a commodity to be exchanged for degrees, salary increments, tenure, promotion, royalties, and privilege. As Marx said in his last thesis on Feuerbach: "The philosophers have only *interpreted* the world; the point is to *change* it."[48]

We really do not need more studies; we need consciousness of our own complicity in the forces of domination and a critical methodology that will inform and be informed by our practice as educators. That critical methodology and practice is social, dialectical, and materialistic. By social I mean only that individuality is only possible because we are, have been, and will be in relation with others and that our fundamental concern is and must be the quality of that social life. Infants and young children partake of our social being. The unfortunate question as to how they become socialized hides that fact. Only our naive and extreme individualism lets us speak of earning a living so we can raise children rather than producing a life for ourselves and others. Our activity and that of the young is part of the continuing transformation of energy and material for the sake of our collective life. To have that activity turned into alienated activity, for someone else rather than for the person and the collective which he or she chooses, is the beginning of distortion of the social relations, of domination, and of language which no longer expresses truth and possibility.

By "dialectical" I mean seeing the part in terms of the totality, the present in terms of the past and the future, and recognizing that contradictions are also a mode of relationship that offer as much understanding of the present moment as cause-and-effect relationships. The child is a part of our whole, a significant part of our past, present, and future, and a source of some of our major contradictions. To speak of adult life without the presence of children is an absurdity; and that absurdity is demonstrated by our efforts to wall them off from our everydayness as adults in schools—public school, preschool, church school, and what have you. Walling them off means that we never have to ask what they mean for us and how much of our productive power should be used for their life. We only need ask what we mean for them and what they must learn, how they must be socialized, how they will inherit our wealth. Dialectical method and practice require that we see the life of the child against the lives of the adults, the activity of children in classrooms against the activities of adults in automobile production plants, banana plantations, cocktail lounges at the top of the World Trade Center, as pushers in Harlem, as prisoners and guards in Attica, and in faculty meetings. The contradictions seen and felt will never be reduced by a curriculum but are the source of consciousness, of class consciousness.

By "materialistic" I intend a concern for the body—the body of the person and the body of the world—and the respect that is due both. Productive interchange between the two is necessary for life. The instruments that have been fashioned to direct this interchange and to increase life's power can be respectful or disrespectful of the body of the person and the body of the world, for the instruments that have been fashioned can indeed alienate individuals, increase collective power, or rape the body of the world. The instruments that have become tools of education are often disrespectful of both, used for profit making, for developing impotence and social weakness, or for producing laborers to do the work of and for others. The schemata of assimilation and accommodation are often for the appropriation of the body of the world for the few; even the public materials for education are often designed for only private gain.

If there is indeed a political economy of the curriculum and of child development, it will not tell us how to educate young people but how the young and the old can live together for mutual benefit and how the current structures of production and consumption intrude upon the social relations among people—young and old, near and far, rich and poor, black and white.

Notes

1. L. Cremin, "Curriculum Making in the United States," *Teachers College Record* 64 (January 1971): 196–200.
2. W. H. Goetzman, ed., *The American Hegelians* (New York: Alfred A. Knopf, 1973).
3. Ibid.
4. G. Novak, *Pragmatism versus Marxism: An Appraisal of John Dewey's Philosophy* (New York: Pathfinder Press, 1975).
5. F. Bobbitt, *The Curriculum* (Boston: Houghton Mifflin Co., 1918).
6. H. Langford, *Education and Social Conflict* (New York: Macmillan, 1935).
7. Z. Slesinger, *Education and the Class Struggle* (New York: Couici-Friedo, 1937).
8. J. S. Mann, "Influences of Marxism on Curriculum Theory" (Paper presented to Professors of Curriculum, New Orleans, April 1976).
9. S. Bowles and H. Gintis, *Schooling in Capitalist America* (New York: Basic Books, 1975).
10. J. Kovel, "The Marxist View of Man and Psychoanalysis," *Social Research* 45 (Summer 1976): 220–45.
11. R. Lichtman, "Marx and Freud," *Socialist Revolution* 30 (October–December 1976): 3–56.
12. W. Reich, *The Invasion of Compulsory Sex-Morality* (New York: Farrar, Straus and Giroux, 1971).
13. M. Horkheimer, "Authority and the Family," *Critical Essays*, trans. M. O'Connor, (New York: Herder and Herder, 1972).
14. J. Piaget, *Biology and Knowledge* (Chicago: University of Chicago Press, 1971).
15. Bowles and Gintis, *Schooling in Capitalist America.*
16. K. Marx, "Theses on Feuerbach," *The German Ideology* (New York: International Publishers, 1947), pp. 195–99.
17. B. Ollman, *Alienation* (Cambridge: Cambridge University Press, 1971).
18. K. Marx, *Capital: A Critique of Political Economy. Vol. I: The Process: Capitalist Production*, ed. F. Engels (New York: International Publishers, 1967).
19. See, for example, Lichtman on this point.
20. Marx, *Capital*, p. 177.

21. K. Marx, *A Contribution to the Critique of Political Economy*, ed. M. Dobb, (New York: International Publishers, 1970), p. 193.
22. Ibid., p. 192.
23. Marx, *Capital*, p. 178.
24. Ollman, *Alienation*, p. 171.
25. Piaget, *Biology and Knowledge*.
26. K. Marx, *The Economic and Philosophic Manuscripts of 1844*, ed. D. Struik, (New York: International Publishers, 1964), p. 110.
27. Marx, *Capital*, p. 184.
28. Ibid., p. 177.
29. Marx, *Economic and Philosophic Manuscripts*, p. 111.
30. K. Marx, *Grundisse*, ed. and trans. D. McLellan (New York: Harper & Row, 1971).
31. Piaget, *Biology and Knowledge*, p. 338.
32. J. Macmurray, *Persons in Relations* (New York: Harper and Bros., 1961), chap. II.
33. M. Lewis and L. Rosenblum, *The Effect of the Infant on Its Caregiver* (New York: John Wiley, 1974).
34. Ibid., p. xv.
35. R. Bell, "Contributions of Human Infants to Caregiving and Social Interaction," Lewis and Rosenblum, *Effect of the Infant*, pp. 1–30.
36. S. Fraiberg, "Blind Infants and Their Mothers: An Examination of the Sign System," Lewis and Rosenblum, *Effect of the Infant*, pp. 215–32.
37. A. Thomas et al., *Temperament and Behavior Disorder in Children* (New York: New York University Press, 1968).
38. Piaget, *Biology and Knowledge*, p. 354.
39. Ibid., p. 345.
40. M. Merleau-Ponty, *The Phenomenology of Perception*, trans. C. Smith (London: Routledge & Kegan Paul, 1962).
41. Ibid., p. 354.
42. Ibid.
43. Horkheimer, "Authority and the Family."
44. M. Schneider, *Neurosis and Civilization, A Marxist/Freudian Synthesis*, tran. M. Roloff (New York: Seabury Press, 1975).
45. J. Habermas, "Toward a Theory of Communicative Competence," in *Recent Sociology*, vol. 2, ed. H. P. Dreitzel (New York: Macmillan, 1970), pp. 114–49.
46. Marx, *German Ideology*, p. 19.
47. Ibid., p. 27.
48. Marx, "Theses on Feuerbach," p. 199.

10 Autobiography and Reconceptualization

Madeleine R. Grumet

Introduction

In this short essay Professor Grumet explains and demonstrates an autobiographical method of curriculum research. This method is research that concretely details an individual's experience of the curriculum in an effort to transform that experience. It is grounded in psychoanalytic theory and the phenomenological tradition.

As you read, consider the differences between this method and viewpoint and both the traditional and conceptual-empirical methods and viewpoints. Certain differences you might note revolve around the general mass and the individual, the abstract and the concrete, the objective and the subjective.

Some economically and politically oriented curricularists have objected to what they have termed the excessively personal character of autobiographical curriculum research. (You will read this dispute in the last section of this text.)
- Do you find this work, as exemplified in the Grumet piece, excessively personal?
- How could one achieve a balance between the personal and impersonal in describing educational experience?

Literally, reconceptualization means to conceive again, to turn back the conceptual structures that support our actions in order to reveal the rich and abundant experience they conceal. To some, this reflexive scrutiny may suggest a relentless descent into abstraction and introspection, and there are

Reprinted, with permission, from *Impact* 14, no. 3 (1978–79), pp. 10–14.

probably moments we can all recall when reflection drew us down and into eddies of confusion and anxiety.

The reconceptualization of curriculum is spared this paralyzing doubt which accompanies an infinite regression of questions because it is firmly anchored in the world. The concrete event that is experienced by a particular person is its mooring. Curriculum is the child of culture, and their relation is as complex and reciprocal as are any that bond the generations. Curriculum transmits culture, as it is formed by it. Curriculum modifies culture, even as it transmits it. Similarly, as with culture, we live curriculum before we describe it. The event and the thought about the event are never simultaneous, never identical. We live curriculum as we drive to work, take a quick stop in the faculty washroom before class, make our way past students stuffing bulky coats into narrow lockers, past tiled walls and display cases into the room where the curriculum we describe is or is not experienced. Curriculum as lived and curriculum as described amble along, their paths sometimes parallel—often not—occasionally, in moments of insight, intersecting. So it is possible that experience and description diverge now and then and the paeans of praise to participative democracy are sung in autocratic classrooms, individualization degenerates into depersonalized programming, and inquiry method requires that I search for answers to someone else's questions.

Reconceptualization of curriculum requires a more than reflexive somersault that scoops up our old flat ideas and turns them over. It is a reflexive project that attempts to reclaim curriculum as we have lived it and to test our conceptual schemes and descriptions of it against the evidence of our experience. Tonight I may find that evidence in the image of my father bending over my textbooks at the dining-room table, covering them with deep red, durable paper, rolled up and carried home from work on the subway just for that purpose. The evidence surprises me, presenting itself abruptly, like the ticket stubs from South Pacific wedged into the pocket of an old purse. Or it may be the memory of the young man with the curly hair and angular face who came to teach us junior high social studies and called us "people." "People, did you finish the assignment" and "I want to ask you people some questions." Or it may be the day he asked us to grade ourselves for the term, and Bobby Aaronson became a hero because he gave himself an F, explaining that he knew he had not done his best. It is Miss Leahy telling a thirsty third-grade classmate to bite his tongue and drink the blood, and it is the penny that glowed in the puddle on Broadway and 118th Street as I walked out into the twilight after hearing Stravinsky's Symphony of Psalms played in class.

My students tell their own stories, of speaking Spanish in a kindergarten where everyone speaks English, of talking to a kid from the "slow" class one

Autobiography and Reconceptualization

day in the girl's bathroom, of understanding the discipline of natural science while rehearsing an ensemble scene from *Richard III*.

The method is autobiography. Curriculum reclaimed in this manner is, of course, inevitably reconceptualized, even in the most meticulous and ingenuous retelling. The selection of some events and the exclusion of others, the repudiation of some feelings and the acknowledgment of others remind us that these accounts can never exactly coincide with our experience. The event-in-itself defies re-presentation, slipping away from our grasp like the landscape outside the window of a railway car. Nevertheless, the abstractions of primary experience presented in these autobiographical reflections are vulnerable to critical scrutiny. The writer can turn back upon her own texts and see there her own processes and biases of selection at work. It is here that curriculum as thought is revealed as the screen through which we pass curriculum as lived. Miss Leahy did make that sadistic comment. The student teacher (was he appended to Miss Leahy?) did call us "people," and my father did cradle his paper for my books under his arm and bring it home, battling the rush-hour crowds and his own fatigue to cover my books. Those things did happen then, but why do I tell them rather than other tales? What principle of selection excludes the story about Mrs. Dobkin who called my mother to urge her to consult another pediatrician when I had been out of school for two or three weeks with a mysterious ailment? Why is Leahy's sadism a more successful candidate for recycling than Dobkin's solicitous concern? Perhaps one question may illuminate another. Why "people"? The designation flattered us, suggesting that we were all peers, even though we knew that the status the student teacher extended to us so generously was tentative because he survived from day to day only by Leahy's (yes, it was Leahy) leave. And even Bobby Aaronson's martyrdom was staged. We weren't real people, and Bobby Aaronson wasn't a real martyr. We played at human dignity, and our gestures confirmed our impotence and degradation. And finally, that's why Dobkin is in the piece, not because she cared enough to call but because she assumed that my parents needed her advice, that her pediatrician would be better than the one they had chosen, and because they resented her patronizing intrusion even as they appreciated her concern. Tales of power, its use and abuse.

The gaps in the tale are brimming with information for the reader who is the writer of such an autobiography. And that information is not about what it was to be seven, nor is it about Leahy and Dobkin. It is information that pulls the past into the present, drawing it together to confirm what I anticipate will be my next move. Today, as I teach students who would be teachers and encourage them to be agents of their own visions and commitments, am I also posturing with my "people" while Leahy smirks?

Through this critical reflection upon educational experience, curriculum is reconceptualized in two ways. The first phase of this reflexive research is free associative. The content that will be specified by that word, *curriculum*, is reclaimed by a reflective process that allows the mind to wander but notes the path and all its markers. In this essay Leahy, Dobkin, "people" are the souvenirs of that side trip. When the method has been extended by any students, they have been asked to write an essay that provides at least three narratives of events in their lives that they would call educational experiences. The stories need not concern schooling, but they may. The persuasion of autobiography resembles that of fiction. Detail is required to demonstrate lawful possession of the tale. It is detail that reveals that my father brought the book covers back from the "place," the term we used to refer to the loft across the river that housed my father's manufacturing company. It is the shelter and authority of the "place" with its slamming presses, piles of cardboard from floor to ceiling that my father applies to the fragile binding of my social studies text. Anything brought home from the "place" contained a potency absent in items purchased at Woolworth's or at the corner candy store. These imports, the five hundred rubber bands, the packing tape, paper clips, the red paper were passports back to the world across the river, to the loading dock, to the union, to the machines, to the business, the commerce, the power of "the place."

This reconceived curriculum is the curriculum reclaimed by what Merleau-Ponty calls the body-subject. It is the relation of the knower to the known (and to the unknown) that is manifested in the concrete images of lived worlds. It is the body-subject who ran her fingers over the sharp folds and hard corners of that book cover, heard the music, felt the rain, and imagined the salty taste of my own blood. It is the curriculum of bitten nails that were noted on the report card, of crayola cranberry vines decorating each page of the report on New England, of singing "The Battle Hymn of the Republic" on the high school steps after chorus rehearsal the night Julius and Ethel Rosenberg were executed. This concrete reclamation reconceptualizes the curriculum, for it literally reconceives it by gathering it from the specific associations that represent our experience of it. The themes repeat themselves—the bitten nails, the energy turned back upon myself, expressiveness shunted into decorative margins. And those early stirrings of political awareness, of identification and protest, sentimentalized and nationalized and moved out of the building, after hours, on to the steps.

As we analyze the narrative, we reveal interests and biases we rarely see because they are threaded through the thick fabric of our daily lives. This is the second phase of reconceptualizing that illuminates the ways we organize and interpret our experience by framing those choices in an aesthetic object, the autobiography. Within those pages those choices, which when embedded in the activity of our daily lives seem obligatory and unavoidable, stand as expressions of our freedom. I organize my story of the past that can tell me where I am and where I am going.

Because I question the reality of my own power, the brave but ultimately hollow gestures return to remind me that oppression is most insidious when the oppressed are placated with the false but flattering slogans and poses that disguise their experience.  The possibility that schools may become places where students understand their own powers is never realized through rhetoric but through the choices and actions that fill the minutes we spend together.

The faculty bathroom is clean and has a door. I enjoy its privacy. The students' bathrooms have no outer doors, and when I visit them, demonstrating my egalitarianism, all conversation stops, cigarettes are quickly flushed, and I destroy whatever privacy peer solidarity and separate facilities have provided.

In schools the exercise of power is institutionalized and disclaimed. Reclaiming it requires attention to the initiatives we take and the responses we make.

If "people" and "the place" have washed up on the shore to remind me of power the child didn't own, power the student merely imitated or borrowed, they also remind me of the power I now claim as teacher and as parent. And if, when I push it and prod it like a jellyfish, it turns out to have a real sting, what use shall I make of it?

I have used this method of reflexive analysis with students in teacher education courses,[1] in theatre courses,[2] and in in-service work.[3] (The theatre students organized their reflective writing around the concept of theatrical experience in one case and around play in another.) While there is initial anxiety, for students have little practice in finding and telling their own stories, there is usually a rush of fluency once the choices are made. It is rare that these pieces are burdened with poor writing. People usually make sense when they know what they are talking about.

I attempt to reply to the pieces in ways that will extend both the concrete and abstract sources of information that the autobiographical exercise can offer. I footnote my comments, which I append on a separate sheet; my questions sometimes request information drawing out the particular details that are not yet visible but may hold, I suspect, the clue as to why the story is important. I may help the writer to ascertain what is missing in the text as well as to recognize patterns and themes that often surface in each of the apparently disparate narratives. The writer of the piece maintains possession and authority over his own prose. He need not respond to any questions which call him into territory he'd rather not tread. It is his recognition and acknowledgement that establishes the authority of any of the interpretations I may offer. The essays initiate reflexive writing in other forms. Journals may be kept. Additional essays may follow.

This work is pursued in the aspiration that it will enable the student to become the active interpreter of his past as well as heighten his capacity to be the active agent of his own interests in a present that he shares with his community. As curriculum is reconceptualized through the selection and criticism that reorders educational experience into a usable past, it may also be transformed into a usable present by students who see themselves as responsible for the shape and texture of their own experience.

Which brings me to the penny in the puddle. I can still see it glimmer, clean rainwater on pebbly cement, its copper purity adding a pecuniary fallacy to the natural one that accompanied Stravinsky. Although it is not without some guilt that I dishonor this cherished moment with condescending labels culled from lit. crit., I cannot make use of this memory as an image of my current concerns. That evening provided the organic continuity that Pepper attributes to aesthetic experience, the music, the city, the rain, the penny all arranged around me, fused and glowing. But now I am the arranger and look to aesthetics not to create perfect wholes but to reveal those cracks in the smooth surface of our conceptual would that may suggest new interpretations of human experience.

Notes

1. W. Pinar and M. Grumet, *Toward a Poor Curriculum* (Dubuque, Iowa: Kendall/Hunt, 1976).

2. M. Grumet, "Songs and Situations," in *Qualitative Evaluation*, ed. G. Willis (Berkeley: McCutchan, 1978).

3. M. Grumet, "Supervision and Situations," *The Journal of Curriculum Theorizing* 1:1 (Winter 1979): 191–257.

Section II
INSTRUCTION

Three Perspectives on Instruction

The section that follows offers different definitions of the term *instruction* drawn from the viewpoints of the traditionalist, conceptual-empiricist, and reconceptualist. Our purpose in presenting these three points of view is to illustrate the alternative meanings associated with this all-embracing educational term. We also hope to broaden the reader's framework for understanding the connections between instruction and the larger educational process.

Educators, however, have rarely understood the multifaceted nature of and diverse meanings associated with the term *instruction*. For example, traditionalists have emphasized the overly practical dimensions of classroom pedagogy to the exclusion of other points of view. "If it works, use it!" has become a dictum of the traditionalist stance on instruction, and all too little attention is given to finding out how and why a particular classroom practice succeeds in the teaching-learning process. Underlying this pragmatic view of instruction is an attempt to translate lofty educational goals into "specific instructional objectives" and reduce the latter into "learning activities" for the practitioner. The primacy of the practitioner as decision maker is highlighted by Klein. By implication, this traditionalist point of view places enormous responsibility for students' learning on the teacher to the exclusion of other equally significant educational influences.

On the other hand, conceptual-empiricists view the practitioner's world as a problem-ridden environment worthy of categorization and investigation. The classification schemes, the teaching-learning models, and the findings of conceptual-empiricists are represented at their best in the readings by Block and Gagné. Block's task-oriented mastery-learning model offers researchers and practitioners opportunities for further study and practice. It ignores, however, questions about the meaningfulness of these tasks and the student's perception of teaching as informed but routinized and potentially regimented learning. Within the same conceptual-empiricist tradition, Gagné offers a near-perfect fit between an information-processing learning model and a model for teaching. These models are internalist in nature; they focus on the relationship between thinking behavior and learning, and they avoid linkages to classroom social phenomena. As such, they offer important but limited perspectives on the teaching process.

The reconceptualist point of reference is more encompassing in its attempts to find new meaning in the term *instruction* and to link instruction ideologically and overtly to the process of schooling and to larger political, economic, and cultural phenomena. This effort is often elusive and has been subjected to protracted and heated debate. The work of Lundgren and his colleagues in Sweden illustrates the reconceptualist's criticism of empirical studies of instruction. As an alternative perspective for understanding instruction, Lundgren offers a system that he identifies as "frame factors." An additional reconceptualist notion for linking the larger society to classroom instruction is illuminated by Giroux and Penna. This notion, reconceptualist only in its political and economic aspects, has been referred to frequently in educational literature as the "hidden curriculum." In other words, reconceptualists examine what is taught to students via the political norms and assumptions that are often tacitly conveyed through the messages embodied in the curriculum, the mode of pedagogy, and the form of evaluation that make up the day-to-day dynamic of classroom life.  This suggests that reconceptualists are concerned not only with what *is* taught through the hidden curriculum but also with what is rejected, redefined, or only partially accepted by teachers and students. In essence, the writings of the reconceptualists generally point out the weaknesses of modes of educational inquiry that fail to link the form and function of classroom instruction to the political and economic values that underlie power relationships in the larger society.

As you read and study this section, you will begin to recognize the complex web of ideas contained in the general term *instruction*. To know it only in its practical sense is narrow, restrictive, and relatively uninspiring. To add limited research findings of the kinds provided by Block and others in this section, for example, expands one's knowledge of teaching and should provide a more informed basis for defining and articulating classroom practice.

Traditionalists

11 Instructional Decisions in Curriculum

M. Frances Klein

Introduction

In this chapter Frances Klein reviews several considerations in instructional decision making. This review is conducted in the traditional mode of anticipating "practical" situations and outlining some resources available. Klein is interested in the "systematic implementation of society's expectations for schooling." Further, she believes that the Goodlad conceptual system "suggests a model for decision making which should help ... replace considerable chaos in curriculum planning with at least a little more order."

As you read, you might consider the following:
- How much room for instructional decision making is left to the individual teacher in the Goodlad-Klein scheme? Is it enough or too much in your estimation?
- What political and ethical critique has Klein utilized to assess "society's expectations for schooling"? Why is that, do you suppose?
- Do you agree that curriculum planning is in "considerable chaos"? If so, what benefits would derive from more orderliness?
- What group (administrators, teachers, students) would gain and what group or groups would lose?

Reprinted from *Curriculum Inquiry*, ed. John Goodlad and Assoc. (New York: McGraw-Hill, 1979), pp. 177–90. Copyright © 1979. Reprinted by permission of McGraw-Hill Book Company.

There are several levels of curricular decision making, as suggested by Goodlad.¹ One level is the instructional one, and because it is so close to students, it is crucial. The teacher performs the transactional role between students and what society wants for them in schools. Presumably, the planning that has occurred at the societal and institutional levels, including all the political and social transactions taking place between levels, gives considerable—if often confusing—guidance and direction to teachers regarding what to do in their classrooms. Certainly, if the ministry or board of education decides that valuing a plurality of cultures is to be one of the educational aims of schools and that study of Spanish and black cultures should be included as part of the elementary school social studies curriculum, teachers must pay attention to these decisions. Aspects of the two cultures must be made available for study by the students, and thus teacher choices as to what to teach are defined. But these directives still need to be refined at the instructional level where teachers make decisions within (and sometimes in spite of) these constraints.

Criteria must be set to suggest what or how students think and feel when they understand and appreciate these cultures. Specific content with which students will be expected to deal must be selected. Then, organizing centers must be devised that allow the student to practice the behaviors and deal with the content of the cultures specified in the objectives. There must be instructional selections of the major elements of the curriculum. Materials appropriate  to the students and to the subject must be chosen from what is available or perhaps created "from scratch." Finally, ways of assessing student progress toward attaining the objectives, as well as when assessment should occur, must be decided upon. The teacher still faces extremely important curricular decisions even though some significant decisions may have been made for him or her at preceding levels of decision making.

There are resources to assist the teacher—and other curriculum makers—in some of the decisions to be made. These resources are defined in the conceptual system developed by Goodlad² at the ideological or ideaistic level—a data source composed of the ideas, concepts, or products of scholars which could be used in making curricular decisions. The use of such a data source should make curriculum processes more thoughtful and thus increase the cumulative impact of the curriculum upon student learning. This chapter identifies some of the resources that may be extracted from the ideological data source and used in curriculum decision making at the instructional level. It describes how teachers utilized one product of such a data source, the now well-known *Taxonomy of Educational Objectives: Cognitive Domain*.³ The *Taxonomy* is a useful tool in dealing with cognitive aspects of objectives in curriculum planning. Six broad categories of cognitive behavior are defined which, in turn, are broken down into twenty-one discrete behaviors. According to a commonly held view, objectives must state the type of behavior the student is expected to develop and specify the content or realm of human activity with which the student is to be engaged.[4] The *Taxonomy* can be used as a definition of cognitive behavior and utilized as a basis for the behavioral part of objectives specifying attainment of cognition.

Some Resources for Instructional Planning

Other, similar resources are available from ideological sources. Also, taxonomies for the affective[5] and psychomotor[6] domains of human behavior exist and can be utilized in determining rather precisely what the student should be able to do in acquiring proficiency in these realms. Conceptualizations of human behaviors expressed as precise objectives are designed to give assistance to educators making decisions at the institutional and instructional levels of curriculum. All of this exists. Whether and how to use them is another matter.

Still other types of resources are available to educators working at the instructional level. To assist them in the selection of educational objectives, the Instructional Objectives Exchange (IOX) has been established.[7] IOX provides a comprehensive list of instructional objectives in several content areas. From these lists of objectives, a teacher is able to select those with which she or he is most concerned and plan an instructional program designed to achieve the selected objectives. Sets of test items are also available. These can be used as diagnostic devices to help determine where instruction should begin for a specific objective and as summative evaluative instruments to determine how well the students achieved.

The large array of instructional materials available today is another resource for educators involved in instructional planning. These materials are a rich storehouse to help implement a program. It appears obvious that materials have a significant impact upon what students learn from the curriculum. Not all learning aids have to be created by each teacher, school faculty, or school district for instructional use. Materials now commercially available give educators an incredible array of choices for what to include in the curriculum. Some materials present traditional curricular areas, such as reading and mathematics, in new formats, through new media, and based on new concepts and processes. In addition, there are disciplines and topics not traditionally included in the elementary and secondary school curricula: anthropology, economics, human relationships, oceanography, global education, and many more. Although these learning materials and programs represent a tremendous resource for instruction, they also present complicated problems of making choices. Not only are there choices regarding which materials to include in the curriculum, but in addition there are choices to be made among competing, comprehensive programs in subject fields. Unfortunately, not all learning materials and programs are planned and evaluated as carefully as they should be, but there are now promising efforts to improve the quality of these materials and, thus, the richness of this resource for educators.[8]

Various directories of available learning materials and curriculum projects exist, some of which analyze and evaluate programs according to selected criteria.[9] These directories are designed to alert teachers to programs prepared for specified objectives and can assist the teacher in selecting those that were developed according to some standards or to meet selected evaluative criteria. All of the preceding resources are representative of what Goodlad defines as the ideological or ideaistic data source for curriculum planning.

Using an Ideological Data Source for Instructional Decisions

The existence of such sources, however, does not automatically result in improved decision making; these sources make a difference only when understood and used by teachers. Teachers do not always understand and sometimes fall far short of using these available resources.[10] Therefore, it appears that teachers should be assisted to use such resources more frequently and wisely. In the project reported here, assistance to teachers was provided in using the *Taxonomy* for curriculum decisions at the classroom level. The project sought to develop and use a test for primary school children based on the *Taxonomy*.[11] The *Taxonomy* had been developed by compiling and categorizing objectives drawn from the upper levels of schooling, but its potential usefulness at the lower levels had not been tested. A curriculum in the social studies was developed to help young students develop cognitive behaviors, and a paper-and-pencil test was devised according to the *Taxonomy* in order to determine the success attained in seeking to elicit these behaviors in children of primary school age.

Prior to the initiation of this project, a small group of educators at the University Elementary School, UCLA, began to investigate extant student understanding of a few selected generalizations (considered to be very important in the social studies program) and the effectiveness of two teaching techniques—discussion and dramatic play—in helping students develop these generalizations. This exploration by a few teachers utilized the *Taxonomy* as a basis for defining the behavioral dimensions of instruction. They attempted to determine the level of cognitive behavior reached by students in their discussions and in dramatic play, instruction having been focused upon the selected generalizations. Simultaneously, the faculty as a whole was considering what the overall objectives of the school should be. The entire faculty was also studying the *Taxonomy* as a tool to help clarify school objectives. Thus, the classroom objectives being explored at the instructional level by a few teachers were derivatives of those being developed at the institutional level by the total staff.

Two outcomes of the exploratory activity led to a later, more structured project. First, even though one of the teachers was highly skilled at leading students in stimulating discussions (during which she *thought* she helped students develop some of the higher cognitive behaviors as defined by the *Taxonomy*), an analysis of tapes of these discussions showed that rarely did the teacher call for student behaviors at the application level or higher.[12] The class discussion usually moved on when at least the most vocal children appeared to have acquired basic information. Second, there had been a prepared, very comprehensive content analysis of a social studies unit called "Boats and Harbors," which outlined specific content to be taught as well as statements of some of the major generalizations about the content of the unit. With these two outcomes in hand, a second project was undertaken.[13]

This subsequent project utilized the extensive content analysis of the social studies unit prepared previously, on the one hand, and the *Taxonomy* as the basis for determining the objectives for the classroom program, on the other. The content analysis of the pilot project about "Boats and Harbors" was supplemented with an analysis of the social living aspects of the social studies curriculum. The concern among the teachers about basic research methodology was also included.

During the semester prior to the implementation of this project, the two teachers who were to teach the curriculum met with this writer in a series of meetings designed to familiarize them with principles of curriculum decision making at the instructional level and the *Taxonomy*. These meetings focused at first on the setting of objectives at every level of cognitive behavior in the *Taxonomy*. Considerable time was spent on understanding the objectives, particularly the behavioral part, and then finally came the acceptance by the teachers of those objectives considered to be both important and applicable in their classrooms. The group also discussed ways in which the organizing centers could be set up so that students would have opportunities to deal with the content and to practice the behaviors specified in the objectives. They spent only a limited time on ways of arranging the organizing elements of the curriculum so as to maximize learning.[14]

The teachers were aware that the writer was constructing a test to determine if the behaviors specified in the objectives were, indeed, elicited through goal-directed instruction in the social studies program, but the actual test items were not discussed with the teachers. The teachers knew that the test was to be administered at the end of the instructional unit and that each of the items was designed to elicit a certain behavior selected from the *Taxonomy* in accord with the teachers' objectives. Test items were developed for every objective previously determined by the teachers (with the help of the *Taxonomy*) for the social studies program. After these discussion sessions, extending over a semester, the teachers embarked upon the instructional implementation of the planned curriculum in a team-taught, nongraded group of forty-eight primary school pupils. The writer provided a modicum of guidance and supervision.

At the conclusion of the semester, the test was administered to the pupils. Meanwhile, the writer had established acceptable levels of validity and reliability for the instrument. Although not all of the specific behaviors sought were elicited among these children, the results were encouraging enough to suggest that the *Taxonomy* can be a very useful tool to assist with curriculum decisions at the institutional and instructional levels for primary schooling. For the most part, behavioral levels were determined to be discrete and internally consistent. Admittedly, most of the behaviors elicited were at the lower levels of cognition—that is, the acquiring and understanding of knowledge—but some of the behaviors were also elicited at the upper levels.

An aside regarding the *Taxonomy* itself is in order. The subcategories under the major six held up very well, seemingly discrete from each other, and—with an exception or two—each properly arranged according to its designated classification. It is a data source worth using *for the purposes for which it was intended.*

From the point of view of usefulness, it should be noted that more children reached higher levels of cognitive performance than had been the case before introduction to and initiation in its use and that the class group spread out over a wider array of categories than before. However, these results were attained at considerable expense of time and effort by the teachers. And they had the help throughout of a person with some considerable understanding of the *Taxonomy*. It is doubtful that many teachers go into such enterprises with similar advantages and equivalent preparation—and yet the difficulties were considerable. Perhaps all this provides at least one explanation for teachers' continuing to use relatively simplistic instructional resources such as textbooks and why publishers enter the multimedia field, for example, with caution. We should have relatively little fear at this time of instructional curriculum planning becoming an overly rational process involving systematic analysis and utilization of well-developed ideological or ideaistic resources.

Problems and Issues at the Instructional Level of Curriculum Decisions

The preceding pages describe a process by which an instructional curriculum was planned, implemented, and evaluated. The problems and successes experienced by the teachers involved and the resources available from the ideological data source used suggest a number of problems and issues that need explicit identification. If the planned curriculum—the set of intended learnings[15]—is to be implemented or made operational in the classroom, a critical factor becomes the understanding of and acceptance by the teacher of other preceding decisions about the curriculum. The teacher can resist, modify, or even openly reject preceding decisions—in which case the curriculum planned at societal and institutional levels may never have a chance of being implemented. But even if the teacher accepts and thinks he understands the curriculum planned at preceding levels, there are likely to be difficulties in translating these formal plans into an operational curriculum in the classroom.  A variety of factors affects this translation, assuming that there have been societal and institutional decisions. Among them are the skills, knowledge, and attitudes the teacher possesses; the materials available for use in refining and implementing the curriculum; the operational definiton of significant elements in the subject matter; the role of the student in the process; formative and summative evaluation procedures and instruments; the organizing centers provided to students; and many more.

Even though the legislature may decree (at the societal level) that the values of society should be taught in the schools and even though the school faculty at the institutional level decides that this should be done through a social studies program embracing objectives dealing with intergroup relations, such goals and substance may never be implemented if the classroom teacher does not know about or fails to understand these expectations. An insecure teacher dealing with a vocal group of parents may back away from dealing with issues of prejudice and discrimination in the classroom. A teacher prejudiced against the rights of others will subvert goals seeking tolerance and acceptance of all cultures, all people. An ill-prepared teacher will not know about the available resources from which to draw. Thus, the skills, knowledge, and attitudes of the teacher are a key in the final determination of what is taught and how.

Another factor affecting curriculum planning at the instructional level is the availability of materials on planned topics. With the advent of an open-door policy on China, let us suppose a new curriculum topic on China has been approved at the societal and institutional levels, and now the classroom teacher confronts the need to teach it. A search for materials yields little on China at the appropriate maturity levels. This hampers the teacher both in setting objectives and in making a daily program operational for children. The actual development of curriculum materials for this new topic is probably an unrealistic expectation to hold for the classroom teacher; an array of learning materials from which to choose would enormously facilitate planning for teaching. Low-level cognitive objectives for children such as recalling information from the teacher's lectures or general readings on China provided by the teacher might be possible, but the provision of much more than this would be unrealistic. And to change children's affective behaviors would require considerable involvement in Chinese studies, with a variety of approaches over a period of time. It is well and good to talk about leaving teachers free to choose, but freedom becomes academic when the choices are limited.

The teacher—or other persons planning the curriculum at the instructional level—is also faced with the dilemma of identifying the significant organizing elements around which to arrange specific topics. Preceding levels of planning usually do not provide enough detail for such a task. From such planning there will be suggested topics for each subject, perhaps broad behaviors desired, and value positions to be incorporated into classroom programs. Presumably, teachers are now to translate these into instruction by emphasizing those most important central concepts, skills, and values contained in such expectations. They must select a little from much to accomplish a great deal. It is to be expected that their choices will be random and perhaps even whimsical, except perhaps in those countries where what is to be taught is specified day-by-day and even hour-by-hour from on high, leaving little choice for teachers. Just how much specificity in societal and institutional planning is helpful and how much is restricting to the point of being harmful to teacher creativity in instructional planning is one of the most critical theoretical and practical issues in the field of curriculum.

Another question confronting curriculum planners at all levels, but especially at the classroom level, is the role of the student. There are very few, if any, schools that grant the student total freedom to plan his or her curriculum. Guidelines, criteria, and decisions established elsewhere and by others usually are present to act as constraints upon the student and to determine the curriculum she or he actually experiences. The identical question raised above for teachers is at issue. To what extent should a student's curriculum be planned for him? What should be his participation in this planning? What kind of data should the student contribute to curriculum planning? Is she only to experience the curriculum and not help plan it? There are many points and ways for students to become involved. They might select appropriate organizing centers based on their own interests for achieving predetermined goals. They might determine some goals of their own, an alternative that is seldom open to them, especially at precollegiate levels of schooling. Or, more conservatively, students might help build alternative activities from which to make choices in working toward groups of objectives. It is my belief that much more meaningful ways of involving the student in curriculum decisions must be identified and used.[16] We are at a primitive stage in the much-lauded quest for student self-guidance in learning.

A very practical problem that the classroom teacher must face is to identify ways of evaluating student progress toward the objectives of the curriculum. Curriculum planning conducted remote from classrooms may propose that students be assisted in developing a meaningful philosophy of life. At the instructional level of planning, the teacher becomes concerned not only with how to make this lofty goal operational in a classroom program but also with ways of evaluating student progress toward such an end. Adequate evaluation procedures and instruments for some new trends and topics in the curriculum simply do not exist. When curricula involve values—creativity or empathy, for example—evaluating student progress may be quite difficult if not impossible at this time. It may be impossible for teachers to determine the impact of the curriculum in seeking to help students achieve some of the most significant objectives. The expectation that they make such evaluations can only be frustrating to teachers.

This chapter suggests that planning appropriate organizing centers at the instructional level is exceedingly complex and difficult to do. For example, in the pilot project reported earlier, the teacher skilled in leading discussions found that she was not developing the higher cognitive behaviors she thought she was. The organizing center—in this case discussion of a topic by an entire class—apparently was not providing the necessary stimulus and sustained practice. The preponderance of low-level telling and questioning exhibited by teachers observed in another study[17] suggests that teaching for higher cognitive behaviors is not often practiced by teachers. One of the persistent problems I have identified in my analysis of curriculum materials is the absence of organizing centers designed specifically to help students attain one set of objectives rather than another (or any). Too often the student is led to a preordained set of conclusions by the author of the materials, or reading and discussion elicit only recall when the stated objectives of the materials specify development of higher cognitive abilities. The planning of appropriate organizing centers designed specifically for clearly differentiated objectives could be of assistance in an area where teachers need considerable help. The improvement of instructional decisions requires, in addition to other things, vast improvement in the quality of societal and instructional decisions.

In summary, this chapter has identified some resources available from ideological curriculum planning which are relevant to instructional planning, described an example of curricular decision making at the instructional level using such a resource, and identified some problems and issues associated with implementing curriculum plans at the instructional level. The instructional level of making curricular decisions is one to be guided by more than teacher intuition if any systematic implementation of society's expectations for schooling is to occur. Decisions may be made by default through letting the textbook become the curriculum or by thoughtless acts of commission. But decision making through omission or commission cannot be considered adequate for helping students build the kinds of skills, attitudes, and knowledge they need now and in the future. The Goodlad conceptual system suggests a model for decision making that should help lay people, educators, and students assess current practices and, perhaps, replace considerable chaos in curriculum planning with at least a little more order.

Notes

1. J. Goodlad, *The Development of a Conceptual System for Dealing with Problems of Curriculum and Instruction* (Los Angeles: University of California Cooperative Research Program USOE Project No. 454, 1966).

2. Ibid.

3. B. Bloom, ed., *Taxonomy of Educational Objectives* (New York: Longmans, Green, 1956).

4. This position is outlined in a basic primer of curriculum: R. Tyler, *Basic Principles of Curriculum and Instruction* (Chicago: University of Chicago Press, 1950). There is currently much discussion, however, on how best to state educational objectives and whether behaviorally stated objectives function as a help or hindrance in the educative process. This controversy has been discussed and a possible resolution suggested by L. Tyler and F. Klein in "Not-Either-Or," a paper delivered at the American Educational Research Association Conference, held in New Orleans, Louisiana, in 1973. Although there are other positions in the literature, the stating of educational objectives in behavioral terms appears to be the most popular as well as controversial extant position.

5. D. Krathwohl, B. Bloom, and B. Masia, *Taxonomy of Educational Objectives: Affective Domain* (New York: David McKay Co., 1964).

6. E. Simpson, "The Classification of Educational Objectives, Psychomotor Domain," *Illinois Teacher of Home Economics* 10 (Winter 1966-1967): 110–44.

7. W. Popham, *Instructional Objectives Exchange Rationale Statement* (Los Angeles: P.O. Box 24095, 1970).

8. See, for example, the following articles: L. Tyler and F. Klein, "Caveat Emptor: Let the Educational Buyer Beware," *Educational Technology* (April 1973): 52–54; F. Klein and L. Tyler, "Curriculum, Bone or Bane?" *Elementary School Journal* (February 1972): 225–29; F. Castan, "The Great Instructional Materials Game," *Scholastic Teacher* (February 1973): 10–16.

9. See, for example, *Alert* (Washington, D.C.: U.S. Government Printing Office, 1972); *CAS Curriculum Advisory Service Quarterly* (Chicago: Curriculum Advisory Service, 1973); *Product Development Reports No. 1-20* (Palo Alto, California: U.S. Department of Health, Education, and Welfare Office of Education, American Institute for Research in Behavioral Sciences, 1972); *Seventh Report of the International Clearinghouse on Science and Mathematics Curricular Developments* (College Park, Maryland: University of Maryland Teaching Center, 1970); and *Social Studies Curriculum Materials Data Book* (Boulder, Colorado: Social Science Education Consortium, 1973).

10. See, for example, the following references which suggest that teachers do not always understand or adequately use the concept of behavioral objectives: E. Baker, "Effects on Student Achievement of Behavioral and Nonbehavioral Objectives," *Journal of Experimental Education* 37 (Summer 1969): 5–8; S. Deno and J. Jenkins, "On the 'Behaviorality' of Behavioral Objectives," *Psychology in the Schools* 6 (1969): 18–24.

The following references suggest that the *Taxonomy*, specifically, is not adequately utilized: M. Marksberry, M. McCarter, and R. Noyce, "Relation Between Cognitive Objectives from Selected Texts and from Recommendations of National Committees," *Journal of Educational Research* 62 (May–June 1969): 422–29; R. McFall, "The Development and Validation of an Achievement Test for Measuring Higher Level Cognitive Processes in General Science, *Journal of Experimental Education* 33 (Fall 1964): 103–06; I. Pfeiffer and O. Davis, Jr., "Teacher-Made Examinations—What Kind of Thinking Do They Demand?" *Bulletin of the National Association of Secondary School Principals* 49 (September 1965): 1–10.

11. A more extensive report on the development of the test instrument can be found in M. Klein, "Use of Taxonomy of Educational Objectives (Cognitive Domain) in Constructing Tests for Primary School Pupils," *Journal of Experimental Education* 30 (December 1972): 38–50.

12. Other evidence that reports a similar finding can be found in D. Tinsley, E. Watson, and J. Marshall, "Cognitive Objectives in 'Process-Oriented' and 'Content-Oriented' Secondary Social Studies Program," *Educational Leadership* 30 (December 1972): 245–48.

13. The pilot project and a discussion of organizing centers in curriculum planning has been reported by J. Goodlad, "The Organizing Center in Curriculum Theory and Practice," *Theory Into Practice* 1 (October 1962): 215–21.

14. The major topics of discussion were those discussed by R. Tyler, *Basic Principles*.

15. Goodlad's definition, *Development of a Conceptual System*, p. 12.

16. This view is supported by other writers in the curriculum field. See, for example, Tyler and Klein, "Not-Either-Or"; R. Ojeman, "Who Selects the Objectives of Learning—and Why?" *Elementary School Journal* 71 (February 1971): 262–73; O. Sand, "Curriculum Change," *The Curriculum: Retrospect and Prospect,* 70th Yearbook, National Society for the Study of Education (Chicago: University of Chicago Press, 1971); J. Macdonald, B. Wolfson, and E. Zaret, *Reschooling Society: A Conceptual Model* (Washington: A.S.C.D., 1973).

17. J. Goodlad, M. Klein, and Associates, *Behind the Classroom Door* (rev. 1974, retitled *Looking Behind the Classroom Door*), (Worthington, Ohio: Charles A. Jones, 1970.)

Conceptual-Empiricists

12 Promoting Excellence Through Mastery Learning

James H. Block

Introduction

Conceptual-empiricists view the curriculum field as an opportunity to plan for future interactions and engagements with learners. To understand curriculum in this way—namely as planned intentions, mediation, and systematic ordering according to acceptable assumptions and principles—is to take us logically from the curriculum mapping activity to the actual engagement and interaction with learners. This latter and now acknowledged critical activity is referred to as teaching and instruction.

Until recently, studies of the teaching process and its relationship to student learning have yielded either negative or ambiguous results. Empiricists found either no statistical or educationally significant results from their many studies, or they were unable to replicate positive findings of teaching effectiveness on student achievement. Such an experience leads to a number of flawed conclusions, namely that systematic manipulation and control of the highly complex process known as teaching was at this point in time impossible or that teaching was not a critical experience in the lives of learners. It seemed that other factors, including family background and income, simply explained more of a student's learning and capacity for additional learning.

In the section that follows, James Block provides the reader with a conceptual and empirically verified model of instruction broadly characterized by its supporters as "mastery learning." Based upon an unconventional model of achievement and an approach to instruction that is made systematically operational, mastery learning offers all teachers a theoretical and practical mode of instruction that appears both easy to learn and easy to implement. But the proponents of mastery learning do not rest their approach to pedagogy merely on its usefulness and uncomplicated design; they arm themselves with a barrage of studies that support their assumptions about the nature of learning, the value of certain forms of classroom management, and the view they hold of knowledge.

As you read this essay, think carefully about the basic assumptions that characterize this approach to teaching. Clearly, questions regarding what mastery learning is as well as how it works, and how successful it is should be investigated.

- What if anything is minimized in this model?
- How does mastery learning address itself to the question of school culture?
- What opportunity is provided for students to capitalize upon their own cultural experiences in dealing with school knowledge?
- How are the questions of power and values dealt with in this approach?

Mastery learning is a topic currently creating much controversy and excitement in national and international education circles. The controversy centers around the mastery learning views about human potential to learn and teach; the excitement around mastery learning classroom practices.

This article provides an introduction to mastery learning.[1] First, the article defines what mastery learning is; then it examines how mastery learning works. Lastly it indicates how well mastery learning works.

What Is It?

What is mastery learning? It is two things.

First, mastery learning is an optimistic theory about teaching and learning. Essentially this theory asserts that any teacher can help virtually *all* students to learn excellently; the teacher can help "dumb" students to learn like the "smart" students, "slow" students to learn like the "fast" students, "retarded" students to learn like the "gifted" students. Such teaching, the theory contends, not only improves many students' chances for long-term social and personal prosperity but many teachers' chances as well. In particular, the students acquire those basic intellectual, manual, and emotional competencies which ensure that they can and want to undertake lifelong learning. And the teachers acquire some basic pedagogical skills and career rewards which ensure that they can and want to keep teaching.

Second, mastery learning is an effective set of individualized instructional practices that consistently help *most* students to learn excellently. Some of these practices are of the group-based/teacher-paced variety where students learn cooperatively with their classmates and where the teacher controls the delivery and flow of the instruction. The genotype for these practices would be Bloom/Block's "Learning for Mastery" (LFM) strategy.[2] The remainder of these practices are of the individually based/student-paced variety where students learn independently of their classmates and where each student controls the delivery and flow of the instruction. The genotype for these practices would be Keller's "Personalized System of Instruction" (PSI).[3]

Like other individualized instructional strategies, such as IPI, IGE, and PLAN,[4] both varieties of mastery learning strategies assume that virtually all students can master a great deal of what they are taught in school if the "instruction is approached systematically, if students are helped when and where they have learning difficulties, if they are given sufficient time to achieve mastery, and if there is some clear criterion of what constitutes mastery."[5] Unlike other individualized approaches, however, mastery approaches are designed for use in the typical classroom situation where the teacher already possesses a curriculum which s/he must get through in a fixed period of calendar time, where inordinate amounts of instructional time cannot be spent in diagnostic-progress testing, and where student learning must be graded. Moreover, mastery approaches rely primarily on human beings for their success rather than on machines and other technological devices; teachers decide what goes on in the classroom and use their own instructional techniques and materials, and students guide their own learning as well as the learning of others. Finally, at least one variety of these mastery approaches, namely the group-based/teacher-paced variety, can be implemented without major structural changes in school and classroom organization.

How Does It Work?

How do mastery learning strategies work? Let us describe the group-based/teacher-paced "learning for mastery" strategy. This strategy reflects all the basic mastery learning concepts and ideas. Moreover, it has proved to be one of the easiest mastery learning strategies to implement. We shall begin by describing the various steps in implementing the strategy. Then we shall examine the basic mastery learning concepts and techniques that underpin these steps.

The learning for mastery strategy is designed for use in instructional situations where the calendar time allowed for learning is relatively fixed and where students must be taught largely in groups. This strategy attempts to minimize the time a group of students needs to learn excellently so that this can occur within the fixed amount of calendar time available for instruction. This is accomplished through two distinct sets of steps. One set—the preconditions—occurs outside the classroom and prior to the instruction; the second set—the operating procedures—takes place inside the classroom and during the instruction.

Preconditions for Mastery Learning

Defining Mastery. The teacher who wishes to use a learning for mastery approach begins by formulating what is meant by "mastery" of the subject. Ideally, the teacher would first define what material all students will be expected to learn. This entails the formulation of course objectives. Next, the teacher would prepare a final or summative examination[6] over all these objectives for administration at the course's close. Last, the teacher would set a summative examination score indicative of mastery performance. Students who perform better than this predetermined standard would be graded "masters"; those who do not would be graded "nonmasters."

In actual practice, though, teachers have found it useful to use their old course achievement tests as working definitions of the material that each student will be expected to master. They have also found it convenient to administer one or more of these tests throughout the course for grading purposes. Finally, rather than grade the student's performance on a mastery/nonmastery basis, the teachers have found it useful to fix an absolute grading scale wherein mastery corresponds to a grade of A and nonmastery corresponds to a grade of B, C, D, or F. The teacher forms this scale by determining the level of performance that students traditionally had to exhibit on the course examinations in order to earn an A, B, C, D, or F. All students who achieve to a particular level using mastery learning methods then receive the grade that corresponds to this level.

Planning for Mastery. Now the teacher breaks the course to be taught for mastery into a sequence of smaller learning units, each of which typically covers about two weeks' worth of material. In practice, these units correspond roughly to chapters in the course textbook or to a set of topics.

Next, the teacher sequences these units. After all, the teacher has broken the whole course into pieces; s/he must now recast the pieces into a whole. Teachers of mathematics and sciences have tended to sequence their units linearly so that the material in each unit transfers directly to the next unit. Teachers of arts, humanities, and social sciences, however, have tended to sequence their units hierarchically so that the material in each unit transfers but not necessarily to the next unit. It may transfer to a subsequent unit.

Then, for each unit the teacher develops perhaps the single most important component of the mastery learning strategy: the unit feedback/correction procedures. These procedures will serve to monitor the effectiveness of the group-based instruction and to supplement it where necessary to better suit the learning requirements of certain students.

First, the teacher constructs a brief, ungraded diagnostic progress test or "formative" evaluation instrument[7] for each unit. These tests are explicitly designed to be an integral part of each unit's instruction and to provide specific information or feedback to both the teacher and the student about how the student is changing as a result of the group-based instruction.

Next, the teacher specifies a score or performance standard on each formative test that when met will be indicative of unit mastery. Usually a score of 80 to 90 percent correct on a formative test indicates that the student is not having learning problems.

Finally, the teacher develops a set of alternative instructional materials and procedures or "correctives" keyed to each item on each unit's formative test. Typically these correctives have consisted of cooperative small-group study sessions, individual tutoring by classmates, or alternative learning aids such as different textbooks, workbooks, audiovisual materials, academic games/puzzles, and affective exercises.

Each corrective is designed to reteach the material tested by certain items on the unit formative test but to do so in ways that will differ from the unit's initial group-based instruction. The correctives may present the material in a different sensory mode or modes or in a different form of the same mode than the group-based instruction. They may involve the student in a different way and/or provide not only different types of encouragements for learning but also different amounts of each type. Hence, should a student encounter difficulty in learning certain material from the group-based instruction unit, he can then use the correctives to explore alternative ways of learning the unmastered material, select those correctives best suited to his particular learning requirements, and overcome his learning problems before they impair subsequent learning.

Operating Procedures for Mastery Learning

Orienting for Mastery. The teacher is now ready to teach. Since students are not accustomed to learning for mastery or to the notion that they all might earn A's, the teacher must usually spend some time at the outset of the course orienting them to the procedures to be used—what they are expected to learn, how they are generally expected to learn it, and to what level they are expected to learn. My experience has been that this orientation period—combined with continual encouragement, support, and positive evidence of learning success—is crucial in developing in most students the belief that they can learn and the motivation to learn.

The typical orientation periods have stressed the following:
1. The students are going to learn by a new method of instruction designed to help all of them learn well.
2. Each student will be graded *solely* on the basis of his performance on the final examination(s).
3. Each student will be graded against a predetermined performance standard and not in relation to the performance of his classmates. The standard of A work has been indicated.
4. Each student who attains this standard will receive an A.
5. There will be no fixed number of A's. Accordingly, cooperation with classmates in learning need not hurt a student's chances of earning an A. If a student and his classmates cooperate, and all of them learn well, then all will earn A's.
6. Each student will receive all the help he needs so as to learn. So if a student cannot learn in one way, then alternative ways will be readily available.
7. Throughout the course, each student will be given a series of ungraded diagnostic-progress tests to promote and pace his learning. He should use the information provided by these tests to locate misunderstandings and errors in learning.
8. Each student with learning problems will be given a number of alternative learning procedures or correctives to help him overcome his particular errors and misunderstandings.
9. The student should use his choice of the suggested correctives to "correct" these errors and misunderstandings before they accumulate and impair his subsequent learning.

Teaching for Mastery. Following this orientation period, the teacher teaches the first learning unit, using his or her customary group-based teaching methods. When this instruction has been completed, and before moving to the next unit, the teacher then administers the unit's formative test to the entire class. Next, each student usually corrects his or her own test. Finally, using a show of hands to discover the test results, the teacher certifies those students who have achieved the unit mastery standard and identifies those who have not. The former students are free to engage in enrichment activities and/or to serve as tutors for their "slower" classmates; the latter are asked to use the appropriate correctives to complete their unit learning.

The teacher then announces when the group-based instruction for the next unit will commence, and both sets of students are given responsibility for making use of the opportunities provided. If the teacher desires to postpone the start of the next unit, the students are given in-class as well as out-of-class time to discharge their respective responsibilities. If the teacher does not desire to postpone the start of the next unit, then the students must use out-of-class time.

The teacher repeats this cycle of initial instruction, diagnostic-progress testing, and certification or individual correction, unit by unit, until all units have been taught. The cycle is paced so that the teacher covers just as much material as would ordinarily be covered. Two pacing options are possible. If all the student enrichment/tutoring or correction responsibilities are to be discharged outside of class, then the teacher may pace each unit's instruction as in the past. However, if some or all responsibilities are to be discharged in class, the teacher can adjust the pace of the instruction, allowing more time for the early units and less time for the later ones. Essentially, the teacher borrows time that would ordinarily be spent on later units and spends this time on the earlier units. The assumption is that this borrowed time will not be needed later if students learn for mastery earlier.

Grading for Mastery. The teacher finally administers the course summative examination and awards A's or their equivalent to all students whose test scores are at or above the predetermined mastery performance standard. Those students who score below this level are awarded grades appropriate to the level they have achieved.

Some Basic Concepts

As noted earlier, some basic concepts about instruction underlie each of the preceding steps. Figure 12-1 indicates these concepts and the associated mastery techniques.

At the most general level, the conceptual level, mastery learning strategies are *systematic* approaches to instruction. They attempt to build a strong bridge between what the teacher desires to teach and whom s/he wants to teach. First, the instruction is matched to the course outcomes the teacher seeks, that is, all mastery strategies are outcome based. Then, the instruction is matched to the learners to be taught, that is, all mastery strategies provide multiple methods for each student to attain each of these outcomes.

At a more specific level, the extra classroom level, mastery learning strategies are *proactive* approaches to instruction. Much of the teacher's time, effort, and energy is spent in planning outside of class for possible inside-of-class contingencies. Thus, when these contingencies occur, the teacher is ready for them. S/he need not waste valuable time, effort, and energy reactively manufacturing all solutions on the spot.

Proactive teaching, from a mastery learning perspective, entails several stages. One stage is the definition of the learning outcomes the teacher is seeking. Obviously if the teacher has no clear idea of where his or her instruction is headed, then s/he is more likely to be seduced by fruitless pedagogical detours.

Outcome definition is a two-step process. First, the practitioner must implicitly define what all students will be expected to attain and at what levels.

Concepts

General

A. Approach instruction *systematically*: It should provide a bridge between *whom* and *what* you teach
   1. Match instruction to *outcomes*
   2. Match instruction to *learners*

Specific: Extra Classroom

B. Be *proactive*, not reactive
   1. Clarify *outcomes*
   2. Provide for appropriate *help* in learning
   3. Provide for appropriate *learning time*

Specific: Intraclassroom

C. Manage *learning*, not learners
   1. Provide *student orientation*
   2. Vary *how* and *how long* each student is taught as necessary
   3. *Personalize grading*

Techniques

→ Base instruction on outcomes
→ Provide multiple instructional methods

→ Predefine mastery and make it explicit
→ Preplan instruction for mastery
→ Preplan instruction for mastery

→ Orient students to mastery learning
→ Use preplanned instruction to teach for mastery
→ Grade for mastery

Figure 12-1
Mastery learning: how does it work?

Second, the practitioner must make his or her implicit definitions more explicit so they communicate clearly to the teacher what must be taught and to the students what must be learned.

Both of these steps are accomplished in mastery learning strategies in the process of defining mastery. When the mastery practitioner formulates the course instructional objectives and constructs a special course final or "summative" examination based upon them, the practitioner has explicated what all students will be expected to attain. And when s/he sets some mastery grading standards on the summative examination, the practitioner has explicated what levels all students will be expected to attain.

A second stage in proactive teaching is the provision of appropriate help in learning. Oftentimes student learning problems at one point in the classroom instruction are caused by unresolved problems from earlier points. So these earlier problems must be identified and corrected as they occur.

This identification and correction is accomplished in mastery learning strategies through the preplanning of the classroom instruction. First, the teacher breaks the entire course into smaller learning units. Each unit is long enough to convey a number of skills, ideas, concepts, and appreciations but small enough to allow the close monitoring of each student's learning as the units, that is, the course, unfolds. Second, the teacher sequences these units so that the material in one unit is used over and over in the subsequent units. This procedure helps ensure that if this material is taught well once, then the material will not be forgotten and will be available for later use. Finally, the teacher formulates a plan of mastery instruction for each unit consisting of (a) the *original instruction*, whereby the unit's material will be taught initially—typically this instruction will be similar in content and delivery, if not identical, to the teacher's customary group-based instruction; (b) a *feedback* instrument (pencil and paper or otherwise) whereby each student's learning from the original instruction can be described diagnostically and prescriptively; (c) a *mastery standard* whereby sufficient and insufficient learning progress can be judged; and (d) the *correction* whereby the unit's material can be taught in a variety of ways different from the original instruction. This plan enables the teacher to monitor student learning as it unfolds on a unit-by-unit basis and to exercise a necessary measure of quality control should the learning ever unfold less than excellently.

A third stage in proactive teaching is the provision of appropriate learning time. Clearly, if each student is to be provided with appropriate help in learning, then sufficient time must be found to make use of this help. All students cannot be allowed the same amount of learning time, if this time is insufficient for most students.

The provision of appropriate learning time is also accomplished through the preplanning of the classroom instruction. This preplanning helps, first, to increase the quantity of time that each student spends in learning. Essentially, it constrains each student to spend as much time as necessary to master the material in one unit before attempting the material in the next one. For many students, this means spending far more learning time in class and/or outside of class than is customary. They can no longer passively settle for mediocrity or worse in their learning; they must actively pursue excellence. The preplanning helps, second, to increase the quality of the time that each student spends in learning. Essentially, it helps to ensure that no student spends unnecessary time learning by methods that are poorly suited to his or her learning requirements. If any student cannot learn excellently from the original instruction, the student can learn excellently from one or more correctives. S/he need not waste time restudying the ineffective original instruction.

At the most specific level, the intraclassroom level, mastery strategies are *management of learning* approaches to instruction. They propose that inside the classroom ". . . the function of the teacher is to specify what is to be learned, to motivate pupils to learn it, to provide them with instructional materials, to administer these materials at a rate suitable for each pupil, to monitor students' progress, to diagnose difficulties and provide proper remediation for them, to give praise and encouragement for good performance, and to give review and practice that will maintain pupils' learning over long periods of time."[8]

The management of learning is executed in three basic stages by mastery practitioners. In the orientation stage, they indicate, in a concrete fashion, how and toward what ends students will be taught. Obviously, no instructional technique can succeed if the ground in which it is sown is not properly prepared.

In the teaching stage, they then vary, as necessary, how and how long each student is taught by using their preplanned instructional units. The original instruction for each unit gives all students a chance to learn excellently from one method of instruction over one period of time. The feedback instrument and mastery standard indicates those students for whom the original instruction and the initial learning time was sufficient and for whom it was not. The unit's correctives provide these latter students with the opportunity to master the material not mastered from the original instruction using additional methods of instruction and additional learning time as necessary.

In the grading stage, the practitioner evaluates students on a more personal basis. Students are graded for what they actually have learned. In short, they are graded for mastery. Such mastery grading is designed to engage what White[9] has called "competence motivation," that is, the intrinsic desire to compete against oneself and the material to be learned, and to disengage what I have alluded to as "competition motivation,"[10] that is, the extrinsic desire to compete against others. From the standpoint of developing the talent of all students rather than a few, the engagement of the former motivation makes much more sense that the engagement of the latter.

How Well Does It Work?

How well, then, does mastery learning work? As numerous practitioners have discovered, mastery learning represents a particular commitment about education, that is, an innovative philosophy and set of practices for its improvement.[11] But is this commitment, like so many others, "attractively argued but unsupported by data"[12] or supported by data that indicates it works 51 percent of the time and fails 49 percent of the other? The answer is no! Mastery learning strategies may not work quite as well as their advocates propose, but they do work very well indeed.

Let us review the mastery learning research according to criteria set out by Dunkin and Biddle[13] for evaluating any commitment. These are:

1. that a given teaching practice is presently occurring in typical classrooms;
2. that an alternative teaching practice can be encouraged by changes in teacher education programs;
3. that the alternative teaching practice produces more desirable classroom processes or (preferably) products in pupil growth than the present practice."[14]

Classroom Usage. There can be no question that mastery learning ideas and practices are presently occurring in many typical classrooms. Indeed, as I note in a special issue of *Educational Leadership* on mastery learning,[15] with the help of dedicated practitioners and administrators, of innovative teacher in-service and preservice programs, or progressive national and international educational organizations (for example, ASCD, NEA, NASA, UNESCO, IEA), of leading educational publishers (for example, McGraw-Hill, SRA, Westinghouse Learning Corporation, Random House), and of powerful news media (for example, the *New York Times*, CBS Television), mastery learning has helped reshape the face of contemporary educational practice. Not only are mastery learning ideas being widely implemented here, they are also being widely implemented abroad.

Two trends in the classroom usage of mastery learning are now obvious. One trend is the growing use of mastery learning ideas and practices on a large-scale basis. Mastery learning is being used with a greater *number* of subjects, classes, teachers, and schools than ever before. Whereas in the early part of the 1970s the typical experiment involved one subject, class, teacher, and school; the current experiments often involve many subjects, classes, teachers, and schools. Indeed, in North America one can find entire school districts (for example, Chicago, Denver, District of Columbia, New Orleans, Philadelphia, Vancouver) actively plumbing the value of mastery learning for their particular educational situation and, especially for purposes of competency-based-education.[16] What is true here is even more true abroad. Countries such as South Korea, Indonesia, and Australia already have large-scale tests of mastery learning under way, with the South Korean tests involving several million students in all the subjects grades 1-9. About ten to twenty other member nations of the IEA (International Study of Educational Achievement) should have additional large-scale tests off the ground by 1981-82.

The second trend is the growing use of mastery learning ideas and practices on a more adaptive basis. Mastery learning is being used by more variety of subjects, classes, teachers, and schools to meet particular needs. Whereas in the early part of the 1970s, the typical experiment involved:
1. subjects that were basic, required, "closed," and oriented toward convergent thinking;
2. classes that were small and "regular";
3. teachers who were inexperienced, behaviorally or cognitively oriented, and "majority" members; and
4. schools that were suburban, elementary level, academically oriented, and public.

The current experiments increasingly involve:
5. subjects that are intermediate or advanced, elective, "open," and oriented toward divergent thinking;
6. classes that are large and "special" (for example, handicapped, bilingual);
7. teachers who are experienced, humanistically oriented, and "minority" members; and
8. schools that are urban and rural, secondary and tertiary level, technically or professionally oriented, and private.

Teacher Training. There also can be no question that mastery learning ideas and practices can be taught to teachers. Teachers both here and abroad have participated in countless local, regional, statewide, and national preservice and in-service teacher training workshops and credentialing courses. Moreover, the experiences gleaned from these workshops and courses have already been packaged in a variety of how-to-do-it manuals, perhaps the best known of which are Block's and Anderson's *Mastery Learning in Classroom Instruction*, Keller's and Sherman's, *The Keller Plan Handbook*, Okey's and Ciesla's, *Mastery Teaching*, and Torshen's, *The Mastery Approach to Competency-Based Education*. More workshops and courses and how-to-doit manuals are bound to appear.

Nor can there be much question that once teachers are taught for mastery they can use their training in the classroom. Okey,[17] for example, taught twenty in-service teachers and twenty preservice interns how to teach for mastery and then followed them back to their classrooms. He found that students noted a perceptible change in their teachers' and interns' behavior when they taught for mastery. For example, students saw the teachers and interns as telling them what they were expected to learn, allowing them different amounts of learning time, and using diagnostic tests to monitor their progress.

But there is a distinct question as to whether inexperienced preservice teachers use their training as effectively as experienced in-service ones do. Okey,[18] for example, found that in-service teachers were far more likely to elicit greater learning from their students under mastery learning conditions than preservice interns. And my own experience, as well as that of others, has been similar. Perhaps this is because learning how to teach for mastery requires less in the way of the acquisition of a whole new set of teaching skills and more in the way of orchestrating and supplementing the skills one already has. Preservice interns would tend to have fewer classroom skills to orchestrate than in-service teachers.

Student Outcomes. Lastly, there can be little question that mastery learning ideas and practices promote student growth. Indeed, the impact that mastery learning ideas and practices have had on student cognitive and affective development has been remarkable.

Consider, for example, a recent review by Block and Burns[19] of some forty rigorous studies of student outcomes under mastery and nonmastery approaches to instruction. These echoed the general findings of earlier and later reviews. Block and Burns reported the following:

Learning effectiveness: Mastery-taught students typically learned more effectively than their nonmastery-taught counterparts. Whether learning was measured in terms of student achievement or in terms of student retention, they almost always learned more, and usually significantly more, and they learned more like one another.

Learning efficiency: Mastery-taught students also typically learned more efficiently than their nonmastery-taught counterparts. Whereas in the nonmastery-taught classrooms some students learned several times as fast as other students, in the mastery-taught classrooms individual differences in learning rate were substantially less. In fact, in these latter classrooms individual differences in learning rate seemed headed toward a vanishing point in which even the "slowest" students would learn roughly as fast as the "fastest" students.

Learner affect: Lastly, mastery-taught students liked their learning, their teaching, and themselves better than their nonmastery-taught counterparts. They virtually always responded more positively than their counterparts, for example, on measures of interest in and attitudes toward the subject matter learned, of self-concept (academic as well as general), of academic self-confidence, of attitudes toward cooperative learning, and of attitudes toward the instruction. Whether their more favorable affective responses were just momentary expressions of enthusiasm or more permanent ones that would carry over into their subsequent work was, however, indeterminable.

Summary

This article has provided an introduction to the topic of mastery learning. Specifically, the article addressed three questions: what is mastery learning, how does it work, and how well does it work?

We have learned that mastery learning is essentially an optimistic theory about teaching and learning and an effective set of individualized instructional practices for implementing this theory in the ordinary classroom setting. At the heart of this theory is the assertion that any teacher can help virtually all of his or her students to learn excellently.

We have also learned that mastery learning works on the basis of three large assumptions about what constitutes teaching for excellence. The most general of these assumptions is that the teacher must approach his or her instruction more systematically in the sense that the instruction should definitely bridge what is to be taught to whom is to be taught. This means that the instruction for mastery learning is outcome based and provides multiple ways for each student to reach each outcome.

A more specific assumption is that the teacher must become more proactive in his or her instruction in the sense that more time, effort, and energy is spent outside of class readying for possible inside-of-class contingencies. This means that the teacher predefines and explicates "mastery" in learning so that the classroom outcomes s/he is seeking are clear. And the teacher preplans the classroom instruction for mastery learning so that it consistently provides appropriate help and learning time for each student.

The most specific assumption is that the teacher must concentrate more heavily on the management of learning in the classroom. This means the teacher orients students to learning for mastery so that they are clear about how and what they will be taught. The teacher also uses the preplanned classroom instruction for mastery learning so that how and how long each student is taught varies appropriately. And the teacher grades for mastery learning so that each student is graded on a more personal and less competitive basis.

Lastly, we have learned that mastery learning has worked very well indeed. Mastery learning ideas and practices are being widely used in classrooms both here and abroad, and their use is on the rise. They are also being widely disseminated to preservice and in-service teachers. When the ideas and practices have been learned and used, they have consistently promoted student growth. Students have not only learned more effectively and efficiently, they have also felt better about their learning, their instruction, and themselves.

Much that we have learned about mastery learning theory, practice, and research will, of course, seem "old hat" to some educators. After all, an optimistic faith in all students' capacity for excellent learning, an approach to instruction that is systematic, proactive, and learning oriented, and an approach that consistently promotes student cognitive and affective growth have long been the trademarks of the *paragons* of the teaching profession. What should be "new hat," however, is the message that mastery learning theory, practice, and research now offers these trademarks of our best teachers to *all* our teachers. Surely, at a time when public confidence in the teaching profession is low, such a message cannot be ignored.

Notes

1. See the following for more detailed treatments: L. W. Anderson and J. H. Block, "Mastery Learning," in *Handbook on Educational Psychology: Instructional Practice and Research*, ed. D. Treffinger, J. Davis, and R. Ripple (New York: Academic Press, 1976); J. H. Block, ed., *Mastery Learning: Theory and Practice* (New York: Holt, Rinehart & Winston, 1971); J. H. Block, ed., *Schools, Society, and Mastery Learning* (New York: Holt, Rinehart & Winston, 1974); J. H. Block and L. W. Anderson, *Mastery Learning in Classroom Instruction* (New York: Macmillan, 1975); J. H. Block and R. B. Burns, "Mastery Learning," in *Review of Research in Education*, vol. 4, ed. L. Shulman (Itasca, Ill.: F. E. Peacock, 1976); B. S. Bloom, *Human Characteristics and School Learning* (New York: McGraw-Hill, 1976); K. P. Torshen, *The Mastery Approach to Competency-based Education* (New York: Academic Press, 1977).

2. Block and Anderson, "Mastery Learning."

3. See F. S. Keller and J. G. Sherman, *The Keller Plan Handbook* (Menlo Park, Calif.: W. A. Benjamin, 1974).

4. See H. Talmage, ed., *Systems of Individualized Education* (Berkeley: McCutchan, 1975); N. Gronlund, *Individualizing Classroom Instruction* (New York: Macmillan, 1974); R. K. Hambleton, "Testing and Decision-making Procedures for Selected Individualized Instructional Programs," *Review of Educational Research* 44 (1974): 371–400.

5. B. S. Bloom, "An Introduction to Mastery Learning Theory," in *Schools, Society and Mastery Learning*, ed. J. H. Block (New York: Holt, Rinehart & Winston, 1974), p. 6.

6. B. S. Bloom, J. T. Hastings, and G. F. Madaus, *Handbook on Formative and Summative Evaluation of Student Learning* (New York: McGraw-Hill, 1971).

7. Ibid.

8. J. B. Carroll, "Problems of Measurement Related to the Concept of Learning Mastery," in *Mastery Learning: Theory and Practice*, ed. J. H. Block (New York: Holt, Rinehart & Winston, 1971), pp. 29–30.

9. R. W. White, "Motivation Reconsidered: The Concept of Competence," *Psychological Review* 66 (1959): 297–333.

10. J. H. Block, "Motivation, Evaluation, and Mastery Learning," *UCLA Educator* 19: 2 (Winter 1977): 31–36.

11. M. J. Dunkin and B. J. Biddle, *The Study of Teaching* (New York: Holt, Rinehart & Winston, 1974).

12. Ibid., p. 51.

13. Dunkin and Biddle, *Study of Teaching*.

14. Ibid., p. 52.

15. J. H. Block, "Mastery Learning: The Current State of the Craft," *Educational Leadership* 37:2 (November 1979): 114–17.

16. W. G. Spady, "The Concept and Implications of Competency-based Education," *Educational Leadership* 36 (1978): 16–22.

17. J. R. Okey, "Development of Mastery Teaching Materials," Final Evaluation, Rep., USOE G-74-2990 (Bloomington, Indiana: Indiana University, 1975).

18. Ibid.

19. Block and Burns, "Mastery Learning."

13 The Learning Basis of Teaching Methods

Robert M. Gagné

Introduction

Information-processing learning theory and research serve as one of the more promising educational efforts in the search for a scientific basis for teaching. In this quest for linkages between human thought processes and teaching processes, conceptual-empiricists have borrowed heavily from the models of human thinking and the findings of research generated by cognitive psychologists.

In an effort to construct a model of instruction that links learning to teaching, Robert Gagné relates information-processing activities to sequential phases of instruction. Gagné's essay identifies eight distinct but hierarchical learning processes: motivation, attention, rehearsal, coding, retrieval, transfer of learning, response, and feedback. According to Gagné, these internal mental activities are influenced by a series of external planned events called instruction. These instructional events in Gagné's model correspond to learning processes, which are: apprehending, acquisition, retention, recall, generalization, performance, and feedback.

Beyond these important connections of learning and instruction, Gagné postulates a dimension of instruction that deals with learning outcomes and argues that there are five varieties: verbal information, intellectual skills, cognitive strategies, attitudes, and motor skills. In all, this detailed presentation examines the internal processes of learning, the external planned instructional environment that interacts with the learner's processing of information, and the outcomes of these interactions.

As you read, think about the following questions:
- What meaning does Gagné assign to each of the learning processes in his hierarchy?

- What is the corresponding relationship of these learning processes to each instructional phase?
- How would you go about the activity of linking a learning process and an instructional phase to a learning outcome?

The practice of teaching incorporates both the planning and delivery of instruction. Teaching in both these aspects may be done with individuals or groups, by the use of a number of different methods and their combinations—lecturing, discussion, tutoring, or the use of games—and by using various media including printed texts, pictures, television, and films. And, of course, teaching is done in connection with a great variety of subjects—from reading in an elementary classroom to the traditional categories of the high school curriculum and to the vocational and avocational pursuits of adult education.

With all of this variety of means and modes, it nevertheless remains true that the central purpose of teaching is the promotion of *learning* in individuals called students. As a consequence, it seems reasonable to expect that, whatever particular method or style the teacher may choose on any given occasion or whatever variation in teaching approach he may consider desirable, he will continue to maintain the support of learning as his primary goal. In pursuit of this goal, it is evident that the teacher must make a host of individual decisions concerning what kinds of stimulation to present to the learner, what communications to make, what questions to ask, what sorts of confirmation of the learner's productions to provide, and many other decisions of this general sort. These decisions are based upon the teacher's understanding of what is happening to the student as a learner; that is, they are influenced by the teacher's conceptualization of the *processes* of learning and the *expected outcomes* to which these processes lead.

Descriptions of the procedures and methods of teaching must likewise take into account the goal of promotion of learning, including remembering and the transfer of learning. The events that are planned by the teacher and responded to by the teacher as parts of the instructional situation are conceptually related to processes that are operating within the student to produce outcomes that are newly learned, retained, and applied. Accordingly, a *model* of these processes provides an essential framework for describing the activities of teaching that are designed to support or otherwise influence them. In the following sections of this chapter, three questions are considered for the purpose of providing a reference framework of learner processes to which the actions of the teacher may be related. These questions are:

1. What are the processes involved in learning, retention, and transfer of learning? (Process of learning.)

Reprinted, with permission, from *The Psychology of Teaching Methods*, Seventy-fifth Yearbook of the National Society for the Study of Education, Part I (Chicago: University of Chicago Press, 1976), pp. 21–43.

2. What is the sequence of transformations brought about by these processes? (Phases of learning.)
3. What kinds of outcomes of learning processes can be inferred from human performance? (Capabilities and dispositions produced by learning.)

Learning Models

A model of learning has the function of identifying the structures and processes that need to be taken into account in giving an adequate rational explanation for the learning event. These structures and their associated processes are derived as hypothetical constructs from empirical research findings by means of rational inference. Their existence as constructs also depends upon continued verification from empirical data. As customarily used, a model serves to identify the structures and processes involved in learning but does not necessarily predict the quantitative values of the operation of these processes. Thus, a model is merely the beginning of a learning theory; in fact, alternative theories of individual processes or combinations of processes may be equally compatible with a given model.

A Prototypical Model

While it seems reasonable that theories of learning that make possible quantitative prediction of learning outcomes may have important implications for instruction, such theories have not yet achieved this state of development. Models that identify learning structures and processes, however, are currently available and appear to have substantial applicability to the understanding of instructional events. There are several such models, employed as frameworks for a variety of theories of human learning and memory.[1] Recent trends in such theories have been reviewed by Greeno and Bjork,[2] who also developed a basic model emphasizing common features of other models. A similar prototype is shown in Figure 13-1.

In brief, the model depicts the following flow of information from one hypothesized structure to another: a stimulus input from the receptors enters the sensory register (a very short-lived memory store) and then the short-term memory, where it persists for about thirty seconds or less. Rehearsal by the learner can maintain information here for longer periods. It is then coded for storage and transferred to the long-term memory, assumed to be a permanent repository. Later the information is retrieved, following a search, and when recovered is transferred again to the short-term memory (in a sense, to the "forefront" of memory). At this point its appropriateness is considered, resulting in a decision for further search or for the generation of responses that result in performance by activation of the response generator. Important components of the model are the executive control processes, by means of which the various kinds of information transfer are activated and modified. A similar

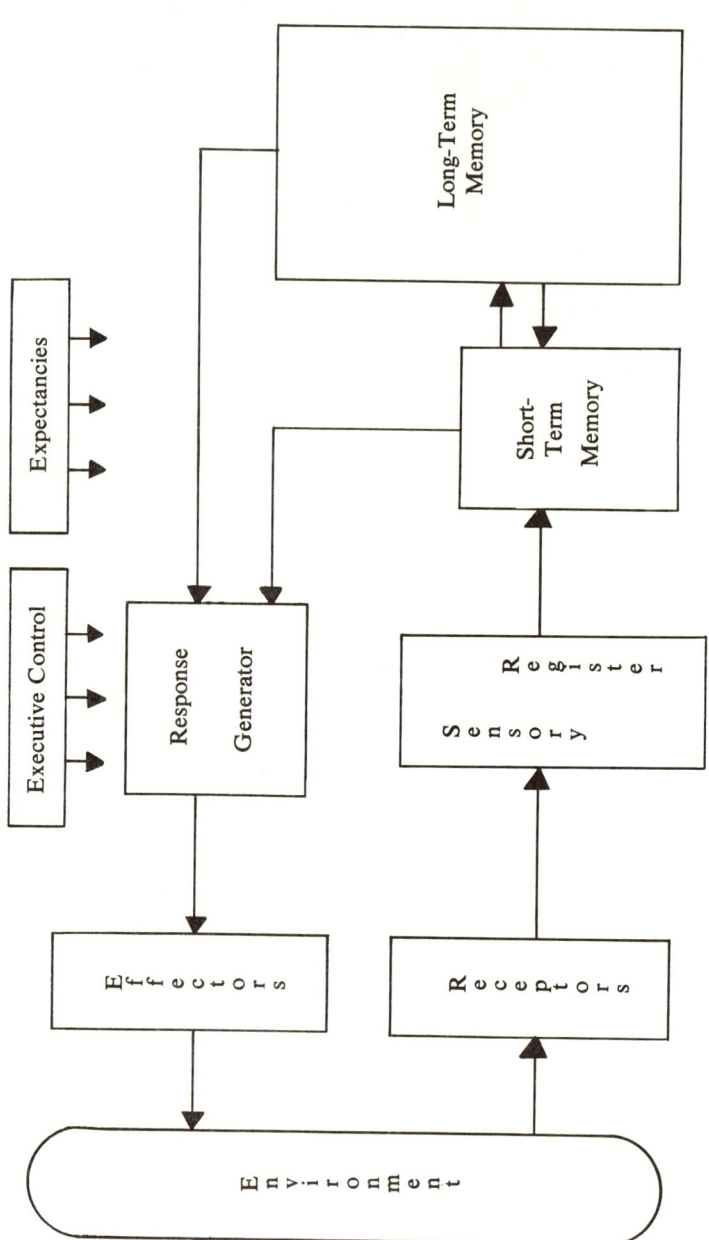

Figure 13-1.
A prototype of models employed by contemporary information-processing theories of learning and memory

function may be proposed for expectancies established in preparation for an act of learning.[3] Specific flow connections of these processes are not indicated in the figure, since most theories do not identify them in detail.[4]

When described in this brief manner, it is evident that the model provides little more than a framework to which descriptions of the processes required to make the necessary transformations of information from one structure to another can be added. It is these processes that are targets of explanation, in part or in whole, for contemporary theories of learning and memory. Accordingly, the model in Figure 13-1 can well serve the purpose of a referent learning model relevant to teaching. A detailed review of research findings relevant to the model has been presented by Kumar.[5]

Learning Processes

The model for learning and memory may be examined to reveal the processes it identifies that occur during an act of learning. Some of these processes are entirely familiar, in the sense that they have been investigated over a period of many years (for example, attention, selective perception). Others, like coding and retrieval, have more recently come into prominence as parts of contemporary theory.

Motivation. As given in Figure 13-1, the model includes the process whereby the motivation of the learner is brought to bear upon learning and memory. It seems reasonable to assume that this process exerts its effects by means of a *set* or *expectancy* established prior to the act of learning itself. Such an interpretation is suggested by Estes.[6] An expectancy set, persisting during the learning act, may be seen as one kind of "executive control process." Such a set may act to guide a number of other processes involved in learning. In particular it may be expected to influence the type of performance that eventuates from learning, thus setting the stage for feedback that serves to confirm the expectancy. The notion of expectancy is associated with the concept of reinforcement, the implications of which for an information-processing model have been examined by Atkinson and Wickens.[7] As will be pointed out later, the process of expectancy is of singular importance in its implications for teaching.

Attention: Selective Perception. These processes (or this process) serve the important function of modifying the information flow from the sensory register to the short-term memory (Figure 13-1). The array of stimulation that reaches the learner through his sensory register is acted upon selectively by means of this process in such a way that certain salient features of it are "attended to" and "perceived." Thus they are "perceptually coded" for storage or further processing in the short-term memory.

Rehearsal. Without further processing, the contents of short-term memory decay fairly rapidly. They may, however, be maintained for longer periods by means of a control process called rehearsal. Since short-term memory is often considered to function as a "working memory,"[8] rehearsal processes are conceived as playing an active role in the relating of new information to that previously acquired.

Coding. The information in the short-term memory is transformed in several different ways for entry into long-term memory. The individual learners may have alternative control processes available that can be utilized for the purpose of coding. Relating the newly learned item to larger organized bodies of information is one example of a coding process; transforming it into an image is another. Most importantly, coding transforms the material into conceptual form for storage as propositions, as conceived by Kintsch[9] or by Anderson and Bower.[10]

Search and Retrieval. Retrieval is generally conceived as a process of search, aided by cues from the learner's environment or from other parts of her memory. Material which is stored in memory becomes "accessible"[11] when revived by such cues. Frequently, selected portions of what has been learned are retrieved and recovered by the short-term memory (the "working memory") where they may be used in further learning or as inputs in response generation.

Generalization: Transfer of Learning. Presumably, the transfer of acquired knowledge to new situations depends in part upon how this knowledge is stored and also upon what cues are available for recovering it in the new situation. This conception implies that there can be "coding for transfer" as one form of "coding for retrieval." It seems likely that the transfer of learning may require processes beyond those of storage and retrieval. Transferability of knowledge and skill is of course a matter of great importance to the design and conduct of instruction.

Response Generation. The contents of long-term memory, or of information recovered to the working (short-term) memory, are transformed into the performances of the learner. It is these performances, of course, that enable the external observer to verify that learning has in fact taken place.

Feedback. An act of learning is completed when the learner receives information to the effect that his performance has met certain expectations. There is, in other words, a confirmation of the expectancy that was activated at the initiation of the learning act. Some theorists interpret feedback in ways that do not involve expectancy confirmation. Virtually all, however, agree in identifying as *reinforcement* those events that provide positive feedback.

Phases of Learning and Phases of Instruction

The processes required to account for the phenomena of learning are *internal* processes, rational constructs of the model builder. Many of them, however—and perhaps all of them—are affected by events that are *external* to the learner, that is, external sources of stimulation from his or her environment. It is these external events that may be planned and executed in ways that serve to activate, maintain, facilitate, or enhance the internal processes of learning. When planned and conducted to promote learning by any of these means, these external events are called *instruction*. They are, accordingly, the particular province of the teacher.

The Phases of Instruction

The sequence of transformational events effected by learning processes follows the sequence in which these processes are listed in the previous section. As these events unfold in the course of an act of learning, they may be influenced to a greater or lesser degree and in a number of different ways by the external events of instruction. Some processes (for example, the establishment of expectancy) are obviously affected by instruction, whereas others (for example, the internal processes of memory storage) may be only indirectly influenced. It seems reasonable, therefore, to distinguish as successive *phases of instruction* those interactions of external stimulation and learning processes that can most clearly alter the course of learning. Designating instructional phases in this way helps to emphasize the function of instruction as supportive of learning and thus to suggest the variety of tasks involved in teaching.

Parenthetically, it may be noted that as the learner develops in sophistication, many of the events of instruction, initially observed as planned external events, come to be accomplished by the learner himself. In other words, to a greater or lesser degree, he becomes a "self-learner." He may supply his own motivation, develop his own system of coding, initiate strategies of search and retrieval, and supply his own feedback. Naturally, the teacher wishes to encourage this growing tendency toward independent learning. This is done in a number of ways, including the progressive reduction in external "cueing" for coding and retrieval processes as the learner develops.

The phases of instruction, as related to the processes of learning previously described, may be identified as follows.

Motivation Phase. The preparation for learning is accomplished by instruction, which activates motivation by appealing to student interests. Communications of the teacher during this phase have the additional purpose of relating these interests to an expectancy of "what the student will be able to do" once he has learned.

Apprehending Phase. During this phase teaching is concerned with arousing attention in a general sense and also with providing stimulation (often verbal), which "directs" attention so that particular features of the stimulus situation are selectively perceived.

Acquisition Phase. This phase of instruction supports the process of entry into long-term store. Coding processes may be provided or suggested. Alternatively, a set to employ a strategy of coding may be activated by communications from the teacher.

Retention Phase. This phase pertaining to "storage" is included for the sake of completeness. The manner in which internal processes of storage (such as interference, simplification, and the like) can be directly influenced by instruction, if indeed they can be, is not entirely clear. It seems evident, however, that indirect influence can be brought to bear by suitable arrangement of learning conditions, as, for example, in presenting dissimilar stimuli together rather than highly similar ones, thus reducing the possibility of interference.

Recall Phase. External instructional events during this phase may take the form of providing cues to retrieval or of monitoring the process of retrieval to insure that suitable strategies of search are employed. Teaching also includes the conduct of "spaced reviews," providing opportunities for retrieval to occur.

Generalization Phase. During the generalization phase, the teacher provides situations (which may be verbally described) calling for the transfer of learned knowledge and skills in novel ways and providing cues for application to previously unencountered situations.

Performance Phase. Instruction oriented to this phase of learning is largely a matter of setting occasions for the student to "show" that he has learned. Obviously, these occasions set the stage for the feedback that comes next.

Feedback Phase. The feedback phase is one in which information is supplied to the student concerning the extent to which his performance has reached or approached a criterion standard reflected in his expectancy. What is accomplished in this phase is the confirmation of the expectancy, affecting the process of reinforcement.

Outcomes of Learning

The processes of learning, supported by events of instruction, result in the establishment of more-or-less permanent states within the individual learner. These states are, of course, inferred from observations of his performances, as these are exhibited in specifiable situations on two or more occasions. To emphasize the learned and also the persisting nature of these states, they may be called *capabilities* and *dispositions*.

It is customary in describing the varieties of outcomes of school learning to deal with them in terms of subject matter. Thus, one may speak of a student's having learned American history or algebra or typing or biology or auto repair. Such categories, however, although they may be necessary for the conduct of logistical operations of school instruction, are grossly inadequate for purposes of differentiating the kinds of outcomes resulting from learning. The reasons are as follows:

1. Learning is not unique to subject matter. There is no sound rational basis for such entities as mathematics learning, science learning, language learning, or history learning, except as divisions of time devoted to these subjects during a school day or term.

Learning Basis of Teaching Methods

2. The same varieties of learning outcome occur in different subjects. For example, the student may learn the fact that Newton invented the calculus in the subject called mathematics, whereas he may learn the fact that Bell invented the telephone in a subject called history.
3. Different varieties of learning outcomes occur within the same subject. In biology, a student may learn a capability, for example, the skill of deriving the expected genetic constitution of the offspring of cross-mated animals. In the same course he may also acquire a disposition, for example, an attitude of avoidance of harmful drugs. The classes of performance that these learning outcomes make possible are distinctly different.

Varieties of outcomes of the learning process are important to teaching because they create different requirements for instruction.[12] While the phases of instruction described in the previous section imply certain general characteristics for the events controlled by the teacher, these events also require more specific design related to the type of learning outcome expected. For example, the acquisition phase of learning is concerned with the coding of stimulation and may be influenced by a means of coding suggested by a teacher or a textbook. Obviously, though, the coding of a motor skill like shooting baskets cannot be greatly influenced by externally suggested codes; the ineffectiveness of verbal guidance in facilitating the learning of motor skills is well known. In contrast, the learning of information, such as the steps in passage of a law by Congress, can be highly influenced by the suggestion of appropriate coding procedures and retrieval cues. Thus the learning of these two kinds of capabilities (motor skill, verbal information) requires two quite different procedures of instruction, even though they both may be undertaken during the acquisition phase.

Varieties of Learned Capabilities and Dispositions

There are five classes of learned capabilities and dispositions, which differ from each other in the essential nature of the performances they mediate, their characteristics in retention and transfer, and the conditions of instruction that may be employed to support or enhance them. These five varieties of learning outcome have been identified as (a) verbal information, (b) intellectual skills, (c) cognitive strategies, (d) attitudes, and (e) motor skills.[13] For present purposes, the most important differentiating feature of these classes of capabilities resides in the fact that they require different approaches to the support of processes involved in learning them. In other words, for each of these classes of learning, something different has to be done about instruction by the teacher, the textbook, the ITV tape, or any other medium.

Verbal Information. The student learns a great deal of information in school—names, facts, generalizations about what things are, what has happened, where things are located, and so on. Information is identified as verbal not because it is necessarily stored that way but because verbal information is the outcome. One knows that the student has learned verbal information because she can *state* it. In a fundamental sense, it has a sentence (or propositional) form.

Presumably, verbal information is often (or perhaps usually) stored in the form of internally organized bodies of knowledge. Various forms of organization have been proposed for such storage, including hierarchical networks and mental imagery.[14] The retrieval of verbal information is greatly facilitated by externally supplied cues, and cues may also be supplied by the learner herself.

Modern research suggests that the most critical feature of instruction for the learning of any item of verbal information is the *provision of a larger meaningful context* with which the item can be associated or into which it can be incorporated.[15] Ausubel proposes that new items of information are "subsumed" into more comprehensive cognitive structures.[16] Another possibility is that verbal information is transformed into visual images.[17] Presumably, whatever the nature of the larger context, it is this that makes it possible for the item of information to be most readily searched for and retrieved. The implication for instruction is clear, at least in a general sense: the teacher and the medium must either separately or together provide a meaningful context at the time a new item or set of items is presented for learning.

Intellectual Skills. The learning of intellectual skills begins with the aquisition of simple discriminations and chains.[18] School learning, although it may sometimes include these simpler forms, is mainly concerned with the learning of *concepts* and *rules*. These are the kinds of capabilities that make it possible for the student to *do* something with the symbols representing his environment. While verbal information has to do with knowing "what," intellectual skills have to do with knowing "how."

Many varieties of intellectual skills are learned in formal education, beginning with the basic skills of manipulating language and number symbols. The concepts and rules that are acquired in the subjects of the curriculum offered in later grades may be viewed as increasingly elaborate and complex forms that incorporate the simpler forms within them. As opposed to information learning, the learning of intellectual skills appears to be cumulative in nature. The learning of a new rule, for example, requires the availability of the simpler rules or concepts that compose it.

Intellectual skill learning requires the "combining" of simpler intellectual skills (rules, concepts), which have been previously learned and can be retrieved. (In terms of the learning model, they must be "recovered" in short-term memory.) The implications for instruction, therefore, are clear. First, the teacher must insure that the prerequisite skills have been learned. This prior learning may have taken place in an immediately preceding lesson or in a lesson that occurred a long time ago. If the necessary prerequisite skills have not been learned, then instruction must be given to establish them. Second, cues must be given to enable the student to retrieve the previously learned skills. And third, some kinds of externally provided cues must usually be offered to suggest the nature of the "combination" to be learned. This function of instruction is most typically performed by verbal means; the new rule or concept is stated verbally. Minimal cues for such learning characterize the method of "discovery learning," an alternative sometimes employed to good effect.

It should be pointed out that although the learning of intellectual skills under ideal conditions appears to be a simple and straightforward matter, their storage and retrieval may involve other complications. For example, the student who has acquired the rule for transforming Fahrenheit temperature into Celsius may know "how" but may find that she has forgotten the formula (information) that enables her to recover the skill. It appears, then, that informational cues often need to be learned besides the skill itself. The full implications of this state of affairs cannot currently be described. However, the importance of *spaced reviews* for retrieval of intellectual skills has more than once been verified.[19]

Cognitive Strategies. Cognitive strategies are internally organized skills that govern the individual's behavior in attending, learning, remembering, and thinking. In terms of the learning model previously described, they are *control processes*. Presumably, some of these processes may be inborn, but most of them are learned. Processes of attention and selective perception may be acquired in perceptual learning, as the work of E. J. Gibson indicates.[20] The operation of strategies for storage and retrieval of word pairs has been investigated by Rohwer and his associates.[21] Strategies of problem solving and thinking are prominently emphasized in the writings of Bruner.[22]

On the whole, knowledge of how cognitive strategies are learned is meager. Accordingly, the arrangement of instruction to promote the learning of these strategies appears correspondingly primitive. The usual recommendation is to provide frequent opportunities for the student to practice the use of cognitive strategies and presumably to refine them by so doing. Thus, provision is often made for the student to solve challenging novel problems, to write original essays or stories, or to undertake projects requiring the application and transfer of knowledge and skills. It is widely believed that such procedures are effective in promoting the learning and improvement of cognitive strategies, although the evidence for this belief is sadly lacking. The importance of this kind of learning objective is universally acknowledged, and the description of increasingly effective instructional methods may be hoped for in the near future.

Attitudes. The school is usually considered responsible for establishing a number of kinds of attitudes in students and for modifying preexisting attitudes. Among other attitudes, self-concept and self-esteem are often considered important by educational scholars. In addition, it is expected that such attitudes as tolerance, consideration for the feelings of others, honesty, kindness, and helpfulness will be acquired and reinforced by school learning experiences. Then there are attitudes toward school subjects, such as a liking for mathematics, literature, music, or sports. Included also are such negative attitudes as aversion to drug abuse and avoidance of accidents and disease. Obviously, this is a very large category of school learning, sometimes referred to as the affective domain.[23] This particular title, however, should not lead us to neglect the behavioral aspects of attitudes.

Attitudes are learned dispositions that influence the choice of personal action toward classes of things, events, or persons. In the terms of a learning model, they bear a resemblance to cognitive strategies in being internally organized control processes. However, since they do not actually determine behavior but only influence it, they may perhaps better be described as "moderator processes." They are often identified as "tendencies," which may be either positive or negative in their influence on actions.

So far as instruction is concerned, a number of techniques for establishing and maintaining attitudes can be employed. Perhaps the first point to be noted is the striking ineffectiveness of verbal communications (in and of themselves) as means of establishing or modifying attitudes. Telling students to "avoid harmful drugs" or "be kind to animals," whether these communications are couched in terms of rational arguments, exhortations, or emotional appeals, is not a technique that changes attitudes. In other words, attitudes cannot be established or changed simply by having the student learn verbal information. This fact has been verified many times.[24]

Attitudes are often learned under conditions in which the student experiences success or receives reinforcement following a choice of action that he deliberately makes. Perhaps equally important for instruction, if not more so, are methods providing vicarious reinforcement by way of a human model, as described by Bandura.[25] The human model may in some circumstances be the teacher. Other possibilities are respected public personalities, sports figures, famous men and women, and (by extension) heroes of literature. Effective conditions for attitudinal change require that the student observe the human model making the desired choice of action (avoiding harmful drugs, being a cautious driver, placing personal trash in a container) and subsequently being rewarded (reinforced) for this action.

Motor Skills. The learning of motor skills, while not a large component of school learning, is nevertheless a part that can readily be identified. Motor skills are prominent in physical education and sports and in a number of specialties of the performing arts and vocational education. They also occur as learning outcomes in such activities as printing letters and words and in the pronunciation of language sounds.

The learning of smoothness and timing of responses is a critical feature of motor skills, and these aspects are influenced by kinesthetic feedback from the muscles and other elements of the response system. Accordingly, instruction mainly takes the form of providing reinforced *practice* of the motor responses.

Sometimes, the learning can be facilitated by arranging conditions so that feedback is made more nearly immediate or more precise or both.

In addition to the learning of increased smoothness and accuracy of responding, motor skills often require that the student acquire a procedure that determines the sequence of his actions. This aspect of motor-skill learning is called an *executive subroutine* by Fitts and Posner.[26] Besides learning to pitch a baseball accurately and smoothly, the pitcher must learn to wind up, check first base, place his foot properly, and so on. A procedure of this sort has the nature of a sequence rule and is presumably acquired as are other intellectual skills. Intellectual skills of this kind can accordingly be influenced by verbal cues as a part of instruction; in contrast, the essential motor skill cannot be so influenced and must be practiced. Of course, both of these components need to be present in instruction of a practically useful skill.

Other Learning Theories

It is not possible within the confines of the present paper to make comparisons of the details of theories that use the information-processing model nor to compare them with other types of learning theories. However, some points of similarity and difference can perhaps be pointed out concerning issues specifically related to teaching. Particularly this can be done in terms of the previously described dimensions of instruction, namely, the phases of instruction and the outcomes of instruction.

The facts seem to be that in their sometimes incidental attempts to suggest the critical variables in instruction, different learning theorists have emphasized different instructional phases. Likewise, they have directed their theoretical ideas toward particular learning outcomes and ignored others. Some examples of theoretical views that are addressed to linkages between learning and instruction may serve to illustrate these points.

Behaviorist Views

One variety of learning theory of the behaviorist type is that of Hull,[27] who accounted for learning in terms of postulated intervening variables affecting the strength of associations (S-Rs). Advocating a "liberalized" version of this basic viewpoint is N. E. Miller,[28] who has described the implications for instruction of learning theory of this general sort.[29] Miller proposes that an effective sequence of instruction, in any medium, includes provision for *motivation, cue, response,* and *reward.* As a first step, instruction must invoke and channel existing motivation of the student. Second, it must aid the student in distinguishing the relevant cues. Third, the student must be given the opportunity to do something, that is, to exhibit his learned response. And finally, knowledge of his achievement must be fed back to the student, that is, reinforcement must occur.

There is obviously a strong resemblance between the implications for instruction described by Miller and those derived from contemporary information-processing theories. Assuming that both accept the necessity of motivation, made explicit by Miller, the two sets of implications begin the same way (with attention) and end the same way (with performance and feedback). The difference lies in the middle—with cue and what follows. For Miller, the externally provided cue serves the primary purpose of supporting attention and perception processes. Information-processing theory, however, expands the notion of cue to encompass the provision of additional context for coding and also for the support of retrieval and transfer. Although they supplement Miller's views in this manner, the proposals of contemporary theory are obviously highly compatible with his.

The brand of behaviorism espoused by Skinner presents a rather different picture.[30] In the first place, Skinner maintains that the internal processes postulated by contemporary information-processing theories are irrelevant for analysis and unnecessary for the prediction of behavior. In brief, he advocates accounting for learning on the basis of external events that act upon the learner, including the arrangement of contingencies for reinforcement.[31]

The implications of these views for instruction, however, do not differ greatly from those of information-processing theory; the differences appear to be largely matters of emphasis. Thus, Skinner provides for the motivation of the learner through initial selection of a preferred activity, which becomes a "reinforcer" for the act to be acquired when set in a contingency sequence. Skinner's next point of emphasis is on the response and feedback phases of instruction, providing the occasion for positive reinforcement to have its effect. Between these two sets of events are "prompting," "fading," and "gradual stimulus change." It is conceivable that these forms of learning guidance, when put into practical usage, sometimes take on the characteristics of coding and of cueing for retrieval. Whereas the coding and cueing functions are incorporated in information-processing theory, they are not explicitly formulated in Skinner's theory nor are they implied as instructional events.

Cognitive Theories

Some cognitive theorists postulate a fairly complex set of internal mechanisms to account for learning and retention. In this respect their theories resemble information-processing theories, even though a different nomenclature is employed. Prominent among such theorists is Ausubel.[32] In brief, Ausubel proposes that the information to be learned must be (a) selectively perceived, (b) meaningfully structured, (c) encoded by being subsumed within a previously learned cognitive structure, (d) differentiated within that structure for later retrieval, and (e) subjected to further consolidation and "reconciliation" to promote transfer.

If one allows for differences in terminology, resemblances between Ausubel's theory and contemporary information-processing models are substantial. Ausubel emphasizes the operational processes of meaningful coding and the storage of information in propositional form. His ideas about the differentiation and dissociability of material stored in memory imply the need for instruction that concerns itself with cueing for retrieval and transfer. In contrast to behaviorist theories previously described, Ausubel's theory focuses on the middle set of events for instruction, that is, on the presentation of stimulus material, its coding and cueing. Not much is said in his theory about the beginning and end of the instructional process, that is, on the establishment of motivation, on the one hand, and the provision of feedback, on the other.

As a cognitive theorist, Bruner presents wide-ranging views, including ideas about the social and biological foundations of education[33] and the cognitive development of children[34] as well as the design of effective instruction.[35] Perhaps the most important point of emphasis, so far as instruction itself is concerned, is the use of discovery methods of teaching,[36] with the aim of developing cognitive strategies.[37] Cognitive strategies are processes by which the learner controls his own attending, learning, and thinking behavior. As a general class, they may be considered equivalent to the executive control processes that form a part of the information-processing model. Although Bruner acknowledges that intellectual skills constitute a substantial part of most school subjects to be learned,[38] it is the strategies of learning and productive thinking that he considers worthy of greatest attention in instruction.

The theoretical ideas advanced by Bruner would apparently not conflict with notions derived from information-processing theories, insofar as the latter concern matters of coding, storage, and retrieval. The contrast is again one of emphasis. Although the information-processing model depends heavily upon the operation of executive control processes, it does not have much to say about how such processes are acquired, developed, stored, or activated by the learner. It is these matters that are of greatest concern to Bruner. His theory implies that the learner must have considerable freedom of exploration to develop these processes and at the same time frequent intellectual challenges to stimulate his thinking and allow discovery to take place.

A Social Learning Theory

Another variety of theory that has significance for instruction is social-learning theory, of which Bandura is a leading proponent.[39] As indicated previously, this theory emphasizes the role of imitation of human models as a mode of learning. Instruction takes the form of demonstration of desired behavior by the model. The student learns by observing the behavior and noting also the evidences of satisfaction and reward to the model. Feedback is provided in this situation as "vicarious reinforcement," which may lead, under suitable conditions, to "self-reinforcement."[40]

Learning by human modeling provides still another example of a theory having instructional implications that do not appear inherently incompatible with those of information-processing theory. Modeling represents a somewhat different way of dealing with motivation, with coding, and with feedback. The major point of difference lies in the area of what is being learned. Most prominently, social-learning theory deals with the learning of attitudes and motor skills, kinds of learning outcomes that information-processing theories have not attempted to encompass.

Learning Theories and Learning Outcomes

The place occupied by Bandura's theory of human modeling—largely outside the purview of contemporary theories of learning and memory—serves to illustrate a more general point about the latter theories. All of them are, in a sense, partial theories. They do not cover the range of learning phenomena that occur in the school and are therefore the concern of the teacher. It is for this reason that, in thinking about instruction in an analytical sense, one needs to bear in mind the total range and variety of learning outcomes described in the previous section of this chapter. In educational environments, students are learning more than information; they are also learning intellectual skills, motor skills, cognitive strategies, and attitudes.

Contemporary information-processing theory concerns itself almost exclusively with the learning and retention of verbal information of the sort that is exhibited as propositional knowledge. Other theorists have given attention to other kinds of learning outcomes they see as relevant to school instruction: Bruner to cognitive strategies, Bandura to attitudes, Gagné to intellectual skills. Evidently, a truly comprehensive theory of human learning will ultimately account for learning processes that are differentially applicable to all of the kinds of capabilities and dispositions that human beings can and do learn.

Summary: Implications for Instruction

As viewed from the standpoint of learning models of the information-processing variety, each act of learning involves the operation of a number of internal processes. The inputs to these processes come partly from the learner himself, that is, they are recovered from his memory and thus depend to a considerable extent upon previous learning. These inputs can also be altered, modified, and enhanced in various ways by stimulation from the learner's external environment. It is these actions that constitute *instruction*.

The essential task of the teacher is to arrange the conditions of the learner's environment so that the processes of learning will be activated, supported, enhanced, and maintained. Thus the teacher needs to be aware of what the processes of learning are and of the specific influences he can exert on them in order to provide successful instruction. It will be convenient for him to look upon an act of learning as having a number of phases, beginning with the arousal of a motivational state of expectancy and proceeding to the point at which feedback is provided to confirm this expectancy. In this view, there are eight phases to learning, each of which may be influenced by events of instruction to a greater or lesser degree and each in a different way.

An orthogonal dimension of instruction to be taken into account in teaching concerns the matter of *what* is to be learned or the nature of the *learning outcome* to be expected. The effects of learning consist in the establishment of human capabilities, of which there are five major varieties: verbal information, intellectual skills, cognitive strategies, attitudes, and motor skills. While the phases of learning that reflect underlying processes are presumably common for all of these learning outcomes, their learning differs with respect to which phases are most subject to external influence by instruction. The coding of verbal information for retrieval, for example, appears to be greatly influenced by externally suggested schemes, whereas coding of the smoothness and timing of motor skills can be influenced little, if at all, by such schemes. Accordingly, it is desirable for the teacher to be aware of, and to make adequate provision for, certain critical conditions of instruction relating to each type of learning outcome.

Models of learning thus make possible a conceptual frame of reference within which learning can be viewed as a set of sequentially ordered processes leading to the establishment and retention of more or less permanent human capabilities. At the same time, these models provide a conceptualization of what instruction can and cannot accomplish when considered as a set of planned external events designed to influence the ongoing processes of learning.

Notes

1. R. C. Atkinson and R. M. Shiffrin, "Human Memory: A Proposed System and Its Control Processes," in *The Psychology of Learning and Motivation*, vol. 2, ed. K. W. Spence and J. T. Spence (New York: Academic Press, 1968), pp. 89–195; D. A. Norman, ed., *Models of Human Memory* (New York: Academic Press, 1970); E. Tulving and W. Donaldson, eds., *Organization of Memory* (New York: Academic Press, 1972); A. W. Melton and E. Martin, eds., *Coding Processes in Human Memory* (Washington, D.C.: Winston, 1972).

2. J. G. Greeno and R. A. Bjork, "Mathematical Learning Theory and the New 'Mental Forestry,' " *Annual Review of Psychology* 24 (1973): 81–116.

3. W. K. Estes, "Reinforcement in Human Behavior," *American Scientist* 60 (November–December, 1972): 723–29.

4. R. C. Atkinson, D. J. Herrmann, and K. T. Wescourt, *Search Processes in Recognition Memory*, Technical Report No. 204 (Stanford: Institute for Mathematical Studies in the Social Sciences, Stanford University, 1973).

5. V. K. Kumar, "The Structure of Human Memory and Some Educational Implications," *Review of Educational Research* 41 (December 1971): 379–417.

6. Estes, "Reinforcement in Human Behavior."

7. R. C. Atkinson and T. D. Wickens, "Human Memory and the Concept of Reinforcement," in *The Nature of Reinforcement*, ed. R. Glaser (New York: Academic Press, 1971), pp. 66–120.

8. Atkinson and Shiffrin, "Human Memory."

9. W. Kintsch, "Notes on the Structure of Semantic Memory," in Tulving and Donaldson, *Organization of Memory*, pp. 247–308.

10. J. R. Anderson and G. H. Bower, *Human Associative Memory* (Washington, D.C.: Winston, 1973).

11. E. Tulving and Z. Pearlstone, "Availability versus Accessibility Information in Memory for Words," *Journal of Verbal Learning and Verbal Behavior* 5 (August 1966): 381–91.

12. R. M. Gagné and L. J. Briggs, *Principles of Instructional Design* (New York: Holt, Rinehart & Winston, 1974).

13. R. M. Gagné, "Domains of Learning," *Interchange* 3:1 (1972): 1–8.

14. G. Wood, "Organizational Processes and Free Recall," in Tulving and Donaldson, *Organization of Memory*, pp. 49–91; G. H. Bower, "Mental Imagery and Associative Learning," in *Cognition in Learning and Memory*, ed. L. W. Gregg (New York: John Wiley, 1973), pp. 51–88.

15. Anderson and Bower, *Human Memory*.

16. D. P. Ausubel, *Educational Psychology: A Cognitive View* (New York: Holt, Rinehart & Winston, 1968).

17. A. Paivio, *Imagery and Verbal Processes* (New York: Holt, Rinehart & Winston, 1971).

18. R. M. Gagné, *The Conditions of Learning*, 2d ed. (New York: Holt, Rinehart & & Winston, 1970).

19. J. H. Reynolds and R. Glaser, "Effects of Repetition and Spaced Review upon Retention of a Complex Learning Task," *Journal of Educational Psychology* 55 (October 1964): 297–308; L. R. Gay, "Temporal Position of Reviews and Its Effect on the Retention of Mathematical Rules," *Journal of Educational Psychology* 64 (April 1973): 171–82.

20. E. J. Gibson, *Principles of Perceptual Learning and Development* (New York: Appleton-Century-Crofts, 1969).

21. W. D. Rohwer, Jr., et al., "Pictorial and Verbal Factors in the Efficient Learning of Paired Associates," *Journal of Educational Psychology* 58 (October 1967): 278–84.

22. J. S. Bruner, *The Relevance of Education* (New York: W. W. Norton & Co., 1971).

23. D. R. Krathwohl, B. S. Bloom, and B. B. Masia, *Taxonomy of Educational Objectives. Handbook II: Affective Domain* (New York: David McKay Co., 1964).

24. H. C. Triandis, *Attitudes and Attitude Change* (New York: John Wiley, 1971).

25. A. Bandura, *Principles of Behavior Modification* (New York: Holt, Rinehart & Winston, 1969).

26. P. M. Fitts and M. I. Posner, *Human Performance* (Belmont, Calif.: Brooks/Cole, 1967).

27. C. L. Hull, *Principles of Behavior* (New York: Appleton-Century-Crofts, 1943).

28. N. E. Miller, "Liberalization of Basic S-R Concepts: Extensions to Conflict Behavior, Motivation and Social Learning," in *Psychology: A Study of a Science*, vol. 2, ed. S. Koch (New York: McGraw-Hill, 1959), pp. 196–292.

29. N. E. Miller, *Graphic Communication and the Crisis in Education* (Washington, D.C.: Department of Audio-Visual Instruction, National Education Association, 1957).

30. B. F. Skinner, *Science and Human Behavior* (New York: Macmillan, 1953).
31. B. F. Skinner, *The Technology of Teaching* (New York: Appleton-Century-Crofts, 1968).
32. Ausubel, *Educational Psychology*.
33. Bruner, *Relevance of Education*.
34. J. S. Bruner, "The Growth of Mind," *American Psychologist* 20 (December 1965):1007–17.
35. J. S. Bruner, *Toward a Theory of Instruction* (Cambridge: Harvard University Press, 1966).
36. J. S. Bruner, "The Act of Discovery," *Harvard Educational Review* 31 (Winter 1961): 21–32.
37. Bruner, *Relevance of Education*.
38. Ibid., pp. 109–10.
39. Bandura, *Behavior Modification*.
40. A. Bandura, "Vicarious and Self-Reinforcement Processes," in Glaser, *Nature of Reinforcement*, pp. 228–78.

Reconceptualists

14 Frame Factors in Teaching

Ulf Lundgren

Introduction

Within the last decade, Ulf Lundgren and his colleagues in Sweden have demonstrated that theory and empirical studies can be used to reconceptualize the nature of the relationship between the schooling process, classroom pedagogy, and the larger society. Lundgren begins this article by claiming that scientific ideas and perspectives within the main tradition of educational research have failed to connect the internal functions and effects of education with explanations of economic, social, and cultural change in the wider society. Or to put it another way, he claims that macrolevel and microlevel studies of schooling and classroom pedagogy have not informed each other in a sufficient way.

Lundgren argues that any educational system operates according to an explicit or implicit definition of its role in society, one that cannot be separated from the nature and function of curriculum theorizing. Thus, educators and educational researchers will have to develop heuristic concepts that serve as theoretical devices to both unpack and explain how the economic and social structure of society relates to and influences the teaching process itself. Lundgren, in part, attempts to fulfill the latter task by developing a number of explanatory insights about the teaching process around the concept of frame system.

As you read this article, take note of how Lundgren defines the concept of frame system.
- How does it differ in its basic assumptions and approach to analyzing the teaching process from the approach provided by the traditional research perspective?

• How might Lundgren's model be used to help you view education as a societal process or to influence classroom practice?

Frame Factors: The First Approximation

If we take the actual teaching as a starting point, we can make a first assumption, namely, that the transactions in the teaching situation are constrained and governed by various political and bureaucratic decisions. Thus, we have to make a distinction between factors that are constraining the process and factors that are governing it. The term *frame* will be used to refer only to the constraints on the teaching situation. The concept of frame has been used both by Dahllöf[1] and by Bernstein.[2] Although their theoretical contexts were different, I shall here expand the definition of this concept using Dahllöf's and Bernstein's works as point of reference.

In Berstein's terminology, frame refers to the options available as to the curriculum content. But in a broader sense, the number of options as to the form of transaction, the methods (instructional and otherwise), and the time that may be devoted to a certain subject (or content unit) during a definable period (for example, a school year) could also be regarded as limited, or "framed."[3]

Dahllöf uses the concept of frame more broadly, in relation to decisions that are outside the teacher's and student's control. This usage thus links the macro- and the microlevel of analysis.[4] It should be remembered, however, that the concept of frame as used by Dahllöf was developed in order to cope with the special problem of ability grouping.

In a study by Lundgren,[5] Dahllöf's earlier findings concerning ability grouping were tested. His conceptual framework was also expanded, and the elaborated model is illustrated in Figure 14-1. The model relates frame factors, steering group, and the nature of the teaching process, as well as indicating the concepts used to describe both frame factors and the teaching process. In the following pages we shall explain the three main demands of this model and describe an empirical study[6] that tested it. The results of this study pinpointed some important shortcomings in the model, which will then be discussed.

As can be seen in Figure 14-1, the model includes three types of frame factors, all of which are interrelated. The first refers to the goals or objectives of teaching and may vary from generally expressed to clearly stated goals of behavior. The second factor refers to the sequence of content units within which these various educational goals may be achieved. This factor varies in relation to the structure of the content taught. The third factor is the time needed by a student to master the content and, hence, achieve the goals. For

---

Reprinted from *Model Analysis of Pedagogical Process* (Lund, Sweden: LWK Gleerup, 1977), pp. 24–38. Reprinted with permission of the author.

Frame Factors in Teaching

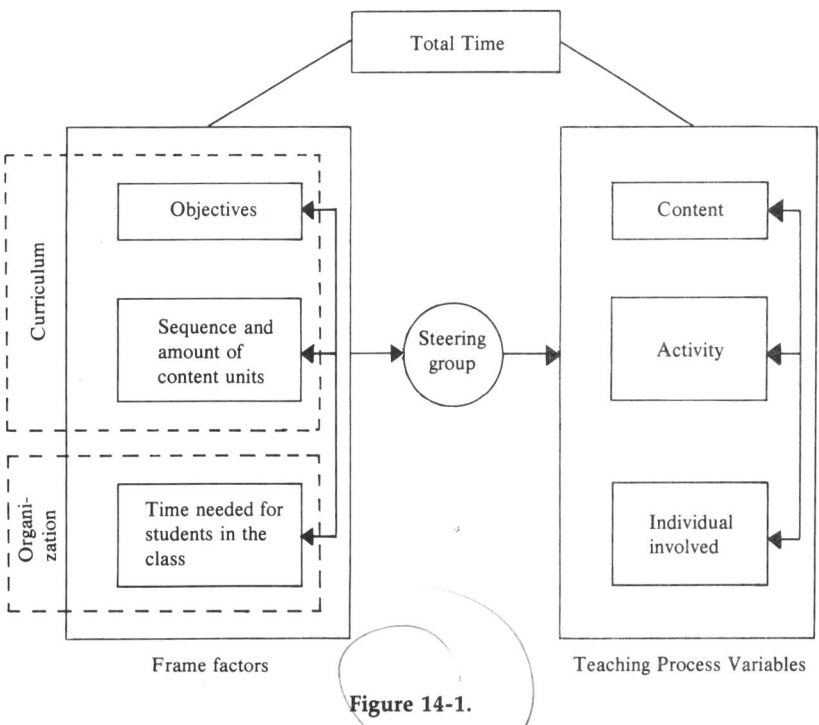

Figure 14-1.
Model of the relationship between frame factors, steering group, and teaching process variables.[7]

each student, the time needed is a consequence of the subject that is taught and how this subject is transformed in the teaching situation. Therefore, the time needed will always be an expression of both learning capacity and the structure of the educational system in relation to the student's experiences. Hence, the model is not restricted to the microlevel, for it can also be used as a description of the curriculum-planning process (that is, at the macrolevel).

The total time available to the teacher can be classified in three ways:
1. The time is sufficient to satisfy the relations between the frame factors.
2. The time is more than is needed.
3. The time is not sufficient.

In the last instance the time will act as a frame factor. In that event the teacher must make various decisions in relation to the frames. Since the total time cannot be prolonged, the teacher must place a priority on certain goals or students or both.

In this sense the creation of a steering group can be interpreted as a solution the teacher can follow when the time is not sufficient. As a criterion for judging when he can finish one section of the syllabus and begin another, the teacher uses the progress of a particular group of students. But at the same time, it is obvious that access to time is not the only explanation for the differentiation by the teacher of students and groups of students. The governing rules of the teaching situation demand such differentiation in the form of achievement scores or grades. Thus, differentiation cannot be explained by the frame system alone; the evaluation system (including rules for control, that is, evaluation procedures and so on) must also be taken into account.[8]

The decisions the teacher takes are also dependent on the curriculum and class organization (ability grouping, class size, and so forth), as well as the teacher's perception of these factors. While the effects of the constraints will be most visible when time is not sufficient, subjective interpretation of these constraints will also determine how time is used. Of course, some may always interpret the time as insufficient because they hold teaching goals that are too ambitious to fulfill. This interpretation is also a consequence of the rules and obligations that the teacher must fulfill. If she is obliged to describe the outcomes of her teaching in terms of student grades, she will then be forced to make a differentiated interpretation of the frame factors (goals, content, and available time). Thus, the combination of an evaluation system according to which the teacher has to make a differentiation between students will always cause a situation in which the time available is not sufficient for some groups of students to achieve the goals. Thus, my second assumption will be that if there is evaluation criteria governing teaching in such a way that the teacher is obliged to present qualitative descriptions of student outcomes, then the time available for subgroups of students will not be sufficient to reach the goals set for other subgroups. These two basic assumptions may seem fairly truistic, but they are necessary in order to classify different groups of factors governing, controlling, and constraining the teaching process. In this way, the assumption of a steering group can now be further explained.

In the model in Figure 14-1, three concepts were used as teaching-process variables: content, activity, and person involved. Using these concepts as a starting point, we conducted an empirical study in which this model was tested.[9] The study was carried out on students in the Swedish high school grade 11 (ages seventeen to eighteen). Two types of data were collected: survey data (the extensive study) and in-depth data (the intensive study). The survey data were collected from a panel study on teaching in forty-six classes in the natural science and social science streams. Five subjects were studied: English, civics, history, mathematics, and Swedish. Questionnaires were sent to the teachers on four separate occasions during the school year. In each questionnaire the teachers were asked to describe how they had actually conducted their classes during the intervening periods and what they had really planned to do. They also answered questions about the teaching methods used, the decisions they made when they had to change their plans, their perceptions of teaching, and the problems they experienced. On three occasions the students were also questioned about their behavior in class, their attitudes towards their teachers, their subjects and their homework, and the reason for their choice of subjects. The in-depth study covered eight classes which were observed a total of fifty-seven times. The unit of analysis was the pedagogical move.[10] In all, a little over 11,000 moves were classified, according to the Bellack system, the VICS-system[11] and Bales's category system.[12]

In the survey study, the textbook was used as a frame of reference. The first step was to analyze the content of the textbooks in relation to the syllabus so that different classes using different textbooks could be compared. Next, the responses of the teachers were used to build up a description of their teaching as it had been conducted and as it had been planned. The third step was to compare the teaching process in different classes. To do this, we assumed that students between the tenth and twenty-fifth percentiles in general intellectual ability formed the steering groups so that classes could be divided into three categories: those in which the steering group had high-average ability, those with a low-average level, and those in between.

Classes with high-ability steering groups and low-ability steering groups were found to follow the planned teaching better than those with a middle-ability group. The interpretation of this was that the teachers of these classes can either follow their plans or can revise them at an early stage and then follow them through. Teachers in the average-level classes that were unable to get through the units originally planned were forced to make a series of decisions: to lower the goals, leave out parts of the syllabus, or let students lag behind.

The fourth step was to analyze the decisions made by the teachers when the pace of the teaching could not be maintained and when different groups of students could not master a certain unit satisfactorily. Up to that point, parts of the first model could be empirically proved, and the assumed relationship held true.

In the in-depth study, data were analyzed in two stages. In the first stage, the relationship between the ability level of the steering group and the relative frequency of various verbal utterances was determined. A markedly significant relationship was obtained, and it was found that the relationship formed a consistent pattern irrespective of the coding system used. When the steering group was made up of students with a high level of general ability, the degree of subject-relevant utterances increased, as did behavioral sequences typical of a traditional style of teaching: the question-answer pattern increased, there was less disruptive behavior, the amount of disciplining decreased, the number of predictable answers increased, the teaching climate became more positive, and the behavior of the teacher more indirect.

In the second stage of the in-depth study, the steering group was redefined. The assumption was that teaching is not directed towards individuals but towards groups of students. The teacher's perceptual grouping of the students was determined and then analyzed in relation to the classroom behavior of the various groups in order to delineate the pattern of student roles.[13]

Although this empirical study verified the assumptions the model in Figure 14-1 made, it went no further in developing the conceptual framework. The basic relationship between frame factors and the teaching process has been

established, but it is also necessary to explain how these relationships are formed and the way in which they affect the teaching process. The limitations of the model can now be clarified with the following points:
1. The frame concept and the concept of curriculum should be separated because the curriculum articulated in the syllabus, textbooks, and teaching materials governs rather than constrains the process. But governing factors are similar to constraining factors in that they are both determined at decision-making levels above the teaching process.
2. In making a distinction between governing and constraining factors, the nature of the governing process must be described in relation to the teaching process, that is, curriculum determines the classroom language. While the constraining factors structure the classroom language, the governing factors (curriculum) determine the content of this language.
3. The distinctions between frames and curriculum are not sufficient to explain the structure of the teaching process. The legislative system regulating the teachers' duties must also be taken into consideration (the marking system, the examination system, and so on).
4. The model should be related to a general theory of education and its function in society.

The final point is the most essential. The internal functions and effects of education cannot be explained without relating them to a basic theory of education and society. This theory must, then, be built on an explanatory model that specifies the determinants of the teaching process.

External and Internal Functions of Teaching

Educational researchers cannot be expected to develop a complete social theory, but on the other hand it is evident that educational research should be based upon the conclusions of the more comprehensive social theories. Although the statements may seem truistic, they have rarely been reflected in research. With the possible exception of central European countries, contemporary educational research is mainly empirical in nature and is heavily influenced by positivistic philosophy. The "narrow view of science,"[14] which conceives science as descriptive, value-free, and nomothetic, is presented as a basis for pedagogical inquiry in standard textbooks on research strategies.[15] According to these sources, research is an "objective" enterprise, and objectivity is in its turn defined with reference to a set of acceptable methods. This concentration upon research methodology can be regarded as the result of long chains of transformations between problems and methods leading to a reification of the problems by perceiving them as purely methodological. One basic assumption is that there exists an objective observational language separated from the theoretical language and that translations between these languages can be performed through the use of a set of translation rules. The consequence of this assumption has been a concentration upon methodology. Science and, thereby, objectivity have been defined in terms of methodology.

In educational research the aim of researchers has been to establish laws through descriptions which have been correlational, experimental, or even quasi-experimental in nature. Also evident in educational research as a further consequence of this basic assumption is the belief that "objective" interpretation can only be achieved through the use of strict rules for the formulation and verification of hypotheses. These rules have been based essentially upon the idea that educational phenomena can be expressed quantitatively.

To summarize: the scientific ideas and perspectives within the main tradition of educational research have been expressed in terms of acceptable research strategies or methods, which then obviously influence the kind of problems that may be studied. One consequence of this scientific perspective, in our view, has been the lack of adequate conceptualizations of pedagogical phenomena that link explanations of economic, social, and cultural change in the society to explanations of the nature of the educational processes.

A concrete illustration of the consequences of this research tradition can be seen in the type of teaching research that has been done. With some few exceptions, this has been based on the view of teaching contained in the curriculum, that is, that teaching leads to the learning of the stated goals.

An educational system operates according to an explicit or implicit definition of its role in society. Clearly, education has external effects in the society, and the assumption is that the inner functions of schooling can be derived from the external functions. From another perspective, the general purpose of all pedagogical processes is to inculcate the value system of the society. There are, of course, different ideas about what the external functions of education are and about the value systems, knowledge, and experiences that should be included. There are also different ideas about the actual correspondence of the internal and external functions. However, many of these ideas are ideological and do not reflect the real relationship between education's internal and external functions.

An empirical educational theory must then be based on data concerning the educational process as it exists in reality and not on analyses of what researchers think these processes ought to be.[16] Such a theory thus constitutes a heuristic device for classroom research by serving as an indicator of important processes occurring in the classroom. The purpose of research should be to examine the various forms in which these processes are manifested. These will be determined by frame factors, in the sense that they define certain allowable "outer limits" seen as necessary for the fulfillment of that process. But the frame factors themselves can, in turn, be derived from the political, economic, and social structure of the society. This is also a consequence of the fact that pedagogical processes are artificial[17] *but not arbitrary and subjective*. The school is an institution that promotes learning in terms of postulated knowledge, skills, attitudes, and values. Legislation and rules prescribe the form of this institution, while the available resources in terms of personnel, teaching aids, and composition of students determine how the actual teaching corresponds to the formal goals and regulations. Curricula, regulations, personnel, and teaching aids as well as available time and the composition and size of classes are the most visible frames and forces constraining and governing the teaching process. These frames are translations of the external functions of education to internal frames, but they cannot of course explain the whole process.

Education has several other functions that are not expressed in any curricula.[18] Abrahamsson[19] and Cohen[20], for instance, have pointed out the following external functions of schooling: reproduction of labor and absorption of labor; social control and selection and individual welfare. Although these factors have not been thoroughly analyzed, they can be used as concrete examples of various functions of education.

The learning of the content of the curriculum within the constraints given by the frame factors is of course not the only type of learning that occurs in classrooms. If research is restricted only to the narrow learning perspective, neglecting the external functions of education, the relationship between frame factors and the teaching process will appear to be fairly random. Obviously, the teaching process is determined and constrained not only by the formal frames but also by many external factors inherent in the cultural context. Many of these external influences operate outside the consciousness of the acting individuals.

This is, of course, neither dramatic nor new in itself. However, existing educational research has been directed towards analyses of the teaching process in terms of the learning of the curriculum content. But in the real teaching situation, the learning of school subjects may actually function as a more general socialization process that bears little relationship to the theories of learning and development formulated on the basis of experimental situations.[21]

We can also illustrate these statements from another point of view. Traditional research on teaching has aimed at the acquisition of knowledge in order to improve the teacher's competency. This has resulted into two research goals—to discover the types of teaching behavior related to student achievement and to isolate those behaviors that it is possible to manipulate. The results obtained have consequently been interpreted in relation to teacher education.[22] Two points must be clarified here. First, although the behavior of the teacher in the classroom is the main source of learning, the teacher is her- or himself part of a wider context. By disregarding this context, researchers have been unable to identify those factors that could be manipulated in order to bring about changes in the teaching process. Second, the link between teacher behavior and teacher education is a complex one, as teachers colleges operate in the same social context as do the schools. Hence, a knowledge of the social context is also necessary to bring about changes in teacher education.

Up to this point I have discussed, albeit broadly, the concept of frame in relation to the educational and scientific perspective in which it must be understood. This was done in order to establish a starting point. Furthermore, the first model (Fig. 14-1) has been developed and expanded with the aid of an empirical study. While this study was shown to confirm some of the basic assumptions and relationships in the model, it also illustrated the need for an expansion of the model. Consequently, a distinction was made between the concept of frame and the concept of curriculum, and successively we have shown the need for another distinction between frames, curriculum, and the formal obligations of teachers.

The definition of frame used up to this point includes any factor that limits the teaching process. However, this definition is rather broad and should be supplemented by a stipulative definition: *frame factors are those factors which are determined outside the teaching process.* Hence, frames are outside the control of the teachers and students.

The next step will thus be to distinguish between three systems that constrain, govern, and regulate the teaching process. From here on, the term *frame system* will be used instead of frame factors. Hence, the three systems are:
the goal system
the frame system
the formal rule system.

The goal system includes the concrete consequences of a specific curriculum, that is, the syllabus, recommendations for teaching, teaching materials, textbooks, and so on. The frame system includes everything that constrains the teaching process that is determined outside teaching. This would include physical equipment such as rooms, organizational arrangements such as size of school and class, ability grouping, time available for teaching, and so forth. The formal rule system includes regulations of a legislative nature concerning the duties of the teacher such as marking systems and rules concerning the employment of teachers such as the required number of lessons per week and demands of competency.

These three groups of systems are linked to three main concepts:
curriculum
the administrative apparatus
school laws and school legislation.
It is usual in the teaching situation that these factors cannot be influenced by either the teacher or the students. The only way of influencing them is through the political process. In turn, then, the curriculum, the administrative apparatus, and the laws of the school can be analyzed and related to the

economic, social, and political structure of the society. The relationship between these concepts would thus be:

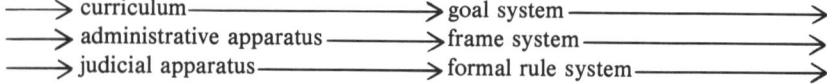

Figure 14-2.
School-society model

In the first model the concepts used were not particularly well defined, mainly because their pedagogical and psychological relevance were mixed. I have discussed only the pedagogical relevance of the concepts. This can lead to a conceptual paradigm in which the teaching process is looked upon as more or less mechanically determined by the structure of society. A purely pedagogical explanation of the educational process, even if it does take into account the social context, is as limited in its usefulness as a purely psychological explanation. This "joining" of a psychological conceptual structure and a pedagogical conceptual structure to explain educational processes is the central idea of the theory being developed here.

The main argument is that to explain any educational process, we must have a conceptual apparatus that relates the economic and social structure of society to the teaching process. This means that we must have concepts on different levels of analyses that can be related to each other using empirical references. But such a conceptual apparatus would constitute only one of two necessary parts of an explanation.

We can use an example to make this more concrete. Both the formulation of a curriculum and its manifestation in a goal system are determined by the particular cultural context. The curriculum will also express the structure of social and economic power in the society. The student's interpretation of the meaning of the teaching process is interpreted by him in relation to the social context in which he lives. His access to the content of the goal system is dependent upon the psychological prerequisites of the student. These prerequisites are not determined by nature alone but are also expressions of the economic, social, and political structure.

To return to the question of ability grouping, it is clear that this must be linked to both a pedagogical analysis of the functions of education and the manner in which these functions are transformed into the frames and curriculum. This idea is the key to our later analysis of educational research.

If we return to our first model (Fig. 14-1), we can now summarize our discussion as follows:

Frame Factors in Teaching

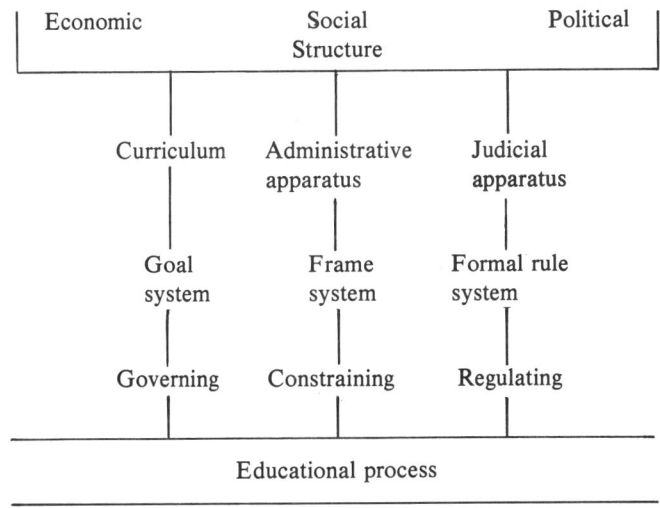

Figure 14-3.
Advanced frame model

Notes

1. U. Dahllöf, *Ability Grouping, Content Validity and Curriculum Process Analysis* (Goteburg: Reports from the Institute of Education, University of Education, 1969); U. Dahllöf, *Ability Grouping, Content Validity and Curriculum Process Analysis* (New York: Teachers College Press, Columbia University, 1971).

2. B. Bernstein, "On the Classification and Framing of Educational Knowledge," in *Knowledge and Control: New Directions for the Sociology of Education*, ed. M. F. D. Young (London: Collier-Macmillan, 1971), pp. 47–69; B. Bernstein, "Class and Pedagogics: Visible and Invisible," *Educational Studies* 1 (1975): 23–41.

3. U. Dahllöf, *Skoldifferentiering Och Undervisningsforlopp* (Stockholm: Almqvist and Wiksell, 1967); Dahllöf, *Ability Grouping* (1969); Dahllöf, *Ability Grouping* (1971); Dahllöf, "Trends in Process-Related Research at Different Problem Levels in Educational Sciences," *Scandinavian Journal of Educational Research* 19: 55–77; D. Kallos and U. P. Lundgren, *En Diskussion av Forutsattningar Och Riktlinger For Forsoksverskamhet Med Individanpassad Universitetsundervisning* (Stockholm: Universitetskanslersambetet, 1972); D. Kallos and U. P. Lundgren, "Evaleuring av Universitetsundervisning Som Pedagogiskt Vetenskapligt Problem," in *Utvardering av Universitet (Evaluation of Universities)*, ed. D. Kallos (Kopenhamn: Nordiska Radet, Nordisk Utredningsserie, 1974), p. 47–57; U. P. Lundgren, *Frame Factors and the Teaching Process: A Contribution to Curriculum Theory and Theory of Teaching* (Stockholm: Almqvist and Wiksell, 1972); U. P. Lundgren, *Pedagogical Frames and the Teaching Process: A Report from an Empirical Curriculum Project*, (Paper read at the annual meeting of the American Educational Research Association in New Orleans, 1973, Goteborg: Institute of Education, University of Goteborg).

4. See, for example, Dahllöf, *Skoldifferentiering;* Dahllöf, *Ability Grouping* (1969); Dahllöf, "Trends in Process-Related Research"; U. Dahllöf and U. P. Lundgren, "Macro and Micro Approaches Combined for Curriculum Process Analysis: A Swedish Educational Field Project" (mimeographed 1970); U. Dahllöf, U. P. Lundgren, M. Sioo, "Reform Implementation Studies as a Basis for Curriculum Theory," *Curriculum Theory Network Monographs Supplement* (1971), pp. 99–117.
5. Lundgren, *Frame Factors;* Lundgren, *Pedagogical Frames.*
6. Lundgren, *Frame Factors.*
7. Ibid., p.43.
8. G. Arfwedson, *Vad Kan Larare Gora? Ett Makroperspektiv Pa Lararnas Arbetssituation* (Stockholm: Pedagogiska Institutionen, Lararhogskolan i Stockholm, Fakta Och Debatt, 1976).
9. Lundgren, *Frame Factors.*
10. See, for example, A. A. Bellack, et al., *The Language of the Classroom* (New York: Teachers College Press, Columbia University, 1966).
11. E. Amidon and E. Hunter, *Improving Teaching: The Analysis of Verbal Interaction* (New York: Holt, Rinehart & Winston, 1967).
12. R. F. Bales, *Interaction Process Analysis* (Reading, Mass.: Addison-Wesley, 1950).
13. See also U. P. Lundgren, "Pedagogical Roles in the Classroom," in *Contemporary Research in the Sociology of Education*, ed. J. Eggleston (London: Methuen Press, 1974), pp. 200–14.
14. H. B. Dunkel, "Wanted: New Paradigms and a Normative Base for Research," in *Philosophical Redirection of Educational Research*, ed. L. G. Thomas (Chicago: University of Chicago Press, 1972), p. 77–93.
15. N. F. Kerlinger, *Foundations of Behavioral Research*, 2d ed. (London: Holt, Rinehart & Winston, 1973); R. M. W. Travers, *An Introduction to Educational Research*, 3d ed. (New York: Macmillan, 1970).
16. R. G. Paulston, *Conflicting Theories of Social and Educational Change: A Typological Review* (Pittsburgh: University Center for International Studies, University of Pittsburgh, 1976), p. 44.
17. See, for example, D. B. Gowin, "Is Educational Research Distinctive?" in Thomas, *Philosophical Redirection of Educational Research.*
18. See, for example, E. Altvater and F. Huisken, *Materialen zur Politischen Okonomie der Ausbildungssektors* (Erlangen: Politladen, 1971); P. Bourdieu and J. C. Passeron, *La Reproduction: Elemente pour une Theorie du Systeme d'Enseigement* (Paris: Edition de Minuit, 1970).
19. B. Abrahamsson, "Utbuildning och Samhalle: Nagra problemomraden," *Skolan som Arbetsplats* (Stockholm: Utbildningsdepartementet, Statens Offentliga Utredningar, 1974), pp. 291–338.
20. Y. A. Cohen, "Schools and Civilizational States," in *The Social Sciences and the Comparative Study of the Educational System*, ed. J. F. Tischer (Scranton, Pennsylvania: International Textbook Co., 1970).
21. See, for example, N. Keddie, "Classroom Knowledge," in *Knowledge and Control*, ed. M. F. D. Young (London: Collier-Macmillan, 1971).
22. See, for example, N. L. Gage, *Teacher Effectiveness and Teacher Education* (Palo Alto: Pacific Books, 1972).

15 Social Education in the Classroom: The Dynamics of the Hidden Curriculum

Henry A. Giroux
Anthony N. Penna

Introduction

In this article Giroux and Penna argue that the debate over the relationship between schooling and the hidden curriculum has been dominated by three contrasting perspectives: a structural-functional view, a phenomenological view, and a neo-Marxist view. After examining the assumptions that underline each of these positions, the authors argue that the neo-Marxist view offers the most comprehensive and useful perspective for understanding the nature of schooling, at least in the political and social sense. Moreover, the authors attempt to demonstrate the importance of the latter view by illuminating how its basic theoretical assumptions can be used to both analyze and overcome the authoritarian effects of the hidden curriculum in the classroom.

As you read the article, examine the basic assumptions of the three traditions that Giroux and Penna outline.
- Which one do you think provides the most useful approach for analyzing the hidden curriculum?
- Would you support the mode of pedagogy suggested by Giroux and Penna? If so, why? If not, why?
- Are some of their suggestions open to criticisms? If so, which ones?
- Can you suggest an alternative approach?

The belief that schooling can be defined as the sum of its official course offerings is a naive one. Yet such an implicit belief served as the theme of the social studies curriculum development reform movement of the 1960s and early 1970s. Developers believed that if they changed the curriculum of the nation's schools, the school's ills would be remedied.[1] In recent years, however, numerous reasons have been offered to explain the seeming inability of the reform movement to penetrate the traditional patterns of instruction in the schools. Inadequate teacher preparation and curriculum materials that overestimated the perceived capabilities of students represent the more familiar, albeit uncritical, explanations offered by educators. Now some of them lend uncritical support for the "back-to-basics" movement in social studies education, assuming once again that new curriculum materials will provide an answer to the question of how to bring about change in social studies education. Attend to the cognitive needs and capabilities of students, they argue, and the failures of the recent reform movement will be overcome.[2]

Unfortunately, such recommendations are based heavily on structural-functional educational models of curriculum theory,[3] which fails to perceive the purpose of social education beyond its limited explicit instructional outcomes. Further, there is a failure to recognize the complex, intimate relationship between the institution of the school and the nation's economic and political institutions. Once the relationship between schooling and the larger society is recognized, questions about the nature and meaning of the schooling experience can be viewed from a theoretical perspective capable of illuminating the often-ignored relationship between school knowledge and social control. By viewing schools within the context of the larger society, social studies developers can begin to focus on the tacit teaching that goes on in schools and help to uncover the ideological messages embedded in both the content of the formal curriculum and the social relations of the classroom encounter.

It is only recently that some educators have begun to raise questions that point to the need for a thorough study of the interconnections between ideology, instruction, and curriculum.[4] For instance, Michael Apple argues that we need to:

... examine critically not just "how a student acquires more knowledge" (the dominant question in our efficiency-minded field) but "why and how particular aspects of the collective culture are presented in school as objective, factual knowledge." How concretely may official knowledge represent ideological configuations of the dominant interests in a society? How do schools legitimate these limited and partial standards of knowing as unquestioned truths? These questions must be asked of at least three areas of school life: (1) How the basic day-to-day regularities of schools contribute to model, students accept social conformity and lose the ability to make meaning for themselves.

The social-phenomenological approach to educational theory, often called the new sociology, moves far beyond the structural-functionalist position in its approach to the study of schooling. The new sociology focuses critically on a number of assumptions about classroom interactions and social encounters. For the new sociologists, any valid theory of socialization has to be seen as "a theory of the construction of social reality, if not of a particular historical social order.[11] They posit a model of socialization in which meaning is made interactively. That is, meaning is "given" by situations but also created by students as they interact in classrooms. Moreover, the social construction of meaning by both teachers and students raises anew questions about the objective nature of knowledge itself. For the new sociologists, the principles governing the organization, distribution, and evaluation of knowledge are not absolute and objective; instead, they are sociohistorical constructs forged by active human beings creating rather than simply existing in the world.

In this approach, the view of students as actors with a fixed identity is replaced by a more dynamic model of student behavior. The new sociologists focus on the participation of students in defining and redefining their worlds. Thus the focus of classroom studies with the rise of the new sociology has shifted from an exclusive emphasis on institutional behavior to a focus on students' interactions with language, social relations, and categories of meaning. The proponents of the new sociology have provided a new dimension to the study of the relationship between socialization and the school curriculum.[12] The new sociology raises to a new level of discussion the relationship between the distribution of power and knowledge. It requires social studies curriculum developers to make problematic many of the truisms that characterized the selection, organization, and distribution of knowledge and pedagogical styles inherent in curriculum development. In one sense, the new sociology has stripped the school curriculum of its innocence.

But the new sociology is not without flaws—flaws that undermine its ability to resolve the very problems it identified. The most thoughtful critique lodged against the new sociology is that it represents a form of subjective idealism.[13] Allegedly, at its core the new sociology lacks an adequate theory of social change and consciousness. While it helps educators to uncover the ways in which knowledge is defined and imposed, it fails to provide criteria for measuring the value of different forms of classroom knowledge. By endorsing the value and relevance of students' intentionality, the new sociology has succumbed to a notion of cultural relativity. It lacks a theoretical construct to explain the role ideology plays in the construction of knowledge by students. It fails to account for the fact that the way students perceive the external world does not always correspond to the actual structure and content of that world. Subjective perceptions are dialectically related to the social world and do not simply "mirror" it. To ignore this, as the new sociology proponents have, is to fall prey to a distorted subjectivism. Sharp and Greene have captured this position cogently.

> The social world is more than the mere constellations of meaning. Although we can accept that the knowing subject acts in the world on the basis of his understanding, that there is always a subjective factor which enters into knowledge of the world, it does not follow from this that the world possesses the character which the knowing subject bestows upon it, that the objects which we know in the social world are mere subjective creations capable of being differently constituted in an infinite variety of ways. The phenomenologist appears to be putting forward what we could argue is an extreme form of subjective idealism. Where the external objective world is merely a constitution of the creative consciousness, the subject-object dualism disappears in the triumph of the constituting subject.[14]

In the final analysis, the new sociology fails in spite of its desire for radical change and fundamental egalitarianism. Its failure lies in its inability to illuminate how social and political structures function to mask reality and promote ideological hegemony.[15] Thus, this position not only fails to explain how different varieties of classroom meanings, knowledge, and experiences arise, it also fails to explain how they are able to sustain themselves. By focusing exclusively on the microlevel of schooling, on studies of classroom interaction, the new sociology falls short of illustrating how sociopolitical arrangements influence and constrain individual and collective efforts to construct knowledge and meaning. These arrangements probably play an important role in influencing the very texture of classroom life.

A third position is a neo-Marxist approach to socialization and social change. While this position is not without its own flaws, its value lies in being able to move beyond the apolitical view of the functionalist position as well as the subjective idealism of the new sociology. At the core of the neo-Marxist approach is a recognition of the relationship between economic and cultural reproduction. Moreover, inherent in this perspective is an intersection of theory, ideology, and social practice. Schools are viewed in this approach as agents of ideological control which function to reproduce and to maintain dominant beliefs, values, and norms. This is not meant to suggest that schools are merely factories that process students and "mirror" the interests of the larger society; such a perspective is clearly mechanistic and reductionist.[16] The neo-Marxist position points out that schools in corresponding ways are linked to the principles and processes governing the work place. The cutting edge of this perspective is its insistence on connecting macro forces in the larger society to microanalysis such as classroom studies.

The neo-Marxist approach, more clearly than the other two approaches identified in this chapter, illuminates how social reproduction of knowledge is related to the notion of false consciousness. While stressing the importance of a student's subjective role in constituting meaning for himself, neo-Marxists are equally concerned with the way in which social and economic conditions constrain and distort social construction of meaning, particularly as mediated through the hidden curriculum. Not only do classroom studies have to be linked to the study of the larger society, they have to be connected to a notion of justice, one that is capable of articulating how certain unjust social structures can be identified and replaced.

School Knowledge and Classroom Relations

While the neo-Marxist perspective provides an important focus on the ideological nature of the process of schooling and the larger social order, it has done little to explicate in specific terms the kinds of knowledge and classroom social relationships that have been used to reproduce the reified consciousness that maintains the cultural and economic interests of a stratified society. This is where the structural-functionalists and new sociology adherents have made valuable contributions to the study of curriculum and social education. By drawing on the insights within a new Marxist framework, we can begin to answer the fundamental question of what is learned in schools.

In response to this question, Robert Dreeben[17] points out that the student learns more than simply instructional knowledge and skills and that the traditional view of schooling as being "primarily cognitive in nature is at best only partially tenable.[18] Stephen Arons reinforces this view by calling school "a social environment from which a child may learn much more than what is in the formal curriculum.[19] Implicit in this analysis of the school and classroom as a socializing agent is an important pedagogical premise. The premise is that any curriculum designed to introduce positive changes in classrooms will fail unless such a proposal is rooted in an understanding of those sociopolitical forces that strongly influence the very texture of day-to-day classroom pedagogical practices.

Since it is not entirely clear to social studies educators that schools are indeed sociopolitical institutions, a case must first be made to validate the position that schools are inextricably linked to other social agencies and institutions within American society. Ralph Tyler[20] highlights the social function of schools by pointing out that all educational philosophies are essentially an outgrowth of one of two possible theoretical perspectives. He claims that a statement of educational philosophy can be built upon one of the following questions: "Should the schools develop young people to fit into present society as it is, or does the school have a revolutionary mission to develop young people who will seek to improve the society?"[21]

Tyler's point about educational philosophy is important for a number of reasons. First, it reinforces the notion that schools have a sociopolitical function and cannot exist independently of the society in which they operate. Second, it suggests that underlying every educational program designed to intervene in the structure of the schools there lies a theoretical frame of reference. Paulo Freire, the Brazilian educator, argues both points in his claim that

> There is no such thing as a neutral educational process. Education either functions as an instrument which is used to facilitate the integration of the younger generation into the logic of the present system and bring about conformity to it, or it becomes the "practice of freedom"—the means by which men and women deal critically and creatively with reality and discover how to participate in the transformation of their world.[22]

Whether they realize it or not, social studies educators work in the service of one of the two positions outlined by Tyler and Freire.[23]

An examination of schooling and its sociological ties to the family and the work place can illuminate the social and political functions of schools. While a number of sociologists convincingly point out that schools no longer assume the role of a surrogate family, they do perform a socializing function that the social structure of the family cannot satisfy. For instance, comparing the functions of the family to those of the school, Robert Dreeben[24] argues that the structural properties of the family, while satisfying specific affective needs of children, cannot adequately socialize them to function in the adult world. According to him, schooling demands the formation of social relationships that are more time bounded, more diverse, less dependent, and less emotive than those of the family. Unlike the family, schools separate performance from emotional expression and perform what is considered their most explicit purpose: "Imparting the skills, information, and beliefs each child will eventually need as an adult member of society."[25]

He argues that schools do more than provide instruction. They provide norms, or principles of conduct, which are learned through the varied social experiences in schools that influence students' lives. Though Dreeben ignores the political nature of these social experiences, he does mention four important norms that students learn: independence, achievement, universalism, and specificity.

Worth noting is Dreeben's failure to mention in specific ideological terms the cultural values that support and give meaning to these norms. Two examples will suffice. Independence is defined as "handling tasks with which under different circumstances, one can rightfully expect the help of others."[26] Achievement is defined so as to assure pupils of the gratification of "winning and losing" and, while not stated by Dreeben, justifies extrinsic rewards and the notion that someone must always come in last.

That students learn more than cognitive skills is illuminated further in Bernstein's analysis which brings into sharp focus some of the features of the political nature of schooling. His analysis argues that students learn values and norms that would produce "good" industrial workers. Students internaliz values that stress a respect for authority, punctuality, cleanliness, docility, and conformity. What the students learn from the formally sanctioned content of the curriculum is much less important than what they learn from the ideological assumptions embedded in the school's three message systems: the system of curriculum; the system of classroom pedagogical styles; and the system of evaluation.[27] In describing what students learn from the school's hidden curriculum, Stanley Aronowitz[28] provides a capsule view of the socializing processes that operate within these "message" systems:

Indeed, the child learns in school. . . . The child learns that the teacher is the authoritative person in the classroom, but that she is subordinate to a principal. Thus the structure of society can be learned through understanding the hierarchy of power within the structure of the school. Similarly, the working-class child learns its role in society. On the one side, school impresses students as a whole with their powerlessness since they are without the knowledge required to become citizens and workers. On the other, the hierarchy of occupations and classes is reproduced by the hierarchy of grade levels and tracks within grades. Promotion to successive grades is the reward for having mastered the approved political and social behavior as well as the prescribed "cognitive" material. But within grades, particularly in large urban schools, further distinctions among students are made on the basis of imputed intelligence and that in turn is determined by the probable ability of children to succeed in terms of standards set by the educational system.[29]

Writers such as Dreeben and Aronowitz[30] have helped to make it clear that the school functions as an agency of socialization within a network of larger institutions. Yet, with few exceptions, the political role of the school and how that role affects educational objectives, methods, content, and organizational structures has not been adequately illuminated by social studies educators.[31]

While commenting on the consequences of ignoring the political nature of education, Jerome Bruner[32] candidly indicates that educators can no longer strike a fictional posture of neutrality and objectivity.

A theory of instruction is a political theory in the power sense that it derives from consensus concerning the distribution of power within the society—who shall be educated and to fulfill what roles? In the very same sense, pedagogical theory must surely derive from a conception of economics, for where there is a division of labor within the society and an exchange of goods and services for wealth and prestige, then how people are educated and in what number and with what constraints on the use of resources are all relevant issues. The psychologist or educator who formulates pedagogical theory without regard to the political, economic, and social setting of the educational process courts triviality and merits being ignored in the community and in the classroom.[33]

As mentioned previously, a serious approach to social studies educational change would have to begin with an examination of the contradictions that exist between the school's hidden curriculum and official curriculum. Any approach to social studies curriculum development that ignores the existence of the hidden curriculum runs the risk of not only being incomplete but also insignificant. For the heart of the school's function is not to be found simply in the daily dispensing of information by teachers but also "in the social relations of the educational encounter."[34]

School Curriculum Organization

But before any study of classroom social relations is put forth, it must be made clear that the content of what is taught in social studies classes plays a vital role in the political socialization of students. For instance, studies by Apple, Anyon, and Popkewitz[35] have pointed out that what counts as "objective" knowledge in social studies textbooks in fact often represents a one-sided and theoretically distorted view of the subject under study. Knowledge is often accepted as truth legitimizing a specific view of the world that is either questionable or patently false. The selection, organization, and distribution of social studies knowledge is hidden from the realm of ideology.[36] In addition to its overt and covert messages, the way knowledge is selected and organized represents a priori assumptions by the educator about its value and legitimacy. In the final analysis, these are ideological considerations that structure the students' perception of the world. If the fragile ideological nature of these considerations is not made clear to students, then they will learn more about social conformity than critical inquiry. To break through the "hidden curriculum" of knowledge, social studies educators must help students understand that knowledge is not only variable and linked to human interest but also must be examined in regards to its claims to validity. Popkewitz has succinctly focused in on this issue for social studies educators with his claim.

Constructing curriculum requires that educators give attention to the social disciplines as a human product whose meanings are transmitted in social processes. Instruction should give serious attention to the conflicting views of the world these crafts generate, the social location and the social contexts of inquiry. To plan for children's study of ideas, educators are compelled to inquire into the nature and character of the discourse found in history, sociology, or anthropology. What problems does each deal with? What modes of thought exist? What are its paradigmatic tasks? What limitations are placed on the knowledge of their findings? Instruction should be concerned with the different perspectives of phenomena that are within each discipline and how these men and women come to know what they know.[37]

Moreover, it follows that equal weight must be given in any analysis of the hidden curriculum to the organizational structures that influence and govern teacher-student interactions within the classroom. For these suggest an

Social Education in the Classroom

ideological character that is no less compelling than curriculum content in the socialization process at work in the classroom encounter. Though distinctly apolitical in nature, Philip Jackson's[38] work represents one important attempt to analyze the social processes that give shape to another dimension of the hidden curriculum. Unlike the official curriculum, with its stated cognitive and affective objectives, the hidden curriculum in this case is rooted in those organizational aspects of classroom life which are not commonly perceived by either students or teachers. According to Jackson, elements of the hidden curriculum are shaped by three key analytical concepts: crowds, praise, and power.

In short, working in classrooms means learning to live in crowds. Coupled with the prevailing values of the educational system, this has profound implications for the social education established in the schools. Equally significant is the fact that schools are evaluative settings, and what a student learns is not only how to be evaluated but how to evaluate himself and others as well. Finally, schools are marked by a basic, concrete division between the powerful (teachers) and the powerless (students). As Jackson[39] points out, what this means "in three major ways, then—as members of crowds, as potential recipients of praise or reproof, and as pawns of institutional authorities—students are confronted with aspects of reality that at least during their childhood years are relatively confined to the hours spent in the classroom."[40]

In more specific terms, especially those that highlight student-teacher interactions, Jackson's analysis of the hidden curriculum proves to be particularly instructive. Learning to live in crowds affects students in a number of important ways. Students have to learn constantly to wait to use resources, with the ultimate outcome being that they learn to postpone or give up desires. In spite of the constant interruptions in the classroom, students have to learn to be quiet. Though students work in groups with other people whom they eventually get to know, they have to learn how to be isolated in a crowd. For Jackson, the quintessential virtue learned by students under these conditons is patience (that is, not a patience rooted in mediated restraint but one that is rooted in an unwarranted submission to authority). "They must also, to some extent, learn to suffer in silence. They are expected to bear with equanimity, in other words, the continued delay, denial, and interruption of their personal wishes and desires."[41]

Praise and power in the classroom are inextricably connected to one another. While students may find themselves in a position occasionally in which they can evaluate each other, the unquestioned source of praise and reproof is the teacher. Though the administration of positive and negative sanctions is the teacher's most visible symbol of power, the real significance of his or her role lies in the network of social relationships and values that are reproduced with the use of that authority. The nature of the hidden curriculum is nowhere more clearly revealed than in the system of evaluation. The potential effect of evaluation comes into sharp focus where one recognizes that what is taught and evaluated in the classroom is both academic and nonacademic, and includes in the latter institutional adjustment and specific personal qualitites.

In fact, some notable studies have been made that support the above hypothesis; Bowles and Gintis,[42] after reviewing a number of studies that link personality traits, attitudes, and behavioral attributes to school grades, reached the following conclusions:

Students are rewarded for exhibiting discipline, subordinacy, intellectually as opposed to emotionally oriented behavior, and hard work independent from intrinsic task motivation. Moreover, these traits are rewarded independently of any effect of "proper demeanor" on scholastic achievement.[43]

In addition, they point out that students who are rated high in citizenship (that is, conformity to the social order of the school), also rated "significantly below average on measures of creativity and mental flexibility."[44] Viewed from the student's perspective, the classroom becomes a miniature work place in which time, space, content, and structure are fixed by others. Rewards are extrinsic, and all social interaction between teachers and students is mediated by hierarchically organized structures. The underlying message learned in this context points less to schools helping students to think critically about the world in which they live than it does to schools acting as agents of social control.

Teachers obviously play a vital role in maintaining the structure of schools and transmitting the values needed to support the larger social order.[45] Lortie's[46] study of teachers indicates that they generally are unable to offset the conservative pedagogical influences accepted by them during their precollege and college schooling. He also claims that "recruitment resources foster a conservative outlook among entrants ... they appeal strongly to young people who are favorably disposed toward the existing system of schools."[47] Lortie's study also found that one of the most severe shortcomings of teachers was their subjective, idiosyncratic approach to teaching. Lacking a thought-out theoretical framework from which to develop a methodology and content, teachers lacked significant criteria to shape, guide, or evaluate their own work. But more importantly, they pass their distrust of theory on to their students and help in perpetuating intellectual passivity.

As mentioned before, at the heart of the social educational encounter is a hidden curriculum whose values shape and influence practically every aspect of the student's educational experience. But this should not suggest that the hidden curriculum is so powerful that there is little hope for educational reform. Instead, the hidden curriculum should be seen not as an *impassable* boundary but as *providing* a possible direction for focusing educational change. For instance, while social studies developers alone cannot eliminate the hidden curriculum, they can identify its organizational structure and the political assumptions upon which it rests. By doing so, they can develop a pedagogy, curriculum materials, and classroom structural properties that offset the most undemocratic features of the traditional hidden curriculum. In doing so, a first but significant step will be made to help teachers and students reach beyond the classroom experience and tentatively move toward changing those institutional arrangements.

Democratic Conditions and Collective Action

Before changes in social education and in social studies development can be undertaken, however, social studies educators will have to develop very specific classroom processes designed to promote values and beliefs which encourage democratic, critical modes of student-teacher participation and interaction. That the traditional hidden curriculum of schooling is inimical to the stated aims of the official curriculum is a fact that no longer escapes astute social analysis.[48] Instead of preparing students to enter the society with skills that will allow them to reflect critically upon and intervene in the world in order to change it, schools act as conservative forces that, for the most part, socialize students to conform to the status quo. The structure, organization, and content of contemporary schooling serve to equip students with the personality requisites desired in the bureaucratically structured, hierarchically organized work force. As Philip Jackson has pointed out:

So far as their power structure is concerned, classrooms are not too dissimilar from factories and offices, those ubiquitous organizations in which so much of our adult life is spent. Thus, schools might really be called a preparation for life but not in the usual sense in which educators employ that term.[49]

The remaining section of this paper will identify an alternative set of values and classroom social processes. In our view, these alternatives represent a basis for formulating a collectivist and democratic social education, stripped of egoistic individualism and alienating social relationships. These values and processes should be used by social studies educators in developing a content and pedagogy which link theory and practice and restore to students and teachers an awareness of the social and personal importance of active participation and critical thinking. While the values will be enumerated at the outset, the classroom processes will be illuminated through an analysis of the specific features that in our judgment should characterize social education.

The values and social processes which provide the theoretical underpinning for social education include developing in students a respect for moral commitment, group solidarity, and social responsibility. In addition, a nonauthoritarian individualism should be fostered, one that maintains a balance with

group cooperation and social awareness. Every effort should be made to give students an awareness of the necessity of developing choices of their own and to act on those choices with an understanding of situational constraints. The educational process itself will be open to examination in relation to its links to the larger society.

Students should experience social studies as an apprenticeship in the milieu of social action, or as Freire has stated,[50] students should be taught the practice of thinking about practice. One way of doing this is to view and evaluate each learning experience, whenever possible, with respect to its connections with the larger social-economic totality. Moreover, it is important that students not only think about both the content and practice of critical communication but recognize as well the importance of translating the outcome of these experiences into concrete action. For example, it is folly in our view to engage students in topics of political and social inequality in the classroom and in the  larger political world and to ignore the realities and pernicious effects of economic and income inequality on the quality of life of substantial numbers of people in schools, communities, and nations. Even when linkage to the larger reality is made, a failure to address and to implement the practical will not provide students with the learning implied in Freire's appeal. In other words, it is important that social studies educators provide students with the opportunity to grasp the dynamic dialectic between critical consciousness and social action. There is a need then to integrate critical awareness, social processes, and social practice in such a way that what is made clear to students is not simply how the forces of social control work but also how they can be overcome. Students should be able to recognize the truth value of Marx's eleventh thesis on Feuerbach ". . . the philosophers have only interpreted the world in various ways; the point is, to change it."[51]

Many liberal social studies educators accept these values and social processes and attempt to develop content-based curriculum that translates them into practice. But, in effect, liberals strip these values and social processes of their radical content by situating them within the framework of social adjustment rather than social and political emancipation. The liberal philosophic stance with its emphasis on progress through social melioration, the value of meritocracy and the professional expert, and the viability of a mass education system dedicated *to serving* the needs of the industrial order fails to penetrate and utilize the radical cutting edge of the values and social processes we support. Elizabeth Cagan captures the contradiction between liberal thought and radical values and social practices in her comment:

While liberal reformers intend to use education to promote equality, community, and humanistic social interaction, they do not confront those aspects of the schools which pull in the opposite direction. Their blindness to these contradictions may stem from their class position: as middle-class reformers they are unwilling to advocate the kind of

Social Education in the Classroom 223

egalitarianism which is necessary for a true human community. Reforms in pedagogical technique have been instituted, but the ... [hidden curriculum] ... remain[s] in effect. This hidden curriculum promotes competitiveness, individualism, and authoritarianism.[52]

The social processes of most classrooms militate against students developing a sense of community. As in the larger societal order, competition and individual striving are at the core of American schooling. In ideological terms, collectivity and social solidarity represent powerful structural threats to the ethos of capitalism. This ethos is built not only upon the atomization and division of labor but the fragmentation of consciousness and social relationships.[53] Whatever virtues about collectivity that are brought to the public's attention exist solely in form and not in substance. Both in and out of schools, self-interest represents the criterion for acting on and entering into social relationships. The structure of schooling reproduces the ethos of privatization and the moral posture of selfishness at almost every level of the formal and hidden curricula. Whether gently supporting the philosophy of "do your own thing" or maintaining pedagogical structures which undermine collective action, the message coming from most classrooms is one that enshrines the self at the expense of the group. The hidden message is one that supports alienation.[54]

The classroom scenario that fosters this unbridled notion of individualism is a familiar one. Students traditionally sit in rows staring at the back of each others' heads and at the teacher who faces them in symbolic, authoritarian fashion or else in a large semicircle with teacher and student space rigidly proscribed. Events in the classroom are governed by a rigid time schedule imposed by a system of bells and reinforced by cues from teachers while the class is in session. Instruction and, hopefully, some formal learning usually begin and end because it is the correct predetermined time not because a cognitive process has been stimulated into action.

Implementation

A number of social processes help to undermine the authoritarian effects of the hidden curriculum in the classroom. Our terminology will be familiar to all social studies developers; liberals among them will espouse the immediate instructional goals, but only reconstructionists will accept the long-range implications of these processes for life in classrooms, schools, and larger social-political institutions.

The pedagogical foundation for democratic processes in the classroom can be established by eliminating the pernicious practice of "tracking" students. This tradition in schools of grouping students according to "abilities" and perceived performance is of dubious instructional value. The justification for this practice is based on traditional genetic theories which have been systematically refuted on intellectual and ethical grounds.[55] A more heterogeneous class provides a better opportunity for flexibility to be manifested. For instance, in the heterogeneous class setting, students who qualitatively perform faster than other students could be given the opportunity to function as peers acting as individual or group leaders for other students. In such a situation, students can act collectively in the process of learning and teaching. As such, knowledge becomes the vehicle for dialogue and analysis as well as the basis for new classroom social relationships. Moreover, not only are more progressive social relationships developed in this context, but traditional notions of learning and achievement are now made problematic. It must be stressed that social education should be based on a notion of achievement that is at odds with traditional genetic theories of intelligence, which serve as the theoretical base to support tracking.

With the elimination of tracking, power is further diffused in a classroom so individuals in both peer and group-leadership roles are able to assume leadership positions formerly reserved for the teacher alone. In other words, with the breakdown of rigid, hierarchical roles and rules, which Basil Bernstein has called strong framing, both students and teachers can explore democratic relationships rarely developed in the traditional classroom.[56] These new relationships will also allow teachers to set the groundwork for breaking down the cellular structure exposed by Dan Lortie's study. The cellular structure refers to the failure of teachers to mutually adapt their task and actions. Most teachers do not share pedagogical strategies; and, thus, they lack any cohesiveness in their professional interpersonal relationships.[57] By sharing their power and roles, teachers will be in a better position to break through the provincialism and narrow socialization that prevents them from sharing and examining their theory and practice of pedagogy with both students and colleagues.

Another important change that such courses should perpetuate centers around the issue of authority and grades. Extrinsic rewards should be minimized whenever possible, and students should be given the opportunity to experience roles that will enable them to direct the learning process independently of the behavior usually associated with an emphasis on grades as rewards. Social relationships in the traditional classroom are based upon power relations inextricably linked to the teacher's allotment and distribution of grades. Grades become in many cases the ultimate discipline instruments by which the teacher imposes his or her desired values, behavior patterns, and beliefs upon students.[58] Dialogical grading eliminates this pernicious practice since it allows students to gain some control over the distribution of grades and thereby weakens the traditional correspondence between grades and authority. We refer to such grading as dialogical because it involves a dialogue between students and teachers over the criteria, function, and consequences of the system of evaluation. The use of the term is in fact an extension of Freire's emphasis on the role of dialogue in clarifying and democratizing social relationships.[59]

While opportunities for dialogue with teachers and peers should be encouraged, they are not conducive to large group settings. In small groups, students should evaluate and test the logic in each other's work. The importance of group work to social education rests on a number of crucial assumptions. Group work represents one of the most effective ways to demystify the traditional, manipulative role of the teacher; moreover, it provides students with social contexts that stress social responsibility and group solidarity.

Group interaction provides students with the experiences that they need in order to realize that they can learn from one another. Only by diffusing authority along horizontal lines will students be able to share and appreciate the importance of learning collectively. Crucial to such a process is the element of dialogue. Through group dialogue, the norms of cooperation and sociability offset the traditional hidden curriculum's emphasis on competition and excessive individualism. In addition, the process of group instruction provides students with the opportunity for experiencing, rather than simply hearing about, the dynamics of participatory democracy.

In short, developing an awareness that is nurtured in a shared task to democratize classroom relationships is imperative for students if they are to overcome the lack of community reminiscent of the traditional classroom and the larger social order. The group encounter provides the social basis for the development of such a consciousness. Under such conditons, social relations of education marked by dominance, subordination, and an uncritical respect for authority can be effectively minimized.

Social relations marked by reciprocity and communality are not the only by-products of the group component. Another important feature centers around giving students the opportunity to serve an apprenticeship in teaching. By evaluating each other's work, acting as peer leaders, participating in and leading discussions, students learn that teaching is not based on intuitive and imitative pedagogical approaches. Instead, by establishing a close working relationship with teachers and peers, students are given the chance to understand that an analytical, codified body of experience is the central element in any pedagogy. This helps both students and teachers to recognize that behind any pedagogy are values, beliefs, and assumptions informed by a particular world view. Most students see teaching in terms of individual personalities rather than the result of a thought-out set of socially constructed pedagogical axioms.[60] By using this course of action, both students and teachers are provided with a "particular" framework for teaching that highlights the theoretical underpinnings of classroom pedagogy.

The concept of time in schools restricts the development of healthy social and intellectual relationships among students and teachers. Reminiscent of life in factories with its production schedules and hierarchial work relationships, the daily routine of most classrooms acts as a brake upon participation and democratic processes. Modified self-pacing is a classroom process that is more compatible with the view that aptitude is the amount of time required by the students to develop a critical comprehension and resolution of the task under study.

It is imperative that students be given the opportunity to work alone and in groups at a comfortable learning pace so as to be able to develop quickly a learning style that enables them to move beyond the fragmented and atheoretical pedagogies that now characterize American education.[61] The flexible use of a mode of self-paced learning could modify these practices.

Self-pacing is important for other reasons. The delay and denial characteristic of most conventional classrooms can be offset by freeing teachers and students to respond to each other almost immediately. Students need not wait to get feedback and communication about their work. This militates against students giving up or postponing their desire to learn or to share and analyze what they have learned with other students. Modified self-pacing allows students to work alone or with other students at a comfortable pace within reasonable bounds mutually agreed upon by teachers and students. Under this format, the clock ceases to shape the pace and character of the class, and the tyranny of a rigid time schedule gives way to a schedule governed by reciprocal exchanges. Moreover, since students have a measure of control over their work, grades, and time, this eliminates pitting students against one another and reinforces the notion that learning is essentially a shared phenomenon.

In political terms, the self-pacing and peer-leader features inveigh against the myth of considering the teacher as the indispensable expert, alone qualified to define and distribute knowledge.[62] Moreover, with the use of peers and modified self-pacing, democratic classroom relationships are developed and the one-dimensionality of traditional classroom social relationships gives way to the possibility of infinitely richer classroom social encounters. These classroom social encounters are reciprocally humanizing and are mediated through an emancipatory conceptual framework.

The peer-leader and self-paced features represent two social processes that significantly offset some of the organizational and structural properties of the traditional classroom. In most traditional classrooms, students work in an isolated and independent fashion. This is usually rationalized by educators on the grounds that it fosters independence. In part, this is true, but it fosters a type of independence that precludes the development of social relationships among age peers and adults that promote opportunities to share and work in an interdependent fashion. Moreover, its function appears to be more ideological than rational and represents a strong pedagogical component in upholding the division of labor characteristic of the larger society. In any case, the traditional notion of independence does not strike a balance between developing one's specific talents and sharing tasks with other students. The self-paced and peer features smoothly reconcile this contradiction. Students not only are given ample opportunity to explore their talents and interests at a pace they can control, they also can share their interests with other people. They get help both from the classroom leaders and from their peers.

Conclusion

This paper provides the groundwork for a new thrust in the task of identifying the dynamics and ideological assumptions underlying specific patterns of socialization in social studies classrooms. By identifying the social processes of classroom and school life which make these patterns operative and highlighting the normative nature of social studies knowledge, it attempts to clarify the dichotomy between the goals of social studies developers and the process of schooling. In our judgment, the recognition of this dichotomy between the official and hidden curriculum will compel social studies educators to develop a new theoretical perspective about the dynamics of educational change, one that penetrates the functional relationships that exist between the institutions of the schools, the work place and the political world. In so doing, they will begin to uncover those social processes in all sociopolitical institutions including the classroom that militate against the creation of a democratic, social education. Further enumeration and elucidation of those processes as well as the search for interconnections among them will become the necessary prerequisites for educators planning to intervene into the educational process.

For the message is a clear one. Social studies educators will run the risk of repeated failure unless they develop a structural foundation that will counter the social processes and values of the hidden curriculum. If social solidarity, individual growth, and dedication to social action are to emerge from social education, the hidden curriculum will have to be either eliminated or minimized as much as possible. There is little room in social education for tracking and social sorting, hierarchical social relationships, the correspondence between evaluation and power, and the fragmented and isolated interpersonal dynamics of the classroom encounter, all of which characterize the hidden curriculum. These classroom processes will have to be replaced by democratic social processes and values that take into consideration the reciprocal interaction of goals, pedagogy, content, and structure.

The above task will not be an easy one; the changes to be made will be difficult and often frustrating but nonetheless necessary. Educational reformers can no longer operate within the limited confines of traditional educational theory and practice. It should be clear that social education is normative and political in essence and at its best can be both emancipatory and reflective. By stepping outside the traditional parameters of educational theory and practice, we can view schooling as inextricably linked to a web of larger socioeconomic and political arrangements. And by analyzing the nature of the relationship between schools and the dominant society in political and normative terms, we can counter a hidden curriculum defined through the ideology of traditional classroom social processes. If social education is in Kant's words to be used to educate students for a better society, social studies educators will even have to go further than democratizing their schools and classrooms. They will have to do more than help develop changes in student consciousness; they will have to help implement the rationale for reconstructing a new social order whose institutional arrangements, in the final analysis, will provide the basis for a truly humanizing education.

Notes

1. C. E. Silberman, *Crisis in the Classroom: The Remaking of American Education* (New York: Random House, 1970); J. Spring, *The Sorting Machine: National Educational Policy Since 1945* (New York: David McKay Co., 1976), pp. 93–139.

2. G. Lyons, "The Higher Illiteracy," *Harper's* 253:15 16 (September 1976), pp. 33–40; B. Brodinsky, "Back to the Basics: The Movement and Its Meanings," *Phi Delta Kappan* 58:7 (March 1977): 522–27.

3. W. F. Pinar, "Notes on the Curriculum Field 1978," *American Educational Research Journal* 7:8 (September 1978): 5–12.

4. P. Bourdieu and J. C. Passeron, *Reproductions in Education, Society and Culture* (London: Sage Publications, 1977); B. Bernstein, *Class, Codes and Control* (London: Collier-Macmillan, 1976).

5. M. Apple, "Curriculum as Ideological Selection," *Comparative Educational Review* 20 (June 1975): 210–11.

6. R. Dreeben, *On What Is Learned in Schools* (Reading, Mass.: Addison-Wesley, 1968); P. Jackson, *Life in Classrooms* (New York: Holt, Rinehart & Winston, 1968); N. Overly, ed., *The Unstudied Curriculum* (Washington, D.C.: Association of Curriculum and Supervision, 1970); M. Apple, "The Hidden Curriculum and the Nature of Conflict," *Interchange* 2:4 (1971); M. Apple and N. King, "What Do Schools Teach?" in *Humanistic Education,* ed. R. H. Weller (Berkeley: McCutchan, 1977), pp. 29–63.

7. P. Stern and J. Yarbrough, "Hannah Arendt," *American Scholar* 47:3 (Summer 1978): 380.

8. T. Parsons, "The School Class as a Social System: Some of Its Functions in American Society," *Harvard Educational Review* 29:4 (Fall 1959): 297–318; R. Dreeben, "The Contribution of Schooling to the Learning of Norms," *Socialization and Schools* (Cambridge: Harvard University Press, 1968).

9. M. Apple, "Some Aspects of the Relationships Between Economics and Cultural Reproduction" (Paper presented at Kent State Invitational Conference on Curriculum Theory, November 11, 1977, p. 29).

10. J. Karabel and A. H. Halsey, eds., *Power and Ideology in Education* (New York: Oxford University Press, 1972).

11. J. O'Neill, "Embodiment and Child Development: A Phenomenological Approach," in *Childhood and Socialization*, ed. H. P. Dreitzel (New York: Macmillan, 1973), p. 65.

12. M. F. D. Young, ed., *Knowledge and Control* (London: Collier-Macmillan, 1976); N. Keddie, ed., *The Myth of Cultural Deprivation* (Baltimore, Maryland: Penguin, 1973); C. Jenks, ed., *Rationality, Education and the Social Organization of Knowledge* (London: Routledge and Kegan Paul, 1977); J. Eggleston, *The Sociology of the School Curriculum* (London: Routledge & Kegan Paul, 1977).

13. R. Sharp and A. Greene, *Educational and Social Control* (London: Routledge & Kegan Paul, 1975); M. Sarup, *Marxism and Education* (London: Routledge & Kegan Paul, 1978).

14. Sharp and Greene, *Educational and Social Control* p. 21.

15. A. Gramsci, *Selections from the Prison Notebooks*, ed. and trans. Q. Hoare and G. Smith (New York: International Publishers, 1971); H. Entwhistle, "Antonio Gramsci and the School as Hegemonic," *Educational Theory* 28:1 (Winter 1978): 23–33.

16. R. LaBrecque, "The Correspondence Theory," *Educational Theory* 28:3 (Summer 1978): 194–201.

17. Dreeben, *On What Is Learned*.

18. Ibid., p. 24.

19. S. Arons, "The Separation of School and State: Pierce Reconsidered," *Harvard Educational Review* 46 (February 1976): 98.

20. R. Tyler, *Basic Principles of Curriculum and Instruction* (Chicago: University of Chicago Press, 1949).

21. Ibid., p. 35. Traditionalists like Tyler raise the question only to ignore it as a focus for investigation.

22. P. Freire, *Pedagogy of the Oppressed* (New York: Seabury Press, 1973), p. 15.

23. Tyler, *Basic Principles* (1949); Freire, *Pedagogy of the Oppressed*.

24. Dreeben, *On What Is Learned*.

25. Ibid., p. 13.

26. Ibid., p. 66.

27. Bernstein, *Class, Codes and Control*.

28. S. Aronowitz, *False Promises: The Shaping of American Working Class Consciousness* (New York: McGraw-Hill, 1973).

29. Ibid., p. 75.

30. Dreeben, *On What Is Learned*; Aronowitz, *False Promises*.

31. M. Apple, "The Hidden Curriculum"; H. Giroux and A. Penna, "Social Relations in the Classroom: The Dialectic of the Hidden Curriculum," *Edcentric* 40:41 (Spring-Summer 1977): 39–47.

32. J. Bruner, *The Relevance of Education* (New York: W. W. Norton & Co., 1973).

33. Ibid., p. 115.

34. S. Bowles and H. Gintis, *Schooling in Capitalist America: Educational Reform and the Contradictions of Economic Life* (New York: Basic Books, 1976).

35. Apple, "The Hidden Curriculum"; J. Anyon, "Elementary Social Studies Textbooks and Legitimating Knowledge," *Theory and Research in Social Education* 6:3 (September 1978): 40–54. T. Popkewitz, "The Latent Values of the Discipline-Centered Curriculum in Social Education," *Theory and Research in Social Education* 5 (April 1977): 41–60.

36. Apple, "The Hidden Curriculum"; Popkewitz, "Latent Values."
37. Popkewitz, "Latent Values," p. 58.
38. Jackson, *Life in Classrooms*.
39. Ibid.
40. Ibid., p. 16.
41. Ibid., p. 18.
42. Bowles and Gintis, *Schooling in Capitalist America*.
43. Ibid., p. 40.
44. Ibid., p. 41.
45. N. Keddie, "Classroom Knowledge," in *Knowledge and Control*, ed. M. F. D. Young (London: Collier-Macmillan, 1971).
46. D. Lortie, *Schoolteacher: A Sociological Study* (Chicago: University of Chicago Press, 1975).
47. Ibid., p. 54.
48. I. Illich, "After Deschooling, What?" in *After Deschooling, What?* ed. A. Gartner, C. Greer, and F. Reisman (New York: Holt, Rinehart & Winston, 1973); R. Bernstein, *The Restructuring of Social and Political Theory* (Philadelphia: University of Pennsylvania Press, 1976).
49. Jackson, *Life in Classrooms*, p. 33.
50. P. Freire, *Pedagogy in Process* (New York: Seabury Press, 1978).
51. K. Marx, "Theses on Feuerbach," in *The German Ideology*, ed. C. J. Arthur (New York: International Publishers, 1972), p. 123.
52. E. Cagan, "Individualism, Collectivism and Radical Educational Reform," *Harvard Educational Review* 48:2 (May 1978): 227–66.
53. H. Braverman, *Labor and Monopoly Capital* (New York: Monthly Review Press, 1974); S. Ewen, *Captains of Consciousness* (New York: McGraw-Hill, 1976).
54. P. Slater, *The Pursuit of Loneliness* (Boston: Beacon Press, 1970); Cagan, "Individualism, Collectivism."
55. N. Daniels, "The Smart White Man's Burden," *Harper's* 247 (October 1973); B. Berger, "A New Interpretation of the I.Q. Controversy," *The Public Interest* 50 (Winter 1978):29–48; J. B. Biggs, "Genetics and Education: Alternative to Jensenism," *Educational Researcher* 7 (April 1978): 11–17.
56. Bernstein, *Class, Codes and Control*, pp. 88–89.
57. Lortie, *Schoolteacher: A Sociological Study*.
58. Bowles and Gintis, *Schooling in Capitalist America*.
59. Freire, *Pedagogy of the Oppressed*.
60. Lortie, *Schoolteacher: A Sociological Study*.
61. S. Aronowitz, "Mass Culture and the Eclipse of Reason: The Implications for Pedagogy," *College English* 38:8 (April 1977): 768–74.
62. I. Illich, *Deschooling Society* (New York: Harper & Row, 1971).

Section III
EVALUATION

Three Perspectives on Evaluation

This section presents readers with examples of how traditionalists, conceptual-empiricists, and reconceptualists use the term *evaluation* in education. As you know from reading the previous sections on curriculum and instruction, the dual concerns of how educators assign values to the quality and quantity of curriculum and instruction and how they validate their work in these areas are basic issues for the educational community.

Issues such as teacher accountability, testing for basic literacy, and cost-benefit calculations as they apply to decisions about school financing, as well as other issues often cloud the educator's need and ability to know more about the operational aspects of the system. Such evaluations cause much debate, some consternation, and not a little alarm about the ideologies and goals of the program evaluations. Evaluations will not, however, disappear from the educational landscape by simply ignoring them.

Educators should be aware of two factors in the evaluation field. First, evaluation gains attention during periods of slow growth or contraction in education. During these periods, administrators make efforts to preserve the conventional modes for operating the educational system. This propensity unfortunately causes some educators to ignore newer and sometimes more promising approaches to long-standing educational problems. It goes without saying that educators need to guard against this tendency, which can become an accepted policy and practice rather quickly when efforts to evaluate are either ignored or noticed only casually.

Second, evaluation is a relative newcomer to the dual fields of curriculum and instruction. There are few evaluation instruments and practices that are applicable to all educational settings and problem areas. In addition there are few findings from evaluation research at the present time that allow us to generalize across the educational spectrum. On the one side, caution is advised in using these findings and practices; on the other, optimism is the proper posture to assume when getting involved in the evaluative process. Your involvement should be enhanced as you read and study the three theoretical positions on evaluation presented in this section.

The traditionalist view presented here focuses the attention of the reader on practical criteria for evaluating school programs and learning experiences and on the precise definition of terminology used by evaluators. For example, Tyler focuses on the need to link objectives with specific kinds of classroom behaviors, to define behavioral objectives clearly, and to develop learning situations that give students the opportunity to display called-for behavior. If the reader is interested in learning about what the present practices are without an inquiry into the origins, philosophy, and limitations of these known procedures, the chapters by Tyler and McNeil respectively satisfy this interest. A caution is offered, however, about an over reliance on present practices. Procedures, criteria, terminology, and evaluation models are all hotly contested among the community of practitioners and researchers engaged in evaluation studies. Little in this field of study is as cleanly divided and as indisputable as the traditionalists imply. The meaning of terminology changes rapidly; and if it remains the same, the value given to it by evaluators seldom remains constant over time.

The conceptual-empiricists represent the leaders in the emerging field of evaluation. Methodologically, they draw on the behavioral and social sciences for both qualitative and quantitative methods of research. Ideologically, technical rationality—with its focus on proof process, validation, and the search for verifiable results and testable hypotheses—represents the underlying basis for much of the present thinking of the conceptual-empiricists. As quantification has lost some of its luster in recent years, an increasing number of conceptual-empiricists have embraced phenomenology as an alternative philosophy. Using both sociological and anthropological methods, a new wave of evaluation research studies has emerged that is both empirical and reconceptual in structure.

The essay by Walker discusses the needed relationship between research and curriculum studies. He argues that curriculum developers have a number of misconceptions about research in education and as a result fail to understand the benefits to be gained from the natural linkage of research to curriculum development. The final selections by the conceptual-empiricists are a debate over the use of the adversary evaluation model. It is especially useful for readers to gain information about a model by learning about it and its critics simultaneously.

The reconceptualist stance on evaluation in education is multidimensional. It is introspective and provocative in that it examines in microscopic fashion the underlying political and ideological values embedded in the dominant and minority cultures, and it traces the manifestations of these values in the discourse, rhetoric, and texts found in schools. Popkewitz's article extracts and illuminates the latent values found in most conceptual-empiricist educational research. He argues that premises and values are at the heart of all research and that they should be made explicit by researchers. Anyon offers a reconceptualist view of the school-society paradigm. She provides empirical support for the notion that schools in industrial societies such as our own offer students from different social classes different types of educational experiences, knowledge, and future work opportunities. Her paper suggests that there is a hidden curriculum in school work which has profound implications for curriculum theory and practice. Donmoyer's article raises issues about the aesthetics of evaluation and one's capacity to think about the evaluative process in artistic rather than in either pure or applied scientific terms.

As you read and study, you will recognize that this emerging field of evaluation will continue to receive more attention from practitioners and researchers as educational problems continue to resist simple solutions.

Traditionalists

16 How Can the Effectiveness of Learning Experiences be Evaluated?

Ralph W. Tyler

Introduction

In 1949 the University of Chicago Press published the first edition of Ralph Tyler's *Basic Principles of Curriculum and Instruction*. Since that time, Tyler's small book has become a classic in the literature on curriculum theory and practice. The following essay is drawn from that book and is an exemplary representation of the traditionalist position on evaluation.

For Tyler, the process of evaluation is grounded in weighing the outcomes of instruction against the objectives that underlie the essential function of the instructional process. That is, the notion of evaluation is tied to measuring changes in students' behavior to see if the latter changes conform to the original objectives designed to modify such behavior via certain predetermined learning experiences.

Tyler's article is very important, not so much because it provides an accurate perspective on the nature of evaluation but because it has exercised a powerful influence on the development of educational research and inquiry. It is for this second reason that you should read this essay with a critical eye.

As you read this essay, try to determine what the basic assumptions are that constitute Tyler's view of evaluation.
- In other words, how is learning viewed in this perspective?
- What is Tyler's view of knowledge?
- How is the notion of values addressed?
- What conception of human nature emerges from this model?
- Where is the political element in Tyler's perspective?

Since we have [in earlier chapters of Tyler's book] considered the operations involved in choosing and formulating educational objectives and in selecting and organizing learning experiences, it may appear that we have completed our analysis of curriculum development. Although the steps previously discussed provide the plans for the day-by-day work of the school, they do not complete the planning cycle. Evaluation is also an important operation in curriculum development.

The Need for Evaluation

The steps thus far outlined have provided us with learning experiences that have been checked against various criteria derived from educational psychology and from practical experience. We also have utilized criteria regarding the organization of these learning experiences. In a sense, then, certain preliminary evaluations of the learning experiences have already been made. We may refer to these as intermediate or preliminary stages of evaluation. The learning experiences have been checked to see that they are related to the objectives set up and to see that they provide for other important psychological principles, so far as these principles are known. However, this is not an adequate appraisal of the learning experiences planned for curriculum and instruction. The generalizations used as criteria against which to check the learning experiences are general principles applying to generalized characteristics of the learning experiences, and they are not highly precise statements of the exact conditions to be met in providing for the learnings desired. Furthermore, any set of learning experiences involves a number of criteria, each of which can only be approximated so that we can only predict in general or with a certain degree of accuracy the likelihood that these experiences will actually produce the effects desired. Finally, the actual teaching procedures involve a considerable number of variables including variations in individual students, the environmental conditions in which the learning goes on, the skill of the teacher in setting the conditions as they are planned, the personality characteristics of the teacher, and the like. These many variables make it impossible to guarantee that the actual learning experiences provided are precisely those that are outlined in the learning units. Hence, it is important to make a more inclusive check as to whether these plans for learning experiences actually function to guide the teacher in producing the sort of outcomes desired. This is the purpose for evaluation and the reason why a process of evaluation is necessary after the plans themselves are developed.

It should be clear that evaluation then becomes a process for finding out

---

Reprinted from Ralph W. Tyler, *Basic Principles of Curriculum and Instruction* (Chicago: University of Chicago Press, 1949). Copyright © 1949 by the University of Chicago Press. Reprinted by permission.

Effectiveness of Learning Experiences

how far the learning experiences as developed and organized are actually producing the desired results, and the process of evaluation will involve identifying the strengths and weaknesses of the plans. This helps to check the validity of the basic hypotheses upon which the instructional program has been organized and developed, and it also checks the effectiveness of the particular instruments, that is, the teachers and other conditions that are being used to carry forward the instructional program. As a result of evaluation, it is possible to note in what respects the curriculum is effective and in what respects it needs improvement.

Basic Notions Regarding Evaluation

The process of evaluation is essentially the process of determining to what extent the educational objectives are actually being realized by the program of curriculum and instruction. However, since educational objectives are essentially changes in human beings, that is, the objectives aimed at are to produce certain desirable changes in the behavior patterns of the student, then evaluation is the process for determining the degree to which these changes in behavior are actually taking place.

This conception of evaluation has two important aspects. In the first place, it implies that evaluation must appraise the behavior of students since it is change in these behaviors that is sought in education. In the second place, it implies that evaluation must involve more than a single appraisal at any one time since to see whether change has taken place, it is necessary to make an appraisal at an early point and other appraisals at later points to identify changes that may be occurring. On this basis, one is not able to evaluate an instructional program by testing students only at the end of the program. Without knowing where the students were at the beginning, it is not possible to tell how far changes have taken place. In some cases, it is possible that the students had made a good deal of progress on the objectives before they began the instructional program. In other cases, it may very well be that the students have very little achievement before they begin instruction, and almost all of that noted at the end took place during the time the instruction went on. Hence, it is clear that an educational evaluation involves at least two appraisals—one taking place in the early part of the educational program and the other at some later point so that the change may be measured.

However, it is not enough to have only two appraisals in making an educational evaluation because some of the objectives aimed at may be acquired during an educational program and then be rapidly dissipated or forgotten. In order to have some estimate of the permanence of the learning, it is necessary to have still another point of evaluation that is made sometime after the instruction has been completed. Hence, schools and colleges are making follow-up studies of their graduates in order to get further evidence as to the permanence or impermanence of the learnings that may have been acquired during the time these young people were in school. This is a desirable part of the evaluation program. In fact, so far as frequency of evaluation is concerned, much can be said for at least an annual appraisal carried on as the children move through the school so that a continuing record of progress can be obtained and evidence accumulated to indicate whether desirable objectives are being realized and to indicate places where these changes are not actually taking place.

Since evaluation involves getting evidence about behavior changes in the students, any valid evidence about behaviors that are desired as educational objectives provides an appropriate method of evaluation. This is important to recognize because many people think of evaluation as synonymous with the giving of paper-and-pencil tests. It is true that paper-and-pencil tests provide a practicable procedure for getting evidences about several kinds of student behavior. For example, if one wishes to find out what knowledge students have, it may be easily gotten from paper-and-pencil tests if the students are able to express their ideas in writing or can read and check off various items in a multiple-reponse test or other similar tests. As another illustration, paper-and-pencil tests are useful devices to get at the ability of students to analyze and deal effectively with various types of verbal problems, with vocabulary, with reading, and a number of other types of skills and abilities easily expressed in verbal form. However, there are a great many other kinds of desired behaviors which represent educational objectives that are not easily appraised by paper-and-pencil devices. For example, such an objective as personal-social adjustment is more easily and validly appraised through observations of children under conditions in which social relations are involved. Observations are also useful devices to get at habits and certain kinds of operational skills. Another method that is useful in evaluation is the interview, which may throw light upon changes taking place in attitudes, in interests, in appreciations, and the like. Questionnaires sometimes serve to give evidence about interests, about attitudes, and about other types of behavior. The collection of actual products made by students is sometimes a useful way of getting evidence of behavior. For example, the collection of themes students have written may serve to give some evidence of the writing ability of students, or the paintings students have made in an art class may serve to give evidence of skill and possibly interests in this area. Objects made in the shop or in the clothing construction course are additional illustrations of the collection of samples of products as an evaluation device. Even records made for other purposes sometimes provide evidence of types of behavior or interest in terms of educational objectives. For example, books withdrawn from the library may provide some indication of reading interests. Menus checked in the cafeteria may provide some evidence of the eating habits of students. Health records may throw some light on health practices. These are all illustrations of the fact that there are many ways of getting evidence about behavior changes and that when we think of evaluation we are not talking about any single or even any two or three particular appraisal methods. Any way of getting valid evidence about the kinds of behavior represented by the educational objectives of the school or college is an appropriate evaluation procedure.

Sampling is another basic notion of evaluation. Sampling is involved in many points. For example, evaluation assumes that it is possible to estimate the typical reactions of students by getting evidence about a sample of his reactions. We do not collect all the written work the students have ever prepared in order to get some estimate of their writing ability. We recognize that it is possible to judge the writing commonly to be expected from this student by examining a proper sample of his writing. Correspondingly, with reference to a student's knowledge, we do not ask him all the questions about all the facts, principles, concepts, and the like that may be involved in his education, but rather we choose a sample of these things to question him about, and we infer from his reaction to this sample how he might react to the total set of items that might be involved in his knowledge. This holds for all types of human behavior, attitudes, interests, intellectual skills, appreciations, and the like. We assume that it is possible to infer the person's characteristic performance by appraising his reaction in a sample of situations where this reaction is involved.

Sampling is not only involved in appraising the individual's behavior, but it may also be involved in appraising the effectiveness of curriculum experiences in use with a group of students. It is not always necessary to find out the reaction of every individual in order to see the effect that the curriculum is producing. It is possible to take a sample of students, and, if this sample is properly chosen, the results with this sample of students may—within small limits of error—properly represent the kind of results that would have been obtained had all the students been involved in the appraisal. Thus, it is possible for an appraisal to be so designed that not too many students need to be interviewed or probed with time-consuming means in order to get some indication of what is happening to the students in terms of the behavior appraised by these means. Correspondingly, when follow-up studies are made to determine the permanency of the learning, it is possible to select a sample of graduates that will be properly representative of the total group and to concentrate a fairly intensive study of the behavior of the sample of graduates in order to draw some conclusions about the permanence of learning, which is probably characteristic of the average graduate of the program.

These are some of the basic notions regarding evaluation that guide in the development of an evaluation program. There are other notions involved in evaluation, but these are among the most important ones. Their implications will be considered further as we examine the procedures for making an educational evaluation.

Evaluation Procedures

The process of evaluation begins with the objectives of the educational program. Since the purpose is to see how far these objectives are actually being realized, it is necessary to have evaluation procedures that will give evidence about each of the kinds of behavior implied by each of the major educational objectives. If, for example, one of the objectives is to acquire important knowledge about contemporary social problems, then it is necessary that the evaluation give some evidence of the knowledge students are acquiring. If another is to develop methods of analyzing social problems and appraising proposed solutions of them, then it is necessary that the evaluation procedures give us some evidence as to the skill of the student in analyzing social problems and appraising suggested solutions to them. This means that the two-dimensional analysis that served as a basis for planning the learning experiences also serves as the basis for planning the evaluation procedures. The two-dimensional analysis of objectives thus serves as a set of specifications for evaluation. Each of the behavioral headings in the analysis indicates the kind of behavior which should be appraised to see how far that kind of behavior is developing; and each of the content headings of the analysis indicates the content to be sampled in connection with the behavior appraisal. Thus, in the case of the objectives regarding knowledge about social problems, the two-dimensional analysis indicates that evaluation of knowledge must be made for the behavior, and the content headings indicate what areas of knowledge should be sampled in order to have a satisfactory appraisal of the knowledge being acquired by the students in this field. Correspondingly, an objective of "Developing Interests in Literature" would require an appraisal of developing interests in students for the behavior aspect, and the content headings would indicate the areas in which interests might be expected to be developed and which should be sampled in order to see whether such interests are actually being developed. In this way a two-dimensional analysis of objectives becomes a guide to the evaluation of the curriculum.

It is, of course, assumed that these "behavioral objectives" have been clearly defined by the curriculum worker. They should have been defined clearly so as to provide a concrete guide in the selection and planning of learning experiences. If they have not yet been clearly defined, it is absolutely essential that they be defined in order to make an evaluation since unless there is some clear conception of the sort of behavior implied by the objectives, one has no way of telling what kind of behavior to look for in the students in order to see to what degree these objectives are being realized. This means that the process of evaluation may force persons who have not previously clarified their objectives to a further process of clarification. Definition of objectives, then, is an important step in evaluation.

The next step in evaluation procedure is to identify the situations which will give the student the chance to express the behavior that is implied by the educational objectives. The only way that we can tell whether students have acquired given types of behavior is to give them an opportunity to show this behavior. This means that we must find situations that not only permit the expression of the behavior but actually encourage or evoke this behavior. We are then in a position to observe the degree to which the objectives are actually being realized. In some cases, it is easy to see the kinds of situations that give students the chance to express desired types of behavior. We are accustomed to stimulating students to express ideas through questions, and it is therefore possible in the question situation to evoke reactions of the students that involve knowledge and ability to deal with verbal materials. When we consider the whole range of desired objectives, we can see that the situations are not all of this type. If we are going to see how children are developing personal-social adjustment, we must use situations that give children a chance to react to other children. This may mean looking for evidence about personal-social adjustment in the nursery school during those periods when children are playing and working together. It may mean that we shall look for evidences of interests in those situations where there is opportunity for free choice of activity. Students may, therefore, freely express their interests. If we want evidence of the student's ability to express himself orally, we must look at those situations which evoke oral expression. The principle is simple enough that any evaluation situation is the kind of situation that gives an oppotunity for the students to express the type of behavior we are trying to appraise. Although the principle is simple, there are still many problems involved in finding situations that are sufficiently under control and permit the teacher or other evaluator to have access to them in order to see the types of behaviors the students are developing. In case some situations are difficult to handle, one of the tasks of the specialist in evaluation is to try to find other simpler situations that will have a high correlation with the result obtained when the situation is used that directly evokes the kind of behavior to be appraised.

It is only after the objectives have been identified, clearly defined, and situations listed which give opportunity for the expression of the behavior desired that it is possible to examine available evaluation instruments to see how far they may serve the evaluation purposes desired. It is not really possible to look at a particular test and to decide whether it would do for appraising a certain educational program until the objectives of the program have been identified and defined and until the kinds of situations that would give an opportunity for this behavior to be expressed have also been identified. After these steps have been taken, one can then examine particular tests and see how far they sample the types of objectives that are to be appraised and how far the tests either use situations which directly evoke the kind of behavior to be appraised or else use situations which have been correlated with the situations that directly evoke the type of behavior. It has too commonly been true that persons have gone to test catalogues or have looked at sample tests and selected them without having these previous steps in mind to serve as the basis for making a wise selection. Just because Test A is the most widely used test in physics or Test B is commonly recommended for art or Test C has been prepared by some widely known specialist in mathematics, these are not indications that these tests may be appropriate ways of getting evidence about the particular objectives that are aimed at in a given educational program. It is very necessary to check each proposed evaluation device against the objectives that are being aimed at and to see whether it uses situations likely to evoke the sort of behavior that is desired as educational objectives.

When available evaluation instruments are checked in this way, it is quite probable that the curriculum constructor will find that there are available instruments that will be quite satisfactory for certain of the educational objectives, that there are other available instruments which can be modified somewhat and made appropriate for certain other educational objectives, and finally, that there are some educational objectives for which no available evaluation instruments can properly be used. For these last, it may be necessary to construct or devise methods for getting evidence about the student's attainment of these objectives. The construction of evaluation instruments can be a very difficult task if the purpose is to get a highly refined instrument, but a great deal of a less refined sort can be done by collecting evidence in rather simple ways relating to these various educational objectives. We shall discuss illustrations of these later.

If it is necessary to construct an evaluation instrument for a particular objective, the next step is actually to try out some of the situations suggested as situations that give the student a chance to express the behavior desired. This tryout provides an opportunity to see whether these situations will serve as convenient ways of getting evidence. Thus, it may appear that the type of situation likely to give students a chance to show their ability to analyze problems is a situation in which a number of problems are presented in written form and the students are asked to analyze them. Situations of this sort can actually be tried out with students to see how far the responses obtained provide an adequate basis for checking the student's ability to analyze problems. Or, a situation that is likely to give students a chance to indicate their interests is to present a questionnaire in which a variety of activities are listed and the students are asked to check those in which they have no interest. If this appears to be a situation likely to give students an opportunity to show interests, then it should be used in trial form to see how satisfactorily it works. This step is a useful one in developing possible evaluation devices into forms where they can be satisfactorily used.

After deciding on certain situations used to get evidence about the behavior of students, it is then necessary to devise a means of getting a record of the student's behavior in this test situation. In the case of a written examination, the student makes his own record in his writing. Hence, the problem of getting a record of his behavior is not a serious one. On the other hand, a situation that gives nursery school children a chance to play and work together may be a good situation to provide evidence of personal-social adjustment, but it is necessary to get some record of the children's reaction in this situation if there is to be an opportunity to appraise this reaction after it has been made. This may involve making a detailed description of reaction by an observer; it may suggest the use of a motion picture or sound recording; it may suggest the use of an observer's check list by which he checks off particular types of behavior that commonly appear; or it may involve some other means of getting a satisfactory record of the children's reaction. This is a step that must be considered in connection with each test situation to be sure that the situation not only evokes the desired behavior but that a record can be obtained which can be appraised later.

The next step in developing an evaluation instrument is to decide upon the terms or units that will be used to summarize or to appraise the record of behavior obtained. This method of appraising the behavior should, of course, parallel the implications of the objective itself. For example, if reading interests as an educational objective are to be defined as the development of increasingly broad and mature interests, it then becomes necessary to decide upon units by which a record of children's reading can be summarized to indicate breadth and maturity. Breadth may be indicated by a number that measures the different categories of reading material included in the youngster's reading for the year. Thus, a child who reads only Wild West stories and detective stories would have his reading list classified under two categories only and the figure 2 would represent a measure of breadth. This would be in contrast to a boy whose reading record could be classified under four categories such as adventure, romance, psychological, sociological. The fact that the second boy read materials classified under a wider number of categories would be represented by the number 4 in contrast to the number 2. Correspondingly, if different reading levels can be classified under different levels of maturity, it becomes possible to summarize a reading record in terms of its average level of maturity and thus to provide a measure of that aspect of reading interest. This illustration has been chosen because it is very different from the problem as it is usually viewed by the person who reads and scores the test; and, yet, essentially all evaluation involves this problem, that is, the decision upon the characteristics that are to be appraised in the behavior and the unit to be used in the measurement or summarization of these characteristics. In the case of reading interests, the characteristics used were range and maturity so that the methods of summarization provided a rating for range and maturity.

The problem is a similar one in summarizing a typical objective type test. Suppose it is a measure of knowledge. The question then to be faced is: Will knowledge be summarized in terms of the number of different items in the sample that the student was able to remember properly, or is it better indicated by some classification of the items so as to indicate which topics he remembers best and which less well, or is there some other way by which the objective of knowledge can be most satisfactorily summarized or appraised in order to serve the purpose of evaluation? Every kind of human behavior that is appraised for its part as an educational objective must be summarized or measured in some terms, and the decision about these terms is an important problem in the development and use of evaluation instruments.

It should be clear that for most purposes the appraisal of human behavior should be an analytic one rather than a single score summary. Simply to know that John Smith made a score of 97 and Mary Jones made a score of 64 on some evaluation instrument used is not an adequate kind of summary likely to be most helpful for improving the curriculum. It is much more useful to have summaries that indicate the kinds of strengths and weaknesses, summaries at least in terms of each objective; and in many cases, it may be desirable to have several scores or summaries for each objective so as to describe more adequately the achievement of this particular sort of objective. Thus, it is useful to know whether the students are making progress in developing a range of reading interests even though they may be making less progress in developing maturity of reading interests. It is helpful to know that students are making progress in their skill of interpretation in reading although their reading interests may not be as satisfactory as hoped. This kind of analytic summary that indicates particular strengths and weaknesses is, of course, invaluable in using the results to improve the curriculum. It means that the plan for appraisal must be developed before scoring and rating is actually made. Decisions about these points are necessary decisions in developing an evaluation program.

The next step in the construction of an evaluation instrument is to determine how far these rating or summarizing methods are objective, that is, to what degree two different persons, presumably competent, would be able to reach similar scores or summaries when they had an opportunity to score or summarize the same records of behavior. If the scores or summaries vary markedly, depending upon who does the scoring or summarizing, it is clearly a subjective kind of appraisal and requires improvement in its objectivity in order to be a more satisfactory means of appraising a human behavior. Sometimes improvement can be made through clarifying the specifications for scoring; sometimes, through getting a more refined record of behavior itself. It is beyond the scope of the present discussion to outline the various techniques for refining and improving the objectivity of the instruments. It is necessary, however, to recognize this problem and to attempt to get a more objective procedure when necessary. When these possible evaluation instruments have been tried out, one cannot only check on the objectivity of the scoring or summary but must also check upon the adequacy of the sample of behavior included in the instrument.

In general, the size of the sample of behavior to be obtained depends upon how variable that behavior is. If one wishes to get evidence about the social attitudes of students and these attitudes are highly consistent in each individual, it takes only a few samples to get a rather dependable indication of the attitude of each student. On the other hand, if there is wide variability in each student's attitudes—for example, if he is highly selfish at some points and highly social at others—it takes a much larger sample of his behavior in order to reliably infer about the degree of his social or selfish attitudes. Hence, it is not possible to be sure in advance how large a sample of behavior must be collected regarding a given objective in order to have a dependable sample from which to draw conclusions about the individual's status. It is possible, after trying out an instrument, to find out what the variation among the items in the instrument is and thus to estimate how reliable the sample is and whether a larger or smaller sample would do satisfactorily. This is the problem of reliability of a test or other evaluation device; and, although it is beyond the scope of this discussion to describe methods of estimating reliability, it is important to recognize what reliability means and to realize that if a given test is too short to provide an adequate sample or if a given set of observations does not cover a large enough span of time to get an adequate sample of the student's behavior, it will be necessary to extend the sample before dependable conclusions can be drawn.

Since we have used the two terms for two of the important criteria for an evaluation instrument, namely, objectivity and reliability, it is necessary to emphasize the third and most important criteria of an evaluation instrument, namely, validity. Validity applies to the method and indicates the degree to which an evaluation device actually provides evidence of the behavior desired. Validity can be assured in one of two ways. One way is by getting directly a sample of the kind of behavior to be measured, as when one directly observes the food children are selecting as the basis for inferring food habits, or one obtains an actual record of reading done as an indication of reading habits, or one presents problems for children to analyze in order to get evidence of their ability to analyze problems. This is know as "face validity"—the evaluation instrument is valid on the face of it because it directly samples the kind of behavior it is desired to appraise. The other way of assuring validity is through correlating a particular evaluation device with the result obtained by a directly valid measure. If it can be shown that the results of a certain reading questionnaire correlate very highly with the results obtained from an actual record of reading, then the reading questionnaire might be used as a valid indication of what children read. It would be valid because the results are shown by experimental methods to correlate highly with the direct evidence. In some cases, persons developing tests find that it is expensive or difficult or otherwise impracticable to get evidence by the direct method, and they try out various possible ways for getting evidence that are simpler and easier to handle. None of these should be used, however, as a valid instrument until it has been shown to correlate highly with the evidence obtained directly, that is, from an instrument that has face validity.

These steps indicate the procedures followed in making an evaluation and in developing an instrument for an evaluation. In case the instrument is found to have too little objectivity or reliability, it is necessary to improve it. It is also necessary to make any other revisions indicated by the preliminary tryout, such as eliminating ambiguities in directions, dropping out parts of the instrument that got no significant reactions from students. In general, then, the result is a continually improved instrument for getting evidence about the degree to which students are attaining given educational objectives.

These instruments are used in order to obtain summarized or appraised results. These results may be in the form of scores or descriptions or both, depending upon the form that can be most satisfactorily used to summarize the behavior in terms that are appropriate for the objectives desired.

Using the Results of Evaluation

Since every educational program involves several objectives and since for almost every objective there will be several scores or descriptive terms used to summarize the behavior of students in relation to this objective, it follows that the results obtained from evaluation instruments will not be a single score or a single descriptive term but an analyzed profile or a comprehensive set of descriptive terms indicating the present student achievement. These scores or descriptive terms should, of course, be comparable to those used at a preceding date so that it is possible to indicate change taking place, and one can then see whether or not educational progress is actually happening. If it is found, for example, that the range of students' interests in reading is no greater at the end of the tenth grade than it was at the end of the ninth grade, it is clear that no appreciable change is taking place in reading interest. Correspondingly, if it is shown that the ability to interpret reading passages critically is no higher at the end of the tenth grade than at the end of the ninth grade, again, no educational change is taking place. It is, therefore, essential to compare the results obtained from the several evaluation instruments before and after given periods in order to estimate the amount of change taking place.

The fact that these are complex comparisons, that they involve a number of points and not a single score, may complicate the process, but it is necessary for the kind of identification of strengths and weaknesses that will help to indicate where the curriculum may need improvement. For example, in connection with one curriculum program that involved the development of a core focused upon contemporary social problems, it was found that at the end of the first year the students had acquired a great deal more information about these

Effectiveness of Learning Experiences

contemporary problems, that they had shifted their social attitudes slightly in the direction of greater social and less selfish attitudes, but that their attitudes were much more confused and inconsistent than before, that they had not gained any skill in analyzing social problems, and that their ability to interpret social data was worse because the students were drawing more unwarranted conclusions than before. Putting all of these things together gave the teachers the chance to see the kinds of strengths, which were largely covering more material and more ideas, and the kinds of weaknesses, which had to do with their greater inconsistencies, less ability to analyze critically and the like. This is more helpful in getting at the seat of the difficulty in this particular core curriculum than if there had been a single score that indicated a small amount of improvement but did not analyze this improvement into a number of different categories.

It is not only desirable to analyze the results of an evaluation to indicate the various strengths and weaknesses, but is also necessary to examine these data to suggest possible explanations or hypotheses about the reason for this particular pattern of strengths and weaknesses. In the case just cited, after examining all the data available, it is suggested that this implied that a great deal more ground was covered and that not enough time was being spent in careful critical analysis. This was checked against the actual amount of reading provided, which turned out to be more than six thousand pages, and the number of social problems dealt with, which turned out to be twenty-one, both of which in the light of these data seemed to be excessive and suggested that a possible explanation for these weaknesses was that too much material was being covered and not enough time devoted to critical analysis, interpretation, and application.

When hypotheses have been suggested that might possibly explain the evaluation data, the next step is to check those hypotheses against the present available data, that is, against additional data that may be available, and to see whether the hypotheses are consistent with all the data then available. If they appear to be consistent with the available data, the next step is to modify the curriculum in the direction implied by the hypotheses and then to teach the material to see whether there is any actual improvement in student achievement when these modifications are made. If there is, then it would suggest that the hypotheses are likely explanations, and the basis for improving the curriculum has been identified. In the case just cited, it was possible to reorganize the course for the coming year and to reduce the number of major problems from twenty-one to seven and to reduce the quantity of reading material by more than half so as to utilize more time in interpreting, applying, analyzing, and otherwise treating the material dealt with. At the end of the second year, it was found that, although the students had not gained quite so much in the range of information acquired, they had gained greater consistency in social attitudes, had gained greater skill in analyzing social problems, and had become able to draw better generalizations from the data presented to them. This would indicate that the hypothesis that what was wrong with the course was that it covered too much ground seemed to be a sound one. This is a typical procedure that can be followed in using evaluation results so as to modify and improve the curriculum and instructional program.

What is implied in all of this is that curriculum planning is a continuous process and that as materials and procedures are developed, they are tried out, their results appraised, their inadequacies identified, suggested improvements indicated; there is replanning, redevelopment, and then reappraisal; and in this kind of continuing cycle, it is possible for the curriculum and instructional program to be continuously improved over the years. In this way we may hope to have an increasingly more effective educational program rather than depending so much upon hit-and-miss judgment as a basis for curriculum development.

Other Values and Uses of Evaluation Procedures

In the foregoing discussion of evaluation, we have concentrated primarily upon the use of evaluation procedures in identifying the strengths and weaknesses of the curriculum program. This is its main function in curriculum work. It also serves other purposes. The very fact that it is not possible to make an evaluation until objectives are clearly enough defined so that one can recognize the behavior to be sought means that evaluation is a powerful device for clarifying educational objectives if they have not already been clarified in the curriculum planning process.

Evaluation also has a powerful influence upon learning. It has been shown in the New York Regents' Inquiry that the regents' examinations, which are the evaluation instruments of the state, have more effect upon what is taught in New York State than course of study outlines as such. Students are influenced in their study by the kind of evaluation to be made, and even teachers are influenced in their emphasis by the sort of evaluation they expect to be made. This means that unless the evaluation procedure closely parallels the educational objectives of the curriculum, the evaluation procedure rather than the curriculum objectives set up may become the focus of the students' attention and even of the teachers' attention. Hence, evaluation and curriculum must be closely integrated so that the effect will not be for the curriculum planning to be ignored in order for diverse objectives appraised by evaluation to be given major attention.

Evaluation procedures also have great importance in the individual guidance of pupils. It is not only valuable to know about students' backgrounds but also to know about their achievement of various kinds of objectives in order to have a better notion of both their needs and their capabilities. Any comprehensive evaluation program provides information about individual students that can be of great value.

Evaluation can also be used continuously during the year as a basis for identifying particular points needing further attention with particular groups of students and as a basis for giving individual help or planning individual programs for students in light of their particular progress in the educational program.

Finally, evaluation becomes one of the important ways of providing information about the success of the school to the school's clientele. Ultimately, schools need to be appraised in terms of their effectiveness in attaining important objectives. This means that ultimately evaluation results need to be translated into terms that will be understandable to parents and the public generally. Only as we can more accurately describe the results we are attaining from the curriculum are we in a position to get the most intelligent support for the educational program of the school. Neither parents nor the public can be satisfied long with reports about the number of children enrolled and the number of new buildings built and things of that sort. Eventually, parents have a right to know what kind of changes are being brought about in their children. Now, most of the reports of this sort that they get are from appraisals that are not fairly made. We hear about the number of persons rejected because of lack of reading ability or lack of physical health in connection with selective service, but we have no means of tracing those cases back to particular schools. Increasingly, we must expect to use evaluation procedures to determine what changes are actually taking place in students and where we are achieving our curriculum objectives and where we must make still further modifications in order to get an effective educational program.

17 Evaluating the Curriculum

John D. McNeil

Introduction

In this excerpt from his book *Curriculum: A Comprehensive Introduction*, John McNeil surveys the mainstream evaluation field. The issue he delineates and the evaluation theorists he cites dominate the evaluation field at the present time. Their work tends to be derived from mainstream social science (or conceptual-empiricism in the curriculum field). We place this chapter under a traditionalist heading as it attempts to present an impartial overview of the field. But, as you will see when you read the reconceptualist section on evaluation, the chapter is neither impartial nor an overview. Aside from a brief reference to the "humanistic," McNeil ignores any treatment of "existential" or political issues, which reconceptualists argue are inextricably present in any evaluation of classroom activity.

As you read take time to decide if you agree with our assessment of this writing.

- Do you (or do you not) see what ties this chapter with earlier examples of traditional curriculum writing?
- What are the strengths in this position?

The word *evaluation* generates a host of responses. Fear of power and control is one. Local communities have been dismayed by those in government saying: Do your own thing, set your own goals; but of course your efforts must be evaluated by standardized tests in areas important to us. Another reaction is

Reprinted from John D. McNeil, *Curriculum: A Comprehensive Introduction*, pp. 133–53. Copyright © 1977 by Little, Brown and Company (Inc.). Reprinted by permission.

that of perceived reassurance. People often expect that evaluation will solve many pressing problems—the public that demand accountability, the decision maker who chooses curriculum alternatives, the developer who needs to know where and how to improve the curriculum product, and the teacher who is concerned about the effect of learning opportunities on individual students—all look to evaluation for their answers.

The field of evaluation is full of different views as to the purposes of evaluation and how it is to be carried out. For example, humanists argue that outcomes are an insufficient basis for determining the quality of learning opportunities. They believe it naively simplistic to measure higher mental functioning, knowledge of self, and other lifelong pursuits at the end of the school year. Curiously, however, they perceive no difficulty in evaluating the existential quality of life in the classroom. For them, the learning experience is itself "the event," not a rehearsal whose values will be known only on future performance. Technologists, on the other hand, perceive evaluation as a set of verified guidelines for practice. They believe that if curriculum workers use these procedures, essential decisions regarding what and how to teach will be more warranted.

The paragraphs to follow contain an examination of the most promising roles of evaluation and illustrations of where they are appropriate and inappropriate. Finally, several important issues in curriculum evaluation are treated. We will look at sampling, the value of behavioral objectives, standardized tests versus criterion-referenced tests, and the ethics of evaluation, including the measurement of affect.

Questions Curriculum Evaluation Must Answer

In a general sense, curriculum evaluation is an attempt to throw light on two questions: (1) Do planned learning opportunities, programs, courses, and activities as developed and organized actually produce desired results? (2) How can the curriculum offerings best be improved? These general questions and the procedures for answering them translate a little differently at macrolevels (for example, evaluating the citywide outcomes from several alternative reading programs) than at microlevels (evaluating the effect of a teacher's instructional plans for achieving objectives of a course). Classroom teachers often have an additional set of evaluation questions to guide them in making decisions about individuals:

1. *Placement.* At which level of learning opportunity should the learner be placed in order to challenge but not frustrate?
2. *Mastery.* Has the learner acquired enough competency to succeed in the next planned phase?
3. *Diagnosis.* What particular difficulty is this learner experiencing?

Decisions and Evaluative Techniques

Evaluation must provide information that is useful to decision makers, and evaluative models should be chosen in light of the kind of decisions to be made. In this connection, a useful distinction is made between formative and summative evaluation. Formative evaluation is undertaken to improve an existing program. Hence, the evaluation must provide frequent detailed and specific information to guide the program developers. Summative evaluation is done to assess the effect of a completed program. It provides information to use in deciding whether to continue, discontinue, or disseminate the program. Summative evaluation is frequently undertaken in order to decide which one of several competing programs or materials is best.

Guidelines for conducting formative evaluation have been given by Lee J. Cronbach in a classic article treating *course improvement* through evaluation. The following prescriptions are among the most important:
1. Seek data regarding changes produced in pupils by the course.
2. Look for multidimensional outcomes and map out the effects of the course along these dimensions separately.
3. Identify aspects of the course in which revisions are desirable.
4. Collect evidence midway in curriculum development, while the course is still fluid.
5. Try to find out how the course produces its effect and what parameters influence its effectiveness. You may find that the teacher's attitude toward the learning opportunity is more important than the opportunity itself.
6. During trial stages, use the teacher's informal reports of observed pupil behavior in aspects of the course.
7. Make more systematic observations only after the more obvious bugs in the early stages have been dealt with.
8. Make a process study of events taking place in the classroom and use proficiency and attitude measures to reveal changes in pupils.
9. Observe several outcomes ranging far beyond the content of the curriculum itself—attitudes, general understanding, aptitude for further learning, and so on.[1]

To achieve the purposes of formative evaluation, it is not necessary or even desirable to ask all pupils the same questions. Rather, as many questions as possible should be given, each to a different sample of pupils. Follow-up studies to indicate the ultimate educational contributions of the course are of minor value in improving the course because they are too far removed in time.

Summative evaluation has several purposes. One purpose is to select from several competing curriculum programs or projects those which should continue and those which are ineffective. To this end, an experimental design is highly desirable. Donald Campbell and Julian Stanley have provided an excellent source for such designs.[2] Also, James Popham has illustrated ways of adapting these designs to meet various practical situations.[3]

For example, there is the *pretest-posttest control group design.* As the design's name suggests, students are pretested on whatever dimensions are sought from the programs. Then, after receiving instruction, students in each of the competing programs are tested for their status on a common set of objectives. That is to say, effectiveness is noted for all objectives for which each program claims superiority. The posttest used must not be biased in favor of one program's objectives. Objectives important to others but not those of the designers of a particular program can also be assessed.

The students are assigned randomly. Each student has an equal chance to be assigned to any of the programs. Differences in the performance of students may be attributed to differences in the programs. However, evaluators may not always know whether the respective programs were carried out as planned. It is desirable to try each of the programs in many settings, since the experimental unit for analysis is likely to be schools or classrooms not pupils. Only in within-classroom experiments in which the pupils receive different programs can the pupil be the unit of analysis.

Donald Horst and colleagues of the RMC Research Corporation have identified twelve hazards in conducting evaluations. Each hazard makes it difficult to know whether or not students do better in a particular program than they would have done without it.

1. *The use of grade-equivalent scores.* One should not use grade-equivalent scores in evaluating programs. The concept is misleading; a grade-equivalent score of seven by fifth graders on a math test does not mean that they know sixth- and seventh-grade math. Such scores do not comprise an equal interval scale and, therefore, "average" scores are not interpretable. Procedures for generating these scores make them too low in the fall and too high in the spring.

2. *The use of gain scores.* Gain scores have been used to adjust for differences found in the pretest scores of treatment and comparison groups. Using them in this way is a mistake because raw gain scores (posttest scores minus pretest scores) excessively inflate the posttest performance measure of an initially inferior group. Students who initially have the lowest scores will have the greatest opportunity to show gain.

3. *The use of norm-group comparisons with inappropriate test dates.* A distorted picture of a program's effect occurs when pupils in the new program are not tested within a few weeks of the norm group's tests. Standardized test developers might collect performance scores in May for the purpose of norming the test. If the school's staff, however, administers the test during a different month, the discrepancy might be due to the date of testing rather than to the program.

4. *The use of inappropriate test levels.* Standardized norm-referenced tests are divided into levels that cover different grades. The test level may be too easy or too difficult and thereby fail to provide a valid

measure of achievement. Ceiling and floor effects may also occur with the use of criterion-referenced tests. Hence, one should choose tests on the basis of the pupils' achievement level not their grade in school.
5. *The lack of pre- and posttest scores for each treatment participant.* The group of students ultimately posttested is not usually composed of exactly the same students as the pretest group. Eliminating the scores of dropouts from the posttest may raise the posttest scores considerably. Conclusion of a program's report should be based on the performance of students who have both pre- and posttest scores. The reason for dropping out should also be reported.
6. *The use of noncomparable treatment and comparison groups.* Students should be randomly assigned to groups. If they are not, students in a special program may do better or worse than those in other programs because they were different to start with.
7. *Using pretest scores to select program participants.* Groups with low pretest scores appear to learn more from a special program than they actually do because of a phenomenon called *regression toward the mean.* Gains of high-scoring students may be obscured.
8. *Assembling a matched comparison group.* The correct procedure for matching groups is to match pairs of pupils and then randomly assign one member of each pair to a treatment or comparison group. If, for example, one wants to control for age, one should choose pairs of pupils of the same age. Each member of the pair must have an equal opportunity to be assigned to a given treatment. Do not consciously try to place one member in a certain group.
9. *Careless administration of tests.* Pupils from both treatment and comparison groups should complete pre- and posttests together. Problems arise when there is inconsistent administration of tests to the two groups. For example, if there is a disorderly situation in one setting and a different teacher present, the results may differ.
10. *The assumption that an achievement gain is due to the treatment alone.* The Hawthorne effects—unrecognized "treatments"—may be responsible for gain. Plausible rival hypotheses should be examined as a likely explanation.
11. *The use of noncomparable pretests and posttests.* Although there are conversion tables that allow one to correct scores on one test to their equivalent on other tests, it is best to use the same level of the same test for both pre- and posttesting. Often it is possible to use the identical test as both pre- and posttest. Obviously, this will not suffice if teachers teach to the test and if there are practice effects from taking the test.
12. *The use of inappropriate formulas to estimate posttest scores.* Formulas that calculate "expected" posttest scores from IQ or an average grade-equivalent score are inaccurate. The actual posttest scores of

treatment and comparison groups provide a better basis for evaluating treatment effects.[4]

Evaluators should not allow ideas about what must happen in a perfect evaluation to discourage them; they should remember that there have been no perfect evaluations. When faced with frustrations, like student absentees or the failure to give tests, they should remember that the curriculum evaluator is only responsible for providing the best information possible under existing circumstances.

One purpose of evaluation is to decide on the value of a curricular intervention. An *interrupted time series design* is useful for this purpose. In this design, a series of measurements are taken both before and after the introduction of the intervention. Nonobtrusive records—absences, disciplinary referrals, requests for transfer—are frequently used with this design, although test scores and other data can also serve. A significant difference in pupil performance during and after the intervention may be taken as evidence that the intervention had a positive effect.

Another important purpose of evaluation is to decide on the long-term value of curriculum offerings. Longitudinal or follow-up studies are undertaken to indicate whether desired objectives are being realized and to reveal shortcomings. One of the better known longitudinal studies was conducted on a national level in Project Talent. This project was initiated in 1960 with the testing of 400,000 secondary school students. Such data as student interests, ability scores, and characteristics of a student's school, including courses offered, were collected. Fifteen years later, a representative sample of these persons was interviewed, and they reported on their satisfaction with their current status on different life activities. One overall generalization from the findings was that educational programs should be improved and modified to enable persons to achieve greater satisfaction in intellectual development and personal understanding.[5] Another example of the findings from Project Talent studies is that, whereas in 1960, 47 percent of the graduating boys and 38 percent of the girls said their courses were not helpful in preparing them for occupations, eleven years later 46 percent of the men and 40 percent of the women still felt high school had been "at best" adequate.

National Assessment of Educational Progress (NAEP) is another assessment plan designed to furnish information regarding the educational achievements of children, youth, and young adults and to indicate both the progress we are making and the problems we face.[6] Unlike Project Talent, NAEP does not follow individual progress but does sample different age groups. The project includes plans for the assessment of each of ten study areas—reading, literature, music, social studies, science, writing, citizenship, mathematics, art, and career and occupational development—on four- or five-year cycles. Test results are reported by age group, sex, region, type of community, racial group, and level of parental education. An illustration of how the NAEP illuminates problems is the 1975 finding that many Americans are unable to use basic math to solve everyday consumer tasks ranging from balancing their checkbooks to deciding which size package is the cheapest. Too many students apparently fail to see the relationship between math courses in school and the use of math in everyday living. Even though 87 percent of the adults said they had managed to balance a checking account before, only 16 percent of those tested could solve a problem that included a subtraction error, a deposit error, service charges, and an outstanding check.

Evaluation Models

Several theorists have put forth their conceptions of what should be involved in evaluating. Most of these schemes advocate more than determining a curriculum program's goal achievement. Robert E. Stake's *Countenance Model*, for example, calls for attending to three phases of an educational program: *antecedent, transaction,* and *outcome* phases. Antecedents are conditions existing prior to instruction that may relate to outcomes; transactions constitute the process of instruction; and outcomes are the effects of the program. Stake emphasizes two operations, descriptions and judgments. Descriptions are divided according to whether they refer to what was intended or what actually was observed. Judgments are separated according to whether they refer to standards used in arriving at the judgments or to the actual judgments. The model is depicted in Table 17-1.

The model is designed to explain the "why" of the outcomes—the antecedents and transactions. Stake believes that evaluators should tell which standards are held by whom. He also believes that the evaluator should be fully aware of and sensitive to the concerns of the many persons affected by the program.

A second example of models for evaluation is the CSE Model, named for its origin at the UCLA Center for the Study of Evaluation. As described by Marvin Alkin, this model has five stages, each related to a particular kind of decision to be made.[7] The first stage is related to *problem selection*, in which the evaluator tries to find out the difference between what is and what is not desired in order to determine educational need and to identify educational goals. The procedures used in this stage are analogous to the curriculum needs assessment model for formulating outcomes. The second stage of the CSE model is related to the *selection of programs* that might be used to close identified gaps. This stage involves the appraisal of available instructional materials that might be used in a program for attaining goals and is analogous to the curriculum task of selecting learning opportunities. In this stage, the evaluator determines the likelihood of success with the different programs. The third stage is related to *modification of the program*. The evaluator provides

Table 17-1

Stake's description of data needed for educational evaluation

	Descriptive Matrix		Judgment Matrix	
	Intents	Observations	Standards	Judgments
Antecedents (student and teacher characteristics, curriculum content, instructional materials, community context)				
Transactions (communication flow, time allocation, sequence of events, social climate)				
Outcomes (student achievement, attitudes, motor skills, effect on teachers and institution)				

Source: R. E. Stake, "The Countenance of Educational Evaluation," *Teachers College Record* 68 (1967). Reprinted by permission of Teachers College, Columbia University.

information on the degree to which the program as carried out corresponds to the plan. Any departure must be duly noted. The fourth stage is also related to program modification. However, in this stage the evaluator tries to find out the relative success of the different parts of the program as it is progressing. The final stage of the CSE model concerns *program certification* or *adoption.* In this stage information on the achievement of goals from stage 1 helps the decision makers to determine whether the program should be modified, eliminated, retained, or disseminated more widely.

Controversial Issues in Curriculum Evaluation

Measurement people, curriculum specialists, teachers, and administrators often disagree regarding which techniques to use in evaluation. Many disputes about procedures occur because the antagonists have different purposes and needs in mind. They argue over the merits of procedures and instruments such as sampling, taxonomies, and formats for stating objectives, prespecifying goals, and norm- and criterion-referenced tests. Their controversies will not be resolved by taking an either-or attitude but by showing the circumstances in which one approach is better than another.

Sampling

Sampling is the practice of inferring an educational status on the basis of responses from representative persons or representative tasks. James Popham has said, "Sampling should make a Scotsman's values vibrate. It is *so* terribly thrifty."[8] It is controversial mainly because it is sometimes imposed in inappropriate situations. For example, when students are to be graded on their relative attainment of common objectives, it is not proper to assess only certain students nor is it valid to test some individuals on one set of objectives and other individuals on another set.

Administrators rightfully use sampling when they estimate the typical reactions of students from a few instances of their behavior. It is not necessary to collect all the compositions students have written in order to judge their writing ability. Samples will suffice—perhaps one at the beginning of the year and one at the end—to show change, if any, as a result of instruction. Similarly, to determine a student's knowledge in one subject, it is not necessary to ask the student to respond to all the items that are involved in this knowledge. A sample of what is involved is enough to draw an inference about the student's status. To find out whether the student can name all the letters of the alphabet, one can present only five letters at random from the alphabet and ask the student to name them. The responses will indicate ability to respond to the total population of letters. If all five are named correctly, there is a high probability that the child could name all of the letters. If the child cannot name one or more of the letters, obviously the objective has not been reached. The controversy over sampling arises because teachers have concerns that do not lend themselves to sampling. If sampling indicates that a child cannot name all of the letters of the alphabet, then the teacher wants to know specifically which ones must be taught. Sampling is unlikely to reveal this information.

Controversy may also arise between legislators who want achievement records of individuals and evaluators who prefer to use a technique like *matrix sampling* to determine the effects of a program. In this sampling technique, randomly selected students respond to randomly selected test items measuring different objectives. Thus, different students take different tests. The advantages of the technique are many: reduced testing time required of the student, attainment of information concerning learners' knowledge with respect to many objectives, reduced threat to students since examinees are not compared. The disadvantage is that sampling does not tell us the status of an individual on all the objectives. But again, this is not necessary to get an indication of abilities within groups of students.

The Form of Objectives

During the last ten years, no issue in curriculum has received more attention than the value of and proper manner for stating objectives. Part of the problem is philosophical. One extreme position is that an objective must specify the exact overt behavior that a learner is to display at the end of an instructional sequence. This overt response is seen as important in itself. A more moderate behavioral position is that the objective must specify behavior that will indicate whether the objective has been attained. This position allows for high-level covert responses on the part of the learner but demands that some overt behavior be specified to indicate whether the desired (perhaps hidden) behavior has occurred. Another extreme position is that there should be no stated objectives at all. It is said that objectives represent external goals and manipulation and that they in no way indicate what a learner actually experiences from a given situation.

Part of the problem is that the protagonists try to judge the form and value of objectives without understanding their purposes. There are many uses for objectives. They can communicate general direction at a policy level, provide a concrete guide for selecting and planning learning opportunities, and set the criteria for evaluating the learners' performance. To illustrate, there are at least four degrees of specificity for an objective. There are very general statements that are useful when trying to get a consensus on direction at a policy level. For this pupose, it is often sufficient to use *general goal statements*: to learn to respect and get along with people by developing appreciation and respect for the worth of individuals; to respect and understand minority opinions; to accept majority decisions.

There are more specific objectives that are useful when planning the learning opportunities for courses or when analyzing instructional materials. These objectives are called *educational objectives* and are illustrated in several taxonomies of educational objectives.[9] These taxonomies treat affective, cognitive, and psychomotor domains. The *Taxonomy of Educational Objectives: Handbook I,* for example, treats cognitive objectives and classifies them using six major categories and several subcategories. Categories range from simple recall of information to critical evaluative behaviors. One such category is *application.* Application is defined as using abstractions in particular and concrete situations. The abstractions may be general ideas, rules of procedures, or generalized methods. They may also be technical principles, ideas, and theories that must be remembered and applied. The taxonomy also gives sample objectives. The level of specificity of an educational objective can be seen in this example: "The ability to predict the probable effect of a change in a factor on a biological situation previously at equilibrium." The objective can be further amplified by an illustration of the kind of test or test item that would be appropriate.

The taxonomies have greatly influenced curriculum making. More attention is now given to affective, cognitive, and psychomotor domains. Also, curriculum workers are now more sensitive to the level of behavior expected from instruction. They are, for instance, more concerned now that objectives and test items treat higher cognitive processes like comprehension, application, and analysis rather than dealing only with recall of information.

There is an even more specific form for an objective; it is called an *instructional objective*. This form is useful when teaching pupils a specific concept. It is often called a Mager-like instructional objective after the person who advocated its use.[10] These objectives specify the behavior to be exhibited by the student, a standard or criterion of acceptable performance, and the kind of situation in which the behavior is to be elicited. One instructional objective might be, "Given a linear algebraic equation with one unknown [the situation or condition], the learner must be able to solve the equation [behavior and criterion] without the aid of references, tables, or calculating devices [additional conditions]."

An additional degree of specificity can be found in the *amplified objective*, which is used when one desires to communicate to writers and consumers of criterion-referenced tests. Amplified objectives represent a set of rules to generate test items.[11] These rules describe (1) the stimuli or testing situations that can constitute or be used in constructing test items, including the potential content from which items can be generated and the directions to be given the learners; (2) the response options, including the nature of the distractors to appear in a multiple-choice test; and (3) the criteria of correctness (the bases for judging an item right or wrong).

Specific behavioral objectives seem valuable in providing guidance for evaluation of instructional materials and student performance. However, the other functions of behavioral objectives, such as giving direction in teaching and aiding learning, arouse much difference of opinion. It is charged that a teacher who uses specific objectives may not give enough attention to the immediate concerns of learners. The research on this issue, however, is inconclusive. Some studies on the effects of behavioral objectives on learning, for example, have shown facilitative effects, but an equal number have not shown any significant differences.[12] Objectives sometimes help and are almost never harmful. They seem to assist students in determining what is expected of them and in discriminating between relevant and irrelevant content. There remains, however, a question regarding the number of objectives provided the student. If the list of objectives is extensive and detailed, the student may be overwhelmed.

Measurement of Intended Outcomes versus Goal-free Evaluation

Years ago Ralph Tyler told evaluators that it was impossible to decide whether a particular test would be appropriate for appraising a certain program until the objectives of the program had been defined and until the kinds of situations that would give an opportunity for this behavior to be expressed were identified. Tyler recommended checking each proposed evaluation device against the objectives and constructing or devising methods for getting evidence about the student's attainment of these objectives.

More recently, Michael Scriven moved beyond Tyler's concern for data about intended outcomes to a concern for all relevant effects.[13] His approach is called *goal-free evaluation*. Such evaluation does not assess a situation only in terms of prespecified goal preferences. It is evaluation of *actual* effects against a profile of demonstrated needs. It is offered as a protection against the "tunnel vision" of those close to the program—against harmful side effects, missed new priorities, and overlooked achievement. To the extent that Scriven's approach is used, more evaluative measures will have to be employed. Selection of these measures will be difficult, for there are thousands of such devices. Practicality will probably dictate the use of measures that assess most intended outcomes and a limited number of possible side effects.

Norm-Referenced Tests and Criterion-Referenced Tests

Standardized achievement tests are norm referenced; that is, they are designed to compare the performances of individuals to the performance of a normative group. The purposes of these tests initially were to find the most able persons and to sort out those who would most likely succeed or fail some future learning situation. Only those test items that discriminate between the best and worst are kept. The assumption that everyone can learn equally well is rejected in norm-referenced testing. These tests, therefore, tend to correlate very highly with intelligence tests. In order to obtain items with high response variance, writers of norm-referenced tests are likely to exclude the items that measure well-taught concepts and skills of schooling.

Although norm-referenced tests do identify persons of different ability, they are of questionable value in curriculum evaluation. They may not accurately measure what educational programs are designed to teach or reveal particular problems that are keeping pupils from achieving. Teachers can sometimes improve scores on such tests, but such improvement usually results from tricks like (1) telling children to respond to all items so that the possibility of getting more right answers is increased (a child needs to get only three to seven more items right to show one-year improvement on typical achievement tests); (2) testing at a different time of the year than previously to show apparent but not real gains; (3) capitalizing on regressing effects that make the poorest scores look better on the second testing; and (4) teaching pupils how to respond to the items themselves and to the test format.

Criterion-referenced tests are meant to ascertain a learner's status with respect to a learning task rather than to a norm. These tests tell what learners can and cannot do in specified situations. The tasks selected can be those which the curriculum emphasizes. The items used in the test match the set of learner behaviors called for in the objective and should not be eliminated, as in the norm-referenced tests, merely because most students answer them correctly. Hence, these tests can be sensitive measures of what has been taught.

Criterion-referenced tests are also useful in showing whether a student has mastered specific learnings. That is why they are popular in instructional settings using continuous-progress plans or other individualized teaching approaches. The tests indicate what instructional treatments are needed by individual learners and also indicate when learners are ready to proceed to other tasks.

Criterion-referenced tests are sometimes faulted because they have been based on objectives that are too narrow. The multiplicity of tests necessary to accompany many objectives has been a management problem to teachers. Trends indicate that particular courses in the future will use perhaps eight to ten very important objective-based tests of high transfer value rather than thirty-five or fifty objective-based tests as is now common. Tests that are curriculum embedded—that is, tests that have items dependent on particular materials or programs—will diminish. Other ways of improving these tests are to include a complete description of the set of learner behaviors that the test is to assess and to increase the number of items for each competency measured in order to have an acceptable standard of reliability.

Tests and Invasion of Privacy

The American Civil Liberties Union has taken up the cause of the students who charge that tests are an invasion of privacy. Students have complained about the use of instruments, usually self-report devices, that probe their attitudes in such areas of self-esteem, interest in school, and human relations. Evaluators want such data in order to assess the effects of schooling. Protests against the use of tests to guide the learning process in academic areas are less frequent. ACLU lawyers argue that authorities have not made it clear that pupils may refuse to take tests that they believe to be invading their privacy. Pupils should also be told that the questions asked in a test might require self-incriminating responses.

This issue is related to a larger problem, that of the effect of tests on students. Do they affect motivation and self-esteem by producing anxiety and encouraging cheating? Do they create labels and determine adult social status? Marjorie C. Kirkland completed an extensive review of the research treating such questions. Her review throws light on test effects. For example, she shows that how individuals think of themselves and what they believe about a test influences their test behavior. Other examples from Kirkland's review show that students' attitudes about tests in general are negative. The more interested persons are in their test results, the more they perceive positive consequences of tests. Systematic reporting of test results helps students to understand their interests, aptitudes, and achievements.[14] Anyone reading Kirkland's review will conclude that the tests are powerful indeed and that their consequences are far-ranging.

Techniques for Collecting Data

Newton S. Metfessel and William B. Michael have published a list of multiple criterion measures for evaluating school programs.[15] The list indicates the great range in ways of collecting evidence. One class of indicators of change in learners is associated with informal, teacher-made devices, incomplete sentence techniques, interviews, peer nominations, sociograms, questionnaires, self-evaluation measures, projective devices, and semantic differential scales. The authors also describe the many ways for assessing the effect of programs without influencing the outcomes. These noninfluencing ways are called *unobtrusive measures;* they include attending to absences, anecdotal records, appointments, assignments, stories written, awards, use of books, case histories, disciplinary actions, dropouts, and voluntary activities.

Creative indicators can be devised if persons will think beyond the use of formal tests. A useful scheme for generating indicators is to reflect on (1) learners' products—such as compositions, paintings, constructions; (2) learners' self-reports on preferences and interests; and (3) how learners solve problems, conduct discussions, and participate in physical games and dances. With these methods, the teacher or evaluator should use an accompanying checklist stipulating behavior to be exhibited by the pupil and the qualities to be found in the pupil's product.

Measuring Affect

Although it is a controversial activity, the assessment of affect is gaining interest. Special techniques are used for this task because it is believed that individuals are more likely to "fake" their attitudinal responses. Hence, mild deception is often used so that learners will not know the purpose of the inquiry or that they are being observed. For example, a student may be asked to respond to several hypothetical situations, only one of which is of interest to the examiner. The examiner may ask, "Where would you take a visitor friend from out of town—to the market, the movie, the school, the library, the bank?" If "school" is the answer, it is presumed that the respondent tends to value that institution. Another, less direct approach is to use high inference and theoretical instruments. The examiner might ask, "Would you play the part of a degenerate in a play?" or "Which of the following names (one of which is the respondent's own) do you like?" (The inference is that sudents with high self-concepts will play any role and will like their names.) Situations are sometimes contrived, and students' reactions are interpreted to indicate particular attitudes. For example, student accomplices may collect unobtrusive data and report their observations later. Audio recordings are sometimes made of student small-group discussions and analyzed later.

Sometimes, too, individuals are offered ways to respond anonymously. It should be clear that in evaluating affective effects of curriculum, individuals need not be identified. One only has to know what effect the curriculum is having on students as a group. Further, the measures or scores obtained with most high-inference instruments are not reliable enough for making predictions about individuals.

In an effort to improve the credibility of their findings, evaluators may use *triangulation* (the use of three different measures in concert). If a similar attitude is found by all three measures, they have more confidence in the findings. Locally developed instruments also are thought to be more valid when two or more persons score student's responses the same and when several samples of student behavior are consistent.

Appraisals of Existing Instruments

There are several sources that both list and evaluate instruments. The Center for the Study of Evaluation at UCLA has four publications that describe and evaluate thousands of tests for elementary and secondary schools.[16] The Social Science Education Consortium has analyzed and cataloged one thousand instruments for use in evaluating programs in the social studies.[17] Many measures of social and psychological attitudes are described in a publication by John Robinson and Phillip Stover of the Survey Research Center Institute for Social Research at the University of Michigan. Data concerning criterion-referenced tests and instructional objectives can be obtained from the Instructional Objectives Exchange.[18] *Tests in Print II*, by Oscar K. Buros, includes a bibliography of most known tests published for use with English-speaking persons, a classified index to the contents of mental measurement yearbooks, descriptions of the population for which each test is intended, and other features. Buros is also the editor of *The Seventh Mental Measurements Yearbook. This yearbook includes, among other things, 798 reviews of 546 tests.*[19]

For those interested in instruments to use in evaluating the interactive phase of instruction, Anita Simon and E. Gill Boyer have edited two good sourcebooks, and a third has been prepared by the Texas Research and Development Center.[20] Excellent criteria for assessing observation instruments have been prepared by John Herbert and Carol Attridge.[21]

Concluding Comments

Measurement is a waste if implications of the data are not drawn and acted on in modifying the curriculum. Looking at test scores and filing them away mocks the evaluative process. Admittedly, there are latent functions for evaluation. Results are sometimes used to gain support of parents and others. Evaluation may be undertaken because it is a necessary basis for requesting federal monies. However, the principal purpose for using the data should be improvement of the curriculum. Hence, some schools now have curriculum groups that study the findings and then make plans both for the whole school and for individual teachers.

Scores or descriptive terms that summarize learner performance give study groups the opportunity to see the strengths and weaknesses of their programs. Analyses of different populations of pupils are done, and teachers attempt to find out from the data what needs individual students have. Diagnosing needs becomes a basis for giving personal help. Study groups also discuss the reasons for a curriculum's strengths and weaknesses. Members try to explain results in terms of particular learning opportunities, time spent on an objective, the ordering of activities and topics, the kinds and frequency of responses from learners, the grouping patterns, and the use of space and interactions with adults. Explanations are verified by seeing whether all the data lead to the same conclusion. Plans are made to modify the curriculum in light of deficiencies noted and the cause of the deficiencies.

The results from evaluation should be used in at least two ways. First, they can be used to strengthen ends. Results can be the basis for inferring new instructional objectives aimed at meeting revealed needs. If evaluation of a program or particular learning opportunities results in the selection of more important objectives than were originally held, the experiences were valuable. Dewey put it well, "There is no such thing as a final set of objectives even for the time being or temporarily. Each day of teaching ought to enable a teacher to revise and better in some respect the objectives arrived at in a previous work."[22]

Results can also be used to revise means. They can serve as a guide to the need for new learning opportunities and arrangements that might close gaps. That is, evaluation pinpoints needs and guides one in the selection of new material, procedures, and organizational patterns. These innovations in turn must be tried out and their results appraised. In short, evaluation is only a link in a continuing cycle.

Questions

1. How would you respond if faced with the choice of getting important data about the learner through deception or getting less important data in a straightforward manner?
2. What kinds of student progress are best revealed by (a) products of learners, (b) self-reports, and (c) observations of pupil behavior?
3. The National Assessment of Educational Progress is a federal project that administers tests called objective-reference exercises to small groups of representative pupils and young adults (a sample) across the country. Many persons, however, do not consider the assessment information help-

ful, saying they can cite no program changes based on assessment reports. Further, the assessment data do not tell whether the results are good or bad nor do they pinpoint the reasons for the percentage scores. What kind of information should national assessment provide if it is to affect the decision-making process?

4. Compare the purposes and manner of construction of norm-referenced and criterion-referenced tests.
5. Think of a learning opportunity that you might select for learners (for example, a particular educational game, lesson, field trip, experiment, textbook article, or story selection). Then indicate what you would do in order to find out whether or not this opportunity produced both intended outcomes and unanticipated consequences.
6. How might a teacher or principal gain information regarding the end-of-year progress of students with respect to a large number of objectives without subjecting students to a great deal of testing?
7. What are the major advantages and disadvantages of objectives from the point of view of *curriculum* (the designation of worthwhile ends), *instruction* (the designing of instructional sequences), and *evaluation* (the determination of accomplishment and judgment of the program's worth)?

Notes

1. L. J. Cronbach, "Course Improvement Through Evaluation," *Teachers College Record* 64 (May 1963): 672–83.
2. D. T. Campbell and J. C. Stanley, "Experimental and Quasi-Experimental Designs for Research on Teaching," in *Handbook of Research on Teaching*, ed. N. L. Gage (Chicago: Rand McNally, 1963).
3. W. J. Popham, *Educational Evaluation* (Englewood Cliffs, N.J.: Prentice-Hall, 1975).
4. D. P. Horst et al., *A Practical Guide to Measuring Project Impact on Student Achievement*, Monograph Series on Education, no. 1 (Washington, D.C.: U.S. Office of Education, 1975).
5. J. C. Flanagan, "Education's Contribution to the Quality of Life of a Sample of 30-Year-Olds," *Education Researcher* 4:6 (June 1975): 13–16.
6. National Assessment of Educational Progress, 1860 Lincoln Street, Denver, CO 80203.
7. M. Alkin and C. T. Fitzgibbon, "Methods and Theories of Evaluating Programs," *Journal of Research and Development in Education* 8:3 (September 1975): 2–15.
8. Popham, *Educational Evaluation*, p. 218.
9. B. S. Bloom, ed., *Taxonomy of Educational Objectives: Handbook I: Cognitive Domain* (New York: David McKay Co., 1956); D. R. Krathwohl et al., *Taxonomy of Educational Objectives: Handbook II: The Affective Domain* (New York: David McKay Co., 1956); A. Harrow, *A Taxonomy of the Psychomotor Domain: A Guide for Developing Behavioral Objectives* (New York: David McKay Co., 1972).

10. R. F. Mager, *Preparing Instructional Objectives* (Palo Alto, Calif.: Fearon Publishers, 1962).

11. Popham, *Educational Evaluation,* p. 147.

12. P. C. Duchastel and P. F. Merrill, "The Effects of Behavioral Objectives on Learning: A Review of Empirical Studies," *Review of Educational Research* 43:1 (Winter 1973): 53–69.

13. M. Scriven, "Pros and Cons about Goal-free Evaluation," *Evaluation Comment* 3:4 (December 1972): 1–4.

14. M. C. Kirkland, "The Effects of Tests on Students and School," *Review of Educational Research* 41:4 (October 1971): 303–51.

15. N. S. Metfessel and W. B. Michael, "A Paradigm Involving Multiple Criterion Measures for the Evaluation of the Effectiveness of School Programs," *Educational and Psychological Measurement* 27 (1967): 931–34.

16. The Center for the Study of Evaluation, 405 Hilgard Ave., Los Angeles, CA 90024.

17. The Social Science Education Consortium, 855 Broadway, Boulder, CO 80302.

18. Instructional Objectives Exchange, Box 24095, Los Angeles, CA 90024.

19. O. K. Buros, ed., *Tests in Print II* and *The Seventh Mental Measurements Yearbook* (Highland Park, N.J.: Gryphon Press, 1974, 1972).

20. A. Simon and E. G. Boyer, eds., *Mirrors for Behavior: An Anthology of Classroom Observation Instruments* (Austin, Texas: Research and Development Center for Teacher Education, University of Texas at Austin, 1975).

21. J. Herbert and C. Attridge, "A Guide for Developers and Users of Observation Systems and Manuals," *American Educational Research Journal* 12:1 (Winter 1975): 1–20.

22. J. Dewey, *The Sources of a Science of Education* (New York: Horace Liveright, 1929).

Conceptual-Empiricists

18 Deep Dark Deficits of the Adversary Evaluation Model

W. James Popham
Dale Carlson

Introduction

The quest for more effective models and research procedures to evaluate instructional and curriculum programs has led some conceptual-empiricists to invent new models as well as adapt existing ones. This movement toward alternatives implies disenchantment with existing designs. The evaluation design that has received considerable criticism, yet continues to be used widely, relies on a quantitative analysis of school, instructional, and curriculum inputs and their impact on learning outcomes. As alternatives, some evaluation researchers have recommended more qualitative, process-oriented designs that study the "workings" of a program while it is operational rather than at its beginning and its end.

One of these process-evaluation models is referred to in the research literature as the adversary evaluation model; it borrows extensively from judicial procedures. These procedures include issue generation and selection, the preparation of arguments and the hearing itself. This final stage attempts to simulate actual courtroom procedures.

Although this evaluation procedure has appealing qualities to an educated citizenry who advocate "due process," the adversary model has received much more critical commentary than would ordinarily be anticipated. This paper by James Popham and Dale Carlson is such a critique. It identifies six major weaknesses, referred to as deficits, of this evaluation process. Briefly, these weaknesses are disparity in prowess, fallibility, excessive confidence, framing difficulties, decision-maker

bias, and excessive costs. Wherever possible, the authors attempt to offer remedies for each of these deficits. As you read this critique, think about the following questions:
- How would you describe the weaknesses identified in this paper?
- In your judgment, are the remedies offered adequate to meet the perceived weaknesses?
- Are any of these weaknesses evident in other evaluation models you have studied or seen in operation?

As a spectator attraction, competition is hard to beat. Whether it is a courtroom drama or a sporting event, we thrill as the contest totters in favor of one side then the other. Perhaps it is the uncertainty of the outcome that fascinates us. But whatever the appeal, it is quite clear that ancient folks, like present-day ones, got genuinely excited by competitive events. The athletic contests of antiquity, whether Greek, Roman, or Mayan, were capable of drawing standing-room-only audiences.

It is not surprising, therefore, that when people recently started touting the adversary model as a novel approach to educational evaluation, many of us were enthralled. After all, this would be a chance to pick up all the dramatic dividends of a competitive event and, if the legal folklore is to be believed, to end up with an objective evaluation in which both sides of a case are most forcefully presented. Oh yes, the adversary evaluation model was quite alluring.

Adversarying under Palm Trees

In spring 1976 we were invited to participate in an adversary evaluation project being directed by the Northwest Regional Educational Laboratory (NWREL) for the state of Hawaii. The focus of the evaluation was a large-scale, team-teaching program for K–3 classes in Hawaii, a program in which three teachers worked with two classrooms full of children, hence the designation: The Hawaii 3-on-2 Program.

Both of us were intrigued by the adversary evaluation model and wanted to learn more about it. And if we were going to learn about the adversary approach, then careful analysis (three seconds) suggested that Hawaii would be a more suitable place to acquire such knowledge than, say, equatorial Africa, Antarctica, or just about any place else we could think of. Adversarying in Hawaii was an offer we just couldn't turn down.

Thus, for the better part of a year, we were intermittently involved in carrying out an adversary evaluation. We were two members of a four-person Advocate Team, the team which, by coin toss, ended up defending the raptures of the

Reprinted, with permission, from *Educational Researcher* 6, no. 6 (1977), pp. 3–6. Copyright © 1979, American Educational Research Association, Washington, D.C.

Adversary Evaluation Model

Hawaii 3-on-2 Program. Another four-person team, designated as the Adversary Team, was charged with attacking it. Staff members from NWREL served as arbiters. A complete report of the evaluation effort is available elsewhere.[2]

The Cream Begins to Curdle

During the early stages of the evaluation, both of us behaved like kittens with bowls full of cream. We were caught up with the glitter of the adversary approach even as we worked out ground rules with our colleagues, and we anticipated the future give and take of the adversarial contest. It seemed, further, like an excellent vehicle for setting forth two partisan but opposing views of the program we were evaluating. Everything was peachy.

But as the months went wandering by and we became more and more conversant with the adversary evaluation model, either our cream began to curdle or we sensed the incongruity of behaving like middle-aged kittens. Now, the evaluation behind us, we want to register downright skepticism regarding the adversary evaluation model, at least insofar as it is applied to education. Its deficits are deep in the sense that they may render the approach essentially inappropriate for any significant applications. Its deficits are dark in the sense that it is hard to detect some of these weaknesses unless you have actually participated in an adversarial evaluative effort and attempted self-consciously to appraise what was going on.

We wish to set forth, therefore, the set of weaknesses that we believe are present in most adversary evaluation approaches. Along the way we will attempt to offer a few suggestions, where warranted, for ameliorating certain of the weaknesses.

Some of the deficits to be discussed in the following paragraphs, obviously, represent more serious difficulties than others. Some, it appears, can be taken care of with either modest or serious effort. Some, in our estimate, are sufficiently formidable that they render the adversary approach ineffectual for educational evaluators.

Because the typical ingredients of adversary evaluation models have been described elsewhere, they will not be recounted here. For those unfamiliar with the adversary approach, an examination of these sources is recommended.[3] Clearly, there are all sorts of variations in the actual way that an adversary evaluation study is carried out.

Deficit Number One: Disparity in Proponent Prowess

If an adversary evaluation model is to function effectively, it is assumed that both sides of an issue will be satisfactorily presented for the consideration of decision makers. This is far easier to assume than to accomplish. And, of course, if one side of a proposition is not adequately defended, then the decision makers may erroneously opt for the other side merely because it appears more compelling.

All too often we see instances in our nation's legal enterprise where one would have to be naive to contend that equality of justice is present. Whereas affluent defendants can have an attorney such as Melvin Belli or F. Lee Bailey, poverty-stricken defendants may be obliged to accept a public defender fresh out of law school. And, notwithstanding a Biblical exception or two, most David-Goliath contests end up in favor of the big fellow.

In the conduct of adversary educational evaluations, it is all too likely that there will also be a disparity in the skill of the two competing teams (or individuals). The danger, of course, is that the effective team may end up defending the weak side of the case, yet do it so well that the decision makers are won over.

Although we all recognize that this happens in the real world, somehow the occasional injustice that stems from mismatched lawyers seems less outrageous than when an incorrect educational decision is made because of a mismatch in adversary skills. In the courtroom, one or two people at most are usually wronged. That's terrible, but we recognize that systems operated by human beings will have their share of failures. We have become inured to an occasional miscarriage of justice. Yet, when the matter at hand is an educational decision that can influence the formative years of essentially unprotected children, all of a sudden the stakes are perceived as much higher. Injustice is unacceptable whenever it occurs, but when it occurs with large numbers of young children, it seems genuinely intolerable.

In the adversary evaluation of the Hawaii 3-on-2 Program referred to earlier, the writers found themselves assigned (via a coin flip) to defend the merits of a program that we became increasingly convinced was not a cost-effective investment for the taxpayers of Hawaii. Primary grade children, we came to believe, were being shortchanged because a program that cost about $10,000,000 annually was not yielding its promised results. But there we were—obliged to defend it. What would happen if we did such an effective job of convincing the Hawaii decision makers that they opted to maintain the 3-on-2 Program in its present form? Our team might win the adversary contest, but the children of Hawaii would experience a decisive loss.

Yet, should we harness our zeal in trying to defend the 3-on-2 Program? Obviously not, since the adversary model would then lose its purported advantage of fully setting forth both sides of a case.

Remedy

In order to cope with this profound weakness of the adversary evaluation model, it is our belief that procedures will have to be employed whereby each adversary team (individual) argues *both* sides of the case at hand. By having each team prepare a pair of reports, one pro and one con, the decision makers would be able to consider two sets of positive and two sets of negative arguments. The more capable team should be able to do a better job defending the more defensible side of the issue.

While this does involve double work for the adversary teams, it should pose no insurmountable intellectual problems. College and high school debaters constantly shift sides of an issue as they wind their way through each year's debate tournaments. If anything, by undertaking to defend both sides of an issue, members of an adversary team should experience less ethical qualms because they can do their best job in defending both the "wrong" and "right" sides of a case.

Deficit Number Two: Fallible Arbiters

Anyone familiar with our courts will instantly concede that judges vary in their abilities. Some people who sit on the bench are actually better suited to dusting or polishing it. But, thankfully, when a judge rules improperly in a trial, that case can be appealed to a higher court where such errors can be rectified.

We don't have an appeals court when we carry out adversary evaluations. If the people coordinating the overall conduct of the evaluation muck up, where is an adversary team to turn? Oh, resigning from the project is always possible, but that hardly seems appropriate in many instances. And merely registering formal protests doesn't do the job if the arbiters rule against you. The situation can become really sticky at times. Let's illustrate.

In the evaluation of the Hawaii 3-on-2 Program, we were obliged to defend 3-on-2. We were certain that if standardized achievement tests were used, there would be no significant differences in favor of the 3-on-2 pupils. Previous evaluations of 3-on-2 had turned out that way. Standardized achievement tests almost invariably result in no significant differences. Why should anything be different in this case? Yet, even though we realized that standardized achievement tests would be used in the 3-on-2 evaluation, for surely our adversary colleagues would insist that they be used, we were prepared to argue against their appropriateness.

In the early stages of the evaluation, as the adversary teams and the arbiters worked out procedural details of the evaluation, one of the ground rules agreed to was that both teams would collaboratively work out the design for the study, then agree not to subsequently criticize that design. It seemed a sensible ground rule.

But our team did not interpret that ground rule to preclude the possibility of criticizing the tests themselves, whereas the arbiters assumed that the "design" included the measuring instruments used. It was an instance of the kind of misunderstanding that often pops up when dealing with such matters. But had the arbiters imposed their interpretation on us, rigidly insisting that we could not attack the testing devices, our case would have been badly damaged. (It was weak enough in any event.) What should we have done?

As it turned out, the arbiters exercised good judgment (in our view) and allowed us to question the suitability of the tests. Yet, there are innumerable points along the way where unwise arbiter decisions can improperly influence the case in one direction or the other. This is particularly true in an embryonic arena where no set of tested ground rules exists for the conduct of such evaluations.

Remedy

Other than striving to secure saintlike individuals to serve as arbiters, we do not have a handy solution to cope with this problem. All of the remedy tactics we considered turned out to be patently inefficient or too elaborate to be practical.

Deficit Number Three:
Excessive Confidence in the Model's Potency

Faced with problems that appear insoluble, people often seek solutions from technologies they don't understand very well. We tend to ascribe unwarranted potency to disciplines that we do not comprehend. Perhaps we think: "If a field is so complex that *I* don't understand it, it must be worthwhile." Surely the deference of many educational practitioners toward statisticians is prompted by the fact that few practitioners have ever ginned up a geometric mean or fondled a canonical correlation coefficient.

Perhaps this same mentality is operative when we assume that adversary evaluation approaches will lead us out of evaluative imprecision and directly into a world of improved decisions. Leon Lipson of the Yale Law School puts it succinctly as he comments on a proposed science court, a scheme analogous to the adversary evaluation model:

... the proposal overestimates the power and efficacy of the adversary process as a means of finding a truth—even current, provisional, working, technical truth—that the "loser" will concede to be truth.[4]

Lipson observes that the recent initiatives to throw a variety of controversies into the mode of quasi-judicial resolution generally came from those whose experience with the law is limited. He concludes his appraisal of such proposals cogently:

The proposal, in sum, rests upon the wistful hope that conflict conducted in the public view on difficult technical and scientific aspects of controversial issues can be leached of its political juices. Do we have to spend years, and millions, to relearn the folly of such a hope? Over the last few years, experts and laymen have found other and better ways of communicating with one another, in a variety of official and unofficial forums. The proposal for a science court appears to be not so much a useful addition to the spectrum of working devices as a quaint fantasy of technical closure in circumstances of disagreement over policies.[5]

Remedy

While there is no certain way to bridle the enthusiasm of recent converts, we must recognize that much of the drum pounding for the adversary evaluation model is emanating from educators who, as Lipson observes, have limited experience with the legal discipline from which it is derived. To balance the well-intentioned zeal of adversary model devotees, we must add occasional dashes of reality to their "quaint fantasy."

Deficit Number Four: Difficulties in Framing the Proposition in a Manner Amenable to Adversary Resolution

Drawing on our familiarity with the courtroom contest, we, too, readily assume that educational issues can be cast in such a way that an advocate-adversary conflict will yield suitable guidance for decision makers. But the decision options facing educational policy makers are often more complicated than can be readily encompassed in the framework of a simple guilty/innocent, winner/loser, or go/no-go adversary contest.

As we became more and more conversant with the intricacies, both educational and political, of the Hawaii 3-on-2 Program, we realized that Hawaii's decision makers should not be forced to deal with a simple save-it-or-scrap-it choice. Middle-ground positions were more sensible. Halfway measures, in this instance, probably made more sense. But there we were, obliged to do battle with our adversary colleagues on the unembellished question of whether to maintain or terminate the 3-on-2 Program. Most issues facing educational decision makers are more similar to the myriad-option 3-on-2 cases than they are to the guilty/innocent courtroom model.

Remedy

Apply the adversary evaluation model exclusively to those educational situations in which it is thoroughly clear that only a binary choice faces decision makers and in which the two decision options are in direct opposition to one another.

**Deficit Number Five:
A Cat's-Paw for Biased Decision Makers**

Although in the abstract we can think of the adversary evaluation model as a crucible from which truth obligingly bubbles forth, in the hands of an unprincipled decision maker, the model can serve a more devious function. Let's say you are a college president who secretly wishes to eliminate a small Germanic languages department so as to use the freed financial resources for other purposes. Now if you commission an adversary evaluation of the merits of saving or squashing the Germanic languages department, you know that you'll get an argument on both sides of the issue. All you have to do is sit back, then assert that you were reluctantly persuaded by the arguments in favor of abolishing the department. For you, it's a no-lose situation. Who is to say you weren't, quite properly, persuaded by the team advocating abolition?

Although it is surely not the case that most educational decision makers are unscrupulous, or that every time an adversary model is employed a biased decision maker is using it as a ploy to support a prejudgment, we must recognize that this possibility exists.

Remedy

We can proffer no way of heading off this misuse of the adversary model other than by requiring potentially evil decision makers to take an extensive course in ethics—and it would have to be awfully well taught. A screening test to detect latent unscrupulousness in decision makers should be developed without delay.

Deficit Number Six: Excessive Costs

It is difficult to conceive of an adversary evaluation project that would cost no more than a conventional evaluation study. The costs of doing an adversary study properly are typically double, at least, the cost of an ordinary evaluation study because two teams and a coordination/arbitration staff are required. Besides the raw staffing requirements, there will typically be a greater demand for data because the two teams will often grasp at straws, any old straws, in an effort to bolster their cases.

In the Hawaii 3-on-2 Program evaluation, for example, we attempted to secure various sorts of attitudinal data from teachers and pupils that had only a very slight chance of turning out in our favor. Yet, because we were obliged to defend a case in which there were no supporting student-performance data, we were desperate. Had we been approaching the evaluation task in a more conventional fashion, it is unlikely that we would have carried out these fishing excursions.

In addition, surely because there are yet no definitive guidelines for the conduct of adversary evaluations, there is an alarming amount of time expended on ground-rule clarification, reclarification, and reconsideration. We spent an inordinate chunk of our time in the Hawaii evaluation trying to work through the various aspects of our operating procedures. This was necessary, to be sure, since we really were obliged to settle these details; but the resolution of procedural matters does bump up the cost of an adversary evaluation effort.

For instance, in December 1976, both 3-on-2 adversary teams met in Portland for a three-day meeting to exchange our initial reports (for the first time) and to prepare initial drafts of rebuttal statements. Of the *three* working days, we spent about *two* days dealing with procedural matters regarding the initial reports and how to handle the reporting formats planned for the following month in Hawaii. While two-thirds of our working time may have been needed for procedural matters, such wrangling obviously increases the cost of the enterprise.

And if, in an effort to reduce the disparity in adversary team prowess, anyone followed our earlier suggestion to have both teams prepare a report on each side of the case, the costs would multiply even further. Clearly, conducting adversary evaluations is costly business.

Remedy

Only entertain the thought of an adversary evaluation approach when you can afford it. Note that we did *not* say only use an adversary evaluation approach when the issue is important enough to warrant the extra costs. The entire thrust of this paper has been to suggest that the adversary model is not an expensive but more effective model to be trotted out only when the stakes are high enough. The higher the stakes, the more queasy we become about becoming adversarial. All we are saying here is, if you can't afford to spend the extra dollars in your evaluation, don't go the adversary route.

Retrospect

When the writers accepted the assignment to work on the Hawaii 3-on-2 Program evaluation, we did so chiefly to learn more about the adversary model. We did not enter into this activity with the thought that we were going to end up disliking the model. Indeed, we both thought we were going to learn more about its intricacies so we could apply it to future evaluations. As the foregoing analysis suggests, our romance with the adversary model soon faded into neutrality, then downright negativism.

What will happen to the adversary evaluation model in the next few years? Well, it's sure to have a champion or two who, considering it their personal hobby horse, will push it for all it's worth. What we have been trying to say, however, is that it is not worth much. The adversary evaluation model brings with it not only a few real (and many imaginary) dividends; it also brings far too many deficits.

Notes

1. Adapted from a paper presented as part of a symposium, *The Adversary Evaluation Model: A Second Look*, Annual Meeting of the American Educational Research Association, New York, April 4–8, 1977.

2. Northwest Regional Educational Laboratory, *3-on-2 Evaluation Report*, 1976–77, vol. I, II, and III. Portland, Oregon, January 1977.

3. See, for example, R. L. Wolf, "Trial by Jury: A New Evaluation Method," *Phi Delta Kappan* 57:3 (November 1975): 185–87; T. Owens, "Educational Evaluation by Adversary Proceeding," in *School Evaluation: The Politics and Process*, ed. E. House (Berkeley: McCutchan, 1973); M. Levine, "Scientific Method and the Adversary Model," *American Psychologist* (September 1974): 666–77; or M. Kourilsky, "An Adversary Model for Educational Evaluation," *Evaluation Comment* 4:2 (1974).

4. L. Lipson, "Technical Issues and Adversary Process," letter to the editor, *Science* 194 (1976): 890.

5. Ibid.

19 What Curriculum Research?

Decker F. Walker

Introduction

Evaluation research has emerged in recent years as a response to a public need to know about the effectiveness of various educational programs. Instructional and curriculum effects on student learning have been among the primary public concerns for they represent two of the most crucial dimensions of formal education. It is no surprise, therefore, that both large-scale evaluations (for example, Head Start and Follow Through) and smaller evaluations conducted at the regional, state, and local levels have been concerned with the impacts of teaching and curriculum on pupil achievement.

In the paper that follows, Decker Walker comments on the paucity of curriculum research, identifies the misconceptions of empirical research, which distracts members of the curriculum field from conducting work in the discipline, and finally addresses many of the misconceptions themselves. Among the important research considerations are those dealing with human behavior, verification and proof, reliability, cause and effect relationships, and control of the experiment.

As you read, think about the following questions:
- What is the basis for Walker's concern about the quality of research in the curriculum field?
- What arguments does he present to elaborate on the basic misconceptions held by professionals in the curriculum field?

Reprinted, with permission, from *Journal of Curriculum Studies* 5 (January 1973), pp. 58–72.

My thesis in this paper is this: We in the field of curriculum have failed to conduct the empirical research needed to clarify the nature of the phenomena and problems we address. This failure is due in part to misconceptions we have uncritically accepted about the nature and aims of empirical inquiry in a field concerned with practice. As one consequence of these misconceptions, we lack faith in empirical inquiry as a means of dealing with our concerns.

Let me clear the way for my main points with some definitions. When I refer to the field of curriculum, I mean the field of professional study and practice in education that emerged from the generalized matrix of pedagogy in the United States around the turn of this century. Its founders and early builders would undoubtedly include Franklin Bobbitt, W. W. Charters, and Harold Rugg. Many others, such as John Dewey, Hollis Caswell, and the McMurrys, are also frequently mentioned as important formative influences. (The early years of the field of curriculum have been chronicled by several authors, including Caswell,[1] Kliebard,[2] and Seguel.[3]

The school curriculum as a subject of study and an object of professional practice is more difficult to define. In the fraction of a century since attempts to distinguish curriculum from other elements or aspects of educational practice first began to be made, no consensus on the proper basis for this distinction has been reached. But all agree that curriculum is to be distinguished from instruction and teaching on the rough basis that it deals with questions of what items of content or skill or experience to include in the educational program, whereas the latter fields deal more with questions of how best to present these items. It is not necessary to go beyond this rough distinction so far as this paper is concerned because the remarks I will make here about curriculum and curriculum research I would also make about instructional research and research on teaching.

In order to define the field in a positive way, rather than by its differences with other fields, I think it is necessary to consider the phenomena and problems of the field. Like medicine, which studies the human body and how to make and keep it healthy, or architecture, which studies shelter and how to build and use it, or horticulture, which studies plants and how to make them grow and contribute to man's welfare, education—and curriculum as a part of education—is defined by what it studies and to what end rather than by the ideas, methods, theories, or techniques it uses or the identity, training, and organizational affiliations of its practitioners.

The phenomena of curriculum include all those activities and enterprises in which curricula are planned, created, adopted, presented, experienced, criticized, attacked, defended, and evaluated, as well as the objects that may be part of a curriculum, such as textbooks, apparatus and equipment, schedules, teachers' guides, and so on.

In addition to these actual objects, events, and processes, the phenomena of curriculum can be—and in my judgment should be—interpreted to include the plans, intentions, hopes, fears, dreams, and the like of agents such as teachers, students, and curriculum developers or policymakers.

The central problem of curriculum I take to be *"What should be taught, studied, and learned?"* This question takes many forms as it is asked in different situations. What should be taught to disadvantaged students? Considering the needs of the students in this community, what should be taught in their schools? Considering the characteristics of this particular topic within a school subject, to whom should it be taught? Given that a community wants this and this and this for its children, what should the school program be like in that community? Answering these basic questions may require us to address other questions, such as, "What has been or is being taught, studied, or learned?" or "What are the likely outcomes of teaching, studying, or learning this?"

Variants of this central problem and related questions of importance to the field include: At what ages are various subjects or topics or skills most efficiently or effectively taught? What patterns of personal characteristics—abilities, interests, and so on—predispose students to what sorts of reactions to studying, learning, or being taught certain subjects, topics, or skills? What do children want to study, learn, or be taught and why do they want this? What do parents, teachers, school board members, and various other publics want children to study, learn, and be taught? Why do they want this? In spite of differences about the proper definition of the field, people who identify themselves with the curriculum field would probably agree that these questions are centrally important.

By empirical research I mean systematic, disciplined study of observable phenomena. I distinguish this from watching or participating in the phenomenon without system and discipline, although such informal activities may lead to understanding and may even be vitally necessary to all inquiry. My definition of empirical research in curriculum also excludes the activities of creating curriculum materials, curriculum planning and policymaking, the implementation of curriculum plans and policies, and the criticism of existing, past, or proposed curricula. That is, these activities in themselves are not what I regard as empirical curriculum research. Research may be done in connection with them, or they may be the objects of research, but in themselves they are not curriculum research. (While I exclude these activities from my definition of empirical research, I accord them high places in the field.) When I speak of empirical research in curriculum, then, I mean systematic, disciplined study of curricular phenomena undertaken in an attempt to clarify our ideas about those phenomena or to help solve some curricular problem.

The Dearth of Curriculum Research

It is my impression that relatively little empirical research is done in the curriculum field. This impression is based on my own experience of reading in the field and of talking with others who identify themselves with the field, though I certainly am not alone in this impression. When the *Review of Educational Research* followed the practice of devoting one issue every three years to a given topic, one of which was curriculum research, the editors of each curriculum issue could be depended upon to bemoan the lack of empirical research in the field during the three-year period covered in their review. Goodlad[4] was "struck in preceding chapters with the paucity of ordered 'findings' from curriculum research—findings in the sense either of scientific conclusions from cumulative inquiry or of tested guidelines for curriculum decisions." Abramson[5] referred to "the continuing paucity of studies which can serve as models for curriculum research." He also claimed that "until recently there was considerable doubt as to whether curriculum research existed as a field at all, as distinguished from educational research in general or from the production of content and materials." Macdonald and Raths said simply, "reports of specific studies designed to attack this problem area (curriculum) are sparse indeed."[6]

Since the *Review* changed its policy two years ago and began to accept reviews individually, regardless of their subject, exactly one article reviewing research in curriculum has appeared. The card catalogue in Cubberley Library at Stanford University shows exactly one collection of research reports with the word "curriculum" appearing in the title. I was unable to find a single book devoted entirely to methods or problems of research in curriculum, though I ran across several such books on instructional research. Three journals published in English regularly feature research reports in curriculum: *Journal of Curriculum Studies, Curriculum Theory Network,* and *Educational Leadership*. At least ten journals are devoted to research on media and methods of instruction. If further evidence of the dearth of empirical research is necessary, it would be easy enough to point to the length of the entries under "curriculum" and "teaching methods" and the number of research studies cited in each in the *Encyclopedia of Educational Research* or the number of papers presented annually in each field at the meetings of American Educational Research Association or any of a dozen other indices. All show the same result; not nearly as many studies are reported in curriculum as in instruction or teaching.

In the final analysis, though, it is not the number of studies that should concern us but the extent to which the studies, few or many, that are actually conducted illuminate the phenomena of concern to the field's practitioners and deal in a satisfactory way with its major problems. Let us, then, examine some of the major phenomena and problems of the curriculum field, looking for the bodies of research that grow up around such foci of attention in fields with vigorous tradition of empirical research.

I suspect many of us would agree with Hollis Caswell's statement that "The fundamental problem facing curriculum specialists is to establish a consistent relationship between general goals, on the one hand, and specific objectives that guide teaching, on the other."[7] Surely this relationship is not a purely logical one. Specific objectives do not follow logically and automatically from larger goals. It is not a matter purely of logic that making a living requires learning to read or that learning to budget one's income requires learning economics or even mathematics. If it were, we could simply deduce the specific objectives from the general goals. So this relationship must be, at least in part, an empirical one to be discovered in actual observations of the outcomes of school programs. But where in our journals are observations reported bearing on the relationship of general goals to specific objectives?

One of the first systematic studies in education in the United States, Joseph Mayer Rice's study of spelling,[8] showed that the ability of students to spell a standard list of words did not increase with the amount of time they spent in school on spelling drills, thus showing that the specific objectives guiding daily teaching were not contributing to the attainment of the general goal of learning to spell. In the second and third decades of this century, Thorndike, Judd, Rugg, and others launched a devastating attack on the doctrine of mental discipline in a series of studies that showed convincingly that the sort of general improvements in ability to memorize and to learn new facts claimed to result from tedious drill in such subjects as mathematics, spelling, and Latin were not produced by these activities.

These are genuine contributions to our understanding of the relationship between general goals and specific objectives. But they are half a century old. We continue to justify our practices by claims of general outcomes: better citizenship, more careful and rigorous habits of thought, greater ability to learn new things, new and more desirable attitudes toward any number of things. Yet we have almost no research that shows any connection between the particular things we do and these general outcomes, certainly nothing comparable in scope and quality to the earlier research on mental discipline.[9]

Let us proceed to another central problem of the field: to assess "the educational potentialities of all fields of study at each level of instruction," to "look impartially at the competing claims of various groups of specialists and to balance these interests in terms of the best service to students and society."[10] Surely this task is in large measure empirical for how, short of looking for them in the actual conduct and consequences of schooling, are these potentialities to be determined? Yet where are the empirical studies that report on the relative benefits of teaching, studying, and learning various subjects, topics, or skills? I have been unable to find even a recent systematic presentation of the arguments for and against the teaching of various subjects, though a model for such a work exists in Gilbert's *What Children Study and Why*.[11] Broudy, in a paper presented to the American Educational Research Association in 1970 and subsequently published in *Curriculum Theory Network*,[12] pointed to a similar lack of research on what he called "the life consequences of school learnings." How can a field comprised of persons professionally concerned with the question "What should be studied, taught, and learned?" not undertake the study of the consequences for life of studying various subjects?

Or consider the problem of sequence in learning: In what order should various subjects, topics, and skills be studied, taught, and learned? Travers judges that "We are probably no nearer today than were the schoolmen of the Middle Ages to finding appropriate subject matter sequences within the disciplines."[13] He adds that "those who talk most about the importance of sequencing subject matter have done little to solve the enormous difficulties that the practical application of this concept involves." I fear this last remark is a direct hit on the curriculum field.

Perhaps these problems are too difficult. Researchers normally attack the most tractable problems first. The important curriculum problem that presents probably the least conceptual and methodological difficulty is the determination of what has been and is being taught (not learned necessarily) in schools. How many students of what kind are being asked to study economics or ecology or filmmaking, or, if the course unit is too large for your taste, the law of supply and demand in a free market or conservation of energy or *Moby Dick* or any of thousands of other topics. Without this basic information we cannot even argue cogently about the balance, comprehensiveness, up-to-dateness, or rate and direction of change in our educational programs. Here, too, the field provides us with a series of models and precedents in older works—Payne,[14] Stout,[15] Bagley and Kyte,[16] Counts,[17] Mann,[18] Bruner,[19] Latimer[20]—that form a veritable research tradition in the field, unfortunately, a neglected one. Economists construct a statistical market basket to represent what people buy so that changes in prices and patterns of consumption can be monitored. Surely the technical and practical problems of constructing a statistical curriculum that represents what we ask our children to study are no greater. Why have we not pursued this traditionally important and accessible area of study?

Finally, consider any of hundreds of important curricular problems that actually arise in practice where they fairly beg to be studied. What are the various responses to being asked to study something that teachers and students judge to be unnecessary, dull, too difficult, or too easy? In short, what are the pathologies of content that we all as students and teachers felt so keenly; what are the responses it is possible to make to these pathologies; and what are the consequences of these responses? Or, to take a different problem in a different realm, how is it that a system which prides itself on diversity and local autonomy seems to have a single curriculum from coast to coast and from year to year? Why is it that the school curricula across the country are swept periodically by great waves of reform and innovation as pervasive and seemingly as permanent as changes in fashions or automobile design? What are the empirical studies that would help us understand these problems?

I have overlooked important studies surely, though inadvertently, in this brief review. But a field of study should be able to exhibit bodies of empirical and theoretical work on the problems that preoccupy its members. And I doubt that I have overlooked several bodies of research.

Doubtless the dearth of empirical research in curriculum has many causes. The problems of curriculum are frequently normative and thought for that reason to be unsuited for empirical investigation. Many of the problems of curriculum also arise in particular situations where research seems uneconomic, because ungeneralizable. And of course we are all keenly aware of the complexity and multifaceted nature of curricular phenomena and problems. But whatever the difficulties that lie in the way of research in curriculum, I cannot believe they are so much greater than the difficulties that confront other fields as to be so unyielding to determined assault by two generations of dedicated researchers. I conclude, therefore, that many of us in curriculum have at best a comparatively weak commitment to empirical research as a means of dealing with our professional problems.

Why have we in curriculum had such a weak commitment to empirical research? One important reason, I believe, is because we have misunderstood the nature and aims of empirical inquiry in education, a contention that I shall elaborate in the remainder of this paper.

Educational research is almost always classified as a branch of the social and behavioral sciences, and our conceptions of appropriate forms of research have come almost entirely from that tradition. Educators generally and we in curriculum in particular have accepted research in the behavioral and social sciences as the proper model of research in education. More accurately, we have adopted as our implicit ideal of empirical research a common but quite unsatisfactory reconstruction of social science research. Having accepted this reconstruction of what behavioral and social scientists do as our idea of what empirical research in curriculum must be, our distaste for and disavowal of empirical research is understandable. Consider some common misconceptions.

1. *We have believed that we must study only overt behavior.* And some of us have interpreted this to exclude even the study of the physical and social conditions under which the overt behavior occurs. So when we think of studying textbooks, say, and how they influence their users, we eschew introspective accounts. And when we study classrooms, we look for "behaviors," since we have been convinced that nothing but behavior is observable. (Ironically, we do this in a time when methodologically rigorous psychologists study dreams, daydreams, fantasy, perception, and other phenomena relying wholly or primarily on introspective accounts.[21])

Our problem here comes from our too ready acceptance of a philosophy of science that regards some data as objective and incorrigible. In physical science these are pointer readings. The pointer readings of behavioral science have been thought to be bodily motions—physical changes in the body. These are observable, objective, and incorrigible. We build our science on them. We have known for some time in the physical sciences that this theory would not do, and we are now well on our way to understanding this in the social and behavioral sciences. Experiments on perception show that strict separation of observation and inference is impossible, that observations are theory dependent from the very beginning. And studies in the history of science have shown that data are ignored, explained away, or reinterpreted to fit conceptions of the world that are powerful and otherwise coherent. So no matter what we do, our observations will be theory dependent. Our motto in this matter might well be: observation is selection in conformity with expectation.

In fact, what we observe are, even accepting philosophical behaviorism, patterns in behavior: structured sequences of bodily motions interconnected with one another and adapted to other physical and behavioral circumstances frequently distant in space and time from the events we are watching. These structured patterns of behavior are more often than not creations or inventions adapted to human purposes and to environmental circumstances. They are, in Herbert Simon's phrase, "artificial," not natural.[22] Some terms commonly used to mark out such artificial behavioral structures are "performances," "practices," "policies," "courses of action," and, misleadingly, "behaviors." Reading, writing, and doing arithmetic are performances, not "behaviors." They are rule-bound patterns of behavior that are what they are because certain people made them that way and others have continued to follow their lead. These structured patterns of action, their influences on students, teachers, and others, and the environmental conditions which sustain and affect them are the legitimate objects of our inquiries—not the bodily motions of students and teachers.

This may seem to be a trivial distinction, but it is really of the greatest importance. Even though the matters we are concerned with in education are all manifest in bodily motions (behavior), the particular patterns of interest to us are not necessarily illuminated or clarified by being treated in behavioral terms. This is a difficult point to grasp, so an analogy may help. All material objects are made of atoms. So, in one sense, all we can observe about the material world are atoms. But an architect, city planner, builder, or interior designer would be ill-advised to think of his or her work as "changing atoms," as would a barber, gardener, painter, dentist, or grocer, though the work of all these jobs can be so described correctly. Nor would the injunction to "state their goals in atomic terms" be generally helpful. An architect deals entirely with atomic material, that is true, but the matters he or she really deals with are better expressed as entrances, exits, steps, doors, windows, roofs, walls, and in general, the myriad terms developed over the centuries to describe the particular sorts of functional patterns of atomic organization of concern to architects. There is no necessary contradiction in maintaining that bodily motions are all we can observe about another person and at the same time using concepts like knowledge, content, topic, life consequences of school learnings, integration or articulation of educational programs, sequence, curriculum design, steering criterion group or any of the other myriad terms developed to describe the particular sorts of "behavior" of interest to people studying the curriculum. Nor are there any genuine problems in the field that are ruled out for study simply because of our incapacity to describe them in terms of bodily motions.

2. *We have believed that research must be entirely a matter of verification and proof.* "We may argue back and forth for years," we say, "but in the end research will show who's right. Research winnows the true from the false." But this view looks at the final stage in a process and lays full credit for the result at the feet of the last step. As William Blake put it two hundred years ago, "What is now proved was once only imagined." If research tests something, it must have something to test. How is this something to be obtained?

If the field of curriculum had a conceptual scheme for dealing with its central phenomena, a conceptual scheme that enabled inquirers to formulate and fruitfully pursue the important questions of the field in a verificational mode, then research-as-verification would be a limiting but not crippling conception. But in the present state of the field, this view strangles inquiry because we do not have the substructure of ideas and concepts needed to provide a rich store of plausible and interesting hypotheses to test. Instead of feverishly trying to think up hypotheses to be tested, would it not be better to do this thinking while observing and manipulating our phenomena and posing our questions rather than in the armchair beforehand?

I believe we must distinguish in our research between the context of discovery or invention and the context of verification or justification. Both are appropriate and necessary if empirical research is to progress. What we in curriculum sorely need are paradigms for conducting research in a context of discovery to match existing paradigms available from the research traditions of the behavioral and social sciences for the context of verification.

3. *We have believed that human judgments are unreliable and therefore not fit objects for empirical research.* When we study curriculum development and planning, we observe people making judgments about the value of certain topics or activities or objectives. Do we treat these judgments as data, as information about the phenomenon we are investigating? Or do we dismiss them as "intuitive," "guesswork," or "personal prejudice"? We do not have to accept these judgments as valid indicators of the objective worth of the matters to which they are applied, but they are (or at least may be under some circumstances) expressions of the values people attach to those matters.

To think that we can study curriculum planning without reference to such judgments is like believing that it is possible to study piano playing without reference to any "arbitrary" human standards of performance. What it means to play a piano well is in large part a matter of human preference. To think of these preferences as inadequate, judgmental indicators of some more objective criterion is a mistake. While people's judgments of the value of curriculum elements are not entirely pure expressions of subjective human preferences, neither are they entirely weak and fallible indicators of some objective values that can be uncovered by empirical study of facts as they are. In dealing with the question "What should be studied, taught, and learned?" we have, I submit, already wandered into the realm of human judgment. We might as well recognize this fact and find ways to study these judgments and the factors that influence them.[23]

4. *We have believed that empirical research (at its best) means searching for isolated causes or cause-effect relations.* According to this view, every event has an explanation in terms of a sequence of prior events each of which caused the next in the chain. And behavioral events are thought to be caused only by physical events, physiological events, or previous behavioral events. The task of empirical science in this view is to uncover the links in the causal chain leading up to the events to be explained. But of course one isolated event never causes another. It is always a complex "initial" situation that leads to a complex "final" situation. Our causal talk is just a convenient shorthand which singles out from the seamless web of events those that for one reason or another seem crucial to important other events. Too often we forget we have introduced this simplification and come to believe that "the curriculum" *caused* this result, when in fact the curriculum is at best a crucial (and complex) factor in a complex situation that leads with some regularity to this result among others. The point here is not to urge abandonment of the search for courses of action that can give us control over educational results but rather to urge acceptance of the view that such courses of action are elements in a larger situation and the "result" produced is part of a pattern of consequence.

We must also remember that we single out parts of the seamless web of events as needing explanation and others as being well enough understood to serve as explanations for them. What serves as explicans from one point of view may be explicandum from another. Thus, some investigators regard the curriculum as a simple fact and seek to explain what social factors account for its being the way it is, while others seek to explain social phenomena by reference to the curriculum. Furthermore, entirely different modes of explanation can be applied to the same sequence of events. For example, a curricular "effect" can be explained as the effect of "studying physics" or of "having been socialized into the norms of physics" or of "having mastered certain cognitive skills required in physics." These explanations (actually brief sketches of explanations) are neither contradictory nor equivalent. They represent different selections from among the various possible self-consistent sets of terms in which an explanation may be couched. They are, in effect, different forms or levels of explanation. But we must live with all the actual consequences of our actions regardless of the particular descriptions given to both actions and consequences in some particular explanatory scheme. In curriculum the phenomena of interest to us are amenable to many forms of explanation—psychological, social, historical, moral, intellectual, physical. A causal shorthand which implies that these phenomena are simple effects of isolated causes is almost certain to have bad consequences serious enought to offset any benefits.

Many important questions in the curriculum field do not lend themselves to a causal formulation—some, for example, because they concern discovery of what people want to happen and why they want it. In those cases where a causal formulation of a problem is appropriate—notably, the study of curricular outcomes—we would do better, I believe, to speak of consequences, determinants, and influences rather than effects and results. The first set of terms should remind us that we must always think of complex situations leading to other complex situations rather than isolated causes leading to isolated results.

5. *We have believed that we must control our phenomena in order to study them scientifically.* So when we puzzled over something like discovery learning, we took it into the laboratory where we could ensure that discovery would occur in only the experimental group. But in fact all that is necessary is control of the inferences we make from our observations. If it were necessary to control the phenomena, astronomy, the oldest of the sciences, would not be a science at all.

We must be able to make and substantiate arguments which show that some observation we have made is more consistent with one interpretation of the situation being studied than it is with another interpretation of this situation. This is the minimum condition for empirically testing such an interpretation. But we meet this condition as much by controlling what, where, when, and how we observe as we do by controlling the phenomenon being observed. And when our efforts to rule out alternative interpretations of a phenomenon interfere in unknown ways with the phenomenon, we are immediately presented with an unforeseen alternative interpretation: that our interference accounts for what we observe.

While controls are not absolutely necessary, they may be extremely useful, so that we would be foolish to give them up altogether. But controls imply a "theory of the phenomenon" that directs us in deciding what actions on the part of the inquirer rule out or make improbable what interpretations of the observed phenomena. Without such a theory, no one can be sure that actions thought to control for some interpretations have not fundamentally altered the phenomenon being investigated.

Relatively uncontrolled approaches to a phenomenon are necessary in order to learn the terms on which the phenomenon will admit of being studied. And in my judgment we do not yet know these terms for curricular phenomena.

6. *We have believed that we must study one small thing at a time.* We cannot study everything at once, so the story goes. We must select bits of our phenomenon for intensive study, forgetting for the moment the other parts of it. So instead of studying a reasonable number of important potential outcomes of a new curriculum we study only end-of-course performance on a standardized achievement test, hoping, perhaps that someone else will study other outcomes later.

Certainly it is necessary and helpful to place some aspects of what you are studying in the foreground of your attention and to relegate the rest to the background. But it is equally necessary to appreciate that one's actions implicate not merely the foreground aspects that one has studied but the whole form from which these aspects were abstracted. Educational policies and practices necessarily operate on the whole child, the whole staff, the whole school, and the whole community, not just on those aspects that were singled out for study.

At some stage in an educational inquiry someone will have to use the knowledge obtained in intensive studies of particular aspects of an educational phenomenon to devise and determine wise policies. When this stage is reached, it will be necessary to weigh in the same scale the results of various studies carried on from different points of view with different techniques and perhaps within the traditions of different disciplines. If each of these studies was conducted in a way that ignored the other, how will this ultimate coordination in use be possible?

This is a major recurring problem in curriculum—indeed, in all fields of practical endeavor. Perhaps medical research offers a useful model and an alternative to the one-variable-at-a-time research strategy. A medical researcher specializing in the gastrointestinal tract is not a biochemist or psychologist or physiologist. But he uses the terms and techniques of these and other disciplines when they illuminate his phenomenon. And when he studies the secretion of the stomach, he is not acting as a biochemist or as anything but a medical researcher honoring his phenomenon and trying to understand it from any vantage point that offers a clear view. Empirical researchers in curriculum seem to me better advised to take the medical specialist as their model rather than his colleagues in the disciplines. (They might copy the medical specialist in another way, too, by working in interdisciplinary teams.)

Significantly, the gastrointestinal specialist and the biochemist have inherited independent traditions of careful data collection and analysis, medicine and the natural sciences, that have over years accommodated themselves to one another in a mutually complementary way. We need to develop a tradition of synthetic and integrative research that will complement the work of our colleagues in related disciplines.

Each of these misconceptions has a legitimate concern behind it. It is important to have objective evidence for empirical claims, and this evidence must ultimately come from observations of people's actions. It is important to conduct research that will verify empirical claims. Human judgments of matters of fact are frequently unreliable. Research should help identify factors that can be manipulated to achieve what we want educationally. Research must control for confounding variables. And we must always limit our attention in any study. Trouble comes when, through excess zeal or lack of insight, we carry these legitimate concerns too far or insist unnecessarily on particular ways of handling them. The restrictions we place on our inquiry in this way can be so great that they make intelligent study of our phenomena and problems impossible.

Is it any wonder really that people who think of empirical research as the search for isolated causes of overt behavior in controlled situations, one variable at a time, for the purpose of verifying hypotheses not concerned with human judgments or preferences find little use for empirical research in their study of the phenomena and problems of curriculum? But empirical research does not have to be this sort of enterprise. In accepting such a conception, we give it power over us. If we reject this image of empirical research and set about finding more appropriate ways of getting and using factual information to help us formulate and resolve our problems, we will find, I believe, that empirical research can be extremely useful. In fact, I believe it to be ultimately indispensable. As S. S. Tomkins put it, "the world we perceive is a dream we learn to have from a script we have not written."[24] The trouble with so much of the literature of curriculum is that the author has written the script, so the dream is entirely a work of imagination undisciplined by reality. Empirical research gives us access to a common source of scripts outside ourselves. We cannot afford to be scared away from that source by the nightmarish image of research that we are told we should honor.

If the field of curriculum is to develop and sustain a rich and vital tradition of disciplined inquiry, those of us who work in the field will have to reverse some trends of the past decades. We will need to develop a stronger commitment to empirical inquiry as a means of dealing with our professional affairs. We will need to discard some widespread misconceptions about the nature and purpose of empirical inquiry and to find or develop modes of inquiry that meet the legitimate concerns that lie behind these misconceptions in ways that are not unduly restricting. We would be wise, I think, to cultivate the research tradition handed down to us from our predecessors and to honor it with criticism, imitation, or revision as circumstances require. Most importantly, we will need to keep our attention fixed on the phenomena and problems of the field at all costs. If we make no progress in elucidating these, if we turn instead to the phenomena and problems of instruction or administration or philosophy or sociology because these seem more accessible, we will have abandoned the most powerful justification for our existence as a field: the importance of the phenomena and problems with which we deal.

Notes

1. H. Caswell, "Emergence of the Curriculum as a Field of Professional Work and Study," in *Precedents and Promises in the Curriculum Field*, ed. H. F. Robison (New York: Teachers College Press, 1966), pp. 1–11.

2. H. Kliebard, "The Curriculum Field in Retrospect," in *Technology and the Curriculum*, ed. P. W. F. Witt (New York: Teachers College Press, 1968), pp. 69–84.

3. M. L. Seguel, *The Curriculum Field: Its Formative Years* (New York: Teachers College Press, 1966).

4. J. I. Goodlad, "Curriculum: State of the Field," *Review of Educational Research* 39 (June 1969): 368.

5. D. A. Abramson, "Curriculum Research and Evaluation," *Review of Educational Research* 36 (June 1966): 388-95.

6. J. B. Macdonald and J. Raths, "Curriculum Research: Problems, Techniques, and Prospects," *Review of Educational Research* 33 (June 1963): 322-29.

7. Caswell, "Emergence of the Curriculum," p. 5.

8. J. M. Rice, "The Futility of the Spelling Grind." *Forum* 23 (1897): 163-72, 409-19.

9. The work based on Gagné's hierarchical task analysis technique is probably the most ambitious modern attempt to deal with the problem of relating specific goals to more general ones. The basic idea in this procedure is to identify simple, specific capabilities that are prerequisite to more complex and general ones. The more complex and general capabilities are then taught by proceeding carefully and sequentially through each of the prerequisite tasks, making sure that the student has mastered the prerequisites for each new task. This is a promising beginning, but it seems to be limited to the teaching of skills and knowledge—it is not clear that attitudes, elements of character, or creative enterprises requiring novel responses can be analyzed in this way—and it needs to be empirically tested. Gagné's own work shows that this sort of analysis can be performed, but whether such an analysis yields curricula that are more effective or efficient than ones produced in some other way is not known.

10. Caswell, "Emergence of the Curriculum," p. 9.

11. C. B. Gilbert, *What Children Study and Why* (Boston: Silver, Burdett, 1913).

12. H. S. Broudy, "Components and Constraints of Curriculum Research," *Curriculum Theory Network* 5 (Spring 1970): 16-31.

13. R. M. W. Travers, "Directions for the Development of an Educational Technology," in *Technology and the Curriculum*, ed. P. W. F. Witt (New York: Teachers College Press, 1968), p. 99.

14. B. R. Payne, *Public Elementary School Curricula* (Boston: Silver, Burdett, 1905).

15. J. E. Stout, *The Development of High School Curricula in the North Central States: 1860-1918*. Supplementary Monographs (Chicago: University of Chicago, 1921).

16. W. C. Bagley and G. C. Kyte, *The California Curriculum Study* (Berkeley: University of California, 1926).

17. G. S. Counts, *The Senior High School Curriculum* (Chicago: University of Chicago, 1926).

18. C. Mann, *How Schools Use Their Time* (New York: Teachers College Press, 1928).

19. H. Bruner et al., *What Our Schools Are Teaching* (New York: Teachers College Press, 1941).

20. J. Latimer, *What's Happened to Our High Schools?* (Washington, D.C.: Public Affairs Press, 1958).

21. E. Klinger, *Structure and Functions of Fantasy* (New York: John Wiley, 1971); J. Singer, *Daydreaming* (New York: Random House, 1966).

22. H. Simon, *The Sciences of the Artificial* (Cambridge, Mass.: MIT Press, 1969).

23. Anyone interested in the systematic study of educational judgments should consult Robert Stake's article, "Objectives, Priorities, and Other Judgment Data," *Review of Educational Research* 40 (April 1970): 181–212. The work reviewed there is a fine start toward the serious study of educational judgments.

24. S. S. Tomkins, *Affect, Imagery, Consciousness* (New York: Academic Press, 1963).

Reconceptualists

20 Educational Research: Values and Visions of Social Order

Thomas S. Popkewitz

Introduction

In this article, Thomas Popkewitz challenges the traditional mainstream assumption that educational research represents, at its best, a form of social inquiry that is objective and value-free. Popkewitz argues that such a view is mistaken in its beliefs and conservative in its practice. Pointing to the various communities of scholars that constitute the research field in education, he claims that educational researchers are members of specific groups whose work contains assumptions, values, and modes of inquiry that are legitimized by the group in question. In other words, rather than being neutral, educational research is marked by a diverse number of competing political and ideological views. The specific views that particular modes of research embody not only structure what is an educational problem but also utilize theories and methods that either affirm or reject existing social values and relationships.

Popkewitz concludes that the political and normative character of educational research makes it imperative that a reflective and critical stance be taken by those engaging in such research. He further argues that educational research, rather than shunning the question of values, should give careful deliberation to the ethical premises and consequences implicit in its view of schooling.

In reading this article you might want to give careful attention to Popkewitz's notion that educational research is a cultural imperative.
- What does Popkewitz mean by community aspect of scientific inquiry?
- How does the latter contribute to educational theory as a form of political affirmation?

- Finally, you might want to consider how educational inquiry, as Popkewitz defines it, can provide a mode of analysis that can illuminate the unintended consequences of classroom practice.

If these conditions [of social science being historically influenced] make trouble for us as social scientists, remember that they are a great advantage to humanity, by leaving men the illusion of choice. I speak of the illusion because I myself believe that what each of us does is absolutely determined.[1]

It is often thought and said that what we most need in education is wisdom and broad understanding of the issues that confront us. Not at all. What we need are deeply structured theories in education that drastically reduce, if not eliminate, the need for wisdom.[2]

The above statements are part of more general treatises about the nature of social research. The authors argue for social/psychological sciences which provide explanatory statements about human behavior.[3] They believe the power of the explanations lies in their objective, culture-free quality. Yet, as the quotes suggest, the very search for scientific reasoning reflects commitments that go beyond the coherence of findings or methods. Underlying the practice of social research are assumptions about society. These assumptions refer to the nature of social control, order, and responsibility. Far from being neutral, inquiry is a human process of understanding that involves hopes, values, and unresolved questions about social affairs.

The purpose of this paper is to explore the values of educational research and its implications for social education. The argument will focus on the social and cultural implications of research. The concern will be how theory and methods give legitimacy to certain educational and cultural patterns. The purpose is to locate the political and sometimes ideological functions of professional work.

Educational Research as a Cultural Imperative

Social research expresses human commitment and value in at least two ways. First, research may respond to our perceptions of social and cultural conditions. It enables us to reconcile possible social contradictions and to consider the consequences of institutional arrangements. Durkheim's studies of religion and education, for example, have social and historical meanings beyond those traditionally associated with their descriptive reliability. Durkheim's studies give focus to his deep moral concern about urban and industrial changes in the late nineteenth century.

Reprinted, with permission, from *Theory and Research in Social Education* 6, no. 4 (December 1978), pp. 20–39.

Second, social research has a highly valued status in society. Many people believe that political, social, and educational issues require scientific solutions. Deliverance from the domination of nature and from social oppression requires expert knowledge. In the following discussion, these two cultural dimensions of social research will be explored.

Much of the sociology of science emphasizes the community aspect of scientific inquiry.[5] A scientific discipline, it is believed, exists as a social organization. It contains certain norms, standards, and lines of reasoning that provide underlying rules for judging the worth of individual research. Individuals are socialized into a particular community and tend to accept the existing definitions of problems and methods. For example, a U.S. economist typically will think about "capital" and "production" and express findings mathematically. A cultural anthropologist, in contrast, documents and interprets events as "culture" and expresses them in narrative form. However, because socialization is not totally coercive, many different points of view may exist within a single discipline. These disagreements can produce intense debate about which research questions and methods of study are appropriate. Mulkay[6] argues that these conflicts and the resultant cross-fertilization of ideas are vital to scientific imagination and creativity.

The conflict within the social sciences should be considered in the larger context of social and cultural commitments. Disciplinary disagreements often involve an interplay of political, methodological, and epistemological issues.[7]

This conflict can be illustrated in recent debates within the field of education. For example, learning psychologists have dominated the intellectual work of education. Educational psychology tends to focus upon student performance and the interchange between students and teachers. Recently, however, sociologists of educational knowledge have challenged the educational psychologists' assumptions about the study of schooling.[8] These sociologists believe that learning psychology deflects attention from the way schools legitimize certain types of cultural knowledge and interests.

The criticism of conventional educational research defines alternative methods. Sociological approaches emphasize the relationship between institutional patterns and individual consciousness. In defining a different purpose and method for study, these criticisms challenge deeply held beliefs about the social meanings and purposes of educational research.

We can illuminate the relationship between research and social conditions more clearly by focusing upon the purpose of research. Rather than a rationalization for existing conceptions, inquiry can be viewed as a search for new metaphors for thinking about everyday affairs. The metaphors are "lenses" which enable people to give coherence to daily events that before seemed incomprehensible or troubling. The genius of Einstein and Keppler, for example, was their ability to put the physical world into sharp focus, different from what others accepted as common sense. The new lenses enabled scientists to consider different forms of questions and produce greater depths of understanding. The importance of the systems of thought provided by Freud, Marx, and Weber, as well, was to orient people to feel, see, and think about their social and personal lives in new and different ways. The metaphors of "unconsciousness," "ideology," or "bureaucracy" permitted people to conceive of social reality as having many different layers of interpretation, some of which were not readily apparent in everyday life. The concepts focus on the pretentions, deceptions, and self-deceptions that people use to cloak their interactions.

Social and cultural affairs influence the search for new metaphors in the social sciences. Töennies's *Gemeinschaft und Gesellschaft*, a classical work in sociology, articulated his sense of a loss of community brought about by industrialization. Weber's notion of bureaucracy reflected an attempt to rationalize social and economic affairs that were occurring. Durkheim's theme of anomie represented a spirit of pessimism, moral uncertainty, and dislocation of norms produced in a period of material progress.[9] In more recent times the Civil Rights Movement and protests against the Viet Nam War brought new themes for study to the research community. For example, political scientists and many social studies educators became concerned about problems of political legitimacy and socialization occurring in this relatively unstable period. Some scholars studied the school practices, curriculum materials, and community life which they thought influenced the learning of minorities. Curriculum designers in social studies education, as well, responded to the conflicts in society by developing value clarification, public issues and citizenship education programs.

Educational researchers are members of their culture and inherit its history.[10] Their work contains assumptions developed and sustained in everyday conversations, behaviors, and events. Social theory, for example, uses language drawn from everyday conversations. The form and content of the language reflect beliefs, commitments, and values. Theories of totalitarianism, important in the 1960s, were built on people's daily experiences. Totalitarian theories grew out of the 1950s debate about a "cold war." People in this country found themselves with allies who had been enemies just a few years before during a large-scale war. The new forces of evil were communism, not fascism. One response to the new situation and its alliances was to generate theories about totalitarianism. These theories not only reflected the changed situation but lent credibility to our new political allies.

This discussion has, to this point, focused upon two cultural dimensions of social research. First, the creativity of inquiry has sociological as well as psychological characteristics. Research exists within and is supported by a community of discourse. Second, the nature and character of scientific work is responsive to the larger social world. The social researcher participates in everyday conversations and uses those dialogues as a background for occupational endeavors. The cultural quality of research, however, is not complete until a third dimension is considered: a scientific community is a product of the social world.

Science does not stand by itself but is a cultural artifact. Status is given to scientific knowledge in business, political and social institutions. Political leaders use scientific techniques to "poll" people about their actions and policies. Industrial psychologists and organizational researchers provide information about how to organize labor. Economic theorists guide peoples' interpretations about the relationship between work, capital, and consumption. Historians interpret America's past, which helps establish a collective identity.[11] Curriculum researchers apply scientific thought for selecting, organizing, and evaluating schooling. In everyday choices, science is viewed as making life more manageable and social problems more solvable. Social science is in demand and seems a necessary component of our everyday consciousness.

The cultural imperative of scientific thought can be illuminated by comparing Western science with the African Azande.[12] The Azande maintain a system of magical thought which constitutes a coherent universe of discourse similar to science. It provides an intelligible conception of reality and a clear way of deciding which beliefs are and are not in agreement with that view of reality. Poison oracles or ghost rites to influence rainfall exist within a context of rules and conventions that gives these actions a sense of significance.

The Azande rationale is no less intelligent than the logic of science practiced by anthropologists who study these people. Its principles and rules arise out of the course of human conduct and are subordinate to existent cultural beliefs. The magic rites explain and justify those beliefs. The way of thinking found in Western science would be incomprehensible to the Azande. In fact, science would seem to have many of the same irrational "magical" qualities that Western anthropologists see in Azande culture when judging solely by logical "scientific" rules. The Azande or the anthropologists' structure of thought is significant only within the context of larger social forms.

Educational Theory as Political Affirmation

At first glance, the suggestion that theory and research methods contain political values may seem misleading, if not in error. Our assumptions "tell" us that theory is objective and neutral. Theories, it is believed, give coherence to data and expression to human regularities. The previous discussion, however, suggests that theories are products of human ingenuity. In this section, the nature of social values in research will be considered by focusing upon how theories justify social action.

Theory has at least three political functions in educational discourse. Theory can (a) provide a rationale for changing social and economic conditions that enables these changes to seem reasonable, (b) provide a mechanism to legitimize institutional interests, and (c) give direction to consideration of alternative social arrangements.

Social theory can provide symbolic coherence to changing social, political, and economic conditions. Alvin Gouldner[13] argues that social theory is not so much a determination of "facts" as an effort to make sense of unresolved experiences and to interpret the meaning of one's life. The dominant sociology of the 1930s, Gouldner argues, was a conservative response to the crisis of the times. The fundamental posture of sociological theory was to accept dominant institutions in order to maintain traditional loyalties and avoid discontinuities. In a similar discussion, Merelman[14] defines social science as a social organization that responds to larger social institutions. This response often creates new symbols of harmony and hope in times of changing social order. The changing political world after the 1930s[15] brought an encroachment of political activities into what had been previously considered private affairs.[16] Government extended its activities by creating social security, unemployment insurance, and corporate and agricultural subsidies. This rapid encroachment brought with it a sense of political impotence to individuals.

Behavioral political scientists provided an organized response to these changing social conditions. Political inquiry created political symbols that reestablished the idea of community. These symbols included political culture, pluralism, and political socialization. Interestingly, many of these symbols are used today to justify educational practices such as decentralization and citizenship education. Political inquiry also developed methodologies that enabled people to believe they were being consulted, such as "polls" or surveys of public opinion. The theory and methods of political science helped reduce strain between the changing role of government and the beliefs people cherished about public life.

The introduction of "new" theories of instruction or curriculum can be a way of helping people to cope with larger crises in social and political conditions. For example, the late 1960s and 1970s have produced a "crisis of values." An Asian war, urban riots, and government lawlessness such as Watergate, FBI, and CIA activities have thrown some of the basic values of American life further into question.

In this social context, many social studies educators have used theories about "moral development" and "values clarification" to orient curriculum development. The concept of "values clarification," for example, helps explain and give coherence to social conditions that otherwise seem without purpose. The theories of values, in turn, serve institutional functions. Value theories justify the use of therapeutic approaches in situations where students and parents have questioned the efficiency of institutions.[17]

The recent and extensive attention to "individualized" education can also be considered within a social and institutional context. The sanctity of the individual has received increasing ideological support since the early nineteenth century. Out of the French Revolution came a definition of the individual as free from religious and feudal restraints. The development of Western industrialization and the fragmentation of community life expanded the need for an ideology of individual inviolability.

The notion of individualism is an increasingly potent symbol in education. The social efficiency curriculum of David Snedden responded to individual "needs" of the early twentieth century.[18] Progressive educators, as well, developed programs to respond to the "uniqueness" of individuals. Criticism in the past two decades has focused upon the routine, standardized nature of instruction. Phillip Jackson,[19] for example, argued that too much of schooling is formed around the grouping process and batching of children. This social organization of schooling eliminates spontaneity, creativity, and the pursuit of individual interests.

"Individualized instruction" is a contemporary response to the belief that social institutions should consider personal fulfillment as essential. The theories of individualization provide ways for individuals to believe that schools are responsive to human differences. Many educators, for example, adopt management and learning theories to provide a rationale for individualized program development. These theories guide educators in identifying "systems" for organizing teaching and instruction. Curriculum content, for example, is subdivided into different levels or degrees of difficulty. Materials are organized sequentially and children paced "individually" through the defined work. A contrasting model of individualized instruction exists in the British Infant School, which stresses the nurturing of "self" through social interaction.

Theories of moral development and individualization have political potency. They provide symbols that help people to express a variety of emotions associated with schooling. These theories enable people to resolve contradictions between the values they hold and the actual conditions of schools. The theories of pedagogy symbolically tie together seeming discontinuities and social strains, bringing reassurances of ethical commitment and institutional adaptiveness. The theories make it appear that professionals have a grasp of what should be done. Reassurances, however, do not necessarily alter or explain what actually occurs in schools.

Theory as Legitimation

Closely tied to the "strain" function of theory is legitimation. Statements that result from educational research enable certain structures and interests in school affairs to seem normal and reasonable. Legitimation occurs in at least two ways. First, theories have underlying values and beliefs that dispose us to act. Second, the organizing categories of theory define what is often taken for granted about institutional life.

The legitimating function of theory can be understood by realizing that theory has different layers of meaning. A typical way of considering theory is through its explicit statements, that is, what is overtly said about schools, curriculum, or students. For example, many recent social studies programs are based on political theories that encourage interest in group participation. Therefore, curriculum developers may propose that: "Students have more positive attitudes about school if involved in decision making." This statement has nonobvious meanings. It contains a series of unpostulated and unlabeled assumptions about the world. The theory of participation, for example, may "treat" the world as highly integrated and people as rational. These assumptions will guide people seeing and experiencing political activities. Participation may be considered to mean rational involvement in publicly sanctioned groups, such as a student council. The assumptions about participation also create attitudes about how institutional structures should be challenged. Lack of participation, for example, may be viewed as lack of individual motivation rather than as an institutional defect. Remedies, then, are those that enable students to feel politically capable, such as courses in student participation "skills." The courses, however, may not deal at all with the structural reasons that some students, such as low-income groups, fail to participate. Such courses may, in fact, increase the students' sense of inadequacy. While designing curriculum, the assumptions and prescriptions of a political theory are treated as "real" and not scrutinized for possible latent implications or consequences.

The social categories researchers accept to guide their inquiry can also serve to legitimize school structures. Often educational research is initiated in response to some administrative action and is guided by the administrator's definition of the problem. Many curriculum research projects accept the objectives of pedagogical programs and are organized to "explain" how the means helped reach the objective. In a social studies curriculum project, for example, the research focused on whether the course material was learned, whether the teachers perceived the material to be clear and easy to use, and how well students understood and achieved project goals.[20] The results of the research did not question but assumed the premises of the project, that is, that knowledge from the social sciences should be distributed equally in schools.[21] The consequence is an ad hoc curriculum theory that justifies the agreed-upon design of the project administrators.

"Basic" research, as well, often assumes that the administrative categories of schooling are nonproblematic. A recent article on teacher pedagogical decisions, for example, was concerned with how teachers make instructional choices based on information processing.[22] The empirical problem was to present a group of graduate students in education with information about student aptitude, children's ages, family status (divorced, number of siblings, and so on), children's use of time in school, and intelligence. Sometimes the information was negative, the child did not do his or her homework or the father was a machinist rather than an engineer. A second session for teachers was held to provide more information. The teachers were asked to revise instructional decisions based on the above information. The conclusion of the study was (a) "subjects may use different kinds of information to make different kinds of decisions"; (b) ". . . decisions at time one and time two were influenced by other factors not measured in this study."[23]

With such commonsense conclusions, one might ask what the function of such research is. The question can be answered in two different ways. Methodologically, researchers tend to believe that through the slow accumulation of data some important generalizations about teaching will be made. Furthermore, there seems to be a technical elegance to the report itself, especially when data collection, literature, and review findings are succinctly and carefully presented, and sophisticated techniques such as path analysis increase data manipulation.

The social impact of the research, however, overshadows its methodological elegance. It has social and political ramifications that are as important as the tests of reliability. First, people tacitly accept institutional assumptions, some of which are defined by school professionals themselves. Achievement, intelligence, and "use of time" are accepted as useful variables for stating problems about schools, and these categories provide the basis for research. Inquiry enables researchers to see how school categories relate, but it does not test assumptions or implications underlying the school categories. For example, there is no question about the nature of the tasks at which children spend their time. Research conclusions are conceived within parameters provided by school administrators. Second, researchers accept social myths as moral prescriptions. Social class, social occupation (engineer or machinist), or divorce are accepted as information that should be used in decision making. These assumptions maintain a moral quality and criteria which may justify social inequality. Third, the research orientation tacitly directs people to consider school failure as caused by those who happen to come to its classes. Social and educational assumptions are unscrutinized.

One could say at this moment that this is *only* research; it is not how people make decisions. I would argue, however, that research often has a way of entering into the domains of school interaction. People adopt the categories and definitions for understanding their own and others' actions. The research orientation defines as well as responds to the school situation. Educational administrators, curriculum developers, and teachers use the research to direct their practical activities, and the effect is to limit and predispose individuals in their actions and conceptions of educational possibilities.

Theory as Alternate Possibilities

Theory can also direct attention to the possibility of alternatives. Open education is a case in point.[24] Its followers have developed a consistent set of statements which orient people to think about different institutional forms. Open education searches for ways in which students could develop more autonomy in social relationships. Mutuality of roles, community and reciprocity of relations are perceived to be central to the structure of school experience and are measures of its outcomes.[25]

Open education theories provoke thought about alternative institutional structures. The North Dakota Study Group on Evaluation, for example, uses theory to develop a consistent relationship between the ethical purposes of schooling, its curriculum methods, and evaluation procedures. It is one of the few attempts to explore systematically the relationship between ideology, practice, and research. Tabachnick[26] has argued that open education theories can direct the formation of social inquiry curriculum. He suggests that there is a mutual relationship between open education and social inquiry in schools, the latter giving emphasis to an active search for knowledge and individual responsibility.

In conclusion, educational theory is a form of political affirmation. The selection and organization of pedagogical activities give emphasis to certain people, events, and things. Educational theory is potent because its language has prescriptive qualities. A theory "guides" individuals to reconsider their personal world in light of more abstract concepts, generalizations, and principles. These more abstract categories are not neutral; they give emphasis to certain institutional relationships as good, reasonable, and legitimate. Visions of society, interests to be favored, and courses of action to be followed are sustained in theory.

Research Practices and Visions of Social Order

Thus far, I have focused the argument upon the implications of educational research. I have considered the cultural nature of inquiry and the politics of educational theory. I would like to focus now upon the practices of study. The purpose is, again, to shift the argument away from conventional discourse about the reliability and validity of scientific endeavors. While important, such scrutiny is unable to shed light upon the cultural values actually represented. If science is a cultural activity, an adequate understanding of the truth of its statements must include discussion of cultural definitions. In particular, questions should be considered which illuminate value statements about social affairs embedded in the practices of study.

As with theory, the suggestion that research practices embody values goes against conventional wisdom. Researchers often argue that methods are the only factors in science. Kerlinger,[27] for example, defines methods of inquiry as procedures in which beliefs have no effects. The character of method, he argues, remains entirely independent of our beliefs, perceptions, biases, values, attitudes, and emotions.

The stance of neutrality is itself a value stance. It expresses a belief and a hope of researchers. As I will argue, the procedures of inquiry contain assumptions about social relationships that are interrelated with theory and human purpose.

One approach to considering values in practice is to look at techniques. In many ways, the techniques of study are treated as skills which exist independently of the purpose or commitment of those who do research. The professional preparation of researchers, for example, consists of courses in statistics, field study, or survey research. It is assumed that these techniques of data collection and analysis can be learned as specialized skills apart from the actual process of inquiry. The techniques, to phrase the problem somewhat differently, are conceived of as neutral to the conduct of study.

A critical scrutiny of techniques yields a different perspective. Techniques emerge from a theoretical position and therefore reflect values, beliefs, and dispositions towards the social world. Factor analysis, for example, was created as a measurement procedure for faculty psychology and was based on the assumption that the mind has different compartments that could be trained as independent units.[28] While faculty psychology has been discredited, its techniques are still in use, thus maintaining the assumptions that the mind is a cluster of parts.

Fox and Hernandez-Nieto[29] argue that mathematical models for research articulate value preference and underlying assumptions about social relations. Conventional statistical techniques, for example, are based on Euclidean geometry, which has linear conceptions of time and space. In contrast, newer mathematical models contain dialectical principles. The development of the new models for research derives, in part, out of a theoretical and value commitment to include dimensions of free will, intention, and historical setting.

The choice of technique is a moral responsibility. Moral questions are deeply intertwined with the general commitments of science. Social scientists, for example, are concerned with developing verifiable knowledge. This interest involves manipulating variables to test outcomes of a hypothesis and the predictive quality of theory. This commitment poses no dilemma to most physical or life scientists—they can change the heating temperature to combine elements or experiment with hybrid feed without any moral guilt. In high energy physics, molecular biology, or medical research, the manipulation of variables often does have direct implications for human beings. Various ethical and legal restrictions have evolved from this research.

Questions of morality and immorality are *always* involved in social research since the "subjects" of social scientists are people. The problem of controlling variables is a moral one. It is immoral, Homans[30] argues, to manipulate people. The alternative is to create statistical techniques that provide scientists with the necessary tools to manipulate data.

It is certainly less easy in the social sciences than in some physical and biological sciences to manipulate variables experimentally and to control the other variables entering into a concrete phenomenon. . . . It is less easy to control the variables because it is less easy to control men than things. Indeed it is often immoral to try to control them: men are not to be submitted to the indignities to which we submit, as a matter of course, things and animals. Hence the relative prominence in some of the social sciences, even increasingly in history, of other methods of controlling variables, methods thought somehow less satisfactory, such as the use of statistical techniques.[31]

Ideology and Methods

The relationship between technique and value implies that educational research is based upon certain background assumptions and consequences. These implications can be illuminated by looking at the particular commitments to science that underlie much conventional research. These commitments are: (a) Social science is to be modeled after the physical sciences. (b) Social science is a deductive system of propositions which reports the lawlike qualities of human affairs. These laws are to explain and predict the actions of individuals in a manner similar to those developed in the physical sciences. (c) Objectivity is important to social science. This is the ability of the observer/recorder to develop techniques that place the data outside (away from) the particular meanings, interpretations, and values of social situations and researchers. (d) Objectivity is obtained through rigorous techniques which produce "hard" data that express events as numbers rather than words. Mathematics is important to these beliefs and commitments to science because it eliminates ambiguities (43 percent *is* 43 percent) and human values.

These commitments and related research practices produce a pattern in which problems, methods, and theory interrelate as a self-sustaining and almost self-justifying system. The significance of this research pattern is that peculiar definitions are given to social problems and social order.

The commitment to rigorous techniques tends to narrow the focus of research to those aspects that can be numerically expressed. In a recent study of teacher effectiveness,[32] for example, the authors discussed student outcomes as involving dimensions such as citizenship, attitude towards learning, conceptions of "self," creativity, and achievement. However, since achievement is the only dimension which has reliable testing, achievement was treated as the primary interest. Rigorous techniques of the study enable us to learn less and less about the social affairs we researched. David Easton[33] argues that an important dimension of educational theory is that it be relevant to social problems. However, as illustrated above, the commitment to rigorous techniques has removed that dimension and, in fact, hinders the search for understanding our human condition. Questions of human values and politics are ignored.

Another consequence of conventional research is related to objectivity. Some researchers maintain the belief that there are regularities or laws of human nature that lie outside personal intentions and motives. The belief in an underlying natural order has a direct impact upon how data are obtained, that is, objective data require mathematical expression which eliminates human values and ambiguity from science. This commitment to objectivity requires a view of the world as certain and crystallized.[34]

The assumption that the world is certain influences social practice. Sociological researchers suggest that people can only pretend to play a role for so long. After awhile, the role becomes real. The form of playing is the reality. The quote by Homans cited at the beginning of this paper suggests that determinism is an a priori value of some research. What was originally a methodological device is now a view of the world that includes definitions of how people should act, believe, and feel.

The pedagogical sciences provide a case in point. Researchers often define the purpose of education as "changing children to some desired end." Educational theories are the technical apparatus that guide the manipulation of children. Experimental techniques are implemented as the means of instruction. Behavior modification is thought of as a teaching strategy. The moral hesitancy of social scientists to intervene in human life is often nonexistent when it comes to schooling.

The belief that teachers are human engineers is exemplified in a popular book on curriculum development entitled *Instructional Product Development*.[35] The authors define curriculum design as a technological problem that involves stating educational results in terms of precise, observable performances of children. For example, an acceptable objective of a history lesson might be to teach a student to "order four wars of the nineteenth century chronologically."[36] The goal of educational research is to find more efficient ways of obtaining correct performances from children. To test these performances, criterion-referenced measures are constructed. They provide clear, precise test items that refer to objectives (that is, a child lists wars chronologically). The authors define professionals as "personnel" whose function is "management of human resources which will lead to more efficient administration of instruction and the greater likelihood that prescribed outcomes will be attained." A professional's task is to measure teaching efficiency and a researcher's task is to identify levels of mastery.

Educational change theories maintain similar assumptions about people, schools, and research. Change oriented research is often concerned with how experts (change agents) can encourage participants in an organization to accept the administrators' reforms.[37] Psychological and organizational research on "change" provides information that enables the change agent to manipulate the people or situation to achieve the desired results. A *healthy* organization is defined as one that accepts the change agent's definitions. A *traditional* organization is defined as one in which there are close, personal ties, and this social affiliation makes it less easily manipulated through outside intervention schemes. Change practices carefully control, through piecemeal additions, the established order of things. People are defined as recipients of values, and human capabilities as functionally related to existing structures. The ethical implications of how educational institutions are organized, or the nature of expectations upon school participants, are not deemed important for scrutiny.

In much curriculum thought and educational reform, the science of education is translated into a technology. Choices exist only when they make the existing system more rational, efficient, and controllable. Science is administration of people; research is a team effort, user-oriented and devoid of the imagination described earlier. The skepticism and self-criticism that characterize science are made irrelevant. Curriculum is no longer an ethical task. In fact, the technical nature of professional work makes the image of the Renaissance man, as Baker and Schultz suggest,[38] an image "for his time, not ours."

The image of educational science exudes a belief that "the laws" of nature or the knowledge of human existence have been discovered and are available to implant in children. Educators manipulate and control children as physical scientists manipulate objects of the physical world. Although the belief that the laws of social life are known is a chimera, human engineers act upon educational affairs as though there were not difficulties or uncertainties. The ceremonies and rituals of research give the practice legitimacy and sanctity. The moral implications of control, dominance, and power are eliminated from discussion when the only problem of schooling is considered to be implementing technologies.

The concept that educational science is similar to the physical sciences is an ideological one. Gouldner[39] argues, for example, that behind methodologies and techniques is a belief that (a) people might unite in order to subdue a "nature" that is regarded as external to man, and (b) technologies might be developed that would transform the universe into a "usable" resource of mankind as a whole. These assumptions led to a belief that people could control the rest of the universe and have the right to use the universe for their own benefit. When the assumptions of the physical sciences were applied to studies of people, specific problems arose.

The humanistic parochialism of science, with its premised unity of mankind, created problems when the effort was made to apply science to the study of mankind itself. It did so partly because national or class differences then became acutely visible, but also, perhaps more important, because men now expected to use social science to "control" men themselves, as they were already using physical science to control "nature." Such a view of social science premised that a man might be known, used, and controlled like any other thing; it "thingafied" man. The use of the physical sciences as a model fostered such a conception of the social sciences, all the more so as they were developing in the context of an increasing utilitarian culture.[40]

Research as a Cultural Imperative Revisited

At this point, one might argue that educational research contains many different approaches and values to study. Within the educational research community, for example, there are Marxists, pluralists, liberals, and so on. The conflict between people of different research orientations would tend to cancel out the importance of any particular intellectual approach in determining social affairs.

The history of science, however, suggests that not all approaches are accepted equally. Marxist analysis, for example, while having a respected tradition in Europe, has not been accepted within the American research community. In contrast, behavioral and management approaches have assumed a dominant position in this country's social scientific community.[41] This dominance makes the pattern of power and authority underlying behavioralism more potent in determining social affairs. Behavioralism is used to sustain and make credible many existing practices. The fact that the values of behavioralism are tacit and not scrutinized makes those values psychologically compelling.

It is important to ask why a particular approach, such as behavioral research, can become dominant. The answer, though, cannot be obtained simply by examining the ideas generated by the approach itself. The conclusions of behavioral education research, for example, often have little practical use as metaphors or as predictors in institutional life. The reasons for accepting a research pattern lie, in part, outside the educational community and within larger historical and political trends.

The acceptance of behavioral research can be related to the rise of professionalism. The drive for professional stature of the managerial and the "helping" occupations occurred at approximately the same historical time. Each sought more control over its domains.[42] The helping professions, in particular, persuaded their clients to rely on scientific technology and the advice of scientifically trained experts. The clients' "needs," however, were not those that emerged from the clients but were often invented by professionals in order to create a demand for their services. The "helping" professionals accepted a technological knowledge that could be centralized and than parceled out in a piecemeal fashion. Professionalism tends to undermine individuals' capacity to provide for themselves and, thereby, justifies the continuing expansion and control of experts into new sectors of society. The values of behavioralism can be viewed as instrumental to this process.

Defining behavioralism as a research approach which influences and is influenced by larger social patterns suggests that a major obligation of researchers is to maintain a critical stance. Whether doing behavioral or other modes of study, such as ethnography or phenomenology, researchers must consider the impact of work beyond its immediate procedures or findings. They must scrutinize the interests, visions, and definitions of power made reasonable by the research approach. Their understanding must include an overview of larger social and political processes and of how they impinge upon research practices.

Conclusions

Educational research involves values that emerge from an interplay of various communities. Research into school affairs is influenced by a community of scholars who follow accepted lines of reasoning, standards of discourse, and definitions of problems. The character of research is also responsive to the issues and dilemmas confronted by the larger society. Research is often initiated to resolve possible institutional contradictions. The study of poverty, deviance, moral development, or sexism are examples of such responses to conflict.

The values affirmed in research *are political*. Theories and methods imply what the customary ways of behaving in society are. Certain ways of participating in social affairs are given emphasis and, hence, preference through research activities. Rather than being aloof and detached, engagement in research affirms social values, beliefs, and hopes.

The values of educational research also have ideological implications. As argued earlier, the perspectives of social science not only describe but also give direction to how social events are to be challenged. The perspectives of research are increasingly incorporated into commonsense reasoning. The theories of social and educational research help to define political, social, and educational problems. The methods of inquiry identify possible solutions. These practices tend to favor certain interests and handicap others in society through the underlying social visions and definitions of power contained in research.

The normative quality of educational research makes it especially potent when applied in schools because it imposes ideas and work patterns upon children. Much of what occurs in schools is justified and made credible by the activities of the educational research community. Scientific evidence provides the rationale for curriculum development, instructional approaches, and evaluation strategies. Theories about social affairs, childhood, and learning guide educators in their choice of content and in the procedures they use to conduct everyday activities at school.

Values in educational inquiry, therefore, pose certain responsibilities for educators when developing and evaluating school programs. First, a self-reflective and critical stance needs to be adopted by educational researchers. The theories and procedures used to study social education programs and to devise curriculum are not neutral. Educators need to consider the social and political implications of educational analysis. It is worth noting that the traditions of objectivity, detachment, and scientific neutrality have undergone a thorough reexamination and redefinition within the philosophies of science. However, little of this discussion seems to have filtered into everyday educational discourse.

Second, educators should extend their notion of "adequacy" in research. In part, acceptable research must conform to scientific procedures for ensuring validity and reliability. These procedures, however, should include careful deliberation about the ethical premises and moral considerations upon which schools are founded. The potential of educational inquiry, I believe, is in its ability to sustain a public discourse about how schools can contribute to a more just and humane society.

Educational inquiry should provide a mode of analysis that can illuminate the unintended and latent consequences of our school arrangements. The ceremonies and rituals of our public institutions create symbolic forms which make ongoing practices seem heroic, institutional structures seem benevolent, and professionals seem competent in maintaining the historic mission of schools. Yet social affairs are filled with pretentions, deceptions, and self-deceptions by which people cloak the meanings and consequences of their arrangements with each other. Our institutional arrangements have become traditional, customary, and seemingly "natural." The unmasking and debunking motif in social inquiry can be a powerful intellectual force in a social world that is built upon beliefs in certainty.[43]

Third, we should reconsider the way in which we proceed when designing curriculum. Many educators consider the idea of scientific method as a superior one in curriculum construction. Our analysis suggests that there is no one scientific method, but rather there are scientific methods that people invent to respond to problems in their social world. Inventions of methods have the characteristic of reflecting different concepts of social order and of disciplined thought. While I have discussed some of the implications of the social nature of knowledge when applied to the problem of social studies curriculum design elsewhere,[44] I would suggest here that to define inquiry as a logical or psychological task (such as analyzing, inferring, or interviewing) is to distort the nature and character of that enterprise as a social endeavor. Logical or solely psychological definitions hide the values and beliefs underlying the forms of content brought into schools and the role of discourse in giving shape to our conceptions of "self" and society.

Notes

1. G. C. Homans, *The Nature of Social Science* (New York: Harcourt, Brace, and World, 1967).

2. P. Suppes, "The Place of Theory in Educational Research," *Educational Researcher* 3 (1974): 3–10.

3. I will use the label *social science* as a general term that includes the traditional social sciences (political science, sociology, psychology, and history). Educational

research is a special type of social science, having an institutional focus on schooling. The generic label, *social science*, gives emphasis to the social nature of all the disciplines.

4. I have explored the social and cultural nature of inquiry in "Myths of Social Science in Curriculum," *Educational Forum* 60 (1976): 317-28; and "Craft and Community as Metaphors for Social Inquiry Curriculum," *Educational Theory* 5 (1977): 41-60.

5. W. Hagstrom, *The Scientific Community* (New York: Basic Books, 1965); W. Storer, *The Social System of Science* (New York: Holt, Rinehart & Winston, 1966).

6. M. J. Mulkay, *The Social Process of Innovation* (New York: Macmillan, 1972).

7. I. Horowitz, *Professing Sociology: Studies in the Life Cycle of Social Science* (Chicago: Aldine Publishing Co., 1968).

8. J. Karabel and H. Halsey, "Educational Research: A Review and an Interpretation," in *Power and Ideology in Education,* ed. J. Karabel and H. Halsey (New York: Oxford University Press, 1977).

9. R. Nisbet, *Sociology as an Art Form* (New York: Oxford University Press, 1976).

10. A. Schultz, "Collected Papers 1," in *The Problem of Social Reality*, ed. M. Natanson (The Hague: Martinus Nithoff, 1973).

11. See H. Zinn, *The Politics of History* (Boston: Beacon Press, 1970).

12. P. Winch, "Understanding Primitive Society," in *Understanding and Social Inquiry*, ed. F. Dallmayr and T. McCarthy (Notre Dame, Indiana: University of Notre Dame Press, 1977).

13. A Gouldner, *The Coming Crisis of Western Sociology* (New York: Basic Books, 1970).

14. R. Merelman, "On Interventionist Behaviorism: An Essay in the Sociology of Knowledge," *Politics and Society* 6 (1976): 57-78.

15. Many of the theoretical perspectives and research techniques developed at this historical time have become important to educational analysis. Among these are the theory of functionalism in sociology and the survey methodology of behavioral science.

16. Merelman, "On Interventionist Behaviorism."

17. A. Lockwood, "A Critical View of Values Clarification," *Teachers College Record* 77 (1975).

18. W. Drost, *David Snedden and Education for Social Efficiency* (Madison, Wisconsin: University of Wisconsin Press, 1967).

19. P. Jackson, *Life in the Classrooms* (New York: Holt, Rinehart & Winston, 1968).

20. S. Angrist, R. Mickelsen, and A. Penna, "Development and Evaluation of Family Life Course," *Theory and Research in Social Education* 4 (1976): 57-79.

21. These assumptions are challengeable. The discipline-centered curriculum tends to provide a crystallized notion of science that distorts its creativity and maintains values that are conservative: N. Keddie, "Classroom Knowledge," in *Knowledge and Control: New Directions for the Sociology of Education,* ed. M. Young (London: Collier-Macmillan, 1971); T. Popkewitz, "Latent Values of the Discipline-Centered Curriculum," *Theory and Research in Social Education* 4:2 (1976): 57-79.

22. R. Shavelson, J. Cadwell, and T. Izu, "Teachers' Sensitivity to the Reliability

of Information in Making Pedagogical Decisions," *American Educational Research Journal* 14 (1977): 83–98.

23. Ibid., p. 95.

24. B. Tabachnick, "Open Education: Ideology and Alternative Visions of Schooling" (Speech given at the National Council of Social Studies Convention, Washington, D.C., November 1976).

25. While the vision of open education does have the potential to guide people in a search for social alternatives, the practice of open education has tended to be nonpolitical. Puppetry, "creative" writing, or stitchery often replace sustained disciplined thought. Mutual satisfaction among class participants becomes the purpose of schooling rather than a search for community in relation to some general intellectual problem or social issue.

26. Tabachnick, "Open Education."

27. F. Kerlinger, *Foundations of Behavioral Research*, 2d. ed. (New York: Holt, Rinehart & Winston, 1973).

28. D. Hamilton, "Educational Research and the Shadows of Francis W. Dockrell and Galton and Ronald Fisher," in *Rethinking Educational Research*, ed. D. Hamilton (London: Hodder and Stoughton, in press).

29. T. Fox and R. Hernandez-Nieto, "Why Not Quantitative Methodologies to Illuminate Dialectic or Phenomenological Perspectives?" Paper presented at the meeting of the American Educational Research Association, New York, 1977).

30. Homans, *Nature of Social Science.*

31. Ibid., p. 22.

32. W. Cooley, G. Leinhardt, and J. McGrail, "How to Identify Effective Teaching," *Anthropology and Education* 2 (1977): 119–26.

33. D. Easton, *The Political System: An Inquiry into the State of the Political Science* (New York: Alfred A. Knopf, 1971).

34. The idea of objectivity in research can be treated in a different manner. In P. Berger and T. Luckmann, *The Social Construction of Reality: A Treatise in the Sociology of Knowledge* (Garden City, New York: Anchor Books, 1967), reality is defined as being socially constructed and maintained through a dialectic, thus arguing against a crystallization of social structures.

35. R. Baker and R. Schultz, eds., *Instructional Product Development* (New York: Van Nostrand Reinhold Co., 1971).

36. Ibid., p. 10.

37. See, for example, T. Popkewitz, "The Ideology of Educational Reform" (Speech given at the National Council for the Social Studies Convention, Washington, D.C., November 1976).

38. Baker and Schultz, *Instructional Product Development.*

39. Gouldner, *Coming Crisis of Western Sociology.*

40. Ibid., p. 492.

41. The assumptions, implications, and consequences of management perspectives in education are discussed in T. Popkewitz and G. Wehlage, "Accountability and Critique and Alternative," *Interchange* 4 (1973): 46–62.

42. C. Lasch, "The Siege of the Family," *New York Review of Books*, November 1977.

43. See, for example, Berger and Luckmann, *Social Construction of Reality*.
44. T. Popkewitz, "Myths of Social Science in Curriculum," *Educational Forum* 60 (1976): 317–28; T. Popkewitz, "Ideology of Educational Reform"; Popkewitz, "Latent Values"; T. Popkewitz, "Craft and Community as Metaphors for Social Inquiry Curriculum," *Educational Theory* 5 (1977): 41–60; T. Popkewitz, "The Craft of Study, Structure and Schooling," *Teachers College Record* 74 (December 1972): 155–66; Popkewitz and Wehlage, "Accountability and Critique and Alternative."

21 Social Class and the Hidden Curriculum of Work

Jean Anyon

Introduction

In this article Jean Anyon argues that schools help to reproduce the existing society by giving students from various socioeconomic classes different types of curriculum knowledge and educational experiences. By examining five elementary schools in contrasting school communities, Anyon offers findings that suggest there is a "hidden curriculum" which prepares students from different social classes for class-specific roles in the dominant society. For instance, she argues that it is evident from her study that working-class students are prepared through their school experience for jobs that are routine and mechanical in nature, whereas students from the upper class are given school work and experiences that prepare them for jobs in the larger society that demand the creativity and the skills necessary for a self-managed existence.

As you read this article, consider the relationship Anyon tries to make between schools and the larger social structure.

- What are the specific classroom mechanisms that constitute the hidden curriculum of schooling?
- How can teachers recognize the effects of "hidden" class-based pedagogy in their own teaching?
- What is the point of both recognizing and identifying such determinants and their effects on the classroom experience?
- What are the implications of Anyon's analysis for curriculum development and practice?

This research was funded by Rutgers University Research Council. Reprinted, with permission, from *Journal of Education* 162, no. 1 (Winter 1980), pp. 67–92.

Scholars in political economy and the sociology of knowledge have recently argued that public schools in complex industrial societies like our own make available different types of educational experience and curriculum knowledge to students in different social classes. Bowles and Gintis,[1] for example, have argued that students from different social-class backgrounds are rewarded for classroom behaviors that correspond to personality traits allegedly rewarded in the different occupational strata—the working classes for docility and obedience, the managerial classes for initiative and personal assertiveness. Basil Bernstein, Pierre Bourdieu, and Michael W. Apple,[2] focusing on school knowledge, have argued that knowledge and skills leading to social power and regard (medical, legal, managerial) are made available to the advantaged social groups but are withheld from the working classes, to whom a more "practical" curriculum is offered (manual skills, clerical knowledge). While there has been considerable argumentation of these points regarding education in England, France, and North America, there has been little or no attempt to investigate these ideas empirically in elementary or secondary schools and classrooms in this country.[3]

This article offers tentative empirical support (and qualification) of the above arguments by providing illustrative examples of differences in student work in classrooms in contrasting social class communities. The examples were gathered as part of an ethnographical study of curricular, pedagogical, and pupil evaluation practices in five elementary schools. The article attempts a theoretical contribution as well and assesses student work in the light of a theoretical approach to social-class analysis. The organization is as follows: the methodology of the ethnographical study is briefly described; a theoretical approach to the definition of social class is offered; income and other characteristics of the parents in each school are provided, and examples from the study that illustrate work tasks and interaction in each school are presented; then the concepts used to define social class are applied to the examples in order to assess the theoretical meaning of classroom events. It will be suggested that there is a "hidden curriculum" in schoolwork that has profound implications for the theory—and consequence—of everyday activity in education.

Methodology

The methods used to gather data were classroom observation; interviews of students, teachers, principals, and district administrative staff; and assessment of curriculum and other materials in each classroom and school. All classroom events to be discussed here involve the fifth grade in each school. Except for that school where only one fifth grade teacher could be observed, all the fifth grade teachers (that is, two or three) were observed as the children moved from subject to subject. In all schools the art, music, and gym teachers were also observed and interviewed. All teachers in the study were described as "good" or "excellent" by their principals. All except one new teacher had taught for more than four years. The fifth grade in each school was observed by the investigator for ten three-hour periods between September 15, 1978, and June 20, 1979.

Before providing the occupations, incomes, and other relevant social characteristics of the parents of the children in each school, I will offer a theoretical approach to defining social class.

Social Class

One's occupation and income level contribute significantly to one's social class, but they do not define it. Rather, social class is a series of relationships. A person's social class is defined here by the way that person relates to the process in society by which goods, services, and culture are produced. One relates to several aspects of the production process primarily through one's work. One has a relationship to the system of ownership, to other people (at work and in society), and to the content and process of one's own productive activity. One's relationship to all three of these aspects of production determines one's social class; that is, all three relationships are necessary, and none is sufficient for determining a person's relation to the process of production in society.

Ownership Relations

In a capitalist society, a person has a relation to the system of private ownership of capital. Capital is usually thought of as being derived from physical property. In this sense capital is property that is used to produce profit, interest, or rent in sufficient quantity so that the result can be used to produce more profit, interest, or rent—that is, more capital. Physical capital may be derived from money, stocks, machines, land, or the labor of workers (whose labor, for instance, may produce products that are sold by others for profit). Capital, however, can also be symbolic. It can be the socially legitimated knowledge of how the production process works, its financial, managerial, technical, or other "secrets." Symbolic capital can also be socially legitimated skills—cognitive (for example, analytical), linguistic, or technical skills that provide the ability to, say, produce the dominant scientific, artistic, and other culture or to manage the systems of industrial and cultural production. Skillful application of symbolic capital may yield social and cultural power and perhaps physical capital as well.

The ownership relation that is definitive for social class is one's relation to physical capital. The first such relationship is that of capitalist. To be a member of the capitalist class in the present-day United States, one must participate in the ownership of the apparatus of production in society. The number of such persons is relatively small: while one person in ten owns some stock, for example, a mere 1.6 percent of the population owns 82.2 percent of *all* stock, and the wealthiest one-fifth owns almost all the rest.[5]

At the opposite pole of this relationship is the worker. To be in the United States working class, a person will not ordinarily own physical capital; on the contrary, his or her work will be wage or salaried labor that is either a *source* or profit (that is, capital) to others or that makes it possible for others to *realize* profit. Examples of the latter are white-collar clerical workers in industry and distribution (office and sales) as well as the wage and salaried workers in the institutions of social and economic legitimation and service (in state education and welfare institutions).[6] According to the criteria to be developed here, the number of persons who presently comprise the working class in the United States is between 50 percent and 60 percent of the population.

In between the defining relationship of capitalist and worker are the middle classes, whose relationship to the process of production is less clear and whose relationship may indeed exhibit contradictory characteristics. For example, social service employees have a somewhat contradictory relationship to the process of production because, although their income may be at middle-class levels, some characteristics of their work are working class (they may have very little control over their work). Analogously, there are persons at the upper income end of the middle class, such as upper-middle-class professionals, who may own quantities of stocks and will therefore share characteristics of the capitalist class. As the next criterion to be discussed makes clear, however, to be a member of the present-day capitalist class in the United States, one must also participate in the social *control* of this capital.

Relationships Between People

The second relationship that contributes to one's social class is the relation one has to authority and control at work and in society.[8] One characteristic of most working-class jobs is that there is no built-in mechanism by which the worker can control the content, process, or speed of work. Legitimate decision making is vested in personnel supervisors, in middle or upper management, or—as in an increasing number of white-collar working-class (and most middle-class) jobs—by bureaucratic rule and regulation. For upper-middle-class professional groups there is an increased amount of autonomy regarding work. Moreover, in middle- and upper-middle-class positions there is an increasing chance that one's work will also involve supervising the work of others. A capitalist is defined within these relations of control in an enterprise by having a position that participates in the direct control of the entire enterprise. Capitalists do not directly control workers in physical production and do not directly control ideas in the sphere of cultural production. However, more crucial to control, capitalists make the decisions over how resources are used (that is, where money is invested) and how profit is allocated.

Relations Between People and Their Work

The third criterion that contributes to a person's social class is the relationship between that person and his or her own productive activity—the type of activity that constitutes his or her work. A working-class job is often characterized by work that is routine and mechanical and that is a small, fragmented part of a larger process with which workers are not usually acquainted. These working-class jobs are usually blue-collar, manual labor. A few skilled jobs such as plumbing and printing are not mechanical, however, and an increasing number of working-class jobs are *white*-collar. These white-collar jobs, such as clerical work, may involve work that necessitates a measure of planning and decision making, but one still has no built-in control over the content. The work of some middle- and most upper-middle-class managerial and professional groups is likely to involve the need for conceptualization and creativity, with many professional jobs demanding one's full creative capacities. Finally, the work that characterizes the capitalist position is that this work is almost entirely a matter of conceptualization (planning and laying out) that has as its object management and control of the enterprise.

One's social class, then, is a result of the relationships one has, largely through one's work, to physical capital and its power, to other people at work and in society, and to one's own productive activity. Social class is a lived, developing process. It is not an abstract category, and it is not a fixed, inherited position (although one's family background is, of course, important). Social class is perceived as a complex of social relations that one develops as one grows up—as one acquires and develops certain bodies of knowledge, skills, abilities, and traits, and as one has contact and opportunity in the world.[9] In sum, social class describes relationships that we as adults have developed, may attempt to maintain, and in which we participate every working day. These relationships in a real sense define our material ties to the world. An important concern here is whether these relationships are developing in children in schools within particular social-class contexts.

The Sample of Schools

With the above discussion as a theoretical backdrop, the social-class designation of each of the five schools will be identified, and the income, occupation, and other relevant available social characteristics of the students and their parents will be described. The first three schools are in a medium-sized city district in northern New Jersey, and the other two are in a nearby New Jersey suburb.

The first two schools I will call *working-class schools*. Most of the parents have blue-collar jobs. Less than a third of the fathers are skilled, while the majority are in unskilled or semiskilled jobs. During the period of the study

(1978—1979), approximately 15 percent of the fathers were unemployed. The large majority (85 percent) of the families are white. The following occupations are typical: platform, storeroom, and stockroom workers; foundrymen, pipe welders, and boilermakers; semiskilled and unskilled assembly-line operatives; gas station attendants, auto mechanics, maintenance workers, and security guards. Less than 30 percent of the women work, some part-time and some full-time, on assembly lines, in storerooms and stockrooms, as waitresses, barmaids, or sales clerks. Of the fifth grade parents, none of the wives of the skilled workers had jobs. Approximately 15 percent of the families in each school are at or below the federal "poverty" level[10]; most of the rest of the family incomes are at or below $12,000, except some of the skilled workers whose incomes are higher. The incomes of the majority of the families in these two schools (at or below $12,000) are typical of 38.6 percent of the families in the United States.[11]

The third school is called the *middle-class school*, although because of neighborhood residence patterns, the population is a mixture of several social classes. The parents' occupations can be divided into three groups: a small group of blue-collar "rich," who are skilled, well-paid workers such as printers, carpenters, plumbers, and construction workers. The second group is composed of parents in working-class and middle-class white-collar jobs: women in office jobs, technicians, supervisors in industry, and parents employed by the city (such as firemen, policemen, and several of the school's teachers). The third group is composed of occupations such as personnel directors in local firms, accountants, "middle management," and a few small capitalists (owners of shops in the area). The children of several local doctors attend this school. Most family incomes are between $13,000 and $25,000, with a few higher. This income range is typical of 38.9 percent of the families in the United States.[12]

The fourth school has a parent population that is at the upper income level of the upper middle class and is predominantly professional. This school will be called the *affluent professional school*. Typical jobs are: cardiologist, interior designer, corporate lawyer or engineer, executive in advertising or television. There are some families who are not as affluent as the majority (the family of the superintendent of the district's schools, and the one or two families in which the fathers are skilled workers). In addition, a few of the families are more affluent than the majority and can be classified in the capitalist class (a partner in a prestigious Wall Street stock brokerage firm). Approximately 90 percent of the children in this school are white. Most family incomes are between $40,000 and $80,000. This income span represents approximately 7 percent of the families in the United States.[13]

In the fifth school the majority of the families belong to the capitalist class. This school will be called the *executive elite school* because most of the fathers are top executives (for example, presidents and vice-presidents) in major

United States-based multinational corporations—for example, ATT, RCA, City Bank, American Express, U.S. Steel. A sizable group of fathers are top executives in financial firms in Wall Street. There are also a number of fathers who list their occupations as "general counsel" to a particular corporation, and these corporations are also among the large multinationals. Many of the mothers do volunteer work in the Junior League, Junior Fortnightly, or other service groups; some are intricately involved in town politics; and some are themselves in well-paid occupations. There are no minority children in the school. Almost all the family incomes are over $100,000, with some in the $500,000 range. The incomes in this school represent less than 1 percent of the families in the United States.[14]

Since each of the five schools is only one instance of elementary education in a particular social class context, I will not generalize beyond the sample. However, the examples of schoolwork which follow will suggest characteristics of education in each social setting that appear to have theoretical and social significance and to be worth investigation in a larger number of schools.

Social Class and Schoolwork

There are obvious similarities among United States schools and classrooms. There are school and classroom rules, teachers who ask questions and attempt to exercise control and who give work and homework. There are textbooks and tests. All of these were found in the five schools. Indeed, there were other curricular similarities as well: all schools and fifth grades used the same math book and series (*Mathematics Around Us*, Scott Foresman, 1978); all fifth grades had at least one boxed set of an individualized reading program available in the room (although the variety and amounts of teaching materials in the classrooms increased as the social class of the school population increased); and, all fifth grade language arts curricula included aspects of grammar, punctuation, and capitalization.[15]

This section provides examples of work and work-related activities in each school that bear on the categories used to define social class. Thus, examples will be provided concerning students' relation to capital (for example, as manifest in any symbolic capital that might be acquired through schoolwork); students' relation to persons and types of authority regarding schoolwork; and students' relation to their own productive activity. The section first offers the investigator's interpretation of what schoolwork *is* for children in each setting and then presents events and interactions that illustrate that assessment.

The Working-Class Schools

In the two working-class schools, work is following the steps of a procedure. The procedure is usually mechanical, involving rote behavior and very little decision making or choice. The teachers rarely explain why the work is being assigned, how it might connect to other assignments, or what the idea is that lies behind the procedure or gives it coherence and perhaps meaning or significance. Available textbooks are not always used, and the teachers often prepare their own dittos or put work examples on the board. Most of the rules regarding work are designations of what the children are to do; the rules are steps to follow. These steps are told to the children by the teachers and often written on the board. The children are usually told to copy the steps as notes. These notes are to be studied. Work is often evaluated not according to whether it is right or wrong but according to whether the children followed the right steps.

The following examples illustrate these points. In math, when two-digit division was introduced, the teacher in one school gave a four-minute lecture on what the terms are called (which number is the divisor, dividend, quotient, and remainder). The children were told to copy these names in their notebooks. Then the teacher told them the steps to follow to do the problems, saying, "This is how you do them." The teacher listed the steps on the board, and they appeared several days later as a chart hung in the middle of the front wall: "Divide, Multiply, Subtract, Bring Down." The children often did examples of two-digit division. When the teacher went over the examples with them, he told them what the procedure was for each problem, rarely asking them to conceptualize or explain it themselves: "Three into twenty-two is seven; do your subtraction and one is left over." During the week that two-digit division was introduced (or at any other time), the investigator did not observe any discussion of the idea of grouping involved in division, any use of manipulables, or any attempt to relate two-digit division to any other mathematical process. Nor was there any attempt to relate the steps to an actual or possible thought process of the children. The observer did not hear the terms *dividend*, *quotient*, and so on, used again. The math teacher in the other working-class school followed similar procedures regarding two-digit division and at one point her class seemed confused. She said, "You're confusing yourselves. You're tensing up. Remember, when you do this, it's the same steps over and over again—and that's the way division always is." Several weeks later, after a test, a group of her children "still didn't get it," and she made no attempt to explain the concept of dividing things into groups or to give them manipulables for their own investigation. Rather, she went over the steps with them again and told them that they "needed more practice."

In other areas of math, work is also carrying out often unexplained fragmented procedures. For example, one of the teachers led the children through a series of steps to make a 1-inch grid on their paper *without* telling them that they were making a 1-inch grid or that it would be used to study scale. She said, "Take your ruler. Put it across the top. Make a mark at every number. Then move your ruler down to the bottom. No, put it across the bottom. Now make a mark on top of very number. Now draw a line from. . . ." At this point

Social Class and Hidden Curriculum

a girl said that she had a faster way to do it and the teacher said, "No, you don't; you don't even know what I'm making yet. Do it this way, or its's wrong." After they had made the lines up and down and across, the teacher told them she wanted them to make a figure by connecting some dots and to measure that, using the scale of 1 inch equals 1 mile. Then they were to cut it out. She said, "Don't cut until I check it."

In both working-class schools, work in language arts is mechanics of punctuation (commas, periods, question marks, exclamation points), capitalization, and the four kinds of sentences. One teacher explained to me, "Simple punctuation is all they'll ever use." Regarding punctuation, either a teacher or a ditto stated the rules for where, for example, to put commas. The investigator heard no classroom discussion of the aural context of punctuation (which, of course, is what gives each mark its meaning). Nor did the investigator hear any statement or inference that placing a punctuation mark could be a decision-making process, depending, for example, on one's intended meaning. Rather, the children were told to follow the rules. Language arts did not involve creative writing. There were several writing assignments throughout the year, but in each instance the children were given a ditto, and they wrote answers to questions on the sheet. For example, they wrote their "autobiography" by answering such questions as "Where were you born?" "What is your favorite animal?" on a sheet entitled "All About Me."

In one of the working-class schools, the class had a science period several times a week. On the three occasions observed, the children were not called upon to set up experiments or to give explanations for facts or concepts. Rather, on each occasion the teacher told them in his own words what the book said. The children copied the teacher's sentences from the board. Each day that preceded the day they were to do a science experiment, the teacher told them to copy the directions from the book for the procedure they would carry out the next day and to study the list at home that night. The day after each experiment, the teacher went over what they had "found" (they did the experiments as a class, and each was actually a class demonstration led by the teacher). Then the teacher wrote what they "found" on the board, and the children copied that in their notebooks. Once or twice a year there are science projects. The project is chosen and assigned by the teacher from a box of 3-by-5-inch cards. On the card the teacher has written the question to be answered, the books to use, and how much to write. Explaining the cards to the observer, the teacher said, "It tells them exactly what to do, or they couldn't do it."

Social studies in the working-class schools is also largely mechanical, rote work that was given little explanation or connection to larger contexts. In one school, for example, although there was a book available, social studies work was to copy the teacher's notes from the board. Several times a week for a period of several months the children copied these notes. The fifth grades in the district were to study United States history. The teacher used a booklet she had purchased called "The Fabulous Fifty States." Each day she put information from the booklet in outline form on the board and the children copied it. The type of information did not vary: the name of the state, its abbreviation, state capital, nickname of the state, its main products, main business, and a "Fabulous Fact" ("Idaho grew twenty-seven billion potatoes in one year. That's enough potatoes for each man, woman, and . . ."). As the children finished copying the sentences, the teacher erased them and wrote more. Children would occasionally go to the front to pull down the wall map in order to locate the states they were copying, and the teacher did not dissuade them. But the observer never saw her refer to the map; nor did the observer ever hear her make other than perfunctory remarks concerning the information the children were copying. Occasionally the children colored in a ditto and cut it out to make a stand-up figure (representing, for example, a man roping a cow in the Southwest). These were referred to by the teacher as their social studies "projects."

Rote behavior was often called for in classroom oral work. When going over math and language art skills sheets, for example, as the teacher asked for the answer to each problem, he fired the questions rapidly, staccato, and the scene reminded the observer of a sergeant drilling recruits: above all, the questions demanded that you stay at attention: "The next one? What do I put here? . . . Here? Give us the next." Or "How many commas in this sentence? Where do I put them . . . The next one?"

The (four) fifth grade teachers observed in the working-class schools attempted to control classroom time and space by making decisions without consulting the children and without explaining the basis for their decisions. The teacher's control thus often seemed capricious. Teachers, for instance, very often ignored the bells to switch classes—deciding among themselves to keep the children after the period was officially over to continue with the work or for disciplinary reasons or so they (the teachers) could stand in the hall and talk. There were no clocks in the rooms in either school, and the children often asked, "What period is this?" "When do we go to gym?" The children had no access to materials. These were handed out by teachers and closely guarded. Things in the room "belonged" to the teacher: "Bob, bring me my garbage can." The teachers continually gave the children orders. Only three times did the investigator hear a teacher in either working-class school preface a directive with an unsarcastic "please," or "let's" or "would you." Instead, the teachers said, "Shut up," "Shut your mouth," "Open your books," "Throw your gum away—if you want to rot your teeth, do it on your own time." Teachers made every effort to control the movement of the children, and often shouted, "Why are you out of your seat??!!" If the children got permission to leave the room, they had to take a written pass with the date and time.

The control that the teachers have is less than they would like. It is a result of constant struggle with the children. The children continually resist the teachers' orders and the work itself. They do not directly challenge the teacher's authority or legitimacy, but they make indirect attempts to sabotage and resist the flow of assignments:

Teacher:	I will put some problems on the board. You are to divide.
Child:	We got to divide?
Teacher:	Yes.
Several children:	(Groan) Not again. Mr. B., we done this yesterday.
Child:	Do we put the date?
Teacher:	Yes. I hope we remember we work in silence. You're supposed to do it on white paper. I'll explain it later.
Child:	Somebody broke my pencil. (Crash—a child falls out of his chair.)
Child:	(repeats) Mr. B., somebody broke my *pencil!*
Child:	Are we going to be here all morning?

(Teacher comes to the observer, shakes his head and grimaces, then smiles.)

The children are successful enough in their struggle against work that there are long periods where they are not asked to *do* any work but just to sit and be quiet.[16] Very often the work that the teachers assign is "easy," that is, not demanding and thus receives less resistance. Sometimes a compromise is reached where, although the teachers insist that the children continue to work, there is a constant murmur of talk. The children will be doing arithmetic examples, copying social studies notes, or doing punctuation or other dittos, and all the while there is muted but spirited conversation—about somebody's broken arm, an after-school disturbance the day before, and so on. Sometimes the teachers themselves join in the conversation because, as one teacher explained to me, "It's a relief from the routine."

Middle-Class School

In the middle-class school, work is getting the right answer. If one accumulates enough right answers, one gets a good grade. One must follow the directions in order to get the right answers, but the directions often call for some figuring, some choice, some decision making. For example, the children must often figure out by themselves what the directions ask them to do and how to get the answer: what do you do first, second, and perhaps third? Answers are usually found in books or by listening to the teacher. Answers are usually words, sentences, numbers, or facts and dates; one writes them on paper, and one should be neat. Answers must be given in the right order, and one cannot make them up.

The following activities are illustrative. Math involves some choice: one may do two-digit division the long way or the short way, and there are some math problems that can be done "in your head." When the teacher explains how to do two-digit division, there is recognition that a cognitive process is involved; she gives several ways and says, "I want to make sure you understand what you're doing—so you get it right"; and, when they go over the homework, she asks the *children* to tell how they did the problem and what answer they got.

In social studies the daily work is to read the assigned pages in the textbook and to answer the teacher's questions. The questions are almost always designed to check on whether the students have read the assignment and understood it: who did so-and-so; what happened after that; when did it happen, where, and sometimes, why did it happen? The answers are in the book and in one's understanding of the book; the teacher's hints when one doesn't know the answers are to "read it again" or to look at the picture or at the rest of the paragraph. One is to search for the answer in the "context," in what is given.

Language arts is "simple grammar, what they need for everyday life." The language arts teacher says, "They should learn to speak properly, to write business letters and thank-you letters, and to understand what nouns and verbs and simple subjects are." Here, as well, actual work is to choose the right answers, to understand what is given. The teacher often says, "Please read the next sentence and then I'll question you about it." One teacher said in some exasperation to a boy who was fooling around in class, "If you don't know the answers to the questions I ask, then you can't stay in this *class*! (pause) You *never* know the answers to the questions I ask, and it's not fair to me—and certainly not to you!"

Most lessons are based on the textbook. This does not involve a critical perspective on what is given there. For example, a critical perspective in social studies is perceived as dangerous by these teachers because it may lead to controversial topics; the parents might complain. The children, however, are often curious, especially in social studies. Their questions are tolerated and usually answered perfunctorily. But after a few minutes the teacher will say, "All right, we're not going any farther. Please open your social studies workbook." While the teachers spend a lot of time explaining and expanding on what the textbooks say, there is little attempt to analyze how or why things happen, or to give thought to how pieces of a culture, or, say, a system of numbers or elements of a language fit together or can be analyzed. What has happened in the past and what exists now may not be equitable or fair, but (shrug) that is the way things are and one does not confront such matters in school. For example, in social studies after a child is called on to read a passage about the pilgrims, the teacher summarizes the paragraph and then says, "So you can see how strict they were about everything." A child asks, "Why?" "Well, because they felt that if you weren't busy you'd get into trouble."

Another child asks, "Is it true that they burned women at the stake?" The teacher says, "Yes, if a woman did anything strange, they hanged them.[sic] What would a woman do, do you think, to make them burn them?[sic] See if you can come up with better answers than my other [social studies] class." Several children offer suggestions, to which the teacher nods but does not comment. Then she says, "Okay, good," and calls on the next child to read.

Work tasks do not usually request creativity. Serious attention is rarely given in school work on *how* the children develop or express their own feelings and ideas, either linguistically or in graphic form. On the occasions when creativity or self-expression is requested, it is peripheral to the main activity or it is "enrichment" or "for fun." During a lesson on what similes are, for example, the teacher explains what they are, puts several on the board, gives some other examples herself, and then asks the children if they can "make some up." She calls on three children who give similes, two of which are actually in the book they have open before them. The teacher does not comment on this and then asks several others to choose similes from the list of phrases in the book. Several do so correctly, and she says, "Oh good! You're picking them out! See how good we are?" Their homework is to pick out the rest of the similes from the list.

Creativity is not often requested in social studies and science projects, either. Social studies projects, for example, are given with directions to "find information on your topic" and write it up. The children are not supposed to copy but to "put it in your own words." Although a number of the projects subsequently went beyond the teacher's direction to find information and had quite expressive covers and inside illustrations, the teacher's evaluative comments had to do with the amount of information, whether they had "copied," and if their work was neat.

The style of control of the three fifth grade teachers observed in this school varied from somewhat easygoing to strict, but in contrast to the working-class schools, the teachers' decisions were usually based on external rules and regulations—for example, on criteria that were known or available to the children. Thus, the teachers always honor the bells for changing classes, and they usually evaluate children's work by what is in the textbooks and answer booklets.

There is little excitement in schoolwork for the children, and the assignments are perceived as having little to do with their interests and feelings. As one child said, what you do is "store facts up in your head like cold storage—until you need it later for a test or your job." Thus, doing well is important because there are thought to be *other* likely rewards: a good job or college.[17]

Affluent Professional School

In the affluent professional school, work is creative activity carried out independently. The students are continually asked to express and apply ideas and concepts. Work involves individual thought and expressiveness, expansion and illustration of ideas, and choice of appropriate method and material. (The class is not considered an open classroom, and the principal explained that because of the large number of discipline problems in the fifth grade this year they did not departmentalize. The teacher who agreed to take part in the study said she is "more structured" this year than she usually is.) The products of work in this class are often written stories, editorials and essays, or representations of ideas in mural, graph, or craft form. The products of work should not be like everybody else's and should show individuality. They should exhibit good design, and (this is important) they must also fit empirical reality. Moreover, one's work should attempt to interpret or "make sense" of reality. The relatively few rules to be followed regarding work are usually criteria for, or limits on, individual activity. One's product is usually evaluated for the quality of its expression and for the appropriateness of its conception to the task. In many cases, one's own satisfaction with the product is an important criterion for its evaluation. When right answers are called for, as in commercial materials like SRA (Science Research Associates) and math, it is important that the children decide on an answer as a result of thinking about the idea involved in what they're being asked to do. Teacher's hints are to "think about it some more."

The following activities are illustrative. The class takes home a sheet requesting each child's parents to fill in the number of cars they have, the number of television sets, refrigerators, games, or rooms in the house, and so on. Each child is to figure the average number of a type of possession owned by the fifth grade. Each child must compile the "data" from all the sheets. A calculator is available in the classroom to do the mechanics of finding the average. Some children decide to send sheets to the fourth grade families for comparison. Their work should be "verified" by a classmate before it is handed in.

Each child and his or her family has made a geoboard. The teacher asks the class to get their geoboards from the side cabinet, to take a handful of rubber bands, and then to listen to what she would like them to do. She says, "I would like you to design a figure and then find the perimeter and area. When you have it, check with your neighbor. After you've done that, please transfer it to graph paper and tomorrow I'll ask you to make up a question about it for someone. When you hand it in, please let me know whose it is and who verified it. Then I have something else for you to do that's really fun. [pause] Find the average number of chocolate chips in three cookies. I'll give you three cookies, and you'll have to *eat* your way through, I'm afraid!" Then she goes around the room and gives help, suggestions, praise, and admonitions that they are getting noisy. They work sitting, or standing up at their desks, at benches in the back, or on the floor. A child hands the teacher his paper and she comments, "I'm not accepting this paper. Do a better design." To another child she says, "That's fantastic! But you'll never find the area. Why don't you draw a figure inside [the big one] and subtract to get the area?"

The school district requires the fifth grade to study ancient civilization (in particular, Egypt, Athens, and Sumer). In this classroom, the emphasis is on illustrating and re-creating the culture of the people of ancient times. The following are typical activities: The children made an 8mm film on Egypt, which one of the parents edited. A girl in the class wrote the script, and the class acted it out. They put the sound on themselves. They read stories of those days. They wrote essays and stories depicting the lives of the people and the societal and occupational divisions. They chose from a list of projects, all of which involved graphic representations of ideas: for example, "Make a mural depicting the division of labor in Egyptian society."

Each child wrote and exchanged a letter in hieroglyphics with a fifth grader in another class, and they also exchanged stories they wrote in cuneiform. They made a scroll and singed the edges so it looked authentic. They each chose an occupation and made an Egyptian plaque representing that occupation, simulating the appropriate Egyptian design. They carved their design on a cylinder of wax, pressed the wax into clay, and then baked the clay. Although one girl did not choose an occupation but carved instead a series of gods and slaves, the teacher said, "That's all right, Amber, it's beautiful." As they were working the teacher said, "Don't cut into your clay until you're satisfied with your design."

Social studies also involves almost daily presentation by the children of some event from the news. The teacher's questions ask the children to expand what they say, to give more details, and to be more specific. Occasionally she adds some remarks to help them see connections between events.

The emphasis on expressing and illustrating ideas in social studies is accompanied in language arts by an emphasis on creative writing. Each child wrote a rhebus story for a first grader whom they had interviewed to see what kind of story the child liked best. They wrote editorials on pending decisions by the school board and radio plays, some of which were read over the school intercom from the office and one of which was performed in the auditorium. There is no language arts textbook because, the teacher said, "The principal wants us to be creative." There is not much grammar, but there is punctuation. One morning when the observer arrived, the class was doing a punctuation ditto. The teacher later apologized for using the ditto. "It's just for review," she said. "I don't teach punctuation that way. We use their language." The ditto had three unambiguous rules for where to put commas in a sentence. As the teacher was going around to help the children with the ditto, she repeated several times, "Where you put commas depends on how you say the sentence; it depends on the situation and what you want to say." Several weeks later the observer saw another punctuation activity. The teacher had printed a five-paragraph story on an oak tag and then cut it into phrases. She read the whole story to the class from the book, then passed out the phrases. The group had to decide how the phrases could best be put together again. (They arranged the phrases on the floor.) The point was not to replicate the story, although that was not irrelevant, but to "decide what you think the best way is." Punctuation marks on cardboard pieces were then handed out, and the children discussed and then decided what mark was best at each place they thought one was needed. At the end of each pararaph the teacher asked, "Are you satisfied with the way the paragraphs are now? Read it to yourself and see how it sounds." Then she read the original story again, and they compared the two.

Describing her goals in science to the investigator, the teacher said, "We use ESS (Elementary Science Study). It's very good because it gives a hands-on experience—so they can make *sense* out of it. It doesn't matter whether it [what they find] is right or wrong. I bring them together and there's value in discussing their ideas."

The products of work in this class are often highly valued by the children and the teacher. In fact, this was the only school in which the investigator was not allowed to take original pieces of the children's work for her files. If the work was small enough, however, and was on paper, the investigator could duplicate it on the copying machine in the office.

The teacher's attempt to control the class involves constant negotiation. She does not give direct orders unless she is angry because the children have been too noisy. Normally, she tries to get them to foresee the consequences of their actions and to decide accordingly. For example, lining them up to go see a play written by the sixth graders, she says, "I presume you're lined up by someone with whom you want to sit. I hope you're lined up by someone you won't get in trouble with." The following two dialogues illustrate the process of negotiation between student and teacher.

Teacher:	Tom, you're behind in your SRA this marking period.
Tom:	So what!
Teacher:	Well, last time you had a hard time catching up.
Tom:	But I have my [music] lesson at 10:00.
Teacher:	Well, that doesn't mean you're going to sit here for twenty minutes.
Tom:	Twenty minutes! OK. (He goes to pick out a SRA booklet and chooses one, puts it back, then takes another, and brings it to her.)
Teacher:	OK, this is the one you want, right?
Tom:	Yes.
Teacher:	OK, I'll put tomorrow's date on it so you can take it home tonight or finish it tomorrow if you want.
Teacher:	(to a child who is wandering around during reading) Kevin, why don't you do *Reading for Concepts*?

Kevin: No, I don't *like Reading for Concepts*.
Teacher: Well, what are you going to do?
Kevin: (pause) I'm going to work on my DAR. (The DAR had sponsored an essay competition on "Life in the American Colonies.")

One of the few rules governing the children's movement is that no more than three children may be out of the room at once. There is a school rule that anyone can go to the library at any time to get a book. In the fifth grade I observed, they sign their name on the chalkboard and leave. There are no passes. Finally, the children have a fair amount of officially sanctioned say over what happens in the class. For example, they often negotiate what work is to be done. If the teacher wants to move on to the next subject, but the children say they are not ready, they want to work on their present projects some more, she very often lets them do it.

Executive Elite School

In the executive elite school, work is developing one's analytical intellectual powers. Children are continually asked to reason through a problem, to produce intellectual products that are both logically sound and of top academic quality. A primary goal of thought is to conceptualize rules by which elements may fit together in systems and then to apply these rules in solving a problem. Schoolwork helps one to achieve, to excel, to prepare for life.

The following are illustrative. The math teacher teaches area and perimeter by having the children derive formulas for each. First she helps them, through discussion at the board, to arrive at $A = W \times L$ as a formula (not *the* formula) for area. After discussing several, she says, "Can anyone make up a formula for perimeter? Can you figure that out yourselves? [pause] Knowing what we know, can we think of a formula?" She works out three children's suggestions at the board, saying to two, "Yes, that's a good one," and then asks the class if they can think of any more. No one volunteers. To prod them, she says, "If you use rules and good reasoning, you get many ways. Chris, can you think up a formula?"

She discusses two-digit division with the children as a decision-making process. Presenting a new type of problem to them, she asks, "What's the *first* decision you'd make if presented with this kind of example? What is the first thing you'd *think*? Craig?" Craig says, "To find my first partial quotient." She responds, "Yes, that would be your first decision. How would you do that?" Craig explains, and then the teacher says, "OK, we'll see how that works for you." The class tries his way. Subsequently, she comments on the merits and shortcomings of several other children's decisions. Later, she tells the investigator that her goals in math are to develop their reasoning and mathematical thinking and that, unfortunately, "there's no *time* for manipulables."

While right answers are important in math, they are not "given" by the book or by the teacher but may be challenged by the children. Going over some problems in late September the teacher says, "Raise your hand if you do not agree." A child says, "I don't agree with sixty-four." The teacher responds, "OK, there's a question about sixty-four. [to class] Please check it. Owen, they're disagreeing with you. Kristen, they're checking yours." The teacher emphasized this repeatedly during September and October with statements like "Don't be afraid to say if you disagree. In the last [math] class, somebody disagreed, and they were right. Before you disagree, check yours, and if you still think we're wrong, then we'll check it out." By Thanksgiving, the children did not often speak in terms of right and wrong math problems but of whether they agreed with the answer that had been given.

There are complicated math mimeos with many word problems. Whenever they go over the examples, they discuss how each child has set up the problem. The children must explain it precisely. On one occasion the teacher said, "I'm more—just as interested in *how* you set up the problem as in what answer you find. If you set up a problem in a good way, the answer is *easy* to find."

Social studies work is most often reading and discussion of concepts and independent research. There are only occasional artistic, expressive, or illustrative projects. Ancient Athens and Sumer are, rather, societies to analyze. The following questions are typical of those that guide the children's independent research: "What mistakes did Pericles make after the war?" "What mistakes did the citizens of Athens make?" "What are the elements of a civilization?" "How did Greece build an economic empire?" "Compare the way Athens chose its leaders with the way we choose ours." Occasionally the children are asked to make up sample questions for their social studies tests. On an occasion when the investigator was present, the social studies teacher rejected a child's question by saying, "That's just fact. If I asked you that question on a test, you'd complain it was just memory! Good questions ask for concepts."

In social studies—but also in reading, science, and health—the teachers initiate classroom discussions of current social issues and problems. These discussions occurred on every one of the investigator's visits, and a teacher told me, "These children's opinions are important—it's important that they learn to reason things through." The classroom discussions always struck the observer as quite realistic and analytical, dealing with concrete social issues like the following: "Why do workers strike?" "Is that right or wrong?" "Why do we have inflation, and what can be done to stop it?" "Why do companies put chemicals in food when the natural ingredients are available?" and so on. Usually the children did not have to be prodded to give their opinions. In fact, their statements and the interchanges between them struck the observer as quite sophisticated conceptually and verbally, and well-informed. Occasionally the teachers would prod with statements such as, "Even if you don't know [the answers], if you think logically about it, you can figure it out." And "I'm asking you [these] questions to help you think this through."

Language arts emphasizes language as a complex system, one that should be mastered. The children are asked to diagram sentences of complex grammatical construction, to memorize irregular verb conjugations (he lay, he has lain, and so on . . .), and to use the proper participles, conjunctions, and interjections in their speech. The teacher (the same one who teaches social studies) told them, "It is not enough to get these right on tests; you must use what you learn [in grammar classes] in your written and oral work. I will grade you on that."

Most writing assignments are either research reports and essays for social studies or experiment analyses and write ups for science. There is only an occasional story or other "creative writing" assignment. On the occasion observed by the investigator (the writing of a Halloween story), the points the teacher stressed in preparing the children to write involved the structural aspects of a story rather than the expression of feelings or other ideas. The teacher showed them a filmstrip, "The Seven Parts of a Story," and lectured them on plot development, mood setting, character development, consistency, and the use of a logical or appropriate ending. The stories they subsequently wrote were, in fact, well-structured, but many were also personal and expressive. The teacher's evaluative comments, however, did not refer to the expressiveness or artistry but were all directed toward whether they had "developed" the story well.

Language arts work also involved a large amount of practice in presentation of the self and in managing situations where the child was expected to be in charge. For example, there was a series of assignments in which each child had to be a "student teacher." The child had to plan a lesson in grammar, outlining, punctuation, or other language arts topic and explain the concept to the class. Each child was to prepare a worksheet or game and a homework assignment as well. After each presentation, the teacher and other children gave a critical appraisal of the "student teacher's" performance. Their criteria were: whether the student spoke clearly, whether the lesson was interesting, whether the student made any mistakes, and whether he or she kept control of the class. On an occasion when a child did not maintain control, the teacher said, "When you're up there, you have authority and you have to use it. I'll back you up."

The teacher of math and science explained to the observer that she likes the ESS program because "the children can manipulate variables. They generate hypotheses and devise experiments to solve the problem. Then they have to explain what they found."

The executive elite school is the only school where bells do not demarcate the periods of time. The two fifth grade teachers were very strict about changing classes on schedule, however, as specific plans for each session had been made. The teachers attempted to keep tight control over the children during lessons, and the children were sometimes flippant, boisterous, and occasionally rude. However, the children may be brought into line by reminding them that "It is up to you." "You must control yourself," "you are responsible for your work," you must "set your priorities." One teacher told a child, "You are the only driver of your car—and only you can regulate your speed." A new teacher complained to the observer that she had thought "these children" would have more control.

While strict attention to the lesson at hand is required, the teachers make relatively little attempt to regulate the movement of the children at other times. For example, except for the kindergartners, the children in this school do not have to wait for the bell to ring in the morning; they may go to their classroom when they arrive at school. Fifth graders often came early to read, to finish work, or to catch up. After the first two months of school, the fifth grade teachers did not line the children up to change classes or to go to gym, and so on, but, when the children were ready and quiet, they were told they could go—sometimes without the teachers.

In the classroom, the children could get materials when they needed them and took what they needed from closets and from the teacher's desk. They were in charge of the office at lunchtime. During class they did not have to sign out or ask permission to leave the room; they just got up and left. Because of the pressure to get work done, however, they did not leave the room very often. The teachers were very polite to the children, and the investigator heard no sarcasm, no nasty remarks, and few direct orders. The teachers never called the children "honey" or "dear" but always called them by name. The teachers were expected to be available before school, after school, and for part of their lunchtime to provide extra help if needed.

Discussion and Conclusion

One could attempt to identify physical, educational, cultural, and interpersonal characteristics of the environment of each school that might contribute to an empirical explanation of the events and interactions. For example, the investigator could introduce evidence to show that the following *increased* as the social class of the community increased (with the most marked differences occurring between the two districts): increased variety and abundance of teaching materials in the classroom; increased time reported spent by the teachers on preparation; higher social-class background and more prestigious educational institutions attended by teachers and administrators; more stringent board of education requirements regarding teaching methods; more frequent and demanding administrative evaluation of teachers; increased teacher support services such as in-service workshops; increased parent expenditure for school equipment over and above district or government funding; higher expectations of student ability on the part of parents, teachers,

Social Class and Hidden Curriculum

and administrators; higher expectations and demands regarding achievement on the part of teachers, parents, and administrato... positive attitudes on the part of the teachers as to the probable occupational futures of the children; an increase in the children's acceptance of classroom assignments; increased intersubjectivity between students and teachers; and increased cultural congruence between school and community.

All of these—and other—factors may contribute to the character and scope of classroom events. However, what is of primary concern here is not the immediate causes of classroom activity (although these are in themselves quite important). Rather, the concern is to reflect on the deeper social meaning, the wider theoretical significance, of what happens in each social setting. In an attempt to assess the theoretical meaning of the differences among the schools, the work tasks and milieu in each will be discussed in light of the concepts used to define social class.

What potential relationships to the system of ownership of symbolic and physical capital, to authority and control, and to their own productive activity are being developed in children in each school? What economically relevant knowledge, skills, and predispositions are being transmitted in each classroom, and for what future relationship to the system of production are they appropriate? It is of course true that a student's future relationship to the process of production in society is determined by the combined effects of circumstances beyond elementary schooling. However, by examining elementary school activity in its social class context in the light of our theoretical perspective on social class, we can see certain potential relationships already developing. Moreover, in this structure of developing relationships lies theoretical—and social—significance.

The working-class children are developing a potential *conflict* relationship with capital. Their present schoolwork is appropriate preparation for future wage labor that is mechanical and routine. Such work, insofar as it denies the human capacities for creativity and planning, is degrading; moreover, when performed in industry, such work is a source of profit to others. This situation produces industrial conflict over wages, working conditions, and control. However, the children in the working-class schools are not learning to be docile and obedient in the face of present or future degrading conditions or financial exploitation. They are developing abilities and skills of resistance. These methods are highly similar to the "slowdown," subtle sabotage, and other modes of indirect resistance carried out by adult workers in the shop, on the department store sales floor, and in some offices.[18] As these types of resistance develop in school, they are highly constrained and limited in their ultimate effectiveness. Just as the children's resistance prevents them from learning socially legitimated knowledge and skills in school and is therefore ultimately debilitating, so is this type of resistance ultimately debilitating in industry. Such resistance in industry does not succeed in producing—nor is it

intended to produce—fundamental changes in the relationships of exploitation or control. Thus, the methods of resistance that the working-class children are developing in school are only temporarily and *potentially* liberating.

In the middle-class school the children are developing somewhat different potential relationships to capital, authority, and work. In this school the work tasks and relationships are appropriate for a future relation to capital that is *bureaucratic*. Their schoolwork is appropriate for white-collar working-class and middle-class jobs in the supportive institutions of United States society. In these jobs one does the paperwork, the technical work, the sales and the social service in the private and state bureaucracies. Such work does not usually demand that one be creative, and one is not often rewarded for critical analysis of the system. One is rewarded, rather, for knowing the answers to the questions one is asked, for knowing where or how to find the answers, and for knowing which form, regulation, technique, or procedure is correct. While such work does not usually satisfy human needs for engagement and self-expression, one's salary can be exchanged for objects or activities that attempt to meet these needs.

In the affluent professional school the children are developing a potential relationship to capital that is instrumental and expressive and involves substantial negotiation. In their schooling these children are acquiring *symbolic capital*: they are being given the opportunity to develop skills of linguistic, artistic, and scientific expression and creative elaboration of ideas into concrete form. These skills are those needed to produce, for example, culture (for example, artistic, intellectual, and scientific ideas and other "products"). Their schooling is developing in these children skills necessary to become society's successful artists, intellectuals, legal, scientific, and technical experts and other professionals. The developing relation of the children in this school to their work is creative and relatively autonomous. Although they do not have control over which ideas they develop or express, the creative act in itself affirms and utilizes the human potential for conceptualization and design that is in many cases valued as intrinsically satisfying.

Professional persons in the cultural institutions of society (in, say, academe, publishing, the nonprint media, the arts, and the legal and state bureaucracies) are in an expressive relationship to the system of ownership in society because the ideas and other products of their work are often an important means by which material relationships of society are given ideological (for example, artistic, intellectual, legal, and scientific) expression. Through the system of laws, for example, the ownership relations of private property are elaborated and legitimated in legal form; through individualistic and meritocratic theories in psychology and sociology, these individualistic economic relations are provided scientific "rationality" and "sense." The relationship to physical captial of those in society who create what counts as the dominant culture or ideology also involves substantial negotiation. The producers of symbolic capital often do not control the socially available physical capital nor the cultural uses to which it is put. They must therefore negotiate for money for their own projects. However, skillful application of one's cultural capital may ultimately lead to social (for example, state) power and to financial reward.

The executive elite school gives its children something that none of the other schools does: knowledge of and practice in manipulating the socially legitimated tools of analysis of systems. The children are given the opportunity to learn and to utilize the intellectually and socially prestigious grammatical, mathematical, and other vocabularies and rules by which elements are arranged. They are given the opportunity to use these skills in the analysis of society and in control situations. Such knowledge and skills are a most important kind of *symbolic capital*. They are necessary for control of a production system. The developing relationship of the children in this school to their work affirms and develops in them the human capacities for analysis and planning and helps to prepare them for work in society that would demand these skills. Their schooling is helping them to develop the abilities necessary for ownership and control of physical capital and the means of production in society.

The foregoing analysis of differences in schoolwork in contrasting social class contexts suggests the following conclusion: the "hidden curriculum" of schoolwork is tacit preparation for relating to the process of production in a particular way. Differing curricular, pedagogical, and pupil evaluation practices emphasize different cognitive and behavioral skills in each social setting and thus contribute to the development in the children of certain potential relationships to physical and symbolic capital, to authority, and to the process of work. School experience, in the sample of schools discussed here, differed qualitatively by social class. These differences may not only contribute to the development in the children in each social class of certain types of economically significant relationships and not others but would thereby help to *reproduce* this system of relations in society. In the contribution to the reproduction of unequal social relations lies a theoretical meaning and social consequence of classroom practice.

The identification of different emphases in classrooms in a sample of contrasting social class contexts implies that further research should be conducted in a large number of schools to investigate the types of work tasks and interactions in each to see if they differ in the ways discussed here and to see if similar potential relationships are uncovered. Such research could have as a product the further elucidation of complex but not readily apparent connections between everyday activity in schools and classrooms and the unequal structure of economic relationships in which we work and live.

Notes

1. S. Bowles and H. Gintis, *Schooling in Capitalist America: Educational Reform and the Contradictions of Economic Life* (New York: Basic Books, 1976).

2. B. Bernstein, *Class, Codes and Control, Vol. 3. Towards a Theory of Educational Transmission*, 2d ed. (London: Routledge & Kegan Paul, 1977); P. Bourdieu and J. Passeron, *Reproduction in Education, Society and Culture* (Beverly Hills, California: Sage, 1977); M. W. Apple, *Ideology and Curriculum* (Boston: Routledge & Kegan Paul, 1979).

3. But see, in a related vein, M. W. Apple and N. King, "What Do Schools Teach," *Curriculum Inquiry* 6 (1977): 341–58; R. C. Rist, *The Urban School: A Factory for Failure* (Cambridge, Mass.: MIT Press, 1973).

4. The definition of social class delineated here is my own, but it relies heavily on my interpretation of the work of E. O. Wright, *Class, Crisis and the State* (London: New Left Books, 1978); Bourdieu and Passeron, *Reproduction in Education*; and R. Williams, *Marxism and Literature* (New York: Oxford University Press, 1977).

5. New York Stock Exchange, *Census* (New York: New York Stock Exchange, 1975); J. D. Smith and S. Franklin, "The Concentration of Personal Wealth, 1922–1969," *American Economic Review* 64 (1974): 162–67; J. R. Lampman, "The Share of Top Wealth Holders in National Wealth, 1922–1956," A Study of the National Bureau of Economic Research (Princeton, New Jersey: Princeton University Press, 1962).

6. For discussion of schools as agencies of social and economic legitimation see L. Althusser, *Lenin and Philosophy and Other Essays*, trans. B. Brewster, (New York: Monthly Review Press, 1971); J. Anyon, "Elementary Social Studies Textbooks and Legitimating Knowledge," *Theory and Research in Social Education* 6 (1978): 40–55; J. Anyon, "Ideology and United States History Textbooks," *Harvard Educational Review* 49 (1979): 361–86.

7. Wright, *Class, Crisis and State*; H. Braverman, *Labor and Monopoly Capital: The Degradation of Work in the Twentieth Century* (New York: Monthly Review Press, 1974); A. Levison, *The Working Class Majority* (New York: Penguin Books, 1974).

8. While relationships of control in society will not be discussed here, it can be said that they roughly parallel the relationships of control in the work place, which will be the focus of this discussion. That is, working-class and many middle-class persons have less control than members of the upper-middle and capitalist classes do, not only over conditions and processes of their work but over their nonwork lives as well. In addition, it is true that persons from the middle and capitalist classes, rather than workers, are most often those who fill the positions of state and other power in United States society.

9. Occupations may change their relation to the means of production over time—as the expenditure and ownership of capital change, as technology, skills, and the social relations of work change. For example, some jobs that were middle-class, managerial positions in 1900 and necessitated conceptual laying out and planning are now working class and increasingly mechanical, for example, quality control in industry, clerical work, and computer programming. See H. Braverman, *Labor and Monopoly Capital.*

10. The U.S. Bureau of the Census defines *poverty* for a nonfarm family of four as a yearly income of $6,191 a year or less. U.S. Bureau of the Census, *Statistical Abstract of the United States: 1978* (Washington, D.C.: U.S. Government Printing Office, 1978) p. 465, table 754.

11. U.S. Bureau of the Census, "Money Income in 1977 of Families and Persons in the United States," *Current Population Reports* Series P-60, No. 118 (Washington, D.C.: U.S. Government Printing Office, 1979) p. 2, table A.

12. Ibid.

13. This figure is an estimate. According to the Bureau of the Census, only 2.6 percent of families in the United States have money income of $50,000 or over. U.S. Bureau of the Census, *Current Population Reports* Series P-60. For figures on income at these higher levels, see Smith and Franklin, "The Concentration of Personal Wealth, 1922–1969."

14. Smith and Franklin, "Concentration of Personal Wealth."

15. For other similarities alleged to characterize United States classrooms and schools but which will not be discussed here, see R. Dreeben, *On What is Learned in School* (Reading, Mass.: Addison-Wesley, 1968); P. Jackson, *Life in Classrooms* (New York: Holt, Rinehart & Winston, 1968); and S. Sarasan, *The Culture of School and the Problem of Change* (Boston: Allyn and Bacon, 1971).

16. Indeed, strikingly little teaching occurred in either of the working-class schools, and this naturally curtailed the amount that the children learned. Incidentally, it increased the amount of time that had to be spent by the researcher to collect data on teaching style and interaction.

17. A dominant feeling, expressed directly and indirectly by teachers in this school, was boredom with their work. They did, however, in contrast to the working-class schools, almost always carry out lessons during class times.

18. See, for example, discussions in A. Levison, *The Working-Class Majority* (New York: Penguin Books, 1974); S. Aronowitz, "Marx, Braverman, and the Logic of Capital," *The Insurgent Sociologist* 8 (1978): 126–46; and S. Benson, "The Clerking Sisterhood: Rationalization and the Work Culture of Saleswomen in American Department Stores, 1890–1960," *Radical America* 12 (1978): 41–55.

22 The Evaluator as Artist

Robert Donmoyer

Introduction

McNeil would probably characterize Donmoyer's article as "humanistic." While Donmoyer might not dispute this judgment, we would propose that the phrase "qualitative evaluation" more aptly describes Donmoyer's work.

The use of the artist as a model for the educational evaluator or "critic" has been developed primarily by Elliot Eisner and his students, such as Donmoyer, McCutcheon, Vallance, and others. Very briefly, the educational critic is to attune her- or himself to classroom activity much as a connoisseur would experience and assess a painting or a dance. The objective is to render what occurs more fully and subtly than quantitative evaluation procedures permit. Donmoyer reports on just such a qualitative evaluation.

- As you read you might ask yourself to what extent is that objective achieved?
- What problems with the artistic analogy come to mind?
- If you recall the history of the field, in particular its close ties to behaviorist psychology and scientific management, you can begin to appreciate some of the theoretical and political difficulties qualitative critics like Donmoyer have faced and face today.

An earlier version of this paper was presented at the 1979 Annual Meeting of the American Eduational Research Association, San Francisco, California. Reprinted, with permission, from *Journal of Curriculum Theorizing* 2, no. 2 (Summer 1980), pp. 12–26.

O wad some pow'r the giftie gie us
To see oursels as others see us!
R. Burns

The limitations of the evaluation field's traditional emphasis on measurement of outcomes in terms of preestablished goals has prompted the development of alternative evaluation models and new roles of the educational evaluator. Levine's adversary model,[1] for example, casts evaluators in the roles of prosecution and defense attorneys. Scriven's goal-free model[2] transforms the evaluator into a sort of latter day philosopher-king. In the illuminative evaluation model of Partlett and Hamilton,[3] the evaluator becomes a quasi-anthropologist sans anthropological theory; and in Stake's responsive approach,[4] the evaluator turns into a quasi-journalist who may occasionally editorialize but, for the most part, simply observes and interviews and then reports his findings.

In addition to these models, an artistic model of educational evaluation, a model rooted in art and literary criticism, has begun to emerge. Mann[5] was the first to utilize an artistic metaphor to conceptualize curriculum evaluation. He suggested that a curriculum might be viewed as a work of art and that the curriculum evaluator might function much as a literary critic does. Willis[6] and Kelly[7] expanded Mann's initial discussion. Advocates of the literary criticism model tended to focus on curriculum in its preactive form; in addition, most of the discussions of the literary criticism model emerged out of a reconceptualist orientation toward the curriculum field, an orientation that is concerned with development of new ways of talking about curriculum and suspicious of the field's traditional ameliorative emphasis.[8]

In the mid 1970s, Elliot Eisner[9] proposed a somewhat different version of the artistic model of curriculum evaluation in his discussions of educational connoisseurship and educational criticism. Eisner's examples were drawn from art rather than literary criticism, yet this difference was not the significant one. More significant was his expanded focus that included the interactive curriculum within the artistic evaluator's field of vision; also significant was Eisner's self-conscious acceptance of both evaluation's traditional ameliorative function and its traditional reliance on social and behavioral science, although both the method of amelioration and the function of social science were somewhat redefined.

This paper focuses largely on the Eisner version of the artistic model, a version that assumes a weaker, more metaphorical relationship between the educational critic and the critic in the arts and in the field of literature. The paper grew out of the realization that while much has been written about educational criticism, there have been few actual examples of educational criticism presented for public scrutiny and even fewer discussions of the problems encountered by the evaluator employing an artistic approach to evaluation in real classrooms to evaluate real programs and real teachers. My plan, therefore, is twofold. First, I will illustrate the central ideas of artistic evaluation with excerpts from and references to critiques of two classrooms. These educational criticisms were part of a more general qualitative evaluation of the implementation of a curriculum in a California school district. Second, I will focus on certain problems with the artistic model of curriculum evaluation that emerged during and after this particular evaluation. Before proceeding, however, it seems important to describe more fully the specific setting and circumstances of the evaluation from which the two criticisms were taken.

The Evaluation: Setting and Circumstances

The Curriculum

The Curriculum that was being evaluated was the City Building Educational Program,[10] a multidisciplinary, experientially oriented curriculum emphasizing group-process skills, problem solving, and the development of intuition. The curriculum that was developed by a team of educators and architectural consultants is organized around activities as opposed to objectives—specifically, activities related to the planning and construction of a city of the future. The particular version of the City Building Educational Program implemented in the evaluated setting emphasized architecture and, in fact, architects and students of architecture served as classroom consultants. The curriculum guide does not designate a specific age group with which the curriculum is to be used, but many of the activities, for example, activities related to scale, require skills that most students do not possess until they reach the upper elementary or middle school years. The curriculum is designed to be somewhat open-ended, however, so in principle it could be adapted to different ages by eliminating or altering some of the activities.

The Curriculum and the School District

The school district where the evaluation occurred was located in a rural area of California with a large percentage of migrant students. The City Building Program in this district was, in fact, partially funded with migrant education funds and was directed by the director of Migrant Education. He was personally enthusiastic about the program's activity-oriented philosophy and felt such an orientation was particularly appropriate to the needs of migrant students. The program was also supported by a grant from the school board. To appeal to this group, the program's name was changed to the "City Building Basic Skills Program," and its potential for helping students learn the 3 Rs was emphasized. In the curriculum guide, this benefit is treated peripherally.

The City Building Program is designed as a one-year curriculum; due to funding delays, it was not implemented in this district until February. The program was implemented by five volunteer teachers in their respective classrooms after a brief in-service training program. Several teachers had previously used the program in the district's summer program for migrant children. The program was implemented at these levels: kindergarten, first grade, third grade, a fifth-sixth grade combination, and seventh grade.

The Evaluation

The evaluation consisted of a qualitative assessment of the curriculum guide itself, educational criticisms of the five classrooms that had implemented the program, and an overview of the program based on issues raised in the specific classroom and curriculum criticisms. The evaluation was conducted by two evaluators from Stanford University. Each evaluator observed and critiqued two or three classrooms individually: the critique of the curriculum guide and the program overview were based on consultation between the two evaluators. Individual classroom criticisms were written after an extremely brief period of observation: two school days in the beginning of June. Budgetary considerations precluded more extended observation time.

The evaluation was to be formative in purpose, and its audience was to be the program's teachers and directors. We were informed, however, that the program participants might opt to distribute the evaluation report to other administrators and to the members of the school board. These groups would decide whether the City Building Program would be continued, terminated, expanded, or altered in some other way.

This cursory description of the evaluation context should be sufficient to serve as a backdrop for the following discussion. The first part of that discussion focuses on the central ideas of artistic evaluation and uses two of the criticisms from the City Building evaluation to illustrate these ideas.

The Evaluator as Artist

Aesthetic Content and Aesthetic Form

The educational critic functions as an artist and art critic in two related ways. First, he or she focuses on the aesthetic aspects, that is, the qualities, of an educational experience. Second, he or she uses aesthetic forms of communication to present his or her findings to the audience.

Langer[11] has emphasized that artistic symbols are presentational in character, that is, their meaning is embodied in their form. Ordinary discourse, as well as discourse in science and mathematics, utilizes representational symbols: "c-a-t" and "1 + 1 = 2" have no meaning in and of themselves. Rather they receive their meaning by conventional association.

Representational symbols and the extended symbolizing process known as reasoning have great utility. Discursive forms, however, cannot accommodate all aspects of experience. Certain aspects of experience, the subjective aspects (that is, "the direct feeling of it") "will not take the impress directly or indirectly of discursive form."[12] The presentational symbol of the artist, however, allows the translation of what is subjective, that is, "unspeakable, ineffable," into a form that is objective and, hence, communicable.

The evaluator as artist, therefore, utilizes artistic symbols and artistic form to communicate those aspects of the educational process that traditional evaluators and even most ethnographers ignore: the qualities extant in a particular educational experience, or—to use Vallance's phrase—the "personal lived-in quality of curriculum"[13]—the qualities of curricular experience as valued both intrinsically and because they impact on future growth.[14]

Metaphor

Because the critic communicates through the written word, metaphorical language is an essential tool for the evaluator as artist attempting to portray curricular experience. Metaphor was used extensively in the educational criticisms prepared for the City Building evaluation. For example, in "Shades of Deja Vu in a Third Grade Classroom," metaphorical language was used to add a qualitative dimension to the physical description of the classroom.

Throughout the room books and papers form unplanned collages on desk tops and shelves. In the back of the room, partially hidden from view by a permanent room divider, large sheets of insulation fall haphazardly against the wall. Nearby commercially prepared ecological activity cards spill out of their package onto countertop and floor, while large cardboard boxes covered with dog-eared black construction paper and white construction paper stripes lay exhausted atop one another like victims of a knockdown, drag-out barroom brawl.

Metaphorical language was also used to portray personal qualities of key participants. In "Democracy and Education is Alive and Well and Living in Mr. Diemo's Seventh Grade City Building Classroom," I attempted to use metaphor to capture qualities that words like charismatic can only point to.

Energizing the activities of all the groups and particularly the activities of the planning commission is the electric personality of the teacher, Mr. Diemo. With his wire-rim glasses, his dark blue corduroy pants, and a blue and white gingham shirt that could easily feel at home on the cover of a John Denver album, Mr. Diemo . . . projects a contemporary image . . . Mr. Diemo is a consummate theatrical performer. His voice sings with a velvet intensity; his movements seem almost dancelike. Even when standing still, talking to students about their various activities, his hips mirror the emotion of his voice, springing or sliding or oozing from side to side, as though under the influence of Bob Fosse's choreography. His arms and shoulders move, too, often in broad, intense, expressively flowing gestures not unlike the gestures of a French cabaret singer.

Metaphor was relied on, too, to characterize the qualitative aspects of interactions. When Mr. Diemo's homework assignment to the class was unclear and the aide supplied by City Building funds interrupted him to inform him of his lack of clarity, this interruption was characterized as being done "with good buddy assuredness." When the third grade teacher, Mr. Nopata, responded to the greetings of students, his response was likened to the response of "a hip Nelson Rockefeller on the stump, acknowledging . . . greetings with the broadest of smiles." Teacher-student interactions within the classroom were also described with the aid of metaphor. Concerning the theatrical Mr. Diemo, I wrote:

Yes, Mr. Diemo is a skilled and energetic performer, yet there is no proceneum arch in sight. Clearly this is not to be a one-man show; rather this is participatory, environmental, improvisational theater. Here, to paraphrase the astute social commentator James Durante, everybody is expected to get into the act.

"Democracy and Education is Alive and Well and Living in Mr. Diemo's Seventh Grade City Building Classroom" also contains the following somewhat more specific but still metaphorical description of student-instructor interactions.

Tom Messanger, the architect consultant for this class is in the front of the room leading the class in solving . . . the problem. His gruff, somewhat ponderous and professorial tone does not appear to command the same sort of natural respect and rapport engendered by Mr. Diemo or Mark. Hints of an us-against-them tug-of-war tension, so commonplace between teacher and students in middle school classrooms and so remarkably absent from this classroom yesterday, now begin to emerge. Students begin talking to each other, seemingly about extraneous matters; individual students begin making audible, joking asides. When these things occur, Mr. Diemo either raises his hands like a cheerleader trying to quiet booing fans at a football game, or he verbalizes what appears to be this classroom's normally unspoken commandment, "Be serious above all." These unobtrusive interventions settle the offenders, and Mr. Messanger and the class can proceed to solve the problem.

Thus, metaphorical language is an important tool for the evaluator as artist. It is not the only tool borrowed from the arts and literature, however. Kelly[15] also emphasizes the importance of plot, theme, and voice.

Voice

Kelly[16] and Willis[17] have emphasized that the adoption of a point of view is inevitable with any form of evaluation. Within the artistic model, however, the subjective dimension of the critique is made readily apparent through the development of voice. As Kelly notes, voice is "a way of expressing the person of the speaker, of letting the reader know where the narrator stands and how he feels about the subject. . . ."[18]

The "person of the speaker" and the personal perspective from which the classroom is being viewed are made quite apparent in the following introspective musings that come near the beginning of "Shades of Deja Vu in a Third Grade Classroom."

As we walk on, I begin to sense that my earlier feelings of deja vu have begun to be warmed by touches of sentiment and nostalgia. Lately I had been in too many classrooms whose curriculum mimicked not only the limited content but also the restrictive form of standardized achievement tests, and I had seen too many teachers behave as cold, detached accountants, unfeelingly prescribing work to robotlike students and then auditing the work the robots produced. Bob Nopata's classroom promised a much-needed respite from these experiences. Here was someone who would return me to the educational values of an earlier era, an era now more distant than the year would indicate. Here was someone who promised to transport me to a time when the excessive order and regimentation that are today's educational virtues would have been seen, to polemicists at least, as symptoms of a "crisis in the classroom"; here was someone who could return me to a time when concern for "why children fail" and "how children learn" took precedence over the mere shaping of behavior; here was someone who could return me to an era when educational attention was not limited to grade equivalency scores but was also focused on "the lives of children."

To my surprise, however, the recollection of these polemics of an earlier era also begins to call up a cool caution to play counterpoint to the warmth of nostalgia. I recall that when polemics were transformed to practice, excessive regulations too often were replaced by the absence of any sort of order, and pedagogical anarchy resulted. I also recall that a myopic concern with thinking and the development of cognitive processes often let poor penmanship, careless arithmetic errors, and other manifestations of sloppiness and carelessness go unnoticed and uncorrected; parents (many of whom were secretaries and accountants whose jobs depended on neatness and accuracy) were legitimately confused and concerned. Finally, I remember that often in the past, concern with the quality of classroom life and a commitment to "love kids" was unaccompanied by a sense of pedagogical responsibility; in such instances children often did not acquire the skills necessary to function in a world where one is not automatically loved. Clearly, educational climates within a nation change for a multitude of reasons, many related more to general political and economic factors than to anything educators do or do not do. Still, as with the reform-minded progressives during the first half of the century,[19] the educational reformers in the sixties must be held partially responsible for their own demise. This thought considerably darkens the feelings of deja vu that just moments earlier had been brightened by nostalgic sentiment.

Plot

Plot is another device the educational critic borrows from the arts and literature. The critic does not simply present a chronology of classroom events (what Kelly would call plot-line) but infuses description with notions of causation and intentionality. The following description of how the City Building Program's emphasis on democratic decision making was actualized in Mr. Nopata's classroom demonstrates the use of plot by the evaluator as artist.

Evaluator as Artist

Ricky, then, in what appears to be a desperate move, spits out that he does not like Lisa because she has freckles. Lisa begins crying.

Bob's rich baritone voice retains its almost singsong, Captain Kangaroo gentleness as he reminds Ricky of the time when Ricky had come to him in tears because some students were teasing him because he was Filipino. He gently prods Ricky to see the relationship between this event and his dislike of Lisa because she has freckles.

Students now pick up on this theme, although not as gently. One boy taunts, "Willie has freckles. Ain't he gonna be your friend anymore?" Other students begin pointing to freckles on their own faces or on the faces of other students. Some students get out of their seats and cross over to Ricky's desk. Before long most of the students are out of their seats displaying the sort of lynch-mob psychology that made Alexander Hamilton distrust democracy.

Faced with the onslaught, Ricky, too, begins to cry. Finally Marshall Bob returns law and order to the classroom by requiring students to take their seats. He gently tells an almost hyperventilating Ricky to step outside with him. Ricky, however, does not move. Bob repeats calmly, "Come on." Ricky manages to emit a hostile, "No!" through the cracks of near frantic inhaling and exhaling. Lisa, still crying, says to Ricky, "Now you know how I feel." She sounds more wounded than bitter. A "yes" manages to squeak out of Ricky's still quite enlarged breaths.

Bob tells Ricky to take deep breaths. Then, as he sits on the desk beside Ricky, Bob repeats rhythmically, calmly, calmingly, "Deep breaths, deep breaths, deep breaths. . . ." As he does this, Bob looks at me, his face glowing like a self-satisfied tap dancer on amateur night who brazenly solicits the audience's approval and applause. Clearly, Bob is sending me a message, a message which I read, "Isn't this great! Isn't this exciting!" I turn away, unsure of the answer I wish to send back. Three minutes more of "deep breaths, deep breaths, deep breaths. . . ." Then when Medea-size rage is finally reduced to muted sobs, it is sermon time. Reverend Nopata's topic is prejudice; his text is an incident which another teacher had that morning related in the teachers' room. He tells how the teacher had always thought someone was stupid and fat and clumsy and how pleased the teacher was when she found out that the person was only fat and clumsy, not stupid.

At the conclusion of this little sermon, Lisa begins to talk about her feelings. Seeming more like an adult participant in a group therapy session than a third grader in a classroom, Lisa coolly discusses how Ricky had hurt her. Ricky, several minutes closer to his optimum point of emotion upset and missing Lisa's verbal prowess must content himself with a "Me, too," after one of Lisa's articulate renderings of the hurt she has felt.

This little drama begins to wander aimlessly, unable to write itself a final act and provide the resolution only final acts can bring.

Theme

Theme also plays a part in the writings of both the art and educational critic. In the two criticisms serving as examples, in fact, theme more than plot provides the organizational focus, the sense of unity. In "Shades of Deja Vu," for example, the dominant theme—that Mr. Nopata's curriculum has the advantages and disadvantages of earlier progressive and open education curricula—emerges at the outset in the description of the classroom and the teacher and reemerges throughout the remaining descriptions as well as in the interpretive and evaluative comments presented in an introspective context throughout the paper. Although no single theme dominates the descriptive section of "Democracy and Education," subthemes such as student involvement, student self-discipline, the teacher as group member and group leader, and improvisation in the classroom can be found. These subthemes are tied together in the subsequent interpretive and evaluative section (in this criticism, conscious interpretation and evaluation generally follow description), which relates classroom practice to John Dewey's educational thought.

Artistic Construction and Reconstruction

The educational critic's role is not only artistic because he focuses on the qualities of experience and utilizes the tools of the artist to communicate these qualities. There is also a less literal, more metaphorical meaning of art that applies to the evaluator as artist. This is the meaning Nisbet[20] employs when he speaks of sociology as an art form and the meaning James[21] uses when he calls teaching an art. This meaning is tied to a constructivist conception of knowledge and action. Constructivists argue that human beings create their world. It is believed that reality is not perceived directly; rather, external reality is thought to be mediated by schemata that are at times the unconscious by-products of social interaction and at other times the result of a more personal construction process analogous to the creative process of the artist. Both types of constructions are relevant to the work of the evaluator as artist.

The Evaluator as Artist and the Process of Artistic Reconstruction

Unlike many other evaluators, the evaluator as artist acknowledges that while "the world of nature ... does not 'mean' anything to molecules, atoms, and electrons,"[22] such is not the case with human beings. Since the meaning people impose upon reality ultimately impacts on the way people think and act, the evaluator as artist is concerned with understanding not only personal meanings of relevant actors but also intersubjective meanings that exist not only in the minds of individuals but also in classroom practice.[23] Such understanding is important for external decision makers; it may also be important to participants since meaning can often be unconscious.

Both criticisms make at least an attempt to describe extant meanings within each classroom. "Shades of Deja Vu," for example, discusses the intersubjective meaning of reading in Mr. Nopata's class by describing both classroom practice (limited time devoted to reading; reading for utilitarian purposes only) and personal perceptions (a female student: "Oh, we don't have time for reading.") In "Democracy and Education," the personal and intersubjective meanings of the traditional skill areas were also probed through observation and interviews.

Evaluator as Artist

Although attempts were made to understand and communicate events from the perspective of participants, the limited amount of time spent in the classroom precluded any sophisticated probing of the deep structure of classroom interaction or individual action. Indeed certain anthropologists have argued that no amount of observation time will lead to an internal understanding. Khleif,[24] for example, argues that since a classroom observer can never really be a participant and since he or she is already familiar with the culture and language of the society, he or she will not undergo "cultural shock," and therefore his- or herself will not undergo the "configuration change" required to see from participants' perspectives. Khleif may overstate this point somewhat; nevertheless, for whatever reason, what I saw in the two classrooms critiqued was as much a result of what I brought to the classroom, both my tacit and propositional knowledge, as what was actually there.

The Evaluator as Artist and the Process of Artistic Construction

From the constructivist perspective, the subjective character of the evaluation is not a weakness but a strength, for evaluation cannot avoid being subjective. For the constructivist, reality is multidimensional and any one vantage point will reveal only partial understanding. The evaluator as artist has the ability to objectify what he sees from the perspective he occupies by virtue of his own unique history. Hence, he or she can help participants and other decision makers to see aspects of the curriculum they may have overlooked and to see things they have seen before from a different angle.

Particularly helpful in this regard are the various theoretical constructions, both scientific, quasi-scientific, and consciously unscientific, supplied by the various disciplines and fields of study. These constructions are not used for purposes of lawlike prediction and control, although they may help approach questions of probable causes and effects more judiciously. Their primary function, however, is to serve as aids to perception. Individually they simplify reality by providing focus and by translating the anticipatory schemata of perception[25] and the tacit knowledge of experience[26] into discursive form. When used in combination with each other, however, these theoretical constructions also help us see more completely.

In addition to tacit knowledge [I had] gleaned from six years as a teacher sympathetic to experientially oriented curricula such as the City Building Educational Program, various theoretical knowledge was employed in interpreting and evaluating events in the two City Building classrooms I critiqued. In "Democracy and Education," for example, Spolin's[27] theory of improvisation for the theater was used to explain why Mr. Diemo's improvisational style of teaching seemed to be working, and James Moffett's[28] theory of language development was used to evaluate certain benefits with respect to language development that might accrue from his interactive style of teaching. In addition, as the title of the criticism implies, the educational thought of John

Dewey (and also criticisms of Dewey's position) was also used extensively to evaluate the City Building curriculum as implemented in this classroom. For example, these comments followed a brief discussion of Dewey's cautionary notes on democratic organization of the classroom:

> Mr. Diemo, too, seems sensitive to the issues Dewey has raised with respect to transporting democratic social organization to the classroom. His use of an agenda indicates a willingness to provide direction and focus, yet the agenda is sufficiently nondirective to allow for student initiative and communal decision making. Similarly, Mr. Diemo does not hesitate to exercise direct authority when necessary. As Dewey predicts, however, such occasions are exceedingly rare; normally the class commandment, "Be serious above all," remains an unquestioned and unspoken rule. When a verbal reminder is called for, Mr. Diemo offers it in the interest of the group and the group's communal purpose, not as an expression of personal power. Mr. Diemo's conversation with Frank at the end of the second day indicates both a willingness to exercise direct authority when necessary and the manner in which such authority is exercised.
>
> Thus Mr. Diemo is both member of the group and, by virtue of his "greater maturity... and... greater knowledge of the world, of subject matters, and of individuals," he is the group's natural leader. His leadership, however, does not appear to inhibit students' perception of themselves as full participants in the group's decision-making processes. In the words of Jeff, "(T)he kids have the power to overtake the teacher if they vote on it or get up a petition.... We could rule out anything Mr. Diemo says, and I think we could do it to most any other teacher if we wanted to." These are not the words of an insurrectionist but of a responsible citizen aware of his potential political power and the socially sanctioned means for exercising it.

Various theoretical perspectives and research findings were also employed in the criticism of Mr. Nopata's classroom. Included were the findings of the effects of individualization reported by Stallings,[29] discussions of the hidden curriculum, Kliebard's[30] discussion of alternative approach to goals in curriculum organization, Eisner's[31] discussion of behavioral and expressive objectives, and cognitive psychologists' discussions of the causes of grooved thinking.[32]

Problems for the Evaluator as Artist[33]

Thus far I have tried to note and exemplify what the evaluator as artist does. Clearly he or she focuses on aspects of curriculum that are often obscured by the methodologies and/or reporting procedures of other evaluation approaches. Because the evaluator as artist illuminates idiosyncrasy, the process of curriculum, and the qualities of the curriculum process, and because he or she uses theory as an aid to perception and action, he or she should provide a valuable supplement to information of other evaluators working with other evaluation models. The evaluator as artist, however, confronts problems, particularly when he or she evaluates curricula in their interactive forms. A reading of the joint committee's proposed evaluation standards indicates that many of these problems are not unique to the evaluator as artist. Even traditional problems are magnified, however, when the evaluator's focus is largely emergent, when the evaluator is his or her own evaluation instrument, and when the evaluator's report strives for the richness and ambiguity of art rather than the precision and sterility of science.

The remainder of this paper, therefore, focuses on seven problems that arose in connection with the artistic evaluation of the implementation of the City Building Educational Program. Most of the discussion is based on information gleaned from interviews with four teachers and two administrators after they had read the evaluation report. Their opinions on the evaluation and the general evaluation approach ranged from enthusiasm to skepticism. With a few exceptions, however, the focus will be on the difficulties raised.

The Problem of Time

A primary concern in evaluating the evaluation was the effect of the limited amount of observation time. Half of the teachers and administrators interviewed found the classroom descriptions amazingly thorough and accurate (that is, the descriptions were in line with their own perceptions) and, hence, did not see the limited observation time as troublesome. The project director, for example, indicated that even negative reactions of some teachers may have resulted primarily from other factors than inaccuracies resulting from limited observation time:

I think a lot of the comments hit home. A lot of things made sense to them. I think that's what hurt them the most. I don't know if it was hurt, but the fact that you had such a deep perception of what they were doing in the class and things that they themselves want to change.

The director also discussed comments about him that were included in the program overview. In this overview I complimented the director for fostering a sense of personal and professional community among program participants but questioned whether group cohesion was not sometimes cemented with an "us-against-them" mentality that stymied external and internal criticism. Concerning these comments, the director said,

The things you said about me were really relevant. You only had about a paragraph devoted to me, but of all the things you could have said, they really made me sit and ponder and reevaluate what I was doing.

In contrast to the director, three teachers tended to be critical of the classroom descriptions, although two of these teachers did not relate their criticisms to the limited amount of time allotted for observation. In fact one of these teachers, Mr. Nopata, reported an ex post facto "ah-ha!" experience after reading the criticism of his classroom similar to the one discussed by the project director in the above quotation. One teacher, however, did see the limited amount of observation time as troublesome. Since her comments were particularly insightful, I include excerpts from the transcript of my discussion with her. The discussion focuses on Mr. Nopata's classroom.

Teacher: I just felt if it's gonna be that subjective—let me word it differently. If you were, say, a chicano college graduate who was raised in a ghetto area and maybe whose parents were illiterate and you came from a different background, I don't think a person like that would have seen things that you saw.
Author: O.K.
Teacher: And I feel like there were a lot of things maybe relevant to this area, this culture, that you didn't see. It's just like somebody coming from the country going to the city, and the things they see are like really out of—they're real, but they're really out of perspective but really not as important as if you were there for three years; then those things would become obsolete. There are more important things going on.
Author: Right, but can you see a benefit from seeing things from an outsider's perspective?
Teacher: Yeah. Like I was saying, maybe there are a lot of people who would react in the same way, and how would you deal with them so they wouldn't get those kinds of feelings?
Author: But is it helpful in the setting? Can you see that it might be beneficial to see things from somebody else's point of view? An outsider's point of view? To see things you may tend to take for granted but which may really be important?
Teacher: O.K. Right. I think maybe if you were here longer and there had been more time, we could have met more often and discussed these things. . . .
Author: O.K., that's the key. . . .
Teacher: We would have learned a lot. . . .
Author: And I would have learned a lot. . . .
Teacher: And you would have learned a lot, and there would have been a lot more going on—the feedback was missing.

This teacher may have exaggerated the effects of limited observation time. I am not at all certain whether my view of Bob's classroom would have been radically altered had I been given more time to observe. I had taught in a school located in a ghetto neighborhood myself, and, therefore, I was not totally naive to the educational implications of poverty. In addition, my impressions were relatively similar to the views expressed by other teachers and administrators

Evaluator as Artist

in the district interviewed both before and after the criticism was written. Indeed, further probing indicated that differences in perception may not have been as great as first thought; the metaphors I had chosen had, at least in this reader's mind, distorted my meaning.

Still, it is important to realize that an outsider may easily bring with him or her an insensitivity to environmental constraints that cannot be overcome during a brief period of observation. More importantly, time is essential for the kind of communication for which the evaluator as artist strives. Since the goal is to help participants see anew, that is, to see through the eyes of another person, time for interaction and feedback—not to mention time to build mutual trust and respect—is essential. When feedback and interaction are not provided for, the message of the critic can easily be distorted, either consciously or unconsciously, and written off as emanating from a totally unsympathetic value perspective. Imprecise, poetical modes of communication are particularly susceptible to such misinterpretation.

What I am saying, then, suggests that the artist as evaluator might work effectively in the context of clinical supervision, a suggestion that has already been made by others.[34,35] In addition, if outsiders are employed to bring a fresh perspective (and one principal repeatedly emphasized the need for periodic external assessment), then the artistic evaluator's role ought to be quite similar to the evaluator's role outlined in the "alternative and extended view" of evaluation discussed by the Stanford Evaluation Consortium.[36] This view states, among other things, that "(t)he evaluator, instead of running alongside the train making notes through the windows, can board the train and influence the engineer, the conductor, and the passengers...." It also notes that "(t)he evaluator should recognize (and act upon the recognition) that systems are rarely influenced by reports received in the mail."[37]

The Problems of Personal Description

The problems of personal description have been recognized by others who have written about artistic approaches to evaluation. Jenkins and O'Toole,[38] for example, raise the following question: "Can cryptic pen portrayals of individuals get close enough to their full, rounded uniqueness as people for the human perspective to be defensible?"[39] In attempting to answer their own question, they distinguish between round and flat characters.

Flat characters are humorous types of caricatures constructed around an idea or quality. Round characters partake of a full imaginative and moral existence. It seems unlikely that the curriculum evaluator will ever compete with the novelist in sheer roundness of characterization. Perhaps the best he can hope for is a few well-chosen suggestive phrases held together by a narrative viewpoint or some sense of an issue that can be sharply personalized (art teaches by example). If so, he is closer to the world of the theater critic than the world of the novelist, and his ethical dilemmas, vis à vis his responsibility to the subjects of the study, are increased rather than diminished.[40]

Jenkins and O'Toole might have added that even great art, with all its complexity and ambiguity, is still an abstraction and therefore an incomplete rendering of reality. To be sure, any focus on curriculum processes must be incomplete, but nobody expects an impersonal Flander's Interaction Analysis, for example, to present a full picture. The power of artistic description, however, results from the illusion of reality it creates.

The personal descriptions were troublesome to half of the teachers in the City Building evaluation. These teachers touched on the problem of multidimensionality discussed by Jenkins and O'Toole. Their primary concern, however, centered on another facet of personal descriptions that Jenkins and O'Toole touch on—the inseparability of public performance and private personality. Many of the teachers asked, "What does hair length have to do with teaching? Isn't such a personal description of me and my actions in the classroom an invasion of my privacy?"

I could certainly make a case for the inclusion of personal description in evaluation. First, I could note that teachers teach themselves as well as the curriculum,[41] and therefore a discussion of personal characteristics and values is a defensible subject for evaluation. I could also note, somewhat defensively, that the personal descriptions I employed in the illustrative criticisms were never done arbitrarily; they always related to some general point (for example, an explanation for Mr. Diemo's success with his students). Finally, I could argue that personal descriptions are important in helping a wider audience understand the qualitative experience of the curriculum, should the evaluation report be released to a wider audience.

These arguments, I believe, are valid. However, they do not obliterate the ethical problem so clearly delineated by Jenkins and O'Toole. There appear to be only two ways out of this dilemma. First, artistic evaluation can be used in the context of clinical supervision with the clear understanding that what the supervisor-critic writes will not be seen by anyone except the teacher being critiqued. Second, if an outside evaluator is used or if the supervisor-critic wishes to release his critique to a wider audience, the teacher must have veto power over the release of any or all of it. In short, questions of ethics as well as questions of utility require the artistic evaluator to initially, at least, play a formative role and write for an audience of one.

The Problem of Metaphor

The problem of personal description is intertwined with the problem of metaphor. Particularly troublesome for some were the following metaphorical sidered the use of metaphorical language a welcome relief from the staid writing of educational scientists, many teachers were bothered by the use of metaphor. Particularly troublesome for some was the following metaphorical allusions to the sixties, which were made in the opening of "Shades of Deja Vu" and which, in fact, introduced the theme that reemerged thoughout the critique.

Evaluator as Artist

Bob Nopata, the City Building Program's third grade teacher, seems like a remnant of the sixties, an aging flower child still managing somehow to bloom and grow in the sunshine despite massive changes in the societal ecology. There are updates, of course. Neat, nondescript slacks and shirt substitute for the outlandish, sometimes slovenly garb of an earlier age; tennis shoes cover what earlier might have been bare feet; a bouncy, almost cocky tennis shoe gait stands in for the sixties' ethereal shuffle. Still certain visual and auditory stimuli—an everpresent guitar, longish black hair pulled back into a ponytail, and a drooping walruslike moustache, hip speech periodically punctuated with the exclamation, "Man!"—combine with less tangible qualities to create feelings of deja vu.

Three of these less tangible qualities—a playful enthusiasm, an ideological self-assuredness, and a distaste for the status quo—begin to emerge during our very first conversation.... We sit together on the floor of Bob's classroom amid a decor that could best be characterized as early Haight-Ashbury cluttered. The bulletin boards show the neglect and decay of tenement slums....

Interestingly, the teachers who were concerned with this section did not generally question the appropriateness of fit between the metaphorical description and the described reality. Some raised the dimensionality problem discussed above, yet even these individuals conceded that Mr. Nopata relished his role as outsider and antiestablishment type and that I had "really picked up on that." Rather than appropriateness of fit, therefore, my critics were more concerned with questions of ethical appropriateness. "Was it justifiable for the evaluator to allude to the personal preference and lifestyle of the teacher even obliquely?" they asked.

Obliqueness, in fact, created difficulties in and of itself. As I discovered when I interviewed the teachers, when one says one thing to mean another, one can easily be "misread." For example, I intended the above description of Mr. Nopata to be read basically as description and not evaluation. Later on in the criticism, I made clear that I personally looked back on the sixties, both professionally and personally, with mixed feelings, just as I saw positive and negative aspects in Mr. Nopata's curriculum. Yet in retrospect, I can understand why Bob Nopata, after reading the first page of my criticism, could say, "This guy is out to get me." Clearly many people, particularly in a conservative school district like the one in which Bob works, do not share my ambivalence toward the age of flower children; to them, my metaphors may say more than I intended. The many positive features of Mr. Nopata's classroom pointed to later in the criticism could easily be obscured by the evocative character of the opening metaphors.

I am reluctant to abandon the use of unconventionalized metaphor. Indeed, the desire to help people to see anew requires new ways of talking. In addition, acknowledging idiosyncracy requires metaphorical description. Metaphor, however, must be used cautiously; the safeguards discussed in the context of personal description must also be employed with all metaphorical descriptions.

The Problem of Plot

The attribution of causation presents other problems. Social psychologists,[42] Jones,[43] for example, speak of the fundamental attribution error, that is, the tendency of individuals to overestimate personality or dispositional characteristics and downplay situational pressure in explaining events. When the evaluator's focus is specifically on the teacher, the evaluator can easily be even more prone than usual to commit the fundamental attribution error.

I may have committed this error in "Shades of Deja Vu." In this criticism, I specifically related many of the difficulties I saw in Mr. Nopata's classroom to Mr. Nopata's tendency to oversimplify complex questions and to his generally uncritical antiestablishment ideology. Although I indicated that the City Building curriculum provided an ideological framework to support Mr. Nopata's view of education and that the perceived "us-against-them" attitude prevalent among City Building personnel may have lent social support, I said nothing about the role Mr. Nopata's school may have played in fostering what I considered to be an uncritical antiestablishment stance.

One teacher I interviewed after the evaluation report was released indicated that Mr. Nopata's attitudes may have been at least in part the product of his situation. Specifically she indicated that all the teachers in his school were hostile toward him and wanted to get him out of the school. He was in fact transferred at the end of the year.

In a sense, the attribution of causality inevitably involves one in a chicken-or-egg type of controversy, and Collingwood's[44] discussion of the relativity of causes indicates this controversy is incapable of solution. In fact, if Collingwood is correct when he asserts that the attribution of causation is inevitably tied to purpose, then an attribution bias in favor of the teacher as opposed to the environment is not only inevitable but also desirable when, as with "Shades of Deja Vu," the designated audience—initially at least—is the teacher. The relativity of causes, however, does provide yet another reason for using artistic evaluation primarily in a formative role and for insuring that if educational criticisms are to be released to summative decision makers, program participants be guaranteed veto power over material describing them and their actions.

The Problem of Distance

Michael Apple[45] raises a related problem in his critique of the qualitative case studies in Willis's *Qualitative Evaluation*. Apple criticizes most of the case-study writers for failing to look beyond the school to the broader political and economic environment and making that broader environment a part of the explanatory framework. As Apple notes, "This very 'external' context provides substantial legitimation for the allocation of teacher time and energies and for the kind of cultural capital embodied in the school itself."[46]

Apple's criticism could be applied to the two educational criticisms being used as examples in this paper. The fault, however, lies not so much with the specific criticisms but with their general ameliorative purpose. Whenever the objective is to help practitioners to improve the curriculum, the evaluator as aritst must focus on what such decision makers have the power to improve. This means that the critic must accept the parameters set by the existing social order and direct his or her attention to options that are possible within those parameters. Thus ameliorative artistic evaluation, just as ameliorative evaluation in general, is inevitably a relatively conservative activity.

Indeed, in the two criticisms being used here for purposes of illustration, social and political forces were referred to, but reference to such forces was made in the context of putting legitimate constraints on classroom practice. Consider, for example, the following reflections on a conversation I had with Mr. Nopata about his reading program.

One could argue . . . that we should not be concerned with decoding skills and, hence, reading until we have helped children develop the cognitive processes that will be brought into play in the process of comprehending what is read. This appears to be Bob's position, so I concede that a case can be made for this position in principle. I note, however, that in this less than best of all possible worlds, social reality dictates that decoding and encoding be emphasized at the outset of schooling. I note that once students leave the confines of Bob's classroom, they will be labeled failures if they cannot read (and, I could have added, write and compute). I also note that statistics indicate that slow readers in the earlier years are almost always slow readers in high school, and I argue that even if this is a result of socially created phenomena, such phenomena must still be accommodated.

The Problem of Logistics

Some of the problems with the evaluation resulted not from the evaluation itself but, as one teacher put it, "from how the evaluation was used." In violation of the agreement between the teachers and the project director and in contradiction to statements the project director had made to us during negotiations, the evaluation report, including the classroom criticisms, was released to other administrators in the school even before the teachers had seen it, much less had an opportunity to decide to release the material. The project director's actions were understandable. He was attempting to salvage the program in the wake of Proposition 13 cutbacks, and he felt that the evaluation, which was balanced but on balance more positive than negative, might be useful. Though understandable, the project director's actions were ethically questionable and point up the need for clear reporting procedures outlined in detail and in writing.

The Problem of the Theoretician-Practitioner Gap

Happily, the problem of the theoretician-practitioner gap was a problem that existed more in my anticipations than in actuality. Even those teachers who felt a gap existed agreed that it could have been bridged with more time and more opportunity for interaction and feedback. To my surprise, no teacher was bothered by the use of theoretical references and specific citations. Eisner has argued that specific references are necessary to provide depth and intellectual support for interpretive and evaluative comments. I have always been concerned that such citations would be perceived by practitioners as an academic affection, or worse yet, as cocktail-party-style theory dropping. The teachers I interviewed, however, indicated they appreciated such citations, and some suggested the references might make an excellent reading list for an in-service seminar.

Thus, in this evaluation, the theoretician-practitioner gap was relatively narrow. Of course, I should add that it helped greatly that both evaluators had relatively extensive classroom teaching experience; the first question the teachers asked us centered on our experience in the classroom, not in the university.

Conclusion

The evaluator as artist brings a touch of humanity to the evaluation process. Not only does he or she remind us that evaluation is a human activity inescapably intertwined with human subjectivity, he or she also reminds us that education itself is rooted in human interaction. What educational practitioners perceive, believe, value, and think impacts not only on the curriculum that is taught but also on the curriculum that is learned; the evaluator as artist offers the educational practitioner an opportunity to step outside of him- or herself and view the personalized curriculum he or she teaches through the eyes of another human being.

The very humanity which is the artistic evaluator's strength, however, also poses unique problems. Seven of these problems have been discussed in this paper. Although these problems have been gleaned from informal interviews with a relatively small number of respondents after an evaluation conducted under less than ideal conditions, common sense indicates that the seven problems discussed here transcend the idiosyncracy of individual and situation. Therefore, it has been suggested that the evaluator as artist adopt primarily a formative role, possibly working within the context of clinical supervision. If the artistic evaluator is an outsider, ample time for feedback and interaction must be provided. In addition, it has been argued that the practitioner who is the subject of the artistic evaluator's criticism must retain veto power over the release of the criticism to summative decision makers or any other individual. Only if these suggestions are adhered to, can the evaluator as artist's work be ethically desirable, politically possible, and practically useful.

Notes

1. M. Levine, "Scientific Method and Adversary Model," *American Psychologist* (September 1974): 666–77.
2. M. Scriven, "Prose and Cons about Goal-Free Evaluation," *Journal of Educational Evaluation* (December 1972): 73–76.
3. M. Partlett and D. Hamilton, "Evaluation as Illumination: A New Approach to the Study of Innovating Programs," in *Curriculum Evaluation Today: Trends and Implications* by M. Partlett and D. Hamilton (New York: Macmillan, 1973).
4. R. Stake, *Evaluating the Arts in Education: A Responsive Approach* (Columbus, Ohio: Charles Merrill, 1975).
5. J. Mann, "Curriculum Criticism," *Curriculum Theory Network* (Winter 1968): 2–14.
6. G. Willis, "Qualitative Evaluation as the Aesthetic, Personal, and Political Dimensions of Curriculum Criticism," in *Qualitative Evaluation*, ed. G. Willis (Berkeley: McCutchan, 1978).
7. E. Kelly, "Curriculum Criticism and Literary Criticism: Comments on the Analogy," *Curriculum Theory Network* 5:2 (1975): 98–106.
8. W. Pinar, ed., *Curriculum Theorizing: The Reconceptualists* (Berkeley: McCutchan, 1975).
9. E. Eisner, " The Perceptive Eye: Toward the Reformation of Educational Evaluation" (Address to the American Educational Research Association, Division B, 1975); E. Eisner, "Educational Connoisseurship and Criticism: Their Form and Functions in Educational Evaluation," *Journal of Aesthetic Education* (1976): 135–50; E. Eisner, "On the Use of Educational Connoisseurship and Educational Criticism for the Evaluation of Classroom Life," *Teachers College Record* 78:3 (February 1977): 375–88.
10. D. Nelson, *The City Building Educational Program* (Hollywood: Center for City Building Program, 1975).
11. S. Langer, *Problems of Art* (New York: Charles Scribner's Sons, 1957).
12. Ibid.
13. E. Vallance, "Scanning Horizons and Looking at Weeds," in *Qualitative Evaluation*, ed. G. Willis (Berkeley: McCutchan, 1978).
14. J. Dewey, *Experience and Education* (New York: Collier Books, 1963).
15. Kelly, "Curriculum Criticism."
16. Ibid.
17. Willis, "Qualitative Evaluation."
18. Kelly, "Curriculum Criticism," p. 121.
19. L. Cremin, *Transformation of the School* (New York: Alfred A Knopf, 1964).
20. R. Nisbet, *Sociology as an Art Form* (London: Oxford University Press, 1976).
21. W. James, *Talks to Teachers* (New York: W. W. Norton & Co., 1958).
22. A. Schutz, "Concept and Theory Formation in the Social Sciences," in *Sociological Theory and Philosophical Analysis*, ed. Emmet and MacIntyre (New York: Macmillan, 1970).
23. C. Taylor, "Interpretation and the Sciences of Man," *Review of Metaphysics* XXV (1:97): 3–51.

24. B. Khleif, "Issues in Anthropological Fieldwork in the Schools," in *Education and the Cultural Process: Toward an Anthropology of Education*, ed. G. Spindler (New York: Holt, Rinehart & Winston, 1974).

25. U. Neisser, *Cognition and Reality: Principles and Implications of Cognitive Psychology* (San Francisco: W. H. Freeman, 1976).

26. M. Polyani. *Personal Knowledge* (New York: Harper & Row, 1958).

27. V. Spolin, *Improvisation for the Theater* (Evanston, Illinois: Northwestern University Press, 1963).

28. J. Moffett, *Teaching the Universe of Discourse* (Boston: Houghton Mifflin Co., 1968).

29. J. Stallings, "Individualization of Instruction" (Menlo Park, California: SRI International, undated).

30. H. Kliebard, "Reappraisal: The Tyler Rationale," in *Curriculum Theorizing: The Reconceptualists*, ed. W. Pinar (Berkeley: McCutchan, 1975).

31. E. Eisner, "Instructional and Expressive Objectives: Their Formulation and Use in Curriculum," in *Instructional Objectives*, ed. J. Popham et al. (Chicago: Rand McNally, 1969).

32. J. Steinburner, *The Cybernetic Theory of Decision* (Princeton: Princeton University Press, 1974).

33. The problems discussed in the following section refer specifically to the use of artistic approaches to research for purposes of evaluation. Elsewhere I have suggested that educational researchers have underestimated the potential of qualitative methodology and artistic modes of reporting for nonevaluative research (see R. Donmoyer, "Logical, Psychological and Phenomological Generalization: Toward a Rationale for the Use of Naturalistic Methodology and Modes of Reporting in Curriculum and Instructional Research," paper presented at AERA annual meeting, April 1979). While the use of artistic methods and modes of reporting in a nonevaluative context is not without problems, those problems are not identical to the problems confronting the artistic endeavor.

34. T. Sergiovanni and R. Starratt, *Supervision: Human Perspectives* (New York: McGraw-Hill, 1979).

35. J. Cross, "Applying Educational Connoisseurship and Criticism to Supervisory Practices" (Doctoral dissertation, University of Illinois, 1977).

36. Cronbach and Ross, 1976.

37. Ibid.

38. D. Jenkins and B. O'Toole, "Curriculum Evaluation, Literary Criticism and the Paracurriculum," in *Qualitative Evaluation*, ed. G. Willis (Berkeley: McCutchan, 1978).

39. Ibid.

40. Ibid.

41. E. Eisner, "Emerging Models for Educational Evaluation," *School Review* 80:4 (August 1974).

42. W. Harvey and J. Kidd, *New Directions in Attribution Research* (Hillsdale, New Jersey: Erlbaum, 1976).

43. E. Jones, *Attribution: Perceiving the Causes of Behavior* (Morriston, New Jersey: General Learning Press, 1972).

44. R. Collingwood, *The Idea of History* (New York: Oxford University Press, 1946).
45. M. Apple, "Ideology and Form," in *Qualitative Evaluation* (Berkeley: McCutchan, 1978).
46. Ibid.

Section IV
DIALOGUE AND DEBATE

23 Curriculum and Its Discontents

Philip W. Jackson

Introduction

This paper was the second annual state-of-the-art address read to members of the Curriculum Division of the American Educational Research Association. Philip Jackson achieved an international reputation with his *Life in Classrooms* (1969). In recent years, he has become less interested in sociology and more interested in curriculum theory. This paper represents his first major statement on the field. Clearly he is ambivalent about the reconceptualization.

As you read, pay particular attention to Jackson's use of humor in making his argument.
- Does it replace or assist logic?
- Attend also to his definition of curriculum and to his objections to past characterizations of the field as moribund.
- From this paper, in which category would you place Jackson? Why?

They had traveled a long way. Their horses bore marks of the journey—flanks caked with mud, manes matted with dust. At last, the end was near. Dismounting, the pair walked the final few yards on foot. At the edge of the cliff, they paused and gazed upon the scene below. The younger of the two, tugging at his partner's arm, broke the silence.

"Behold," he said, gesturing at the view that lay before them, "Yon lies the field of curriculum. So vast and inviting. Such a worthy object of contemplation. So ready for the harvest, ripe for the hands of willing workers. But wait! What's this? Can it be? Why

---

Presented as the invited address to Division B of the American Educational Research Association, San Francisco, April 1979. Reprinted from *Curriculum Inquiry* 1, no. 1 (1980), pp. 28–43. Reprinted by permission of John Wiley & Sons, Inc.

is there not more movement? Why does it lie so still? Tell me, good father, is it . . . is it alive? Or is it . . . could it be . . . (gulp!) . . . dead?"

The introductory vignette is sheer hokum, of course, inspired at some subconscious level, I suspect, by memory traces left over from viewing *Star Wars* a couple of years ago. The speaker's query, however, is not a figment of my imagination. Oddly enough, a question very much like the one raised by our fictitious traveler has been preying on our collective mind of late, or so it would seem if we were to judge by the writings of several educators, including at least two who have had the honor of addressing this division of AERA in recent years.

To the best of my knowledge, my former colleague Joseph Schwab was the first one within the recent past to raise this ominous query. (The adjective *ominous* seems necessary because, through our exposure to B-rated movies and other forms of melodrama, we have come to expect the worst when circumstances require determining whether death is apparent or real.) Actually, Schwab answered the question without even bothering to ask it in the opening lines of his widely read essay "The Practical: A Language for Curriculum." The year was 1970. Herewith, Schwab's delivery of the bad news.

"I shall have three points," he began, innocently enough. "The first is this: The field of curriculum is moribund. It is unable by its present methods and principles to continue its work and contribute significantly to the advancement of education."[1]

For all its starkness, Schwab's health bulletin did contain a ray of hope, though its light was faint indeed. As we know, the word *moribund* allows within its meaning for the possibility of a miraculous recovery, but as we also know, the chances of that happening are mighty slim. In short, the message could hardly be called optimistic. The field of curriculum may not have been completely gone at the time Schwab took its pulse, but if we were to believe his prognosis, its end was close at hand.

Just how close the end really was back in 1970 has been brought into question by subsequent readings of the vital signs. Consider, for example, Dwayne Huebner's address to this division six years after Schwab's gloomy pronouncement. Huebner's debt to Schwab's initial pessimism was made explicit in the title of his paper—"The Moribund Curriculum Field: Its Wake and Our Work."[2] But the title also revealed Huebner's basic uncertainty about whether the patient was yet alive or had long since crossed the bar. For if the field was in fact still moribund, as Huebner described it, why talk about a wake? A death watch, perhaps, or even a vigil might sound all right. But "The Moribund Curriculum: Its *Wake* . . ."? That did seem to be rushing things, or so I felt on first pondering the meaning of Huebner's title.

In the body of his paper, Huebner went on to clarify the matter somewhat, though there, too, a trace of ambiguity continued to nag the close reader. For example, toward the end of his remarks Huebner emphatically declared, "the curriculum field of the past one hundred years is not just moribund; for all practical puposes it is dead."[3]

"Fair enough," the consciousness behind my skimming eye replied, "time to exchange the physician for the mortician." "But wait a minute," a reflective thought broke in, "what about the maddening phrase 'for all practical purposes'? What does that mean? Is Huebner, with that qualifier, trying to make the distinction we hear so much about these days—that between real death and clinical death? Is he saying that the curriculum field has no more brain activity but with artificial help its heart beats on?"

Almost as if he had heard my question, Huebner proceeded to speak like a man who had surreptitiously pulled the plug. The telltale sign of his guilt was a sudden switch in verb tense, from present to past. He turned to the question of why the field of curriculum *died*. He went on to assure his readers that there could be no hope of a renaissance. The only consolation he offered to those who grieved was some vague talk about the possibility of a reincarnation, but to follow these thoughts would take us deeper into the body of his thesis than present purposes allow. This passing comment on his paper is merely intended to show that Huebner, like Schwab, found it useful to muse on the question of whether the curriculum field was alive or dead. Also like Schwab, he arrived, with some waffling I fear, at a gloomy conclusion.

In 1977 and again in 1978, William Pinar of the University of Rochester delivered two papers at the annual meeting of the AERA, each of which helped to keep alive the question of the curriculum field's state of health. In the first of these, entitled "The Reconceptualization of Curriculum Studies," Pinar[4] referred specifically to the earlier observations of Schwab and Huebner, though in doing so he seemed as confused as I have been about their final judgment. When it came to reporting on what Schwab and Huebner had said, Pinar could not decide whether or not a definitive judgment had been reached. So he decided to play it safe by noting that the traditional curriculum field had been declared "terminally ill *or* already deceased."[5]

As for himself, however, Pinar seemed resigned to the more severe of the two judgments, for in the sentence immediately following the one with the ambiguous "or," he referred to the field's "demise." He then talked about an "heir to the field," thus introducing thoughts of wills, last testaments, and the like. Such talk leaves little doubt that Pinar either believed the end was past, or, like Huebner's wake, was rushing things a bit. Whichever interpretation we accept, Pinar's 1977 pronouncements could hardly be called gay spirited. If not overtly mournful, they were at least draped in black.

By last year, however, in his state-of-the-art address to Division B of the AERA, Pinar[6] was in a more cheerful mood. In his remarks he made no mention of death and dying. Instead, he described the state of the field as being "fragmented and arrested." "The state of the field is arrest," he reiterated in his concluding paragraph, thus seeming to abandon all reference to the earlier worry. Yet, for me, its echo could be heard in that final judgment, for is there not something deathlike in the word *arrest*? Perhaps I have become hypersensitive to such imagery through exposure to the views already discussed, but Pinar's words suggest the most final of all diagnoses: a cardiac arrest. Thus, the thanatotic fantasy, which Pinar had entertained earlier and which seems to have captured the imagination of Schwab, Huebner, and others, was gone perhaps but not forgotten.

My impatience with this lugubrious talk about the curriculum field's last gasps should be obvious by now. In fact, if my impatience had a voice of its own and if it were allowed to join the morbid musing long enough to have its say, it would sound something like this: "Away vultures, away! No more black garb and muted organ music. Let's pull back the velvet drapes and let some light in. The place reeks of calla lilies and smelling salts!"

"All right, all right," a calmer voice from somewhere else inside of me intones. "Settle down now, no need to be distraught. Your vexation comes through loud and clear. But what is not so clear is what really upsets you. Is it the deathbed imagery itself with its gloom and doom? Or is it the message that imagery is intended to convey? Are you seeking to defend the counterclaim that the field of curriculum is alive and well? Is that it?"

"No, that is not it," I reply, the real me speaking now. "I have no desire to debate the messengers of gloom in their own terms. I shall leave that task to more official conveyors of good cheer, such as the officers of professional societies or the authors of textbooks that deal with curricular matters."

Incidentally, one of the latter was apparently so worried about the negative effect the Schwabian diagnosis might have upon budding young teachers enrolled in education courses that he decided to end his book with an explicit rejoinder to that view. "All in all," he assured his readers in the last sentence of the text, "there is plenty of evidence that the curriculum field is not moribund but very much alive and well."[7] Can't you just hear the students in Education 101 heaving a massive sigh of relief as they read those parting words?

Regrettably, perhaps, for those who seek some bucking up, no such Panglossian heartiness guides my pen. Rather, I insist the terms themselves, the illness metaphor and all the ratiocinations that trail in its wake (no pun intended), are either silly or misleading or both. In fact, my complaint goes deeper than that. Truth be known, I am unhappy with those who speak as though there *were* such a thing as a *field* of curriculum. But talk about that deeper complaint can come later. First, some comments about the business of whatever-it-is being ill. At the risk of sounding like a teacher of English, which I am not and never was, allow me to remind us all that when we speak of the curriculum field's health, we are already guilty of a *faux pas* in the minds of sentinels who guard against lapses of grammatical or linguistic propriety. We have committed a mixed metaphor! Just think of the fun our linguistic watchdogs can have with us now.

"A sick and dying field?" someone snickers, "How would you find out if a field were alive or dead? By putting your ear to the ground? By keeping an eye out for the heaving of turf that comes with frost or by sniffing the rising vapors that the poet transforms into the breath of spring? Do living things, like earthworms and crickets, quit a dead field, or does life attack it more virulently after death than before, like maggots hungrily devouring carrion?"

We might, with effort, prevent our puckish questioner from getting after us that way. Perhaps if we were pontifical enough at the start, such quirky thoughts would never enter his head. But he does have a point. It is a bit of a trial, you must admit, trying to be serious about a sick field.

And the hidden humor concealed in the mixed metaphor and lying ready for use by the first critic who comes along is only the beginning of what we must contend with if we expect our listeners to accept such an image as more than a piece of rhetoric, a casual ornament of speech, and a rather shopworn one at that. Having introduced the thought of illness, we are practically forced to follow where it leads, regardless of whether or not movement in that direction is heuristically valuable.

And where does the thought of a sick field take us? Consider, as a start, all the associated worries and unanswered questions that crowd the mind and press for answers at the mere suggestion of someone or something (even a field) being terminally ill. "How did it get that way?" we ask. "Who is qualified to make the judgment?" "What is to be done about burial?" "Is there anything to be bequeathed?" And on and on our thoughts race, hardly knowing when or where to stop.

Of course, the skilled user of a metaphor does know where to stop, and the three authors I have mentioned all seem to use the device skillfully and with good taste. None, for example, gets into the nitty-gritty of what to do with the remains. All have the good sense to say nothing about the graveside ceremony.

Nonetheless, I cannot help wondering whether some of the metaphor-inspired questions they raise are worth asking. Take, as an example, Pinar's talk about an heir to the field. Such talk fits perfectly, of course, within the mental set created by thoughts of moribundity. But is that what those of us who care about the curriculum of our schools should be worrying about? I wonder. Remove the metaphor, and the question of who shall be the heir goes with it.

Even more important, perhaps, than the danger of being led to unproductive questions is the associated possibility of the metaphor dictating harmful attitudes about the real world. For example, the deathbed image seems to encourage a feeling of there being a sharp break between the present and the past, a sense, in other words, of historical discontinuity. Now none of our three authors explicitly condoned such an attitude, and I suspect all three would strongly oppose its creation, but in a sense the deathbed metaphor did the dirty work without their complicity.

Schwab, for example, tells us that he recoils at the thought of counting all the people and books devoted to restating the Tyler rationale or the case for behavioral objectives or the virtues and vices of John Dewey. "Me too," I want to reply, "Enough, already." At the same time, I have this nagging unease about saying that we've heard enough about Tyler or behavioral objectives or Dewey: in doing so *within the context of the "dead field" frame of mind*, we encourage those who might heed our words to turn away completely from a contemplation of and a building upon our own past. The temperament of educators is notoriously fickle already, without our acting in ways that might make it more so.

My unease must not be understood to be an argument against using metaphors to enlighten educational thought. I love metaphors. They are, if I may speak metaphorically on their behalf, among our most useful tools of thought. But, like all tools, they can be abused and do damage when used improperly. And that's what worries me.

I have no real proof, I must admit, that all this talk about the demise of the curriculum field has done any harm to anyone or anything. Quite possibly it has not. Yet when it continues for almost an entire decade, when a prominent textbook writer feels obliged to assure his readers that the field is alive and well, and when I feel my own thinking pulled along by the sheer drama of the question, I begin to wonder whether it's time to end such talk.

I have the same feeling, as I have already said, about the other half of the mixed metaphor—the idea of there being such a thing as a curriculum *field*. But I hesitate to talk in public about my misgivings, for fear of being run out of town on a pole. Even the slightest hint of an attack on such a time-honored way of thinking is bound to rub a lot of people the wrong way. It probably sounds to them as though I were out to rob folks of something of value, something that gives them status.

Think of them all—curriculum designers, curriculum developers, curriculum evaluators, professors of curriculum, curricularists (a generic term that Pinar seems to have invented to cover just about everybody), and plain old curriculum persons (the tag Huebner seems to prefer) with its down-home flavor and explicit appeal to our antisexist sentiments—what in heaven's name would all those folks do if it were discovered that there was no such thing as a field of curriculum? Talk about the hullabaloo triggered by the announcement that the emperor had no clothes! Declaring curriculum a nonfield would have even worse effects. Such a declaration would send shock waves throughout the pedagogical kingdom. "Besides," the wounded would complain, "no one seems to be toying with the idea of depriving psychologists or historians or physicists or mathematicians of *their* fields. Why, then, pick on the poor old curriculum workers?"

Fair enough, I'm willing to drop the issue. I'm not looking for a fight. So keep your field, curriculum people. Enjoy it. But remember, it exists only in your head. It is a figure of speech, not a territory to be defended; a mental fiction, not something that can truly be trespassed by poachers.

We know these things, of course, and therefore there is no need to say them. Yet as I read the papers by Schwab, Huebner, and Pinar, I noticed how natural it seemed for them to elaborate on the field metaphor and how easily my own imagination was engaged by their elaboration. Schwab complained about curriculum workers "fleeing the field," and I began to wonder if they were wayward sons or runaway slaves. Huebner pleaded for a "return to our roots" and a vision of migrant laborers distracted momentarily by an airplane overhead arose before my mind's eye. Pinar, convinced that the present owners of the land were dead or nearly so, mumbled something about becoming heir to the property; and in the darker regions of my mind, where the memory of a country kitchen still survives, I saw a younger me edging nervously toward the corner in which the shotgun is kept. Field. Fieldhands. Property. Heirs. Metaphors all, and all, like my dimly remembered firearm in the kitchen, to be handled with care.

So much, then, for the dangers of talking about the dead or dying curriculum field. If these words of mine are of any help in ridding us of such talk, I shall be pleased. Yet my remarks, even if successful, cannot end here, for still to be addressed is the important question of what stirred such talk in the first place. What, in other words, is the reality behind the metaphor?

My answer to that question begins in full agreement with the trio whose ideas I have been discussing. For though I do not fully share Schwab's or Huebner's or Pinar's view of the matter, I do agree with all three that there is something out there to be viewed, something worth pondering and discussing. That something, and on this the four of us also seem to agree, has chiefly to do with the intellectual outlook and occupational activity of those people who are or have been professionally engaged in speaking and writing about the curriculum of schools and closely related topics. This is a rather long-winded and loose definition of the "reality" in which we are jointly interested, but anything more precise begins to exclude things that I believe all four of us want to discuss. Also, I admit to sharing in the general confusion over what to call all those people who have something important to say about curricular matters, but rather than offering yet another neologism to pin on that amorphous glob, I shall dodge the issue.

Now when it comes to saying what it is about the outlook and activity of these speakers and writers and practitioners that is worth pondering and discussing, Schwab, Huebner, Pinar, and I begin to drift apart, not only them from me but each from the other. Yet even then I suspect we might still be in enough agreement to speak in a single voice on one additional point, which is that some important changes seem to be occurring within our loosely defined reality. More precisely, a growing number of people within my unlabeled glob seem to be unhappy about what other members of the glob, perhaps the majority, are doing or have done. Our reality, in other words, is permeated by a widespread spirit of discontent.

Why this is so, and what if anything can or should be done about it are the two most important questions to ask. I suspect that Schwab, Huebner, and Pinar would agree. Beyond this point, however, the four of us seem to part company. But rather than attempting any further specification of the differences between my view and theirs, I would prefer to concentrate on what I perceive to be true and my own interpretation of that perception. Disagreements with others will likely be evident in my discussion, so I won't bother to point them out.

If, as I claim, a spirit of discontent is sufficiently widespread to be commented upon by almost any thoughtful observer, then this must mean there is a potentially identifiable person or, more likely, group of persons responsible for generating and disseminating it. Who are they? Who are these people whom I have labeled "discontents" in the title of this paper? And what are they discontented about?

My answer to the first of these key questions is aided by spreading out the map of the United States and Western Europe that most of memorized as children and that we continue to keep tucked away in our heads for just such an occasion. On it I locate three centers of activity from which the clearest or at least the loudest expressions of discontent seem to emanate. Two of these are in England, and the third is in the United States.

The precise location of one of the British centers I would place at the Institute of Education of the University of London. The other I would place, with somewhat less confidence, at the University of East Anglia. The American center is not as easy to pinpoint, beyond saying that it lies somewhere west of New York City and east of the Mississippi. If I had to stick a tack in a map to give this center a home, I suppose I would close my eyes and aim for Hershey, Pennsylvania, or thereabouts. But don't ask me why I chose that location. Hershey just feels right. Perhaps it has something to do with my childhood love of chocolate, I'm not sure.

From each of these three centers, I see in my mind's eye lines—many of them transatlantic—connecting individuals from far-flung spots to one or another of the nuclei, thus forming three webs of overlapping and crisscrossing strands. Finally, I also envision a scattering of single, unconnected dots representing individuals who seem to be unaffiliated with any of the three centers of activity but whose voices are clearly part of the general chorus of discontent. These solitary dots are too numerous and widespread to arrange mentally, so I will simply ask that you pepper to taste your own imaginary map.

My justification for thinking of the discontents as being concentrated in this way rests on the fact that each of the three centers had spawned one or more edited volumes containing collections of essays that share a more or less common outlook on educational matters. As the best single example of the work emanating from each location, I would nominate *Knowledge and Control*,[8] edited by Michael F. D. Young of the University of London, *Beyond the Numbers Game*,[9] edited by David Hamilton of the University of East Anglia and four other British educationists, and *Curriculum Theorizing*,[10] edited by William Pinar of the University of Rochester (a bit north and west of Hershey). These three volumes, though representative, do not begin to exhaust the list that could be compiled for each cluster. They should suffice, however, to give some bibliographic justification for the divisions.

By mentioning specific books I do not mean to imply, of course, that an intellectual affiliation with any of the three clusters is necessarily defined by authorship in one or more of its publications. Some contributors to the volumes associated with one of the clusters would doubtlessly complain about being identified with the dominant perspective of the book in question. Others whose writings do not appear there might well seek to be so identified. For these reasons, it makes little sense to attempt a roster of who is in or out of any of the three foci of activity.

For similar reasons, I think it unwise to name the individuals whose work is salient within the total corpus of writings that deal with curricular matters but who would not appear on any one of the three rosters were I to attempt them—the solitary dots on our mental map. Suffice it to say that the group would include individuals as physically separate as Joseph Schwab in California and Ulf Lundgren in Sweden and as ideologically distant as Elliot Eisner and Henry Levin, both of Stanford University.

As I tune in, figuratively speaking, to the chorus of complaints issuing from both the clusters and the individuals, what sounds at first like a cacophonous babble later becomes slightly melodious. The same note is struck by more than one person, motifs issuing from one location are picked up in another, and contrapuntal harmonies emerge. The sense of listening to a babble never disappears completely, but, later, portions of the sound become familiar enough to hum to oneself. These humable passages, at least the ones that I have managed to select, comprise a sort of litany, containing the following set of verses (to be authentic, you should chant them, I suppose, in a minor key):

The Tyler rationale is out-of-date, and we have little or nothing to replace it with.

Our present ways of thinking and talking about schools and schooling do not do justice to the complexity and dignity of the human condition.

The control of the curriculum is in the hands of technologists, test makers, textbook publishers, and school administrators.

Our schools are losing sight of humanistic values and goals.

Curriculum workers have little to offer teachers that is of direct help to them.

The aesthetic, ethical, and spiritual dimensions of the educational experience are being ignored.

Our schools are damaging to many students, particularly to children of the poor and oppressed minorities.

The Tyler rationale is out-of-date, and so on.

Doubtlessly, there are other lines that should be inserted, and I may not have gotten the words exactly right in the ones I have given, but the sense is there. Furthermore, though no single contributor to the writings from which I have culled the above list would be likely to nod in agreement to the total set of assertions, I would bet that the majority of the discontents would go along with most of them. In fact, there may be no one who could not find something, perhaps even a great deal, to agree with on that list, which may not mean that the list itself is defective as a portrayal of the complaints to be found in the curricular writings I have studied, but that there is a bit of discontent in us all.

Our probable agreement with some of the items on the list also means that the total set of complaints cannot be discarded as crank letters. In fact, I fear that my flippant use of the liturgical imagery may already have created the impression that I believe these complaints are not to be taken seriously. If so, I must hasten to correct it, for my wisecrack about the complaints forming a litany was merely a crude attempt to inject a note of levity into a topic that might otherwise become intolerably grave. In truth, I see most of the items pointing to serious problems that are worthy of our genuine concern.

Because these individual problems are too numerous to treat in a single essay and the proposed solutions put forth in the writings in question are even more so, I shall now concentrate on what I perceive to be the two most general suggestions for change emanating from the discontents. The first has to do with a proposed shift in scholarly allegiances from one intellectual tradition to one or more others. The second has to do with a proposed change in the relationship between those who talk and write about curricular matters and those who are closer to educational practice, including, especially among the latter, classroom teachers. After describing each of these sets of suggestions more fully, I will close with a few caveats of my own.

The proposed shift in scholarly allegiance is away from what is increasingly referred to as "mainstream social science," a term that is usually intended to be interpreted pejoratively, and toward a wide assortment of intellectual traditions that have not heretofore been drawn upon heavily by persons interested in educational and curricular topics. These comprise, in the main, existential, phenomenological, and Marxist thought, but they also include, somewhat less prominently, the contributions of literary critics, psychoanalysts, and even a philosopher of science or two. The key ideas being drawn upon are distinctly European in flavor, with French and German influences predominating. Besides Marx and Freud, others that are frequently cited in this literature include Heidegger, Husserl, Merleau-Ponty; Sartre, Schutz, Gramsci, Polanyi, and Habermas. Taken as a whole, the ideological bias of the sources drawn upon most heavily is decidedly left of center. The major argument in support of drawing upon these new sources of ideas (new for educators, that is) is, as I understand it, that they are more helpful in thinking about and understanding the richness and complexity of educational phenomena than are the intellectual frameworks that have till now dominated educational thought. So much then for a thumbnail sketch of the first major proposal that flows from the writings of the discontents.

The second proposal, that having to do with a change in the relationship between those who talk and write about curricular matters—let's call them the academics—and those who are closer to educational practice—the practitioners—is really split into two subproposals that move in opposite directions. The first calls for a *closer* relationship between academics and practitioners; the second, for a *more distant* one. Though supporters of both subproposals can probably be found in all four quadrants of our imaginary curricular map, I see the argument for a closer relationship concentrated in our East Anglia center and that for a more distant relationship concentrated in London. I can't quite figure out how our Hershey, Pennsylvania, folks vote on this split (I suspect they are not certain either), so I'll just leave a question mark there.

The argument on behalf of a closer relationship between academics and practitioners is probably the easier of the two to understand, for it has been around a long time. Since at least the turn of the century, and probably long before that, both academics and practitioners have lamented the gap of communication and understanding that separates them and have sought, through various schemes, to close it. That desire is still very alive in many quarters.

The most recent set of suggestions for closing the gap requires giving teachers a greater sense of partnership in educational research undertakings, even making them the dominant partners. Teachers are to participate in defining the potential problems and to be active in all phases of the investigation, from data collection (usually by naturalistic observation) through analysis and interpretation. As might be expected from what has been said so far, they are also thought to be the chief beneficiaries of what is learned.

The last point raises a question that seems to be answered satisfactorily, if not actually dodged, by advocates of the let's-team-up-with-teachers proposal. This has to do with whether the *only* beneficiaries of a particular investigation are the teacher-participants (and to a lesser extent, presumably, the collaboraing academics or research technicians) or whether it is hoped that nonparticipating teachers might also benefit indirectly through reading a report of the investigation in the form of a case study. In other words, are the outcomes of these efforts purely for local consumption or can they be generalized? On the basis of all I have read so far, I remain puzzled. On the one hand, the mere fact that a lot of the case study material has already been published makes it clear that persons other than the participants are expected to gain something from reading it, though that something may be nothing more than the technique of producing a case study. On the other hand, there is much talk among advocates of this position about helping teachers solve particular problems in real situations, together with derisive comments about more traditional research approaches that seek generalizations and principles that are trans-situational. Thus, this brief sketch of the argument for a closer working relationship between practitioners and academics closes on a note of ambiguity.

Those who advocate a more distant relationship between practitioners and academics do so because it promises to afford those adopting it greater objectivity in their examination of educational and curricular matters. Until recently, so the argument goes, academics interested in the operations of our schools—educational psychologists, sociologists, historians, and the rest— have allowed their inquiries to be guided if not dictated by the needs and perceptions of practitioners themselves. Hog-tied, as it were, to the practitioner's view of things, the academic was not free to take a critical stance about the operation of the schools. As a consequence, the argument continues, most efforts at curricular or educational change or reform amounted to little more than tinkering with the system to make it work better. What is sought, therefore, is a perspective that allows those adopting it to see beyond the officially sanctioned view of schools and their operation.

The benefits that such a view might yield for practitioners themselves is not entirely clear from the argument itself, nor is it made clearer by the reports that claim to be the result of having adopted such a perspective. On the one hand, there is much vague talk about such a view being "liberating" or "emancipatory" for all who achieve it. This would include practitioners as well as their critics. On the other hand, in almost all the exemplary instances of having taken such a view that I have encountered, the practitioners are portrayed in a poor light. It could be argued that everyone benefits from having his mistakes pointed out and, less painfully, from having the mistakes of others laid bare for all to see. But somehow that argument leaves me with an uneasy feeling of the sort aroused by the parent who claims that the spanking about to be delivered will hurt the grown-up more than the child. So, like its predecessor, this brief sketch of the proposal to back off from the world of educational practice, at least in the sense of terminating any "sweetheart" deals that may have come into being, also ends on a note of uncertainty.

The only question remaining, for which time is scant, has to do with my reactions to the two trends—the turning toward new intellectual traditions and the call for an altered relationship between practitioners and those of us who study what they do. What do I make of them?

A partial answer to that question has doubtlessly been revealed in much that I have said so far, for there is no such thing, I suspect, as a completely neutral description of anything, at least not of anything as complex as the phenomena under discussion. It should come as no surprise, then, if I were to sum up what has been revealed already and what has yet to come with the single wishy-washy word *ambivalence*. That's how I feel toward the discontents. And, given the sheer bulk and complexity of the writings covered by my blanket term, what else could you expect?

On the positive side, there is something refreshing, even at times heady, about the attempt to gain a new perspective on educational matters by drawing upon intellectual traditions that heretofore have been overlooked or ignored. Thus, there is much about this body of writing that is intellectually stimulating and challenging. It is also better written, for the most part, than the average fare to be found within educational journals; faint praise, I realize, but still to be counted on the plus side.

But counterbalancing the refreshment that comes from the introduction of new ideas and the pleasure of readable prose is the annoyance created by too many signs of in-groupiness and too many lapses into a sophomoric profundity, characterized by half-baked thoughts and a vulgar display of partially digested knowledge. Terms like *hegemony* and *hermeneutics* get tossed around as though everybody but a fool is intimately familiar with their meaning. *Lebenswelts* and *weltanschaungs* and *geisteswissenshaftens* are plopped like German dumplings into the thin broth of Anglo-Saxon prose in the hope, I suppose, of thickening it. Buzz words from the writings of some of the European intellectuals I have named are inserted almost surreptitiously into the middle of sentences, like sly winks to the *cognoscenti*.

Again speaking positively, I certainly share what seems to be an almost universal rejection of the narrow-minded empiricism that has dominated educational inquiry throughout this century. I, too, have had my fill of studies whose triviality is cloaked by the mantle of scientistic mumbo jumbo and all gussied up with numbers that add up to nothing. These we can do without.

At the same time, I suspect that the more extreme critics among our discontents would not be satisfied with the elimination of trivial or poorly conducted empirical studies but, rather, would like to throw out both the baby and the bath. In this extreme view, all attempts at quantification are seen as violating the complexity of reality. From this perspective, science—with all its talk about reliability, objectivity, and the rest—is reduced to little more than vain posturing. I strongly disagree with this extreme view and find it troubling.

One of the things that troubles me most is that some extreme advocates of the antiscientific or antiempirical position continue to make claims about educational matters whose truth value could only be established, it seems to me, by using the methodology being rejected. When, for example, an author talks about American schools as being institutions in which intellectual development is arrested, he or she is under some obligation to substantiate such a sweeping charge. And two or three anecdotes involving teacher sadism or some other kind of folly will not do. Empirical claims demand empirical support. If the latter cannot be provided, the former should not be made. This allows plenty of room for personal impressions, conjectures, and other forms of guesswork that require some investigation by others or by the guesser at some later date. But some of the writings I have encountered, particularly by a few authors who claim to be taking a "liberated" and, hence, critical view of our educational enterprise, go far beyond such tentative pronouncements, while at the same time they appear to be thumbing their noses at the very procedures that might help to make their accusations stick. When that happens, I get nervous.

Finally, I sense a youthfulness in this body of curricular writings that is at once bracing and disconcerting. I need hardly explain the bracing quality, for that is what youthfulness is all about. It's full of life, feisty, and has a sparkle in its eye. What I find disconcerting about this quality, however, is that it seems to be conjoined with a spirit of intergenerational conflict that diminishes its initial attractiveness. Perhaps this, too, is an inevitable aspect of youthfulness, but I suspect it's not. My suspicion returns my thoughts to the deathbed metaphor and to Pinar's talk of becoming an heir. The occupant of that bed, come to think of it, cannot be just any aged person. It almost has to be a relative, and probably a parent at that. An ancient fantasy, Freud reminds us. As common as acne among the young. Enough talk about my own ambivalence. I suspect that many of the discontents feel it as well.

Meanwhile, back on the cliff at the end of the trail, the older traveler turned and looked incredulously at his younger companion. "What's got into you, son?" he asked. "That ain't no field of curriculum. Them is plain old summer squash as far as the eye can see. Field of curriculum! Well, I never! All that university book-learning must have gone to your head. Well, you're home now, son, so you can talk normal again. Just mind your words and speak up loud and clear. You should have plenty to talk about."

After a long pause the older man again broke the silence. "Let's go now," he said.

The pair turned, walked back to their horses, remounted, and began the long descent into the valley. Neither spoke on the way down.

Notes

1. J. Schwab, "The Practical: A Language for Curriculum," in *Science, Curriculum and Liberal Education*, ed. I. Westbury and N. Wilkof (Chicago: University of Chicago Press, 1978).
2. D. Huebner, "The Moribund Curriculum Field: Its Wake and Our Work," *Curriculum Inquiry* 6:2 (1976): 153–76.
3. Ibid.
4. W. Pinar, "The Reconceptualization of Curriculum Studies," *Journal of Curriculum Studies* 10:3 (1978): 205–14.
5. Ibid.

6. W. Pinar, "Notes on the Curriculum Field 1978," *Educational Researcher* 7:8 (1978): 5–12.
7. J. McNeil, *Curriculum: A Comprehensive Introduction* (Toronto: Little, Brown & Co., 1977).
8. M. F. D. Young, *Knowledge and Control* (London: Collier-Macmillan, 1971).
9. D. Hamilton et al., eds., *Beyond the Numbers Game* (Berkeley: McCutchan, 1977).
10. W. Pinar, ed., *Curriculum Theorizing: The Reconceptualists* (Berkeley: McCutchan, 1977).

24 Emancipation From Research: The Reconceptualist Prescription

Daniel Tanner
Laurel N. Tanner

Introduction

In this article Daniel and Laurel Tanner attack what they view as the central tenets and characteristics of the "reconceptualist movement." They charge that reconceptualist work, specifically Pinar's work, is bad scholarship, antiresearch, and finally mystical. Further they charge there is no reconceptualist movement.
As you read, pay particular attention to the tone of this article.
- How would you characterize it? Is it scholarly for instance? You have read several examples of reconceptualist scholarship in this text.
- Do you tend to agree with the Tanners? If so, why; if not, why not?

Recalling the late 1960s, when our nation was beset with social upheaval and student protest, Harry Reasoner, the newscaster, said "The past is like a foreign country; they do things differently there."[1] For most of us, the era of New Left ideology and campus confrontation is like a foreign country, and for many the distance is agreeable. For some individuals in the curriculum field, however, it is still the late 1960s. The radical countercultural rhetoric of the late 1960s echoes again in the late 1970s, but this time it is sounded by a small cadre of curricularists who call themselves "reconceptualists."[2] According to their chief spokesman, the ultimate aim of the reconceptualists is self-reflective "emancipation" from distortions of communication imposed by technological control.[3]

Reprinted, with permission, from *Educational Researcher* 8, no. 6 (June 1979), pp. 8–12. Copyright © 1979, American Educational Research Association, Washington, D.C.

It will be recalled that emancipation from the domination of science and technology was a major theme of the New Left. In his analysis of student protest (and faculty sympathy), Lipset[4] found the antitechnology theme to be a reflection of the resentment of scholars in the humanities toward the growing emphasis on *intellectual* technology: systematic and quantitative social science. He concluded:

> The differentiation of social science knowledge into distinct fields of technical expertise has sharply undermined the role of the humanist intellectual who has traditionally claimed the right to comment on and influence public policy.[5]

Certainly, simplistic ideological solutions for reforming society do not fare well against arguments derived from specialized knowledge. And "general" (humanistically oriented) intellectuals have had to face the added insult of seeing government contracts in social research awarded to scholars in the policy-relevant fields. Moreover, Lipset's analysis seems to be borne out by the disproportionate number of student activists from the humanities and "softer" social sciences.[6] However, the point of the foregoing analysis is that the leftist antitechnology theme, which is a backlash against scientific scholarship in policy-relevant fields (economics, for example), has been portrayed by the reconceptualists as a curriculum theory. The themes of existentialism, political consciousness, and "cultural revolution" dominate reconceptualist literature.[7]

Despite the expanding literature labeled "reconceptualist" in recent years, the adherents or proponents of the reconceptualist view are difficult to identify; most of the literature is either written or edited by William Pinar, and much of this edited literature bears only a tacit linkage with the reconceptualist views as espoused by Pinar. For example, *Curriculum Theorizing: The Reconceptualists,* edited by William Pinar, is a collection of previously published articles, most of which are addressed to topics having little or no bearing on reconceptualism. Here one finds articles by Lawrence Cremin and Herbert Kliebard, whose writings are not even remotely related to "reconceptualism."

Pinar tells us that the reconceptualists are "heirs" to the curriculum field,[8] but an analysis of reconceptualist writing reveals the reconceptualists as radical critics and not the curriculum theorists they claim to be.

Just as paranoid phraseology characterized the rhetoric of student demogogues and radical critics of the 1960s, so paranoid phraseology suffuses much of reconceptualists' "theoretical" writing. In *Curriculum Theorizing: The Reconceptualists,*[9] Pinar writes that through schooling one

> loses one's life's blood, is filled with embalming fluid, which is the alien that is the estranged self, the self fabricated by unaware compliance and collusion with significant others
> [and,]
> The cumulative effect is madness.[10]

Pinar provides no documentation of the effects of schooling on the "self." We are left to depend on his rhetoric. Nevertheless, Pinar does quote from Adler, Allport, Jung, Sullivan, and Fromm—none of whom say that schooling drives children mad. Only Pinar says this, admitting that his psychological analysis is "overly simple to be sure, but the point is there nonetheless."[11]

Similarly, Murphy and Pilder, also writing in *Curriculum Theorizing*,[12] tell us that schools are formal bureaucratic organizations that "deny the highest possibilities for human development by colluding with a society based on the same denial."[13] Both critiques refer to "collusion" by institutions against individuals. This is rhetoric rather than rigorous analysis and is reflective of the psychopathology of the radical left. To say that schools collude with society is to overlook the fact that the educational system is conducted by society. To present the relationship between school and society as an undercover for deliberately repressive measures and to say that one can only find the "real" reasons behind the educational process by using psychological or economic analyses merely echoes the rhetoric of the radical left, straight out of the 1960s. Ravitch[14] describes the radical left of the 1960s in the words:

> A correlate of the radical left's disavowal of the political system was the belief that American history was composed of legends that justified the status quo. Thus one could understand events only by looking beneath the surface for purposely obscure patterns, and both Freudian and Marxist analyses provided the intellectual tools for doing so. Whether the "real" reason for some event was psychological or economic, it seemed that things were never what they appeared....[15]

Criticism Promulgated as Theory

One might reasonably assume that as "heirs" to the curriculum field, reconceptualists would not stop with criticism but would translate their concern into an actual undertaking: the development of reformist curricula. However, this appears not to be the case; reconceptualists show surprisingly little interest in the curriculum. Pinar even argues that "an intellectual and cultural distance from our constituency (school practitioners) is required for the present in order to develop a comprehensive critique and theoretical program to be of any meaningful assistance now or later."[16] This notion would have been an anathema to Dewey,[17] who wrote of the "indispensable necessity" for "some kind of vital current flowing between the field worker and the research worker. Without this flow," Dewey warned, "the latter is not able to judge the real scope of the problem to which he addresses himself."[18]

An in-depth study, "Schooling in America" directed by John Goodlad, has found the education profession "badly segmented" with "researchers and practitioners often at odds." According to Goodlad, this is the major problem with which the profession must contend.[19] An "intellectual distance," as prescribed by Pinar, could only exacerbate the problem.

By effectively removing himself from the world of action, Pinar provides the clue to his identity. Pinar is a radical not a reformer. As Ravitch has pointed out, "the reformer is one who grapples with political and social problems and seeks solutions," while the radical remains "aloof from the system and from any ultimate reponsibility for its success or failure."[20]

Maxine Greene[21] sees this problem clearly in Pinar's orientation. Criticizing his "lack of concern for social injustices, the damages inflicted by poverty, the tracking of children, the neglect of children's rights," she notes that "he is interested in . . . and committed to radical critique."

Pinar characterizes the reconceptualists as a movement,[22] but the evidence is otherwise. A movement must meet all of the following requirements: an identifiable theory, a group of identifiable adherents to that theory, and a significant impact in the world of practice. As one reviews the work of William Pinar, nothing is more striking than the absence of an identifiable reconceptualist theory. Pinar's theoretician is the German neo-Marxist philosopher Jurgen Habermas, who argues that class antagonisms have been displaced by technological "domination" as the fundamental problem of mankind.[23] (Habermas's theoretician is Herbert Marcuse.) The democratic decision-making process is an impossibility within the confines of a rational-bureaucratic technology where politicians are the agents of a scientific intelligentsia.[24] Technology has replaced rationalization, and only free communication can emancipate humanity from technical control, contends Habermas. For this to come about, there must be a dualism between "work" (instrumental action) and symbolic interaction, between science and technology on the one hand and communication on the other.[25] This is dangerous because what is being called for is a split between the two cultures. If we cannot make decisions on the basis of the best available evidence, how do we make them—through mere dogma, convention, faith, or superstition?

The Habermas analysis is highly appealing to humanist intellectuals who are concerned about the declining status of diffuse intellectualism. Its appeal for curriculum theorists who seek to develop the understandings that citizens must share as members of a joint culture (humanistic and scientific) is incomprehensible. Yet the obverse of the needed unification and synthesis is put forward as a theory of curriculum by Pinar. Reconceptualism pits the humanities and sciences against each other and seeks to widen the gap (with cheers for the former and hard words for the latter). It favors mystical illumination ("heightened consciousness") over reason and is therefore not curriculum knowledge but a promiscuous enthusiasm for whatever advertises itself as counter to our culture.

For Habermas, education is a key structure for legitimizing economic and social inequities.[26] But Habermas is a German sociologist and writes from the vantage points of the cultural, social, and economic elements in his own society. The German experience turned education into a civic function with the subordination of the individual in service to the nationalistic state as the measure of citizenship. In America, whatever gaps and contradictions there may be between ideology and practice, the tradition of education and citizenship is exemplified by the precepts of democratic theory in which a cosmopolitan humanitarian element is dominant. In this element, personal development and individual rights are regarded as essential to the well-being of society as a whole.

Pinar gives no recognition to the complexities and differences in capitalistic societies. "Society" is treated as a monolith. Pinar's attempt to project a German radical critique of knowledge as a theory of curriculum is a reflection of the reductionist character of radical thought.

But beyond this is the larger question of the nature of educational theory. To say that a neo-Marxist analysis is not an educational theory does not do away with this question. A theory of education, like the problems of educational science, must emerge from the educational situation. As Dewey[27] observed, the various disciplines (sociology and psychology, for example) are sources of educational science, but each can provide only partial insights into the problems that reveal themselves in educational practice.[28] Dewey was adamantly opposed to using the answers from other fields to define educational problems. Reconceptualism is an attempt to substitute a radical critique of society for a curriculum theory, and this is testimony to its atheoretical character. For as Cremin[29] tells us, "the strictures John Dewey advanced almost a half century ago in *The Sources of a Science of Education* remain as pertinent as ever.[30]

Of profound importance in any discussion of educational theory is Kuhn's view of scientific development. "Science," Kuhn points out, "is a highly cumulative enterprise."[31] The natural scientist is concerned with the behavior of nature. Hence "a new theory is always announced together with applications to some concrete range of natural phenomena; without them it would not even be a candidate for acceptance."[32] The point may be generalized to the curriculum field. A new curriculum theory must have applications to educational phenomena. It is clear that reconceptualism does not meet this criterion and would be unacceptable to the community of curricularists. More importantly, the term *theory* is used all too loosely in the field of curriculum. A doctrine is not a theory.

At best, reconceptualism is a remnant of the broader countercultural and student protest movement of the 1960s and early 1970s, which has all but disappeared from pedagogy. Having failed to meet the first criterion for a movement—that is, failing to posit an identifiable theory—the reconceptualists must fail to meet the second criterion, adherents to the theory. Moreover, since its theoretical postulates remove it from the world of action, reconceptualism fails to meet the third criterion—an impact in the world of practice (the schools).

Finally, the publications of the reconceptualists are disjointed and do not convey an impression of movement toward some definite end.

Fictional Categories

Claiming to use Habermas as the framework for his classificatory scheme, Pinar marks off the curriculum field into "traditionalists," "conceptual-empiricists" and "reconceptualists." Curiously, Pinar does not go to primary sources (the works of Habermas himself) but uses Bernstein's *The Restructuring of Social and Political Theory* as his "source book."[33] This becomes even more curious in view of Bernstein's conclusion, which questions the tenability of Habermas's thesis regarding the alleged categories of knowledge and inquiry: "It is a fiction—and not a useful methodological one—to suggest that there are categorically different types of inquiry and knowledge."[34]

In what Habermas calls a "radical critique of knowledge,"[35] which is part of his attempt to develop a "critical theory of society," he argues that man has three discrete cognitive interests: technical, practical, and emancipatory. Corresponding to these interests are three types of science.

> The approach of the empirical-analytic sciences incorporates a *technical* cognitive interest; that of the historical hermeneutic sciences incorporates a *practical* one; and the approach of critically oriented sciences incorporates the *emancipatory* cognitive interest.[36]

Empirical-analytic sciences are oriented toward technical control; historical-hermeneutic sciences, toward mutual understanding (free, nondistortive communication) in practical affairs; and the critically oriented sciences, toward emancipation. The natural sciences and "hard" social sciences represent man's technical interest; sociology, history, and political science are examples of historical-hermeneutic sciences. Freud's psychoanalysis and Marx's theory and practice of critique are the emancipatory disciplines and form the basis for Habermas's "critical theory of society."[37] Habermas's "critical theory" is highly programmatic. Its objective is open communication and political action based on unconstrained consensus rather than on technical knowledge. Habermas is attempting to restore "practical" discourse as a basis for decisions in the policy realm.[38]

But as Bernstein[39] points out, the empirical-analytic sciences cannot be characterized as representing a technical interest, "for at their very foundation they require interpretative principles and a rational resolution of the conflict of interpretations." Moreover, the "philosophy and history of science is deeply questioning the categorical distinctions that separate even the hard natural sciences from what Habermas calls the historical-hermeneutical disciplines."[40]

In a fascinating essay, "Objectivity, Value Judgment, and Theory Choice,"

Kuhn[41] argues that "the choices scientists make between competing theories depend not only on shared criteria—those my critics call objective—but also on idiosyncratic factors dependent on individual biography and personality."[42] Thus we see that actual practice lessens a separation between the empirical-analytic sciences and the critically oriented sciences (one of which is psychology). Furthermore, as Bernstein argues, the boundary between the "information" that Habermas calls the output of empirical-analytic sciences and practical knowledge is nonexistent.[43]

If Habermas's scheme is a fiction, however, so is the outcome of what Greene[44] calls "Pinar's idiosyncratic handling of the Habermas constructs."[45] In Pinar's reductionist scheme, the traditionalists represent the practical interest; the conceptual-empiricists represent the technical interest; and the reconceptualists represent the emancipatory interest.[46] And whereas Habermas's technical interest corresponds with the objectivity of science (the techniques and outcomes of scientific research), Pinar arbitrarily reduces this to a narrow and simplistic conceptual empiricism. Moreover, although the experimentalists in the curriculum field have long been distinguished for their commitment to a unity between the theoretical and the practical in educational research and to making curricular decisions according to the best available research evidence, Pinar portrays them as being concerned almost exclusively with the practical—to the detriment of theory and research.

According to Pinar, the traditionalists (he names Tyler, Taba, Smith, Stanley, Shores, and the present authors) "have not been theoretical ... in their books they have focused on schoolpeople ... and 'kids'." Pinar contends this lack of conern for theory caused the narrow discipline-centered curriculum reforms of the 1960s.[47] The fact that these reforms were conceived and promoted by university scholar-specialists in the academic disciplines and that a number of curricularists whom Pinar labels as "traditionalists" were among the most outspoken critics of the disciplinary reforms[48] is conveniently ignored by Pinar. He goes on to claim that in the discipline-reform movement, the curricularists adopted a social science model, and the conceptual-empiricists, who had social science backgrounds (and consequently knew nothing about the history of the curriculum field), dominated the scene. The conceptual-empiricists were even worse than the traditionalists when it came to technical control, argues Pinar. We are told that in Beauchamp's *Curriculum Theory* "the practical becomes even more the technical."[49] This claim is followed by rhetoric but no analysis.

According to Pinar, in the 1970s the field of curriculum took a turn for the better with the arrival of the reconceptualists. Their allegiance is not to practitioners or "kids"; they aspire to an "emancipatory discipline" of curriculum. "What would an emancipatory discipline of curriculum look like?" asks Pinar. "This is not clear to me, although my sense is that the movement in the field that is the reconceptualization aspires to such work."[50]

Pinar has no difficulty with the ambiguity of the rationale of reconceptualism, for an emancipatory discipline of curriculum is essentially radical criticism in the guise of "critical theory." As with other radical tracts, it is based on selected constructs from Marx and Freud. And in the vein of the counterculture of the 1960s, scientific inquiry is rejected as these constructs are alchemized by a process of inner-centered contemplation, which is somehow to move through a transcendental-existential levitation to bring about the promised emancipation. After telling us of his devotion to Zen Buddhism and Hatha Yoga postures, Pinar describes the emancipatory process in these words:

This process of turning inward to examine one's *currere* will lead to a generalized inner-centeredness and hopefully initiate or further the process of individuation, leading to the gradual formation of the transcendental ego.[51]

Aside from this mystical alchemy, Pinar's classificatory scheme for the curriculum field bears no relation to reality. It is an invention to suit his own purposes. Consider, for example, his classification of Tyler as a "traditionalist" (a leader of an atheoretical, ahistorical group). Tyler was dean of Social Science at the University of Chicago and was the first director of the Center for Advanced Study in the Behavioral Sciences, where he served in this capacity from 1953–1967. Tyler was director of evaluation for the Eight-Year Study in which he and his associates systematically assessed the outcomes of progressive curriculum designs that rejected the traditional college preparatory programs of the high schools.

Hilda Taba's research on the development of critical thinking and her efforts to apply scientific principles to the techniques of curriculum planning and evaluation made significant contributions to the body of concepts in the field of curriculum.[52]

Smith, Stanley, and Shores[53] constructed a theoretical framework for curriculum based on the development of a critical intelligence and the ability to solve social problems. The theoretical principles in their classic work on curriculum development fell squarely in the realm of social policy. Interestingly, too, Dewey and the progressivists viewed ideas as the outcome of a community of minds ("Communicative competence," or undistorted communication, did not originate with Habermas.) But Dewey believed that the test of ideas is in their practical consequences.

What is most striking about Pinar's portrayal of the curriculum field is its atheoretical and ahistorical character. Pinar has used Habermas as a way of seeing the curriculum field and, as Greene observes, the grid "exerts its own demands."[54] Fact and fancy are deliberately blurred and interchanged to fit convenient labelings and categories in a repository of doctrine, and so progressives and experimentalists are labeled and categorized as "traditionalists." Natural science and social science are reduced to a narrow empiricism.

The entire culture is caricatured as being in an arrested condition. According to Pinar:

> The point for curricularists is this: the generally debilitating, arrested condition of American culture forbids profound intellectual movement and achievement.

and,

> For movement to occur, we must shift our attention from the technical and practical, and dwell on the notion of emancipation.[55]

How this "emancipation" will derive from reconceptualist ideology is never made clear. We are simply expected to accept the notion that the curriculum field, and indeed the entire culture, will be emancipated somehow by the new alchemists and concierges of countercultural ideology who call themselves reconceptualists.

Notes

1. H. Reasoner, "1968," CBS News, 25 August 1978.
2. W. Pinar, "Notes on the Curriculum Field 1978," *Educational Researcher* 7:8 (September 1978): 5-12.
3. Ibid., pp. 9-11.
4. S. Lipset, "The possible effects of Student Activism on International Politics," in *Students in Revolt*, ed. S. Lipset and P. Altbach (Boston: Houghton Mifflin Co., 1969).
5. Ibid., pp. 505-06.
6. Ibid.
7. Significant here is the title of the book, *Heightened Consciousness, Cultural Revolution, and Curriculum Theory*, ed. W. Pinar (Berkeley: McCutchan, 1974).
8. Pinar, "Notes on the Curriculum Field 1978," p. 7.
9. W. Pinar, ed., *Curriculum Theorizing: The Reconceptualists* (Berkeley: McCutchan, 1975).
10. Ibid., pp. 361 and 374.
11. Ibid.
12. W. Pilder and W. Murphy, "Alternative Organizational Forms, Cultural Revolution and Education," in Pinar, *Curriculum Theorizing*.
13. Ibid., p. 347.
14. D. Ravitch, *The Revisionists Revised: Studies in the Historiography of American Education* (Proceedings of the National Academy of Education, 1977).
15. Ibid., p. 7.
16. Pinar, "Notes on the Curriculum Field 1978," p. 6.
17. J. Dewey, *The Sources of a Science of Education* (New York: Liveright, 1929).
18. Ibid., p. 44.
19. H. Shane, "A Preview of 'Schooling in American' " (Interview with John Goodlad), *Phi Delta Kappan* 60:1, p. 50.
20. Ravitch, *The Revisionists Revised*, p. 8.

21. M. Greene, "A Response to 'Curriculum Knowledge and Cacophony' by John D. McNeil and 'Notes on the Curriculum Field 1978' by William F. Pinar" (Paper presented at the Annual Meeting of the American Educational Research Association, Toronto, Canada, March 27, 1978).
22. Pinar, *Curriculum Theorizing,* and Pinar, "Notes on the Curriculum Field 1978."
23. J. Habermas, *Toward a Rational Society* (Boston: Beacon, 1970), pp. 81–122.
24. Ibid., pp. 107–22.
25. J. Habermas, *Knowledge and Human Interests* (Boston: Beacon, 1971).
26. J. Habermas, *Legitimation Crisis* (Boston: Beacon, 1975), p. 77.
27. Dewey, *Sources of a Science of Education.*
28. Ibid., pp. 73–75.
29. L. Cremin, *Public Education* (New York: Basic Books, 1976).
30. Ibid., p. 48.
31. T. Kuhn, *The Structure of Scientific Revolutions* (Chicago: University of Chicago Press, 1970), p. 52.
32. Ibid., p. 46.
33. R. Bernstein, *The Restructuring of Social and Political Theory* (New York: Harcourt Brace Jovanovich, 1976), p. 5.
34. Ibid., p. 223.
35. Habermas, *Knowledge and Human Interests*, p. vii.
36. Ibid., p. 308.
37. Ibid., pp. 214–310.
38. Ibid., pp. 316–17.
39. Bernstein, *Restructuring of Social and Political Theory.*
40. Ibid., p. 222.
41. T. Kuhn, *The Essential Tension* (Chicago: University of Chicago Press, 1977), p. 222.
42. Ibid., p. 329.
43. Bernstein, *Restructuring of Social and Political Theory*, p. 222.
44. Greene, "A Response."
45. Ibid., p. 7.
46. Pinar, "Notes on the Curriculum Field 1978."
47. Ibid., p. 6.
48. D. Tanner and L. Tanner, *Curriculum Development* (New York: Macmillan, 1975).
49. Pinar, "Notes on the Curriculum Field 1978," p. 9.
50. Ibid., p. 9.
51. Pinar, *Curriculum Theorizing*, pp. 358 and 410.
52. See the works of H. Taba: *Curriculum Development* (New York: Harcourt Brace Jovanovich, 1962), *Thinking in Elementary School Children* (San Francisco: San Francisco State College, 1964), and *A Teacher's Handbook to Elementary Social Studies: An Inductive Approach* (Reading, Mass.: Addison-Wesley, 1971).
53. B. Smith, W. Stanley, and J. Shores, *Fundamentals of Curriculum Development* (New York: Harcourt Brace Jovanovich, 1957).
54. Greene, "A Response," p. 8.
55. Pinar, "Notes on the Curriculum Field 1978," p. 10.

25 A Reply to My Critics

William F. Pinar

Introduction

In this short paper Pinar replies to articles by Philip Jackson and Daniel and Laurel Tanner. He attempts to shift the argument from specific charges made by these critics to what he sees as a broader issue involving "disciplinary conversation."
- Is Pinar successful in this effort, in your judgment, or does he appear to be only evading the Tanners' charges?
- Do these articles suggest to you a disciplinary conversation?
- What is absent, if you think not, and what is present if you did view these exchanges as advancing the field?
- What is your assessment of the generational issue?
- If you tend to agree that the generational issue is probably at work in this dispute, do you think it illumines or obscures the disagreements to shift the argument to it?
- Do you find yourself "taking sides" in this debate and, if so, which "side" has your sympathy and why?

We can gauge the vitality of a field by the quantity and quality of scholarly production. The caliber of minds in a field; the degree of institutional, governmental, and foundational support; and the quality of disciplinary conversation—all contribute to its well-being. In this brief article, I wish to concentrate on only one of these issues, that of disciplinary conversation. More specifically, I

Portions of this article are reprinted from: William F. Pinar, "Letter to the Editor," *Educational Researcher* 8:9 (October 1979), p. 6.

Reprinted from *Curriculum Inquiry* 10, no. 2 (Summer 1980), pp. 199–205. Reprinted by permission of John Wiley & Sons, Inc.

will address this issue as it has been raised by two recent articles: "Emancipation From Research: The Reconceptualist Prescription" by Daniel and Laurel Tanner[1] and "Curriculum and Its Discontents" by Philip W. Jackson.[2]

Two aspects of disciplinary conversation[3] interest me. The first is the excitement the solitary researcher experiences as he investigates that which is interesting and important to him and his communication of the investigations. The second is the response of his colleagues to these communications. Traditionally in the academy, such responses are infrequently laudatory. The frequency of "critical response" derives from our obligation to point to the incompleteness of any specific investigation or to flaws in its reasoning. One kind of critical response is born of an interest in assisting the work under scrutiny to become more complete, more sophisticated. This is the criticism of a pedagogue who wants to improve the work.

There is a second kind of critical response, however, that is not born of a pedagogic interest but of a cathartic one. It is ill-tempered and results not in the development of the other's work but in silence. Perhaps this silence is angry and defiant or intimidated and self-crippling. But it tends to be silence because this criticism cannot be integrated by the other. Both the Tanner-Tanner and Jackson articles are of this sort. But I must press through the angry silence these articles produced. I must reconceive what they write and in so doing escape the anger, else my own response is also catharsis; it perpetuates monologue and inhibits disciplinary conversation. I want to return to this matter of reconceiving, but now I wish to point to the most basic errors in these two articles.

In the Tanners' article, the first fundamental misunderstanding occurs in the title. No reconceptualist has ever "prescribed" an "emancipation from research." Such distortion could be made only by a positivist of the narrowest sort. One must repeat what is by now tiresome to repeat. Namely, research in the contemporary academy takes several forms; one of the most historically recent and epistemologically questionable is that conducted by mainstream social scientists. To state that reconceptualist work is not research only underscores the intellectual parochialism of some who have evidently forgotten that the term is not their invention. There are research traditions centuries older, traditions such as the hermeneutical one[4] that many in the humanities and the arts still work in. Literary criticism, art history and criticism, philosophical inquiry, historical analysis—all are forms of research, forms that reconceptualist work is derived from. I know of no "reconceptualist prescription" for freeing anyone from research.

A second misunderstanding is indicated in the use of the term *reconceptualism*. I have never used this term. In fact, in one article I explained why others should not.[5] The term is a misnomer because it connotes a degree of unity (conceptual and methodological) nonexistent among reconceptualists. I used the term *reconceptualization* to indicate a fundamental reconceiving of the field. This fundamental reconceiving of the field is indicated by the growing presence of work quite different in form and objective from traditional work. Merely glancing through *Curriculum Theorizing: The Reconceptualists* or *The Journal of Curriculum Theorizing* confirms this. Yet the writing that functions to reconceptualize the field is quite diverse. It is one literature insofar as it functions to alter fundamentally the conceptual and methodological shapes of the field. Of course there is no "reconceptualist theory." There is no reconceptualism. And there is no "movement" in the sense in which the Tanners stipulate that term's definition.

The Tanners look for a movement similar to the student movement of the 1960s. There are, I hope, no "adherents" in the curriculum field. Scholars and theoreticians are individualists. It is astonishing and demeaning to suggest there could be adherents. To repeat the obvious, reconceptualization is not a movement comprised of "leaders" and "adherents" but a term used to describe a fundamental shift—a paradigm shift—in the orders of research conducted by diverse curricularists, the common bond of which was opposition to the traditional field. Because the term *reconceptualization* is historical in nature, the duration of its appropriateness is limited. There will come a time when it is no longer a useful term. But surely no reasonable observer can deny that a reconceptualization of the curriculum field is occurring.[6] There are those who believe it has occurred already, but I believe this pushes events somewhat. Where the field will stabilize and what will constitute the next major paradigm remain open questions.

The tripartite schema I devised to help describe this shift—traditionalists, conceptual-empiricists, reconceptualists—has produced anger, the Tanners following Philip Jackson and Maxine Greene. It is interesting that the response *has* been anger and not dispassionate disagreement. The schema has hardly been ignored. It is difficult not to conclude that one has "hit a nerve." While part of the anger, I speculate, is a healthy refusal to be labeled (any labeling scheme blurs fine distinctions and tends to be reductive), much of it is in the service of psychological denial. No field wishes to acknowledge moribundity.

The categories are broad and overlapping. Like "reconceptualization," they are historically contingent. In fact, it is probably no longer very useful to think in these terms. Given the state of the field in the early and mid 1970s, a field still dominated by traditional work, such broad strokes were descriptive. Now that reconceptualization is occurring, more subtle distinctions are appropriate, particularly among those who have been labeled "reconceptualists."

These two misunderstandings—one based on a narrowly positivistic view of research, the other on the illusion of "reconceptualism"—are fundamental. Had the Tanners read anything I wrote after 1974 (in addition to "Notes on the Curriculum Field 1978"), these misunderstandings as well as their exaggerated view of my ties to the 1960s, could have been avoided. As an undergraduate then, I was deeply influenced (as were many) by the events of that time. It should not be surprising that the anger which characterized that period should enter a critique of schooling written in 1971, the year "Sanity, Madness, and the School" was written.[7] That essay was the end of an emotional time that began in the mid 1960s. It was the beginning of a search for new ways in which schooling could function. This effort to reconceptualize the experience of schooling resulted in the formulation of an autobiographical method for examining and transforming educational experience, the method of *currere*.

This method, and the view of curriculum embedded in it, are developed to considerable theoretical maturity in *Toward a Poor Curriculum*[8] and in ensuing essays.[9] While this work does not represent a comprehensive theory of a curriculum, it is certainly a partial one. (Let me note again that I am using the term *theory* as it is often used in the humanities and the arts and not as Ernest Nagel or, in the curriculum field, George Beauchamp would.) Had the Tanners read this material, they could not have tried to reduce my work to warmed-over sixties critique. Further, they could not have misunderstood my discussion of "transcendental ego" as merely mystical insight. It is the term Husserl used to suggest the fact of self-reflexivity in human life, the possibility of essential knowledge. Sartre argued against the term in his famous essay "The Transcendence of the Ego," insisting that one need not posit a second ego (the first being the everyday "natural ego") to describe self-reflexivity. I used the concept to evoke the developmental possibilities of self-investigative work. Had the Tanners had even superficial knowledge of the phenomenological tradition, they could not have attempted to reduce my discussion to "mystical alchemy."

Clearing up misunderstandings is not terribly interesting; it feels like work one could have avoided had one's readers been more studious. What does interest me about the Tanners' article is the tone. It is not a reasonably argued piece. *Ad hominem* describes it. It is not the sort of argument or analysis that spurs on a reply or generates questions. Rather, it is a diatribe that tends to result in silence.

This is what I regret about the Tanners' article. It is not an effort to begin or continue a conversation but to stop one. They offer no advice or instruction as to how one is to proceed. And so, silence prevails. The Tanners do not disagree with what I have written on theory and practice, distance from practitioners, the reconceptualization, and other issues; they misunderstand what I have written. That they misunderstand can be forgiven given the hiatus between traditional views of the curriculum field and views being developed by reconceptualists. That they seem to have little interest in understanding illustrates a generational division that is accompanying the shift in paradigms. Philip Jackson's article makes this generational issue explicit.

In the 1979 state-of-the-art address to Division B of the American Educational Research Association, Philip Jackson discusses "Curriculum and Its Discontents." In a clever, humorous, but finally demeaning way, Jackson criticizes Schwab's, Huebner's, and Pinar's analyses of the field.[10]

The criticism is literary, focused upon the danger of the moribundity metaphor, although only one of these is ever identified.[11] The criticism is psychological as well, as the following passage illustrates:

> My impatience with this lugubrious talk about the curriculum field's last gasps should be obvious by now. In fact, if my impatience had a voice of its own, and if it were allowed to join the morbid musing long enough to have its say, it would sound something like this: "Away vulture, away! No more black garb and muted organ music. Let's pull back the velvet drapes and let some light in. The place reeks of calla lilies and smelling salts!"[12]

Such criticism is humorous but insubstantial. It is "impatience" that moves Jackson to ridicule the moribundity metaphor. He has no counterclaim. Instead, he suggests there is no curriculum field, calling it a "figure of speech" and "mental fiction."[13] Soon afterward, however, Jackson does acknowledge that there is in fact a field, although he prefers what is by his own account a "rather long-winded and loose definition."[14]

> ... I do agree with all three [Schwab, Huebner, Pinar] that there is something out there to be viewed, something worth pondering and discussing. That something, and on this the four of us also seem to agree, has chiefly to do with the intellectual outlook and occupational activity of those people who are or have been professionally engaged in speaking and writing about the curriculum of schools and closely related topics.[15]

Why he chose to attack the idea that there is a field is not clear. Nor is it clear why he objects to discussion of heirs to the field.[16] As is commonplace knowledge after Kuhn's work, a field is a sociopolitical group as well as an intellectual tradition. Accepting that a field is comprised of concrete individuals as well as abstract ideas, it is hardly extraordinary to note that the history of a field has its generational aspects. Given that the field is well into a paradigm shift and given that the traditional paradigm is associated with many in a generation now within fifteen or fewer years of retirement, it is appropriate to note that the current situation of conflict and fluidity has its generational aspect. This aspect is evident in the conclusion of Jackson's article:

> Meanwhile, back on the cliff at the end of the trail, the older traveler turned and looked incredulously at his younger companion. "What's got into you, son?" he asked. "That ain't no field of curriculum. Them is plain old summer squash as far as the eye can see. Field of curriculum! Well, I never! All that university book-learning must have gone to your head. Well, you're home now, son, so you can talk normal again. Just mind your words and speak up loud and clear. You should have plenty to talk about."
> After a long pause the older man again broke the silence. "Let's go now," he said.
> The pair turned, walked back to their horses, remounted, and began the long descent into the valley. Neither spoke on the way down.[17]

It is no wonder why. The father does not ask why the son sees the curriculum field. Rather, he berates him, suggesting his vision is only personal delusion. Note the father's categorical, monological pronouncement "that ain't no field of curriculum." There is no interest in conversation here. Note the demeaning phrase "them is plain old summer squash," indicating something indistinct, common, unworthy of serious interest. One can only think of those who have devoted their lives to that which Jackson jocularly dismisses as "summer squash." Next comes the father's admonition to the son to talk, now that the son has been effectively silenced. It is the father who decides they will leave. Neither speaks on the descent.

This image captures something of the severity of the generational conflict in the curriculum field. Daniel Tanner, Laurel Tanner, and Philip Jackson refuse to engage in dialogue, refuse to question, refuse to answer with the care one might expect from pedagogues, from intellectual parents. The Tanners attempt to annihilate the son with anger; Jackson makes the attempt with patronizing humor.

This point about the monologic quality of the Tanner-Tanner and Jackson articles must not be construed as perpetuating that quality. My interest is not to punish (as it appears to be for the Tanners) or to use the occasion for self-aggrandizing humor (as it appears for Jackson). Of course, it is impossible to escape feeling some anger at each. I acknowledge this anger to exorcise it. I am interested in conversation. I do not regard my work as fixed, apart from time and historical circumstances. That means I am open to its transformation in conversation with those who see its limitations, its possible errors. But such openness requires of the other a minimal civility, a pedagogic orientation, and a willingness to regard one's own work as capable of limitation and error. It cannot be only the sons (and daughters) who must change. Dialogical encounter means each is willing to be transformed by the other.

Shouting brings silence. It is possible, however, to work through that silence and one's anger. Through such work one transforms the shouting into new questions. This is a process of reconceptualization, of using text, using curriculum to suggest new texts, new curriculum. One pushes oneself to integrate information—in this case information born in vindictiveness—and to generate questions that can be answered, questions that sustain disciplinary conversation.

To reconceive the Tanner-Tanner and Jackson articles only partially involves responses to specific issues raised in those articles. One must refrain from counterattack, a mode of response that only perpetuates shouting and monologue. One must use that information to raise a more general issue and, in the present case, the issue of conversation. Conversation cannot occur unless the participants are willing to maintain a minimal civility, a pedagogic orientation, and a willingness to be changed by the other. With such conditions present, a vital conversation, indicative of a vital field, can occur.

I, for one, am open to being influenced by my critics. And so I invite Daniel Tanner, Laurel Tanner, and Philip Jackson to critique my writing once again or other reconceptualist writing but with one stipulation: that they cast their critiques in terms that I and others can use. This openness, it seems to me, is a prerequisite for not only individual development, but—writ large—the advancement of a field as well. Those of us who care for the field will cultivate it.

Notes

1. D. Tanner and L. Tanner, "Emancipation From Research: The Reconceptualist Prescription," *Educational Researcher* 8:6 (June 1979): 8–12.

2. P. Jackson, "Curriculum and Its Discontents, *Curriculum Inquiry* 10:2 (Summer 1980): 159–72.

3. "Disciplinary conversation" connotes too casual an exchange to describe the often ill-tempered argumentation common among students of a field, but it does suggest a fluidity and civility that I think is essential to an energetic, yet not incautious, disciplinary dialogue.

4. There are many explications of this tradition; a recent and particularly fine one is S. Bauman, *Hermeneutics and Social Science* (New York: Columbia University Press, 1978).

5. W. Pinar, "The Reconceptualization of Curriculum Studies," *Journal of Curriculum Studies* 10:3 (1978): 205–14.

6. Indices of reconceptualization include (a) a rapidly expanding literature, (b) yearly national conferences, (c) the appearence of the *Journal of Curriculum Theorizing*, and (d) increasing graduate student interest as evidenced by dissertation studies and correspondence.

7. W. Pinar, "Sanity, Madness and the School," in *Curriculum Theorizing: The Reconceptualists*, ed. W. Pinar (Berkeley: McCutchan, 1975).

8. W. Pinar, *Toward a Poor Curriculum* (Dubuque: Kendall/Hunt, 1976).

9. W. Pinar, "The Concept of Class in Educational Theory," in *Sex, Race, Ethnicity and Education*, ed. M. Belok and R. Shoub (Meerut, India: Annu Prakashan, 1977); W. Pinar, "Currere: A Case Study," in *Qualitative Evaluation*, ed. G. Willis (Berkeley: McCutchan, 1978); W. Pinar, "The Abstract and the Concrete in Curriculum Theorizing," in this text.

10. J. Schwab, "The Practical: A Language for Curriculum," in *Science, Curriculum and Liberal Education*, ed. I. Westbury and N. Wilkof (Chicago: University of Chicago Press, 1978); D. Huebner, "The Moribund Curriculum Field: It's Wake and Our Work," *Curriculum Inquiry* 6:2 (Summer 1976): 153–76; Pinar, "Reconceptualization of Curriculum Studies."

11. This danger, Jackson writes, is creating ". . . a sharp break between the present and the past, a sense, in other words, of historical discontinuity. Now none of our three authors [Schwab, Huebner, Pinar] explicitly condoned such an attitude, and I suspect all three would strongly oppose its creation but, in a sense, the deathbed metaphor did the dirty work without their complicity." In Jackson, ibid. My view is the opposite. It is acknowledgment of the field's moribund state that has spurred increased historical scholarship and increased the sense of a continuous disciplinary history. A substantial portion of the *Journal of Curriculum Theorizing* is devoted to historical work, for instance.

12. Jackson, "Curriculum and Its Discontents," p. 161.
13. Ibid., p. 164.
14. Ibid., p. 165.
15. Ibid., pp. 164–65.
16. Ibid., p. 161.
17. Ibid., p. 171.

26 Hegemony, Resistance, and the Paradox of Educational Reform

Henry A. Giroux

Introduction

In this article Henry Giroux points out that there are three dominant positions that characterize the new sociology of curriculum movement, both in the United States and abroad. He argues that while all of these movements provide some insight into the relationship between schooling and the larger social order, each of them eventually fails to provide the theoretical framework needed to develop an adequate foundation for a critical model of pedagogical reform.

Note the critique that Giroux makes of each of the three positions he analyzes. It might be particularly useful to examine how he defines the concepts of ideology, hegemony, and resistance—especially since he claims the latter are central to a critical theory of educational change. In the last section of the article, he lays out a number of general suggestions that might be helpful in developing progressive classroom practices.

- Are his suggestions enlightening? Impractical?
- What are the limits to his suggestions?
- How does Giroux's analysis differ from, let's say, that of Ralph Tyler or George Beauchamp?

In the current debate over the political, social, and economic functions of schooling, the discourse of radical educational theory appears to be caught in a paradox that allows it to simultaneously criticize and strengthen the existing relationships between schools and other more powerful institutions in the dominant society. Sharply critical of schools as social sites that function in

Reprinted, with permission, from *Interchange* 12, nos. 2 and 3 (in press).

response to the logic of capital, radical theories of reproduction provide both institutional and interactional analyses of the process of schooling. Through these forms of analyses, such studies have revealed the economic and political character of education. That is, by examining schools against the landscape of capitalist social relations and economic life, such theories have illuminated the deep structure and grammar of class domination and inequality that bear so heavily on the purpose and processes of day-to-day classroom experiences.

In stressing the determinant nature and primacy of either the state or political economy in educational theory and practice, reproductive approaches have played a significant role in exposing the ideological assumptions and processes behind the rhetoric of neutrality and social mobility characteristic of conservative as well as liberal views of schooling. Yet while such approaches represent an important theoretical break from idealist and functionalist paradigms in educational theory, they still remain situated within a problematic that ultimately supports rather than challenges the logic of the existing order. The point here is that there are some serious deficiencies in existing theories of reproduction, the most important of which is the refusal to posit a form of critique that demonstrates the theoretical and practical importance of counterhegemonic struggles both within and outside of the sphere of schooling.

By failing either to acknowledge the degree to which the oppressed are *not* constituted by capital or to recognize those aspects of daily life to which capitalist ideology is indifferent, reproductive theories have been trapped within a reductive logic that appears at odds with the aim or even the possibility of developing a radical theory of education. In other words, neither the promise of oppositional teaching nor the more encompassing task of radical social change represent important moments in these perspectives. The implications that these approaches have for a model of radical pedagogy seem obvious. For between the fact of class and gender domination and the promise of counterideologies embedded in the contradictions and tensions of classroom experiences, reproductive theories posit models of domination that appear so stark that even references to resistance or social change sound like a weak utterance inscribed in madness. In the end, abstract negation gives way to unrelieved despair, and the discourse of radical reproductive approaches points to a mode of theorizing that belongs to the rationality of the existing administered system of corporate domination.

The shortcomings of such approaches to radical pedagogy are not new. Earlier criticisms of theories of reproduction have pointed to their one-sided determinism, somewhat simplistic view of social and cultural reproduction, and their often ahistorical mode of theorizing.[1] What is disconcerting is that radical educational critics, especially in the United States,[2] have failed to abstract and develop those partially articulated elements with existing theories of reproduction that offer a concrete possibility for developing a theory of radical pedagogy: in this case, a theory of pedagogy that accounts for the connection between structure and intentionality on the one hand and points to the need for a connection between critical theory and social action on the other. It is imperative that such a pedagogy be informed by a political project that speaks not only to the interest of individual freedom and social reconstruction but also has immediate relevance for educators as a mode of viable praxis. This essay attempts to develop the groundwork for such a project.

Theories of Reproduction

There are three major positions that emerge from the broad range of reproductive approaches that presently rely upon macrosociological models to analyze the relationship between schooling and the capitalist societies of the advanced industrial countries of the West. These include: (1) theories of social reproduction, particularly the work of Althusser[3] and Bowles and Gintis;[4] (2) theories of cultural reproduction, with a primary focus on the work of Bourdieu and his cohorts[5] and Basil Bernstein;[6] (3) theories of resistance, with this approach most directly linked to the work of Willis[7] and the more recent scholarship in cultural studies that has been developing in the United Kingdom.[8]

Theories of Social Reproduction

The starting point for theories of social reproduction rests with the emphasis on the relationship between the process of schooling and the relationships of economic life in capitalist society. Though Althusser[9] and Bowles and Gintis[10] view the latter issue in different ways, they do share the assumption that the economy-school nexus represents the most important element in the reproduction of class relationships in industrialized capitalist societies. In analyzing these positions, I will first examine the work of Althusser before I look at the work of Bowles and Gintis and the implications that the work of these two perspectives has for a radical theory of pedagogy.

Louis Althusser

Broadly speaking, Althusser attempts to tackle the difficult question of how a labor force can be constituted to fulfill the important material and ideological functions necessary for reproducing the capitalist mode of production. For Althusser, this involves not only training workers with the skills and competencies necessary for working *within* the process of production but also ensuring that workers will embody those attitudes, values, and norms that provide the required discipline and respect essential for the maintenance of the existing relations of production. Like Gramsci,[11] Althusser believes that the maintenance of the existing system of production and power arrangements depends both upon the use of force and the use of ideology. Thus, for Althusser the reproduction of the "conditions of the conditions of production"[12] rests upon three important interrelated moments in the process of production, capital accumulation, and reproduction of social formations characteristic of industrialized societies. These are: (1) the production of values that support the relations of production; (2) the use of force and ideology to support the dominant classes in all important spheres of control; and, (3) the production of knowledge and skills relevant to specific forms of work.

Jettisoning more vulgar interpretations of the base-superstructure issue in Marxist theory, Althusser argues that the role of the economic base to the institutions of civil society cannot be reduced to a simple cause and effect determination. Instead he claims that the legitimizing principles of capitalist industrialized societies are rooted in the self-regulating practices of the state that consist of the *repressive state apparatus*, which rules by force and is represented by the army, police, courts, and prisons, and the *ideological state apparatus*, which primarily rules through consent and consists of schools, the family, the legal structure, the mass media and other agencies. Though Althusser insists that in the final analysis the economic realm is the most important mode of determination, he manages to escape from an orthodox reading of this issue. He does this by claiming that within particular historically located societies there is a displacement of the logic of determination and domination from its primary contradiction in the economic sphere to other levels of determination within the social totality. For instance Althusser argues that at the present moment, the primary determination in reproducing capitalist societies rests with institutions in the ideological state apparatus, particularly the school. And it is here that Althusser's notion of schooling becomes important.

Althusser argues that schools within advanced capitalist societies have become the dominant institution in the ideological subjugation of the work force. For it is the schools that teach both the skills and the know-how that constitute the subjectivity of future generations of workers. As Althusser writes, ". . . one ideological state apparatus certainly has the dominant role, although hardly anyone lends an ear to its music; it is so silent! This is the school."[13]

The notion of ideology is central to Althusser's analysis of social reproduction. For it is through the force of ideology that schooling functions as an agent of reproduction. Defined in part as "the imaginary relationship of individuals to their real conditions of existence,"[14] ideology functions within schools to constitute subjectivity as well as to socialize students into the dominant society. Thus, ideology is viewed not only as a manipulative set of imposed ideas, which embody class-specific roles; it also is viewed as being constitutive of subjects themselves.[15] Thus, hegemony in Althusser's account points to a link between the mode of production and ideology. In this account, human beings become role bearers, and, as Richard Johnson points out: "The whole sphere of the cultural/ideological, the very processes by which subjectivities are formed, are subsumed within a single function: the reproduction of the conditions of capitalist relations."[16]

There is a curious paradox underlying Althusser's account. On the one hand, he raises the central question at the heart of any attempt to unravel the processes of domination and social reproduction: the question of how a particular form of subjectivity is constituted in schools and other ideological sites. On the other hand Althusser ignores any sustained analysis of day-to-day classroom practices and in doing so fails to address the question. Similarly, he provides a conceptual notion of ideology which presupposes that if such a question were answered, it would do little to contribute to a liberating mode of radical pedagogy. For what we end up with in Althusser's analysis is a notion of ideology that exists without the benefit of human agents. Domination appears to be helplessly reduced to the prison house of the ideological state apparatus, and as a result the conditions or even possibility of transcendence get lost in a grimly mechanistic notion of social reproduction. This is an important issue, for it suggets that Althusser sacrifices the possibility for human struggle and resistance within a notion of hegemony that is as pessimistic as it is conceptually limited.[17] Rachel Sharp[18] captures the contradictions and limitations of Althusser's position in her comment:

It suggests a determinist reproduction of the relations of production by the educational system which tends to contradict Althusser's own thesis of the relative autonomy of the ideological and political levels and lead to a form of reductionism. It also provides no hope that subjects can ever escape from ideology.[19]

Bowles and Gintis

Bowles and Gintis[20] share Althusser's basic notion of the role of schooling in capitalist society. As Madeleine MacDonald writes: "Both see the reproduction of the social relations found in the production process as the central function and determining force in the shaping of schools within capitalism."[21] That is, like Althusser, Bowles and Gintis believe that schools serve two functions in capitalist society. One essential function is the reproduction of the labor power necessary for capital accumulation. This is provided for in schools through the differential selecting and training along class and gender lines of students with the "technical and cognitive skills required for adequate job performance"[22] in the hierarchical social division of labor. The second essential function requires the reproduction of those forms of consciousness, dispositions, and values necessary for the maintenance of "institutions and social relationships which facilitate the translation of labor into profit."[23]

Unlike Althusser, Bowles and Gintis do not focus upon ideology as the central dynamic in the process of social reproduction. Instead, they emphasize the structural relationship between schools and the "relationships of dominance and subordinancy in the economic sphere."[24] At the heart of their account is what has been called the correspondence theory. Broadly speaking, the correspondence theory posits that the hierarchically structured patterns of values, norms, and skills that characterize the work force, and the dynamics of class interaction under capitalism are mirrored in the social dynamics of the daily classroom encounter. Schooling in this view functions through its classroom relations to inculcate students with the attitudes and dispositions necessary for them to accept the social and economic imperatives of a capitalist economy. Bowles and Gintis clearly articulate the nature of their structural analysis when they write:

The educational system helps integrate youth into the economic system, we believe, through a structural correspondence between its social relations and those of production. The structure of social relations in education not only inures the student to the discipline of the work place but develops the types of personal demeanor, modes of self-preservation, self-image, and social identifications which are crucial ingredients of job adequacy. Specifically, the social relationships of education—the relationships between administrators and teachers, teachers and students, students and their work—replicate the hierarchical division of labor.[25]

While Bowles and Gintis are helpful in pointing to the social relations of the classroom as social processes that link schools to determinant forces in the work place, they eventually end up with a theory of social reproduction that is much too simplified and overdetermined. Not only does their argument point to a spurious "constant fit" between schools and the work place, it does so by ignoring important issues regarding the role of consciousness, ideology, and resistance in the schooling process. In other words, hegemonic control in this view is dominated by a model of analysis that "forgets" that social structures such as schools and the work place represent ". . . both the medium and the outcome of reproduction practices."[26] The notion that human action and structure presuppose one another is ignored by Bowles and Gintis in favor of a model of correspondence in which the subject gets dissolved under the weight of structural constraints that appear to form both the personality and the work place exhaustively.[27]

Lacking a thought-out theory of consciousness or ideology, Bowles and Gintis grossly ignore what is taught in schools as well as how classroom knowledge is either mediated through the schools' culture or given meaning by the teachers and students under study. Bowles and Gintis provide no conceptual tools to unravel how knowledge is *both* consumed and produced in the school setting. What we are left with is a theoretical posture that reinforces the notion that there is little that educators can do to change their circumstances or plight. In short, not only do contradictions and tensions disappear in this account but also the promise of critical pedagogy and social change.

Summary

In summary, both Althusser and Bowles and Gintis fail either to define hegemony in terms that posit a dialectical relationship among power, ideology, and resistance or to provide a framework for developing a viable mode of radical pedagogy. Both views relegate human agency to a passive model of socialization and overemphasize domination at the expense of those contradictions and forms of resistance that also characterize social sites such as schools and the work place. Moreover, both views stress the notion of social reproduction at the expense of cultural reproduction, and in spite of Althusser's insistence upon the role of ideology as a mechanism of domination, the concept ends up as a cheap prop that mystifies rather than explains how people resist, escape, or change the "crushing" weight of the existing social order.

It is also important to note that in these accounts not only are the specificities of the mechanisms of power and domination either underdeveloped or ignored but also that they fail to consider that domination is never total or that power itself is something other than a negative force reducible to the economic sphere or state apparatus. Lost from this perspective is any serious consideration of schools as social sites that produce and reproduce ideologies and cultural forms that stand in opposition to dominant values and practices. By ignoring the notion that dominant ideologies and social processes have to be mediated rather than simply reproduced by the cultural field of the school, social reproduction theorists exempt themselves from one of the central questions in any theory of reproduction, that is, the question of explaining both the nature and existence of contradictions and patterns of opposition in schools. The existence of such patterns suggests that dominant educational values and practices have to be viewed in such a way that their determinate effects can neither be guaranteed nor taken for granted.[28]

A more viable approach to understanding the role schools play in the process of social reproduction of class and gender relationships would have to focus on the role that the cultural field of the school plays as a *mediating* force within the complex interplay of reproduction and resistance. It is at this juncture that we can turn to theories of cultural reproduction.

Theories of Cultural Reproduction

Theories of cultural reproduction are also concerned with the question of how capitalist societies are able to repeat and reproduce themselves. But the focus of their concern regarding issues of social control centers around either an analysis of the principles underlying the structure and transmission of the cultural field of the school or questions concerning how school culture is produced, selected, and legitimated. In other words, the mediating role of culture in reproducing class societies is given priority over the study of related issues such as the source and consequences of economic inequality. The work of Pierre Bourdieu and his cohorts[29] in France and the work of Basil Bernstein[30] in England represent two instrumental perspectives for studying the cultural reproduction position.

Pierre Bourdieu

Pierre Bourdieu and Jean-Claude Passeron have made a sustained effort to develop a sociology of curriculum that links culture, class, and domination on the one hand and schooling, knowledge, and biography on the other. Bourdieu and Passeron reject reproductive accounts that view schools simply as a mirror of society and argue that schools are relatively autonomous institutions that are only indirectly influenced by more powerful economic and political institutions. Rather than being directly linked to the power of an economic elite, schools are seen as part of a larger universe of symbolic institutions that, rather than impose docility and oppression, reproduce existing power relations through subtle means via the production and distribution of a dominant culture that tacitly confirms what it means to be educated.

Bourdieu's theory of cultural reproduction begins with the assumption that class-divided societies and the ideological and material configurations on which they rest are mediated and reproduced, in part, through what he calls "symbolic violence."[31] That is, class control is not simply the crude reflex of economic power imposing itself in the form of overt force and restraint. Instead it is constituted through the more subtle exercise of symbolic power waged by a ruling class in order "to impose a definition of the social world that is consistent with its interests."[32] Culture in this perspective becomes the mediating link between ruling class interests and everyday life. It functions so as to present the economic and political interests of the dominant classes, not as arbitrary and historically contingent, but as necessary and natural elements of the social order.

Education is seen as an important social and political force in the process of class reproduction. For by appearing to be an impartial and neutral "transmitter" of the benefits of a valued culture, schools are able to promote inequality in the name of fairness and objectivity. This is an important point in Bourdieu's analysis because through this argument he rejects both the idealist position, which views schools as independent of external forces, and orthodox radical critiques, in which schools merely mirror the needs of the economic system. In contrast to these positions, Bourdieu argues more specifically that it is precisely the relative autonomy of the educational system that "enables it to serve external demands under the guise of independence and neutrality, that is, to conceal the social functions it performs so as to perform them more effectively."[33] Moreover, it is in analyzing how the school actually performs the functions of cultural reproduction that we begin to benefit most from this analysis.

The concepts of cultural capital and habitus are central to understanding

Bourdieu's analysis of how the mechanisms of cultural reproduction concretely function within schools. The first concept, cultural capital, refers on the one hand to those different sets of linguistic and cultural competencies that individuals inherit by way of the class-located boundaries of their family. In more specific terms, a child inherits from his or her family those sets of meanings, qualities of style, modes of thinking, and types of dispositions that are accorded a certain social value and status as a result of what the dominant class(es) label as the most valued cultural capital. Schools play a particularly important role in both legitimating and reproducing the dominant culture. For schools, especially at the level of higher education, embody class interests and ideologies that capitalize upon a kind of familiarity and set of skills that only specific students have received by means of their family backgrounds and class relations.[34] For example, those students whose families have a tenuous connection to forms of cultural capital that are highly valued by the dominant society are at a decided disadvantage. Bourdieu sums up the process well when he argues that the educational system:

. . . offers information and training which can be received and acquired only by subjects endowed with the system of predispositions that is the condition for the success of the transmission and of the inculcation of the culture. By doing away with giving explicitly to everyone what it implicitly demands of everyone, the educational system demands of everyone alike that they have what they do not give. This consists mainly of linguistic and cultural competence and that relationship of familiarity with culture which can only be produced by family upbringing when it transmits the dominant culture.[35]

But Bourdieu attempts to do more than link power and culture. He also demonstrates how the social practices of a dominant social structure are reproduced outside of the boundaries of a vulgar determinism or abstract voluntarism. To do this he points to the concept of habitus. According to Bourdieu, the habitus refers to those subjective dispositions, which reflect a class-based social grammar of taste, knowledge, and behavior, inscribed permanently in the "body schema and the schemes of thought"[36] of each developing person. The habitus, or internalized competencies and sets of structured needs, represents the mediating link between structures, social practice, and reproduction. That is, the system of "symbolic violence" does not mechanically impose itself on the oppressed; it is, in part, reproduced by them since the habitus governs practices that assign limits to its "operations of invention."[37] In other words, objective structures (language, schools, economics) tend to produce dispositions, which in turn structure social experiences that reproduce the same objective structures.

The value of Bourdieu's analysis is that it exposes the political nature of the false distinction between power and knowledge and in doing so clearly illustrates that any theory of knowledge "is a dimension of political theory because the specifically symbolic power to impose the principles of the construction of reality—in particular social reality—is a major dimension of political power."[38] Moreover, unlike Althusser, Bourdieu addresses the question of how a certain form of subjectivity is imposed on people. But Bourdieu seems to have gotten carried away with the latter issue, and in the final analysis the concept of habitus appears somewhat one-dimensional and overdetermined. While habitus is helpful in pointing to a mode of domination in which it is illustrated how the oppressed contribute to their own subjugation through the processes of socialization and self-formation, in the end the concept emerges *only* as a form of hegemony for those under the sway of ruling-class interest. In the final analysis, the notion of habitus smothers the possibility for social change and is reduced to a mode of management ideology. For example, Bourdieu ignores the notion that reflexive thought on one's part may result in social practices that qualitatively restructure one's disposition or structure of needs, that is, habitus.[39] Consequently, Bourdieu ends up with a notion of hegemony irreversibly rooted in the personality structure, and in doing so, he appears to short-circuit the hope for individual and social transformation. In spite of the value of much of Bourdieu's work, ultimately it reduces its author to a prophet of gloom. This may not be too surprising since there is little room in his work for either historical analyses or a theory of consciousness, both of which are necessary elements in developing a theory of human agency and social reconstruction.

Basil Bernstein

At the core of Bernstein's analysis of education and the role it plays in the cultural reproduction of class relationships is a theory of cultural transmission. Bernstein points to the problematic at the center of this theory in his comment:

How a society selects, classifies, distributes, transmits, and evaluates the educational knowledge it considers to be public reflects both the distribution of power and the principles of social control. From this point of view, differences within, and change in, the organization, transmission, and evalution of educational knowledge should be a major area of sociological interest.[40]

Arguing that education is a major force in the structuring of experience, Bernstein attempts to illuminate how curriculum, pedagogy, and evaluation represent message systems whose underlying structural principles represent modes of social control rooted in the wider society. In investigating the question of how the structure of education shapes both identity and experience, Bernstein develops a theoretical framework in which he claims that schools embody an educational code. Such a code is important because it functions to organize how authority and power are to be mediated throughout all aspects of the school encounter and experience.

The dominant educational code in Bernstein's typology consists of either a collection code or an integrated code, the meanings of which are directly connected to the concepts of classification and framing. In brief, classification refers "not to what is classified but to the relationship between contents."[41] In other words, classification refers to the strength or weakness in the construction and maintenance of the boundaries that exist between different categories, contents, and so on. Boundary strength in Bernstein's perspective is a critical feature that underlies the division of labor at the heart of the educational experience and wider society. On the other hand framing refers to the pedagogical relationship itself and the issue of how power and control are invested and mediated between teachers and students. Or as Bernstein puts it, framing refers "to the degree of control teacher and pupil possess over the selection, organization, pacing, and timing of the knowledge transmitted and received in the pedagogical relationship."[42] Either or both concepts can be strong or weak in different combinations and thus constitute the dominant educational code. For example, the collection code refers to strong classification and framing and could take the form of a traditional curriculum characterized by rigid subject boundaries and strong hierarchical teacher-student relationships. Whereas an integrated code, characterized by weak classification and weak framing, represents a curriculum in which subjects and categories become more integrated and teacher-student authority relationships become more negotiable and open to modification. What is important to understand is that both codes are tied to modes of social reproduction, although Bernstein believes that the integrated code contains more possibilities for a progressive pedagogy.

By using this typology, Bernstein has attempted to conceptualize the structural features that link schools and the mode of production as they function to reproduce class relationships. Power and control in this perspective are embedded in the structuring devices that shape the experiences and consciousness of human beings as they pass through social sites such as the family, the school, and the work place. While Bernstein rejects any form of mechanical correspondence among these different social sites, nevertheless, he tends to assume that regardless of the *form* of social control they perpetuate, all of these social spheres share in the reproduction of class control and the maldistribution of power that underlies the existing mode of production. Thus, in the end, Bernstein argues that educational reforms that call for a change in the *form* of social control pose little threat to the class basis of power and will do just as little to effect social change.

Bernstein's work is particularly useful in identifying how the principles of social control are coded in the structuring devices that shape the messages embedded in schools and other social institutions. But in the final analysis, Bernstein's work does not go far enough as a theory of radical pedagogy. While he points to the importance of a semiotic reading of the structural features that shape knowledge, classroom social relationships, and organizational structures in the day-to-day functioning of schools, he does so at the expense of analyzing the lived experiences of the actors themselves. That is, Bernstein ignores how different classes of students, teachers, and other educational workers give meaning to the codes that influence their daily experiences. By ignoring the production of meaning and the content of school cultures, Bernstein provides a weak and one-sided notion of consciousness and human action. Needless to say, by ignoring the production of meaning, whether in the self-constituted acts of discourse, social practices, or in the school materials themselves, Bernstein escapes the tricky question of how the state and other powerful capitalist institutions such as the corporate conglomerates influence school policy and curriculum making through the production of *specific* ideologies and cultural materials.[43]

Summary

In short, both Bourdieu and Bernstein surrender to a version of hegemony in which the cycle of reproduction appears unbreakable. Not only do social actors as possible agents of change disappear in these accounts but also instances of conflict and contradiction. In spite of the insistence of both theorists on the relative autonomy of the educational system and their similar rejection of imposition theories, they both end up ignoring the notions of resistance and counterhegemonic struggle and are reduced to empty chatter when we look to their work for a theory of radical pedagogy.[44] Macdonald sums up this position cogently:

In both theories there is a sense in which socialization is nearly total, the gap between socially determined action and individual freedom of action is small if not insignificant. . . . The view which comes across is that power is exerted down from the macrolevel of societal structures and class domination to the individual through school experience, and the possibilities of social change through the creation of a radical consciousness are denied. The individual is seen more as a social product of the structure than an active creator of "reality."[45]

Theories of Social and Cultural Reproduction

Though there are notable differences between theories of social and cultural reproduction, they do share a number of commonalities that tie them to the logic of the corporate state. Both positions view class domination as the central element underlying the mechanisms of social and cultural reproduction. Yet, rather than viewing class domination as only *one* mode of oppression, they have fallen into the reductive position of seeing it as the *only* mode. Consequently, there is little or no treatment of patriarchy as a related but distinct and powerful moment in the process of social domination. Moreover, as previously mentioned, the notion of domination at the heart of these two sets of theories is one-sided and undialectical. On the one hand, power is seen as a purely negative instance. Whether it be located in the state, the mode of production, the cultural sphere, or in the structural principles that shape knowledge, a notion of power emerges in these accounts in which it is viewed merely as a form of imposition. Power as a form of production, invention, and resistance *as well as* a form of domination is lost here. As Foucault points out, "Power is never monolothic; it is never completely controlled from one point of view. At every moment, power is in play in small individual parts."[46] The insight that power both forms and works through the individual, that power is desirable and not just constraining has not been acknowledged adequately in either theory of reproduction. The result has been that both positions have given secondary importance to the concepts of resistance, conflict, and struggle. Where conflict or resistance is recognized, its potential for radical pedagogy is ignored. As a result, when the focus moves from domination to resistance, it gets subsumed in a form of "conflict functionalism"[47] that subordinates all elements of struggle to the crushing weight of existing power relations. Put another way, concepts such as conflict and resistance are useful in these analyses only as theoretical tools to *highlight* structures of domination, but they play little or no role in the development of a viable pedagogical strategy to overcome them.

In the final analysis, none of these positions develops an adequate theory of ideology, hegemony, or resistance. For example, ideology is either ignored altogether in the account provided by Bowles and Gintis, given a one-sided treatment, as in Bourdieu's notion of habitus and Bernstein's focus on structuring principles, or is reduced to a monolithic vehicle of domination that constitutes subjectivity, as in Althusser's account. Thus, in all of these cases, ideology becomes indistinct from hegemony, which in turn is viewed in reductive and incomplete terms. For instance, hegemony as a field of struggle, a mode of domination that has to reconstitute itself continually, disappears in these accounts. What finally emerges as a commonality in these perspectives on reproduction is a one-sided emphasis on the systemic and deterministic aspects of social and cultural reproduction in capitalist societies. Not only are the voluntaristic aspects of struggle and change missing here but also any hope or optimism for social change.

Theories of Resistance

If theories of social and cultural reproduction exclude from their respective problematics the issue of conflicts and consciousness, theories of resistance make the latter the starting point for a critical study of the relationship between schooling and capitalist society. In doing so they have focused primarily on detailed studies of both the conflicts and tensions that mediate school culture and the role of youth subcultures within and outside of schools. Combining ethnographic studies, and grounded in a neo-Marxist perspective, with more recent European cultural studies, Willis,[48] Hall and Jefferson,[49] and others[50] have attempted to demonstrate that the mechanisms of social and cultural reproduction are never complete and are always faced with partially realized elements of opposition. Furthermore, these approaches have developed a dialectical model of reproduction in which the domination of the working class is viewed not only as the result of capital and its institutions but is also linked to the dynamics of self-formation within the working class itself. That is, a mode of analysis emerges in this approach in which the self-formation of the working class is grounded not only in acts of resistance but also in a limited political awareness of the nature and possibilities of such resistance.

What is significant about this work is that in pointing to the gaps and tensions that exist in social sites such as schools, it successfully undermines versions of the correspondence theory that support a "constant fit" between the school and the work place. Moreover, it further undermines oversocialized and overdetermined models of imposition theory, so fashionable among leftist pedagogues. On another level, these studies provide a notion of culture in which the production and consumption of meaning are connected to specific social spheres and traced to their determinate sources in historically and class-located parent cultures. Simply put, culture is not reduced to an overly determined, static analysis of dominant cultural capital, that is, language, cultural taste, and manners. Instead, culture is viewed as a system of practices, a way of life, that constitutes and is constituted by a dialectical interplay between the social-specific behavior and circumstances of a particular social group and those powerful ideological and structural determinants in the wider society. Hall and Jefferson express this clearly:

Culture is the distinctive shapes in which the material and social organization of life expresses itself. A culture includes the "maps of meaning" which makes things intelligible to its members. These "maps of meaning" are not simply carried around in the head: they are objectivated in the patterns of social organizations and relationships through which the individual becomes a social individual. Culture is the way the social relations of a group are structured and shaped, but it is also the way those shapes are experienced, understood, and interpreted.[51]

Theories of resistance take as their major objective a study of the way in which class and culture combine to offer the outlines for a cultural politics. Central to such a politics is a semiotic reading of the style, rituals, language, and systems of meaning that constitute the cultural field of the oppressed. Through such a reading, it becomes possible to analyze what counterhegemonic elements such cultural fields contain and how they tend to get incorporated into the dominant culture so as to be stripped of their political possibilities. Implicit in such an analysis is the need to develop strategies in schools in which oppositional cultures might provide the basis for a viable political force. Willis sums up this position when he writes:

We must interrogate cultures, ask what are the missing questions they answer, probe the invisible grid of context, inquire what unsaid propositions are assumed in the invisible and surprising external forms of cultural life. If we can supply the premises, dynamics, logical relations of responses which look quite untheoretical and lived out "merely" as cultures, we will uncover a cultural politics.[52]

Theories of resistance perform a theoretical service in their call for forms of political analyses that take as their object of study and transformation the radical themes and social practices that make up the class-based cultural fields and details of everyday life. Willis is stunningly accurate in his perception that if radical social theory is to investigate how "the detailed, informed, and lived can enjoy its victory in a larger failure,"[53] such theories will have to develop strategies that link a politics of the concrete not just with questions concerning reproduction but also with the issue of social transformation. Moreover, rather than seeing culture simply as the reflex of hegemony and defeat, Willis and others have illuminated it as a social process that both embodies and reproduces lived antagonistic social relationships.[54] This points to the importance of studying schools as social sites that contain levels of determination that have their own specificity and rather than reflect the wider society only have a particular relationship to it. But there are also weaknesses in this approach that must be overcome if a viable theory of radical pedagogy is to be developed.

First there is a strong tendency in these positions to underplay the role of the state in influencing both schools and in shaping those hegemonic practices that don't show up in the most immediate experiences of the actors. Secondly, the concept of resistance and the form it takes is sometimes overly romanticized in these accounts. Similarly, not only are the material forces that constrain both individual and group resistance underplayed, but the "dark side" of the form and content of modes of opposition that are studied are not readily acknowledged. That is, anticapitalist values do not lead inexorably toward socialism or to the dead end of alienating labor; the latter also contain a logic that links them to the fascism of the Ku Klux Klan or other such movements. This oversight, in part, may explain the refusal of many theorists who study resistance to treat seriously either the sexual divisions that characterize working-class subcultures or those forms of resistance displayed by working-class women.[55] There is a disturbing quality about the silence that accompanies these accounts regarding the violence that underpins the discourse and social relationships that male subcultures display toward the women that share their experiences. It is a silence that suggests that such theorists are not aware of their own connections to capitalist rationality and the equally insidious moments of class and sexual domination at its core. In addition, there is a tendency in these approaches to ignore those segments of the working class that accept the logic of domination, those who have, as Freire[56] points out, internalized the oppressor. How do we account for their incorporation into the logic of defeat and exploitation? If hegemony in all of its facets is to be understood, the answer to such a question is crucial.

Finally, there is a misplaced pessimism that stands between the critical

Marxist orientation of these accounts and their focus on the existential dimensions of working-class life. It is misplaced in the sense that beneath the celebration of resistance that it points to in schools there is a refusal to develop concrete strategies that might help to move countercultural groups from the politics of oppositional style to the terrain of political struggle for power. Thus, in the end, resistance gets subsumed within the rationality of domination. For example, though theories of resistance argue that the logic of capital and its institutions are formed not in passivity but, in part, in opposition, the model that emerges still ends up serving the logic of the capitalist state.

Before proceeding to the next section in which I attempt to spell out what the theoretical components of a radical pedagogy might look like, I want to make it clear that the previous analysis of theories of reproduction is not meant to summarily dismiss whatever value they may have. The point is that these positions need to be read critically so that we can abstract from them those critical elements necessary for a more viable theory of radical pedagogy. In addition, the central task is to move beyond their weaknesses by developing perspectives and strategies that they have hitherto ignored. Central to such an approach will be a more complete analysis of the concepts of ideology, hegemony, and culture and the implications these have in developing a critical theory of pedagogy. It is to the latter task that I will now turn.

Ideology

If ideology is to become a useful construct in the service of radical pedagogy, it will have to be rescued from the restrictive meanings that presently dominate its use. Unfortunately, the contemporary usage of the concepts of ideology is one that often abstracts it from the critical tradition given to it by Marx,[57] Kosik,[58] Lukacs,[59] and other Western Marxists. That is, the concept of ideology appears to be caught in a paradox that limits its meaning either to a mode of false consciousness, system of myth, or even as an expression of the totality of an age. Ideology as false consciousness is tied to a reflectionist epistemology and dissolves both the subject and the notion of active consciousness in a medicinal bath of class-based illusions. On the other hand, ideology as the expressive totality of an age or as a system of myth or social reconstruction lacks a rigorous systematic investigation of ideology as a form of consciousness and activity that is related to the politics of class domination, material production, and social conflict. In other words, there is no sense in these perspectives of how ideology is constituted within both society and the subject or how, in the dialectical relationship between subject and society, ideology is both acted upon and transformed in the ongoing dynamics of daily life.

People in capitalist societies live out their everyday lives within specific material and social relationships informed by relations of subordination and domination and mediated by the unequal distribution of power. Any notion of ideology has to speak, then, to the material practices, modes of consciousness, and sedimented biographies that produce as well as reproduce such a society. Marx provided the basis for such a task in his somewhat differing treatment of ideology in *The German Ideology* and in *Capital*.[60] In Marx's work there is a treatment of ideology that speaks to both critique and the possibilities inherent in consciousness. On the one hand, ideology typified forms of consciousness and discourse made false by the social and material conditions in which they emerged. At the same time, ideology was viewed as a system of ideas that distorted reality in order to serve the interest of a dominant class. Furthermore, ideology took on the meaning of a mode of consciousness that falsely construed the representation of history. On the other hand, Marx's view of ideology delineated a form of ideology-critique and a call for political action. That is, "ideology becomes a mode of penetrating beyond the consciousness of human actors and of uncovering the 'real foundations' of their activity, this being harnessed to the end of social transformation."[61] What is useful about Marx's underdeveloped notion of ideology is that it calls into question the nature of consciousness and provides a productive starting point for analyzing the historical and contemporary processes whereby existing beliefs and practices function as legitimations of a given society.

Both the notion of ideology and ideology-critique have been further developed by George Lukacs,[62] who extended Marx's notion of commodity fetishism into the important concept of reification, the process whereby concrete relations between human beings are made to appear as objectified relations between things. According to Lukacs, reification was both a moment of consciousness and an objective moment in the process of its production. Central to the notion of reification is the critique of both the social relations of production and those forms of everyday consciousness that "freeze the moment," that accept the factuality of a given world without either questioning its mediations or tracing them back to their determinate sources in the wider society.[63]

Reification as a form of ideology signifies both the limits and interconnections that exist between consciousness and capitalistic society. Its value lies in its analysis of how consciousness becomes "trapped" within a social reality that views social relations as objects. Its value for radical pedagogy is implicit in its call for a mode of subjectivity that links mediation with totality in order to break through the false world of appearances and to change the social reality that needs them. Lukacs's theoretical quest for a more profound understanding of the mediations that penetrated the reifying immediacies of capitalist society prefigures a dialectical conception of ideology that strips it of its narrow definition as simply false consciousness.

But ideology is more than reification of consciousness and social relations; it is also consciousness struggling to constitute itself against the objectified nature of social life; it is ideology as thought production. In other words, human beings in the course of their work and everday lives are never reduced to objective representations of a reified social order. As Giddens points out:

> There is no circumstance in which the conditions of action can become wholly opaque to agents, since action is constituted via the accountability of practices; actors are always knowledgable about the structural framework within which their conduct is carried on because they draw upon that framework in producing their action at the same time as they reconstitute it through that action.[64]

This insight extends the notion of ideology-critique by restoring subjectivity to its critical position as an active element in the production of historical conditions and social reality. For Giddens and others, the promise of ideology-critique is that it not only points, once again, to the active nature of consciousness, but it also focuses on how distorted messages and images become embedded in different modes of communication and social practices, which often carry meanings that must be made subject to criticism. Furthermore, this position points to the problematic relationship that exists between the consciousness of everyday life and those mediations that tie it to a social reality, which disclaims the radical possibilities that have been the legacy of history itself. In other words, ideology-critique also offers the possibility of restoring historical consciousness as an important dimension of critical thinking.

In short, political education needs a more dialectical notion of ideology. In this case, one that stresses it as a mode of consciousness and practice that is related to specific social formations and movements. The latter is particularly important if radical pedagogy is to move beyond the false notion that schools are mere sites that impose dominant hegemonic meanings and values upon relatively passive students and teachers. What is needed is a notion of ideology that provides an analysis of how schools sustain and produce ideologies as well as how individuals and groups in concrete relationships negotiate, resist, or accept them. This means analyzing the way in which domination is concealed at the institutional level. It suggests looking at the way a dominant ideology is inscribed in the form and content of classroom material, the organization of the school, the daily classroom social relationships, the principles that structure the selection and organization of the curriculum, and the discourse and practices of even those who appear to have penetrated its logic. This points to two different but related ideological elements. The first is situated in the relationship of schools to the state and other powerful institutions in the process of social control and class domination. The second exists in the practices and consciousness of individuals and social groups who produce and experience their relationship to the world in social structures that are only partly their own making. If we are to understand not only the distinction but the relationship between these two ideological instances, we will have to extend the definition of ideology to include the concept of hegemony.

Hegemony

Though there exists no fully developed theory of hegemony, the starting point for studying the concept has to begin with the work of Gramsci.[65] For Gramsci, neither political force nor the logic of capitalist development provided the theoretical basis for fully understanding or changing the nature of capitalist society. Gramsci believed that a more suitable approach would have to take the notion of consciousness more seriously. That is, the assumption that human beings become political actors as they move through and create the "terrain on which men move and acquire consciousness of their position, struggle."[66] It is this link between struggle, domination, and liberation on the one side and Gramsci's view of the power of consciousness and ideology on the other that establishes the problematic for understanding his notion of hegemony.

Hegemony as it is used by Gramsci appears to have two meanings. First, it refers to a process within civil society whereby a fundamental class exercises control through its moral and intellectual leadership over allied classes. In this perspective, an alliance is formed among ruling groups as a result of the power and "ability of one class to articulate the interest of other social groups to its own."[67] Gramsci appears very clear in pointing out that the intellectual and moral leadership exercised by the dominant class does not consist of the imposition of its own ideology upon allied groups. Instead, it represents a pedagogic and politically transformative process whereby the dominant class articulates a hegemonic principle that brings together common elements drawn from the world views and interests of allied groups. The second use of the term takes on a much more dynamic character. Hegemony, as it is used in this case, points to the relationship between the dominant and dominated classes. In other words, hegemony involves the successful attempts of a dominant class to utilize its control over the resources of state and civil society, particularly through the use of the mass media and the educational system, to establish its view of the world as all inclusive and universal. Through the dual use of force and consent, with consent prevailing, the dominant class uses its political, moral, and intellectual leadership to shape and incorporate the "taken-for-granted" views, needs, and concerns of subordinate groups. In doing so, the dominant class not only attempts to influence the interests and needs of such groups, it also contains radical opportunities by placing limits on oppositional discourse and practice.

One important feature of hegemonic rule is that it refers to more than the institutionalization and framing of specific modes of discourse; it also includes the messages inscribed in material practices. In other words, hegemony is rooted in both the meaning and symbols that legitimate dominant interests as well as in the *practices* that structure daily experience.

In schools, as in other institutions, the production of hegemonic ideologies "hides" behind a number of legitimating forms. Some of which include: (1) the claim by the dominant classes that their interests represent the entire interests of the community; (2) the claim that conflict only occurs outside of the sphere of the political, that is, economic conflict is viewed as nonpolitical; (3) the presentation of specific forms of consciousness, beliefs, attitudes, values, and practices as natural, universal, or even eternal.

To suggest that hegemony is entered into by both the dominated and the dominant classes raises significant questions about the role that the dominated play in contributing to their own oppression and about the nature of hegemony itself. But in order to unravel such questions, the contradictory nature of ideological hegemony must be laid bare. That is, it is important to demonstrate that hegemony in any of its forms does *not* represent a cohesive force. Instead, it is riddled with contradictions and tensions that open up the possibility for counterhegemonic struggle as well as reinforce the distinction between hegemony and ideology.

Similarly, hegemony is a mode of control that has to be fought for constantly in order to be maintained. It is not something "that simply consists of the projection of the ideas of the dominant class into the heads of the subordinate classes."[68] The terrain on which hegemony moves and functions has to shift ground in order to accommodate the changing nature of historical circumstances and the demands and reflexive actions of human beings. This view of hegemony redefines class rule and also reveals a relationship between ideology and power that is viewed not simply as imposition but, as Foucault points out, as "a network of relations, constantly in tension, in activity, rather than a privilege one might possess . . . power is exercised rather than possessed."[69] Power as used here is a form of production, which, rather than constraining the subject, becomes its constituting feature. Ideology as an element of hegemony points, then, to one's limited perception of the world and to social practices that mold and shape the structure of dispositions and needs as well. Thus power represents both a negative and positive moment. As a negative moment, it strips ideology of its critical possibilities and institutionalizes it as a form of hegemony. As a positive moment, it refers to latent and manifest modes of critical discourse and practices that constitute the core of ideology.

The duality of power and control represents a crucial concept for viewing sites such as schools as instances of both hegemonic and counterhegemonic struggles. Gramsci's notion that hegemony represents a pedagogical relationship through which the legitimacy of meaning and practice is struggled over makes it imperative that a theory of radical pedagogy takes as its central task an analysis of both how hegemony functions in schools and how various forms of resistance and opposition either challenge or help to sustain it.

Hegemony and ideology represent important concepts in educational theory and practice because they expose the political nature of schooling and point to possibilities for developing alternative modes of pedagogy. But as helpful as these concepts are, in the end they are incomplete because they do not provide the theoretical framework for developing a notion of totality that reveals how a society reproduces and mediates a wide range of conflicting social formations, ideologies, and structures that either give it a specific historical location or expose its underlying determinations. For this we have to turn to the concept of culture.

Culture

Traditionally divorced from class, power, and conflict, the concept of culture has been reduced to an anthropological or sociological object of study that has not only obscured more than it has revealed but also, more often than not, has tilted over into an apology for the status quo. A more fruitful starting point would politicize culture by acknowledging that the distinction between power and culture is a false one. At the core of such an acknowledgment lies a redefinition of the concept itself, one in which culture would be grounded within the category of society. Rather than viewing culture as either the general expression of society or as existing beyond its significations and material imperatives, culture would be defined in terms of its functional relationship to the dominant social formations and power relations in society. That is, a politicized notion of culture will have to include the dialectical character of the relationship between ideology and the socioeconomic system on the one hand and "the dialectical character of the relation between critical and apologetic elements with the culture"[70] on the other.

Culture, in this sense, would be defined not simply as lived experiences functioning within the context of historically located structures and social groupings but as "lived antagonistic relations" situated within a complex of sociopolitical institutions and social forms that limit as well as enable human action. These "antagonistic relations" at the heart of any definition of culture suggest that it is more than an expression of experiences forged within the social and economic spheres of a given society. It is a complex realm of antagonistic experiences mediated by power and struggle and rooted in the structural opposition of labor and capital, as one instance, and, in another, as the transformative ability of human beings to shape their lives while only being partially constrained by the social, political, and economic determinants that place interventions on their practice.

Culture is the instance of mediation between a society and its institutions like schools and the experiences of those who are in them daily, such as teachers and students. But since culture is informed by the way power is used in a given society, the notion that culture is the "instance" of a particular social practice that becomes objectified and produces meaning has to be qualified in order to become meaningful. Instead, it is more appropriate to view culture as a number of divergent instances in which power is used unequally to produce different meanings and practices, which finally reproduces a particular kind of society that functions in the interest of a dominant class. Thus it is more appropriate to speak of cultures rather than culture. That is, in a class-specific society, one speaks of dominant and secondary cultures, not to reduce consciousness and practice to the simple reflex of class as much as to point to the organizing principle in which "lived antagonistic experiences" emerge. There is no homologous relationship between class and culture, but there are powerful determinations in a class-based society that roughly structure different cultural experiences along class lines. It is the nature of these determinations and the mechanisms by which they function in different social spheres such as schools that should be the object of a study of culture as a political concept.

To rethink the concept of culture and its political implications is thus to attempt to articulate not only the experiences and practices that are distinctive to a specific group or class but also to link those experiences in both their transformative and passive relationships to the power exercised by the dominant class and the structural field over which the latter exercises control. Similarly, it is important to stress that underlying the complex of dominant and secondary cultures is a range of historical sediments, values, and attitudes that cannot be reduced to the category of class or to the logic of capital. As mentioned previously, issues regarding gender, ethnicity, as well as the dynamics of nature cannot be framed exclusively within class definitions. Class definitions do not adequately explain the power and workings of gender or ethnicity issues, just as the dialectics of nature cannot be reduced to historical laws or class analysis, although of course none of the latter can be viewed outside of the societal landscape against which they move. Accordingly, it is against the dynamic image of this historical and contemporary landscape that we see the gaps, tensions, and contradictions that contain but do not promise the possibilities for changing the schools and the larger society.

In summary, I have stressed that the concepts of ideology, culture, and hegemony as reconstructed provide the theoretical basis for examining the dialectical relationship between the general relations of society and the process of schooling and provide the starting point for developing a more useful theory of radical pedagogy; it is with a general treatment of the latter issue that I will conclude.

Towards a Radical Theory of Classroom Pedagogy

Within theories of reproduction, there has been a tendency to reduce social reality to a dualism. This has taken the form of either macro- or microlevels of analyses in which structure and action appear as antinomies. If we are to move beyond such accounts, a more dialectical perspective is needed, one which demonstrates how human agents and structures interpenetrate each other within historically located modes of activity. This suggests a view of structure, agency, and power in which structures are viewed as both enabling and constraining elements with a social totality. In other words, structures become social sites mediated by forms of domination *and* resistance—that is, social sites where human agents constantly interact with, shape, and respond to objective forces that represent aspects of the broader social structure. This is an important point because theories of reproduction cannot explain the relationship of schools to the wider society either by limiting their analyses to the explication of subjectivity and the role of teachers and students within classroom settings *or* by focusing exclusively on analyses of the objective structural determinants that influence the process of schooling. A more appropriate approach would view human agents as actively involved in the dialectical construction of social reality. Such a view would take as its starting point an analysis of the interface between structure and agency, subjectivity and social practice. In this case the critical moment of such an analysis consists in developing a theory of pedagogy that analyzes the conditions under which reproduction and transformation interconnect within the lived experiences of those classes studied. The message here is that theoretical constructs that deal with reproduction and schooling must be returned to "their" living context.

But it is important to stress that a viable theory of radical pedagogy demands more than an analysis of the dialectical self-formation of human agents within wider structural contexts. What is also needed is a historical account of the dynamics of reproduction *and* transformation within and outside of schools. Such a view demands a theory informed by historical accounts that reveals and explains why different social classes have fought and struggled over specific concerns within contexts such as schools. Institutions, social classes, social issues do not exist in a vacuum; what is needed is an account of their genesis and development. For example, when theories of reproduction make the claim that schools contain gaps and contradictions, they provide a valuable but limited insight; but they move from description to critical analysis only when they can illuminate the historical and sociological determinants that produce the gaps and contradictions under study. Moreover, it is imperative that such theories provide analyses that make distinctions among the relative strengths and degrees of "mediation" on which their insights depend. Clearly, if theories of reproduction are to become useful in the developing of a radical pedagogy, they will have to provide an account of how different mediations and determinations change over time, as well as an assessment of the possibility of using such determinations in promoting counterhegemonic struggles both within and outside of the classroom. Finally, a theory of radical pedagogy must include a historical account that links the development of a given class to those social and economic forces that were instrumental in forming it. Ozolins[71] puts the point well in his study of working-class curriculum.

> Understanding the working class is impossible without understanding the history of the social pressures and conflicts which formed that class, but these relations must be

traced through to the present . . . rather than just a study of working-class culture and working-class life; the way or forces by which their relationship is created and maintained can be investigated, questioned, and eventually transformed.[72]

A critical theory of pedagogy will also have to acknowledge that within certain historical contexts concepts such as cultural reproduction, social reproduction, hegemony, and resistance may belong to the logic of abstract negation. In other words, though they provide powerful analytic tools to critique the capitalist imperatives that underlie its institutions and social relations, such concepts often take a mere negative stance toward the existing social order and "fail to show that something else is possible, that changes can take place."[73] It is important not to forget that we live at a time when radical critique of this sort quickly lends itself to the logic of management ideology if it doesn't understand its own limits.[74] For instance, within the last decade there has been a major decline in the American public's confidence in the ethos of capitalism and its major institutions. Simply put, a crisis of legitimacy permeates this country. Unfortunately, the crisis that capitalism faces has not translated itself into large-scale political opposition; instead, it has developed into massive and pervasive forms of cynicism.

Given the current mood of cynicism, despair, and defeatism, it is important for radical educators to move beyond theories of reproduction that do nothing more than either analyze the contradictions that exist in schools or point to the way in which schools are influenced by structural determinants in the wider society. If we are going to take the concept of class struggle seriously, it makes more sense to heed Horkheimer's[75] suggestion that theoretical concerns get translated into viable pedagogical tools for social change. He writes:

The theoretician and his specific object are seen as forming a dynamic unity with the oppressed class, so that his presentation of societal contradictions is not merely an expression of the concrete historical situation but also a force within it to stimulate change.[76]

As crucial as this issue is, it is imperative that theories of reproduction move beyond a paradox that prevents them from being able to deal with the issue of radical pedagogy constructively. On the one hand most theories of reproduction recognize the need to understand how hegemony functions before it is possible for them to expose and challenge it in the wider society and the schools. On the other hand the importance of such a critique remains in question unless the spirit of relentless criticism can be used to examine what kind of relationship a particular theory of reproduction has to the rationality underlying the modes of hegemony under study. In other words, what must also be investigated is how a particular theory of reproduction, in spite of its own claims, may lend support to the logic of hegemony. To pursue a critical analysis of the dominant society without the benefit of self-criticism places any theory of reproduction in the paradoxical position of possibly serving the very system of domination that it intends to overcome.

Theory of Domination

A more viable theory of domination, particularly as it addresses itself to schools, would have to examine how hegemonic ideologies get mediated in school discourse, materials, social relationships, and school rituals. Moreover, it would have to examine the different ways in which such ideologies become part of the body and character structure of students from various classes.[77] Existing reproductive theories are too cognitive and say too little about the violence that is waged against the body, psyche, and emotional needs of many students. Thus what is needed is a form of social analysis that points to both consciousness and needs as important sites in which ideology presents itself as lived experience.

Theory of Resistance

Ideology as thought production suggests that contradictions exist not only between social sites but also within them. No social site is ever free from some form of opposition and resistance. What is needed for a radical theory of pedagogy is a notion of resistance that is capable of recognizing both its strengths and weaknesses, particularly as these translate themselves into viable classroom practices. For instance, Willis[78] demonstrates that there are forms of resistance that end up serving the existing mode of domination in capitalist societies. What is needed is a clearer understanding of what resistance actually is and how the lived experiences that inform it can become part of a theory of radical pedagogy. For example, it is important to acknowledge that the connection between domination and resistance represents a contradiction within the oppressed themselves. Too often only one side of this contradiction is focused on by radicals. In these studies, "working-class" students are celebrated for their oppositional language, yet it is conveniently forgotten that the language is sexist or racist or does violence to other human beings. As mentioned previously, such theories forget that class domination is not the only form of domination or what may appear to be "resistance" in the most immediate sense may represent a form of domination in the long run. All forms of social domination have to be studied against the assumptions and practices they produce and the distinct forms of resistance that contest them. By identifying the limits of certain forms of resistance, it becomes easier to develop strategies that work toward extending their political potential.

Beyond Resistance and Domination

It is in the interface of domination and resistance on the one hand and structure and human agency on the other that a strategy for a radical pedagogy must be grounded. Central to such a pedagogy is a mode of critique that is informed by a faith in the possibility of empowering both teachers and students with a hope that change is possible. In addition to the need for a vision that suggests that a qualitatively better society is possible, there is also the need for a radical pedagogy to develop a theory of intellectual struggle. That is, if teachers and students are going to examine their own lives in order to understand the ways in which they have been formed within the context of the ideological and material practices that dominate the wider society, a viable theory of pedagogy will have to take seriously the question of cultural capital as a form of pedagogical and political capital. What this means is that radical pedagogy will have to give due weight to the life experiences of those students who are the object of its analysis. For instance, at the level of classroom pedagogy, it is imperative that the concepts and tools used in the pursuit of social and self-analyses by students be rooted in the cultural capital that constitutes and mediates the latter's relationship to the world. In the case of working-class students, this does not mean, as some have suggested,[79] an unqualified celebration of the meanings, lifestyle, manners, or history of such students. Instead, it suggests that for the notion of intellectual struggle to become productive, it must be recognized that any form of pedagogy "has to become meaningful before it can become critical."[80] In more specific terms, this means that for students who have been relatively voiceless within institutions such as schools, it is vital that their experiences be given some form of validation. Thus, working-class cultural capital should become a vehicle both for self-affirmation and for providing the grounds for learning and not simply the object of unqualified and uncritical celebration. Learning, as such, involves not only a process of appropriating one's own history; it also means becoming conscious of the forces that have shaped it so that its own limitations can be understood and reconstructed.[81]

The notion of radical pedagogy, of course, raises serious questions regarding what constitutes appropriate knowledge for working-class students. In the most general sense, any approach to knowledge aimed at working-class students must take seriously the concepts of work, class, and gender. This is not a call to ignore traditional humanistic disciplines and subject matter as much as it represents a more selective concern about what kind of knowledge is really useful for students traditionally excluded from the privileges of power and self-determination. Clearly students need to learn those skills that are necessary for a self-managed existence in this society, but they also need to go beyond learning literacy skills or the traditional academic disciplines. In addition they need to learn how knowledge is produced and reconstructed, how to theorize, and how to judge knowledge useful from a class and political perspective. Put another way, working-class students need to learn the kind of knowledge that both promotes social analysis and points to transformative action.[82]

Knowledge for working-class students must relate and illuminate the themes that dominate their lives through the use of pedagogical approaches that contribute simultaneously to the awakening of their political consciousness. Similarly, working-class students must learn to respect their own language and traditions while at the same time learning how to master the knowledge codes and skills appropriated by the dominant classes. Hopefully, working-class students who have been historically excluded from the dominant discourses will be able to master the critical elements inscribed in traditional culture and disciplines and use them for their own individual and class benefit. A theory of radical pedagogy, for instance, must critically understand and demonstrate how specific knowledge codes effect the nature of pedagogical understanding and practice. The relationship between a self-reflexive mode of pedagogy and how it might be used to help empower students to think critically is captured in Feinberg's comment:

It would mean that learning theory and research would try not only to account for how those differences influence the way in which various groups of youngsters come to understand their own role in the larger scheme of things. It would examine the way in which knowledge in the classroom is defined for different groups of students and the influence that this has on their self understanding, on their understanding of the kinds of people and learners they are, and how this understanding may or may not facilitate their later acceptance or rejection of their social role.[83]

Needless to say, the hegemonic nature of schooling is also rooted in those forms of classroom social practices that sustain capitalist social relations. Forms of organization and social processes need to be developed that promote individual and collective affirmation, provide social relationships that eschew racist and sexist messages, and provide students with the possibility for dialogue and reflective struggle. Students need to experience and critically engage social experiences that both promote critical reflection and demonstrate alternative ways of collective learning.

It is also important to stress that radical strategies of intervention at the classroom level perceive acts of resistance as more than an index to register and chart opposition to the dominant school culture. Such resistance can be used to provide the basis for furthering political understanding it if is utilized "to direct students towards an active explanation of *why* the social world resists and frustrates their wishes and how social action may focus upon such constraints."[84] Students can also be shown through studies of people's history,[85] third-world history, women's history, and popular socialist movements that alternative social relationships have existed and do exist. For instance, the latter studies can be used to demonstrate that possibilities for "new relationships in the family, the work place, the schools, the neighborhood, etc. . ."[86] have existed in the past and that such alternatives exist as real possibilities in the present. Similarly, these studies can be used to indicate that people have the power to both change and make history through collective struggle.[87]

Finally, it must not be forgotten that radical approaches to education are doomed to isolation and failure if cut off from wider political analyses and struggles. In general terms, this suggests that the dynamics of classroom pedagogy cannot be understood if abstracted from a theory of the state, a theory of capital accumulation and reproduction, and a theory of institutions. Similarly, the ultimate purpose of radical pedagogy is not simply one of changing people's consciousness or restructuring schools along more democratic principles; the latter aims are important but are reformist in nature and incomplete when viewed within a radical problematic. At the core of any radical pedagogy must be the aim of empowering people to recognize and work for a change in the social, political, and economic structure that constitutes the ultimate source of class-based power and domination. The latter perspective is crucial because it reminds us that schools represent only one but very important site to be used in the search for truth and the struggle for power.

Notes

1. G. Whitty and M. Young, eds. *Society, State and Schooling* (Sussex, England: Falmer Press, 1977); H. A. Giroux, "Beyond the Correspondence Theory: Notes on the Dynamics of Educational Reproduction and Transformation," *Curriculum Inquiry* 10:3 (1980): 225–47.

2. Of course, there are exceptions to this, and these include a number of radical theorists, the most notable being Apple, Anyon, and Feinberg. See M. W. Apple, *Ideology and Curriculum* (Boston and London: Routledge & Kegan Paul, 1979); J. Anyon, "Social Class and School Knowledge," *Curriculum Inquiry* 11:1 (1981): in press; W. Feinberg, "Educational Studies and the Disciplines of Educational Undertanding," *Educational Studies* 10:4 (1980): 375–91.

3. L. Althusser, "Ideology and Ideological State Apparatuses," in *Lenin and Philosophy and Other Essays* by L. Althusser, trans. B. Brewster (New York: Monthly Review Press, 1971).

4. S. Bowles and H. Gintis, *Schooling in Capitalist America: Educational Reform and the Contradictions of Economic Life* (New York: Basic Books, 1976). Needless to say, this position is especially prevalent among radical educators in the United States. Other examples include M. Carnoy and H. M. Levin, *The Limits of Educational Reform* (New York: David McKay Co., 1976); K. Wilcox and P. Moriarty, "Schooling and Work: Social Constraints on Equal Educational Opportunity," in *Education: Straitjacket or Opportunity?* ed. J. Benet and A. Daniels (New Brunswick, N.J.: Transaction Books, 1980).

5. P. Bourdieu and J. Passeron, *Reproduction in Education, Society, and Culture* (Beverly Hills, Calif.: Sage Publications, 1977); P. Bourdieu, *Outline of Theory and Practice* (Cambridge, London: Cambridge University Press, 1977).

6. B. Bernstein, *Class, Codes, and Control, vol. 3 Towards a Theory of Educational Transmission,* 2d ed. (London: Routledge & Kegan Paul, 1977).

7. P. Willis, *Learning to Labour: How Working Class Kids Get Working Class Jobs* (England: Saxon House, Teakfield Ltd., 1977); P. Willis, *Profane Culture* (Boston and London: Routledge & Kegan Paul, 1978).

8. See P. Cohen and D. Robins, *Knuckle Sandwich: Growing Up in the Working Class City* (Middlesex, England: Penguin Books, 1978); P. Corrigan, *Schooling the*

Smash Street Kids (London: Macmillan, 1979); D. Hebdige, *Subculture: The Meaning of Style* (London: Methuen, 1979).

9. Althusser, "Ideology and Ideological Apparatuses."
10. Bowles and Gintis, *Schooling in Capitalist America.*
11. A. Gramsci, *Selections from Prison Notebooks*, ed. and trans. P. Hoare and G. Smith (New York: International Publishers, 1971).
12. Althusser, "Ideology and Ideological Apparatuses," p. 127.
13. Ibid., p. 155.
13. Ibid., p. 162.
15. Ibid., p. 171.
16. R. Johnson, "Histories of Culture/Theories of Ideology: Notes on an Impasse," in *Ideology and Cultural Production*, ed. M. Barrett et al. (New York: St. Martin's Press, 1979), pp. 69–70.
17. For some excellent critiques of Althusser on these issues, see E. P. Thompson, *The Poverty of Theory and Other Essays* (New York: Monthly Review Press, 1978); M. Erbeen and D. Gleeson, "Education as Reproduction: A Critical Examination of Some Aspects of the Work of Louis Althusser," in Whitty and Young, *Society, State and Schooling*; M. Best and W. E. Connolly, "Politics and Subjects: The Limits of Structural Marxism," *Socialist Review* 9:6 (1979): 88–89.
18. R. Sharp, *Knowledge, Ideology and the Politics of Schooling* (Boston and London: Routledge & Kegan Paul, 1980).
19. Ibid., p. 163.
20. Bowles and Gintis, *Schooling in Capitalist America.*
21. M. Macdonald, "Socio-Cultural Reproduction and Women's Education," in *Schooling for Women's Work*, ed. R. Deem (London: Routledge & Kegan Paul, 1980), p. 18.
22. Bowles and Gintis, *Schooling in Capitalist America*, p. 129.
23. Ibid.
24. Ibid., p. 125.
25. Ibid., p. 13.
26. A. Giddens, *Central Problems in Social Theory: Action, Structure, and Contradictions in Social Analysis* (Berkeley: University of California Press, 1979), p. 5.
27. Best and Connolly, "Politics and Subjects."
28. R. Moore, "The Value of Reproduction," *Screen Education* 29 Winter 1978/79): 49.
29. Bourdieu and Passeron, *Reproduction in Education*; Bourdieu, *Outline of Theory and Practice.*
30. B. Bernstein, *Class, Codes, Control.*
31. P. Bourdieu, "Symbolic," *Critique of Anthropology* 4:13 and 14 (Summer 1979): 77–85.
32. Ibid., p. 80.
33. Bourdieu and Passeron, *Reproduction in Education*, p. 178.
34. For an especially good treatment of this issue, see P. Vogt, "The Inheritance and Reproduction of Cultural Capital," *The Review of Education* 4:3 (1978): 219–28.
35. P. Bourdieu, "Cultural Reproduction and Social Reproduction," in *Power and Ideology in Education*, ed. J. Karabel and A. H. Halsey (New York: Oxford University Press, 1977), p. 494.

36. Bourdieu, *Outline of Theory and Practice*, p. 15.
37. Ibid., pp. 94–95.
38. Ibid., pp. 165–66.
39. A. Heller, *Theory of Needs in Marx*. (London: Allison and Busby, 1976).
40. Bernstein, *Class, Codes, and Control*, p. 85.
41. Ibid., p. 88.
42. Ibid., p. 89.
43. The importance of this kind of analysis is demonstrated in S. Harty, *Hucksters in the Classroom: A Review of Industry Propaganda in Schools* (Washington, D.C.: Center for the Study of Responsive Law, 1979).
44. A comprehensive analysis of theories of cultural reproduction can be found in M. Macdonald, *The Curriculum and Cultural Reproduction* (Milton Keynes, England: Open University Press, 1977); and Sharp, *Knowledge, Ideology*.
45. Macdonald, *Curriculum and Cultural Reproduction*, p. 44.
46. M. Foucault, *Power, Truth, and Strategy* (Sydney, Australia: Feral Publication, 1979), p. 60.
47. E. Bredo and W. Feinberg, "Meaning, Power, and Pedagogy," *Journal of Curriculum Studies* 11:4 (1979): 324.
48. Willis, *Learning to Labour*; Willis, *Profane Culture*.
49. S. Hall and T. Jefferson, eds., *Resistance Through Rituals* (London: Hutchinson Press, 1976).
50. For some excellent examples of this kind of work see Giddens, *Central Problems in Social Theory*; S. Aronowitz, *False Promises* (New York: McGraw-Hill, 1973); S. Aronowitz, "Technocratic Rationality and the Politics of Schooling," *Social Practice* 14 (Spring 1980): 28; Feinberg, "Educational Studies."
51. Hall and Jefferson, *Resistance Through Rituals*, pp. 10–11.
52. Willis, *Profane Culture*, p. 172.
53. Ibid., p. 176.
54. Willis, *Learning to Labour*; T. Bennet, "Popular Culture: A Teaching Object," *Screen Education* 34 (Spring 1980): 17–29; H. A. Giroux, *Ideology, Culture and the Process of Schooling* (Sussex, England: Falmer Press, 1981).
55. A. McRobbie, "Settling Accounts with Subculture," *Screen Education* 34 (Spring 1980): 37–49; Macdonald, "Socio-Cultural Reproduction."
56. P. Friere, *Pedagogy of the Oppressed* (New York: Seabury Press, 1973).
57. K. Marx, *Capital Vol. I*, ed. F. Engels, trans. S. Moore and E. Aveling (New York: International Publishers, 1967); K. Marx, *The German Ideology* (New York: International Publishers, 1972).
58. K. Kosik, *Dialectics of the Concrete* (Boston: D. Reidel Publishing Co., 1976).
59. G. Lukacs, *History and Class Consciousness* (Cambridge, Mass.: MIT Press, 1968).
60. Marx, *The German Ideology*; Marx, *Capital*.
61. Giddens, *Central Problems in Social Theory*, pp. 166–67.
62. Lukacs, *History and Class Consciousness*.
63. A. Arato and P. Breines, *The Young Lukacs and the Origins of Western Marxism* (New York: Seabury Press, 1979).
64. Giddens, *Central Problems in Social Theory*, p. 145.
65. Gramsci, *Selections from Prison Notebooks*.

66. Ibid., p. 377.
67. C. Mouffe, "Hegemony and Ideology in Gramsci," in *Gramsci and Marxist Theory* (London: Routledge & Kegan Paul, 1979), pp. 182-83.
68. K. Nield and J. Seed, "The Theoretical Poverty or the Poverty of Theory: British Marxist Historiography and the Althusserians," *Economy and Society* 8:4 (1979): 408.
69. M. Foucault, *Discipline and Punish: The Birth of the Prison* (New York: Pantheon, 1977), p. 26.
70. H. P. Dreitzel, "On the Political Meaning of Culture," in *Beyond the Crisis*, ed. N. Birnbaum (New York: Oxford University Press, 1977), p. 85.
71. U. Ozolins, "Lawton's 'Refutation' of a Working-Class Curriculum," (*Melborne Working Papers*, 1979).
72. Ibid., p. 50.
73. H. Zinn, *The Politics of History* (Boston: Beacon Press, 1970), p. 47.
74. P. Dreier, "Socialism and Cynicism: An Essay on Politics, Scholarship, and Teaching," *Socialist Review* 10:5 (1980): 105-31.
75. M. Horkheimer, *Critical Theory* (New York: Seabury Press, 1972).
76. Ibid., p. 215.
77. Bourdieu, *Outline of Theory and Practice*; Heller, *Theory of Needs in Marx*.
78. Willis, *Learning to Labour*.
79. H. Entwistle, *Antonio Gramsci: Conservative Schooling for Radical Politics* (London: Routledge & Kegan Paul, 1979).
80. G. Whitty, "Society, Societal Justice, and Social/Political Education" (Paper presented to a conference of the Social Science Education Consortium, University of Surrey, Guildford, England, 1980), pp. 8-9.
81. C. Gould, "The Dialects of Questions to Social Critique: Proposals for a Concrete Phenomenology of Education," *Philosophical Forum* 6:1 (1974): 15-39.
82. Giroux, *Ideology, Culture and the Process of Schooling*; Freire, *Pedagogy of the Oppressed*.
83. Feinberg, "Educational Studies," p. 387.
84. Whitty, "Society, Societal Justice," pp. 16-17.
85. H. Zinn, *A People's History of the United States* (New York: Harper & Row, 1980).
86. Dreier, "Socialism and Cynicism," p. 113.
87. Anyon, "Social Class and School Knowledge."

27 The Abstract and the Concrete in Curriculum Theorizing

William F. Pinar

Introduction

In the first section of this essay, you will be introduced to a disagreement among the reconceptualists themselves. This disagreement has been between those focusing on the experience of the individual and those focusing on the economic and political determinants of that experience. In the first part of Pinar's piece, he answers an earlier criticism by Michael Apple and in the next part illustrates what he views as work that weds the concrete with the abstract.

How does Pinar define *abstract* and *concrete* and what are his objections to what he sees as an excessively abstract view?
- What is the tone of the first part; Do you find it effective or ineffective and why?
- What is the tone of the second part, and how do you find yourself responding to it? Why?
- On which "side" of this dispute do you find yourself and why?

There is a madness of those who treat the world as a dream, and there is a madness of those who treat the inner life as a phantom. The second lunatic is scarcely less frightening than the former. But whereas the former gets locked up in an asylum, the other slowly acquires an ascendency amongst men who forget what it is to be a man.[1]

Accompanying the stasis of the present historical period[2] is disembodied rhetoric from both the Right and the Left. The Right reaffirms the family and biblical values while attacking abortion, homosexuality, and social welfare programs. The Left reaffirms the necessity of structural transformation of society, a vision of socioeconomic and political justice, while attacking political privilege, corporate profits, and the smug self-righteousness of the bourgeoisie. Both Left and Right have enemies and loyalties. As these enemies and loyalties take exclusively abstract form, they function in antidialectical fashion. Without explicit grounding in the concrete (the abstraction "abortion" matched to a particular woman in particular circumstances), the abstraction becomes only an extension of the speaker, a sign for something of oneself that is hated or loved. In order for dialectical movement to occur, one must abandon the solipsistic world of abstraction and enter the material world of concrete individuals.

Abstractions unmatched to concrete referents signify private hatreds and loves, although the private character of the emotion is hidden in its usually strident public expression: "Ban the murder of unborn children!" Because the abstraction's referent is private, it is inaccessible. The person who so abstracts cannot see the concrete fact; that person sees only the abstraction. The fact of individual physicians performing abortions for particular women in particular circumstances for particular reasons is occluded by the abstraction "abortion."

This historical situation involves more than, in Sartre's phrase, the loss of the man into the idea. However it is this dimension of which critical discussion can serve two appropriate and related functions. One is illumination of the difficult term *liberation*. The other is examination of several problems in what has been characterized as "politically and economically oriented curriculum scholarship."[3]

The somewhat loose definition of liberation with which I am beginning is this: a process of freeing—oneself and others—from political, economic, and psychological inequities. Thus the term is multidimensional in meaning. As well it is inherently temporal; that is, liberation does not suggest something finished or static. There can be no "liberated" nation, institution, or person in a final or absolute sense. There are gradations of liberation, as even a cursory consideration of the term reveals. For instance, European countries rescued from Nazi control were described as liberated, as they were. Of course economic inequities remained that came sharply into focus after the war had receded into memory to some extent. What at one time is a liberated country at another time can be viewed as an unjust and unfree one. Another illustration may emphsize the relative and graduated character of liberation. A Soviet dissident who escapes his native country can find the United States a relatively free country. The gross order of restriction he faced in the Soviet Union is absent here. Yet for many native Americans, our country cannot be regarded as free. More subtle yet real forms of opposition are detectable. The point here is that liberation is a process and one which has gradations of realization.

Abstract and Concrete in Curriculum Theorizing 433

The order of liberative work I wish to describe and illustrate may seem to some a too-subtle order of work, one whose political import is invisible. To some extent this is the case. I will argue, however, that its apparent invisibility does not render it politically insignificant. Further, I want to argue that liberative work can and must occur along several dimensions and that the success of work in any given dimension—say the economic—is dialectically related in important ways to work in other—political, psychological, sexual—dimensions. This is an "ecological" view of the human and natural world, a view in which action in one domain affects the character of the others. Work in isolation cannot occur except in a superficial sense. Work focused on the individual has inescapable social consequences.

Relatedly, I want to focus on the problem identified at the outset of this discussion, namely the tendency toward abstraction, although I will restrict my examination to its expression in the curriculum field. Such a tendency, visible in traditional, conceptual-empirical, and politically and economically oriented curriculum work, contributes to the stasis of the field, a condition mirroring the stasis of the historical situation.[4] I seek some liberation from abstraction through recovery of immediate individual experience, of a lived—in contrast to an exclusively conceptual—sense of self and world. Abstractions would hardly disappear as a consequence of such work, but they would become increasingly situated in the context of individual lives. The inversion of the concrete and the abstract, succinctly captured in the phrase "loss of the man into the idea," can be corrected, and a contribution to the field's movement made.

Traditionalists in the field have tended to focus upon "principles" of "curriculum and instruction," phenomena that can somehow be studied and formulated independently of the specific individuals whose use of them gives them life. Even the concept of the individual in the traditional literature tended to portray an abstract idea only, just as curriculum that attempted to function humanistically was described as personless processes. The politically oriented scholars continue the same reduction of the concrete to the abstract, as they speak of "the distribution of cultural capital"[5] and "analyzing hegemony,"[6] phrases and accompanying analyses that omit individual experience as they focus exclusively upon structural relations constituent of society. Such work tends to reduce the individual to the network of structural relations which, presumably, constitute his context. "There are three aspects of the program that need to be articulated here: (1) the school as an institution, (2) the knowledge forms, and (3) the educator him- or herself. Each of these must be situated within the larger nexus of relations of which it is a constitutive part."[7] First, the reader notes that the three aspects are not of the same conceptual or ontological order. Both number one and two represent complex codifications created by the third. To situate all three into a "larger nexus of relations" completes a conceptual and ontological confusion that has potentially pernicious political as well as conceptual consequences, consequences to be sketched later.

What is problematic about this reduction of concrete beings to an idea is the distortion of human life it sustains. The idea becomes larger than the living species who conceive it. The idea becomes more real than the concrete; it becomes a source for explanation and, worse, action. As ideas become more "real" than concrete human beings, the capacity to sacrifice the latter for sake of the former is more possible and likely. Whether the conceptual idols be the "master race" from the Right or "the people" from the left, the fact of accepting human sacrifice remains.

In their adherence to abstraction, in their disinterest and misunderstanding of the concrete existing individual, the politically oriented curricularists become, curiously enough, some kind of idealists, in the philosophic sense. That is, such writers reduce human experience to ideas of it and in this effort parallel the work of mainstream social scientists. The individual is presented as an illustration of the general. One begins with the concrete and moves to the abstract, and as Piaget's theory of cognitive development correspondingly suggests, the greater the degree of abstraction, the greater the degree of profundity and accuracy. Such assumptions—we may term them pretheoretical—often lead to distortion of human experience. What is central to human experience is its particularity, in a sense even its eccentricity. Scientific laws and abstractions cannot capture the singularity of individual experience.

William Earle develops this point, arguing that what is essential to human life is not what is common to individuals, although knowledge of what is common is often interesting and useful. However, such knowledge cannot escape the status of the superficial. What is profound about human life can only be found in the realm of the singular. Mounier discusses the matter this way.

He is a Frenchman, a bourgeois, a socialist, a catholic, and so on. But he is not a Bernard Chartier, he is Bernard Chartier. The thousand ways in which I can distinguish him, as *an* example of a class may help me to understand him, and above all to make use of him; they show me how practically to behave toward him. But these are merely sections taken, in each case, through one aspect of his existence. A thousand photographs put together will not amount to a man who walks, thinks, and wills.[8]

The point is not to acknowledge "individual differences." Such a phrase is possible only from a perspective that retains the superiority of the common, the general, over the unique and irreplicable. What is necessary to portray human activity and experience more accurately is descriptions of particular individuals, on particular days, in particular circumstances. Economic and political structural relations achieve actuality—and escape idealism—as they configure in the concretely existing individual. Put another way, in the singularity that is an individual alive on a certain day during a certain moment

Abstract and Concrete in Curriculum Theorizing 435

is a complex configuration of political, economic, and indeed cultural forces. This certain moment, which can be likened to a crystal with its many facets, all present and interrelated but significant only as they are just facets of a single unique crystal, can be revealed in part through the report of the individual himself. Earle notes, somewhat adamantly, in this regard:

What I am for myself has an absolute priority over what I am for another. . . . And though at the same time I may be indirectly apprehended as an object by someone else, my possible objectification to another can have no effect on my own first-personal subjectivity. My subjectivity therefores underlies any derived objectification and remains logically and ontologically prior to any of its derived appearances or modes.[9]

Earle speaks in absolute terms. In relative, everyday terms, another's objectification of oneself often does take precedence over one's "first-personal subjectivity." In an outer-directed culture, children are socialized from early on to care very much about others' objectifications. While the content of objectifications may vary according to class, the fact of vulnerability to others' characterizations does not. Perhaps those who objectify me are not traditional authorities (such as parents and teachers); perhaps they are peers. The fact of outer-directedness remains the case. What is described in the above passage is a developmental possibility. Those who can free themselves from the power of others' objectifications without trading their outer-directedness for a form of autism can achieve a degree of independence that is political as much as it is social.

Of course, there is no attempt here to deny that the individual is a cultural, political, economic being or that these dimensions cannot be investigated fruitfully. These dimensions are extremely important, and calling attention to them in itself as been an important contribution of the politically oriented curricularists. However, what is clearly ignored in the work of this group is the inescapable fact that these dimensions are rooted in the lives of concrete individuals, and it is this biographic context that must take logical, as well as ontological, precedence. To insist that the individual is primarily an economic being, primarily a social animal, primarily the persona created through conditioning, through the accumulated objectifications of others, is finally to make an autobiographical statement. What many Marxists—I suppose "vulgar" is an appropriate although curiously bourgeois, aesthete term—are telling us when they insist upon the primacy of economic and political determinants of human life is that they themselves are so conditioned. They have lost touch with "first-personal subjectivity," with the self behind the persona, behind the social mask created through complex social interactions. Having lost contact, they have become social animals, vulnerable through their outer-directedness to social winds. Structurally they are no different from their counterparts on the Right. Both confess their vulnerability to the social by their preoccupation with it. Human beings are what they are in public, and the rest of human life is reduced to the public or dismissed as "private life" or "subjectivism." This inversion of what is the case characterizes, to some extent, politically and economically oriented curriculum scholarship.

There is a further tendency in this work to judge all other work according to the degree it acknowledges economic and political factors. There is a tendency to insist on a kind of recitation of structural analysis. By such insistence, this work produces its own form of hegemony. To the extent that it insists upon the superiority of its own view—rather than viewing itself as a constituent element in a larger dialectic, the syntheses of which will be formulated in years to come and perhaps by individuals not yet on the scene—this work functions in antidialectical, politically reactionary ways. It aggrandizes itself into a kind of litany to be murmured endlessly by the faithful.

Rather than adherence to seemingly apolitical, seemingly theoretical principles of curriculum and instruction, we are now asked to submit to an equally abstract and ideological perspective. No longer can we feel the naive hopefulness of the traditional ameliorative orientation (let's roll up our sleeves and improve these schools!). Nor can we believe the bourgeois abstraction "the individual," whose claimed independence was in effect a disguise for self-aggrandizement at the cost of community. From the false safety of "principles" and amelioration and pseudoindividualism, we are now offered another set of abstractions—"mechanisms of cultural and economic preservation and distribution"[10]—equally divorced from the realities of everyday life. While political and economic analyses of curriculum have clearly advanced the field from the naive views of traditionalism and conceptual-empiricism, they have reached their own liberative limits as they establish themselves as "the final word." It is in this appraisal of all work according to its own theoretical emphases that it becomes doctrinaire.

The power of the political focus is not in dispute here, only its excesses. The concrete is lost to the abstract; the relationship between consciousness and matter deformed. Mounier states this relation succinctly.

One cannot speak of any object, still less of a world, except in relation to a consciousness that perceives it. It is therefore useless to seek to reduce matter to a network of relations. . . . The dialectical relation between matter and consciousness is as irreducible as is the existence of the one and the other.[11]

In order to honor the dialectical relation between consciousness and matter, the latter must be explicitly linked to the former. Such linkage has been an aspiration of my work. "*Currere:* A Case Study"[12] is an early attempt to portray curriculum—in this instance one particular text—in dialectical relation to consciousness—in this instance the consciousness of a particular student. Descriptions of his response, a response that includes both dialogue with the text and with himself, concretize abstractions such as "consciousness" and phrases like "the response of the reader." Similarly, the descriptions of that reader's conflict over political, spiritual, and social issues also portray these very issues in the context of a concretely existing individual in the midst of his life, facing certain biographic issues. I submit that it is in such a context that concepts like "network of social relations" have reality or do not.

By focusing upon the individual, it is possible to reclaim the abstractions and begin to extricate oneself from capture by ideology. One's voice becomes discernible. By working regressively, progressively, analytically, synthetically,[13] one begins to reclaim himself from intellectual and cultural conditioning. It is work to initiate a dialectical (rather than passive) relation to scholarly work, to oneself, to the world. Such work is hardly political withdrawal or psychological narcissism. Quite the contrary. The method of *currere* is one way to work to liberate oneself from the web of political, cultural, and economic influences that are perhaps buried from conscious view but nonetheless comprise the living web that is a person's biographic situation. The complex configuration of political, economic, and cultural life converges on this "spot" in the lives of concrete individuals. It is individuals' unconscious perpetuation of static structural relations that in part constitutes the present period. Of course collective political action is necessary. Cultural action is necessary as well. Unless "the people" are prepared—psychologically, intellectually—for the equality of a just political and economic order, they retain the same passivity to authority, their same status as functionaries of the state— as the case of the Soviet Union certainly appears to document.

While the stated message of some politically oriented curriculum scholars differs from their counterparts on the Right, their "hidden curriculum" is not so easily distinguishable. We observe the same loss of self to abstraction. We observe the same interest in social control and management. Worse, we can observe the same biographic functions of scholarship, that is, as a tool of professional aggrandizement. Theory ungrounded in the individual life of the theoretician easily functions for that theoretician as does the expertise of any professional in a capitalistic order—as trade to be bartered. Thus while a socialist message is intended, a capitalistic one is received. From the speaker's jokes we infer that he views his radical scholarship finally as the intellectual equivalent of stock, which he has invested carefully, the final importance of which is its "return," that is visibility and professional acclaim.

Self-reflexive examination of the biographic functions of one's intellectual work makes its unconscious use less likely. When its use is relatively unconscious, it is more likely that it will perpetuate dominant cultural themes, that is, scholarship as economic investment. Further, one begins to glimpse how autobiographical work of this nature, as it transforms individual consciousness, must transform as well the material structures of the culture. While the linkage between specific individual's work and material transformation cannot be explicit, we know—given the inseparable and dialectical relation between consciousness and matter—that self work has its material consequences. What is perhaps easier to comprehend is that individual work necessarily contributes, microscopically although not negligibly, to the transformation of the cultural *weltanschauung*.

It is appropriate here to dwell for a moment on the notion of *weltanschauung*. A culture can be said to possess a conception of what is possible, a kind of "limit situation," in Freire's phrase. Views of what is possible and legitimate politically and economically can be represented by the term *weltanschauung*. This term is associated with historical time, and a particular *weltanschauung* is linked with a "historical moment." Any socioeconomic order changes, and in ways and at rates that cannot be predicted. The point here is that such historical movement, if examined from the view of consciousness and matter, involves movement of each. Work that transforms one necessarily transforms the other, although rarely in measurable, obvious ways. Yet the fact of mutual determinacy is indisputable. Work in the one domain is necessary to work in the other. Conventional political action to alter political and economic structures has as its correlative action individual work to transform consciousness or, writ large, the *weltanschauung*. Yet it is acknowledgment of this fact that politically oriented curricularists seem unwilling to offer.

The unquestionable successes of politically oriented curriculum scholarship have now become its limits. It rightly pointed to the inescapably political character of curriculum, to its status as a kind of "cultural codification." It rightly situated curriculum studies in an interdisciplinary effort to assess the significance of economic structure upon the theoretical formulations that constitute a field of study. It rightly pointed to the delusion of individuality that is the bourgeois individual, who lacks psychological or intellectual agency and yet uses his monadic status to deny the web of social and economic relations and further his own position in that web. And it layed bare the importance of theorists' and practitioners' commitment to social and economic justice. These are major successes.

For some of us who came of intellectual age with such views and commitments, the limits of this view have already been reached. This recognition hardly makes illegitimate the political-economic emphasis. Nor does it suggest political withdrawal. Conventional political action as well as continuing commitments to socioeconomic justice remain prerequisites to responsible professional life. Yet there are orders of understanding not yet achieved. Now that we know the staggering significance of economic structure in the determination of cultural and intellectual life, what next? Of course, political action. Of course, the kind of didactic instruction in which Professor Apple, for instance, is well practised. But what else?

Clearly one next step in the dialectic that is the abstract and the concrete is reclamation of the individual, not as an apology for bourgeois self-aggrandizement but as a concrete, irreducible expression and determiner of economic and political structure. I noted earlier that economic and political structure is dialectically associated with *weltanschauung*. Individuals are producers as well as products of the culture that permeates them. We understand, in large part due to the careful work of Marxist scholars and theoreticians, the order of structural transformation necessary to seriously honor commitments to human rights and justice. We understand to a considerable extent what order of collective political action is necessary to initiate such transformation. While this collective work continues today, there is a companion effort that to date, politically oriented curricularists have refused to appreciate. This is individual work.

In a sense I am speaking of Freire's *conscientizao* or learning to perceive social, political, and economic considerations and to take action against oppressive elements of reality. As Freire's pedagogy demonstrates, praxis (thought and action) can occur only as these contradictions are understood in the context of immediate individual and social life. Freire alludes, for instance, to analyses of peasants' afternoon drinking. What is necessary is that the peasants analytically grasp the political meaning of this drinking; that is, it is born in frustration that cannot be politically expressed or materially remediated. The necessity of matching abstractions such as "oppression" to concrete incidents (such as compulsive drinking or "horizontal violence") is clear. This work is, in some measure, autobiographical. It aspires to assist the student to return from submersion in reality to a distanced, self-reflexive comprehension of his life and its relation to cultural and economic life. Such work may initially occur by didactic instruction but only initially. In didactic instruction the student remains passive. In Freire's term, the procedure is "banking education."[14] It is, in extreme, indoctrination. Extrication from reality, from unconscious, conditioned participation in oppressive political reality to self-reflexive, active movement in order to alter that reality is an important function of the autobiographic work that is the method of *currere*.

Liberative activity very quickly—especially when espoused by educators caught in a scientific understanding of the relation of theory to practice—becomes something they do to and with others. When it is only that, when it is reduced to a mode of social interaction, even when it is characterized by "dialogical encounter" in which both self and other are transformed by the encounter, an important order of liberative work is lost. This order of work involves the relation of self to self, of self to work, of self to others, relations which can be progressively uncovered and progressively transformed by careful work with oneself. This order of investigation is necessary given the individual's and the group's seemingly infinite capacity to delude itself as to the function of its activity. Humanistic rhetoric can easily function in politically and intellectually reactionary ways. The content of any statement or position is secondary to its function for its maker. The function of work for the worker requires self-reflective examination to uncover.

Apple[15] misunderstands my focus on the individual for two reasons. One is that the individual, as treated historically in the field, has been without conceptual content or ontological fact; it becomes finally only a slogan. The second reason is perhaps more germane to the present discussion. He misunderstands "*Currere:* A Case Study," relegating it to aesthetic significance only because the individual is an abstraction in his work. In this regard his work differs little from the work of traditionalists and conceptual-empiricists. Despite allusions to "consciousness of people in a precise historical or sociohistorical situation[16] and "day to day practices,"[17] neither are ever described. His concern is finally theoretical explanation in the tradition of mainstream social science, a tradition that—like academic philosophy— "apes the natural and mathematical sciences."[18] It is a tradition concerned preeminently with discovering nomological knowledge of human behavior and action, knowledge that will enable us to comprehend action in reliable enough ways to permit its prediction. In this respect, politically oriented scholarship does not reconceptualize the field. In this respect, such scholarship tends to function in politically and intellectually reactionary ways, as it continues the reduction of the concrete to the abstract, as it continues the reduction of concretely existing individuals to evidence for theoretical explanation. Such a focus maintains subservience of individuals to theory, subservience of individuals to vertical "superiors" generally. It is little gain if the working classes shift their passive allegiance from the bourgeoisie to economic and political theory, which not incidentally is by and large promulgated by members of the bourgeoisie. The capacity for passive allegiance— the structure of oppression—is left undisturbed.

Needless to say, politically oriented scholarship does not function only in reactionary ways. Insofar as it forces awareness of economic and political determinants of curriculum and of curriculum theorizing, and insofar as it represents a fundamental shift in focus and method of theorizing, it does indeed contribute to a reconceptualization of the field. However, to the extent that it insists upon the omission of the individual and refuses to situate its grand abstractions in the lives of those concrete individuals they are presumably in the service of, to the extent that it insists that all other curriculum scholarship conform to its thematic contours, then politically oriented scholarship will function in reactionary ways. Liberation must not be permitted to be reduced to a slogan, another meaningless abstraction, acting as a Maypole around which curriculum writers dance in service of their careers. For liberation to escape such a fate, it must be examined carefully as to its function in professional lives and projects as well as grasped analytically. Without question, the concept implies economic, political, and social justice. It implies as well individual justice, working to extricate the individual from the psychological and intellectual inequities of child rearing and schooling, working to release the individual from characterological limitations. The two orders of liberative work—collective and individual, matter and consciousness—are correlative.

They are companion efforts that ought not to be at war with each other, one attempting to reduce the other.

For the individual, what can liberative work mean? There are many forms, of course, including the various orders of psychotherapy, spiritual practice, and physical therapies.[19] In an educational sense, it can mean work with texts, teachers, other students, and naturally oneself. The method of *currere* is one strategy for conducting this work. For the remainder of this essay I will focus on one variation of the method, noting procedural as well as theoretical considerations.[20]

This particular variation emphasizes textual and autobiographical analysis. It is portrayed in "*Currere:* A Case Study," in "Life History and Curriculum Theorizing" and "The Voyage Out: Curriculum as the Relationship between the Knower and the Known."[21] After describing procedure, I will illustrate it by including a fragment from the last-named article. One proceeds as follows. While carefully reading a particular text, one underlines or stars sentences and passages that in some way strike him, in some way "stand out" from the remainder of the text. This requires quiet, cautious reading of the text as well as constant attention to one's response. The gestalt notion of figure-ground is useful here. The text becomes figure, that to which one is primarily attentive, and one's response becomes ground. The ink on the page, the book as physical object occupy attention, yet the connection of the physical object to the physical body of the reader is not ignored. In this simple connection is suggested the relationship we hope to uncover. Just as there is one physical continuum between the text and the body of the reader, there is a lived continuum between the text, the reader's immediate response to the text, and his biographic situation. (I am not interested in literary criticism here. I am not attempting to portray phenomenologically the act of reading, insofar as that act involves an "empty" self, an unself-conscious reader giving himself to the voice become print on the page. Such reading is necessary when the motive is only clear comprehension of the text. To understand the relation of the text to the reader, to suggest in what sense reading can be liberative activity, involves a subtle shift of focus from the text itself to the continuum that is the text, the reader's immediate response, and his biographic situation.)

Why the biographic situation? I shall discuss this momentarily. For now let us note that it is one end of the continuum, the other end of which is the text. First the text, then the noted passages. Fourth, one examines the passages, discerning themes that link them. For instance, in the list of passages I wrote after reading Virginia Woolf's *The Voyage Out*[22] are "Music," "Happiness," and "The Social." Using pertinent passages in each category, I then wrote short conventional papers on each subject, loosely in the tradition of literary studies. The focus in each of these pieces remains on the text, although I have shaped this focus by using passages that struck me as interesting or somehow important. Their importance to the text is another matter and not of interest here. The movement here—if we think of the physical image of a reader holding a book—is away from the text and toward the reader. At this moment of the work, perhaps we are midpoint between text and reader. I have written pieces about certain themes in the novel, but they originated in passages selected as important to the reader.

The next "section" of the continuum from text to reader we pass over for the moment and move—for reasons that will become apparent—to the last procedural step of this variation of the method of *currere*. This last step, the end of the continuum, is the reader himself. Just as one cannot peer directly into the sun but can more easily examine the earth it lights, so one cannot easily peer directly into the self. We look also to the ground, to the lights and shadows created by the self's "light" on material surface: the biographic situation. It is useful—in order to escape a taken-for-granted view—to attempt to describe this situation as free associatively as possible, although an initial focus on items such as where one is living and with whom can be helpful. In describing the situation, one works to unself-consciously portray one's experience. The focus is upon lived experience, emphasizing concrete elements ordinarily taken for granted. There is a tendency, particularly among intellectuals, to immediately abstract from the concrete situation and begin analysis. One's effort is always to return to "the things themselves," to experience that which is "preconceptual." The aspiration is to unearth material hitherto submerged in unconsciousness. In the final moment of the work, one returns to the step skipped, the "section" between the short literary pieces and the description of the biographic situation. The student now examines these pieces and then the description of the biographic situation and analysis begins. Before discussing briefly what we have discovered performing this work at the University of Rochester, I will illustrate the procedure by printing three moments (or steps) of the work with *The Voyage Out*.

I will omit the first step—the passages identified as significant to the reader—as these are contained in the short literary pieces. The one included here is entitled "The Social." The next step is a description of the biographic situation; only the pertinent section is printed. The final step or moment is analytic.

June 12, 1974

The Social

"Cows," [Hewet] reflected, "draw together in a field; ships in a calm; and we're just the same when we've nothing to do. But why do we do it?—is it to prevent ourselves from seeing to the bottom of things" (he stopped by a stream and began stirring it with his walking stick and clouding the mud), "making cities and mountains and whole universes out of nothing, or do we really love each other, or do we, on the other hand, live in a state of perpetual uncertainty, knowing nothing, leaping from moment to moment as from world to world?" (p. 127).

Such is the view of the social in *The Voyage Out*. It is surface, it is public; we know it is there, we can see it, participate in it, and it is secure. I can rest on it and, by looking at it, I cannot look beneath it, which is to say, inside. My focus is on the form, and I work to create artful forms. Of Mr. Flushing it is noted: "He knew very well how to make a luncheon pass agreeably, without being dull or intimate" (p. 237). The "calm" passes smoothly, without disrupting waves from the ocean's floor. He is not intimate; he does not threaten evocation of internal material from his companions. He stays on the surface, keeps one's attention on the surface, and entertains one subtly, mildly, not so much as to provoke strain but in a balanced, muted way.

To focus inordinately on the outer is dependence, forcing one to insist upon external order so that internal order is maintained. Mrs. Eliot is said to have "depended so implicitly upon one thing following another that the mere glimpse of a world where dinner could be disregarded or the table moved one inch from its accustomed place filled her with fears of her own stability" (p. 129). The other characters' reliance upon social order is generally not as extreme; nonetheless the routine of life at the hotel and the formfulness of their conversation indicate their "needs"; for custom, culture, tradition. It becomes savored, as the old, the familiar, the constant, as counterpoint to the unknown interior region. Yet upon reflection that social existence that seems so established and real is found to be artibrary and contingent:

How odd! How unspeakably odd! But she could not explain to herself why suddenly as her aunt spoke the whole system in which they lived had appeared before her eyes as something quite unfamiliar and inexplicable, and themselves as chairs or umbrellas dropped about here and there without any reason (p. 36).

When cultural customs become removed from the internal, the historical period can be said to be one of estrangement and incongruence. That which is public and observable no longer corresponds adequately to that which is private and now hidden. As social forms become discontinuous from internal experience, one withdraws and watches. Rachel:

It appeared that nobody ever said a thing they meant, or ever talked of a feeling they felt, but that was what music was for. Reality dwelling in what one saw and felt, but did not talk about, one could accept a system in which things went round and round quite satisfactorily to other people, without often troubling to think about it, except as something superficially strange (p. 37).

Rachel dwells elsewhere than in the social; she has little opportunity to express what she feels and sees. It is music that permits her some social expression of her condition.

The novel is in one sense Rachel's voyage out of herself. She begins to speak from her experience, less from expectations of what is appropriate. She becomes more the agent, less the observer. Helen Ambrose understands that her condition is one of withdrawal and repression and that movement from inside out is necesary. "Talk was the medicine she [Helen] trusted to, talk about everything, talk that was free, unguarded. . . ."(p. 124). Such expression can be likened to catharsis, of language linked to emotion, so that release of the former is release of the latter. Expression of what has been kept hidden is an almost common element among psychotherapeutic strategies.

The culture of early twentieth-century England that we observe in *The Voyage Out* is to some degree schizoid. Social form and personal meaning do not necessarily coincide. The Dalloways comment on dinner as if it were a theatrical event and they are now critics (p. 50). The sense one has of all the visitors is ("the voyage out" refers as well to English tourists traveling by ship to South America, where they stay and holiday) one of varying degrees of self-conscious conformity to imagined social expectations. A disparity between the private and the public is tacit throughout; it is poignantly present in the following passage.

All round her [Rachel] were people pretending to feel what they did not feel, while somewhere above her floated the idea which they could none of them grasp, which they pretended to grasp, always escaping out of reach, a beautiful idea, an idea like a butterfly. One after another, vast and hard and cold, appeared to her the churches all over the world where this blundering effort and misunderstanding were perpetually going on, great buildings, filled with innumerable men and women, not seeing clearly, who finally gave up the effort to see, and relapsed tamely into praise and acquiescence, half-shutting their eyes and pursing their lips (p. 228).

The church service is social custom, presumably standing for something genuine but now a shadow, an empty form without content. The service goes on; the security of tradition and ritual supplants fidelity to the inner condition, and people become actors, estranged from themselves, playing always to an imagined audience, harboring a private life, shared sometimes to some extent with one other. Such a culture is moribund, and the sensitive young see past the public forms; Hewet wants to write a novel to be entitled "Silence," "about the things people don't say"; Rachel is withdrawn and undeveloped. The voyage out is to the primitive, uncultured "new world," where, we are told, "nothing was private" (p. 100). It is flight from social forms that are extant but dead to the creation of more congruent ones. Yet the journey, as we are to see, is perilous and guarantees nothing. The old are not fools.

June 23, 1974

Description of Biographic Situation

Willa, John, and I went to Mendon Park today and walked and walked. I'm tired now but don't want to sleep. Thinking about this work and how to proceed.

What I'm considering is writing a journal with the idea that my situation will present itself more honestly, more artlessly, if I write about what occurs day to day than if I begin to summarize and analyze. I would still need to do that and make explicit any connection between *The Voyage Out* and my situation.

Judy phoned a few minutes ago. How quickly I begin to feel pressed by her. I require distance at this point.

Stephen Spender's photograph appeared on the front page of today's *New York Times Book Review*. All the lines, creases, the flesh sagging, and eyes, slightly dull, vacant, looking past the photographer. Remembering Virginia Woolf's remark about the lines on the faces of the middle aged makes one think they see something horrible the young can't yet see. My own face and body will age like that; already it begins. When I've a lot to drink—like last night—I can see the tiny lines coming and the face aging. It awes me, and I suppose somewhere deeper I'm frightened. Always wanted to age slowly, as if I were getting away with something, as if I had avoided some of the harsher effects of being alive. The one incontestable thing I've learned these past few years is that life mustn't be avoided, that the pain of trying to avoid the pain is—as Kafka noted—the only pain that might have been avoided.

Joseph just here. Thursday night after Jim's I told him I responded to him with anger. Today he asked me why; I told him. It feels as if he doesn't take me seriously. I'm sure it's complicated why he doesn't—cross transference, so on—and I don't care to unravel it with him. Nor does he.

Oh yes, yesterday I bought a piano. An old upright; it comes Tuesday. Later in the afternoon I played my saxophone for the first time in nearly ten years.

A cabin on Keuka Lake. With Paul. It's a relief to be away from Brighton Street; maybe now I can write about it. Such a relief in fact that I remind myself to be cautious, not to ride too far this wave and prepare for its conclusion, a landing on some beach. Thoughts of moving out as soon as I return and of working in the office on campus. The book has been stalled; I've been stalled.

It's curious, but the writing has been like a magnet, drawing to itself all aspects of my life, pinpointing in one effort the multidimensional dilemma I face. Naturally both of us are stalled.

The cast of characters at Brighton Street: Johanna, who has her own room; Willa and John, who sleep together in her room; and me. (I realize I'm reticent to write about Johanna and Willa. How expressive of my partial isolation there.)

Johanna is big. She must be 5'10" at least, and while she keeps her weight a secret, she must weight two hundred pounds, maybe a little more. She came to Rochester from New York to lose weight and she has, thirty-five pounds since last October. She came to stay with Willa, although Willa confides she didn't realize Johanna regarded her as a friend until she rang up last fall, inviting herself.

Johanna grew up in New Jersey in a strict and moneyed Catholic family. She started school at NYU in theater but soon found sex and drugs more interesting. Although I do recall she did at some point play a minor role in a movie and in an off-Broadway piece. After two years she left school, took her own apartment, and began making love and taking drugs in earnest.

I'm usually awake in the morning when Johanna rises at nine or nine-thirty—I'm propped up in bed, sipping coffee, looking at my plants and the rest of the room somewhat blankly. Johanna struggles sleepily in, sits on the bed and begins talking—rubbing her eyes—about the night before, the day ahead, her last lover (or lack of them recently), and part of this talk is invariably complaint. I listen responsively. I tend to give her support, rarely disagree and feel warmly toward her, as a brother would for his sister. Her feeling for me is essentially similar, although she makes it clear she is not respectful of the incest taboo.

What I like about Johanna is finally what I don't like: she is unedited. That is, she speaks her mind honestly, without much speculation as to its consequences for the listener. This isn't totally so, and she would probably deny that it is, but I would maintain my view. She expresses the variety of human emotion easily, at times powerfully. Anger, sadness, depression, joy: all are expressed clearly, without subtlety. One never need guess what she's feeling; she invariably volunteers the information, often in considerable detail.

This self-expression involves a degree of insensitivity to me. If I were equally as expressive, if I took perpetual note of my emotional state, then Johanna . . . well, I'm not sure what it would be like. As it is, I don't and so much of the time my state goes unacknowledged.

Willa. Willa and I lived together (and Nancy with us for two months) for five months in 1972. Then again a year later, when I joined her and Johanna on Brighton Street.

Willa is a work of art. The way she looks, moves, talks, sings—in the way she lives. She's tall, an inch or so taller than Johanna, and slender. Her face is striking, oval, clear-cream skin, large oval green eyes, a large nose, and short curly hair. At first blush it is possible to be unsure of her sex; the shorter her hair, the greater the ambiguity. When she wears a skirt (usually long pieces of cloth drapped around her), she becomes more feminine it seems—she moves more slowly, more softly, her gestures less pointed, mores sliding sweeps of the arms, fewer slices from the elbow. This sexual blend causes no awkwardness; she wears it naturally. It tends to heighten the feeling that one is in the presence of a remarkable being.

Her eyes are wide open. She talks only occasionally, with large spaces of silence in between. When she does talk, it is nearly never about the small events of the day (as with Johanna) but about her emotional state at the time. Sometimes she inquires into others. She has practiced zazen for several years, and one senses that she has evolved to the state where she never quite loses touch with the present moment and the rhythm of her breathing. Her observations of others and herself seem regularly insightful and balanced. Sometimes she consciously abandons this attitude in order to release unconscious material. To do so, in her view, requires plunging into material, releasing whatever is under the surface. Necessarily she loses her calm and becomes passionate.

Partly because she espouses self-conscious aims of evolution and development, she possesses considerable knowledge of emotional states, and she is able to make use of this knowledge to assist others to see what they are estranged from in themselves. I think she is sort of "known" for this ability, and on occasion others ring her up or come over to ask her to work with them. She also uses this knowledge unfairly at times, especially with men she is involved with. I don't believe she is fully aware of this, although she has commented on it in ways that indicate at least partial awareness. She becomes involved with men who tend to be repressed (an easy requirement for us to meet) and laudably attempts to assist them in establishing deeper contact with themselves. Inevitably this altruism is rooted in her own need to have a companion who can experience the range of emotion of which she is capable. Frustrated because no man she has met is so developed (it may be hers is a requirement that cannot be met), she tends to express her frustration, anger, and disappointment in her analysis of the other. Thus her analytic knife cuts deeper and with coarser movements than such a delicate operation properly allows, and some injury and bleeding occur. So it was with me, with Joseph (they were together earlier in the year), and so it is now with John.

John started coming over in April, maybe the very end of March. Joseph was still dropping in for brief rash moments, marching into the kitchen where we were all preparing supper, very nervously handing the slightly startled Willa a rose, muttering "fuck you," and marching out again. John—thin, no taller than Willa, with deep brown eyes often half-closed by lids with long lashes—would sit in the living room, silent. He would greet us when he arrived, but would then say little, often nothing for several hours, not even noticeably observing us, although he maintains that was his motive. Johanna and I concluded it was neither of us who provoked his interest, and assumed it was Willa. After a week or ten days of silent living-room sitting, this was confirmed. He began sitting part of the time in her room, and the two began to talk.

July 1, 1974

John. We've become friends. We complain to each other, joke with each other, take long walks, and often have dinner together. He is gentle, intelligent, artful. He describes his dreams to me; I offer interpretations. He reads my papers and gives criticism. It is a satisfactory friendship.

John, like Willa, is a member of the Zen Center, although, also like Willa, he is near being dropped from the membership rolls due to inactivity. He reports he hasn't been to the center in two years, doesn't consider the Roshi Kapleau his spiritual teacher any longer, and finds deficiencies in his old friends.

The other primary physical locus of my current situation is the university. As soon as I write that, emotions surface.

The past two years my office has been on the third floor of the engineering building. The building from the outside is a modest, slightly tasteful brick structure dating from the late 1950s. Inside, the walls are cement blocks, the floors are tile, and both are kept spotless and polished. The stairs from one floor to another are contained in a chamber airtight enough so that footsteps as one ascends reverberate for a floor or two. The doors leading out are thick metal, reminding me of doors to supermarket freezers, and they strike a final-sounding click when they close.

My office is large as offices go. A large window is at one end of the rectangular room that must be fifteen to twenty feet long and seven or so feet wide. The ceiling is high, fifteen feet maybe, and has pipes, painted light blue, as are the cement blocks that comprise the walls. I have eight or nine Klee prints on these, which help keep my attention off the blue and the cement. The lights are many and bright, and when I use them (infrequently), I imagine I am in a hospital operating room or in a police interrogation chamber.

Socially speaking, I find the university odd. More strikingly than I experience it at Brighton Street, when I walk onto campus I have walked onto a stage. It is true my movements quicken, I tighten and congeal inside, and I feel efficient, guarded, ready. These are fairly subtle behaviorally; once when John accompanied me onto campus he noticed no change in me until I described it afterward. Then he recalled noticing. (He went through his own changes, which kept him occupied.) This state makes facile my entry into the social system indicated in part by the use of "doctor" and "professor." I experience it as being lifted onto a chair that floats in space of its own accord; I need steer it only gently. The burden of existence, in other words, is lightened. The parameters of social possibility are fairly set; we all know, or act as if we do, why we're here and what we're doing. This is the power of tradition, of conditioning, of people who share, at least in idea, some common intentions.

June 11, 1976

Analysis

After rereading the piece on the text, I see that the university functioned similarly for me as English culture—at least her parents' generation of it—functioned for Rachel. For both of us, the outer forms—customary talk and interpersonal modes—were incongruent with felt reality. Rachel's comment could have been mine: "Reality dwelling in what one saw and felt, but did not talk about, one could accept a system in which things went round and round quite satisfactorily to other people, without often troubling to think about it, except as something superficially strange." Such was my experience of the university during my initial years. The way it made my life easy was exactly the way it was unreal. Only in my life away from school did something firmer—what felt like reality—seem possible. Yet the attraction to campus remained, not unlike Rachel's attraction to her aunts, to the Dalloways. Let me look at the biographic description now.

June 23 entry. I mention that John, Willa, and I walked but nothing else. We walked out of convenience, out of habit. Momentary intrusions in the same entry from Judy and Joseph. Then I mentioned I'm in a cabin on a lake with Paul. And that's the last I speak of him. There is no development of social relations in any of this.

Reading the description of those with whom I lived: I was reacting against the social as habit, as "cows . . . draw together in a field." I distrust the social, it seems to function primarily as a way of forgetting oneself, a way of not paying attention to immediate experience, a way of playing tapes recorded long ago and only vaguely appropriate now. To guard against those possibilities, I developed . . . what? How would I characterize those relationships? A mix of distance and intimacy. Familiarity and strangeness. We lived together for convenience's sake. Willa wanted to replace someone moving out, and she asked me. I met Johanna at a party a few days later, and yes we seemed compatible; I was ready for a move (I'd been living with Chip and Doreen for the past six months). My acceptance of her invitation had an automatic quality to it, but as I think of it, not the sort of quality that characterized exchanges among most adults in the novel. Their exchanges seem dissociated from their immediate experience. In contrast, it feels as if my attraction to Willa and Johanna was based in experience, as if it were intuitive. Now I would see it as meaningful not fortuitous; I was drawn to individuals who had certain biographic functions to perform in my life, as I had for them. Moving to Brighton Street was my next step. It seems to me, in contrast, that the characters in *The Voyage Out* have frozen themselves into a pseudostability that precludes biographic movement. That's a difference between the social in the text and in my situation. But the correspondences are there as well: a sense of the automatic, the unconscious, of "cows." Does aspiration to become conscious necessarily involve such disdain of the social?

"What I like about Johanna is finally what I don't like; she is unedited. That is, she speaks her mind honestly, without much speculation as to its consequences for the listener." Finding this passage is helpful. It confirms the fact of my ambivalence in this matter. There is a part of me that is attracted to the predictable, to parameters of social exchange that are known in advance. Such exchanges proceed smoothly, as one experiences a pleasure from the smoothness, permitting all involved a sense of satisfaction, of something done nicely. "He knew very well how to make a luncheon pass agreeably, without being dull or intimate." In contrast, while precedents exist, at home much feels possible and unpredictable. In fact, as I think of it, Willa and I consciously cultivate a sense of possibility. But only so much of this sits easily with me; then to campus and to what is known.

Soon after: "If I were equally as expressive, if I took perpetual note of my emotional state, then Johanna . . . well, I'm not sure what it would be like." There's a fear here and a projection onto Johanna of uncertainty over myself. Writ large, it occurs to me, this is the same order of uncertainty others feel when they speak of the necessity of social order and law. The truth is that unedited emotional expression is possibly dangerous. People do hurt each other during "loss of temper." Yet I am convinced such "losses" would diminish in magnitude as one refused to hoard one's anger over time. Expressed as it occurs and in ways that claim it as one's own material maintains an internal flow, preventing "dams" being built up and then broken.

Regarding the university: "Socially speaking, I find the university odd. More strikingly than I experience it at Brighton Street, when I walk onto campus I have walked onto a stage. It is true my movements quicken, I tighten and congeal inside, and I feel efficient, guarded, ready." What I don't claim in 1973 is that not only do I appreciate that stage, I seem to require it.

I think of the interview with Sartre on the occasion of his seventieth birthday, printed in the *New York Review of Books*. I am paraphrasing, but he argued that historical movement has to do with the species' willingness to increasingly disclose the character of its lived worlds. I believe he used the image of a card game in which the card players told more and more of what constitutes their "hand" and, in so doing, transformed the "game." I share this view and this sense of the political power of self-disclosure.

In investigations at the University of Rochester, of which the preceding is a brief illustration, we have tended to find obvious links between response to the text—captured in the short literary pieces (such as "The Social")—and the biographic situation. These links appear to be lived ones, not conceptually

Abstract and Concrete in Curriculum Theorizing

superimposed. What becomes evident is a biographic continuum between text and reader corresponding to the physical continuum of the reader holding the text. What seems clear at this time is that biographic preoccupations—suggested by this reader's issues with Johanna and Willa—are symbolically expressed in scholarly and theoretical work. A text becomes interesting not only due to its beauty but due as well to its capacity to articulate aspects of the reader's biographic situation that are probably hidden from conscious view. What seems clear is that not only a single text but an entire field of study is often chosen according to its developmental capacity for the student. The biographic issues that comprise a situation, which give it meaning and tension, can resolve themselves through intellectual work. Thus, those who do not engage in explicit work with self can move through the thematic content of their lives symbolically.

However, at this stage of the investigation, my impression is that without awareness of this symbolic function of intellectual interests one is more vulnerable to intellectual "blocks." After the brilliant first book, the scholar writes monographs elaborating this aspect and that aspect of the original thesis, but no further profound intellectual movement occurs. Such an individual suffers from the intellectual equivalent of emotional block or resistance. Arrested movement occurs from time to time in all, but for those who can comprehend the fact of a block and its constitution, including its relation to biographic situation, it is probably more possible to move through the block. Such movement involves dissolution of the resistance, the order of dissolution often described in psychoanalysis. Surfacing of hitherto buried material (in the present case elicited by a text and by the description of situation), its naming and the correct interpretation of its significance can permit material to dissolve, allowing the patient/student to move into new material, including new intellectual interests. With this movement can come heightened awareness of one's biographic issues and those of others. While clearly some of those who have been analyzed continue, perhaps in more subtle ways, to misinterpret the significance of their behavior, often through rigid adherence to the conceptual categories of psychoanalysis, the fact of some movement for many is unquestionable. As Habermas suggests, it is the structure of psychoanalysis, not its conceptual categories, that can inform an understanding of liberative activity, individual and social.

The method of *currere* mirrors psychoanalysis in structure while disowning most of its conceptual categories, particularly those obviously culturally conditioned and contingent, such as "penis envy." Structural concepts, that is, concepts essential to the structure of a self-reflexive method, such as "unconscious," "manifest," and "latent," are retained. The aspiration is not only to correct the idealism that characterizes much curriculum writing by portraying particular individuals in particular situations responding to particular items of curriculum. It is as well to offer a strategy by means of which the interested student can work to transform the very situation he has described and analytically grasped.

Part of what is uncovered during this work is the individual's participation in mainstream culture, his participation in the maintenance of present economic and political structures. Release from biographic situation permits release from his historical situation. This extrication permits him to live in a next stage biographically and historically. As increasing numbers of individuals so move, the *weltanschauung* begins to shift, and historical movement—with corresponding transformation of political and economic structures—occurs. This historical situation is dialectically related to innumerable biographic situations, and change in either finally precipitates change in the other.

It should be obvious I am hardly taking a "spiritualist" view that the material world is but a reflection of a real yet invisible world. I am underscoring the inseparable and dialectical relation between consciousness and matter and redressing what I see as an imbalance in certain curriculum writing toward excessive emphasis on the latter. Economic and political structures are associated with certain conceptions of what is possible and legitimate, and collectively these conceptions help constitute a *weltanschauung*. Further, oppressive economic and political structures are associated with oppressive, nonreflexive self-self relationships. By altering economic structures, one can provoke profound alteration of the *weltanschauung* and of self-self relations. What appears to be forgotten in some materialist tracts, such as politically oriented curriculum scholarship, is that it is possible and in fact necessary to work the other way. By working with the individual's lived material in ways that initiate transformation of such material, the self-self relationship is transformed as well as the thematic content of the material. One individual transformation means a microscopic but *not* negligible shift in *weltanschauung* and in material structure.

This individual work need not, of course, necessarily take the form of the method of *currere*. It may take the form of "dialogical encounter," as in Freire's pedagogy. It may take the form of journal keeping and dialogue with a teacher, as in the work of Madeleine R. Grumet. The journal work of Ira Progroff[23] should be noted in this regard. The development of "subjective criticism," in the work of literary scholar and critic David Bleich, is pertinent also.[24] Other such strategies can be formulated.

Part of what is salient about these efforts is their focus upon individual experience, a focus that permits return of abstractions to their concrete life. By such work it is possible to retrieve free-floating abstractions from reified oppressive "existence," returning them to the individual whose life gives them substance. This work is in part political in consequence, as the psychological and intellectual agency of the individual is heightened. Increasingly he understands his participation in oppressive cultural structures, and increasingly he is able to extricate himself from such participation, freeing him to demonstrate "by example" a being living in a next historical stage. This is the convergence of life history and historical movement.[25] As the *weltanschauung* shifts, so do political structures. The individual shifts from product of structure to producer of structures. In this sense, naming is indeed changing the world, as the naming tranforms both the being who names and the world that is named. In this sense individual intellectual work is political action.

Notes

1. E. Mounier, "Be Not Afraid," quoted in T. Roszak, "The Third Tradition: The Individual, the Collective, the Personal," *New American Review* (Fall 1977).
2. I am referring to a rather small lapse of time, the past three to five years.
3. A phrase Michael Apple uses to describe his work. I use it to refer to all curriculum writing that emphasizes the political.
4. *Situation* here refers to the past three to five years and a continuing sense of stasis. The world economic situation continues to slowly deteriorate, as does the political situation in Africa and the Middle East. A pervasive sense of "viscosity," of inability to move through present issues, is discernible.
5. J. Rosario, "Aesthetics and the Curriculum: Persistency, Traditional Modes and a Different Perspective," *The Journal of Curriculum Theorizing* 1:1, in press.
6. M. Apple, "On Analyzing Hegemony," *The Journal of Curriculum Theorizing* 1:1, in press.
7. Ibid.
8. E. Mounier, *Personalism* (London: Routledge & Kegan Paul, 1952), p. ix.
9. W. Earle, *Autobiographical Consciousness* (Chicago: Quadrangle, 1972), p. 55.
10. Apple, "On Analyzing Hegemony."
11. Mounier, *Personalism*.
12. G. Willis, ed., *Qualitative Evaluation* (Berkeley: McCutchan, 1978), pp. 316–42.
13. W. Pinar and M. R. Grumet, *Toward a Poor Curriculum* (Dubuque, Iowa: Kendall/Hunt, 1976).
14. P. Freire, *Pedagogy of the Oppressed* (New York: Seabury Press, 1973).
15. M. Apple, "Ideology and Form in Curriculum Evaluation," in Willis, *Qualitative Evaluation*, pp. 492–521.
16. Apple, "On Analyzing Hegemony."
17. Ibid.
18. Earle, *Autobiographical Consciousness*, p. 33.
19. Various forms of psychotherapy—psychoanalysis, behavior therapy, gestalt, among many others, and schools within these three forms—are well known. The varieties of spiritual and physical work are perhaps less known: Zen practice, *Gurdjieff* work to name two of the former and Rolfing and Hatha Yoga to mention two of the latter. There are those who argue cogently, though finally mistakenly, that psychotherapeutic work functions in politically conservative ways. See, for instance, C. Lasch, *Haven in a Heartless World* (New York: Basic Books, 1977).

20. See "The Method" in *Toward a Poor Curriculum* for an exposition of the basic method.

21. *"Currere"* is available from the author. "The Voyage Out," *Journal of Curriculum Theorizing* 2:1, in press.

22. V. Woolf, *The Voyage Out* (New York: Harcourt, Brace and Co., Copyright 1920 by George H. Doran Company). The numerals in parentheses refer to this edition.

23. I. Progroff, *At a Journal Workshop* (New York: Dialogue House, 1975).

24. D. Bleich, *Subjective Criticism* (Baltimore: John Hopkins University Press, 1978).

25. E. Erikson,*Life History and Historical Moment* (New York: W. W. Norton & Co., 1975).

28 Politics and Higher Education in the 1980s

Stanley Aronowitz

Introduction

In this article, Stanley Aronowitz argues that the curriculum field's current emphasis on teaching basic skills represents, on the one hand, the failure of the alternative school movement of the 1960s and 1970s to confront its own political assumptions regarding the relationship between schools and the wider social order. Unable either to understand or meet the needs of students from working-class and minority backgrounds, most alternative schools were reduced to "islands of privilege" inhabited primarily by children from the middle class.

On the other hand, the current focus in education stems from the increasing influence of the supporters of the "old curriculum" who have recycled and repackaged their assumptions in rhetoric that calls for a military model of learning designed to fit the needs of a shrinking economy and to allay the anxiety of a populace plagued by excessive property taxes and a shrinking job market.

What is unique about Aronowitz's article is that he not only exposes the theoretical and ideological underpinnings in both the liberal and conservative positions on schooling, he also points to the need for a new model of pedagogy, one that takes both the life experiences of students as well as the tenets of critical inquiry seriously. Building upon Paulo Freire's notion of dialogic education, Aronowitz argues for a mode of curriculum grounded in ideological presuppositions that link the political with the interpretive. Pedagogy, in this instance, closes the gap between critical thinking and the social action. In doing so, Aronowitz points to a model of schooling that defines itself *not* in sterile instrumental terms, but in terms that speak to the goal of developing a more humanistic and just society.

As you read this article, consider some of the following questions.
- What are some of the basic misconceptions that Aronowitz claims characterized the liberal model of pedagogy?
- What are the basic assumptions behind the conservative model of pedagogy?
- What are the strengths and shortcomings in Aronowitz's model of pedagogy?
- What are the latter's implications for curriculum development?

A decade ago, American education seemed on the verge of a renaissance commensurate to the era of progressivism of the 1920s and 1930s. Practical innovations dotted the landscape; experimentalism from Montessori to free schools (often student controlled) succeeded in forcing a modicum of school reform in the public sector from the outside. At the beginning of the 1970s, education officials in cities and towns throughout the country had decided that it was necessary to create alternative elementary and secondary schools *within* the established order. The motivating power for starting these programs was by no means altruistic or a farsightedness by educational professionals. They were simply persuaded, either by the example of successful projects outside the system or the eloquence of educational planners and critics, that certain problems of the schools could at least be ameliorated, if not solved, by educational innovations.

Building on the example of the community-controlled districts in New York elementary and junior high schools, big city boards of education moved into the new decade with plans to encourage neighborhoods and educators to begin experiments in alternative high schools as well. In most cities, the conservative boards felt their backs to the wall: enrollments were exploding, but school attendance was dropping among many segments of the cities' high school population. The metaphor of *seige* was widely employed to describe the atmosphere in the schools with teachers steadily losing ground to more confident young guerila warriors. Employers and colleges complained that applicants lacked the needed skills to perform jobs or do "college" work. These skills deficits were defined as literacy as well as good work habits.

The legitmacy of schools as *educational* institutions was challenged by low attendance and plummeting test scores. Parents, especially those from minority communities and the remaining white middle classes in the cities, began demanding educational changes, the content of which remained unspecified. Neil Postman, George Dennison, Jonathan Kozol, and other "radical" writers may not have become gurus for the establishment,but their ideas were seriously considered in the quest for stability in schools.

In March 1970, I joined a small staff of educational planners, parents, and liberal reformers on New York's upper east side and East Harlem who managed to extract a mandate from the board to start an experimental public high school. The nature of the experiment was not clear at the outset and, indeed, was never clarified beyond a few well-worn cliches: this was to be a "community" controlled school within the limits set by state and city laws governing such issues as credentials for teachers, minimum requirements expected of students, and, importantly, the requirement that the head of the school be qualified by board licensure. Each of these boundaries presented difficulties for the Committee for a Comprehensive Education (the group endowed with the essential power to organize the school). But it was not bureaucratic restrictions that played the major role in transforming the school from a promising experiment into a slightly more gentle version of a New York City public high school. The story of Park East High School, which opened for students in February 1971, is the story of the demise of the new progressivism that accompanied the beginning of the 1970s. Although the political climate of rebellion and reform that marked the 1960s was responsible for the impulse for change, it was not only a changed political climate that ultimately undermined the forward march of educational reform. As the decade wore on, the rise of the new conservatism in educational policy reflected a pervasive retreat among progressive forces.

It was a combination of wrongheaded concepts among most educational innovators that were easily refuted or at least repudiated by the opposition. An effective counterattack by the conservatives *at the ideological level* must be held accountable for the reversals that have marked the recent past.

At Park East we shared all of the misconceptions of the rest of the movement. We attributed alienation to the "straight curriculum" of the public schools, their authoritarian style of leadership, and the failure of the schools to inspire teachers to dedicated pedagogy. Our view was that the curriculum and governance had to (a) be relevant to students' lives by becoming more practical without succumbing to the anti-intellectualism of vocational education; (b) become less rigid to allow students a wider range of learning options; (c) involve students as well as parents in the processes of school governance. Of course, we made no political analysis of the reasons the old curriculum was inadequate or administration had become arbitrary. We attributed its inadequacy merely to the fact that it was imposed from above, without regard to student needs. In short, we accepted the canons of student-centered education but, at the same time, made the claim that such an orientation had outcomes that would satisfy the concerns of parents, college admission criteria, and employers. We claimed that students could master the three Rs without recourse to teaching and curriculum styles that "turned them off." We accepted the implicit assumption that a "caring" learning environment was often the sufficient condition for motivating students to learning. At no time in our ruminations over the crisis in learning did it occur to us that the problem might be broader than the power of the schooling environment. We assumed that good teachers and excited students, given their autonomy by an activist but nondirective administration and political support from parents and other community organizations, would reverse the tendency of schooling to grow more distant from education. Of course school reformers and innovators in that period were dimly aware that among the reasons for the estrangement of Black, Hispanic and working-class white students from schools was their perception that the routes to opportunities to escape ghetto life were paved with nails. We knew that there was reason for kids to doubt that a degree from high school would pay off in concrete economic terms. Despite the boom engendered by the Vietnam War, the lives of those stuck in sub-working-class communities was little changed by Great Society programs. Yet, we were believers in the power of schools to provide these communities with a fair chance in the scramble for mobility for those historically excluded from the ball park, much less allowed to play the game.

Of course, we were wrong. All the alternative-school movements accomplished was to give a few kids the chance to climb into the Black or Hispanic middle class which, in the last analysis, was the objective of Great Society programs. We became unwitting agents (when successful) of the need for a new middle class of ghetto administrators, minority corporate public relations men and women, line supervisors in plants, stores, and government agencies, and subprofessionals in education and social welfare sectors. Alternative education in the sixties and early seventies was a way to find a safety valve to place the most active, disruptive, and talented kids away from the mainstream. It was also a way to return them to the mainstream as trained professionals who acted as mediators between their communities and the corridors of power. They were signs to the community of the reality of mobility promises and interpreters to the powerful. For the mass of the disenfranchised, the alternative schools were confusing. Most of them never saw the inside of these weird places and for many who did, the free or alternative school was a scam, a way to avoid the heavily guarded prisonlike atmosphere of regular high schools. Moreover, after a few years it became painfully obvious that free schools were designed for the linguistically literate. The nondirective character of the school ambience abetted the self-motivated, those for whom traditional schools were actually a retardant. But for many who needed *a reason* to become educated in the ways of industrial or postindustrial society, there was nothing self-evident about either the canons of mathematical calculation or of bourgeois humanistic traditions.

The experiments came to a more or less abrupt ending in the public sector as some of its opponents mounted an effective attack on the ground that it was immoral, and even racist, when the child was Black or Hispanic to permit a ten-year-old to remain a nonreader. Only a reversion to the old curriculum could remedy the situation, according to advocates of "basic" education. Using the rhetoric of the civil rights movement's antielitism, educational conservatism took over in the mid 1970s, leaving fervent ideologues of educational reform such as Jonathan Kozol bewildered and ashamed. Soon even those who began the free-school movement were uttering their *mea culpas*. Administrators and teachers who had furiously tried to "retool" in the hectic sixties breathed a sigh of relief and set out to invent a new ideology of learning that stressed "standards." Among these, the writing of E. D. Hirsch was particularly refreshing because it attempted to incorporate the notion of standards into the concept of rhetoric akin to ancient meanings: rhetoric was not a means of persuasion alone; it was a way of knowing. Thus, expression had a cognitive content. In the manner of some modern students of language, the new drive for literacy found theoretical legitimacy in the unity of utterance and thought, a refusal of the ideas of such sociolinguists as William Labov who argued that forms of Black speech could be transcoded into logical thought commensurable in every respect with canonical expression. The conservatives' insistence that standard English simply connoted the appropriate thought content against colloquialism that was fraught with illogicality convinced both professionals and laypeople that these hard times of stiffening competition for fewer jobs, the nadir of industrial work and its replacement by administrative and technical labor, and the dropping performance of students in schools demanded the end to a crippling permissiveness that had held sway for a decade.

Today free schools are no longer in evidence. They have been incorporated as vestigial structures into "alternative" programs or schools within conventional systems. Like the earlier movement, progressive education, the principles of these experiments exist as "traces" within a system that is moving rapidly towards a definition of educational excellence that antedates the older progressivism. The "new curriculum" devalues social learning as a content in education, replacing this notion with a much more direct concept: social reproduction. The schools are being mobilized to insure the reproduction of a society as a whole. Even though the slogan "critical thinking" has not disappeared from the discourse, it cannot be said that it has any practical influence over the curriculum. In short, the "hidden curriculum" of American education, preparing students to take their place in the corporate order as disciplined, subordinate workers, has now become overt. The counterattacks against the old new progressivism went much further than trying to correct some weaknesses in that palpably middle-class educational paradigm. The conservative onslaught argued explicity for a restoration of old modes of administrative authority within schools, but not for its own sake. Instead the cry "illiteracy" became the rubric under which all forms of repression were subsumed. The old liberalism had swept the rebellion of the young against the arbitrary authority of school officials under the rug by labeling the rebels "hyperkinetic" (a reference to the growing use of psychological categories to eliminate opposition from the subject-objects of schooling, the young). The new conservatives found in "permissiveness" (an explicit attack against liberal notions of rehabilitation and against the critique of authority as a causal agent of the school crisis) a convenient target for justifying the return of the old order.

There are two main things to be said about the current state of education before discussing its future. First, it is perfectly true that progressives have placed entirely too much faith in its elementary principles, particularly the ideas of learning by doing and its view that authority relations that are not legitimated by democratic means are barriers to learning. To be sure, experience-based pedagogy is grounded in a theory of learning which argues that the separation of form and content and, specifically, the bifurcation of knowledge from its consequences is deleterious to learning. Goal-oriented learning that goes beyond intellectual achievement and enters the realm of status, honor, job advancement, and personal pride has already been adopted by the schools as one of the fragmented parts of progressivism consistent with their objectives. But the new conservative curriculum has posed a serious challenge to the epistemological assumptions of liberal educators. The new order argues that the authority of the *word* can be imposed without the crutch of instrumentalism if only the administration, teachers, and parents hold firm: "you shall learn because we say so." Moreover, if you don't, it is curtains for a decent life. America is the land of opportunity only if you do what we say.

Now, it must be admitted that the military model of learning works. Punishment is an effective tool of the reproduction of a hierarchical order, as well as one in which its subjects possess competencies. Of course, one would have to renounce critical thought as a goal of education or the effort to establish a democratic society in order to get kids to read and write under this regime. Or to be more exact, critical and democratic ideas would be produced as an outcome of the rebellion of kids against the authoritarian school, just as in the days before modern progressivism.

The second problem with the old liberal model is that it was based on the assumption of an expanding economy, one that may not be held as a basis for educational policy in the future. If jobs with mobility chances become scarce in the next decade, two consequences might follow. One that is already upon us is that students who believe they have acquired some literacy and cultural skills at home will become more obedient to school authorities and their methods, whether they like them or not. In this sense the conservative program in the new conditions may be far more effective than a liberal position might offer. In this culture competitive practices in all spheres and examinations are accorded preeminence as a criterion of competence. Learning how to pass the exam and getting good recommendations from school authorities take on pronounced importance.

Another consequence is the cleaning out of colleges and universities of those students who have been admitted under affirmative action programs including those called "open admissions." Even many liberals would agree with their antagonists that colleges are no place for the illiterate. So, tightening admissions criteria made necessary by fiscal crises (themselves the result of economic decline) will reduce the initiative of students in lower grades to seek higher education. Those who do not respond to the military/basic education model would be adjudged genetically (in the metaphoric sense of the word) incompetent, strengthening the moves towards a further vocationalization of education in the primary and secondary schools. Here the ideas of Plato's *Republic* seem already to have gained some currency among educators. Even more pronounced than the tracking system, the most recent policy has begun to exclude liberal arts from the lower rungs of the schooling hierarchy. A grotesque appropriator of the surface ideology of the old progressivism is the concentration of schools on technical subjects. The subordination of literature and history to "skills" acquisition and the introduction of "hands on" subjects in the lower grades is all justified as a type of learning by doing as much as a different answer to the cry for relevance that pierced traditional curricula in the sixties and early seventies. What can be more relevant to the lives of students than a curriculum that stresses job preparation in an era that limits opportunities and is, at the same time, increasingly oriented to technique? The new conservatism, in short, preys on the anxiety of a generation that has finally got the news that America in the new era is *hard times*. At a time when colleges face declining enrollments, not because of the famous "demographic shift," but because those who might enter are persuaded by the argument that the liberal arts offer no definite payoff, even the institutions of higher learning are attempting to become "relevant" rather than remain academic. If the size of state colleges and universities does not shrink, say administrators, it will be a measure of the degree to which they can make their programs more practical (real job-preparation oriented).

Thus, a major consequence of the drift (no, gallop) towards a reversal of the old liberal education, in both ideological and formal terms, will be to remove the elements of critical thinking that are inscribed in the traditional curricula. There is an irony here. The free- or alternative-school movement rose on the flag of relevance, as much as learning by doing. The argument of the new conservatives hinges on the appropriation of progressive ideology as much as its repudiation. All the conservatives had to do was to *redefine* the meaning of a few terms and combine them with a concrete alternative to the alternative that answers the objections of those for whom alternatives did not work.

What of the decade that is already upon us? We are in for a heavy dose of the new technicalization of the curriculum corresponding to development within the labor market. The whole task set by contemporary educational policy is to keep up with rapidly shifting developments in technology. The only generalizing emphasis that has conquered so far is the now generally accepted campaign to improve reading and writing skills. There are many issues encapsulated in this back-to-basics movement. First, the theoretical assumptions of the new gurus of the movement are not commensurate with the ideology upon which the movement rests. The movement triumphed on the basis of its claim that neither the traditional nor its alternative curricula were relevant to the new age. But the dominant mode of inquiry that had led to writing and composition programs at all levels, and focused on the three Rs, etc., is highly abstract. On the one hand, learning by doing is repudiated by reference to rhetorical studies, concepts such as standards, focus on parts of speech, vocabulary, basic math, etc. On the other hand, there are some doings under way in high schools, particularly the rapid spread of practically oriented vocational and technical education. Yet, if the former suffers from its other worldliness, the latter's practical claims are defeated by the incredible degradation, segmentation, and reduction of skills in the job market. More importantly, the fact that entry level jobs proliferate faster than any others in the new technology and these require a minimum of training because *scientific* knowledge (not taught in the back-to-basics movement) is inscribed in a few machines and not in their operation. Those who design, maintain, and market these machines are a relatively small proportion of the labor force.

Second, the new learning ideology is encountering a major overhaul of educational resources in America. In the wake of sharply higher defense costs, taxpayers' revolts, and economic stagnation and decline, teaching has become nightmarish. Many classrooms that are overcrowded, lack books and other materials and are led by administrators and teachers who are weary after years of constant warfare and upheaval caused not so much by the kids as by the budget cutters.

Of course, the quest for literacy is paramount in any democratic society, not so much for vocational reasons (it's only during growth periods that genuine skills become in short supply), but for more important reasons. Self-management of society at the political as well as social and economic levels requires a population possessed of detailed and complex knowledge of scientific and technological processes as well as the elements of policy. The issues in a society wishing to widen participation in its key decisions is whether these can be grasped by ordinary people, and reading and writing are essential elements of this process.

But the military model cannot insure democratic participation. On the contrary, it encourages subordination of a *conceptually* illiterate population whose skills extend to the technical plane. They are able to follow orders under the direction of managements that are responsive to bureaucracies and capital, but unable to critically examine public and private life, to determine how and what should be produced and by whom, and to make the public choices that become policy.

There is, of course, a serious problem with the literacy of the American people. Some aspects of this question reside in elementary skills. But, for the most part, this is a misplaced emphasis, a slogan that is oriented to promoting fear and anxiety so that a new wave of school policy may be accepted. Most Janey's and Johnny's can follow written orders, read newspapers, and make calculations in hundreds of thousands of jobs.

Our problem is—who can think through what's going on in the world, the changes in our lives under way as a result of decisions made at the political level? More importantly, the changes in our ways of working and living, the relation of the United States to the rest of the world, especially those parts of it suffering from chronic privation, are changing. Our problems are preeminently public ones, for the gulf between the private and the public is no longer so wide that one may pursue his destiny without regard to institutional and political choices. Neither the old way, the alternative movement, nor the neoconservative back-to-basics movement, propose to deal with the problem of citizenship, the formation of a public that acts for itself, the dangerous centralization of power in American life.

The illiteracy to which I refer can only be addressed in the context of social movements that wish to make serious social changes. The other model of rapid learning for whole populations is the *ideological* model. In a country lacking the conditions for rapid economic growth or the motivating force to accept a highly militarized educational process as grounds for learning, the only alternative is to argue for literacy on radical foundations. Democratic self-determination of all social institutions has been adequate as a spur to incredible advances in literacy conceived in both senses discussed here. The most recent example, Nicaragua, has embarked on such a campaign with revolutionary participation as the fundamental argument. This, of course, does not relieve educators of the responsibility to address specifically cognitive issues, the politics of learning itself. But given the objective of democracy, the abstract "standards" oriented proposals of conservative education cannot suffice. To be sure, language itself has a structure that must be mastered, or, to be more exact, our structural capacity to generate grammar must be given an environment that transforms itself into the symbolic forms of speech and writing, and this task is somewhat distinct from practical and social applications. But as Wittgenstein has remarked, language is—*a* form of life, not *the* form of life. It is bound up with social relations, entwined with the ways of the world of which it is both an expression and through which the world lives. Therefore, the concept of relevance requires still another specification, one that insists that students must learn to examine their own lives, the ways in which they have been part of the system of social reproduction. Language learning is a way of distancing oneself from the self-evident, to discover the sense in which we have all been formed within the context of material practices of which schools as well as discourses are an essential aspect.

It may be that the autobiographical mode of inquiry is a way to help students discover their own relation to school and to language. They may see the ways in which the texts of everyday life such as family, peer relations, and mass culture are not merely activities or institutions "out there" but become fragments of that praxis by which we form ourselves. And, as Paul Willis has shown,[1] self-formation does not occur merely mimetically but also in the process of rebelling against the institutions that have the dominance over our existence. The task of critical thinking, of course, does not end with the recognition that we are part of the system that has shaped us.

Critical education then proposes, not a student centered, practical step, but one that can only be directed, as it were, from without by persons (teachers) who share the goals of the students. But they are better able to guide them towards historical understanding and acquiring a critical scientific knowledge of the social and external, natural world, to see the ways that these may be changed by changing the ways people have conceptualized them over time.

And, of course, an ideological education that wishes to examine critically its own presuppositions must show the ways in which ideology is defined not merely as a system of values and beliefs inculcated from above. Rather the job is to help students see ideology as lived experience, in literature, music, painting, and social interaction, without regard to distinctions between great canonical literature and the art of contemporary popular forms. For, those who despair that students may no longer yield with awe and wonder to the lyrical Keats because the poison of our technological culture has occluded such a possibility have already entered a judgment which is at once problematic on two counts: first as to Keats as a priori superior to anything produced today by popular lyrics in songs and second that technological domination subsumes all but a small avant-garde in recent art. The first responsibility of the educator is to validate the experience of the student, including her aesthetic experience, and then to be willing to learn from students. This view corresponds to Paulo Freire's notion of dialogic education, which is not the same as the old concept of student centeredness.

Critical education remembers that students, especially working-class and third-world kids, have been voiceless in this culture except in popular forms such as play and song (even commercial music allows the voice of the young to shine forth). Voicelessness presupposes powerlessness, but it does not follow that the learning environment of schools can either abdicate to students or impose standards from without. If the objective of education is to empower students intellectually and, to some extent, emotionally, their voice must receive validation. This entails *both* a critical stance towards their already acquired voice, obtained from the contradictory sources of mass culture and peer interaction, as well as an effort to enrich this voice with historical and critical dimension.

Thus the antinomy between critical education and neoconservatism does not engage at the level of the struggle for literacy. Critical education agrees that the problem exists; but it is less a question of *functional* illiteracy than historical and critical/conceptual illiteracy. The trend of current education policy seeks to persuade us that the basics movement can solve the economic crisis for students since it assumes that the problem of dead-end jobs, low income, and insecurity resides with the individual. The critical movement (still incipient but possessing some critical mass) reverses the causal relation. Functional illiteracy is produced by the constitution of the job market, by economic and social inequality, and by political powerlessness. To combat this inequality, students require knowledge (of which skills are derivative) and, most of all, hope in their collective powers to change the world so that democratic power replaces corporate control.

Notes

1. P. Willis, *Learning to Labour* (England: Saxon House, 1977).